AF411911

Foreign Direct Investments from Emerging Markets

The Challenges Ahead

Edited by Karl P. Sauvant
and Geraldine McAllister,
with Wolfgang A. Maschek

Para mamãe, em reconhecimento por sua profunda afeição e generosidade e constante apoio.

Karl P. Sauvant

For my family, thank you for everything

Geraldine McAllister

Meiner wunderbaren Familie gewidmet, insbesondere meiner Mutter.

Wolfgang A. Maschek

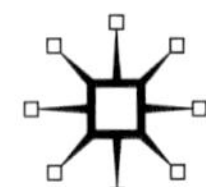

FOREIGN DIRECT INVESTMENTS FROM EMERGING MARKETS
Copyright © Karl P. Sauvant, Geraldine McAllister, and
Wolfgang A. Maschek, 2010.

All rights reserved.

First published in 2010 by
PALGRAVE MACMILLAN®
in the United States—a division of St. Martin's Press LLC,
175 Fifth Avenue, New York, NY 10010.

Where this book is distributed in the UK, Europe and the rest of the world,
this is by Palgrave Macmillan, a division of Macmillan Publishers Limited,
registered in England, company number 785998, of Houndmills,
Basingstoke, Hampshire RG21 6XS.

Palgrave Macmillan is the global academic imprint of the above companies
and has companies and representatives throughout the world.

Palgrave® and Macmillan® are registered trademarks in the United States,
the United Kingdom, Europe and other countries.

ISBN: 978–0–230–10021–3

Library of Congress Cataloging-in-Publication Data

Foreign direct investments from emerging markets : the challenges
ahead / edited by Karl P. Sauvant with Geraldine McAllister and
Wolfgang A. Maschek.
    p. cm.
Includes bibliographical references and index.
ISBN 978–0–230–10021–3
    1. Investments, Foreign—Developing countries. 2. International
business enterprises—Developing countries. I. Sauvant, Karl P.
II. McAllister, Geraldine A. III. Maschek, Wolfgang A.

HG5993.F657 2010
332.67'3091724—dc22   2010000834

A catalogue record of the book is available from the British Library.

Design by Newgen Imaging Systems (P) Ltd., Chennai, India.

First edition: September 2010

10 9 8 7 6 5 4 3 2 1

Printed in the United States of America.

Contents

Conclusion

Foreword

Foreign direct investment (FDI) is no longer an activity exclusively undertaken by firms from developed countries. The growth of multinational enterprises (MNEs) from emerging markets has begun to focus attention around the world on the role of these new players.

The rise of outward investment from emerging markets has contributed to the growth in FDI globally. In 1980, global FDI outflows totaled US$52 billion; emerging markets accounted for only 6% of this figure. By 2007, global FDI outflows were over US$2 trillion, and emerging markets accounted for over 15% (or US$300 billion) of the total.

The first conference in the Five-Diamond Conference cycle in April 2008 at Columbia University, *Thinking Outward: Global Players from Emerging Markets*, dealt with a range of issues related to the key players in this process—firms, home countries, and host countries:

- *Firms*: Like their counterparts from developed countries, emerging market MNEs seek to develop a portfolio of locational assets as a source of their international competitiveness. What drives their transnationalization process and what strategies are such firms pursuing to maximize their efforts to deliver goods and services to foreign markets through direct investment? In particular, what internal and external obstacles do firms face and what support do they receive from their home country governments?
- *Home countries*: Most emerging market governments restrict outward FDI and, in any event, often have no clear policy in this area (contrasting sharply with inward FDI, where virtually all countries have an enabling framework in place and investment promotion agencies seeking to attract investment). A few emerging markets, however, have not only liberalized their outward FDI frameworks, but have put in place a coherent policy framework; some of them actually promote outward FDI in the interest of competitiveness of their firms and the performance of their economies (e.g., China's "Go Global" policy). What experiences have emerging markets and developed countries had in developing their outward FDI policies? What lessons can be learned from these experiences to plan the sequencing of such policies for governments of emerging markets wanting to help their firms by allowing outward FDI?
- *Host countries*: Global players from emerging markets are creating tension in host countries (particularly in the case of cross-border mergers and acquisitions), in both developed and developing regions. What do such reactions mean for the transnationalization of emerging market firms? What influence do such reactions have on the policies of emerging markets?

These issues are also addressed in the present volume.

The financial crisis of 2008 and the ensuing economic recession has impacted foreign direct investment. In 2008, global FDI inflows declined by about 10%, to US$1.7 trillion, and in 2009 they declined a further 40%. Whereas many argue that emerging markets are better able to weather this economic storm than they were ten years ago, and that overall their economies are faring better than those of advanced countries, the reality is that, as banks and investors retrench, and governments seek to finance budget and current account deficits, access to capital will prove challenging. Though the precise effects are yet to be determined, there is no question that this adds to the challenges facing the key players in the outward FDI process. This volume touches on these additional challenges, and a number of the original chapters have been updated in light of the changed economic reality. Ultimately, however, many of the challenges that were identified prior to the current crisis remain relevant, and will remain relevant, even if the crisis has changed the order of priority.

This conference volume offers important information and analysis for all those involved or interested in outward FDI from emerging markets, whether they are corporate executives, academics, or government officials. The experiences of, and lessons from, specific markets will no doubt prove instructive for others. It is important to acknowledge that this is a relatively new field, as reflected in the scarcity of data in some areas as well as in some chapters. This, of course, presents its own set of challenges, but challenges that a number of chapter authors in this volume have chosen to grapple with, and which MNEs and governments must deal with on a regular basis.

This volume is of critical importance to Columbia University, Fundação Dom Cabral, Fudan University, and the Indian School of Business, as it helps equip the leaders of tomorrow with the skills necessary to address and overcome the challenges they face in the globalizing world economy.

New York, April 2009

EMERSON DE ALMEIDA, XIONGWEN LU,

AJIT RANGNEKAR, AND DAVID M. SCHIZER

Preface

The spread of multinational enterprises outward from emerging markets is an increasingly important phenomenon. This volume shows that we are just beginning to come to grips with the most important analytical and policy issues that affect the world community.

What are the basic data surrounding emerging market multinationals? What sectors and home countries exhibit fastest growth? What are the most important rankings for emerging market multinationals? Where are there signs of slowing? Might the phenomenon of global investment from developed as well as developing countries even be overstated, as most companies retain a regional focus?

Are multinationals from emerging market countries driven by similar motivations to OECD multinationals, or do they pursue different distinctive rationales? Do we need a new theory to understand the dynamics of international investment on the part of emerging market multinationals, or do their actions fit within subcategories of well-understood theory?

Do international investors from China, India, Russia, Brazil, South Africa—and elsewhere—behave like each other, or are there identifiable home country patterns of action? Does home country government ownership make a difference? Within the major categories of foreign direct investment (FDI)—FDI in the extractive sector, FDI in infrastructure, FDI in agribusiness, FDI in manufacturing, FDI in services—do emerging market multinationals resemble their counterparts from the developed world? Is there convergence among privately owned international investors, or not?

Do emerging market multinationals convey special advantages or benefits when they enter host countries, whether developed or developing? Or, might they bring noticeable disadvantages or dangers? Do they show the same kinds of core competencies and competitive advantages as developed country multinationals, or are their firm-specific capabilities different? Are emerging country multinationals open to closer relations with host country authorities, communities, and nongovernmental organizations? Or, as UNCTAD warns, do they carry the potential to undermine hard-won global standards, and lead a race-to-the-bottom in corporate governance?

What are appropriate home developing country policy approaches to outward investors? Should they promote outward investment, guide it, or inhibit it? Can developing country policies toward outward investors learn from—or should they mimic—developed country policies toward outward investment?

How should developed countries react to inward investment by emerging market multinationals? What constitutes developed country "protectionism"? What constitutes legitimate developed country concern about national security?

Are some developed country responses (e.g., EU toward Gazprom of Russia) more justifiable than other developed country responses (e.g., U.S. toward CNOOC of China)?

These are just some of the important questions that arise. This conference volume introduces the dilemmas, the controversies, the disputes—and many of the opposing points of view. The reader cannot fail to be drawn into the heart of many of the most important issues surrounding the spread of global players from emerging markets.

THEODORE H. MORAN
Marcus Wallenberg Professor of International Business and Finance
Georgetown University
Non-Resident Senior Fellow,
Peterson Institute of International Economics

Acknowledgments

This volume consists of the papers prepared for, and finalized in light of, the first Five-Diamond International Conference entitled *Thinking Outward: Global Players from Emerging Markets,* held in April 2008 at Columbia University, New York. The conference was organized by the Vale Columbia Center on Sustainable International Investment and its partners, in collaboration with the Special Unit for South-South Cooperation, United Nations Development Programme.

We would like to thank our partners: without their support the event itself, and hence this volume, would not have been possible. It is thanks to the participants in the conference and the contributors to this volume that we hope to advance the international debate on the growing role of multinational enterprises from emerging markets and the issues to which this gives rise.

We also would like to thank everyone who attended the conference for their active participation and the chairs for guiding the discussion expertly: Lisa Anderson, Alan Beattie, Georges Blanc, and Manfred Schekulin.

The conference itself was organized expertly by Michael B. O'Sullivan, Chrysilla Bautista, Maria Estenssoro, and André Almeida. They were supported by Edward Platt, Chris Kaminker, Besnik Hyseni, Dingding Sun, Demis Mavrellis, Carlos Mauricio Mirandola, and Xiaodong Liu. Their efforts ensured the smooth proceeding of the conference. Tatyana Gershkovich and Oleksiy Kononov helped us greatly in finalizing this volume.

Thank you very much indeed to all of them!

New York, May 2010
KARL P. SAUVANT, WOLFGANG A. MASCHEK,
AND GERALDINE MCALLISTER

Contributors

Matthew B. Adler is a PhD candidate in economics at the University of Maryland and a JD candidate at the Georgetown University Law Center. Previously he worked on international trade, finance, and investment as a Research Analyst at the Peterson Institute for International Economics. His publications cover issues ranging from NAFTA, the effect of preferential trade on multilateral trade liberalization, foreign direct investment, and the consequences of globalization. Mr. Adler holds a BA in mathematical economics from Oberlin College. Email: mba29@law.georgetown.edu.

Yair Aharoni is Professor Emeritus at Tel Aviv University where he served as the first dean of the faculty of management. He was instrumental in establishing the Israel Institute of Business Research and the faculty's Top Executive Program, of which he was the first director. He was also Chief Executive Officer of the Jerusalem Institute of Management and served for five years as the Rector of the College of Management in Rishon LeZion, Israel. Mr. Aharoni was the Daniel and Grace Ross Professor of International Business and later the Issachar Haimovic Professor of Business Policy, both at Tel Aviv University. He was the J. Paul Stitch Visiting Professor of International Business at Duke University (1987–1995) and the director of the Center of International Business Education and Research (CIBER) (1989–1995). He has also held visiting appointments at numerous other universities in the United States and Europe. Mr. Aharoni has published extensively. In addition to his books he has edited and coedited numerous volumes and published more than 100 papers in various journals and 150 case studies. In 2010, he was awarded the Israel Prize for his contributions to management science in Israel and abroad. Email: yairah@post.tau.ac.il.

André Almeida is a researcher at the International Business Center of Fundação Dom Cabral, Brazil, where he has coauthored a number of publications including: *Ranking of Brazilian Transnational Corporations* (2007), in conjunction with the Vale Columbia Center on Sustainable International Investment; *Outward Foreign Direct Investment from Brazil* (2007), Fundação Dom Cabral and United Nations (UNCTAD); *The Brazilian Case on International Good Practices on TNC-SME Linkages*, Fundação Dom Cabral and United Nations (UNCTAD); and *Internationalization of Brazilian Firms: Perspectives and Risks* (Elsevier, 2006). Mr. de Almeida holds a bachelor's degree in international relations from Pontifícia Universidade Católica de Minas Gerais, Brazil. Email: andres@fdc.org.br.

José E. Alvarez is the Herbert and Rose Rubin Professor of International Law at New York University School of Law. He was formerly the Hamilton Fish

Professor of International Law and Diplomacy at Columbia University School of Law. He is a graduate of Magdalen College, University of Oxford, and Harvard Law School. He was law clerk to Judge Thomas Gibbs Gee, U.S. Court of Appeals for the Fifth Circuit, and was in private practice at Shea & Gardner. Formerly an attorney-adviser at the U.S. Department of State, Office of the Legal Adviser, he has also held appointments at Georgetown University Law Center, George Washington University Law School, and the University of Michigan Law School. Mr. Alvarez is an International Affairs Fellow at the Council on Foreign Relations, where he is a member, and served on the Board of Editors of the *American Journal of International Law* and the *Journal of International Criminal Justice*. He has been a member of the Department of State Advisory Committee on International Law. His principal areas of publishing and teaching are international law, especially international organizations, international tribunals, war crimes, international legal theory, and foreign investment. Email: jose.alvarez@nyu.edu.

Harry G. Broadman is Managing Director of The Albright Group LLC, a global strategy firm, and Chief Economist of Albright Capital Management LLC, a registered investment advisory firm focused on emerging markets. Immediately prior to his current positions, Mr. Broadman was a senior official at the World Bank Group, working in several regions, including East Asia and the Pacific; Eastern Europe and the former Soviet Union; and sub-Saharan Africa. Before joining the World Bank, he served as Assistant United States Trade Representative in the Executive Office of the President. Earlier, Mr. Broadman worked in the White House on the President's Council of Economic Advisers as the Chief of Staff and Senior Staff Economist. Previously he was Chief Economist of the U.S. Senate Committee on Governmental Affairs. Prior to his government service, Mr. Broadman worked at the Rand Corporation; Resources for the Future, Inc.; and the Brookings Institution. During his academic career, he served on the faculties of Harvard University and the Johns Hopkins University. Mr. Broadman received an AB in economics and history, *magna cum laude*, from Brown University and a PhD in economics from the University of Michigan. He is a member of the Council on Foreign Relations and the Bretton Woods Committee. Email: hbroadman@thealbrightgroupllc.com.

Peter J. Buckley is Professor of International Business and Director of the Centre for International Business at the University of Leeds (CIBUL), recently rated as the world's leading international business research group. He has published extensively, including twenty-four books, and more than 150 articles that have appeared in European, American, and Japanese journals, including the *Journal of International Business Studies*. In 2006 the *Times Higher Education Supplement* listed Mr. Buckley as one of the most "successful Academic Writers." Mr. Buckley was Vice President of the Academy of International Business (AIB) from 1991 to 1992 and was elected a Fellow of AIB in 1985 for "outstanding achievements in international business." He is a Fellow of the British Academy of Management, a Fellow of the Royal Society of Arts, and a Fellow of the European International Business Academy. In December 1998 he was made an Honorary Professor at the University of International Business and Economics, Beijing, China. He was President of the Academy of International Business from 2002 to 2004 and served as "Immediate Past President" from 2004 to 2006. In 2006, Mr. Buckley was awarded the Viipuri Prize for his "outstanding record in the field of international business research." Email: P.J.Buckley@lubs.leeds.ac.uk.

Jeremy L. Clegg is Jean Monnet Professor of European Integration and International Business Management at the Centre for International Business at the University of Leeds (CIBUL), where his Chair is supported by the European Commission. His research interests include the determinants of foreign direct investment by, and into, developed and developing countries, and the impact of European and foreign-owned firms on the productivity and performance of Chinese firms. His current research focuses on the determinants of productivity, and international productivity differences, in the retailing industry and, in particular, in food retailing. Previously, he held appointments at the universities of Bath, Reading, Swansea, and Exeter, in the United Kingdom. From 2001 to 2007, Mr. Clegg served as Chair of the Academy of International Business, United Kingdom & Ireland Chapter. Email: ljc@lubs.leeds.ac.uk.

Judith Clifton is Senior Lecturer at the University of Cantabria, Spain, where her research interests include privatization, regulation, liberalization, and internationalization of enterprises. Prior to joining the University of Cantabria, she lectured at various universities in Europe, including Oxford, Leeds, The Open University, the European University Institute, and Oviedo. In 2007, Ms. Clifton coedited one of the first published volumes on the phenomenon of the transnationalization of network services: *Transforming Public Enterprise in Europe and North America: Networks, Integration and Transnationalization* (Palgrave Macmillan, 2007). Ms. Clifton holds a DPhil in political economy from the University of Oxford. Email: judith.clifton@unican.es.

Adam R. Cross is a Senior Lecturer in International Business at the Centre for International Business (CIBUL) and Director of the Centre for Chinese Business and Development (CCBD) at the University of Leeds. He has published two books, and contributed to over thirty academic papers and books, focusing on cross-border licensing, intellectual property as a business asset, and outward direct investment from emerging markets, with China an important country focus for much of this work. Email: A.R.Cross@lubs.leeds.ac.uk.

Emerson de Almeida has been Dean of Fundação Dom Cabral, Brazil, since its establishment in 1976. He led the negotiations to implement alliances with INSEAD (France), Kellogg (USA), and UBC (Canada), and is currently working toward creating a network among business schools in Latin America and the BRIC countries. Mr. de Almeida has directed the implementation of Fundação Dom Cabral's partnership projects with companies; there are over 300 such partnerships with associated companies in existence today. He is the author of *Fundamentos da Empresa Relevante: Meu aprendizado na FDC* (Campus Press, 2006) and numerous articles. Mr. de Almeida is a member of the International Advisory Council of Guanghua Business School (Peking University), a member of the international INSEAD Council, and a permanent member of *Gazeta Mercantil's* Entrepreneurial Leaders Forum. In 2006, the Forum de Líderes—*Gazeta Mercantil* elected Mr. de Almeida the National Entrepreneurial Leader for the Education Sector. He holds a bachelor's degree in economics from the College of Economic Sciences, Universidade Federal de Minas Gerais, and a maîtrise from the Institut Français de Presse, University of Paris. Email: ealmeida@fdc.org.br.

Filip De Beule is Assistant Professor of International Business at Lessius University College, Antwerp, Belgium, and has been Visiting Professor at the University of Antwerp and the Catholic University of Leuven. He is an affiliate researcher at the LICOS Centre for Institutions and Economic Performance at the Catholic University of Leuven, where his research focuses on multinational enterprises and emerging markets. Mr. De Beule is a member of the Academy of International Business and the European International Business Academy (EIBA) and serves on the board of EIBA as national representative for Belgium. He holds bachelor's and master's degrees in economics from Universitaire Faculteiten Sint-Ignatius Antwerpen (UFSIA), and an MBA from the University of Antwerp Management School (UAMS). He received his PhD from the University of Antwerp. Email: filip.debeule@lessius.edu.

Daniel Díaz-Fuentes is Professor of Economics at the University of Cantabria, Spain. He has lectured at the universities of Oxford, London School of Economics, Manchester UMIST, and Carlos III University of Madrid. His research interests include economic development, public sector economics, central banks, trade, and foreign direct investment. Mr. Díaz-Fuentes assisted UNCTAD in the preparation of the World Investment Report 2008. His latest publication is *Transforming Public Enterprise in Europe and North America: Networks, Integration and Transnationalization* (Palgrave Macmillan, 2007), coedited with Judith Clifton and Francisco Comín, which deals with the internationalization of infrastructure services and its consequences. Email: daniel.diaz@unican.es.

Art Durnev is Assistant Professor of Finance in the Faculty of Management at McGill University, Montreal, where he teaches undergraduate and graduate students, PhD candidates, and executives. Mr. Durnev's research interests are focused primarily on corporate finance, governance, and financial markets development. His work involves empirical investigations of firm governance structures, disclosure policies, insider trading regulation, and idiosyncratic volatility. He has published in the *Journal of Finance, Journal of Accounting Research, Michigan Law Review,* and *Economics of Transition.* His recent work focuses on firms' adaptation of better governance and disclosure practices in countries where investor protection laws are weak. Mr. Durnev, a native of Russia, received an MA in economics from the New Economic School in Moscow and Pennsylvania State University, and a PhD in finance from the University of Michigan Business School. Email: art.durnev@mcgill.ca.

Persephone Economou is a Senior Consultant at the World Bank Multilateral Investment Guarantee Agency (MIGA). Prior to joining the World Bank, Ms. Economou worked on a variety of FDI-related issues at the United Nations in New York and Geneva. She has been involved in the editorial process of the *Transnational Corporations Journal* and the *Journal of International Business Studies,* where she coedited a special issue on International Business Negotiations. Email: peconomou@worldbank.org.

Bingjie Han joined the Shanghai Stock Exchange's postdoctoral program in 2009, having received his PhD from Fudan University. He has published in leading journals such as the *Economic Research Journal* (Chinese) and the *Journal of World Business.* Mr. Han's research interests center on knowledge transfer, the organization and management of multinational enterprise, and the impact of corruption on business in emerging markets. At present, he focuses on the mergers and acquisitions of Chinese listed companies and advises Chinese policy makers. Email: puritan6980@yahoo.com.cn.

Gary Clyde Hufbauer is Reginald Jones Senior Fellow at the Peterson Institute for International Economics. Previously he was the Marcus Wallenberg

Professor of International Financial Diplomacy at Georgetown University, and served in the U.S. Treasury Department from 1974 to 1980. His coauthored publications include *Global Warming and the World Trading System* (Peterson Institute for International Economics, 2009), *Economic Sanctions Reconsidered*, third edition (Peterson Institute for International Economics, 2007), *US Taxation of Foreign Income* (Peterson Institute for International Economics, 2007), *US-China Trade Disputes: Rising Tide, Rising Stakes* (Institute for International Economics, 2006), and *NAFTA Revisited: Achievements and Challenges* (Institute for International Economics, 2005). Mr. Hufbauer holds an AB from Harvard College, a PhD in economics from King's College at Cambridge University, and a JD from Georgetown University Law Center. Email: ghufbauer@petersoninstitute.org.

Andreja Jaklič is Associate Professor and researcher at the Center of International Relations at the Faculty of Social Sciences, University of Ljubljana where her teaching and research focus on internationalization, foreign direct investment, multinational enterprises, and their effects on growth, productivity, and innovation. She has been involved in several international research projects, consulting to international organizations such as UNCTAD and the OECD, as well as to national governmental agencies, and business. Her publications include *Enhanced Transition through Outward Internationalization: Outward FDI by Slovenian Firms* (Ashgate Publishing, 2003), coauthored with Marjan Svetličič; several chapters in volumes published by Routledge, Edward Elgar, Palgrave Macmillan, and Ashgate, among others; and articles in *Transnational Corporations*, *The Services Industries Journal*, *Eastern European Economics*, *Economics and Business Review*, *Journal for East Management Studies*, and others. Email: andreja.jaklic@fdv.uni-lj.si.

Kalman Kalotay is Economic Affairs Officer at the Division on Investment and Enterprise of the United Nations Conference on Trade and Development (UNCTAD). He has been a member of UNCTAD's *World Investment Report* team since 1996. He served as deputy editor (2003–2004) and associate (1996–2003) of UNCTAD's *Transnational Corporations* journal. Previously, he worked on issues related to economic cooperation among developing countries in the UNCTAD secretariat (1990–1996). Before joining the United Nations, Mr. Kalotay taught international economics at Corvinus University, Budapest, Hungary (1983–1990). He holds a PhD in international economics from the same university. His current work and publications focus mainly on the analysis of foreign direct investment in various regions, especially in economies in transition.

Henry Loewendahl is senior adviser to the Financial Times Ltd. on foreign direct investment and is one of the leading international authorities on foreign direct investment trends and investment promotion. After completing a Volkswagen-sponsored PhD on German and Japanese investment, he was a corporate strategy consultant at PricewaterhouseCoopers before becoming manager of inward investment in IBM, managing director of OCO Consulting's investment products division, and product director at the Financial Times. He has worked with some 100 IPAs and multinational enterprises and extensively with UNCTAD, the World Bank, and World Association of Investment Promotion Agencies (WAIPA).

Xiongwen Lu is Dean of Fudan University's School of Management where his research is focused primarily on China's immature market, service and internet marketing and enterprise reorganization. He has been Visiting Scholar at Tuck School of Business, Dartmouth College; Sloan School of Management, MIT; and Fisher College of Business, Ohio State University. He has published more than forty papers and has authored and coauthored numerous books, including *Retaking the Economic Center Stage: Transformation and Integration of the Yangtze Delta Economy* (coauthor, Shanghai People's Press, 2007); *Democratic Management*; *Services Marketing in Asia,* second edition (coauthor, Prentice Hall, 2004); and *Corporate Strategic Management* (coauthor, Fudan University Press, 2004). Mr. Lu holds a PhD in economics from Fudan University. He is a member of the board of directors of several leading companies in China and has served as advisor and consultant to many leading multinational enterprises.

Wolfgang A. Maschek is Counsel and Director for International Regulatory Affairs at Western Union International. Until 2006, he served as a representative of the Oesterreichische Nationalbank (Central Bank of Austria) to the European Union in Brussels. He is a graduate of Columbia Law School's LLM program and holds a master's degree in law from the University of Vienna as well as a master's degree in economics from Vienna University of Economics and Business Administration. Email: wolfgang.maschek@gmail.com.

Geraldine McAllister is a Visiting Scholar at the Institute for Social and Economic Research and Policy, Columbia University, currently focusing on regulation of the financial sector in the United States. She is coauthor with David Epstein and Sharyn O'Halloran of *Delegation and the Regulation of Finance in the United States Since 1950* (forthcoming). Ms. McAllister has over ten years of business development experience in the emerging markets of East-Central Europe, the CIS, and Middle East. She holds a master's degree in international affairs from Columbia University. Email: gam2116@columbia.edu.

Theodore H. Moran holds the Marcus Wallenberg Chair at the School of Foreign Service, Georgetown University, where he teaches and conducts research at the intersection of international economics, business, foreign affairs, and public policy. He is founder, and serves as Director, of the Landegger Program in International Business Diplomacy there. His most recent books include *Three Threats: An Analytical Framework for the CFIUS Process* (Peterson Institute for International Economics, 2009); *Harnessing Foreign Direct Investment for Development: Policies for Developed and Developing Countries* (Center for Global Development, 2006); and *Does Foreign Direct Investment Promote Development?* (coedited with Magnus Blomstrom and Edward Graham, Institute for International Economics, 2005). Mr. Moran received his PhD from Harvard University in 1971. He is a Non-Resident Fellow at the Institute for International Economics and at the Center for Global Development. He is consultant to the United Nations, to diverse governments in Asia and Latin America, and to the international business and financial communities. Email: morant@georgetown.edu.

Andreas Nölke is Professor of International Political Economy at the Goethe University, Frankfurt, Germany. He has taught at the Universities of Constance, Leipzig, Utrecht, and Amsterdam, and served as consultant for the German Agency for Technical Cooperation (GTZ), the European Commission, and the World Bank. Mr. Nölke is a member of the Amsterdam Research Centre for International Political Economy and leads a European research network on non-

Triad multinational enterprises, together with Heather Taylor. His publications have appeared in journals such as the *Review of International Political Economy, World Politics,* and the *Journal of Common Market Studies.* Email: a.noelke@soz. uni-frankfurt.de.

Anthony O'Sullivan is Head of Private Sector Development Division at the Organisation for Economic Co-operation and Development (OECD) and associate professor at Sciences Po, Paris, France. He started his career as a consultant at Accenture, specializing in mergers and acquisitions and postmerger integration in the pharmaceuticals and fast-moving consumer goods sectors, both in Europe and internationally. Pursuing his work on strategy and M&A, he then joined Michael Porter's Monitor Group, where he also developed his credentials on country competitiveness. Mr. O'Sullivan went on to become a founding partner of Adcore, specializing in due diligences and business creation for high-tech investment funds. Before moving to the OECD in 2005, Mr. O'Sullivan spent three-and-a-half years at A.T. Kearney, as a senior manager in strategy, and as the European representative for the Global Business Policy Council, a leading global think tank on government strategy and country competitiveness. Email: Anthony.OSULLIVAN@oecd.org.

Shameen Prashantham focuses on international strategy at the University of Glasgow Business School's Centre for Internationalisation and Enterprise Research (CIER). He pursues research on the internationalization of smaller, knowledge-intensive firms, particularly in the Bangalore software industry. He also has research interests in strategy-making. His work has been published in *California Management Review* among other journals. He has published *The Internationalization of Small Firms: A Strategic Entrepreneurship Perspective* (London: Routledge, 2008). Email: s.prashantham@lbss.gla.ac.uk.

Jase Ramsey is Professor in Organizational Behavior and International Business at Fundação Dom Cabral (Brazil). Prior to joining Fundação Dom Cabral, he was a professor of Organizational Behavior and Educational Statistics at the University of South Carolina (USA). Mr. Ramsey's research interests are focused on organizational behavior and international business, and he has published several papers in international journals. He received his PhD in management from the University of South Carolina and a master's degree in international management from Thunderbird, The American Graduate School of International Management (United States). Email: jase@fdc.org.br.

Ajit Rangnekar is Dean of the Indian School of Business (ISB) and was Deputy Dean from 2003 to 2009. Before joining the ISB, he was Country Head, for Pricewaterhouse Consulting and then for PwC Consulting, in Hong Kong (China) and the Philippines. He was head of the telecom and entertainment industry consulting practice for PwC in East Asia (China to Indonesia). Mr. Rangnekar has over thirty years of experience in East Asia and India in the areas of business strategy, new business creation, systems implementation, and performance improvement in a variety of industries including telecoms, utilities, energy, chemicals, and shipping in the private and public sectors. He also has extensive operations management experience of business start-ups in the manufacturing, trading, and professional services sector in Hong Kong (China) and India. He holds an undergraduate degree from the Indian Institute of Technology, Bombay, and a postgraduate degree from the Indian Institute of Management, Ahmedabad. Email: Ajit_Rangnekar@isb.edu.

Paulo Resende is Associate Dean for Research and Development, and Professor of Logistics, Transportation and Supply Chain Management at Fundação Dom Cabral, Brazil. He is coordinator of the Center for Logistics and Supply Chain Studies, and coordinator of the master's degree programs of Fundação Dom Cabral and the Catholic University of Minas Gerais, Brazil. Mr. Resende is the author and coauthor of numerous publications, including the most recent edition of the book, *Mejores Practicas de Logistica na America Latina*. He is a consultant to several multinational enterprises and the World Bank in Latin America. Mr. Resende is a Senior Member of the Institute of Transportation Engineers; a member of the Federal Highway Administration (USA); the Supply Chain Council (USA); and the Transportation Research Board (USA). He holds a doctorate in planning and logistics from the University of Illinois at Urbana-Champaign, a master's degree in planning and transportation engineering, Memphis State University, Tennessee, and a degree in civil engineering from Fundação Mineira de Educação e Cultura (FUMEC), Brazil. Email: pauloresende@fdc.org.br.

Alan M. Rugman is Professor of International Business at the Henley Business School of the University of Reading (UK) and the Director of Research in the School of Management. Previously he held the L. Leslie Waters Chair of International Business at the Kelley School of Business, Indiana University, 2001–2009. Mr. Rugman has published widely: his recent books include *Inside the Multinationals* (reissued by Palgrave Macmillan on its 25th anniversary in 2006); *The Regional Multinationals* (Cambridge University Press, 2005), and *Regional Aspects of Multinationality and Performance* (Elsevier, 2007). He has served as a consultant to major private sector companies, research institutes, and government agencies, and as an outside advisor on free trade, foreign investment, and international competitiveness to two Canadian prime ministers. From 2004 to 2006, Mr. Rugman served as President of the Academy of International Business (AIB). Email: a.rugman@henley.reading.ac.uk.

Huaichuan Rui is Senior Lecturer of International Business and Strategy at Royal Holloway, University of London, and Research Team Member of the "China Africa Leadership Programme," University of Cambridge, and of the "Political Economy of Global Energy Market," Stanford University. She has conducted extensive research on the global strategies of multinational firms and their impact on development. Since 2005, she has conducted pioneering research on China's investments in Africa, including fieldwork in Sudan in 2008. Ms. Rui has been invited to present her research findings at institutions such as the United Nations. She has published a dozen books and papers, including *Chinese Multinationals: The Resource Sector* (Routledge, December 2010), which analyzes the strategy and behavior of the ten most important Chinese multinational enterprises. Her current research projects include "Strategic Intent of Chinese Multinationals," "How the EU and China Work Together towards Africa," and "Chinese Investment and Poverty Reduction in Africa: Focus on Natural Resources." Email: Huaichuan.Rui@rhul.ac.uk.

Jeffrey D. Sachs is the Director of The Earth Institute, Quetelet Professor of Sustainable Development, and Professor of Health Policy and Management at Columbia University. He is also Special Advisor to United Nations Secretary-General Ban Ki-moon. From 2002 to 2006, he was Director of the UN Millennium Project and Special Advisor to United Nations Secretary-General

Kofi Annan on the Millennium Development Goals, the internationally agreed goals to reduce extreme poverty, disease, and hunger by the year 2015. Mr. Sachs is also President and Cofounder of Millennium Promise Alliance, a nonprofit organization aimed at ending extreme global poverty. He is author of hundreds of scholarly articles and many books, including the *New York Times* bestsellers *Common Wealth: Economics for a Crowded Planet* (Penguin, 2008) and *The End of Poverty* (Penguin, 2005). Prior to joining Columbia, he spent over twenty years at Harvard University, most recently as Director of the Center for International Development. A native of Detroit, Michigan, Mr. Sachs received his BA, MA, and PhD from Harvard. Email: cpaladines@ei.columbia.edu.

Karl P. Sauvant is the Founding Executive Director of the Vale Columbia Center on Sustainable International Investment, Lecturer in Law at Columbia Law School, and Codirector of the Millennium Cities Initiative. He is also Guest Professor at Nankai University, China. Until 2005, he was Director of UNCTAD's Investment Division, where he created (in 1991) the annual United Nations publication *World Investment Report,* of which he was the lead author until 2004, and (in 1992) the journal *Transnational Corporations,* serving as its editor until 2005. He provided intellectual leadership and guidance to a series of twenty-five monographs on key issues related to the international investment agreements (which were published in 2004/2005 in three volumes), and he edited (together with John Dunning) a twenty-volume *Library on Transnational Corporations* (Routledge). Mr. Sauvant received his PhD from the University of Pennsylvania. Email: Karl.Sauvant@law.columbia.edu.

David M. Schizer is Dean of Columbia Law School and the Lucy G. Moses Professor of Law. Prior to his appointment, he served as the Wilbur H. Friedman Professor of Tax Law at Columbia Law School, where students awarded him the Willis L.M. Reese Prize for Excellence in Teaching. Prior to joining the Columbia Law faculty in 1998, he worked at Davis Polk & Wardwell. He clerked for U.S. Supreme Court Associate Justice Ruth Bader Ginsburg for the 1994–1995 term, and for Judge Alex Kozinski of the U.S. Court of Appeals for the Ninth Circuit for the 1993–1994 term. Mr. Schizer serves on two corporate boards, the Tax Club, the Tax Forum, and on the executive committee and as cochair of the Committee on Financial Institutions, N.Y. State Bar Association Tax Section. He has written more than twenty-five books and articles on taxation, financial instruments, and regulation. He is a graduate of Yale University where he earned his BA, MA, and JD degrees. Email: dschiz@law.columbia.edu.

Marjan Svetličič is Professor and Head of the Center for International Relations at the Faculty of Social Sciences, University of Ljubljana. He is Vice President of the EU FP7 Advisory Group for International Scientific Cooperation and a Fellow of the European Academy of International Business (EIBA). In 2000, he received the award of "Ambassador of Science of the Republic of Slovenia." Mr. Svetličič has been Dean of the Faculty of Social Sciences, University of Ljubljana; President of EIBA; and a member of the Steering Committee of the Standing Group of the European Consortium for Political Research (ECPR). His publications include *Enhanced Transition through Outward Internationalization: Outward FDI by Slovenian Firms* (Ashgate Publishing, 2003), coauthored with Andreja Jaklič; *Facilitating Transition by Internationalization: Outward Direct Investment from the Central European Economies in Transition* (Ashgate Publishing, 2003), coedited with Matija Rojec; and *Small Countries in a Global*

Economy (Palgrave, St. Martin's Press, 2001), coedited with Dominick Salvatore and Jože P. Damijan. Email: Marjan.Svetlicic@fdc.uni-lj.si.

Heather Taylor is Research Associate at the Goethe University, Frankfurt, Germany, specializing in International Political Economy, and focusing on the impact on work systems and industrial relations of the postacquisition strategies of Indian multinational enterprises. Ms. Taylor's publications include several chapters in volumes and journal articles on this subject. Recently, she completed a research fellowship at the Sardar Patel Institute for Economic Research, India, and has also worked with the Friedrich Ebert Foundation, Germany. With Andreas Nölke, she is co-organizer of a European research network on non-Triad multinational enterprises. Email: taylor@soz.uni-frankfurt.de.

Stephen Thomsen is Senior Economist at the OECD Directorate for Financial and Enterprise Affairs. He has worked as a consultant based in France and as a Research Fellow at Chatham House in London. He has published widely on foreign direct investment, with particular emphasis on its impact on economic integration and development and its relationship with trade. In addition to several books, articles have appeared in such journals as the *Columbia Journal of World Business, Foreign Policy, Harvard International Review, International Affairs, International Investment Perspectives, Journal of Common Market Studies,* and *The World Economy.* Mr. Thomsen holds a doctorate in international economics from the Graduate Institute of International Affairs, Geneva, Switzerland. Email: stephen.thomsen@oecd.org.

Daniël Van Den Bulcke is Emeritus Professor of International Management and Development at the University of Antwerp, Belgium. He was Director of the Centre of International Management and Development Antwerp (CIMDA) from 1989 to 2006, and President of the Institute of Development Policy and Management from 1996 to 2000. Mr. Van Den Bulcke has lectured and served as Visiting Professor at numerous academic institutions in Belgium, Europe, Asia, and South America. He is the author and coauthor of many books and articles on foreign direct investment issues and the activities of multinational enterprises in Europe and Asia, especially China. He has participated in research projects for numerous international organizations. Mr. Van Den Bulcke was Chairperson of the European International Business Academy (EIBA), as well as President. He has served as Chairperson of the Western European Region of the Academy of International Business (AIB) and was Vice President between 2000 and 2004. He was elected Fellow of AIB in 1992 and of EIBA in 2003. Since 2002 Mr. Van Den Bulcke has served as Vice President of Global Knowledge Forum (New Delhi, India). He holds a PhD and a BA in economics from Ghent University, Belgium, and an MA in international economics from the University of Toronto. Email: daniel.vandenbulcke@ua.ac.be.

Rob van Tulder is Professor of International Business-Society Management at Rotterdam School of Management, Erasmus University. He is coordinator of the ERIM research project "International Business-Society Management," and the SCOPE databank project, which, in collaboration with UNCTAD, compiles the listings of the world's largest multinational enterprises from developed and developing countries. Mr. van Tulder is cofounder of the Expert Centre on Sustainable Business and Development Cooperation and rotating chair of the Department of Business-Society Management. Mr. van Tulder's latest publications include: *Skill Sheets: An Integrated Approach to Research, Study and Management* (fifth revised edition, Pearson, 2007); *International Business-Society Management: Linking Corporate Responsibility and Globalisation* (Routledge, 2006).

Hinrich Voss is a Research Councils UK Academic Research Fellow on "Future Energies and the MNE" at the Centre for International Business at the University of Leeds (CIBUL). His research is organized around the questions of how the business strategies of multinational enterprises from developed and developing countries are affected by climate change policies; how they adapt their international business configuration; and how they help to distribute clean technologies globally. He is also conducting research on the internationalization and the international competitiveness of mainland Chinese companies. This research strand incorporates the influence of China's institutions on the international investment behavior of Chinese firms. Mr. Voss holds a PhD from the University of Leeds. Email: H.Voss@leeds.ac.uk.

Qiuzhi Xue is Associate Dean and Citibank Professor of International Business at Fudan University's School of Management. He has been Visiting Professor at several universities, including Sloan School of Management, MIT (USA); McMaster University (Canada); University of Zurich; and City University (Hong Kong [China]). Mr. Xue's research interests include the organization and management of multinational enterprise and the marketing behavior of multinational corporations in China. He advises several leading Chinese and international companies, particularly in areas relating to his current research, serving both as a board member and as a consultant and management advisor. Mr. Xue's book publications include *Behavioral Economics: Theory and Application* (with Peiyan Huang, Zhi Lu, Xiaorang Zhang, Fudan University Press, 2003); *Managing International Banking* (with Fie Yang, Fudan University Press, 2002); *Multinational Enterprises in the Chinese Market,* (Shanghai People's Publishing House, 2001); *International Marketing Management* (with Weijia Shen, Fudan University Press, 1999); *Boundary-less Business,*(Shanghai Translation Publishing House, 1999); and *Chinese Enterprise Overseas Financing,* (Shanghai Foreign Language Education Press, 1997). He has authored and coauthored more than eighty chapters and articles in professional books and journals and has been awarded numerous research grants from such institutions as the National Research Fund. Email: qzxue@fudan.edu.cn.

George S. Yip is Dean of Rotterdam School of Management, Erasmus University, one of Europe's top business schools. He is a Fellow of the Advanced Institute of Management Research (U.K.); the Academy of International Business; and the International Academy of Management. He has been a Professor at the University of Cambridge, London Business School, and UCLA, and has held visiting professor and other positions at numerous institutions including Harvard, Stanford, the University of Oxford, and the China-Europe International Business School. His extensive business experience includes being Vice President and Director of Research & Innovation at Capgemini Consulting. Mr. Yip's books include *Managing Global Customers* (Oxford University Press, 2007), *Total Global Strategy* (Prentice Hall, 1992, 2003) and *Asian Advantage* (Addison Wesley/Perseus Books, 1998, 2000), and he has published numerous journal articles. Email: gyip@rsm.nl.

Overview

Chapter 1

Foreign Direct Investment by Emerging Market Multinational Enterprises, the Impact of the Financial Crisis and Recession, and Challenges Ahead

*Karl P. Sauvant, Wolfgang A. Maschek, and Geraldine McAllister**

Introduction

The global market for foreign direct investment (FDI) has undergone significant changes in recent years, with the increasingly important role played by emerging market multinational enterprises (MNEs) being one of the most important among them. While outward FDI (OFDI) from these countries, in itself, is not new, the magnitude that this development has achieved has raised a host of issues, which we will examine in this volume. This opening chapter presents the factual background of this phenomenon, the impact of the financial crisis and recession on FDI flows, and the issues and challenges related to emerging markets' high FDI flows.

1.1 The Rise of Emerging Market Foreign Direct Investment in Context

1.1.1 The Rise of Global OFDI Flows

The rise of global OFDI over the past three decades has been remarkable. Since 1980–1985, when global OFDI flows averaged roughly US$50 billion per year, OFDI flows have grown by a factor of forty, to surpass US$2.1 trillion in 2007. In 2008, due to the financial crisis and the global economic downturn, global OFDI flows fell by roughly 10% to US$1.9 trillion (figure 1.1 and table 1.1).

Direct investment flows from developed countries'[1] multinational enterprises (defined as firms controlling assets abroad) have grown by roughly 40% on average from 2003 to 2007 (figure 1.1), supported by high economic growth in key host economies and strong corporate performance. In 2008, due to the financial crisis and the global economic downturn, OFDI flows

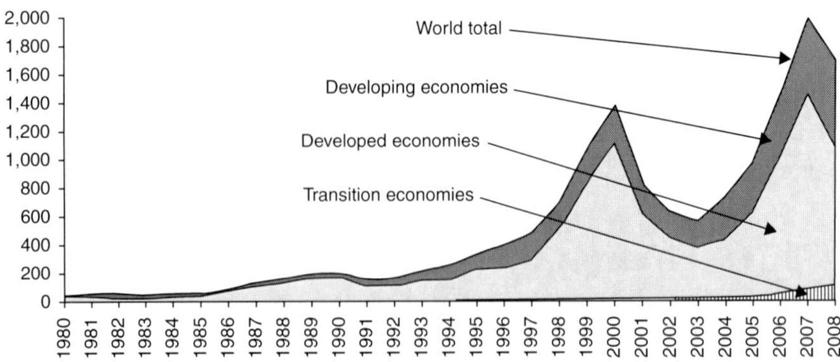

Figure 1.1   FDI outflows, globally and by group of economies, 1980–2008 (US$ billions)
Source: UNCTAD, WIR (2009h).

Table 1.1   FDI outflows and cross-border M&A, by region and major economy, 2007–2008 (US$ billions)

Region/economy	FDI outflows			Cross-border M&A purchases[a]		
	2007	2008	% change	2007	2008	% change
World	**2,146.5**	**1,857.7**	**−13.5%**	**1,031.1**	**673.2**	**−34.7%**
Developed economies	**1,809.5**	**1,506.5**	**−16.7%**	**842.0**	**598.0**	**−29.0%**
Europe	1,270.5	944.5	−25.7%	569.4	333.5	−41.4%
United States	378.4	311.8	−17.6%	179.8	72.3	−59.8%
Japan	73.5	128.0	74.1%	30.4	54.1	78.0%
Developing economies	**285.5**	**292.7**	**2.5%**	**139.7**	**99.8**	**−28.5%**
Africa	10.6	9.3	−12.3%	9.9	8.2	−17.1%
Latin America and the Caribbean	51.7	63.2	22.2%	38.5	2.6	−93.3%
Asia and Oceania	223.1	220.2	−1.3%	91.3	89.0	−2.5%
West Asia	48.3	33.7	−30.3%	37.1	20.5	−44.7%
South, East, and Southeast Asia	174.7	186.5	6.7%	54.2	68.8	26.9%
Transition economies	**51.5**	**58.5**	**13.6%**	**21.7**	**20.6**	**−5.0%**

Source: UNCTAD, WIR (2009g).

[a]Net purchases undertaken by region/economy of the ultimate acquiring company.

from developed countries fell by almost 17% from US$1.8 trillion in 2007 to US$1.5 trillion. Globally, the number of MNEs rose to more than 80,000 in 2007, with more than 800,000 foreign affiliates spread all over the world.

OFDI flows from developed economies, in particular from the European Union (EU) and the United States, represented roughly 84% of total OFDI flows in 2007 and 81% in 2008 (versus 90% between 1995 and 2000). Such investment from developing countries amounted to roughly 12%–13% of total OFDI flows (10%–11% between 1995 and 2000), dominated by Asian MNEs. OFDI flows from transition economies grew strongly and represented 2.4% of total OFDI flows in 2007 and 3.1% in 2008, up from 0.3% on average between 1995 and 2000 (UNCTAD 2008, 2). Roughly two-thirds of global OFDI flows in 2007 were directed toward developed countries, about one-quarter to developing countries (in particular to Asia), and roughly 5% to transition economies.

The global environment for OFDI is changing rapidly. Various "traditional" factors, among them the continuing liberalization of FDI regimes worldwide, competition among firms from all parts of the world, and technological and logistical advancements, influence and support global OFDI flows from both developed and emerging market MNEs. In the future, however, several "nontraditional" factors might additionally shape the FDI landscape, as Jeffrey D. Sachs argues (chapter 2). Sachs looks at the changing FDI landscape from a macroperspective and discusses natural resource constraints and the challenge of sustainable economic growth. The inelastic supply of critical resources—food, oil, metals—has an immediate impact on commodities prices; climate shocks damage the world's food supplies. The scarcity of water and arable land has already led to an increased FDI into the agricultural sector of several developing and least developed countries (see Cotula 2009). Sachs argues that these patterns will become more frequent in the future and will influence the economic determinants of FDI. In order to reconcile the huge global potential for dynamic economic growth with the limited global resource base, new technologies, new forms of cooperation, and new kinds of global arrangements are required.

The dramatic changes in the FDI landscape in the past four decades are the subject of discussion in Yair Aharoni's contribution to this volume (chapter 3). The sectoral composition of global FDI flows has undergone considerable change: while FDI into services made up roughly 25% of global FDI stocks in the early 1970s, services now account for almost two-thirds of global FDI flows. In addition, FDI into the infrastructure sector (e.g., electricity, telecommunication) has been rising strongly. The strong competitive pressures generated by the globalization process force firms to internationalize increasingly early, sometimes already at the moment they are established ("born global"), thereby requiring a revision of the traditional view that firms internationalize gradually and in a sequence that begins with exports. In light of these changes, Aharoni questions whether some of the existing theories that have explained the internationalization process of MNEs are now obsolete.

The rise of global OFDI flows came to a temporary halt in 2008 and 2009, when the financial crisis and the global economic downturn had a negative impact on global FDI flows, in particular on OFDI flows from developed countries. Despite the global downturn, OFDI flows from emerging markets s rose in 2008, albeit marginally (table 1.1), but before declining in 2009 . Given the financial crisis and recession's effects on global FDI flows, section 1.2 of this chapter examines their impact on the FDI flows of both emerging markets and developed countries.

1.1.2 *The Rise of OFDI Flows from Emerging Markets*

OFDI flows from emerging market MNEs (that is, firms from both developing countries and transition economies) have shown particularly dynamic growth rates of roughly 82% on average since 2003, to reach approximately US$351 billion in 2008 (US$293 billion from developing countries and US$58 billion from transition economies). This growth has been driven partly by strong OFDI growth from transition economies, in particular from the Russian Federation (table 1.2).

The regional distribution of emerging market OFDI has undergone considerable change over the past three decades: Asia has overtaken Latin American and the Caribbean to become the dominant region for MNEs engaged in OFDI. While emerging market MNEs have become important investors in many other developing countries, they also increasingly invest in developed countries. Most of this investment is in services, including those that support trade. Natural resources firms, too, are important outward investors.

The overall number of MNEs from developing countries has been rising in line with total OFDI flows: in 2008, UNCTAD counted more than 21,000 MNEs from developing countries and nearly 2,000 from transition economies. This number reflects not only the growing ownership advantages of these firms but also the pressure on firms everywhere to acquire a portfolio of locational assets as a source of international competitiveness. Of the 21,000 MNEs from developing countries, approximately 3,500 were from China, about 1,000 from Russia, 815 from India, and 220 from Brazil (UNCTAD 2009h; Panibratov and Kalotay, forthcoming).[2]

The relatively small number of BRIC[3] country MNEs is also reflected in the list of the twenty largest nonfinancial MNEs from emerging markets by foreign assets for the year 2006 (table 1.3). Only six are from BRIC countries: two from China, two from Brazil, and two from Russia. Out of the "Top 100" nonfinancial MNEs from developing countries, nine hail from China, three from Brazil, and two from India.

A recent feature of OFDI from emerging markets is the involvement of sovereign wealth funds (SWFs). Several Asian, Middle Eastern, and oil-rich

Table 1.2 FDI outflows, by home region and BRIC economy, 1980–2008 (US$ billions)

Region	1980	1990	2000	2001	2002	2003	2004	2005	2006	2007	2008
World	51.5	239.1	1,231.6	751.3	537.4	562.8	920.2	880.8	1,396.9	2,146.5	1,857.7
Developed economies	48.4	227.2	1,093.7	665.7	483.2	507.0	786.0	748.9	1,157.9	1,809.5	1,506.5
Developing economies	3.2	11.9	134.8	82.9	49.6	45.0	120.0	117.6	215.3	285.5	292.7
Brazil	0.4	0.6	2.3	−2.3	2.5	0.2	9.8	2.5	28.2	7.1	20.5
China	–	0.8	0.9	6.9	2.5	2.9	5.5	12.3	21.2	22.5	51.2
India	0.0	0.0	0.5	1.4	1.7	1.9	2.2	3.0	14.3	17.3	17.7
Transition economies	–	0.0	3.2	2.7	4.6	10.7	14.1	14.3	23.7	51.5	58.5
Russian Federation	–	–	3.2	2.5	3.5	9.7	13.8	12.8	23.2	45.9	52.4

Source: UNCTAD, WIR (2009g).

Table 1.3 Top twenty nonfinancial MNEs from emerging markets, ranked by foreign assets, 2006 (US$ millions)

Corporation	Home economy	Industry	Assets		Employment		Number of affiliates	
			Foreign	Total	Foreign	Total	Foreign	Total
Hutchison Whampoa Limited	Hong Kong, China	Diversified	70,679	87,146	182,149	220,000	115	125
Petronas-Petroliam Nasional	Malaysia	Petroleum	30,668	85,201	3,965	33,439	4	78
Samsung Electronics Co.	Republic of Korea	Electrical and electronic equipment	27,011	87,111	29,472	85,813	78	87
Cemex S.A.	Mexico	Nonmetallic mineral products	24,411	29,749	39,505	54,635	493	519
Hyundai Motor Co.	Republic of Korea	Motor vehicles	19,581	76,064	5,093	54,711	19	28
Lukoil	Russia	Oil/gas	18,921	48,237	22,000	148,000	182	…
Singtel Ltd.	Singapore	Telecommunications	18,678	21,288	8,606	19,000	103	108
CITIC Group	China	Diversified	17,623	117,355	18,305	107,340	12	112
Formosa Plastic Group	Taiwan Province of China	Chemicals	16,754	75,760	671,229	89,736	11	12
Jardine Matheson Holdings Ltd.	Hong Kong, China	Diversified	16,704	20,378	58,203	110,125	108	126
LG Corp.	Republic of Korea	Electrical and electronic equipment	15,016	53,915	36,053	7,000	3	12
Vale	Brazil	Mining and quarrying	14,974	60,954	3,982	52,646	17	52
Gazprom	Russia	Oil/gas	10,572	204,228	5,470	432,000	105	…
Petrobas	Brazil	Petroleum	10,454	98,680	7,414	62,266	7	74
China Ocean Shipping (Group) Co.	China	Transport and storage	10,397	18,711	4,432	69,549	245	947
America Movil	Mexico	Telecommunications	8,701	29,473	27,506	39,876	16	33
Petroleos De Venezuela	Venezuela	Petroleum	8,534	60,305	5,373	49,180	30	65
Mobile Telecommunications Co.	Kuwait	Telecommunications	7,968	12,027	975	12,700	37	40
Capitaland Ltd.	Singapore	Real estate	7,781	13,463	16,261	382,000	25	233
Hon Hai Precision Industries	Taiwan Province of China	Electrical and electronic equipment	7,606	19,223	322,372	382,000	82	94

Source: The authors, based on UNCTAD, WIR (2008), 223, and SKOLKOVO-CPII 2008 ranking of Russian multinational enterprises, available at http://www.vcc.columbia.edu/projects/documents/SKOLKOVO-CPIIPressReleaseEnglish_000.

economies, whose foreign currency reserves have risen as a result of high commodity prices and current account surpluses, have pooled part of these reserves in SWFs. The volume of funds under SWF management is estimated to be around US$5 trillion globally (end-2008), of which US$4 trillion are controlled by emerging markets (UNCTAD 2008, 20).

Although FDI via SWFs was negligible in comparison to FDI by other types of investors[4] or the role of state-owned enterprises (SOE) in the OFDI activities of some emerging markets (e.g., China), the negative political reaction to FDI by SWFs—and, for that matter, by SOEs—was considerable.[5] The fear of foreign control over critical domestic infrastructure and strategic industries, and the implications for national security, were at the forefront of a lively discussion. It intensified in 2007 and 2008, when SWFs from Southeast Asia and the Gulf Region bought large portfolio stakes in ailing flagship U.S. and European financial firms such as Morgan Stanley, Merrill Lynch, UBS, and Citigroup, or into U.S. private equity funds such as Blackstone, Carlyle, and Apollo (UNCTAD 2008, 24).

Growing OFDI from emerging market firms, and from BRIC countries' MNEs in particular (section 1.1.3), has given rise to the question of whether these "new kids on the block" are fundamentally different from their developed countries' peers. Part I of this volume ("The Lay of the Land") is devoted to a discussion of the theoretical foundations of emerging market OFDI.

Rob van Tulder (chapter 4) opens the discussion and analyzes emerging market OFDI based on the existing theoretical framework. He finds that the country- and firm-specific advantages of emerging markets do not require the development of a completely new theory, but can be explained by amending existing frameworks (such as the eclectic theory by John H. Dunning and the related concept of the investment development path). Van Tulder even discourages the quest to find an explanation for all emerging market MNEs: given the immense differences in this group, he regards such an endeavor as ill-advised. However, a separate theoretical approach can—and perhaps must—be adopted to explain MNEs from the BRIC countries. Van Tulder identifies and discusses four elements of renewal: the relationship with the *home country government*, the importance of *market power* in the home market, a reappraisal of the impact of *economic size* and its relationship with political power, and a reappraisal of the *general theory of the firm*. He finally refines the *investment development path* with a mesoeconomic layer of analysis in order to explain better OFDI from the BRIC countries.

Alan M. Rugman (chapter 5) takes the discussion a step further and analyzes the firm-specific advantages and disadvantages of emerging market MNEs. In line with van Tulder, Rugman does not support a major change in the existing theoretical framework for FDI. Most country- and firm-specific advantages of, for instance, Chinese or Indian MNEs, can be explained by economies of scale, fueled by the abundance of cheap labor, natural resources, and possibly cheap money. Art Durnev (chapter 6) critically reflects on Rugman's analysis and finds distinct features in some emerging market countries, such as the lack of "soft" financial infrastructure (e.g., credit rating agencies, managerial skills), the nonexistence of appropriate investor protection mechanisms or a lack of transparency (e.g., opaque regulatory and business environment).

1.1.3 OFDI Flows from the BRIC Country Group

The BRIC country group—Brazil, the Russian Federation, India, and China—was one of the driving forces behind the rise of emerging market OFDI flows. With OFDI flows of roughly US$141.7 billion in 2008, this group accounted for approximately 40% of total OFDI flows from emerging markets (table 1.2 above).

Looking at the development of OFDI flows from the BRIC countries since 2000, it is noticeable that Russian MNEs increased their OFDI markedly Russian OFDI stock reached a value of US$255 billion by end-2007, followed by Brazil with roughly US$130 billion, China with approximately US$96 billion, and India with roughly US$30 billion. Part II of this volume is devoted to an analysis of emerging market OFDI from a country perspective, with a particular focus on the BRIC country group ("Gaining Ground: The Expansion of Emerging Market Multinationals").

Brazilian MNEs engaged in OFDI activities in the amount of roughly US$7 billion in 2007, down from the high level reached in 2006 (US$28 billion); the decline was mainly due to one large acquisition undertaken in 2006 (see Lima and de Barros 2009).[6] Preliminary data for 2008 shows an OFDI volume of US$21 billion. Overall, however, OFDI has been rising appreciably in recent years in line with the internationalization plans of Brazilian firms striving for leadership mainly in oil and gas, metal, mining, cement, steel, and food and beverages industries, and helped by the appreciation of the Real (UNCTAD 2008, 60). Paulo Resende et al. (chapter 7) provide a closer look at the transnationalization process of Brazilian MNEs and argue that foreign barriers encouraged OFDI in some sectors (e.g., Brazilian steel companies trying to circumvent target country quota systems). Based on surveys, the authors demonstrate which factors mainly drive the internationalization process of Brazilian MNEs from the executive managements' point of view: better market access, the potential to increase sales internationally, as well as the utilization of economies of scale.

Russian MNEs continued to intensify their OFDI activities, which amounted to US$46 billion in 2007, thereby surpassing the combined OFDI flows from the other three BRIC countries. Data for 2008 shows an OFDI volume of US$52 billion. Russian firms have mainly engaged in resource-seeking FDI projects in pursuit of raw materials and access to strategic commodities. However, they have suffered from a poor image abroad due to the perceived commingling of public and commercial interests. Kalman Kalotay (chapter 8) provides an overview of the main drivers and salient features of Russian OFDI, including its geographical patterns, a panorama of the largest Russian MNEs, and a discussion on the role of government policies (see Panibratov and Kalotay, forthcoming). In his discussion of salient features, Kalotay underlines that Russia, despite its status as a lower-middle-income country, has become a net capital exporter. In fact, several Russian firms, such as Gazprom, Lukoil, Norilsk Nickel, and Severstal, have attained global status. Although Russian MNEs are a heterogeneous group, they do share several commonalities, such as their "leapfrogging" onto the global stage (leveraged by natural resources incomes), their strong link with the natural resources sector, and the strong and growing role of the Russian government.

OFDI by *Indian* MNEs amounted to roughly US$17 billion in 2007, and their OFDI stock represents a value of US$30 billion, approximately 3% of India's gross domestic product (GDP) (see, for example, Pradhan 2009). Data for 2008 show an OFDI volume of US$18 billion. Both OFDI stock and flows are small in comparison with India's BRIC peers, in particular when compared with China and Russia, partly reflecting India's political hesitance to allow OFDI on a larger scale. However, several prominent foreign acquisitions by such Indian firms as the Tata Group, Infosys, and Wipro have brought Indian MNEs into the academic and political limelight. Andreas Nölke and Heather Taylor (chapter 9) analyze OFDI from India in a broader context, distill salient features of this investment, and present the driving forces and enabling conditions behind them. Among the most striking features of Indian MNEs is their preference for mergers and acquisitions (M&As) in the triad region (United States, Western Europe, Japan/Australia). In addition, Indian MNEs have focused their acquisitions on high-tech, knowledge-intensive industries such as pharmaceuticals and information technology services. The authors discuss the liberalization of the Indian OFDI framework in the early 1990s and the role it has played in facilitating Indian OFDI, in particular from industry players that enjoyed regulatory protection and supportive industrial and technological policies.

Chinese OFDI flows have been rising strongly and reached US$23 billion in 2007, thereby adding to the Chinese OFDI stock of US$96 billion. In 2008, they more than doubled to US$51 billion. Driven by strong demand for natural resources, in particular oil, China became an increasingly important source of investment for many resource-rich countries in Africa, Central Asia, and Latin America. In addition, Chinese banks have started to acquire stakes in the financial sector of developed countries.[7] Huaichuan Rui et al. (chapter 10) provide an insight into the motivation, characteristics, and issues of selected Chinese OFDI transactions (acquisition projects of Nanjing Automobile, Lenovo, and Huawei Technology). The authors directly compare these transactions with OFDI projects of Indian competitors (automaker Maruti, IT companies Wipro and Infosys) of these Chinese MNEs in order to distill the key drivers and challenges of these particular acquisitions, based on interviews conducted with the executive management of these firms. Based on the findings concerning the Chinese firms, and the fact that all three had previously formed joint ventures with Western partner firms before engaging in these OFDI transactions, the authors question the current wisdom that allows both partners access to existing knowledge. Also, Chinese firms experience increasingly fierce competition in their "backyard," pushing these firms to internationalize rapidly.

An interesting comparison to the experience of BRIC countries' MNEs is provided in Andreja Jaklič's and Marjan Svetličič's analysis of key features, drivers, and challenges of MNEs from Slovenia (chapter 11), a country that joined the group of developed countries only recently. The authors underline the importance of human resources and managements skills for the success of Slovenia's MNEs, a lack of which can represent a major OFDI constraint. Concerning OFDI barriers, the authors identify various home country as well as internal firm barriers. The late liberalization process and the lack of government support are among the most challenging external barriers. The key internal barriers are related to the "human factor": a lack of management experience and internationalization knowledge. In addition, fast-paced globalization does not allow for an organic approach to deal with these deficiencies.

The BRIC country group shares some common patterns with regard to their OFDI activities. Among the commonalities is the preferred OFDI market entry mode: the country-specific analyses in chapters 7–10 illustrate that all BRIC countries have shown a preference for M&As versus greenfield investments.

However, with regard to a number of other salient features, OFDI from the BRIC countries shows a variety of specific choices, also in comparison to other emerging markets. To begin with, only China and Russia have a substantial SOE involvement in their OFDI. In Russia, the role of the government has been large and growing since 1999; SOEs now account for 26% of total foreign assets held. In China, SOEs account for 80%–90% of the country's OFDI (Cheng and Ma 2007). SOEs also dominate cross-border M&As: out of the fourteen largest foreign investments of Chinese financial institutions, nine were undertaken by state-owned entities. Some studies argue that 75% of all outbound M&A activities from Chinese firms have involved government controlled entities (Deutsche Bank Research 2009b, 34), which seems consistent with the high percentage of state ownership in both financial and nonfinancial corporations.

Moreover, whereas emerging market OFDI has typically followed a South-South investment pattern, Brazil, India, and recently Russia have shown a preference to acquire assets in developed countries, in particular in the United States and Western Europe. The notable exception is China: a majority of the country's OFDI has been directed toward other developing countries. However, the recent rise of Chinese direct investments into developed countries might indicate a change in its previous investment behavior.

No uniform pattern emerges with regard to the sectoral distribution of BRIC country OFDI. Brazil and the Russian Federation have shown a preference for the natural resources sector; China and India have mainly acquired foreign assets in the services sector; and Indian firms target knowledge- and technology-intensive industries, such as pharmaceuticals and automobile and automobile parts.

On the policy side, China's and India's OFDI is supported by the domestic policy framework, whereas no such framework exists yet in Brazil and Russia. Both China and India have adopted "go global" policies at the turn of the century, with noticeable impact on the outward investment strategies of domestic firms. This contrasts sharply with the fact that all four countries have a sophisticated regulatory regime governing inward FDI (IFDI). China's OFDI framework is the most sophisticated among the BRIC countries. Qiuzhi Xue and Bingjie Han (chapter 15) describe its evolution in some detail, from the early 1980s to the current "Going Global" policy framework that explicitly fosters Chinese OFDI. The authors also explain the complex interactions between the main regulatory authorities involved (e.g., the State Council, the Ministry of Commerce, and the State Administration of Foreign Exchange) and thus provide an insight into the approval mechanisms for OFDI transactions in practice.

From an international perspective, the volume of OFDI stock and flows from the BRIC countries remains modest: the BRIC "market share" in global OFDI stock was a mere 3% (US$510 billion) in 2007, and 5% with regard to OFDI flows (US$90 billion)—far below their market share in terms of GDP (Deutsche Bank Research 2009a, 1). Their share of emerging market OFDI total (US$2 trillion) stock was 16% at end-2007, and 15% with regard to total (U$304 billion) OFDI flows.

The catch-up potential for OFDI from the BRIC countries can be gleaned when comparing the OFDI stock to GDP ratios. Whereas developed countries show (on average) an OFDI stock of approximately one-third of GDP, Russia's OFDI stock amounts to roughly 20% of its GDP and Brazil's stock represents 10% of GDP. China's OFDI stock as a percentage of GDP has been growing from 2.5% in 2005 to 3% in 2007. India's OFDI stock grew from a mere 1.2% in 2005 to 2.6% in 2007. China and India thus show the biggest gap, but also catch-up potential, within the BRIC country group.

Despite the negative impact of the current financial crisis and recession on global OFDI flows (see the following section), OFDI flows from emerging markets, including the BRIC countries, are likely to resume their strong growth in the future.

1.2   The Impact of the Financial Crisis and Recession on FDI from Emerging Markets

What is the impact of the 2008–2009 financial meltdown and recession likely to be on FDI outflows from emerging markets? Given the magnitude of the crisis and the impact it is having on worldwide FDI flows (Fujita 2009; Sauvant 2008; UNCTAD 2009a), this issue deserves special attention, as the crisis will invariably affect OFDI from emerging markets as well.

Naturally, the answer to this question has to be speculative, as we are still in the middle of this crisis, and it is not yet known how severe it will be in the end, how long it will last, and how widespread it will be. Any impact works through the three sets of the principal FDI determinants: the economic situation, the regulatory framework for FDI, and investment promotion (UNCTAD 1998).

The most important FDI determinants are the economic factors, once the regulatory framework is enabling for such investment. One of the most critical among these factors is economic growth, as economic growth—or lack of it—influences the demand side for investment and for the goods and services produced by foreign affiliates. In 2009, world output declined by 0.6% (International Monetary Fund 2010, 2). Declining demand discourages investment (domestic and foreign), including by MNEs from emerging markets.

The crisis—and especially the financial crisis with its associated credit crunch—also affects the ability of emerging market firms to invest abroad. Put differently, even if MNEs were not deterred by the deteriorating economic situation in foreign markets, the supply-side for FDI has deteriorated sharply. In particular, the capacity of firms to finance M&As and greenfield investments has declined. Among other reasons, this is the case because international finance is harder to come by due to the credit crunch—a serious bottleneck for firms (e.g., from India) that finance their foreign expansion largely through credits. Declining earnings, weakening balance sheets, and the need for deleveraging accentuate this difficulty. Furthermore, the collapse of the commodity boom empties the coffers of some of the largest emerging market MNEs and hence restricts their ability to expand abroad (although there are some signs of recovery). In fact, a number of emerging market MNEs already had to divest themselves of foreign affiliates or repatriate a larger share of their foreign earnings in order to shore up their balance sheets (see Kalotay 2009; Mortimore and Razo 2009; *PiB* 2009; Pradhan 2009; UNCTAD 2009a).[8] Even sovereign wealth funds have curtailed their investments abroad: because earlier investments performed very poorly,[9] the value of their portfolios declined, the growth of their resources slowed down considerably, suspicion in developed countries regarding direct investments made by them rose,[10] and they need to shore up domestic firms and the domestic economy (see, for example, Setser and Ziemba 2009).

Not all emerging market MNEs, however, will be hamstrung by the current crisis. SOEs in countries with high foreign currency reserves, in particular, remain in a position to expand abroad, the regulatory environments of host countries permitting. Their ability to take a long-term horizon helps in this regard, and the fact that asset prices in a number of potential host counties are low or in distress encourages cross-border M&As (see, for example, Zhan and Ozawa 2001).[11] This factor could be quite important as SOEs account for a significant share of OFDI in a number of emerging markets. In the case of China, such enterprises were responsible for 83% of FDI outflows in 2005 and some 84% of the country's OFDI stock (see Cheng and Ma 2007, 10). Furthermore, future Chinese OFDI finds support in a stable currency value and the availability of domestic liquidity. The appreciation of the Renminbi vis-à-vis the dollar and euro facilitates Chinese acquisitions of dollar- and euro-denominated assets. Chinese domestic liquidity is partly fueled by a US$2 trillion large foreign reserves pool, of which some US$400 billion are under the management of several Chinese SWFs (IFSL Institute 2008).

The worsening economic situation and the unfavorable position in which many emerging market MNEs find themselves may be further complicated by a FDI regulatory framework that is becoming less welcoming worldwide, especially for state-controlled entities from emerging markets. Thus, the percentage of annual changes in FDI laws across the world that went in the direction of making the investment climate less welcoming for MNEs went from 6% during the period 1992–2002 to 12% from 2003–2004 and 21% from 2005–2007 (see UNCTAD 2008). In fact, the share of world FDI flows affected by countries making at least one unfavorable regulatory change during 2006–2007 was 40% (see Sauvant 2009, 239–40). A number of these unfavorable changes involve the increased screening of M&As by state-controlled entities from emerging markets (see Sauvant 2009; Fagan 2010; OECD 2009; UNCTAD 2009c).

In other words, the rise of FDI protectionism may make it more difficult for emerging market MNEs to expand their international production networks. A deepening crisis may well lead to more FDI protectionism[12] and, at least on the margins, discourage OFDI from emerging markets.

Still, the national FDI regulatory framework in virtually all countries remains overwhelmingly favorable. It is further enhanced by a dense network of bilateral investment treaties (BITs) (and double taxation treaties), whose main purpose is to protect foreign investors. By the end of 2008, 37% of the total number of BITs (2,676) had been signed between emerging markets (UNCTAD 2009e).

Moreover, it is quite possible that countries will strive to counteract the forces depressing FDI flows by increasing their investment promotion efforts, including, in particular, by seeking to retain the investments they have already secured. Investment promotion agencies of a number of developed countries, in particular, have already established offices in key emerging markets to attract direct investment from them. Such efforts can help to sustain OFDI flows from emerging markets, but their effectiveness is largely dependent on the nature of the much more powerful economic FDI determinants.

How will these various factors balance each other? Given the dominant importance of the economic FDI determinants, OFDI from emerging markets during at least 2009–2010 will be largely a function of economic growth in important host countries and the ability of emerging market MNEs to finance their own expansion. In 2008, these conditions were still favorable, as reflected in the fact that OFDI from this group of countries remained at the all-time high of US$351 billion, while world FDI outflows declined by 13%. In 2009 (and perhaps in 2010), however, it is most likely that OFDI flows from emerging markets will decline significantly. Global inflows declined by almost 40% in 2009; global outflows may decline by a similar percentage (see UNCTAD 2010; UNCTAD 2009a; UNCTAD 2009b).[13] For the BRICs, the outlook is mixed, judging from data for the first few months of 2009 (table 1.4). In the end, the extent of the decline will mostly be a function of the depth, length, and widespread nature of the economic crisis and associated difficulties, mirroring the decline of FDI flows worldwide.

At the same time, however, this does not change the fact that MNEs from emerging markets have become—and will remain—important players in the

Table 1.4 Outward FDI flows from the BRIC countries, 2008 and 2009 (US$ billions)

Country (Period)	2008	2009	Percent Change
Brazil (January–May)	7.5	0.9	–87
China (January–June)[a]	25.7	12.4	–52
India (January–March)	5.7	4.8	–16
Russia (January–March)	15.8	12.9	–18

Source: EIU database.

[a]Nonfinancial sector.

world FDI market. This in turn raises a number of issues for the host and home countries of emerging market MNEs, several of which are discussed in this volume.

1.3 Global Players from Emerging Markets: Challenges Ahead

The current financial and economic crisis presents significant challenges for emerging market MNEs and governments alike, as section 1.2 detailed. In the short term, the attentions of key actors will doubtless be focused on responding to these challenges. While the current crisis may have changed, at least temporarily, the order of priorities, numerous other challenges, inherent in the rise of these new global players, persist. This section addresses a number of these challenges from the perspective of MNEs, home countries and host countries, and considers the path ahead and the investment promotion, economic and legal challenges that emerging market MNEs should anticipate.

1.3.1 Key Strategy Challenges for Emerging Market MNEs

Perhaps the single most important challenge that emerging market MNEs face relates to their human resources. Building a successful, integrated international production network is a formidable challenge. To do so through the successful integration of acquired firms is an additional challenge. It places considerable demands on their human resources, in particular on their managerial skills and capacity. Moreover, the scale of the challenge is relatively greater for emerging market MNEs: internationalizing often at an early stage in their development, they have had less time to develop such skills and capacities.

Those emerging markets that have a longer and greater experience with OFDI have distinct advantages in this area. As already touched upon in section 1.1.3, Jaklič and Svetličič (chapter 11) underline the importance of human resources in the success of Slovenia's leading MNEs. The fact that most Slovene MNEs are not "transition babies" (chapter 11, 198) has enabled them to develop management skills, expertise, and an understanding of international markets, especially of those of the former Yugoslavia. The authors consider management expertise to have played a crucial role in

OFDI. In particular, familiarity with the western Balkans and the ability to adapt management styles to the particular context and business culture of these markets has been critical to the success of Slovene MNEs. However, a certain lack of mobility among managers, sometimes unwilling to disrupt a comfortable life in their home country to work abroad, threatens the continued success of Slovenian MNEs.

Emerging markets MNEs that have undertaken OFDI more recently are less likely to have built up expertise and capacity in integrating acquisitions and managing foreign affiliates, a gap that may be further compounded by an unwillingness to hire nonnational managers. Resende et al. (chapter 7) highlight the fact that levels of foreign employment among leading Brazilian MNEs are almost half those of the 100 largest developing country MNEs. This low level is the result of a combination of two factors: family-controlled MNEs seeking to avoid any dilution of their control and high levels of "in-group collectivism" (chapter 7, 104). Such limitations in building an international management network do not bode well for the ability of those MNEs to create integrated international production networks.

There are also broader challenges. MNEs face the continuous challenge of balancing opportunities and risks. The rapid pace of globalization and industry consolidation has led in many cases to a mind-set of "hunt or be hunted" (Price Waterhouse Coopers 2007, 5). One illustrative industry in this respect is mining, where record commodity prices facilitated the paying down of debt incurred to pursue acquisitions. Industry players saw consolidation as essential to achieving economies of scale and synergies in operations. Today, however, the dominance of resource based firms in the OFDI of a number of emerging markets brings its own set of challenges, as highlighted for instance by Kalotay (chapter 8, section 8.5): natural-resource-based firms account for four-fifths of the foreign assets of the top twenty-five Russian MNEs, and their rapid expansion took place on the back of high commodity prices. High levels of debt coupled with falling commodity prices make for an uncertain future, in which divestiture and further industry consolidation may be the only options available.

Having developed in riskier political and economic environments, emerging market MNEs' notions of risk can be very different from those of developed countries' MNEs. The greater the level of political risk in the home country, it appears, the greater the tolerance for risk that MNEs develop. The Multilateral Investment Guaranty Agency (MIGA) (chapter 12) outlines the factors that shape perceptions of political risk for "south based" MNEs. These include the location, sector, and size of an investment, as well as the home country environment and the MNEs' experience and history in outward investment. Interestingly, in terms of entry mode, while greenfield investments are considered economically more desirable and less politically risky in developed countries, emerging market MNEs consider them more risky in other emerging markets since "the presence of a domestic partner tends to reduce risk perceptions" (chapter 12, 228).

Corporate social responsibility, the means by which MNEs may balance their increasingly important role in economic development with their growing responsibilities toward the country in which they operate, is another area that presents potential challenges for emerging market MNEs. As George Kell and John Gerard Ruggie stated (1999, 15), "Globalization may be a fact of life, but it remains highly fragile. Embedding global market forces in shared values and institutionalized practices, and bridging the gaps in global governance structures are among the most important challenges faced by policy makers and corporate leaders alike." For the leaders of emerging market MNEs seeking to invest in developed countries, this challenge is potentially even greater. Their ability to adapt to and successfully negotiate the cultural references, standards, and practices of developed markets is critical to their success in these markets—and may ultimately have spillover effects in the home country, leading, in the longer term, to harmonization of standards upward.

1.3.2   Challenges for Home Country Policies

Today, while the landscape of home country OFDI policies is very uneven, the vast majority of emerging markets do not provide a supportive environment for the OFDI activities of their firms, placing them at a competitive disadvantage vis-à-vis their developed country counterparts. The principal challenge for home country policy in emerging markets is, within the constraints of limited resources and widespread needs, to create an environment and policy framework that supports domestic firms. This framework should enhance their competitiveness, enable them to compete effectively in the global arena and, ultimately, secure the benefits of OFDI for the home country. Certainly, the substantial rise in outward investment from emerging markets is a relatively new phenomenon, and national policy is not written or rewritten overnight. On the one hand, if emerging market firms are disadvantaged by a continued lack of supportive policies, and thus are hampered in their competition on the world market, they may, in extreme cases, shift their base to another country in order to stay competitive. On the other hand, the scope of government action and policy-making is constrained by economic reality—limited resources, scarce foreign reserves, and potential concerns over the export of capital and jobs.

The lack of a supportive policy framework in developing countries stands in contrast to developed countries, which have built an extensive and comprehensive policy framework over decades, policies that have evolved in tandem with, and complement, their economic situation. The result has been a gradual but persistent shift in home country policy from restricting and controlling OFDI, to permitting it, and finally to promoting OFDI actively, reflecting the recognition that, in a global market, firms must be globally competitive, with OFDI being one source of such competitiveness.

The experience of developed countries in building a policy framework for OFDI offers lessons for policy makers in developing countries. Peter Buckley et al. (chapter 13) examine this question. In the aftermath of World War II, early restrictions on OFDI focused on capital and foreign exchange controls. Gradually phased out by the early 1980s, these controls were finally eliminated as a global capital market became reality. From restrictions on OFDI, developed countries adapted policies to shape and, ultimately, promote OFDI. The authors group these measures into seven categories: "(i) the provision of information and technical support, (ii) financial support, (iii) fiscal incentives, (iv) investment insurance and guaranteed, (v) support of national champions, (vi) international investment related concordats and agreements, and (vii) official development assistance (ODA) programs" (chapter 13, 262). However, as the authors note, even with a detailed understanding of the policies implemented in developed countries, challenges remain for emerging markets. While the lack of a clear policy framework leaves domestic firms at a competitive disadvantage, changing the situation is not without its own challenges, given the lack of domestic experience and competence in this area, the risks of regulatory capture, and the absence of a significant social safety net. Importantly, the authors note that "[i]n many respects, the lessons for emerging markets are…less in terms of policy and more in terms of management and other types of human capital augmentation at home" (chapter 13, 271).

Information on the experiences of developed countries and the different policy options available is useful for emerging markets, but how applicable is it? Furthermore, even with this information, the challenge of sequencing shifts in policy remains. Filip De Beule and Daniël Van Den Bulcke (chapter 14) address the challenge that such shifts present for emerging markets, acknowledging that the fact that emerging market MNEs may be "born global" or may skip stages of development and internationalization does nothing to lessen the complexity of the policy makers' task. Despite greater access to global capital markets and the reduced importance of capital controls, for instance, emerging markets must still address real concerns over capital flight. They must try to minimize the undue influence of firms whose close links with government allow them to shape policy to their advantage. Overall, rapid globalization and the early internationalization of emerging market MNEs render redundant some of the policy lessons from developed countries. It seems likely that emerging markets, rather than moving neatly from one distinct phase to the next on the "restriction-permission-promotion" scale will instead combine elements of policy from different stages, the selective promotion of OFDI, for example, with retaining elements of control.

China is an example of how one particularly important emerging market has addressed the challenges for home country policy and, in particular, the shift from OFDI restriction to promotion. Qiuzhi Xue and Bingjie Han (chapter 15) offer a detailed examination of the nature and evolution of China's government policy. China's OFDI policy has evolved in three phases from 1984 to 2008. Adopted largely out of economic necessity in 1984, early policy involved strict controls on OFDI: from project approval by the National Planning Commission or State Council to limits on project value and the repatriation of all foreign profits. By 1991, the domestic policy environment had liberalized gradually, and OFDI's role in economic growth was endorsed. From 1991, OFDI policy focused on large SOEs, which, under close government supervision, became the primary actors in Chinese OFDI. Even though capital and currency controls were slightly loosened, the government delineated the areas of foreign activity, with approval required for all projects above

US$1 million. In 2000, funds were established to encourage the internationalization of small and medium-sized firms. The year 2000 also saw the unveiling of China's "Going Global" policy and the differentiation of OFDI policies into policies of regulation, guidance, and support. This involved the simplification of the approval process; an increase in the threshold value of projects for which approval was required; the dissemination of information on investment projects; the development of government guidelines; and the dissemination of information on problems previously experienced. China offers a particularly interesting example: it embraced "Open-Door" policies only three decades ago but, in a relatively short period, OFDI flows have grown considerably, from only US$44 million in 1982 to US$51 billion in 2008. Furthermore, the prominent role of SOEs in the Chinese economy and the country's OFDI allows the government a degree of direct influence, impossible for most other national policy makers. Yet, despite the highly structured process and policies in place in China, the authors acknowledge that this remains a "trial and error path" (chapter 15, 318).

The term "emerging markets," the grouping together of developing countries and transition economies, risks giving the impression, falsely, of a homogenous group of countries. It should also remind us of the limitations inherent in any attempt to construct one policy framework that fits all emerging markets. The key to successful policy is to ensure that it is appropriate to the stage of development of the national economy. In the case of South-South OFDI, policies adopted include the creation of dedicated Export-Import (EXIM) banks and development finance institutions (DFIs). In 2006, a "Global Network of Export-Import Banks and Development Finance Institutions" was launched "…to boost agreements between developing-country EXIM Banks and DFIs to reduce costs of trade between the world's poorer nations…spur cross-border investment, make financing more readily available to new and innovative business …" (UNCTAD 2006, 218). Moreover, in many cases South-South investments enjoy preferential treatment, and the cost of doing business is reduced with the provision of political risk insurance through MIGA.

Until recently, the challenges presented by political risk have been viewed largely in the context of MNEs from developed countries investing in emerging markets. MIGA (chapter 12), presents the results of recent surveys undertaken in this regard. Interestingly, whilst most actors anticipate an increase in political risk in the years ahead and, in the case of investments in developing countries, consider political risk to be a greater challenge than economic risk, the reverse holds true for MNEs from emerging markets: these are more concerned with economic factors, such as exchange-rate risk. Fortunately, governments, alone or in conjunction with the private sector, possess the ability to minimize the impact of political risk on investment decisions through the provision of insurance, a policy tool that should become an increasingly important element of home country policy in emerging markets. For home countries, this raises the question of whether they should offer their own insurance schemes for OFDI, to complement what MIGA offers (and similar to what most developed countries and China do).

Where national champions or SOEs from emerging markets undertake OFDI, this poses potential political challenges for the home country as much as for the host country. Whilst a relatively small share of total OFDI in most emerging markets, as SOEs move abroad and "grow up," they will seek greater independence in determining their own economic future, free from political constraints. Harry G. Broadman (chapter 16) addresses the quandary for home country policy makers of retaining control without hindering the competitiveness of the MNE. He surmises that, as they mature, emerging market MNEs will seek to define objectives and strategy based on economic rather than political considerations. The question of how the home country will respond remains unanswered. Moreover, should state and business interests diverge, the role to be played by public opinion—on which little information is available today—remains unclear. Broadman does offer some evidence of public resistance to the outward investment activities of emerging markets. This suggests that concerns over the export of jobs not only outweigh notions of "national victories," but are as relevant in emerging markets as in developed countries—something policy makers will find increasingly difficult to ignore.

1.3.3 Challenges for Host Country Policies

The rise of outward investment from emerging markets presents its own set of challenges for host country policies, the greatest of which is increasing FDI protectionism, particularly in the case of emerging markets MNEs making acquisitions in developed countries. That the firms being acquired may be deemed to be part of a "strategic sector," thereby raising concerns over national security, and the acquiring firm is a state-owned enterprise or a sovereign wealth fund, only amplifies host country concerns. Host country apprehension—founded or not—that certain acquisitions are driven by political rather than commercial concerns will do nothing to reduce levels of protectionism. Unchecked, this rise in protectionism could inflict damage on the continued integration and smooth functioning of the global economy. Protectionism on the part of developed countries, the main proponents of liberalization, as a response to the emergence of new players would smack of hypocrisy and would deprive host (developed) economies of the widely recognized benefits of FDI. Restricting the access of these new players to developed markets would deny their firms vital access to new skills, technologies, and markets, and, ultimately, would deny opportunities for growth and development—both for the firm and the home economy.

The theory of FDI states that, through positive spillovers and backward linkages, FDI is an important means by which host countries acquire, for instance, technological assets, new management techniques, and skills (see UNCTAD 2001). FDI may improve overall efficiency and, through exports, facilitate entry into new markets. In short, FDI is the "passport" into the international division of production, which can improve the economic performance and competitiveness of the host country and indigenous firms. These are all considerations of particular importance to developing countries when it comes to admitting emerging market MNEs.

In light of ever-stronger competition for reduced FDI flows globally, however, there is concern that host countries will be tempted to lower regulatory standards and increase financial and fiscal incentives. Policy makers and decision makers, however, must use such scarce resources prudently, carefully focusing on sectors that could benefit most from FDI. The extent to which a host country can secure benefits depends on the type of FDI it receives, its level of development, its absorptive capacity, and, finally, host country policies. The promotion of FDI and the financial and fiscal incentives offered should be carefully measured against investments in training and building the necessary skill sets, capabilities, capacity, and infrastructure in the host country.

In spite of the broad acceptance of the benefits of FDI by all actors, economic nationalism is increasingly apparent in host country policies, most visibly in the broader use of the term "strategic assets" and in the decision by more countries to introduce U.S.-style approval bodies.[14] The rise of global players from emerging markets—the "new kids on the block" or "global upstarts"—is likely only to feed this trend: where foreignness is considered a liability, they are viewed as even more foreign.

Judith Clifton and Daniel Díaz-Fuentez (chapter 17) consider the response of the EU to the rise of outward investment from emerging markets. They find that resistance is not limited to FDI originating in emerging markets: individual EU members are showing themselves to be equally resistant to certain investment from other EU markets and to pressure from the European Commission to continue liberalization. This resistance stems from a reluctance to liberalize investment in sectors in which "national champions" play a role, as these are often deemed to serve political economy and national welfare purposes. Despite this resistance and differences between the degree of openness of individual member states and across sectors, the EU has one of the world's most open investment regimes. Complicating the situation is the fact that national security policies, established at the national level, stand alongside single-market policies developed and monitored at the level of the EU institutions. The current economic downturn is likely to delay further harmonization of policy and policy-making.

The rapid rise in OFDI from China in the past decade and the dominant role played by SOEs in this outward investment represents a challenge to host country policy, especially for the United States. China is the U.S. government's largest creditor; it holds approximately US$1.5 trillion in dollar assets and has total foreign reserves of at least US$2 trillion. In the ten years to end-2007, China has invested almost US$79 billion abroad (http://stats. unctad.org/FDI/), and nowhere has this generated more debate and discussion than in the United States. The fact that the vehicle of choice for most of this OFDI has been mergers and acquisitions only exacerbates tensions. As Karl P. Sauvant explains (chapter 18), policy in the United States has become more cautious in recent years, especially with regard to Chinese firms. National security concerns play a more important role in shaping this policy, fed by fears that Chinese investment decisions are driven as much by strategic and political motivations as by economic motivations. This situation is not completely new, however. Japanese investment once stirred up similar fears, which were successfully allayed when Japanese firms worked closely with the different stakeholders in order to become "insiders" (Milhaupt, 2010).

The need to address and allay concerns that feed growing economic nationalism and FDI protectionism is not limited to MNEs, home and host country governments: this situation highlights the important role that international organizations must play if the international investment regime is to remain relatively open, transparent, and stable. Critics of FDI frequently speak of a race to the bottom in terms of national standards, taxation regimes, et cetera, and a race to the top in terms of financial and fiscal incentives, all to the detriment of the host country (Dorgan and Brown 2006). These voices have become louder with the current financial and economic crisis as competition for FDI flows has become stiffer. (See, for example, the Statement by Supachai Panitchpakdi, Secretary-General of UNCTAD, May 4, 2009f.) (Contradictory as it may appear, we are witnessing an increase in economic protectionism at the same time as countries compete ever more fiercely for declining FDI flows.) With the rise of global players from emerging markets, FDI's critics add that emerging markets will apply their lower domestic standards in the host country to the detriment of workers, local firms, and the environment (Dorgan and Brown 2006). Whilst this argument is refuted by those (Fletcher 1999) who claim it is merely sophisticated protectionism, it is evident that an international framework, establishing best practices and minimum standards, and bringing greater transparency to the now truly international investment regime, is to the benefit of all actors.

Anthony O'Sullivan (chapter 19) considers how trust can be returned to the international investment regime, and looks at the facilitating role that the Organisation for Economic Co-operation and Development (OECD) can play. He outlines proposals that would ensure that "freedom of investment" is the case in all countries and for all firms, in order for the potential benefits of FDI to become a reality. These steps include the use of the OECD's forum for intergovernmental dialogue, which seeks to reconcile continued freedom of investment with concerns over national security, by OECD members and nonmembers alike. Foreign investment that makes, and is seen to make, consequential economic contributions in the form of, among other things, employment, innovation, and value added, will reduce support for economic nationalism. However, if the OECD is to retain credibility within emerging markets and successfully to engage global players from emerging markets, it must seek greater involvement of emerging markets in the evolution of policy instruments and agreements.

1.3.4 *The Path Ahead*

Twenty years ago, outward investment from developing countries accounted for less than 5% of total outward investment (table 1.2). The Soviet Union had just reintroduced the right of private ownership in an attempt to stimulate its economy. A decade later, the Asian financial crisis devastated economies across the region and beyond. Today, as global players from emerging markets appear on the world stage, the world is suffering another financial and economic crisis. Looking ahead, what are the challenges facing FDI and the main actors in this process? Will the current economic downturn require the main players simply to ride out this crisis, with normal business resuming as soon as possible? Alternatively, will the combination of the rise of global players from emerging markets and the current financial downturn require that the rules of FDI be rewritten?

Securing inward investment at a time of decreasing FDI flows and increasing competition for these flows represents a significant challenge for investment promotion agencies (IPAs). Significant as they are, these are not, however the only challenges facing IPAs. As discussed in section 1.1, an ever-greater share of FDI flows now comes from markets in which IPAs have had little experience to date, and this at a time when IPAs face budget and resource constraints. As if this did not render the task at hand sufficiently complicated, Henry Loewendahl (chapter 20) identifies additional challenges for IPAs in the changing global economy. IPAs must broaden their focus from greenfield investments to include also strategies for attracting and integrating M&As as well as joint ventures, alliances, and partnerships. In terms of potential sources of funding and backing of FDI, IPAs should also revise their strategies to incorporate the increasingly important role of sovereign wealth funds and the diaspora—especially important with regard to India and China. Finally, identifying and exploiting growth sectors remain as important as ever, albeit more difficult in an economic recession, when investment and research and development spending is often cut back.

The growing importance of OFDI from emerging markets not only increases competition, it also changes the very nature of this competition. Gary Hufbauer and Matthew Adler (chapter 21) underline some of the immediate effects that this new competition will have on other markets, both emerging and developed. Lower costs and lower taxes can no longer be the key selling points for host countries seeking to secure FDI from emerging markets, in a situation in which MNEs already enjoy low costs and low taxes in their home countries. Moreover, for developed country MNEs, competing directly with emerging market MNEs in acquisitions (and possibly losing) is an unfamiliar situation and, in some cases, has resulted in accusations of "subsidized capital." This may be the case when SOEs and SWFs, whatever their country of origin, are behind an acquisition. But it is difficult to determine how much merit this argument holds; it is even more difficult to prove it and to advance remedial action. It may be that this situation will become more familiar in the years ahead.[15] As FDI grows further in importance, this will contribute to the regular challenges that any phenomenon of this size poses, now and in the future.

On the scale that we see today, emerging markets as sources of investment are relatively new, but FDI itself is not new. It is one of the most important means of transferring technology and know-how around the globe. It dwarfs trade in terms of the sale of goods and services in foreign markets, involving, as it does, more than 800,000 foreign affiliates around the globe. José E. Alvarez (chapter 22) outlines the changing legal framework for investment, including the characterization of emerging market MNEs as more tolerant of risk and, therefore, less demanding of the legal system; increasing political and regulatory risk; the rising number of investor-state investment disputes; and resistance in some quarters to the shape of new investment law. Anticipating the possible impact of this changing legal background, he rejects the notion that a country's legal infrastructure is of limited importance to investors from emerging markets, arguing that it is an integral part of a country's infrastructure and contributes to the predictability with which MNEs can do business there. Furthermore, he suggests that, amongst other changes, the fact that emerging market MNEs internationalize at an earlier stage of their development, will thus do not want to "offend their hosts by filing a formal complaint" (chapter 22, 437), and are less "lawyered up," will make them more likely to follow a conciliation rather than arbitration route. This stands in contrast to the actions of MNEs from the most established home countries, the United States and Western Europe. Despite being long-time proponents of free trade and FDI, the increasing influence of politics on their rule-making risks reversing decades of progress in this area, setting a poor example for new players, and consolidating a recent trend of legislation that restricts, rather than enhances, FDI. At the same time, however, the international investment regime must take into account the interests of all its principal stakeholders if it is to maintain its legitimacy.

Conclusions

This chapter has sought to place the rise of emerging market MNEs in context, examining the role of these new global players in global FDI flows, how this is likely to evolve in light of the current economic downturn, and the challenges inherent in their rise for MNEs themselves as well as for home and host countries. Whatever the tensions and temporary setbacks, the great number of firms undertaking FDI will build an ever more interconnected and integrated international production system. The final chapter (chapter 23), by Stephen Thomsen, looks at many of the same issues related to the emergence of an integrated international production system from a thematic angle, bringing in insights from the discussions at the Conference on which this volume is largely based. In particular, he underlines that OFDI from emerging markets is "different only by degree" (chapter 23, 459)—despite the rapidity of its growth and the fact that many emerging market MNEs lack comprehensive proprietary assets. Furthermore, rather than focusing on differences between emerging market MNEs and their developed country counterparts, it is vital to understand why different emerging market MNEs adopt different approaches to OFDI, as well as their effects.

Thomsen highlights the risks inherent in OFDI unless emerging market MNEs acquire new skills, both organizational and political, and adopt the principles and practices of corporate social responsibility: in short, past progress is no guarantee of continued success. Finally, Thomsen identifies areas in which further research is essential if we are to deepen our understanding of OFDI from emerging markets. These include the effects of the different ownership structures and funding systems and the advantages that such investments can transfer from MNE to host country.

All this, finally, needs to be seen against a basic fact: countries do not look at FDI as an end in itself. Rather, it is seen as a tool to advance their development, be it as a home country or host country. As part of that, FDI is a powerful means to help countries in their integration into the world economy. In addition, economic development through integration into the world economy is one of the means by which countries lift themselves out of poverty. Much progress has been made in recent years (some of this threatened by the current economic and financial crisis), yet much remains to be done—and the greater the number of firms involved in this process the better it is for all of us.

Notes

*The helpful comments of Masataka Fujita and Oleksiy Kononov, and the assistance of Lisa Sachs and Ingrid Bandeira are gratefully acknowledged.

1. According to UNCTAD terminology, the group of "developed economies" comprises the twenty-seven member States of the European Union, plus Australia, Bermuda, Canada, Gibraltar, Iceland, Israel, Japan, New Zealand, Norway, Switzerland, and the United States.

    "Emerging markets" comprise both "developing countries" and "transition economies." The "transition economies" group consists of the six countries of Southeast Europe (Albania, Bosnia and Herzegovina, Croatia, The FYR of Macedonia, Montenegro, and Serbia) as well as the twelve countries of the Commonwealth of Independent States (CIS): Armenia, Azerbaijan, Belarus, Georgia, Kazakhstan, Kyrgyzstan, the Republic of Moldova, Russian Federation, Tajikistan, Turkmenistan, Ukraine, and Uzbekistan. All other countries are "developing countries."

2. See also the overview of the twenty-five largest Russian MNEs compiled by the Skolkovo Moscow School of Management and the Vale Columbia Center, available at http://www.vcc.columbia.edu/documents/2008RussiaRankings—SKOLKOVO.pdf.

3. The BRIC country group comprises Brazil, the Russian Federation, India, and China.

4. According to UNCTAD, SWFs invested US$10 billion in OFDI projects in 2007. Private equity funds invested more than US$460 billion in OFDI projects during the same year (UNCTAD 2008, 20).

5. For a discussion, see Sauvant (2009). But this negative reaction has abated in light of the financial crisis and recession; see Fotak and Megginson (2009).

6. Vale acquired Inco, Canada's second largest mining company, for US$18.9 billion in October 2006.

7. For an illustrative list of cross-border M&A deals of Chinese financial institutions, see Deutsche Bank Research (2009b, 34). See also the list of Chinese OFDI transactions in table 10.1 of chapter 10.

8. It is, however, difficult to determine whether a specific divestment is caused by the crisis or is part of the normal course of action as part of a broader corporate strategy.

9. See, for example, the criticisms in the Chinese media of the acquisition of a stake in Blackstone by the Chinese Investment Corporation, *Securities Times*,

October 17, 2008 (http://www.howvc.com/Html/economy/macro/china-road/82605.html).

10. But this may be changing slightly: see Fotak and Megginson (2009).

11. During the Asian financial crisis at the end of the 1990s, a number of MNEs headquartered in developed countries acquired firms in the affected countries, sparking a discussion about fire-sale prices. Looking back at 2008, there are examples of what appeared to be bargain asset purchases, such as the sale of the European and Asian operations of Lehman Brothers to Nomura Holdings, Mitsubishi UFJ Financial Group's investment in Morgan Stanley (UNCTAD 2009a, 32). Even earlier, and at less distressed prices, several (portfolio) investments by SWFs into the U.S. financial sector had taken place, albeit below the 10% equity/voting rights threshold, above which an investment was regarded as the acquisition of "control" and thus subject to screening by the Committee on Foreign Investment in the United States (see Plotkin and Fagan 2009, 2).

12. The Group of 20 recognized this possibility in its Communiqué adopted November 15, 2008 when it called for a one-year moratorium on protectionist measures. See, Group of 20, "Declaration: Summit on Financial Markets and the World Economy," November 15, 2008, athttp://www.globalpolicy.org/images/pdfs/1115g20.pdf This call for a moratorium was repeated in the Group of 20, "The Global Plan for Recovery and Reform," April 2, 2009 (available at http://www.g20.org/Documents/final-communique.pdf). There is also the possibility of OFDI protectionism; i.e., governments of emerging markets restricting or discouraging OFDI by firms from their countries.

13. A survey undertaken by UNCTAD during February–May 2009 (to which 241 responses from firms were received) concluded, among other things, that "Firms are very concerned about the short-term evolution of their business environment. Almost 90% of them are pessimistic or very pessimistic about global FDI prospects for 2009.…About 58% of the respondents reported their intention to reduce their FDI abroad in 2009 compared to 2008, with nearly one-third of them anticipating a large decrease (more than 30%) compared to 2008" (UNCTAD 2009h, 2). For an analysis of FDI prospects based on the number of greenfield projects, see (Loewendahl 2009).

14. Committee on Foreign Investment in the United States (CFIUS).

15. MNEs from developed countries also enjoy various forms of support by their home country governments.

References

Cheng, Leonard K. and Zihui Ma (2007). "China's outward FDI: past and future," available at http://www.nber.org/books_in_progress/china07/cwt07/cheng.pdf, last visited June 23, 2009.

Cotula, Lorenzo (2009). "Land grab or development opportunity? International farmland deals in Africa," *Columbia FDI Perspectives*, No. 8, June 22.

Davies, Kenneth (2009). "While global FDI falls, China's outward FDI doubles," *Columbia FDI Perspectives*, No. 5, May 26.

Davis, G.F., M.v.N. Whitman, and M.N. Zald (2006). "The responsibility paradox: Multinational firms and global corporate social responsibility," University of Michigan, Ross School of Business Working Paper No. 1031, April.

Deutsche Bank Research (2009a). "BRIC outward FDI: the dragon will outpace the jaguar, the tiger and the bear," *Talking Point*, February 9, available at http://www.

dbresearch.com/servlet/reweb2.ReWEB?addmenu=false&document=PROD00
00000000237372&rdLeftMargin=10&rdShowArchivedDocus=true&rwdspl=2
&rwnode=DBR_INTERNET_EN-PROD$NAVIGATION&rwobj=ReDisplay.
Start.class&rwsite=DBR_INTERNET_EN-PROD, last visited June 23, 2009.
——— (2009b). "China's financial markets: a future global force?" *Current Issues,*
March 16, available at http://www.dbresearch.com/PROD/DBR_INTERNET_
EN-PROD/PROD0000000000238901.pdf, last visited June 23, 2009.
Dorgan, Byron and Sherrod Brown (2006) "How free trade hurts," *Washington
Post,* December 23, p. A21, available at http://www.washingtonpost.com/wpdyn/
content/article/2006/12/22/AR2006122201020.html, last visited June 23, 2009.
Economist (2008). "A bigger world: a special report on globalisation," September 20.
——— (2009). "Not quite so SAFE," April 25.
Fagan, David (2010). "The U.S regulatory and institutional framework for FDI," in
Karl P. Sauvant, ed., *Investing in the United States: Is the US Ready for FDI from
China?* (Cheltenham: Edward Elgar).
Fletcher, Susan R. (1999). "Environment and the World Trade Organization (WTO)
at Seattle: issues and concerns," *CRS Report for Congress,* available at http://
ncseonline.org/nle/crsreports/international/inter-46.cfm, last visited June 23,
2009.
Fotak, Veljko and William Megginson (2009). "Are SWFs welcome now?" *Columbia
FDI Perspectives,* No. 9, July 21.
Fujita, Masataka (2009). "Impact of the financial and economic crisis on FDI"
(Geneva: UNCTAD), June 29, mimeo.
International Financial Services London (2008). "Sovereign Wealth Funds
2008," April, available at www.ifsl.org.uk/upload/CBS_Sovereign_Wealth_
Funds_2008.pdf, last visited June 22, 2009.
International Monetary Fund (2010). *World Economic Outlook: Rebalancing Growth*
(Washington, DC: International Monetary Fund).
Kalotay, Kalman (2009). "Take-off and turbulence in the foreign expansion of
Russian multinational enterprises," in Karl P. Sauvant with Wolfgang A. Maschek
and Geraldine McAllister, eds., *Foreign Direct Investment from Emerging Markets:
The Challenges Ahead* (New York: Palgrave Macmillan).
Kell, Georg and JohnG. Ruggie (1999). "Global markets and social legitimacy: the
case of the 'Global Compact,'" available at http://www.unglobalcompact.org/
NewsandEvents/articles_and_papers/global_markets_social_legitimacy_york_
university.html, last visited April 15, 2009.
Lima, Luis Alfonso and Octavio de Barros (2009). "The growth of Brazil's out-
ward investment and the challenges it faces," *Columbia FDI Perspectives,* No. 13,
August 17.
Loewendahl, Henry (2009). "Foreign direct investment landscape 2009–2013:
insights and intelligence from the Financial Times Ltd," February 16 (London:
FDI Intelligence), mimeo.
Milhaupt, Curtis (2010). "Is the U.S. ready for FDI from China? Lessons from Japan's
experiences in the 1980s," in Karl P. Sauvant, ed., *Investing in the United States: Is
the U.S. Ready for FDI from China?* (Cheltenham: Edward Elgar), chapter 7.
Mortimore, Michael and Carlos Razo (2009). "Outward investment by Trans-Latin
enterprises: reasons for optimism," *Columbia FDI Perspectives,* No. 12, August 17.
OECD (2009). "Status report: inventory of investment measures taken between 15
November 2008 and 15 June 2009" (Paris: OECD).
Panibratov, Andrei and Kalman Kalotay (forthcoming). "Outward investment from
Russia and the global crisis," *Columbia FDI Perspectives.*

PiB (2009). "Brazilian enterprises go international: time to trim the sails," 3, May/ June, pp. 20–21.

Plotkin, Mark E. and David N. Fagan (2009). "The revised national security review process for FDI in the US," *Columbia FDI Perspectives*, No. 2, January 7.

Pradhan, Jaya Prakash (2009). "Indian FDI falls amid global economic crisis: Indian multinationals tread cautiously," *Columbia FDI Perspectives*, No. 11, August 17.

Price Waterhouse Coopers (2007). *Mine—Riding the Wave*, available at http:// www.pwc.com/extweb/pwcpublications.nsf/docid/2C084C2F146F2DEFCA2 5731600264F77, last visited June 11, 2009.

Sauvant, Karl P. (2008). "The FDI recession has begun," *Columbia FDI Perspectives*, No.1, November 22.

——— (2009). "Driving and countervailing forces: a rebalancing of national FDI policies?" in Karl P. Sauvant, ed., *Yearbook on International Investment Law & Policy 2008–2009* (New York: Oxford University Press), pp. 215–72.

Setser, Brad and Rachel Ziemba (2009). "GCC sovereign funds: reversal of fortune," Council on Foreign Relations Working Paper, New York.

UNCTAD (1998). *World Investment Report 1998: Trends and Determinants* (Geneva and New York: United Nations).

——— (2001). *World Investment Report 2001: Promoting Linkages* (Geneva and New York: United Nations).

——— (2003). *World Investment Report 2003: FDI Policies for Development: National and International Perspectives* (Geneva and New York: United Nations).

——— (2006). *World Investment Report 2006: FDI from Developing and Transition Economies—Implications for Development* (Geneva and New York: United Nations).

——— (2008). *World Investment Report 2008: Transnational Corporations and the Infrastructure Challenge* (Geneva and New York: United Nations).

——— (2009a). *Assessing the Impact of the Current Financial and Economic Crisis on Global FDI Flows* (Geneva and New York: United Nations), April.

——— (2009b). "Global FDI flows halved in 1st quarter of 2009, UNCTAD data show; prospects remain low for rest of the year," UNCTAD/PRESS/ PR/2009/024 June 24, 2009.

——— (2009c). "Investment policy developments in G-20 Countries" (Geneva and New York: United Nations).

——— (2009d) (WIR database), http://stats.unctad.org/FDI/TableViewer/ tableView.aspx, last visited June 23, 2009.

——— (2009e). "Recent developments in international investment agreements," UNCTAD/WEB/DIAE/IA/2009/8 (Geneva and New York: United Nations).

——— (2009f). "Statements by Supachai Panitchpakdi, Secretary-General of UNCTAD," Investment, Enterprise and Development Commission, May 4, available at http://www.unctad.org/Templates/webflyer.asp?docid=11479&int ItemID=3549&lang=1&print=1, last visited June 23, 2009.

——— (2009g). *World Investment Report 2009: Transnational Corporations, Agricultural Production and Development* (Geneva and New York: United Nations).

——— (2009h). *World Investment Prospects Survey 2009–2011* (Geneva and New York: United Nations).

——— (2010). 'Global and Regional FDI Trends in 2009', UNCTAD Global Investment Trends Monitor, No. 2 (Geneva: United Nations).

Utting, Peter (2003). "Promoting development through corporate social responsibility: prospects and limitations," *Global Future*, Third Quarter (a World Vision publication).

Zhan, James and Terutomo Ozawa (2001). *Business Restructuring in Asia: Cross-Border M&As in the Crisis Period* (Copenhagen: Copenhagen Business School Press).

Chapter 2

Will Natural Resource Constraints Derail Long-Term Global Growth?*

Jeffrey D. Sachs

We are certainly living in turbulent times. At the time of this conference, we discussed the thrilling possibilities for dynamic global development fueled by technological advances. Technology diffuses from one place to the other at lightning speed. The possibility for any place that was unproductive to become productive quickly in five, or ten, or twenty years, is greater than ever before in history, and China serves as an exemplar of this. At the same time, we caught glimmers of the steepest short-term business downturn in recent memory. In my observations, I will keep my eye on the medium term, the next ten to forty years, after we have ridden the waves of the current economic storm.

From a perspective of the past thirty years, China's economic development has simply been remarkable: 1.3 billion people achieving an average economic growth of 10% per year. This means doubling of the Chinese economy roughly every seven years—more than four times within three decades—amounting to around a twentyfold increase from the time that Deng Xiaoping came to power, opened the economy, and legitimized the pursuit of wealth in post-Maoist China. This is a very positive development, and China's role in the world is soaring. China is playing and will play a constructive role in the world in the years to come, even if growth might slow down a bit in light of the financial crisis and the recession. India too has been achieving very rapid growth, not quite as fast as China, but still rapid enough to reduce poverty rates and raise incomes dramatically.

The global economic environment has recently worsened in the wake of the financial crisis and recession, and most discussions deal with the harsh consequences and ways to move out of the crisis quickly and sustainably. The financial crisis and recession have already taken their toll on the foreign direct investment (FDI) activities of multinational enterprises (MNEs) from both emerging markets and developed countries. While FDI flows to developing countries declined by almost 30% in 2008, flows to the larger emerging markets, such as Brazil, China, India, and Russia, continued to increase (UNCTAD 2010b). Initial figures for 2009 indicate that the dramatic 40%

decline in inflows to developed countries is mirrored in emerging markets, where inflows fell by 35% (UNCTAD 2010a). The main problem is that economic growth is a key determinant for attracting FDI and, as the economy slows down, FDI flows are likely to follow this trend.

Until recently, at least, we have seen a booming world economy achieving a growth rate on average of approximately 4% to 5% per year for the 6.8 billion people on the planet, which means a doubling of the global economy in less than twenty years. This is an impressive rate of growth that has brought the world an average output of about US$10,000 per person, measured at purchasing power parities. Growth will slow sharply in the next year or two, but the era of rapid growth is not over, merely in abeyance. We will return soon to rapid catching-up growth in the developing countries.

This positive development, even if it is temporarily derailed by the financial crisis, comes with a tremendous risk for the longer term: because of this dynamism, we are pushing up against the constraints of the physical world as never before. The implications of a global economy of US$70 trillion, weighing on the earth's ecosystems and available resource base, make it clear that resource scarcity and ecosystem degradation threaten us in a number of ways: before the economic downturn set in, the inelastic supply of critical resources—food, oil, and metals—sent commodities prices soaring. Climate shocks impaired the world's food supplies and created major localized crises in hard-hit regions. These are patterns that will become much more frequent in the coming years.

Thus, we face both a huge potential for dynamic economic growth and the challenge of the limited global resource base. Consider the following: to power the US$70 trillion global economy, we are currently emitting thirty billion tons of carbon dioxide every year through fossil fuel use (with a further six billion tons or so from deforestation). We are now increasing the atmospheric concentration of carbon dioxide by more than two parts per million (ppm) each year. Today's concentration of nearly 390 ppm compares with the preindustrial level of 280 ppm. We are likely to breach 400 ppm within a decade, and could easily reach 500 ppm or more by 2050. Yet, climatologists tell us that dangerous climate change is already underway, that carbon concentrations above 350 ppm are already pushing humanity and the earth into uncharted territory, in which climate will change the planet in ways we have not seen during the entire history of the human species. Clearly we are on an unsustainable trajectory.

We will have to find new ways to reconcile global economic growth, especially growth in the emerging markets and in today's poorest countries, with the world's resource base. If the rest of the world catches up to the high income standards of, for instance, the United States, with about US$40,000 per capita, from the current world average of US$10,000 per capita, that would be a fourfold increase. As much as this would be a desirable development, the world could not survive a fourfold increase in carbon emissions to, for example, 120 billion tons each year. Current technologies cannot support such a scale of global economic activity. The earth's ecosystems and key resources (such as conventional oil) simply cannot resist such a multiplication of economic activity if carried out with current technologies.

Even worse, there are places in the world that have not yet been part of economic growth and development at all, and they urgently need to accelerate their economic growth, including their use of global resources. Many places in Africa still have no roads, no electricity, no clinics, and no schools, and children under the age of five are dying at a rate of 200 per thousand. Market forces by themselves will not overcome these deficiencies. There are places that have been trapped in extreme poverty even though the world economy has been growing.

How are we going to power the world economy, find the scarce resources, maintain sufficient political stability, ensure that there is room for everybody in this economy, and not, at the same time, destroy the physical earth in the process? A comprehensive strategy has yet to be plotted out, but we can sketch what such a strategy would include.

Part of the answer is technological advance. We will need substantially more energy from alternative sources. Large-scale solar power plants may be one solution. The total solar radiation hitting the planet is approximately five or six thousand times the current global energy use. If we can make use of a modest part of the incoming solar radiation at costs that are within striking distance of fossil fuels, solar power can become a major part of a new sustainable global energy system. Engineers are indeed confident that they can continue to drive the cost of solar power down far enough that it will substitute for fossil fuels on a large scale.

Another example will be new automobile technologies; for example, plug-in hybrids will greatly conserve increasingly scarce oil by turning to electricity powered by alternative energy sources. Plug-in hybrids should soon achieve 100 or 150 miles per gallon, with the first forty miles or so each day on battery power It is not only the engineering challenges that will determine the uptake of this new technology but also the incentives as determined by public policies. If we do not act in time, we will soon go from around 800 million cars to perhaps 1.5–2 billion cars on the planet based on traditional technologies, adding to the oil squeeze and to environmental destruction. India's new Tata Nano, at a retail price of around US$2,500, is an engineering triumph as well as a warning of the coming explosion of automobile use. Car use will soar. The challenge is to make sure that the cars of the future cut emissions sharply compared to today's automobiles.

Large-scale global technological change—to renewable energy, safe nuclear power, high-mileage automobiles, green buildings, and more—will require an unprecedented degree of global cooperation. Countries around the world will need to adopt fiscal incentives for technological transformation and reduced greenhouse gas emissions. Rich countries will have to share sustainable technologies with poor countries, and will have to finance their uptake in the poorest countries. Such cooperation will have to occur among governments, and between governments and the business sector.

In conclusion, and returning the discussion to FDI, I hope that the new U.S. administration and partner countries will resist the protectionist proposals currently debated in the context of the financial crisis and recession, and honor the international promises made at the G-20 meeting in November

2008 ("Commitment to an Open Global Economy") to keep markets open for FDI, including, in particular, such investments to and from emerging markets. FDI has contributed to global economic growth and prosperity both in the developing and the developed world. FDI will be needed to disseminate a new generation of sustainable technologies. "Turning inward" in times of financial uncertainty and recession would cripple growth and undermine the global cooperation needed to achieve a new era of sustainable development in the coming generation.

Note

*Based on a luncheon speech given on April 29, 2008, at the Five-Diamond International Conference on "Thinking Outward: Global Players from Emerging Markets."

References

UNCTAD (2010a). "Global and Regional FDI Trends in 2009," UNCTAD Global Investment Trends Monitor No. 2 (Geneva: United Nations).
UNCTAD (2010b) (WIR database), http://stats.unctad.org/FDI/TableViewer/tableView.aspx?ReportId=3084, last visited May 7, 2010.

Part One

The Lay of the Land

Chapter 3

Reflections on Multinational Enterprises in a Globally Interdependent World Economy

Yair Aharoni

Introduction

The importance, diversity, and scope of the operations of multinational enterprises (MNEs) in the global economy have grown exponentially. In 1960, the value of worldwide sales of foreign affiliates was about one-half of world exports. By 1982, the worldwide sales of foreign affiliates totaled US$2.7 trillion, roughly comparable to worldwide exports of goods and non-factor services of US$2.4 trillion. By 2007, worldwide affiliate sales stood at US$31 trillion, which was almost twice as much as world exports of US$17 trillion (UNCTAD 2008, 10). Two-thirds of world trade involves MNEs and their affiliates as buyers or sellers, and one-third takes place among units of the same MNE corporate system. In 1982, the ratio of outward foreign direct investment (OFDI) to worldwide gross fixed capital formation was just 1%. In 1999, it had risen to approximately 14% (UNCTAD 2000, 4), and in 2007 it stood at 16.2% (UNCTAD 2008, 10). World foreign direct investment (FDI) outward stock, expressed as a percentage of world gross domestic product in current prices, increased rapidly, from 4.8% in 1982 and 10.8% in 1990, to 28.6% in 2007 (UNCTAD 2008, 10). In fact, global FDI inflows reached a historic high of $1,979 billion in 2007 (UNCTAD 2009). Amid a global financial and economic crisis, inflows declined by 14% to $1,697 billion in 2008 (UNCTAD 2009). This decline continued into 2009, with added momentum: preliminary data suggest that in the first quarter of 2009, inflows fell a further 44% compared with their level in the same period of 2008. A slow recovery is expected in 2010, gathering speed in 2011. The crisis has also changed the investment landscape, with developing and transition economies' share in global FDI flows surging to 43% in 2008 (UNCTAD 2009). Furthermore, the first survey of MNEs carried out by the United Nations in 1973 (United Nations Department of Economic and Social Affairs 1973) identified sixteen countries as having OFDI. In the 1970s, only 678 MNEs had operations in ten or more countries. By

2007, the number of MNE home countries had grown to 135, including eighty-nine developing countries, and nine members of the Commonwealth of Independent States (CIS) and South-East Europe (UNCTAD 2008, 211–12).

Another striking trend is the increase in the number of small and medium-sized enterprises that are multinationals. In the 1970s, multinationals were regarded as giants, with sales erroneously presented as larger than the gross national product (GNP) of most countries. Over twenty years later, David Saari still claimed that "[M]ost businesses are small businesses. This fact is mostly false for globalizing corporations that are very large" (Saari 1999, 307). In fact, today, the vast majority of firms considered MNEs by UNCTAD are small in size. Worldwide, by 2008, the number of MNEs mushroomed to no less than 82,053 parent corporations that controlled 807,353 foreign affiliates around the world. Of these parent corporations, only 2,418 were from the United States, compared to 21,425 from developing countries (UNCTAD 2009, 222–23). The total number of MNEs increased more than elevenfold between 1969 and 2008. The majority of these firms are certainly not giants, and the number of firms does not necessarily translate into significance in terms of sales. Many U.S.-based MNEs remain large and therefore powerful entities, as are MNEs from other developed countries. These MNEs also have special skills, new technologies, or product differentiation—all of which sustain and reinforce their oligopolistic nature. Yet, few industries are dominated by giant firms, even global industries, defined by Porter (1986) as industries in which competition is for world market share. In professional business services, there are a small number of large networks (the "Big Four" in accounting, for example) as well as thousands of small firms with mostly domestic operations.

A third and relatively new trend is that many firms have internationalized early in their evolution, sometimes even at their founding ("born global"), making the slow and gradual model of internationalization obsolete (Knight and Cavusgil 1996). Firms become MNEs not only to seek resources, but also to access new markets, increase efficiency, access and absorb new knowledge from their networks of affiliates, or to be service centered.

The sectoral composition of FDI has also changed dramatically. In the early 1970s, services accounted for approximately one-quarter of FDI stock. By 2002, services rose to approximately 60% of world FDI stock. Between 1990 and 2002, the world stock in services of both inward foreign direct investment (IFDI) and OFDI more than quadrupled, and services came to account for almost two-thirds of world IFDI in 2006. Based on the share of services in GNP, one may expect a further significant increase in the share of service-related FDI. Within services, between 1990 and 2002 the share of trade and finance in FDI stock decreased from approximately two-thirds to less than half, while that of business services increased significantly. Furthermore, since the 1990s, the share of FDI in infrastructure has been increasing. In 2007, the value of total cross-border M&As in the electricity, gas, and water industries rose to US$130 billion (8% of total sales), compared to US$63 billion (6% of total sales) in 2006 (UNCTAD 2008, 9 and Annex

Table B.6). Of course, certain services (such as defense and other government services) may remain domestic for political, cultural, or social reasons.

Another relatively recent phenomenon is the increasing number of MNEs based in developing countries, transition economies, and small countries. The *World Investment Report* for 2008 shows 950 MNEs based in Finland, 991 in Belgium, 3,429 in China, 2,428 in Turkey, and 204 in Tanzania. Thus, there are many more MNEs, and they come from all parts of the globe. In addition, what political scientists had termed the periphery is now becoming the center, or at least a part of a network. Aharoni and Ramamurti (2008) identified four waves of internationalization: (1) European firms in the nineteenth century; (2) U.S. firms essentially from 1950 onward; (3) Japanese firms primarily after the 1980s; and (4) small and large firms from many countries, including emerging markets, from the 1990s. From a negligible share in 1990, OFDI from developing countries accounted for over one-tenth of the world's total OFDI stock and 16% of total world FDI flows in 2006.

Overall, the MNE today is a very diverse species, originating from a large number of home countries, spawned in many industries, and starting at earlier stages of the firm's evolution. Both the size-distribution and the national origin of multinationals have broadened considerably. These phenomena are the result of major shifts in the global political and economic environment—shifts in government policies, attitudes toward MNEs, and new technologies. Advancements in information and communication technologies and transportation have brought almost seamless and low-cost global connectivity. This is also fueled by the process of learning within firms. MNEs have learned how to manage across national borders and how to adapt to different markets and cultures. They have learned how to collaborate in strategic alliances rather than seeking to be "stand-alone superstars." They have learned to scan the world for new ideas, acquire start-ups, and absorb knowledge gained in all parts of the firm. Since the end of World War II, many MNEs have moved from seeking natural resources and markets to seeking ideas, knowledge, and innovation. Their competitive advantages are based less on hard assets (such as factories, inventories, and production skills) and more on intangibles (such as knowledge, intellectual property, and relationships).

Furthermore, we have moved from a reliance on competition toward attempts to achieve cooperation among firms. Nonequity forms of FDI (such as subcontracting, management contracts, turnkey arrangements, franchising, licensing, and product sharing) as well as different forms of strategic alliances have all increased in importance, even if they are not recorded as FDI. In many service industries, nonequity forms are much more important than equity investments are. In the hotel industry, for example, it is common practice for the hotel operator to enter into management contracts without ownership of the real estate. In professional services, the ownership advantage of the firm is reflected in intangible assets such as reputation or organizational capabilities, information processing, or managerial skills and knowledge (Aharoni 2000b). For very different reasons, airlines are globalizers that are not allowed to globalize. IFDI in airlines has been constrained by ownership requirements in bilateral Air Service Agreements. They are therefore forced to use code sharing and other forms of strategic alliances to augment their international competitiveness (Aharoni 2002a, 2002b, 2004). The number of airline alliances has risen markedly, from around twenty in the early 1990s, to 1,221 in 2001 (UNCTAD 2004). However, FDI stock and flow data do not capture these activities.

The growth of FDI has generated increasing interest in MNEs and in their impact on both home and host countries. Rigorous research on this important global institution was pioneered in the 1960s by scholars in Europe and the United States. Perhaps the most influential among these studies were those based on the data bank created under the guidance of Raymond Vernon. Vernon was interested mainly in what he saw as the "basic asymmetry between multinational enterprises and national governments..." (Vernon 1971, 284), "that is, the capacity of the enterprises to shift some of their activities from one location to another, as compared with the commitment of the government to a fixed piece of national turf" (Vernon 1991, 517). Since then, a large number of studies have sought to understand issues such as how nations can enhance their competitive advantages, why and how firms internationalize, how MNEs can gain and sustain competitive advantage, and the causes and consequences of FDI.

To be sure, the growth of FDI was fuelled by relatively high economic growth and strong corporate performance. In 2007, world FDI flows reached an all-time high of US$1.8 trillion (UNCTAD 2008, 1). Since then, faced with the credit crisis and recession, these inflows have declined—and a much larger decline is expected in 2009.[1] This decline may conceivably be larger among MNEs from developed countries than for MNEs from China. Indeed, developing countries have weathered the crisis relatively well. The decline in the supply of FDI is likely to result in heightened competition for these inflows among governments in emerging markets. MNEs are also accused of avoiding the cost of complying with extensive regulations by moving to other markets. Developed countries may be more suspicious of FDI inflows, in particular when they take the form of acquisitions of domestic firms.

In this chapter, we focus on several key issues that must be understood and researched given the new and emerging trends in the size, distribution, and modes of operations of MNEs. Section 3.1 shows that competition has become much less segmented by countries. It analyzes the consequences of globalization for nonmultinational domestic firms. Section 3.2 points out that firm-specific advantages, while still critical to the success of MNEs, are much less of a barrier to acquisition by governments or foreign firms. Perhaps the opposite holds true, with the successful and efficient MNE becoming a more desirable acquisition target. Section 3.3 ponders the relevance of the home country, posing two related questions: why do MNEs start in certain countries, and what are the implications of different home countries for the strategy of MNEs and for the balance of costs and benefits to the nation in which the MNE is headquartered? Section 3.4 notes that much of the received theory on MNEs comes from business schools, and is therefore based on certain axioms that are less and less acceptable to others. Section

3.5 speculates on the possible political reactions in developed countries to changes in the relative power of different nations, in particular given the changing role of government as a result of the world's financial crisis and recession. The concluding section proposes an agenda for further research.

3.1 Changing Environment: A Move to Globalization

Only a few decades ago, almost all business was conducted within national borders. The world was segmented, with each country treated as a separate market and market share calculated on a country level. Import substitution and capital controls prevailed. Capital markets were regulated, and exchange rates pegged. Financial experts believed that one could significantly reduce risk through geographic diversification. Many scholars were puzzled by the clear home country bias manifested in portfolio investment. MNEs were relatively few in number and even they viewed competition in terms of segmented country markets. These firms were often headquartered in the United States or Western Europe and transferred technology, management expertise, and capital from the home country to foreign affiliates—many of which were created in order to access markets. MNEs were forced to jump tariffs walls and other barriers to entry. In so doing, they established often inefficient assembly plants. Indeed, most markets were protected by governments, using both tariff and nontariff barriers. The world was divided into developed, communist, and third-world (underdeveloped) countries, or between core and periphery. A country manager was responsible for operations in his or her market. Knowledge accumulated in one affiliate was rarely transferred to another affiliate. For example, cars made in the United Kingdom were designed for that market, and the knowledge accumulated rarely reached Detroit. MNEs placed primary emphasis on exploiting opportunities in the more affluent parts of the world.

When the Berlin Wall crumbled in November 1989, the former Soviet Empire broke apart, and its former member states moved toward liberal economic policies. At about the same time, India and several Latin American economies began to cut government spending and subsidies, privatize state-owned firms, and deregulate industry. Import substitution was discontinued, and governments adopted export-oriented free market strategies.

With the renaissance of market-based economic systems in the 1990s, governments made strenuous efforts to upgrade indigenous institutions to enhance the competitiveness of domestic firms and to attract IFDI—deemed essential for national competitiveness. The risks to the domestic economy or to the political, social, and cultural fabric of the host countries were ignored. Meanwhile, MNEs learned how to manage global operations and how to transfer knowledge across their network. Today, MNEs absorb knowledge from all affiliates and transfer this knowledge to all parts of the organization, rather than simply transferring technology from headquarters to affiliated subsidiary. It is generally agreed that most MNEs, certainly those in high technology fields, are built on knowledge, of supreme importance in such organizations. We are witnessing the transition from the industrial and service economy to the knowledge economy and from an economy of objects to an economy of ideas.

In this global arena, MNEs today compete over a global market share, or at least a regional share, acquiring each part of the value chain where its acquisition is optimal—from outside sources or by production within the MNE network. Indeed, globalization compels almost all firms to organize all value-added activities in a global manner. MNEs offshore and outsource activities, and enjoy considerable latitude as to where they locate each part of the value chain (Gereffi, Humphrey, and Sturgeon 2005). Facing saturated markets in developed economies, MNEs have shifted, or at least broadened, their attention to emerging markets, which constitute more than half of the world's population. One result has been a need to grapple with the growing complexity of marketing operations. Contrary to what Theodore Levitt (1983) predicted, globalization does not, in fact, necessarily imply economies of scale for a standardized product and brands. It has become imperative to establish a global market presence, but also to retain flexibility, to cope with cultural diversity, and to tailor products to local needs, local contexts, and diverse legal requirements. As suggested by Pankaj Ghemawat (2001), there are four dimensions of distance that must be considered: cultural, administrative, geographic, and economic. All point to the need for local responsiveness. Recently, MNEs have been encouraged to combine local responsiveness with international economies of integration by adopting the transnational solution (Bartlett and Ghoshal 1989).

When competition is global, or even regional, domestic firms are no longer immune to foreign competition. Instead, they are vulnerable to competition from giant MNEs and to the acquisition attempts of such MNEs. In this environment, being more efficient than local competitors is no longer sufficient. Firms must compete effectively on the world market and on the local market. This often necessitates achieving greater scale and scope. In many cases, domestic firms catering solely to the local market face a crucial choice between becoming a multinational and creating an alliance with one: acquire or be acquired. This situation is a straightforward result of global competition and seamless markets, and the question of regional versus global, repeatedly stressed by Alan M. Rugman (2005), is irrelevant. The need to become an MNE, or at least to compete effectively on the world market and perhaps become a supplier to an MNE or an affiliate of a foreign MNE, is the same whether the MNE pursues a regional or global strategy. In the world of the twenty-first century, few firms can hide behind tariff walls and import restrictions, or find protection in differences of culture, language, social norms, or local tastes. Firms must compete with foreign multinationals operating in their industry. Domestic markets have ceased to be a relevant unit of analysis. To quote Andrew Grove, "We live in an age in which the pace of technological change is pulsating ever faster" (Grove 1996, 5). Changing technologies enabled globalization, but a combination of global competition and accelerated technological change mean that the survival of even the largest firms cannot be taken for granted.

3.2 Rethinking the Consequences of
Firm-Specific Advantages

How an MNE competes with domestic firms, given the additional costs of conducting business abroad, has been a fundamental issue in international business theory since Stephen Hymer (1960/1976). Hymer suggested that the MNE enjoys certain advantages; for example, superior technology. Peter Buckley and Mark Casson (1976), in a seminal work, noted that firms internalize certain transactions and, by so doing, can develop and exploit firm-specific advantages. Rugman (1981) distinguished between firm-specific advantages and country-specific advantages. A general consensus emerged that an MNE must enjoy firm-specific advantages in order to compete and compensate for the additional cost of doing business abroad—what Srilata Zaheer termed the "liability of foreignness" (1995). To be sure, Hymer focused on the MNE's additional costs of operations, and primarily of information, compared to domestic firms, whilst Zaheer stressed hazards stemming from discrimination or unfamiliarity.

John Dunning, in his eclectic paradigm (Dunning 1979), termed the firm-specific advantages "ownership advantage," consisting of capabilities, processes, skills, physical assets, or knowledge held by the firm and unique to the firm. Similarly, resource-based theory scholars assert that in any given industry different competitors do not have access to the same capabilities and resources. Jay Barney (1991) advocated the VRIO mode (value, rarity, imitability, and organization). Firms achieve competitive advantage through the accumulation of resources and capabilities that are not only valuable and rare but also inimitable. Furthermore, the policies and procedures of the firm are organized to exploit these valuable, rare, and difficult-to-imitate resources. The successful firm's strategy is based on the exploitation of these resources and capabilities to achieve a competitive advantage. This is in contrast to the emphasis on the industry in which the firm operates (Porter 1980). This is also in contrast to the assertion that institutions determine directly how firms formulate and implement strategy (Peng, Wang and Jiang 2008).

The nature of firm-specific advantages may be different, but the very idea that, without such advantages, an MNE cannot compete outside its home market is a generally accepted axiom. In other words, to become an MNE, the firm must possess some specific advantages relative to its foreign competitors.

Whether or not the world is completely flat, as argued by Thomas Friedman (2005), or still replete with obstacles to the free movement of factors of production, there is no denying the dramatic increase in the size, scope, and complexity of MNE operations. International business scholars have understood that the MNE is a "social community whose productive knowledge defines a competitive advantage" (Kogut and Zander 1993, 626). The MNE is a learning organization, a major advantage of which is its ability to generate knowledge and transfer it across borders. Knowledge transfers are not solely from headquarters to affiliate—new technologies are developed across the network of affiliates. In fact, the challenge for MNEs is "to innovate by learning from the world" (Doz, Santos, and Williamson 2001, 1). More importantly, MNEs often achieve growth through acquisitions, obtaining access to new technologies, providing knowledge of different products, markets, and insights into operating in different institutional frameworks. The firm-specific advantage of many firms appears to be their ability to identify candidates for acquisition, acquire them, and absorb them into their networks. They may also develop and nurture cooperative processes with other firms to build network linkages and foster organizational learning. Such cooperative strategies may result in different governance structures—from collaborative ventures such as code sharing or strategic alliances, to less formal relationships with suppliers, banks, major customers, or other businesses that are part of a relational network, where different parts of the value chain are produced wherever it is most efficient to do so. One result of this is the relocation of a wide range of corporate functions. Firms create and accumulate firm-specific advantages in the identification of trustworthy suppliers, retailers, or other entities, such as research laboratories. They develop long-term cooperative relations, cultivating and nurturing trust, and avoiding opportunistic behavior. Most major multinationals have ceased to rely solely on internal research and development (R&D) efforts as a source of competitive advantage. Instead, the source of competitive advantage is shifting toward an ability to establish and coordinate a network of global partners. The U.S.-based Procter and Gamble expects half of its future products to be based on technologies and concepts it will acquire from third parties, and it has created an organizational structure to achieve these specific goals (Huston and Sakkab 2006). To design and fabricate its 787 Dreamliner airplane, Boeing combined the efforts of fifty partners across 130 locations (MacCormack 2007). Many other MNEs work with a plethora of alliances such as joint ventures, licensing and franchising agreements, strategic supply chain contracts, joint R&D, co-marketing, and code sharing. Perhaps the more MNEs learn how to manage networks, the less important ownership control will become, and the more firms will employ flexible, collaborative ventures with independent domestic suppliers, and other partners, creating larger network of interlinked companies. As firms retreat from internalization to core competencies (Pralahad and Hamel 1990) they outsource activities to reliable partners. Social relations within the network, long-term memory, and reputation are then crucial to achieve trust and cooperation.

Given this new reality, it is conceivable that firm-specific advantages can be acquired through the acquisition of an MNE. A firm from China or the Gulf, for example, which enjoys access to abundant capital, may acquire a large, established and successful MNE, headquartered abroad. By so doing, the established MNE thereby becomes part of an emerging market MNE. Management scholars may argue that such a possibility is unrealistic, arguing that emerging market MNEs lack the managerial skills necessary to manage such a firm or even to identify the appropriate acquisition target. The counterargument is that all of these skills can be bought in the free market. Indeed, the history of existing MNEs shows that they can employ experts from different countries that would efficiently execute such tasks. Parenthetically, in a world of dispersed ownership, a block of 15% of shares may be sufficient to achieve control of the board of directors. To be sure, many studies have shown that a significant portion of mergers and acquisitions fail to achieve the expected goals. However, the possibility of being successful does exist. Whilst it may be impossible to imitate firm-specific advantages, they can nevertheless be acquired. Furthermore, such an acquisition may not even entail a change in strategy. Such a possibility raises the obvious question: how relevant is the home country in understanding the strategy and the benefits of an MNE?

3.3 How Relevant Is the Home Country?

By definition, an MNE operates in more than one country. In each country, it employs human and other resources and few if any expatriates. The MNE and its employees are managed by headquarters, located in a certain home country. Received international business theory assumes that the home country of the MNE is relevant, even important, for several reasons. Primarily, the home country was considered the source of the MNE's ownership advantages. Robert Aliber (1970) suggested that the home country's advantage is related to the strength of its currency. However, today an MNE can and does access funds throughout the world.

Technology was considered to be an additional source of home country advantage and was assumed to have been developed in the home market. The knowledge acquired would then be transferred to other markets (Vernon 1966). It was asserted that the MNE headquarters transfers not only technology, but also management expertise and capital from the home country to the affiliates. In the 1970s, this line of thought led to much discussion over the degree to which the technology transferred from developed countries is appropriate and suited to less developed countries, where capital and labor costs differ significantly. Only much later did certain researchers recognize that an MNE could be a knowledge-seeker as well as a knowledge-creator. As shown above, established MNEs actively seek out technologies, ideas, and products from beyond their home country. They augment their knowledge with knowledge generated abroad, gained, for example, through the acquisition of a foreign firm. MNEs participate in different types of localized knowledge simultaneously (Rugman and Verbeke 2001). The acquired knowledge is then transferred from one affiliate to another, and to headquarters. MNEs no longer secure an advantage from home country invention and development. Instead, the advantage is often derived from the ability to coordinate development efforts across many markets.

A further predominant theme has been the assertion that firms go abroad only after they have exploited all growth opportunities in the home market. The experience and knowledge gained in the home market form the basis of the firm's ability to compete in other markets. One expression of this line of thinking is Porter's (1986) "demand conditions," a vital part of his "diamond," where firms must have a large home base if they are to develop the skills required to successfully manage an MNE. They gain firm-specific advantages from home operations that are transferred to a network of subsidiaries in other locations.

Rugman and Verbeke (1993), having examined the Canadian experience, pointed out that firms may draw on the strengths of the "diamond" of more than one nation, leading to the development of "double diamond" or even "multiple diamond" perspectives. Such perspectives appear useful primarily when analyzing firms from small open economies (Van Den Bulcke and Verbeke 2001). The experience of several small countries demonstrates that a large home market is not a prerequisite for the creation of an MNE. On the contrary, the small size of the home market may be a major incentive for domestic firms to become MNEs, allowing them to cater to much larger foreign markets (Aharoni, 2009). To cite one example, for the Finnish firm, Nokia, domestic sales account for less than 3% of worldwide sales. Firms can and do develop competitive strengths unrelated to the locational advantage of their home country. They achieve economies of scale by treating the world as their "oyster." They raise capital in foreign markets, while retaining headquarters and senior management in the home country.

Home country origin may influence the firm's strategy. The strategy (and behavior) of U.S. MNEs was assumed to be different from that of European MNEs (Franko 1976), UK. MNEs (Stopford 1974), and Japanese MNEs (Yoshino 1976; Tsurumi 1976). According to Doremus et al. (1999), MNEs continue to be shaped by the policies and cultures of their home country, even as they globalize. Yet here again the situation has changed, and dramatically so. If a firm is acquired by a foreign MNE, does its culture change to that of the foreign MNE? Does it matter, for instance, that American firms (Ford and General Motors) acquired the Swedish car firms Saab and Volvo? Is Volvo less Swedish today?

In what other ways does ownership matter? Robert Reich (1990, 1991) claimed that what really matters is the country in which the firm creates employment. For him, a Japanese firm producing in the United States benefits the U.S. economy more than a U.S. firm producing (and thus creating employment) in Asia does. In Reich's terms, the home country is irrelevant. However, a country does expect benefits that go beyond employment generation. MNEs are expected to benefit the economy through the demonstration of best practices, by teaching improved management practices, by remitting profits, and so on. Perhaps if the headquarters of an MNE was located in Country X, one would expect this firm to show some preference to Country X, or at least the right of first refusal in creating employment, in bringing technology, or in remitting profits. Perhaps the U.S. firm, Intel, would be more readily close a factory in Israel than an Israeli-owned firm would. These, however, are hypotheses that require careful consideration and further testing. The results of such research are extremely important for gauging the benefits of OFDI. Furthermore, existing theory seems less than clear on why some countries have become home countries and others have not. What, precisely, were the factors that allowed this proliferation of home countries? Theory also fails to explain what exactly should be expected from a home country; it is certainly neither technology nor capital, but neither is it simply employment generation.

It is less and less clear today, that the location of an MNE's headquarters in a particular country is a source of additional advantage for that country, an advantage that the country would not otherwise have obtained. As an extreme example, assume that an MNE's headquarters are located in country A, but the shareholders reside in other countries. Clearly, the benefits of dividends would, therefore, accrue to citizens of other countries, rather than to the home country. By definition, a globally integrated firm leverages talent, knowledge, and physical assets across value chains and geographies. The MNE can locate functions and operations anywhere in the world to optimize the right skills, costs, and business environment. It brings together a variety of capabilities, in order to deliver value to clients, but it can also disband quickly when the need no longer exists. In fact, an MNE may relocate even its headquarters to another country for tax purposes. When the role of the home country is discussed, the theory of international production cannot rely solely on economic factors. Other factors, such as culture, the behavior of managers, the impact of governmental policies, and political factors, must be considered; analysis that focuses solely on economic factors may result in unsound conclusions.

3.4 Using the Relevant Yardsticks

Many business school professors tend to share with businesspeople a value system that prioritizes efficiency and profits. As a result, they tend to ignore the role of considerations such as culture, religion, beauty, helping the poor, conserving the environment, or the security of the nation. When such variables are said to be taken into account, they are measured by alternative costs. For others, there is no limit to what they feel should be done (and paid) for love, social justice, beauty, cultural heritage, religious needs, social solidarity, rural development, or equity in the distribution of benefits.

Indeed, the objectives of individuals are wider and more varied than implicitly assumed by international business theory. Affluent citizens from rich countries may seek a sustainable environment, clear air, and fair income distribution; poorer citizens from developing countries seek more than purely economic goals. There is a pervasive sense that the impersonality of the market is somehow wrong.

Most economists seem to agree today that the benefits of FDI exceed the costs (Oxelheim and Ghauri 2004, 10; Lall 1995), and that both IFDI and OFDI are beneficial, contributing to growth that might otherwise not occur (Moran et al. 2005; Kokko 2006). Indeed, the experience of the past decade would appear to show that globalization and the spread of MNEs have helped increase global efficiency. However, not all citizens have benefited from these trends, and the poor in developing countries have largely been excluded. Indeed, a major challenge for policy makers is to enable a more equitable division of the benefits of FDI, while minimizing the potentially negative effects on competition and the social, political, and cultural fabric. Hernando De Soto (2000) emphasizes the need to strengthen property rights so that all segments of society can share in the fruits of globalization. Concerns over the operations of MNEs stem from what Robert Gilpin (2000, chapter 10) calls the "communitarian perspective"; that is, concerns shared by environmentalists or human rights advocates over issues such as global warming, poverty alleviation, or the just and equitable distribution of benefits.

Antiglobalization activists are concerned that globalization harms more than it benefits. They expose the glaring shortcomings of global governance. They rally against large MNEs, blamed for financial instability and the decline of the bargaining power of labor, given that capital is highly mobile and labor is not. They are concerned about the growing inequalities between nations and classes and the disruption of traditional social values and cultural norms. They portray a "struggle between people and corporations" (Monbiot 2000, 17). Observers such as Richard Barnet and John Cavanagh claim, referring to sales rather than value added, that the "emerging global order is spearheaded by a few hundred corporate giants, many of them bigger than most sovereign nations. Ford's economy is larger than that of Saudi Arabia and Norway. Philip Morris's annual sales exceed New Zealand's gross domestic product" (Barnet and Cavanagh 1995, 14). Subsequent analysis by UNCTAD that compared the value added of MNEs to gross domestic product (GDP), demonstrated that, in fact, only two of the world's fifty largest economies in 2000 were MNEs: Exxon Mobil, (number forty-five) and General Motors (number forty-seven) (UNCTAD 2002). Antiglobalists insist that the most disturbing aspect is:

> ...that the formidable power and mobility of global corporations are undermining the effectiveness of national governments to carry out essential policies on behalf of their people...Business enterprises...are linking far-flung pieces of territory into a new world economy that bypasses all sorts of established political arrangements and conventions...Tax laws...full employment policies, and old approaches to resource development and environmental protection are becoming obsolete, unenforceable or irrelevant. (Barnet and Cavanagh 1995, 19)

As a solution to the asymmetric power of MNEs and host governments, Saari (1999) proposed a limit on the maximum size of a corporation, in order to reduce "the brazen political implications of the corporate ideology of restructuring, privatization, deregulation and dismantling of democratic rule" (3). The issue, according to him, is the following: "Can 185 nations allow 750 giant corporations to invest the profits of the corporations solely in a way they can see fit—or must public authority of 185 nations be used to check, structure and confine investment decisions by 750 corporations as they move around the globe?" (5).

Joseph Stiglitz (2006) views globalization as advancing corporate interests at the expense of the well-being of ordinary citizens, and working for the rich countries and not for poor developing nations. He thinks that forcing developing countries to open their financial markets would result only in large international banks, interested primarily in their multinational clients, putting many local banks out of business and depriving the poor of access to credit. He argues that rich countries profess to help emerging markets but in fact seek to gain access to third-world markets, while protecting their own markets, for instance, by refusing to liberalize import rules in sectors such as construction or shipping, those very sectors where third-world nations are particularly competitive.

Can the market's strengths be united with the strengths of the universal ideal? Can they be reconciled with the requirements of future generations—as Kofi Annan challenged in his speech to the World Economic Forum, in Davos, in 1999? (Cited in Adler 2008, 328.) The protesters in Seattle and Prague and at the World Economic Forum certainly did not think so. Many of those advocating for social responsibility by business to all stakeholders do believe that such a lofty ideal is possible. For them, globalization does not have to damage the environment, increase inequality, or weaken cultural diversity. Unfortunately, economists do not have the necessary tools in their arsenal to recommend the optimum size of welfare budgets, or even the optimum size of a police force. Much multidisciplinary research is greatly needed, if we are to wrestle with these complex issues.

Furthermore, business school professors tend to exaggerate the degree of globalization, interdependence, and free trade that exists today, as well as the extent of harmonization of international standards and rules, including in the area of intellectual property rights protection. To be sure, the investment climate in most countries today tilts much more toward liberalization, dismantling restrictions on foreign ownership, and attracting FDI, in many economic fields. However, for many products market access is still denied, mainly in agriculture, but also in services. Export support, in the form of state trading enterprises, subsidies, export credits or food aid, is still widely used. After years of extenuated negotiations and countless meetings of ministers and trade representatives, the so-called Doha Development Round is still far from reaching an agreement or convergence. In fact, the differences remain irreconcilable. Even if a compromise were reached, it would certainly entail many restrictions that would distort free trade in agriculture, allow some level of domestic support and many special safeguard mechanisms, and prevent the full enforcement of intellectual property rights. Service agreements were reached only after allowing numerous exemptions on cultural and other grounds. Parenthetically, only 153 of the more than 200 countries in existence today, are members of the World Trade Organization (WTO). Governments perceive themselves as guardians of the national interest and do not voluntarily limit their freedom of action. Even though governments generally abide by agreed rules (but loathe outside scrutiny) they tend to oppose any proposed rules that are deemed contrary to the national interest.

Unfortunately, since the seminal work of Vernon (1971), international business scholars seem to have neglected the study of the determinants of adversarial relationships between MNEs and nation-states, and how such antagonism can be minimized. In 1991, Vernon observed, "governments are becoming reconciled to a modified concept of sovereignty in the economic field. They are aware, for example, that without international cooperation, none of them is any longer capable of ensuring the existence of secure banks or of policing their security markets against fraud" (Vernon 1991, 193). Other scholars have preached for a seamless world and greater cooperation and a spirit of partnership between MNEs and governments. Most scholars simply ignored the issue, which seems to have disappeared from the research agenda. The recognition of globalization led to an almost universal urge to limit the extent of government intervention in the management of resource allocation, to harmonize rules, and to coordinate economic policies, recognizing the fragility of the international financial system. The options open to national governments are said to be severely constrained. Most wealth-creating assets—and—people can easily move across national borders. Governments are expected to encourage free trade, investment, and flows of capital, to concentrate on the maintenance of law and order and on investments in human capital through improved education. However, they may restrict outward investments that impinge on national security; though defining the national security interest is often controversial. In the United States, the International Traffic in Arms Regulations control the international trade of defense-related articles and services. These regulations restrict collaboration across national borders even within the same enterprise. Other countries have established similar arms control restrictions; for example, the Wassenaar Arrangement and the Australia Group. Politically, a government may opt for distribution policies that enhance social cohesion, protect natural habitats, or seek to achieve any other number of cultural and social goals. These lofty ideals are too often interpreted as succumbing to the demands of powerful, vested interests for protection in the name of fairness or security. Yet it is crucial to gauge to what degree cooperation can be achieved, in which economic sectors, and the circumstances that enable such partnerships. The trade-offs between social, cultural, and economic goals are not easy to establish. Scholars from a variety of academic disciplines must wrestle with these issues and propose policy options. Perhaps governments are willing to limit their economic freedom when they are sure the nation will benefit. Weak states are thus less inclined to accept free trade and investment. If this is so, the changing balance of power and the rapid growth of MNEs from emerging markets may lead to a major change in the rules of the game.

3.5   Some Consequences of the Changing Balance of Power

The growth of MNEs has meant, among other things, that the interests of the MNE's network rather than of individual host countries have guided decisions on output, wages, prices, and research. In the 1960s and 1970s, MNE control over resources and its perceived ability to evade national governmental controls, evoked fear and distrust in the minds of the public and the media in many countries. Some saw the MNE as contributing to global welfare; many viewed it as a dangerous tool of imperialism, oppression, and injustice (Vernon 1977) or as a new form of colonialism (e.g., Levitt 1970; Saari 1999, 2). Many scholars portrayed national governments as pawns in the hands of powerful MNEs: impotent, and incapable of achieving national goals (Barnet and Müller 1974). Some observers even claimed that powerful MNEs would bring about the end of the nation-state, rendering it impotent (see Gilpin 1975, 220).[2]

In Europe and around the world, the growing power of U.S. MNEs caused much anxiety. In the developing world, that anxiety applied to foreign MNEs of all stripes. By the 1970s, the climate for MNEs had become quite hostile. Dozens of developing countries that had recently gained their economic independence were reluctant to allow FDI and were fearful of the perceived might of the largest MNEs. MNEs were also criticized over the appropriateness of their technology and transfer-pricing policies, as well as other practices. They were generally perceived as a threat to the sovereignty of the nation-state. The rallying cry was the fear that MNEs would dominate the weaker and less sophisticated nation-state. The ability of MNEs to move resources across borders or to use transfer pricing to minimize tax liabilities created resentment. Jean-Jaques Servan-Schreiber (1967), in his best-selling book, *Le Défi Américain,* warned that U.S. MNEs would take over the French economy. Latin American economists railed against *dependencia* (e.g., Evans 1979), and others feared MNE control of the commanding heights, or the strategic sectors, of the economy. Such fears also led to the nationalization and expropriation of MNE assets. A number of formal and informal initiatives were undertaken to understand, identify, and improve what were perceived as the negative aspects of FDI. The United Nations probed the operations of MNEs, and declared a "New International Economic Order." One result was the creation of the United Nations Centre on Transnational Corporations, which became the Division on Investment, Technology and Enterprise Development (DITE) of the United Nations Conference on Trade and Development (UNCTAD).

MNEs have continued to grow in numbers and importance and, since the 1980s, new views of the economic order have taken hold. MNEs have been increasingly recognized as a vital factor and a prime engine in the fostering of long-term economic development. The potential of FDI to inject capital without debt service obligations, create jobs, transfer technology (including management skills), enhance exports, and raise productivity is now widely acknowledged. Restricting IFDI in the "commanding heights" of an economy seems to have lost much of its appeal. In fact, these industries are no longer the purview of the state. Instead, states have sought FDI in infrastructure, assuming the role of a regulator of private sector activity.[3] The possible disadvantages of FDI, or the possible power struggle between MNEs and nation-states, seem to have been forgotten or are assumed to be manageable.

From a reliance on government to manage national economies and strategic sectors, there has been a shift toward reliance on markets and competition to deliver better and more efficient outcomes. The welfare state and the state-owned national champion have lost their allure as agents of reconstruction, modernization, and economic development. In one country after another, the notion has taken hold that government failures can be much worse than the market failures that they sought to remedy. Deregulation, privatization, and competition have become major slogans everywhere. The collapse of communist regimes and the breakup of the Soviet Empire silenced any remaining skeptics of the wisdom of relying on free markets and competition. As a result, nations compete intensively with each other to persuade MNEs to locate value-added activities within their borders. So-called investor targeting by investment promotion agencies has replaced the tug of war between privately owned MNEs and governments. In developing countries, the advantages of additional jobs, technology transfers, exports, and knowledge creation are perceived as outweighing the risks such as loss of national sovereignty, tax evasion through transfer pricing, crowding out of local private enterprise, suboptimal technology choices, or other negative spillovers in the host economy—even security concerns. UNCTAD has documented the proliferation of investment promotion agencies, the mushrooming of bilateral investment treaties, and the tendency to create a more hospitable environment for MNEs through regulatory change. By the end of 2008, 5,754 investment agreements existed, of which 2,676 were bilateral treaties, 2,805 were double taxation treaties, and 273 were free trade agreements and economic cooperation agreements containing investment provisions (UNCTAD 2009). The general trend in FDI policies remained one of greater openness, and compared to 2007, the percentage of less favorable measures for FDI remained unchanged.

Until recently, much less attention was paid to the possibility of encouraging domestic firms to transform themselves into MNEs, with a home base in their country of origin. In fact, in many economies, until quite recently, the prevalence of foreign exchange controls and other governmental restrictions made the creation of home-based MNEs difficult if not impossible.

The United States, as a hegemon, preached free trade and championed international openness. Yet, even at the height of its power, it continued to protect agriculture, resisting any international agreement on free trade in this sector. It also protected other industries such as aerospace, defense, shipping, and airlines. Developing countries felt compelled to accept U.S. conditions. In the 2008 Doha round of negotiations, China and India were much less willing to acquiesce in what they saw as the directives of developed countries.

The acquisition of firms in developed countries, by firms from emerging markets, has generated opposition for several reasons. The foreign owner may be accused of competing unfairly, damaging the environment, transferring jobs from the United States or Europe to low-wage workers in the new home country, or of being unqualified to manage the operations acquired. A major concern is that the acquisition would threaten national security, especially if the MNE was to come under the control of a foreign government. When Lenovo (China) acquired IBM's global PC business in December 2004, the risks of China acquiring dual-use technologies, or obtaining a U.S. platform for industrial espionage, were among the primary concerns of the Committee on Foreign Investment in the United States (CFIUS), a multiagency federal panel. Dubai Ports World, a firm owned by the government of the United Arab Emirates, received swift CFIUS approval for its indirect acquisition of U.S. ports when it purchased the British firm P&O Steam Navigation Co., but it later ran into a storm of protest from Congress and had to abandon the deal. In many other cases, a CIFIUS investigation has resulted in the foreign investor's withdrawal, even before an official decision was reached. Ironically, calls to tame the power of MNEs are heard today in developed countries more than in the developing or transition economies. These calls intensify even as MNEs themselves have lost much power. If they were once destructive to labor, to the environment, and to democracy, the very increase in their number, the diversity of MNE home nations, and the large number of small and medium-sized MNEs has reduced their oligopolistic power.

The potential loss of jobs to developing countries is a major source of anxiety for developed countries, and it is claimed that workers in developing countries do not enjoy basic social benefits or rights and, therefore, compete unfairly with their counterparts in developed countries. Of course, such job losses are not necessarily related to foreign MNEs. Rather, as domestic firms become MNEs, every function is potentially subject to relocation from the home country to locations with lower costs, less stringent regulations, or lax environmental policies. Offshoring is no longer confined to the outsourcing of unskilled, repetitive manufacturing jobs. Digitization, codification of jobs, the ability to move data cheaply and instantly, and improvements in communications, all allow services to be offshored, including knowledge-intensive activities, even sophisticated R&D, blood tests, x-ray diagnoses, and computer-development tasks. All are susceptible to the "great unbundling" (Baldwin 2006). In the nineteenth century, people moved freely across borders in search of jobs and better opportunities. Millions migrated from Europe to the United States, without being constrained by visas. During the 1890s, 9% immigrated to the United States, 26% to Argentina, and 17% to Australia (Baldwin and Martin 1999, 19). In the century after 1815, approximately sixty million people left Europe in search of better lives in America, South and East Africa, and Oceania (Hirst and Thompson 1999, 23). In the twenty-first century, technology, capital, and certain products and services move freely across borders, even as the movement of people has become ever more restricted. In such a world, blue-collar and white-collar workers in developed countries fear that the trickle of jobs transferred offshore will become a flood, with ever more aggressive moves to areas where functions can be performed at the lowest cost, thereby hollowing out industries in developed countries.

Until now, protectionism manifested itself more in the area of investment than on the trade front. Both U.S. and European governments have sought to check takeover bids, citing security reasons. One may expect developed countries to try to restrict what they may perceive as the takeover of their "precious assets" by foreign firms. They would welcome globalization in industries in which they feel they enjoy advantages, and would attempt to restrict other industries on the grounds of market failure, national security considerations, cultural sensitivities, or special safeguard mechanisms. The lofty ideals that call for liberalization of the economic rules of the game are often forgotten when domestic interests are perceived as threatened. This issue has become even more sensitive as a consequence of the global financial crisis.

Conclusions and Further Questions

International business is about the behavior of firms and the decisions of managers. The firm learns it is operating within *an environment* and a *political and institutional regime*. In all of these dimensions, with the possible exception of the way managers make decisions, there have been fundamental changes in the past few decades. MNEs are very different today. They operate in a much altered environment, the result of the rapid pace of technological advances, which will surely further accelerate. With information and communication technologies providing low-cost and easy global connectivity, globalization is reaching a new era. Furthermore, in the twenty-first century, more and more developing countries are fostering the internationalization of formerly sheltered industries. Their firms have felt compelled to master the art of integrating operations, managing across borders and across cultures. Cutting costs and achieving efficiency is essential to succeed in an era of ever-greater global competition. International agreements covering FDI in goods and services are proliferating at the bilateral and regional level, but less so at the multilateral level. To be sure, to date members of the WTO have failed to reach an agreement on agriculture or to bridge gaps in several other areas.

One result of this unprecedented change is that many theories, taken for granted in the past, have turned out to be obsolete under these new circumstances. Of course, the assumptions of neoclassical economics of trade among atomistic traders, and between nations in predominantly market-determined transactions, are tenuous. Today, MNEs are major engines of both international trade and investment. The so-called obsolescing bargain model (Vernon 1971), is also much less relevant as a picture of the world today. The advantages of MNEs today are less based on factors vulnerable to rapid obsolescence and more on their capability to innovate, generate new technologies, and manage knowledge across a global network. The MNE is therefore welcomed as a major engine of development in a knowledge-based global economy. The product life cycle theory is also obsolete, as are descriptions of organization of the MNE such as that portrayed by John Stopford and Luis Wells (1972) and the idea that firms internationalize in a gradual process and in incremental stages over a long period of time (Johanson and Vahlne 1977, 1990).

The "expansion" of globalization since the end of the Cold War was seen by some scholars as rendering the nation-state obsolete. Yet, the past century has seen the amalgamation of states into larger blocs (such as the European Union) as well as the fragmentation of states into smaller countries. Kenichi Ohmae described the nation-state as "increasingly a nostalgic fiction" (Ohmae 1995, 12) and announced "The End of the Nation State" (Ohmae 1995), but the number of countries has more than doubled in the past three decades of the twentieth century, rising from 96 in 1960 to 192 in 1998, to more than 200 today. At the same time, the number of countries with a population of less than one million has almost tripled—from fifteen to forty-three. The relationship between globalization and the role of the nation-state thus deserves more research. National sovereignty may be in retreat, but predictions of the demise of the nation-state, and the creation of a borderless world, have not been realized. Expectations that national business systems would converge to form a seamless global system have not materialized. Rather, the recent severe financial crisis has highlighted the fact that, even as the free movement of factors of production across borders has had many positive consequences, it also makes it much more difficult for governments to protect their economies from the consequences of a U.S. problem. To be sure, the interdependence was long recognized, as manifested by the statement that "when the U.S. catches a cold, the rest of the world suffers from pneumonia." Yet the rate of movement was neglected in theory. We have very little theoretical understanding of the impact of the financial economy on the real economy.

The problems revealed by the current crisis have evoked scores of proposals for action—many of which may result in a downward spiral of protectionism that will deepen and lengthen the current crisis, and result in retaliation. The general aversion to government intervention has been replaced by calls for more government intervention. The mistrust of government, and the famous dictum of Lord Acton that power corrupts, seem to have been forgotten, at least for the present. Unfortunately, personal values and narrow interests seem to dominate decisions over the most appropriate course of action. Theory is silent on the right blend of regulation, governmental action, and free market operation—or even on the role of ethical beliefs as constraints on power.

Most previous research on MNEs concentrated on large firms. Vernon based his seminal work (Vernon 1971) on U.S. MNEs, on a database of the U.S. *Fortune 500* companies, 187 of which were found to be MNEs using Vernon's definition. More recently, Rugman (2005) studied the world's 500 largest firms, based on the *Fortune 500* list, treating all as MNEs. In both cases, large firms tend to be based in large developed countries. Yet, there are approximately 82 053 MNEs, most of which are small and medium-sized (UNCTAD 2009). We should study these firms, to understand if they face different problems and obstacles in their path toward globalization. As long as government policies in small countries create the proper environment for local entrepreneurs, firms may thrive in global markets if they make the right strategic choices and are well managed. They may not possess the capabilities to build global consumer brands, but they can thrive by dominating a well-differentiated niche (Aharoni 2000a, 2006). To be sure, many firms failed in their attempt to become MNEs, even when they possessed innovative technologies because they lacked expertise in marketing or in managing the growth processes (Aharoni 1994). Others succumbed to acquisitions by a large European or U.S.-based MNE. Yet the tiny size of the home market is a major incentive to create home-based MNEs, catering to large foreign markets. Even if the largest MNEs account for 90% of global FDI stocks, international business theory should also be able to explain the internationalization of small firms and of firms from small open economies, which present different challenges to those of large economies. By definition, large MNEs from small countries account for a significant part of GNP. They thus enjoy greater political as well as economic influence (Aharoni 2006). At the same time, MNEs from small countries carry out most of their operations beyond their home country. They tap capital required for operations or expansion into a foreign market. Perhaps one can learn from outliers more than from a study of averages and populations. Further, it may be hypothesized that relatively small firms from small counties are perceived as less of a threat to the nation-state.

Hopefully, researchers will update their theories, sharpen their analytical tools, and propose ideas and policies for the world of many and very heterogeneous MNEs, many of which will achieve competitive advantage by cooperation with other firms rather than by internalizing operations. Indeed, for too long firms were portrayed as black boxes. We know very little about the determinants of success in managing a MNE and integrating its activities across the globe or within a region. The ownership advantage alluded to as a factor for success, is not easily defined. Research on the inner working of the MNE is essential. Such research should shed light on differences by sector, by industry, by size of firms, by the nationality of the home country, and by experience in international operations. Service-industry MNEs are not the same as manufacturing-industry MNEs (Aharoni 2000c), policy issues are poles apart, and treatment cannot be the same across different types of industry. These problems are augmented by the difficulties inherent in reaching a satisfactory legal definition of complex economic issues. Therefore, scholars should study not only the inner working of firms but also their interaction with their environment—in particular with government.

Each of the areas discussed in this chapter offers many opportunities for fruitful, future research. The possibility of acquisitions of large MNEs, the precise relevance of the home country, the yardsticks by which progress is measured, the trade-offs between competition and cooperation, and the ways to avoid a backlash by making interdependence resilient, all raise many important research issues, and all call for interdisciplinary work. Such work should also analyze the limits to globalization, investigate the connection between private capital and the governance of countries, and attempt to determine the optimum balance between the incentives necessary to attract FDI and the regulation required to defend the public interest.

Notes

1. See related discussion of the financial crisis and recession on FDI from emerging markets by Karl P. Sauvant, Wolfgang Maschek, and Geraldine McAllister in chapter 1, section 1.2 of this volume.
2. For a description and rebuttal of these arguments, see Wolf (2004), chapter 1.
3. See part II of *World Investment Report* (2008) for more details.

References

Adler, Nancy J. (2008). "International business scholarship: contributing to a broader definition of success," in Jean Boddewyn, ed., *International Business Scholarship: AIB Fellows on the First 50 Years and Beyond* (Volume 14 of Research in Global Strategic Management; Editor-in-Chief: Alan Rugman). (Bingley, UK: Emerald Group), pp. 327–37.

Aharoni, Yair (1994). "How small firms can achieve competitive advantages in an interdependent world," in Tamir E. Agmon and R. Drobbnick, eds., *Small Firms in Global Competition* (New York: Oxford University Press), pp. 9–18.

——— (2000a). "Globalization and the small, open economy," in Tamar Almor and Niron Hashai, eds., *FDI, International Trade and the Economics of Peacemaking Papers in Honor of Seev Hirsch* (College of Management Academic Division), pp. 90–116.

——— (2000b). "Introduction," in Yair Aharoni and Lilach Nahum, eds., *Globalization of Services: Some Implications for Theory and Practice* (London: Routledge), pp. 1–23.

——— (2000c). "The role of reputation in global professional business services," in Yair Aharoni and Lilach Nahum, eds., *Globalization of Services: Some Implications for Theory and Practice* (London: Routledge), pp. 125–41.

——— (2002a). "European air transportation: integration, globalization and structural changes," presented at European Integration in Swedish Economic Research, Molle, May 14–17, 2002, Swedish network for European Studies in Economics and Business.

——— (2002b). "The globalizer that cannot globalize—the airline transportation-industry," EIBA Annual Conference Athens, December.

——— (2004). "The race for FDI in services—the case of the airline industry," in Lars Oxelheim and Pervez Ghauri, eds., *European Union and the Race for Foreign Direct Investment in Europe* (Amsterdam: Elsevier), pp. 381–406.

——— (2006). "Helping the little guys," *CIIM Management Review* 2 (2), pp. 10–15.

——— (2009). "Israeli multinationals: competing from a small open economy," in Ravi Ramamurti and Jitendra. V. Singh, eds., *Emerging Multinationals from Emerging Markets* (Cambridge: Cambridge University Press), pp. 352–96.

Aharoni, Yair and Ravi Ramamurti (2008). "The internationalization of multinational," in Jean Boddewyn, ed., *International Business Scholarship: AIB Fellows on the First 50 Years and Beyond* (Volume 14 of Research in Global Strategic Management; Editor-in-Chief: Alan Rugman). (Bingley, UK: Emerald), pp. 177–201.

Aliber, Robert Z. (1970). "A theory of foreign direct investment," in Charles F. Kindleberger, ed., *The International Corporation* (Cambridge, MA: MIT Press), pp. 17–34.

Baldwin, Richard E. (2006). "Globalisation: the great unbundling(s)," *Prime Minister's Office: Economic Council of Finland*.

Baldwin, Richard E. and Philippe Martin (1999). "Two waves of globalization: superficial similarities, fundamental differences," *National Bureau of Economic Research Working paper 6904*, National Bureau of Economic Research.

Barnet, Richard J. and John Cavanagh (1995). *Global Dreams: Imperial Corporations and the New World Order* (New York: Simon and Schuster).

Barnet, Richard J. and Ronald E. Müller (1974). *Global Reach: The Power of the Multinational Corporations* (New York: Simon and Schuster).

Barney, Jay B. (1991). "Firm resources and sustained competitive advantage," *Journal of. Management* 17 (1), pp. 99–120.

Bartlett, Christopher A. and Sumantra Ghoshal (1989). *Managing across Borders: The Transnational Solution* (Boston: Harvard Business School Press).

Buckley, Peter and Mark Casson (1976). *The Future of the Multinational Enterprise* (London: Palgrave Macmillan).

De Soto, Hernando (2000). *The Mystery of Capitalism: Why Capitalism Triumphs in the West and Fails Everywhere Else* (New York: Basic Books).

Doremus, Paul, William W. Keller, Louis W. Pauly, and Simon Reich (1999). *The Myth of the Global Corporation* (Princeton: Princeton University Press).

Dunning, John H. (1979). "Explaining changing patterns of international production: in defense of the eclectic theory," *Oxford Bulletin of Economics and Statistics* 41 November, pp. 269–95.

Doz, Yves, José Santos, and Peter J Williamson (2001). *From Global to Metanational: How Companies Win in a Knowledge Economy* (Boston: Harvard Business School Press Books).

Evans, Peter (1979). *Dependent Development* (Princeton: Princeton University Press).

Franko, Larry G. (1976). *The European Multinational: A Renewed Challenge for American and British Big Business* (Stamford: Greylock).

Friedman, Thomas L. (2005). *The World Is Flat* (New York: Farrar, Straus&Giroux).

Gereffi, Gary, J. Humphrey and T.J. Sturgeon (2005). "The governance of global value chains," *Review of International Political Economy* 12 (1), pp. 78–104.

Ghemawat, Pankaj (2001). "Distance still matters: the hard reality of global expansion," *Harvard Business Review* 79 (8), pp. 137–47.

Gilpin, Robert (1975). *U.S. Power and the Multinational Corporation* (New York: Basic Books).

——— (2000). *The Challenge of Global Capitalism* (Princeton: Princeton University Press).

Grove Andrew S. (1996). *Only the Paranoid Survive: How to Exploit the Crisis Points that Challenge Every Company and Career* (New York: Currency Doubleday).

Hirst, Paul and Grahame Thompson (1999). *Globalization in Question: the International Economy and the Possibilities of Governance,* 2nd ed. (Cambridge: Polity Press).

Huston, Larry and Nabil Sakkab (2006). "Connect and develop: inside Procter and Gamble's new model for innovation," *Harvard Business Review* 84 (3), pp. 58–69.

Hymer, Stephen H. (1960/1976). *The International Operations of National Firms: A Study of Direct Foreign Investment,* reprint of a doctoral dissertation, Department of Economics (Cambridge, MA: MIT Press).

Johanson, Jan and Jan-Erik Vahlne (1977). "The internationalization process of the firm: A model of knowledge development and increasing foreign market commitments," *Journal of International Business Studies* 8, pp. 23–32.

——— (1990). "The mechanism of internationalization," *International Marketing Review* 7 (4), pp. 11–24.

Jolly, Vijay K., Matti Alahuta, and Jean-Pierre Jeannet (1992). "Challenging the incumbents: how high technology start-ups compete globally," *Journal of Strategic Change* 1, pp. 71–82.

Knight, Gary A. and S. Tamer Cavusgil (1996). "The born global firm: a challenge to traditional internationalization theory," in L. Lindmark, P.R. Christensen, H. Eskelinen, B. Forsstrom, O.J. Sorenson, and E. Vatn, eds., *Advances in International Marketing* 8, pp. 11–26.

Kogut Bruce. and Zander U. (1993). "Knowledge of the firm and the evolutionary theory of the multinational enterprise," *Journal of International Business Studies* 24 (4), pp. 625–45.

Kokko, Ari (2006). *The Home Country Effects of FDI in Developing Economies* (Stockholm: European Institute of Japanese Studies), mimeo.

Lall, Sanjay (1995). "Industrial strategy and policies on foreign direct investment in East Asia," *Transnational Corporations* 4 (3), pp. 1–26.

Levitt, Kari (1970). *Silent Surrender: The Multinational Corporation in Canada* (New York: St. Martin's Press).

Levitt, Theodore (1983). "The globalization of markets," *Harvard Business Review* 61 (May–June), pp. 92–102.

MacCormack, Alan D. (2007). "Best practices of global innovators," *Harvard Business School Working Knowledge*, available at http://hbswk.hbs.edu.item/5750, last visited on June 23, 2009.

Monbiot, George (2000). *Captive State: The Corporate Takeover of Britain* (Basingstoke: MacMillan).

Moran, Theodore H., Edward M.Graham, and Magnus Blomström, eds. (2005). *Does Foreign Direct Investment Promote Development?* (Washington, DC: Institute for International Economics).

Navaretti, Giorgio Barba and Anthony J. Venables (2004). *Multinational Firms in the World Economy* (Princeton: Princeton University Press).

Ohmae, Kenichi (1991). *The Borderless World: Management Lessons in the New Logic of the Global Market Place* (New York: Harper Collins).

——— (1995). *The End of the Nation State: The Rise of Regional Economies* (New York: Free Press)

Oxelheim, Lars and P. Ghauri, eds. (2004). *European Union and the Race for Foreign Direct Investment in Europe* (Oxford: Elsevier).

Palmisano, Samuel J. (2006). "The globally integrated enterprise," *Foreign Affairs* 85 (May–June), pp. 127–36.

Peng, M.W., Denis Y.L Wang, and Yi Jiang (2008). "An institution-based view of international business strategy: a focus on emerging economies," *Journal of International Business Studies* 39 (5), pp. 920–36.

Porter, Michael E. (1980). *Competitive Strategy* (New York: Free Press).

——— (1986). *Competition in Global Industries* (Boston: Harvard Business School Press).

Pralahad, C.K. and Gary Hamel (1990). "The core competence of the corporation," *Harvard Business Review* (May–June), 68 (3), pp. 79–91.

Reich, Robert B. (1990). "Who is us? (The Changing American Corporation)," *Harvard Business Review* 68 (1), pp. 53–64

——— (1991). *The Work of Nations: Preparing Ourselves for 21st Century Capitalism* (New York: Alfred Knopf).

Rugman, Alan M. (1981). *Inside the Multinationals: The Economics of Internal Markets* (New York: Columbia University Press).

——— (2005). *The Regional Multinationals: MNEs and "Global" Strategic Management* (Cambridge: Cambridge University Press).

Rugman, Alan M. and Alain Verbeke (1993). "Foreign subsidiaries and multinational strategic management: an extension and correction of porter's single diamond Framework," *Management International Review* 33 (2), pp. 71–84.

——— (2001). "Subsidiary specific advantages in multinational enterprises," *Strategic Management Journal* 22 (3), pp. 237–50.

Saari, David J. (1999). *Global Corporations and Sovereign Nations: Collision or Cooperation?* (Westport, CT: Quorum Books).

Servan-Schreiber, Jean Jacque (1967). Le *Défi Américain* (Paris: Denoel).

Stiglitz, Joseph E. (2006). *Making Globalization Work* (New York: W.W. Norton).

Stopford, J.M. (1974). "The origins of British based multinational enterprises," *Business History Review* 48, pp. 303–35.

Stopford J.M. and Louis T. Wells Jr. (1972). *Managing the Multinational Enterprise* (New York: Basic Books).

Tsurumi, Yoshi. (1976). *The Japanese Are Coming: A Multinational Interaction of Firms and Politics* (Cambridge, MA: Ballinger).

UNCTAD (1983). *Transnational Corporations in World Development Third Survey* (New York: United Nations).

——— (2000). *World Investment Report 2000: FDI and the Challenge of Development* (New York and Geneva: United Nations).

——— (2002). "Are transnationals bigger than countries?" (Geneva: UNCTAD), Press release TAD/INF/PR/47 (December 8, 2002), available at http://unctad.org/Templates/Webflyer.asp?docID=2426&intItemID=2068&lang=1, last visited on June 23, 2009.

——— (2004). *World Investment Report: The Shift Towards Services* (New York and Geneva: United Nations).

——— (2006). *World Investment Report: FDI from Developing and Transition Economies: Implications for Development* (New York and Geneva: United Nations).

——— (2007). *World Investment Report: Transnational Corporations, Extractive Industries and Development* (New York and Geneva: United Nations).

——— (2008). *World Investment Report: Transnational Corporations and the Infrastructure Challenge* (New York and Geneva: United Nations).

United Nations Department of Economic and Social Affairs (1973). *Multinational Corporations in World Development* (New York: United Nations).

Van Den Bulcke, Daniel and Alain Verbeke (2001). *Globalization and the Small Open Economy* (Aldershot: Edward Elgar).

Vernon, Raymond (1966). "International investment and international trade in the product life cycle," *Quarterly Journal of Economics* 80, pp. 190–207.

——— (1971). *Sovereignty at Bay: The Multinational Spread of U.S. Enterprise* (New York: Basic Books).

——— (1977). *Storm over the Multinationals* (Cambridge, MA: Harvard University Press).

——— (1991). "Sovereignty at bay: twenty years after," *Millennium Journal of International Studie*s 20 (2), 191–95.

Wolf, Martin (2004). *Why Globalization Works* (New Haven: Yale University Press).

Yoshino Michael. Y. (1976). *The Japanese Multinational Enterprises* (Cambridge, MA: Harvard University Press).

Zaheer, Srilata (1995). "Overcoming the liability of foreignness," *Academy of Management Journal* 38 (2), pp. 341–63.

Chapter 4

Toward a Renewed Stages Theory for BRIC Multinational Enterprises? A Home Country Bargaining Approach

Rob van Tulder

Introduction: New Players, New Theory?

The recent emergence of a number of high-profile multinational enterprises (MNEs) from emerging markets has triggered considerable research and debate on how to understand and appraise this phenomenon. This is notwithstanding the fact that in relative terms, measured as a share of total international foreign direct investment (FDI), the magnitude of the phenomenon remains relatively modest. The challenge for empirical research includes the question of whether the strategies and motives for the internationalization of these MNEs can be considered *fundamentally* different from the strategies of firms from developed countries (Luo and Tung 2007), or whether their ownership advantages are fundamentally different from those of developed country MNEs (Mathews 2002; Luo and Tung 2007; Buckley et al. 2007; Li 2007). Increasingly described as "springboarding" (Luo and Tung 2007), the internationalization strategies of emerging market firms are characterized by their high-risk, aggressive, and "boom-and-bust" or radical nature, while targeting many customers in many foreign markets at once, in a strategy of entrepreneurial venturing (Yiu et al. 2007). Comparing developed country MNEs of the 1960s, with emerging market MNEs in the 2000s, Dunning, Kim, and Park (2008) identified a number of additional differences. These include forms of entry (alliances); motivation (asset augmentation); managerial approach (regional and geocentric); role of home governments (more active than in the past); regional destination; institutional triggers of internationalization rather than traditional motives related to neoclassical models; and the lack of firm-specific ownership advantages (177).

These are interesting empirical observations, since most of the existing International Business (IB) theories are based on explorations and explanations of the internationalization strategies of these "traditional multinationals" under "normal" institutional circumstances. Does this, therefore, imply that theoretical lines need to be redrawn and new general theories need to be designed in order to explain the new breed of multinationals? Or are we, on the contrary, simply facing a new phase of the world economy, one which applies to all multinationals and which could lead, perhaps, to some modifications, but not to a fundamental change in existing theoretical approaches?

In terms of the stages theory of the international firm of the Uppsala school (Johanson and Vahlne 1977) and the learning school (Kogut and Zander 1993), for instance, the prime theoretical modification seems to be that emerging market MNEs must learn and build up their capacities more quickly, in order to gain competitive advantage and international presence. No major alterations required here. The internalization approach to IB as pioneered by Peter J. Buckley and Mark Casson, stresses the limited value of neoclassical models for understanding the existence of multinational enterprises. This observation still holds (as the contribution by Buckley et al. in chapter 13 of this volume illustrates). An updated internalization approach would have to add a number of additional observations to explain the differences in entry-mode choice by emerging market MNEs, while targeting developed countries in search of strategic assets (Buckley et al. 2007). The extension of the internalization theory by Alan M. Rugman in his FSA-CSA framework, makes the link between firm-level analysis and country-level analysis, something that appears extremely important in explaining the current emergence of new MNEs from countries that barely participated in the world economy forty years ago. A specific subcategory in this group is represented by the so-called BRIC countries, which comprises Brazil, Russia, India, and China (such as the BRIC countries, for various reasons). Rugman in particular (2008; chapter 5 of this volume) is very outspoken on the question of whether a new theory is needed to explain emerging market MNEs. No, the country-specific advantages (CSAs) of emerging markets do not need separate explanation—being based on cheap labor, natural resources, and cheap money—which also leads to firm-specific advantages (FSAs) in the resulting economies of scale.

Finally, as regards the eclectic theory of John H. Dunning, and the related concept of the investment development path (Dunning and Narula 1996) some modifications have been proposed, but no major revisions. Studies by Dunning, Kim, and Park (2008) and Dunning and Lundan (2008) stress that there is, perhaps, need for a more evolutionary and institution-based theory of international business. The investment development path, which is intended to explain the emergence of new players on the global investment scene—and thus of particular potential benefit in the analysis of emerging market MNEs—has also recently undergone slight modification, in particular in its periodization of the net balance between outward foreign direct investment (OFDI) and inward foreign direct investment (IFDI) (cf. Dunning, Kim, and Park 2008).

Most modern IB theorists have either denied that there is need for new approaches, or have slightly modified their approach, not to explain for emerging market multinational specifically, but rather to include some of the characteristics of globalization in general. This chapter, however, proposes a more heterodox approach. It searches for a number of idiosyncratic elements in internationalization strategies of BRIC MNEs and the relationship with home country policies. This approach implies that a number of traditional approaches are renewed and rephrased. In particular, four elements of renewal will be addressed: (1) the relationship with the *home government,* which implies a renewal of Raymond Vernon's obsolescing bargain; (2) the importance of *market power* in the home market, which involves a renewal of Stephen Hymer's market power approach; (3) a reappraisal of the impact of *economic size* and its relationship with political power, which implies that there is need for separate studies of (comparative) BRIC MNEs; (4) a reappraisal of the *general theory of the firm,* as, for instance, pioneered by Edith T. Penrose (1959), which involves looking at the social responsibilities or the fiduciary duties of the firm as precondition and factor for its continued growth and international expansion; finally leading to (5) a reformulation of the *investment development path* as a BRIC-specific explanation of development at the micro/mesolevel of analysis. The conclusion will be that a new theory on IB is not necessarily mandatory, but that (1) some of the old insights into the study of multinationals should be dusted off, while (2) some of the existing approaches require a change in emphasis, in order to (3) document adequately and assess the present stage of globalization in general, and the impact of strategies of BRIC economies and their MNEs in particular. This may also have an impact on the historic study of developed country MNEs.

4.1   An Obsolescing Bargain…Vis-à-Vis Home Governments

The present stage of globalization can be characterized as a transition phase, in which the traditional hegemonic powers from the developed world are increasingly challenged by new powers from the developing world. This applies in particular to the four BRIC countries that combine populous countries with relatively rapid and sustained economic growth. Earlier contenders from the developing world (the Middle East in particular), derived their influence primarily from their possession of resources, but this did not result in the birth of MNEs from these countries. In contrast, the rise of BRIC MNEs has been accompanied—and can be partly explained—by the rise of assertive, and often self-confident, national governments. Along the existing orthodoxy of the Bretton Woods institutions, these governments have started to open their borders to IFDI, accompanied, in many instances, by significant entry conditions. This was possible because of the BRICs' size and their attractiveness as potential markets for developed country MNEs. In the classic obsolescing bargaining model of Vernon and its applications (cf. e.g., Gomez-Casseres 1990) the relationship with *host* country governments, and host country policies, has been the prime object of research, while the direction of the investment flows researched was from developed to developing countries. Initially, these strategies were strongly stimulated by the home country governments (as in the United States in the 1950s, Japan in the 1960s and 1970s, or the United Kingdom and France toward their former colonies in the same period). They were also almost always accompanied by strict regulation of inward FDI in the country. In later phases, developed country governments lowered their leveraging activities for outward FDI considerably.

A traditional characteristic of BRIC MNEs has also been a relative preference for investments in less developed or peripheral countries (cf. Lall 1983; UNCTAD 2007), but recently these firms also started to invest in developed countries. Part of the explanation lies in the already mentioned firm-specific characteristics: asset augmenting, alliance seeking, and ownership advantages. But a considerable part of the explanation can also be found in the relationship with the domestic (home) government. First, this is explained by the adoption of "go global" policies by China and India, in particular, in the course of the 1990s. Initially rather general and passive, but by the twenty-first century, more specific and active, these policies had a noticeable impact on the outward internationalization strategies of firms (cf. Buckley et al. 2008). The governments of Brazil and Russia have been far less accommodating in general to outward investment, so this cannot be applied as a general framework for the BRIC countries (although there are indications that the BRIC policies are also converging in this respect).

Second, the home BRIC governments have remained relatively restrictive toward foreign entries. Other than smaller developing countries, such as Malaysia and South Africa, these countries have used their bargaining power to create substantial entry barriers for foreign MNEs or to strike beneficial deals for local corporations (that consequently could ally with these new entrants on relatively favourable conditions). Contrary to what the obsolescing bargain model would predict, the bargaining position of the government therefore has been strong from the start, and has remained relatively strong throughout the present era. Contrary to what some of the *dependencista* theorists in the 1960s predicted, national governments did not become an "annex" (comprador bourgeoisie) of foreign capital. As a result, and due to sustained institutional barriers, some foreign entries found it extremely difficult to sustain their investment, and consequently had to sell off their BRIC subsidiaries. In the literature we can find this under the heading of "exit," "retreat," or "deinternationalization" strategies (Benito and Welch 1997), but studies have basically been applied to document and explain this retreat from developed economies. It is highly likely that developed country multinationals have found it particularly difficult to sustain their investment in the BRIC economies, due to institutional difficulties (essentially meaning, sustained transaction costs involved in continuous bargaining with the national governments).

Third, strong and assertive home governments at the same time also speeded up the internationalization strategies of dominant national firms. In the resources sector, this has been the case for obvious strategic reasons. Most of the leading resources-based outward investments from the BRIC economies have been performed by state-owned companies. The traditional motives for internationalization of MNEs, thus, have to be complemented by geopolitical motives of the home governments for the BRIC MNEs. The BRIC governments have also increasingly proven themselves prepared to bargain directly with host country governments, which explains the rapidly increasing number of bilateral investment treaties with developing countries.

This indicates that the four leading motives for internationalization, as introduced by Dunning and summarized in numerous popularizations of his work (market/asset/efficiency/resources-seeking), also require updating. For instance, in his original work, under the heading of "other motives," Dunning listed "escape investments" (Dunning and Lundan 2008). In most of the popularizations of his work, this motive has largely disappeared. However, in case studies and narratives on the motives of internationalization by leading BRIC MNEs, the escape motive reappears prominently again: Brazilian firms that internationalize to regional tax havens; Indian firm that seek to escape government restrictions; Russian firms that seek to avoid domestic regulatory constraints (Dunning, Kim, and Park 2008). Recently, the escape response to home constraints has received renewed attention in general (Witt and Lewin 2007). The relationship with the home government and its bargaining dynamics, in any case, appears to be an important factor in explaining the characteristics, as well as the success and failure, of OFDI by BRIC MNEs. Next to firm intrinsic motives, extrinsic motives are increasingly important (Van Tulder with Van der Zwart 2006).

The relationship with policies and policy makers at home and abroad is also the topic of this volume. Table 4.1 summarizes the balancing act, as developed by home country governments toward inward and outward foreign direct investment. It is partly based on the papers by Buckley et al. (chapter 13) and De Beule and Van Den Bulcke (chapter 14). Smaller developing countries—as well as developed countries—have adopted relatively liberal inward FDI policies, combined with very modest stimuli or leveraging activities in support of OFDI. Most developed countries in the past, as well as the BRIC countries at present, have adopted considerable and sustained restrictions. Brazil and Russia have only recently started to develop policies in support of OFDI; while India and China did so slightly earlier. All try to link their outward investment to domestic growth policies.

Table 4.1 Home country FDI policies: a balancing act between stimulus and control

	Stimulus/Leveraging OFDI	
	High	Low
High	United States in 1950 Japan in 1960s/1970s	Developed countries in 1980s Emerging markets: Brazil, Russia, China, India
Low	Malaysia, Singapore, Republic of Korea, South Africa	The neoclassical approach (no real world examples)

Source: Author.

4.2   Timing and the Importance of Regaining the Domestic Market

Internationalization theory has primarily focused on the when, why, and how of internationalization: the timing, the motives of firms in moving abroad, and the competitive causes and consequences. However, this has not considered in detail the relationship with the industry or studied the internationalization trajectories of individual firms over a longer period of time (Maitland, Rose, and Nicholas 2005). Classical macroeconomic approaches suggest that OFDI appears only when a country has reached a certain level of development, without specific reference to industries and industry dynamics. Anecdotal evidence of the specific internationalization strategies of BRIC MNEs ((cf. Fortanier and Van Tulder 2009), however, may indicate a need for different explanations. The recent investment paths of BRIC MNEs, such as Lenovo, Tata, Gazprom, as well as some of the larger Indian pharmaceutical companies, such as Dr. Reddy's, were also triggered by first acquiring in the domestic market, the remnants of developed country firms that had previously invested in these countries. This has already been experienced in the oil industry after nationalizations in an earlier phase.

The factors behind the relative "failure" of these developed country investments deserve particular attention. The literature on retreat and withdrawal strategies is not particularly well developed in the IB literature, certainly not from the perspective of the host country. The question of "international overstretch" in the internationalization strategies of MNEs therefore becomes increasingly relevant. In this case, two dimensions are worth stressing. Both apply in particular to the BRIC countries. First, the pace and motives of internationalization, combined with misconceived opportunities. In particular, the promise of a sizable market in the recently opened BRIC countries of India and China has often been overstated, which has resulted in a serious mismatch between the intention and the reality of the developed country investors. Returns on investment in these culturally and institutionally distant markets proved difficult to achieve, resulting in many loss-making activities. Second, the entry has often been in alliance with an often sizable local partner. This entry strategy may reduce the external institutional uncertainty toward governments, but also makes the long-term success of the investment dependent upon the nature of the cooperation with the local partner. A number of European MNEs have already decided to invest in Europe instead of in Asia, due to the loss of intellectual property to local partners. In the process of offshoring and outsourcing, some studies have also noted that many firms suffer from "overstretch," which has prompted them to substitute distant suppliers for local suppliers or face bankruptcy. The obsolescing bargaining model for the BRIC countries in particular, must be complemented by a firm-firm bargaining/alliance model.

Current IB theory tends to stress the "asset-augmenting" intention of the takeover strategies of emerging market MNEs, and suggests that this goes together with OFDI. However, particularly for BRIC MNEs, this process seems to be *preceded* in many cases, by a strategy of partly regaining control over the domestic market, by acquiring the knowledge through joint ventures in the domestic market first, which hollows out the competitive advantage of these firms and ultimately leads to their withdrawal from the BRIC market. In this sense the classical thesis of Hymer, which stresses that firms internationalize after they have gained sufficient market power in their domestic market (and gain sufficient firm-specific advantages in Rugman's terms), holds. Hymer, however, did not really consider the practical question of *how* firms gain this oligopolistic position in the domestic market. Hymer's thesis for BRIC MNEs can therefore be extended by looking at the way these firms first pick up the pieces (or gain strategic assets) of the retreating firms that operated in their markets. Some of the firms have followed up these domestic repositioning activities, by acquiring even the parent company in the developed market. Indian pharmaceutical and steel companies illustrate this mechanism.

The experience of BRIC MNEs shows that it is important to adopt a sectoral/industrial approach to OFDI and IFDI flows, in order to understand the dynamics of the whole industry and the conditions under which specific firms gain competitive advantages. Ownership advantages play an increasing role. Many of the leading BRIC MNEs are either state-owned or family-owned conglomerates, which is an organizational type of MNEs that has long been deemed inappropriate for rapid internationalization— which requires easy access to capital through the stock market. In particular, family-owned and state-owned firms would seem to be best equipped to gain a dominant position in the domestic market. They have the institutional embeddings and the governance structure to prevent takeover by foreign firms, while at the same time having access to sufficient means to finance rapid takeovers and internationalization strategies.

4.3   The Renewed Importance of Size

Size has always mattered in international business, and it is likely that this also applies to emerging market economies. MNEs from smaller countries tend to be more international and have become international in a much earlier phase of their existence than MNEs from larger countries. Relatively speaking, in terms of the Transnationality Index,[1] BRIC MNEs are less international than their counterparts from smaller developing countries. Moreover, all BRIC economies remain relatively closed, with low penetration ratios of IFDI and a net negative balance of outward to inward FDI (see table 4.2).

Table 4.2   BRIC OFDI/IFDI ratio, various years (percentage of GDP)

Country	1990	2000	2006
Brazil	1.1	0.5	0.4
Russian Federation	n.a.	0.6	0.8
China	0.2	0.15	0.25
India	0	0.1	0.26

Source: UNCTAD, WIR (2007, 264), measured by FDI stocks as a percentage of GDP.

For the largest firms in the BRIC countries, therefore, the domestic market still provides sufficient expansion potential to invest in, and this is certainly the case, where the domestic market is growing rapidly. The domestic market also provides the capabilities to profit from controlled outward expansion (Cantwell and Barnard 2008), while at the same time creating sufficient institutional protection against foreign acquisitions, without debilitating growth possibilities—as long as the domestic economy grows at a sufficient pace. Their relative large size and smaller degree of internationalization, also makes BRIC MNEs more difficult to take over. Consequently, they are less likely to suffer from internationalization overstretch. Internationalization is less necessary to gain access to rapidly growing markets, while resources-seeking investment are often strongly backed by the national government. The exception to this rule may be a number of the smaller and medium-sized firms that recently internationalized through rapid and very risky M&As—and which are therefore incorrectly considered to represent the new model of emerging market MNEs. There are signs that some of these firms (such as the well-publicized but relatively small firms Lenovo [China] and Dr. Reddy's [India]) are already experiencing substantial overstretch problems, which could lead to a declining internationalization path and which would fit in the learning models of internationalization by Vermeulen and Barkema (2002).

The large size of the domestic BRIC market, as well as the institutional backing of the respective large or powerful governments, also provides an excellent ground for relatively controlled—but sizeable—cross-border mergers and acquisitions by BRIC MNEs. BRIC MNEs dominate cross-border M&A statistics. In 2006, the M&As activities of Brazilian firms accounted for 20% of total Latin American and Caribbean cross-border M&As by number, but 64% by value (UNCTAD 2007, 273ff.). Comparable figures exist for Russian (59% by number and 67% by value of all foreign purchases by CIS and transition economy firms), Indian (97% by number and 99% by value, of purchases by South Asian firms) and Chinese firms, including Hong Kong (China) (87% by number and 94% by value, of all M&As in East Asia). A representative measurement, therefore, of M&A activity from emerging markets largely reveals the BRIC perspective. This is something to take stock of.

Finally, size certainly matters in international political fora. The bargaining position of the BRIC governments has considerably increased since the mid-1990s in bilateral, regional, and multilateral institutions. This position may be considered an extension of the relationship between home government and core domestic players. As a consequence, BRIC MNEs may be considered better represented in international fora than the average emerging market MNE, and perhaps even better represented than many developed-market MNEs. The obsolescing bargaining model, as well as a stage model of internationalization, should therefore not only include home governments, but also their position in international fora.

4.4 The Increasing Importance of Corporate Responsibility

The international expansion path of BRIC MNEs is strongly affected by their attitude toward corporate social responsibility—more so than for MNEs from emerging markets generally (Van Tulder with Van der Zwart 2006). The resources on which the growth of large firm is based (Penrose 1959) are increasingly found in intangible assets, including the firm's reputation with a large number of stakeholders from around the world. Most BRIC MNEs represent flagship or core firms (Rugman and D'Cruz 2000; Van Tulder with Van der Zwart 2006), which makes them very focal and vulnerable to stakeholder influence.

Important questions in IB research into corporate responsibility-related topics have focused, in particular, on whether MNEs have a positive or negative impact on their recipient economies (Fortanier 2008). This body of research primarily relates to developed country MNEs. The success of BRIC MNEs, in particular, will be increasingly influenced by their position on corporate responsibility. First, they are leading firms in their own countries, and are often heralded as the carriers of the developmental model (and success) of the country. Focal firms are always more prone to public pressure. The BRIC governments are building sustainable development strategies, often in collaboration with their most important stakeholders (local MNEs), which thus have considerable opportunity to cocreate those domestic institutions that are particularly conducive for their competitive position.

Second, their size, and backing by their home governments, makes the expansion strategies of BRIC MNEs in developed countries especially dependent on their (perceived) legitimacy with influential stakeholders. In this respect, there exists a particular "liability of foreignness" (Zaheer 1995), for BRIC MNEs that is probably greater than for emerging market MNEs in general. Developed country governments, increasingly use corporate social responsibility (CSR) strategies, including trademarks, codes, and governance principles, as a means of protecting their industrial models—sometimes with good reason, sometimes as outright protectionism, but always with the result that BRIC MNEs, in particular, must increase their CSR activities.

Third, CSR strategies have proven to be an excellent entry strategy in specific industries, or a way to break the oligopoly of existing industries. The pharmaceutical industries of India and Brazil have used their bargaining power in the international patenting regime—making use of exemption rules—to provide a niche for generic drug manufacturers that consequently have conquered part of the global pharmaceutical market. A new coalition appeared, for instance, in the case of generic medicines for the treatment of HIV/AIDS: an alliance between influential nongovernmental organizations (NGOs) such as Oxfam, large pension funds such as Calpers, and the governments of South Africa and Brazil. The challenge for BRIC MNEs, thus, is how to incorporate corporate responsibility into mainstream strategy, rather than something that is simply an add-on dimension or limited to corporate philanthropy.

4.5 A Different BRIC Investment Development Path?

The previous comments on BRIC-specific patterns and explanation models are bound to lead to a revised investment development path. This is the final challenge addressed by this chapter. The original investment development path (next to comparable development models such as the flying geese model) links stages of economic development to the balance of IFDI and OFDI (Dunning and Narula 1996). A renewed investment development path (Dunning and Lundan 2008, 330) also attempted to incorporate trade and industrial structural change into the analysis, while linking this to the ownership, location, and internalization (OLI) model. The investment development path reflects the changing competitive advantages of firms vis-à-vis their foreign competitors, but in its most popular adaptation and applications, does this only at a macroeconomic level, while the exact picture and dynamism at the micro- (industry) and mesolevel (firm) of analysis is more or less unstudied. Stage 1 is primarily resource based; stage 2 is investment driven; stage 3 occurs when developing countries reach maturity and become innovation driven; stages 4 and 5 mark an increasingly knowledge- and service-intensive economy. At the end of stage 2, the negative balance between OFDI and IFDI reaches its lowest point, after which firms from the recipient country engage in outward investment to such an extent that the balance slowly starts to improve.

However, even recent modifications in the investment development path have difficulty in explaining the departures in the original predictions of the model, and some of the idiosyncrasies of the BRIC countries, in particular because several developing countries have engaged in OFDI at a much earlier phase than would have been predicted by the investment development path. The turning point in the net balance between OFDI and IFDI might already arrive in stage 1, while IFDI flows are considerably lower than expected in the investment development path. An application of the investment development path approach that includes the specific experience of the BRIC economies and their MNEs, is bound to result in a more meso- (sectoral-industry) or even microeconomic elaboration. This has the advantage of presenting a greater understanding of the firm strategic and home country bargaining dynamism of this process. The prime objective of this exercise should be to zoom in on what might explain the bend or turn in the first downward line toward a more upward line. Figure 4.1 gives a tentative shape of the redrawn BRIC investment development path, with some indicators that explain changes in the nature of the balance between OFDI and IFDI.

Earlier observations in this contribution suggest that the first bend in the investment development path curve might also be the result of real outward investments, as the result of a takeover strategy of failed IFDI by foreign entrants. In this stage, the BRIC government sustains rather rigid regulation; for instance, by allowing foreign firms to enter solely through joint ventures, which ultimately will discourage IFDI in some industries, and slows the pace of IFDI flows. Only BRIC governments are able (and willing) to define such entry barriers; none of the other developing countries have exercised

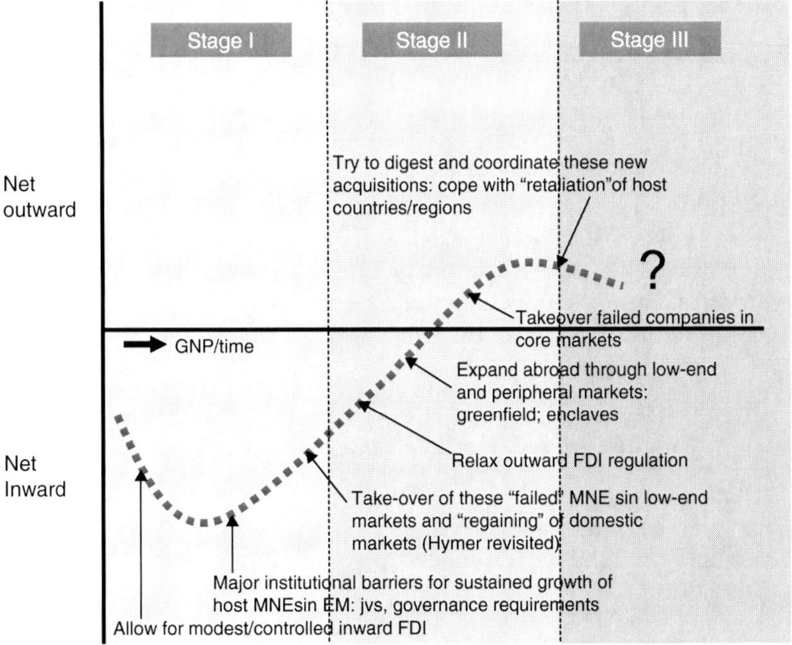

Figure 4.1   Meso investment development path for BRIC firms
Source: The Author.

comparable bargaining power over new entrants. Where home country governments also apply strict limitations on the outward investments of domestic firms, a further bend of the curve toward a less negative balance can be hampered. The curve bends slightly in case of internationalization overstretch by the foreign investors which lead to a slightly better OFDI-IFDI balance, without, however, involving substantial OFDI. Only when the home government relaxes OFDI restrictions, can the upward curve gain pace. This has lead to an expansion of the most competitive (mostly smaller) BRIC MNEs into low-end and peripheral markets, often in the same region (Lall 1983; Rugman, chapter 5 of this volume). Only after the home government starts to stimulate significantly OFDI ("go global" policies), for its largest firms, in particular for resource seeking motives in combination with geopolitical motives, will the balance become positive. This has not yet happened for the BRIC economies as a whole and is not likely to happen in the near future (with the probable exception of Russia, see table 4.2).

What happens in stage 2 remains rather unclear for three reasons. First, this is because few sectors of the BRIC countries have reached a positive OFDI-IFDI balance, making it difficult to reach conclusions. Second, many of the BRIC companies will be confronted with substantial opposition in the recipient countries. Where they can develop sufficiently convincing CSR strategies (including acceptable and transparent governance structures) they might expand unhampered, and evade retaliation. Where they cannot, there will be clear limits to their expansion strategies in OECD countries, as is already the case in a number of strategic industries. Third, the rapid take-over strategy of smaller BRIC MNEs, in particular, remains extremely risky. It is uncertain whether these firms have the managerial capacities to digest their new acquisitions, and whether the remaining competitors in these markets will not try to regain hold of their own domestic market, in the same vein as these firms have done in their home markets. The contribution of the Multilateral Investment Guarantee Agency (MIGA) in this volume (chapter 12) points at a comparable process, supported by a number of interesting cases with regard to the growing importance of political risk. MIGA's conclusion is that the sustainability of the expansion of Indian firms, in particular, is questionable, due to their low perception of political risk. Thus the expansion process may stall.

Conclusion: A Specific Framewok for BRIC MNEs

This chapter has argued that we do not need a completely new theory for emerging market multinationals. This effort to reach one explanation for all emerging market MNEs is ill-founded, given the immense differences in this group of countries. This contribution, however, has illustrated that a separate approach can—and perhaps must—be adopted to explain in particular MNEs from the BRIC countries. BRIC MNEs present a separate and highly instructive research agenda in which political and economic factors play an equally important role. Political factors are not merely external institutions and are not linked to the national level of analysis alone. Economic factors are not just firm specific and related to internalization and learning, they are increasingly becoming prone to strategic and geopolitical considerations in which escape motives may be equally important, as firms become a function of the national policy agenda of emerging world powers. The success of BRIC MNEs can be explained by a combination of firm-specific and policy-specific factors (and their interaction), next to the more traditional factors.

This chapter has outlined a number of the specific dimensions that must be considered when studying BRIC MNEs. Interestingly, in outlining this approach, a number of theories, parts of theories, and empirical angles that have become relatively lost in mainstream IB studies were reappraised. This resulted in emphasizing dimensions that have largely been absent in mainstream studies: home country relations, intergovernmental relations, the regaining of domestic markets, the controversial nature of foreign acquisitions, and the importance of stakeholders. It has resulted in a rudimentary new stages theory of BRIC MNEs at the mesolevel of analysis, in which these elements were—albeit it briefly and intuitively—given consideration. Applying this renewed development path might also be useful for historical studies, leading perhaps to a reappraisal of the exact factors behind the emergence, the subsequent internationalization trajectories, and the relative success over longer periods of time, of developed country MNEs—starting forty years ago (Jones and Khanna 2006; Maitland, Rose, and Nicholas 2005).

In the development course of a scientific approach to international business, the area has slowly changed from international political economy (with strong relations with international economics) in the 1950s and 1960s, via an emphasis on international business (with strong emphasis on internalization and industrial effects) in the 1970s and 1980s, toward international management (with an emphasis on learning and headquarter-subsidiary relationships) in the 1990s and early twenty-first century. As such, the discipline has gained scientific legitimacy, in particular in the management sciences, but has also lost some of its managerial and societal relevance, as well as scientific legitimacy in adjoining areas such as international economics and international relations theory. The emergence of BRIC MNEs in particular will hopefully stimulate a renewal of some of the old approaches to international business, which might lead to a bridging of the traditional divide not only between international political economy, international business and international management, but also with the other scientific disciplines.

Note

1. As documented annually in the *World Investment Report,* on the basis of the joint Erasmus University and UNCTAD research that compiles the internationalization profiles of the largest MNEs from developing and developed countries.

References

Benito, G. and Welch, L. (1997). "De-internationalisation," *Management International Review,* 37 special issue, pp. 7–25.

Buckley, P., Jeremy L. Clegg, A. R. Cross, H. Voss, Mark Rhodes, and Ping Zheng (2008). "Explaining China's outward FDI: an institutional perspective," in Karl P. Sauvant, ed., *The Rise of Transnational Corporations from Emerging Market: Threat or Opportunity?* (Cheltenham: Edward Elgar), pp. 107–57.

Buckley, P., Jeremy L. Clegg, A. R. Cross, X. Liu, H. Voss, and P. Zheng (2007). "The determinants of Chinese outward foreign direct investment," *Journal of International Business Studies* 38, pp. 499–518.

Cantwell, J. and Helen Barnard (2008). "Do firms from emerging markets have to invest abroad? Outward FDI and the competitiveness of firms," in Karl P. Sauvant, ed., *The Rise of Transnational Corporations from Emerging Markets: Threat or Opportunity?* (Cheltenham: Edward Elgar), pp. 55–85.

Dunning, J., C. Kim, and D. Park (2008). "Old wine in new bottles: a comparison of emerging-market TNCs today and developed-country TNCs thirty years ago," in Karl P. Sauvant, ed., *The Rise of Transnational Corporations from Emerging Markets. Threat or Opportunity?* (Cheltenham: Edward Elgar), pp. 158–80.

Dunning, J. and R. Narula (1996). *Foreign Direct Investment and Governments* (London and New York: Routledge).

Dunning, J. and S. Lundan (2008). *Multinational Enterprises and the Global Economy,* 2nd ed. (Cheltenham: Edward Elgar).

Fortanier, F. (2008). *Multinational Enterprises, Institutions and Sustainable Development* (Amsterdam: University of Amsterdam Business School, Ph.D. thesis).

Fortanier, F. and R. van Tulder (2009). "Internationalization trajectories—a cross-country comparison: are large Chinese and Indian companies different?" *Industrial and Corporate Change* 18 (2), pp. 223–47.

Gomez-Casseres, B. (1990). "Firm ownership preferences and host government restrictions: an integrated approach," *Journal of International Business Studies* 21 (1), pp. 1–22.

Hymer, Stephen H. (1960). *The International Operations of National Firms: A Study of Direct Foreign Investment* (Cambridge, MA: MIT Press).

Johanson, J. and J.-E. Vahlne (1977). "The internationalisation process of the firm—a model of knowledge development and increasing foreign market commitments," *Journal of International Business Studies* 8 (1), pp. 23–32.

Jones, G and T. Khanna (2006). "Bringing history (back) into international business," *Journal of International Business Studies* 37 (4), pp. 453–68.

Kogut, B. and U. Zander (1993). "Knowledge of the firm and the evolutionary theory of the multinational corporation," *Journal of International Business Studies* 4, pp. 625–45.

Lall, S. (1983). *The New Multinationals: The Spread of Third World Enterprises* (Chichester: John Wiley).

Li, P. (2007). "Towards an integrated theory of multinational evolution: the evidence of Chinese multinational enterprises as latecomers," *Journal of International Management* 13, pp. 296–318.

Luo, Y. and R. Tung (2007). "International expansion of emerging market enterprises: a springboard perspective," Journal *of International Business Studies* 38, pp. 481–98.

Maitland, E., E. Rose, and S. Nicholas (2005). "How firms grow: clustering as a dynamic model of internationalization," *Journal of International Business Studies* 36, pp. 435–541.

Mathews, J. (2002). *Dragon Multinationals* (Oxford: Oxford University Press).

Penrose, E.T. (1959). *The Theory of the Growth of the Firm* (Oxford: Basil Blackwell).

Rugman, A and J. D'Cruz (2000). *Multinationals as Flagship Firms: Regional Business Networks* (Oxford: Oxford University Press).

UNCTAD (2007). *World Investment Report. Transnational Corporations, Extractive Industries and Development* (Geneva: United Nations).

Van Tulder, R. with A. Van der Zwart (2006). *International Business-Society Management* (London and New York: Routledge).

Vermeulen, F. and H. Barkema (2002). "Pace, rhythm, and scope: process dependence in building a profitable multinational corporation," *Strategic Management Journal* 23 (7), pp. 637–54.

Vernon, R. (1999). "The Harvard multinational enteprise project in historical perspective," *Transnational Corporations* 8 (2), pp. 35–50.

Witt, M. and A. Lewin (2007). "Outward foreign direct investment as escape response to home country institutional constraints," *Journal of International Business Studies* 38 (4), pp. 579–94.

Yiu, D. C. Lau, and G. Bruton (2007). "International venturing by emerging economy firms: the effects of firm capabilities, home country networks, and corporate entrepreneurship," *Journal of International Business Studies* 38 (4), pp. 519–40.

Zaheer, S. (1995). "Overcoming the liability of foreignness," *Academy of Management Journal* 38 (2), pp. 341–63.

Chapter 5

The Theory and Regulation of Emerging Market Multinational Enterprises

Alan M. Rugman

Introduction

In this chapter, we use the logic of international business strategy to demonstrate that examples of worldwide integration are special cases that ignore the empirical realities of multinational enterprises (MNEs). In particular, simplistic thinking on globalization does not apply to MNEs from emerging markets. We briefly review empirical evidence that demonstrates that the world's largest MNEs (including those from emerging markets) do not operate globally, but sell and produce the vast majority of their output within their home region of the triad. We develop an analytical framework which takes into account country-level and regional-level barriers to integration, and is useful in explaining the activities of MNEs from emerging markets. We explore the nature of the firm-specific advantages (FSAs) of emerging market MNEs but find that most of these firms rely on home country-specific advantages (CSAs) at this stage of their development. We finally apply this framework to issues in public policy toward foreign direct investment (FDI). We conclude that, from the viewpoint of international business strategy, prescriptive thinking is misleading if it is believed that MNEs from emerging markets can follow a global strategy of economic integration and assume market access to North American and European economies. Instead, MNEs from emerging markets need to develop strategies to accommodate the realities of intraregional integration and to overcome increasing host country regulations affecting inward FDI.

5.1 Globalization and Emerging Market MNEs

A large academic literature in the international business field suggests that MNEs are the key drivers of globalization (Rugman 1981, 2006). Yet many popular books on globalization fail to recognize the nature, extent, and business reality of MNEs as leaders of globalization. Perhaps the most influential of these books is *The World Is Flat,* by *New York Times* journalist Thomas Friedman (2003). Basically, Friedman argues that today a large proportion of international business takes place through offshoring. There are two main sites for offshoring. First, much manufacturing and cost innovation takes place in China. Second, many service sector activities, especially in information technology sectors, take place in India. While both types of offshoring certainly exist (and are explained by factor cost conditions), it is apparent that Friedman vastly exaggerates the importance of offshoring beyond the information-technology-related area.

Friedman develops an argument that today the world is characterized by Globalization 3.0. This is a situation in which individuals are empowered to run global businesses. They can process information and organize activities with the use of personal computers and the Internet. This type of globalization has replaced Globalization 2.0, in which MNEs organized international activity. During this era of Globalization 2.0 (which lasted from 1800 to 2000), MNEs grew and benefited from falling transportation costs (the development of railroads, bulk shipping lines, jet aircraft) and falling telecommunications costs. Previous to this type of globalization, according to Friedman, there existed Globalization 1.0. This lasted from 1492 to 1800. International exchange was organized across and between countries. International trade was largely explained by labor cost differentials and the existence of natural resources.

The theoretical logic behind Friedman's flat world model (to the extent that there is any theory) would be as follows: Globalization 1.0 is largely explained by international economics and the principle of comparative advantage. Countries that intensively utilize their abundant factor (e.g., cheap labor or mineral deposits) specialize in the export of goods. Globalization 2.0 is explained by theories of international business (MNEs internalize knowledge advantages and control these FSAs within wholly owned subsidiaries). Globalization 3.0 essentially has no theoretical support. It appears to assume that information exchange is free and that there are no barriers to entry for doing business anywhere in the world. Clearly Globalization 3.0 presents many challenges to MNEs from emerging markets, and these are discussed in more detail later in this chapter.

5.2   The FSA and CSA Framework

It is useful to reinterpret Friedman within the basic model used in the field of international business. This matrix relates country to firm factors, as first developed in Rugman (1981). This is reported in figure 5.1, where CSAs are shown on the vertical axis and FSAs on the horizontal axis. It is incorrect to generalize the country effect (the CSAs axis in figure 5.1) and make it the sole explanation of globalization. Instead, the firm effects need to be brought together, as in cell 3 of figure 5.1. It can be seen that Friedman's book is mainly about cell 1, and that he presents no evidence of the way FSAs can be developed such that CSAs in China and India are transformed by emerging market MNEs into cell 3 firm-specific attributes.

This analysis counters the simplistic notions of writers such as Thomas Friedman. The world is not flat. International business suggests that there

Firm specific advantages

		Weak	Strong
	Strong	1	3
Country specific advantages			
	Weak	2	4

Figure 5.1 The FSA/CSA matrix

Source: Rugman and Collinson (2006, 49).

remain strong barriers as a business attempts to cross the boundaries of triad regions. It is pointless to assume globalization; instead, it is necessary to investigate the manner in which a firm's business model may need to be adapted such that its FSAs can overcome the liability of interregional foreignness.

In an earlier influential book, *The Lexus and the Olive Tree,* Friedman used the Lexus as a symbol for economic integration (Friedman 1999). In contrast, the olive tree is a symbol for the historical, political, religious, and social aspects that present obstacles to economic integration. Therefore, the logic of the Lexus view of globalization and economic integration would fit on the vertical axis of figure 5.1, whereas the olive tree would be assigned to the horizontal axis, representing a FSA in national responsiveness. Friedman himself discussed the extreme cases of the Lexus in cell 1 and the olive tree in cell 4. However, based on our analysis of figure 5.1 it is apparent that cell 3 represents another interesting case, in which both the CSA of economic globalization and the FSA of national responsiveness are equally important. The other point is that figure 5.1 is a strategy diagram, to be put into operation by managers of MNEs (or other firms). Therefore, it is the interpretation of the FSA and CSA axes that is important for strategic management. A potential for strategy in cell 3 of figure 5.1 would require that an MNE is able to organize itself to cope with both axes. For example, MNEs from emerging markets may need to develop FSAs in business-government relations in order to gain access to the U.S. market in the face of political and/or regulatory barriers (where the latter are a type of negative host country CSA).

5.3 Regionalization and Emerging Market MNEs

The geographic sales of the world's 500 largest MNEs have been studied by Alan Rugman (2005), and this has been applied to emerging market MNEs in Rugman (2008). Briefly, in Rugman (2005) there is information for the year 2001 on the geographic sales of 380 of the world's 500 largest firms. Of these, 320 average 80% of their sales in their home region of the triad. From a North American perspective, using updated information, again for this set of 380 firms, for the year 2006, 348 provide information on their sales in North America (see table 5.1). Of these firms, 154 are North American MNEs (mostly from the United States). These 154 firms average 75% of their sales in North America, 15.6% in Europe, and 7.5% in Asia Pacific. In contrast, the 194 European and Asian MNEs average 17% of their sales in North America. Of these, 127 European MNEs average 64% of their sales in Europe. The sixty-seven Asian MNEs average 76% of their sales in Asia Pacific.

The average size of the two sets of firms is approximately the same. The 154 North American MNEs average US$44.1 billion in sales, whereas the 194 non-U.S. MNEs average US$44.8 billion in sales. There are over forty North American firms with 100% of their sales in North America (i.e., they are purely home-region triad based). These include retail firms such as Kroger, Walgreens, Sears Roebuck, Target, Federated Department Store, and Safeway; financial firms such as State Farm, Allstate, Aetna, Wachovia, U.S. Bancorp; and utility firms such as Sunoco or EnCana.

Over half of the 154 North American firms have over 80% of their sales in North America. Only two European firms (Delhaize "Le Lion" and Royal Ahold) can match their focus on North America. Indeed, many European and Asian firms have less than 20% of their sales in North America, which is too low a percentage to be of much strategic significance to these firms. However, some seventy non-U.S. firms have more than a 20% presence in North America. These firms are the key rivals of North American firms in the North America region. But they include very few from emerging markets. This is shown in table 5.2, which reports the sales of the twelve emerging market firms (from the top 500 of 2001) potentially active in North America. Three Korean firms (Hyundai Motor, LG Electronics, Samsung Electronics) have large sales in North America (over 20% of their total sales). Otherwise,

Table 5.1   Sales of MNEs in North America, 2006

Company name	Number of MNEs	Average revenue in US$ billions	North America % of total	Europe % of total	Asia-Pacific % of total
Total 500 MNEs	348	44.4	42.6	35.1	26.3
North American MNEs	154	44.1	**75.1**	15.6	7.5
European and Asian MNEs	194	44.8	17.0	47.2	37.8
European	127	48.2	19.6	**64.3**	9.8
Asian	67	38.4	12.1	9.6	**75.9**

Source: Author's calculation based on Rugman (2005).

Note: The values are calculated only when an MNE reports its regional sales in North America. Due to the fact that some firms do not report regional sales, the sum of the three regions cannot be equal to 100%. (Bold denotes the home region's share of sales.)

Table 5.2 Firms from emerging markets, 2006

Company	Country	Revenue (US$ billions)	North America sales (US$ millions)	Intraregional sales (% of total)	North America (% of total)
Bank of China	China	30.8	0.0	98.5	0.0
China National Petroleum	China	110.5	0.0	85.7	0.0
China Telecommunication	China	24.8	0.0	100.0	0.0
Hyundai Motor	Republic of Korea	66.7	1,614.5	62.4	24.2
LG Electronics	Republic of Korea	68.8	1,410.7	50.3	20.5
POSCO	Republic of Korea	27.1	63.9	89.5	2.4
Samsung	Republic of Korea	16.8	127.4	81.7	7.6
Samsung Electronics	Republic of Korea	89.5	1,883.8	53.2	21.1
SK Networks	Republic of Korea	16.7	5.5	90.6	0.3
Carso Global Telecom	Mexico	16.1	1,178.0	73.4	73.4
Lukoil	Russia	54.5	0.0	100.0	0.0
Flextronics International	Singapore	15.3	329.6	56.1	21.6

Source: Authors' calculation based on Rugman (2005).

Note: The values are calculated only when a firm reports its regional sales in North America. Such data are not available for another five firms (two from China; one from India; two from the Republic of Korea; and one from Malaysia).

only Flextronics from Singapore is an Asian player in North America. None of the three Chinese firms report sales in North America (Lenovo and Haier are too small to be listed in the top 500).

The above data are for MNEs for one year. We have been able to update these data for the world's largest 500 MNEs for the seven-year period, 2000–2006 (Rugman and Oh 2007). In this section we provide new data across two dimensions. First, we update the sales data, which now provides data for a seven-year period for a large number of the world's largest 500 firms. It helps us answer the question about whether there is a trend toward globalization or regionalization. Second, we provide data on assets as well as sales. This is done in order to provide clues about the nature of the upstream activities of these firms. Some theories suggest that there may be a possible global supply chain, and the asset data should therefore provide some more details about this aspect of globalization than the sales (downstream) data previously reported in Rugman and Verbeke (2004a) and Rugman (2005). Yet, as will be seen, the addition of information on assets provides essentially the same conclusion as for sales: most large firms are home-region based.

In table 5.3, we break the data into two categories for each year: manufacturing and services. The number of firms remaining in the population over the seven-year period varies by year. Due to mergers and acquisitions, entry and exits according to changes in total revenues, there are 697 firms listed for 2000–2006. In table 5.3 (panel A), there are 437 firms in 2000 but 503 in 2006. These numbers reflect the numbers reporting geographic segment information on sales in each year. In table 5.3 (panel B) there are fewer firms providing data on their geographic segments for assets.

Table 5.3 (panel A) shows that the average intraregional sales figure for all firms is 76.2%, with a plus-or-minus variation by year of less than 2%. There is no significant difference over time, and hence no evidence of a trend toward the globalization of international business activity. However, services average 84% home-region sales as against 66% for manufacturing. This is a statistically significant difference. In panel B of table 5.3, there is, again, no trend toward globalization, but there is a similar statistically significant difference in the average intraregional assets of services (84%) and manufacturing (71%).

The interpretation from both panels of table 5.3 is that services are even more home-region oriented than manufacturing across both downstream (sales) and upstream (assets) activities. These data, for the world's largest 500 firms, show that MNEs, in both services and in manufacturing, remain based in their home regions. There is no evidence to support a trend toward globalization in either the upstream or downstream end of MNE activity.

Table 5.3   Intraregional sales and assets of the top 500 firms, 2000–2006

Panel A. Intraregional Sales

		Intraregional sales (%)		
Year	Number of firms	All industries	Manufacturing	Services
2000	437	77.17	67.30	84.20
2001	511	76.73	66.03	84.25
2002	514	76.50	65.93	84.09
2003	513	76.48	65.61	84.31
2004	526	76.14	65.30	84.05
2005	529	75.54	65.06	83.31
2006	503	74.82	64.62	82.63
Weighted average		76.17	65.60	83.86

Panel B. Intraregional Assets, 2000–2006

		Intraregional assets (%)		
Year	Number of firms	All industries	Manufacturing	Services
2000	358	78.37	70.57	84.45
2001	413	77.44	70.40	83.27
2002	427	77.73	70.48	83.82
2003	431	77.98	70.87	83.91
2004	452	78.30	70.95	84.28
2005	461	78.29	71.18	84.08
2006	435	77.99	71.07	83.83
Weighted average		78.01	70.77	83.97

Source: Annual reports for 2000–2006. Sample firms are listed any year of *Fortune Global 500* during 2000–2006. Data include firms that report intraregional sales.

5.4   What Regionalism Means for Emerging Market MNEs

Given the above theoretical and empirical analysis, we now focus upon the implication of this work for emerging market MNEs. To summarize, our analysis of figure 5.1 shows that emerging market MNEs tend to cluster in cell 1 of the matrix. Yet, this is not the optimal cell for MNEs that wish to move beyond FSAs based upon low cost and economies of scale. In particular, emerging MNEs in cell 1 of figure 5.1 have not developed the tacit knowledge and internal managerial skills necessary to compete with Western MNEs.

Using Friedman's logic, MNEs from emerging markets will aspire to move from cell 2 to cell 1. Cell 1 can be regarded as suitable for small and medium-sized firms. Friedman assumes that the smaller firms are more nimble and that they can operate globally through use of the Internet. This argument has also been developed by C.K. Prahalad (2005), who argues that entrepreneurship is facilitated (especially in India) through the use of the Internet by small businesses. In contrast, China's firms, especially in state-owned industries, are flat footed and slow to respond to the knowledge skills required to operate globally using Internet-type operations. MNEs from India are also suitable candidates for cell 1 in figure 5.1. However, this path to success is much more difficult than imagined, and there is little evidence that other than a handful of India's MNEs have developed the rich managerial and knowledge skills to succeed in cell 3 of figure 5.1.

In figure 5.1, it has already been shown by Rugman and Doh (2008) and Rugman (2008) that MNEs from emerging markets can be found in cell 1. Their success depends upon their internalization of CSAs in cheap labor, cheap money, natural resources, et cetera. These firms do not have sustainable FSAs except in economies of scale. Yet the industries with economies of scale tend to be in natural resources and are often commodity-type businesses. By definition, a commodity-type business does not yield a FSA, so it is placed in cell 1, not cell 3. It has been shown that China's MNEs have characteristics which place them in cell 1. My interpretation of Nolan (2004) and Thun (2005) is that they find that Chinese firms lack FSAs, especially the skills in management and systems integration that are required for cell 3.

To summarize, in figure 5.1, we would again position MNEs from the emerging markets in cell 1. Their FSAs rely upon economic integration achieved through country-specific factors. These emerging market MNEs lack skills in national responsiveness. They rely on scale economies and do not adapt their products for consumers in host country markets. They lack the management systems to develop internal knowledge FSAs across a network of foreign subsidiaries (Rugman and Doh 2008). In general, MNEs from China rely on scale economies due to their home country advantages in cheap labor, national resources, and cheap money. The cheap money assists in takeovers in acquisitions, but these are unlikely to yield knowledge-based FSAs. Even the Lenovo acquisition of IBM personal computers has not led to significant development in new tacit know-how (Rugman 2008); it is in cell 1 of figure 5.1. However, if Lenovo is thought of as having skills in business-government relations and related legal expertise to enter the U.S. market, then this type of FSA may place it in cell 3 of figure 5.1.

The academic literature on emerging market MNEs has been greatly influenced by the thinking associated with Friedman (2003). This academic work tends to argue that emerging market MNEs are latecomers and that a new theory is required to explain their success. Prominent advocates of this view are John Mathews (2006a, 2006b) and Michael Hobday (1995). While some academics have acknowledged the need for new thinking about emerging market MNEs (Dunning 2006; Brouthers, O'Donnell, and Hadjimarcou 2005; Zeng and Williamson 2007), it is apparent that the logic of this chapter denies the need for any new theory. It has been shown that existing international business theory fully explains the nature and positioning of emerging market MNEs in the relevant figure 5.1.

Figure 5.1, using internalization theory as popularized by Rugman (1981), is the basic model for the international business field with its focus on FSAs and CSAs. It suggests that emerging market MNEs lack FSAs in managerial knowledge. Similarly, figure 5.1 contains key ideas popularized by Christopher Bartlett and Sumantra Ghoshal (1989). This analysis suggests that emerging market MNEs are lacking in the systems integration skills to develop FSAs in adapting products and services. This thinking also applies when other variants of modern international business theory are considered, such as the eclectic model of Dunning (1981). In this context, Rajneesh Narula (2006) argues that latecomer MNEs are fully explained by conventional theory.

The conclusion of this section is that emerging market MNEs are operating in a more complex situation of globalization than is widely understood. The world is not perfectly integrated as assumed by Friedman or even more distinguished thinkers, such as Joseph Stiglitz (2002). The MNEs from emerging markets can develop FSAs based upon economic integration, but such advantages are limited to the home region of their triad. Latecomer MNEs will be explained by conventional international business theory. Their FSAs in scale economies depend upon country factors. They lack the sophisticated managerial skills in knowledge and system integration and cannot compete in these areas with Western MNEs that have developed such FSAs. It will take many years before these emerging market MNEs will develop these managerial and knowledge skills.

5.5 Implications for FDI Policy

The growth of MNEs from emerging markets provides interesting challenges for those concerned with public policy toward FDI. In the past, some of the countries that are now the homes of emerging market MNEs (such as India and Brazil) were opposed to policies of trade and investment liberalization. Now that their firms are seeking access to the markets of North America, Europe, and Japan, it can be presumed that their governments will be more supportive of policies to liberalize trade and investment. Yet, as the previous attempt to adopt a multilateral agreement on investment at the Organisation for Economic Co-operation and Development (OECD) was unsuccessful, it is unlikely that any major new multilateral initiatives to liberalize FDI (either inward or outward) will be successful. Instead, it is more likely that liberalization of investment will occur through the process of bilateral investment treaties. In this connection several problems arise, which can be usefully analyzed within the framework developed earlier.

In terms of regulations affecting FDI, the basic concept to govern both inward and outward FDI is the principle of national treatment. MNEs from emerging markets should be allowed to enter the markets of the core triad (North America, the European Union, Japan) and then be afforded transparent and equal treatment under the laws and regulations of those countries. This practice of nondiscrimination in the application of domestic law has long been the cornerstone of policy toward FDI. For example, national treatment has been adopted by the United States since the 1980s and has been incorporated into the investment provisions of the North American Free Trade Agreement (NAFTA). However, even in NAFTA many service industries are exempted from the national treatment provisions (Rugman and Gestrin 1994). In addition, national treatment has sometimes been made contingent upon perceptions of national security; for example, in the awarding of research and development subsidies to high-tech firms (Warner and Rugman 1994).

What does this mean for policy affecting emerging market MNEs? In general, these firms can expect to be able to enter and to conduct business in the markets of the core triad. If the firms have FSAs, then their entry is highly unlikely to be questioned. This is because emerging market MNEs with genuine FSAs (in cell 3 of figure 5.1) help to upgrade the host country economy, perhaps through transfers of technology, technical skills, or other valuable business process and practices. However, if emerging market MNEs have no FSAs and are relying on its home country CSAs, then entry may be restricted. For example, Chinese state-owned firms with domestic monopoly positions, especially if they are in energy and in infrastructure, may well face problems as they seek to enter triad markets. In particular, energy firms may not be able to satisfy the requirements of the Committee on Foreign Investment in the United States (CFIUS) or the equivalent screening agencies in Canada or the European Union. It is even possible that firms in manufacturing building on a home country CSA in cheap labor will be denied entry due to political pressure from trade unions and nongovernmental organizations (NGOs) in triad markets.

Another new problem potentially facing MNEs from emerging markets is the unfortunate manner in which investor-state provisions have been implemented under NAFTA and in some of the bilateral investment treaties (BITs). The basic principle of investor-state legal provisions is sound in that a firm now has rights to seek legal redress for loss of business due to adverse host government policy. Such "regulatory undertakings" first arose in cases under NAFTA affecting the natural environment (Soloway 2002). Previously, firms could not bring actions against governments. Instead, they had to lobby their home government to bring a case against the host government. This escalated business concerns into diplomatic incidents.

The first investor-state provisions were introduced in NAFTA to satisfy the environmental side accord insisted upon by the Clinton administration (after completion of the initial negotiations) in order to have the agreement passed by the U.S. Congress. In an assessment of the application of the resulting chapter 11 disputes, it was found that there were only a handful of cases in the first five years of NAFTA (Rugman, Kirton, and Soloway 1999). However, two of these cases gained a disproportionate amount of publicity (the Canadian PCB and MMT cases) such that environmental NGOs argued that the environmental laws of Canada might possibly be overturned through pressure from U.S. MNEs, which might be able to receive awards from the Canadian Government when their businesses were adversely affected by a trade-related environmental policy. Yet this is misinterpreted by NGOs (Soloway 2002). The compensation paid in the MMT case was a small amount, and a government retains full sovereignty in the administration of its domestic environmental policy (Rugman 1999; Rugman and Verbeke 2004b).

While it is possible that the volume of legal activity involving investor-state conflicts will increase in the future, this should not be a major problem for emerging market MNEs. They only account for less than 1% of inward stock of FDI in core triad markets as of 2008. Even with tremendous growth of such FDI over the next five to ten years there are unlikely to be more than a handful of cases involving emerging market MNEs. Of course, the faster that emerging market MNEs shift from CSAs into FSAs, the more likely it is that they can avoid investor-state conflicts and potentially adverse decisions by review agencies such as CFIUS.

This conclusion is based on two key principles. First, policy on FDI should be based on the data. The data indicate that inward FDI from emerging markets is not a large component of inward FDI. Therefore there should be relatively few disputes. The second principle is that policy should build on good theory. Theory indicates that emerging market MNEs will eventually transfer from CSAs into FSAs. The sooner they do that, the lower the probability of adverse legal procedures in triad markets. If this prediction is incorrect, there is an intermediate solution. In the face of politicization by the U.S. Congress of the CFIUS review process (in which the administration of CFIUS is conducted by the executive branch, which is generally less protectionist than Congress) and an increase in investor-state dispute cases, the solution for MNEs from emerging markets is to develop FSAs in business-government relations. This is a pure knowledge-based FSA, propriety to the top management team. It involves securing expert in-house legal advice and competence on investment provisions and in the successful preemption of a negative CFIUS-type review. In the past such FSAs in business-government relations have been analyzed for Canadian MNEs by Rugman and Verbeke (1990).

Conclusions

In *The World Is Flat* (2003), Friedman argues that the olive tree is no longer relevant and that the world is flat in the sense that only economic integration matters. Friedman is mainly interested in outsourcing and the related labor cost aspects of economic integration, where the latter is driven by the Internet and individual use of personal computers such that business can be undertaken globally by small firms. By reverting to analysis of only the vertical axis of figure 5.1, Friedman has ignored the business strategy complexities of globalization, in particular the benefits of managerial skills in national responsiveness or in business agreement relations. Firm-level data confirm the fact that the world is regional rather than global (Rugman 2005). MNEs from emerging markets cannot expect to "go global." Indeed, they are expanding on an intraregional basis (Rugman 2008).

In this chapter, an analysis has been presented to demonstrate that MNEs from emerging markets tend to lack advanced managerial skills in internal knowledge generation and in the systems integration required to develop FSAs across a network of foreign affiliates. Instead, these MNEs at best enjoy economies of scale based on home country CSAs in cheap labor (even cheap skilled labor, as in India's case), natural resources, and/or possibly cheap money (as in China's case). No new theory is needed to explain CSAs and the resulting FSAs in economies of scale. Furthermore, these FSAs of emerging market MNEs tend to be confined to intraregional operations. The strength of the regional effect is such that analysis of international business strategy for emerging market firms needs to focus on regional strategy rather than the global strategy espoused by Friedman. Due to increased regulations and review of FDI by the European Union and in North America, it is good advice for emerging market MNEs to develop FSAs in business-government relations. Such FSAs may help to preempt negative decisions by review agencies such as CFIUS in the United States or equivalent agencies in Canada and the European Union.

Note

Helpful comments were made by Karl P. Sauvant and the participants at the Five-Diamond International Conference on "Thinking Outward: Global Players from Emerging Markets," Columbia University, April 28–29, 2008.

References

Bartlett, Christopher A. and Sumantra Ghoshal (1989). *Managing across Borders* (Boston: Harvard Business School Press).

Brouthers, Lance Eliot, Edward O'Donnell, and John Hadjimarcou (2005). "Generic product strategies for emerging market exports into triad nation markets: a mimetic isomorphism approach," *Journal of Management Studies* 42 (January), pp. 225–45.

Dunning, John H. (1981). *International Production and the Multinational Enterprise* (London: Allen & Unwin).

Dunning, John H. (2006). "Comment on dragon multinationals: new players in 21st century globalization," *Asia Pacific Journal of Management* 23 (June), pp. 139–41.

Friedman, Thomas L. (1999). *The Lexus and the Olive Tree* (New York: Farrar, Straus & Giroux).

Friedman, Thomas L. (2003). *The World Is Flat* (New York: Farrar, Straus & Giroux).

Hobday, Michael (1995). "East Asian latecomer firms: learning the technology of electronics," *World Development* 23 (7), pp. 1171–93.

Mathews, John A. (2006a). "Dragon multinationals: new players in 21st century globalization," *Asia Pacific Journal of Management* 23 (March), pp. 5–27.

Mathews, John A. (2006b). "Response to Professors Dunning and Narula," *Asia Pacific Journal of Management* 23 (June), pp. 153–55.

Narula, Rajneesh (2006). "Globalization, new ecologies, new zoologies, and the purported death of the eclectic paradigm," *Asia Pacific Journal of Management* 23 (June), pp. 143–51.

Nolan, Peter (2004). *China at the Crossroads* (Cambridge: Polity Press).

Prahalad, C.K. (2005). *The Fortune at the Bottom of the Pyramid* (Upper Saddle River, NJ: Wharton School/Pearson).

Rugman, Alan M. (1981). *Inside the Multinationals: The Economics of Internal Markets* (New York: Columbia University Press).

Rugman, Alan M. (1999). "Negotiating multilateral rules to promote investment," in Michael R. Hodges, John J. Kirton, and Joseph P. Daniels, eds., *The G8's Role in the New Millennium* (Aldershot: Ashgate), pp. 143–57.

Rugman, Alan M. (2005). *The Regional Multinationals* (Cambridge: Cambridge University Press).

Rugman, Alan M. (2006). *Inside the Multinationals: The Economics of Internal Markets*, 25th anniversary ed. (Basingstoke, UK: PalgraveMacmillan).

Rugman, Alan M. (2008). "How global are TNCs from emerging markets?" in Karl Sauvant, ed., *The Rise of Transnational Corporations from Emerging Markets: Threat or Opportunity* (Cheltenham, UK: Elgar), pp. 86–106.

Rugman, A.M. and S. Collinson (2006), *International Business*, 4th ed. (London: Pearson/Prentice Hall).

Rugman, Alan M. and Jonathan Doh (2008). *Multinationals and Development* (New Haven, Conn.: Yale University Press).

Rugman, Alan M. and Michael Gestrin (1994). "NAFTA's treatment of foreign investment," in Alan M. Rugman, ed., *Foreign Investment and NAFTA* (Columbia: University of South Carolina Press), pp. 47–79.

Rugman, Alan M., John J. Kirton, and Julie Soloway (1999). *Environmental Regulations and Corporate Strategy: A NAFTA Perspective* (Oxford: Oxford University Press).

Rugman, Alan M. and Chang Hoon Oh (2007). "Multinationality and regional performance, 2001–2005," in Alan M. Rugman, ed., *Regional Aspects of Multinationality and Performance* (Oxford: Elsevier), pp. 31–43.

Rugman, Alan M. and Alain Verbeke (1990). *Global Corporate Strategy and Trade Policy* (London and New York: Routledge).

Rugman, Alan M. and Alain Verbeke (2004a). "A perspective on regional and global strategies of multinational enterprises," *Journal of International Business Studies* 35 (January), pp. 3–18.

Rugman, Alan M. and Alain Verbeke (2004b). "Toward a theory of multinational enterprises and the civil society," in Abby Ghobadian, Nicholas O'Regan, David Gallear, and Howard Viney, eds., *Strategy and Performance: Achieving Competitive Advantage in the Global Marketplace* (New York: Palgrave Macmillan), pp. 35–53.

Soloway, Julie (2002). "Environmental expropriation under NAFTA chapter 11: the phantom menace," in John J. Kirton and Virginia W. Maclaren, eds., *Linking Trade, Environment and Social Cohesion: NAFTA Experiences, Global Challenges* (Aldershot: Ashgate), pp. 131–44.

Stiglitz, Joseph E. (2002). *Globalization and its Discontents* (New York: W.W. Norton).

Thun, Eric (2005). *Changing Lanes in China: Foreign Direct Investment* (Cambridge: Cambridge University Press).

Warner, Mark A.A. and Alan M. Rugman (1994). "Competitiveness: an emerging strategy of discrimination in U.S. antitrust and R&D policy," *Law and Policy in International Business* 25 (3) Spring, pp. 945–82.

Zeng, Ming and Peter J. Williamson (2007). *Dragons at Your Door: How Chinese Cost Innovation Is Disrupting Global Competition* (Boston: Harvard Business School Press).

Chapter 6

Comment: Do We Need a New Theory to Explain Emerging Market Multinational Enterprises?*

Art Durnev

Introduction

In chapter 5, Alan Rugman argues convincingly that existing theories of globalization cannot be simply transplanted onto multinational enterprises (MNEs) from emerging markets. Rugman's main conclusion is that, from the viewpoint of international business academic research, it is misleading to believe that emerging market MNEs can, in their pursuit of European and North American markets, follow the same strategies as MNEs from developed economies. Rather, emerging market MNEs must develop strategies to expand within their geographic regions.

Rugman contrasts his arguments with opinions in Thomas Friedman's influential book "The World Is Flat," which suggests that the role of MNEs in the world economy is declining as a result of the Internet and the ability of individuals to conduct commerce from personal computers. Rugman contends that Friedman's choice of examples, manufacturing outsourcing in China and service outsourcing (specifically information technology) in India, cannot be generalized to apply to international business at large, and that Friedman makes idealistic assumptions regarding both the state of technology across the globe and firms' access to financing. Using revenue data for the period 2000–2006, from developed and developing market MNE statistics, Rugman further demonstrates that significant regionalization still exists.

While I do not dispute Rugman's contentions in general, there are additional factors that emerging market MNEs and global policy makers should consider. Of particular importance is the lack of "soft" financial infrastructure, often taken for granted by managers and investors in developed markets, such as credit rating agencies and managerial skills developed through business schools. Compounding the problem is the existence of predatory governments that hinder the successful growth of businesses and an opaque regulatory and business environment. The current global economic and financial crisis only amplifies the difficulties that emerging market MNEs face in accessing external finance and further hinders their growth.

The current crisis is already reshaping the global economic map for emerging market MNEs. One of the greatest risks that they face is the dearth of capital, foreign and domestic, available to finance operations. This lack of credit is already taking its toll on many previously successful MNEs, from many parts of the world and especially those from Eastern Europe. As credit becomes scarce, MNEs find it increasingly difficult to refinance old debt or to raise additional funding for further expansion. This will drive less successful MNEs into bankruptcy and slow down the expansion of more successful MNEs. The current crisis raises a number of important issues for managers, scholars, and policy makers.

6.1   The Need for a Proper Financial Infrastructure

In order to be efficient, emerging markets require third-party institutions, such as credit rating agencies, to facilitate the free flow of reliable information, so that investors can make informed decisions. Emerging markets often lack these institutions, and investors are often incapable of accurately finding this information independently, and in a timely manner that allows them to keep pace with modern business. Credit rating agencies, when fair and unbiased, reduce transaction costs by lowering the cost of capital and increasing the efficiency of investment, at the individual, institutional, and corporate levels.[1] For example, without credit rating agencies even simple transactions, such as leasing property, become difficult as landlords, incapable of assessing the risk of potential clients, may decide not to lease the property or to do so at a higher than "equilibrium" price, leading in turn to excess supply.

Business education is a second area in which emerging markets lack "soft" institutions. While business school graduates are not a replacement for seasoned managers, business schools do provide a foundation for highly qualified and trained individuals and offer a certain certification of quality. In the absence of executive education, corporations commonly act as training schools, which may be costly. I fail to see how average individuals can acquire this "know-how" independently, which Friedman (2005) contends is the case.

The lack of financial development in emerging markets increases transaction costs. As a result, corporations often act as "mini-financial markets." As individuals and smaller corporations lack access to capital at a "reasonable" cost, larger firms and MNEs often diversify into industries in which they have little experience and in which they are unable to create operational synergies, simply because they have the resources necessary for expansion, rather than focusing on their core businesses. It is difficult to profitably execute strategies of unrelated diversification, as the 1970s showed. As there is little operational rationale for diversification decisions, it would be more efficient for larger firms to pursue opportunities related to their core businesses.

6.2 Call for Governance Reforms

Emerging markets, such as Russia, often lack the legal tradition to protect adequately the property of investors and firms. A quote from *Vedomosti,* a Russian newspaper (Yavlinsky 2007), illustrates how the limited protection of property rights influences the decisions of firms:

> Even the most successful individuals understand that their prosperity is provisional, and if their assets happen to catch the eye of someone who is stronger and more influential at the moment, they won't have any defence against inevitable requisition. However, even people who aren't business owners understand that their ownership of any property is only provisional, that is, they own it until someone stronger and more aggressive wants to take it away, as long as the size of the property can cover the costs of the process of taking it away.

Related to this lack of property rights in emerging markets is a lack of transparency. Efficient markets rely on transparency and the availability of timely, accurate information. Firms, or investors, who know that their profits can be seized by more powerful parties, are unlikely to disclose in full relevant or accurate information, which in turn inhibits the development of financial markets. Adam Smith also makes this point in his seminal "Wealth of Nations" (1776, 31): "In those unfortunate countries, indeed, where men are continually afraid of the violence of their superiors, they frequently bury and conceal a great part of their [capital] stock." Firms in these markets often adopt poor corporate governance practices that discourage outside investment and hinder global financial market integration, further showing how the world is still "round" and not "flat."

Predatory governments find it slightly more difficult to expropriate the assets of MNEs that have a greater international presence and are unable to expropriate those assets held abroad. Often, emerging market MNEs acquire assets abroad precisely to avoid the risk of government expropriation. By investing abroad, they transfer capital away from the domestic market, a market in which they are generally in a better position to serve; as a result it is not fully developed. The situation is similar for individual investors, with the result that capital flows out from the domestic market, reducing the amount of financing available domestically. As mentioned above, the underdevelopment of domestic financial markets reinforces the idea that large firms are mini-financial markets, which perpetuates this cycle.

Although many emerging economies have implemented governance reforms aimed at strengthening the protection of property rights, introducing better accounting standards and improving shareholder protection, the path they have taken is far from exemplary. There is plenty of evidence that emerging market MNEs are often engaged in "tunneling" activities, such as excessive managers' pay, bribery, and outright theft of corporate resources.

However, there is some hope that emerging market MNEs can overcome weak regulatory environments in home and host countries. As well as the quality of investor protection laws and the efficiency of domestic courts, the MNEs' own motivation to practice good corporate governance is important. In a *Journal of Finance* paper, Art Durnev and E.H. Kim (2005) dispel the stereotype that firms from emerging markets uniformly suffer from poor corporate governance. They show that, with the right incentives (e.g., when firms have good investment opportunities and must raise external financing), firms practice good governance voluntarily. Fortunately for emerging market MNEs, the effort is worth the cost, and good corporate governance is rewarded by shareholders. In Durnev and Kim's study, a ten-point increase in a firm's governance score, out of a maximum of 100 points, increased the firm's market value by 9%. *Thou shall not steal and thou will be rewarded:* a positive message for MNEs from countries with poor investor protection and inefficient court systems.

6.3 The Role of the Current Economic Crisis: Directions for Future Research

There is abundant anecdotal evidence that the expansion of emerging market MNEs, especially MNEs from China and Russia, is largely politically driven, and that their acquisition of foreign assets is often inefficient. In the current financial crisis, earlier investment errors are harshly punished by stock markets. For example, consider the case of Oleg Deripaska, once the richest of Russians, who invested over US\$1.54 billion in Magna International Inc., Canada's largest automobile parts manufacturer, in a highly leveraged deal backed by his own shares. As Magna International Inc.'s share price plunged in October 2008, Deripaska was forced to divest his 20% stake and consequently suffered substantial losses to his personal wealth.

Another very alarming development that may slow down or completely eliminate outward FDI expansion is the rise of FDI protectionism (see, for example, Sauvant 2008).[2] It is becoming clear that many governments, even in developed countries, have implemented protectionist policies as a precondition for bailout packages.

Nevertheless, the global financial crisis, which struck most national and regional economic systems in 2008 and 2009, offers new learning opportunities for emerging market MNEs. It will also provide academic researchers with the opportunity to investigate a number of interesting topics. They include: the impact of the crisis on MNE activity and the strategies that emerging market MNEs implement to mitigate the adverse effects of the crisis; the characteristics of MNEs that risk bankruptcy; specific country risks that may affect MNEs; and the question of nondiscrimination treatment by host country governments. Other questions that arise include: do emerging market MNEs play an active role in crisis resolution? Do they change their consumer and labor policies? Do they change their currency risk policies? Do they change their location of operation? How do MNEs deal with protectionism? What challenges do MNEs face when they deal with local governments? Will MNEs coordinate their policies and put pressure on home and host governments to reform institutional environment?

In other words, the financial crisis and recession offer a host of opportunities to examine or reexamine a range of issues faced by emerging market MNEs and their home countries. The proper understanding of these issues may well be crucial for the future success of multinational enterprises from emerging markets.

Notes

*This manuscript was prepared as a discussion of Alan M. Rugman's paper and a summary of the author's presentation at the Five-Diamond International Conference on "Thinking Outward: Global Players from Emerging Markets," held at Columbia University, April 28–29, 2008. I would like to thank Karl P. Sauvant, Wolfgang A. Maschek, and Geraldine McAllister for their helpful comments.

1. Even in developed countries, major credit rating agencies are blamed for being biased because of the overly optimistic ratings they assigned to mortgage-backed securities.
2. In particular, see chapter 5, "Driving and Countervailing Forces: A Rebalancing of FDI Policies."

References

Durnev, A. and E.H. Kim (2005). "To steal or not to steal: firm attributes, legal environment, and valuation," *Journal of Finance* 60, pp. 1461–93.

Friedman, Thomas (2005). *The World Is Flat: A Brief History of the Twenty-First Century* (New York: Farrar, Sraus & Giroux).

Sauvant, Karl P. (2008). *Yearbook on International Investment Law & Policy 2008–2009* (New York: Oxford University Press), pp. 215–72.

Smith, Adam (1776). *An Inquiry into the Nature and Causes of the Wealth of Nations,* available at http://www.econlib.org/library/Smith/smWN.html, last visited June 22, 2009.

Yavlinsky, Grigoriy (2007). "Property and vulnerability: expropriation can happen to anyone," trans. A. Gorev, *Vedomosti*, August 15, p. 3.

Part Two

Gaining Ground—The Expansion of Emerging Market Multinational Enterprises

Chapter 7

The Transnationalization of Brazilian Companies: Lessons from the Top Twenty Multinational Enterprises

Paulo Resende, André Almeida, and Jase Ramsey

Introduction

Emerging market multinational enterprises (MNEs) have had difficulties making decisions involving their international strategic plans. These difficulties stem largely from the lack of a historical foundation for making decisions on international trade and investment, due to the relatively recent appearance of these firms as important players in the international arena. This makes it difficult to predict what might become a future success or failure in global markets. Brazilian MNEs are also experiencing these same obstacles, related to a lack of familiarity with the transnationalization process. However, in recent years, their degree of transnationalization has increased, as evidenced by a number of companies that appear regularly in the "Top Twenty Brazilian MNEs" ranking.

The measurement of Brazilian MNEs' transnationalization has become established in recent years. This synchronization of methodology yields models and performance indicators that focus on different variables that are now available. Therefore, multidimensional patterns of transnationalization can now be analyzed, resulting in conclusions that are not limited to a single criterion (e.g., foreign assets). Recent work on the ranking methodology of transnationalization has demonstrated the benefits from a multidimensional approach (Kumar and Singh 2008; Sullivan 1996). The result of this approach is a criterion based principally on foreign assets, number of employees in foreign countries, and foreign sales (Sullivan 1994; Ramaswamy, Kroeck, and Renforth 1996). These three variables are the criteria that have been used to measure the transnationalization of Brazilian MNEs. While the ranking of these firms serves as the basis for this chapter, a richer examination of the underlying changes affecting the companies will be undertaken. We seek to demonstrate the most important results of the Brazilian MNEs ranking, based on data from their 2006 activities, and compare these with data from

2004 and 2005 where appropriate.[1] For example, analysis is presented on regional distribution of foreign activities, foreign assets by industry, foreign employment, and foreign sales.

The purpose of this chapter is to discuss the transnationalization processes of Brazilian MNEs, based on their 2006 ranking positions. In the next section, a presentation of the top twenty Brazilian MNEs, based on foreign assets is presented. This section will shed light on the process of transnationalization. The next four subsections are focused on the regional distribution of foreign activities, foreign-asset allocation, foreign employment, and foreign sales, respectively. Subsequently, a discussion on mergers and acquisitions is presented, as they were of vital importance to the transnationalization process in the 2006 ranking. Finally, we provide a summary of the topics discussed, with the goal of tying together the various parts of the Brazilian transnationalization process.

7.1 Brazilian Companies: An Overview of the Transnationalization Process

Brazil is a country experiencing the transnationalization of its major companies. Brazil's top MNEs have largely contributed to the country's rise to the position of second largest outward investor among developing countries, behind only China and Hong Kong (China) in terms of outward foreign direct investment (OFDI) in 2006 (UNCTAD 2007). It had more than twice as much OFDI as fellow BRIC country India, and 30% more than Russia. Moreover, Brazil's top twenty MNEs have a stock of US$56 billion of assets abroad, virtually half of the country's total OFDI stock (US$114 billion). The top twenty MNEs produced and sold goods and services worth approximately US$30 billion and employed 77,000 people abroad. This shows a magnitude comparable to some developed countries (e.g., Australia, Ireland, the Netherlands) (ibid.), further consolidating a process not likely to be reversed. However, geographical expansion brings with it uncertainty and risk. Therefore, Brazilian MNEs have experienced tension between the option of reproducing what they have successfully built in their internal market, and creating new solutions for each foreign market. That is why transnationalization efforts are still focused on Latin America. Its relative liability of foreignness is less than that of other parts of the world, such as Asia and East Europe.

Foreign barriers of entry sometimes force the transnationalization of Brazilian firms. For example, a Brazilian steel company purchased production facilities in the United States in order to circumvent quotas in the host country. Thus, Brazilian MNEs grow by expanding into markets that may be quite different to their home market.

According to the 2006 ranking, about half of Brazilian MNEs focus on their home region, Latin America, where, compared to other regions, they are present in the greatest number of countries (see figure 7.1). The linear trend lines based on twenty-six years of data show both OFDI and inward foreign direct investment (IFDI) growing, with a particular focus on IFDI. This phenomenon of rapid growth in IFDI began in 1995 with the adoption of the Real

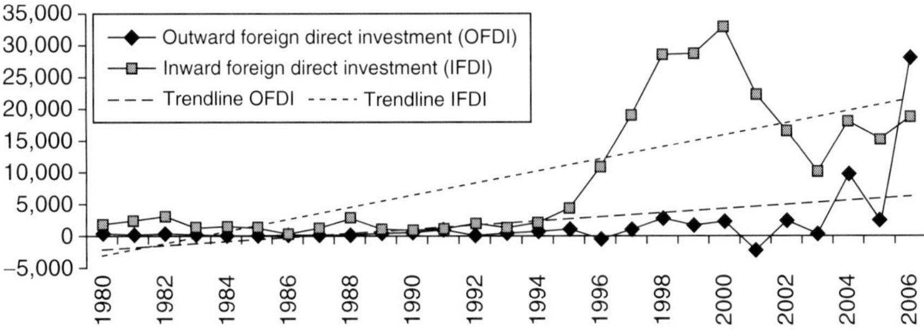

Figure 7.1   Evolution of Brazilian FDI flows, 1980–2006 (US$ millions)

Source: Central Bank of Brazil (balance of payment statistics).

Plan, which incentivized international capital flows to Brazil by increasing the interest rate and controlling inflation. The peak of the inversed U-curve IFDI line around the year 2000 is largely due to a number of large privatizations in the telecom, transportation, and energy industries. And, finally, the huge spike in OFDI from 2005 to 2006 is primarily due to the acquisition of the Canadian firm Inco by Vale for an estimated US$17 billion.[2] Indeed, Vale's acquisition was the largest ever by a Latin American firm.

Natural-resource firms are primarily responsible for the impressive growth of Brazilian MNEs and account for about two-thirds of the total foreign assets of the top twenty Brazilian MNEs. Vale leads the group of firms in the 2006 ranking in terms of foreign assets. In general, the group of companies includes several industrial groups, heavy construction companies, and some high-tech groups (e.g., EMBRAER, Itautec). The high concentration of industries in the primary sector, including oil and gas, minerals, steel, and agribusiness highlights the challenge Brazilian MNEs face in adding value within the domestic market. It also establishes a strategic position from which Brazilian MNEs may base future value-added activities while operating in foreign countries.

Table 7.1 shows the ranking of the top twenty Brazilian MNEs by foreign assets and provides the respective industry of each company. Note the presence of commodity-based companies, as shown by the top three companies that operate primarily mining and metals, oil and gas, and steel, respectively.

Not all of the companies listed are active primarily in the commodities industry. For instance, the service sector is important, with industries related to construction, such as Norberto Odebrecht and Andrade Gutierrez. Also, a number of high-tech companies, such as Datasul, Natura, and Lupatech are active in more sophisticated sectors. In summary, while there are firms moving up the value chain, international activities are still primarily connected to exporting strategies, dominated by fixed assets from Brazilian headquarters.

In order to better understand the drivers of OFDI, we conducted a follow-up survey with company executives. In this survey, we asked executives about the motives behind internationalization. Specifically, we asked them to rate twelve reasons on a six-point Likert-type scale (1 = completely disagree, 6 = completely agree).[3] The results show that Brazilian firms internationalize

Table 7.1 The top twenty Brazilian MNEs, ranked by total foreign assets, 2006 (US$ millions)

Rank	Name	Industry
1	Vale	Mining and metals
2	Petrobras S.A. (Petróleo Brasileiro S.A.)	Oil and gas
3	Gerdau S.A.	Steel
4	EMBRAER - Empresa Brasileira de Aeronáutica S.A.	Aviation
5	Votorantim Participações S.A.	Diversified
6	Companhia Siderúrgica Nacional (CSN)	Steel
7	Camargo Corrêa S.A.	Diversified
8	Odebrecht S.A.	Construction and petrochemicals
9	Aracruz Celulose	Pulp and paper
10	Weg S.A.	Electro-mechanical
11	Marcopolo S.A.	Transport
12	Andrade Gutierrez S.A.	Diversified
13	Tigre S.A. Tubos e Conexões	Construction
14	Usinas Siderúrgicas de Minas Gerais S.A.-Usiminas	Steel
15	Natura Cosméticos S.A.	Cosmetics
16	Itautec S.A.	IT
17	America Latina Logística S.A.	Logistics
18	Ultrapar Participações S.A.	Diversified
19	Sabó Indústria e Comércio de Autopeças Ltda.	Automobile parts
20	Lupatech S.A.	Electro-mechanical

Source: Fundação Dom Cabral—Vale Columbia Center on Sustainable International Investment survey of Brazilian multinationals.

for three primary reasons (based on a rating higher than 5.0). First, firms seek access to new markets. Indeed, the possibility of greater sales is the primary driver of trends toward internationalization. Second, the vision and desire of owners (including stockholders) and managers to internationalize are important. The significance of this reason was unexpected, given that it is largely the result of personal factors. It appears that a global mindset has taken hold in Brazil. Finally, firms seek out economies of scale. Many of the benefits attributed to economies of scale, such as lower unit costs, have motivated executives to invest abroad.

Within the top twenty Brazilian MNEs, as measured by foreign assets, half the firms surveyed are headquartered in São Paulo state. Brazil's colonial history helps explain this concentration of headquarters locations. Beginning in the 1500s, Brazil has primarily been a source of precious metals, wood, sugar cane, and coffee, with all of these materials exported to Portugal. Naturally, goods were exported from the most convenient coastal locations. Once industrialization began, labor migrated to coastal cities, reinforcing the need for headquarters to locate there. One interesting note is an explanation for the headquarters locations of the five companies in the far south of Brazil. These states have a large concentration of European descendants, historically disposed to international trade. The only company whose location is not accounted for by these two explanations is Petrobras, a state-owned company, and thus headquartered in the national capital of Brasilia.

Table 7.2 Snapshot of the top twenty Brazilian MNEs, 2004–2006 (US$ billions)

Variable	2004	2005	% Change	2006	% Change
Assets (US$ billions)					
Foreign	24	27	13	56	107%
Total	190	215	13	277	29%
Ratio of foreign/total	13	13		20	
Employment					
Foreign	32.645	41.284	26	77.058	87%
Total	312.306	330.689	6	405.817	23%
Ratio of foreign/total	10	12		19	
Sales (Excluding Exports [US$ Billions])					
By foreign affiliates	23	26	13	30	15%
Total	148	167	13	190	14%
Ratio of foreign/total	16	16		16	

Source: Fundação Dom Cabral—Vale Columbia Center on Sustainable International Investment survey of Brazilian multinationals.

Finally, before we begin to analyze the details of the Brazilian MNE process, a macrolevel analysis of the core transnationalization variables from 2004 to 2006 is presented (table 7.2). Three particular items stand out. First, the percentage change in foreign assets from 2005 to 2006 (107%) is much larger than the previous year's change (13%). This increase is explained largely by the acquisition of Inco by Vale. Had Vale not acquired Inco, the percentage change would have been a more modest 44%. Yet, even without the Vale acquisition, the percentage change is still quite large. The Vale acquisition largely explains the second noteworthy point, the percentage change in foreign employment from 2005 to 2006, of 87%, compared with 26% for the period from 2004 to 2005. The approximately 12,000 employees that Vale "acquired" increased the percentage change for 2006 by 30%. The final issue is the lack of a corresponding increase in foreign sales from 2005 to 2006 (14%). Indeed, table 7.2 demonstrates that these figures remain largely unchanged between 2004 and 2005 (13%). This can be partially explained by the time lag in foreign sales being booked by Vale.

7.2   The Regional Distribution of Brazilian MNEs

The foreign affiliates of the top twenty Brazilian MNEs have a wide geographic spread; they are present in fifty-one countries. On average, each Brazilian MNE was established in three host countries; Votorantim, Camargo Correa, Odebrecht, and Weg lead the way with each present in twelve countries outside Brazil.

A "Regionality Index" is calculated by taking the number of host countries in which a Brazilian MNE is located in a given region as a percentage of all host countries in which it is located (Sullivan 1994). This index shows that about half of the top twenty Brazilian MNEs have most of their activities in Latin America, with a few focusing their attention on Europe and

Asia (table 7.3). In short, in line with firms from other OFDI countries, most Brazilian MNEs are regional firms.

The Regionality Index yields some noticeable results. First, Vale's index in Asia is a very significant 60%. This is due to the company's aggressive stance on further integrating into the supply chain of a primary market. The rapid expansion of Asian firms has produced a huge demand for ore, Vale's principal product. Another surprising finding is that so many firms are in Africa, a continent which, historically, has not accounted for a significant share of a firm's business. The fact that Mozambique and Angola both have a Portuguese heritage (and languages) has helped to facilitate the entry of Brazilian MNEs into these markets. Furthermore, South Africa has a large mining industry, which is a specialty of Brazilian firms.

Table 7.3 Regionality Index, 2006

		Regionality Index				
Rank	Name	Africa	Asia	Europe	Latin America	North America
1	Vale	10	60	10	10	10
2	Petrobras S.A (Petroleo Brasileiro S.A)	22	–	33	33	11
3	Gerdau S.A.	–	–	9	73	18
4	EMBRAER—Empresa Brasileira de Aeronáutica S.A.	–	40	40	–	20
5	Votorantim Participações S.A.	–	25	33	25	17
6	Companhia Siderurgica Nacional (CSN)	–	–	50	–	50
7	Camargo Corrêa S.A.	17	–	8	67	8
8	Odebrecht S.A	17	8	8	58	8
9	Aracruz Celulose	–	–	40	40	20
10	Weg S.A.	8	17	33	33	8
11	Marcopolo S.A.	14	29	14	43	–
12	Andrade Gutierrez S.A.	–	–	13	88	–
13	Tigre S/A. Tubos e Conexões	–	–	–	86	14
14	Usinas Siderúrgicas de Minas Gerais S.A-Usiminas	–	–	–	–	–
15	Natura Cosméticos S.A.	–	–	14	86	–
16	Itautec S.A.	–	–	25	63	13
17	America Latina Logistica S.A.	–	–	–	100	–
18	Ultrapar Participações S.A.	–	–	–	100	–
19	Sabó Indústria e Comércio de Autopeças Ltda.	–	27	55	9	9
20	Lupatech S.A.	–	–	–	50	50

Source: Fundação Dom Cabral—Vale Columbia Center on Sustainable International Investment survey of Brazilian multinationals.

While the Regionality Index demonstrates a focus and concentration on Latin America, we expect that these figures will change over the coming years, the result of new Brazilian MNE "frontiers" in Africa, Eastern Europe, and Asia. These regions have experienced the allocation of a considerable amount of resources. Furthermore, the increase in political risk in South America further incentivizes Brazilian MNEs to spread their risk by diversifying into other regions.

7.3 Foreign Assets

The foreign assets held by Brazilian MNEs more than doubled between 2005 and 2006 (112% increase), signaling the reinvigoration of the top twenty Brazilian MNEs. This growth was due in part to Vale's US$17 billion acquisition of Inco (Canada). A partial explanation of this high growth is the ability of these firms to draw on foreign pools of capital to finance their expansion. For instance, eight of the top ten MNEs are listed on both the New York Stock Exchange and the São Paulo Stock Exchange. Table 7.4 shows the absolute figures of foreign and total assets of the top twenty.

The foreign assets of these firms as a percentage of total assets range from 1% to 46%, while only two MNEs have more than US$10 billion in foreign assets. For the group as a whole, foreign assets were 20% of total assets in 2006, compared to 12% in 2005. (This increase is largely the result of Vale's acquisition of Inco.) This compares to 33% for the 100 largest MNEs from developing countries in 2005—indicating that Brazilian MNEs still have some way to go to catch up with the average of their (especially Asian) competitors.[4]

The history of the ranking of Brazilian MNEs overall shows that the position of companies such as Vale, Petrobras, Gerdau, and Embraer in the foreign-asset ranking comes as no surprise. In contrast, the ranking of companies such as Marcopolo and Sabó is surprising. In 2006, Marcopolo had the highest percentage of foreign assets (30%) among the lower sixteen companies. Marcopolo is located in five regions of the world, where activities range from sales to final assembly and procurement. Sabó (16% of whose total assets are foreign) is also present in five regions of the world, with all business activities, except research and development, represented in foreign markets. Figure 7.2 shows the distribution of foreign assets of the top twenty Brazilian MNEs with respect to their primary role in the value chain.

Vale, Aracruz, VCP, Klabin (cellulose and paper sector), Sadia, and Perdigão (agribusiness sector) are companies with traditional export strategies, supported by commercial subsidiaries. For them, Brazil's comparative advantage does explain a certain concentration of domestic versus foreign assets.

7.4 Foreign Employment

In line with the increase in assets, the total foreign employment of the top twenty Brazilian MNEs almost doubled from 2005 to 2006 (87%). Three

Table 7.4   The top twenty Brazilian MNEs, by foreign assets, 2006 (US$ millions)

| Rank | Name | Assets | | Ratio |
		Foreign	Total	Foreign/ total
1	Vale	26.016	56.556	46%
2	Petrobras S.A. (Petróleo Brasileiro S.A.)	na	na	na
3	Gerdau S.A.	4.842	12.381	39%
4	EMBRAER—Empresa Brasileira de Aeronáutica S.A.	na	na	na
5	Votorantim Participações S.A.	2.360	45.779	5%
6	Companhia Siderúrgica Nacional (CSN)	2.016	11.507	18%
7	Camargo Corrêa S.A.	1.923	7.346	26%
8	Odebrecht S.A.	1.617	10.618	15%
9	Aracruz Celulose	845	4.403	19%
10	Weg S.A.	419	1.721	24%
11	Marcopolo S.A.	197	662	30%
12	Andrade Gutierrez S.A.	180	4.983	4%
13	Tigre S.A. Tubos e Conexões	na	na	na
14	Usinas Siderúrgicas de Minas Gerais S.A.-Usiminas	88	8.724	1%
15	Natura Cosméticos S.A.	75	339	22%
16	Itautec S.A.	74	401	19%
17	America Latina Logística S.A.	na	na	na
18	Ultrapar Participações S.A.	na	na	na
19	Sabó Indústria e Comércio de Autopeças Ltda.	34	213	16%
20	Lupatech S.A.	27	262	10%
	Total	56.426	276.618	20%

Source: Fundação Dom Cabral—Vale Columbia Center on Sustainable International Investment survey of Brazilian multinationals.

Note: NA—Not available.

Brazilian MNEs, led by Odebrecht, have more than 10,000 employees abroad. The ratio of foreign employment to total employment for the top twenty Brazilian MNEs was 19% in 2006, compared to 39% for the 100 largest MNEs from developing countries, over the same period. Some two-thirds of foreign employment was located in Latin America. The CEOs of all top twenty were Brazilian; only five of the 157 board members were non-Brazilian (3%). Eight of the top twenty Brazilian MNEs reported that they have Spanish and/or English as official language(s) in addition to Portuguese.

Two correlated explanations exist for why there is such a concentration of Brazilians in the top positions of these firms. First, many of the largest businesses are family controlled (e.g., WEG, Gerdau, Odebrecht). Foreigners reaching the top ranks would dilute family control over the firm. Second, as evidenced by the GLOBE studies, Brazil ranks as one of the highest countries in in-group collectivism (see House, Javidan, and Dorfman 2001). This means that individuals are relatively predisposed to trust people close to them, and this increase in trust results in the allocation of positions of influence to others in their "in-group." We refer to these explanations as being

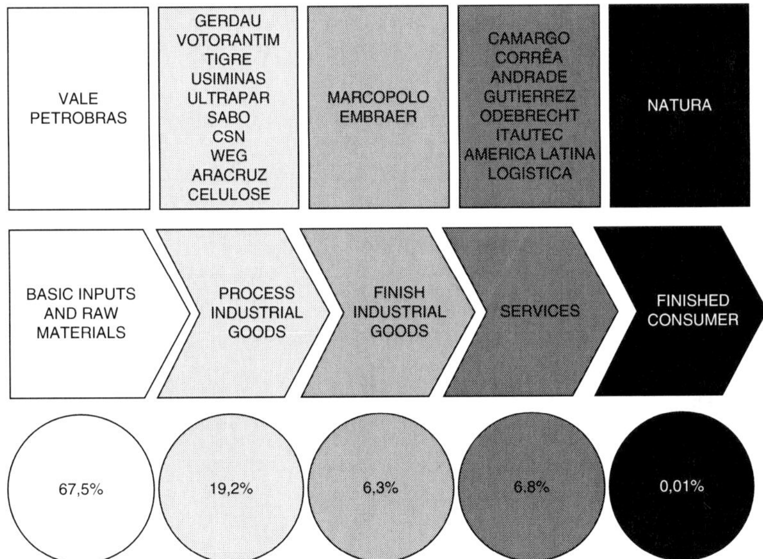

Figure 7.2   Distribution of foreign assets of the top twenty Brazilian MNEs, by industry, 2006

Source: Fundação Dom Cabral—Vale Columbia Center on Sustainable International Investment survey of Brazilian multinationals.

positively correlated, since families are a type of "in-group," and thus understanding one explanation adds meaning to the other.

Furthermore, Brazilian MNEs face important challenges related to the employment of expatriates, in part due to the total absence of governmental support for foreign employees. Brazil does not have official policies to guide and help structure Brazilian MNEs' foreign employment, and this lack of structure often translates into a detrimental career move for would-be expatriates. Brazilian business schools have begun to help firms address the challenges of expatriation by preparing their employees for encounters with foreign cultures and different corporate and societal values. Similar to the findings of Andrea Jaklič and Marjan Svetličič in Slovenia (chapter 11), Brazilians enjoy a high standard of living in Brazil, and unless a foreign assignment offers first-world living conditions, the expatriation of successful employees will remain a challenge.

7.5   Foreign Sales

In 2006, foreign sales represented about one-sixth of total sales for Brazilian MNEs. Six firms had foreign sales of over US$1 billion, and one firm, Petrobras, had foreign sales in excess of US$10 billion. Foreign sales rose by 15% in 2006, in line with the 2005 increase of 13%. Foreign sales of the top twenty Brazilian MNEs were the equivalent of approximately one-fifth of Brazil's total exports in 2006, making OFDI increasingly important for Brazil in terms of delivering goods and services to foreign markets (Central Bank of Brazil balance of payment statistics). If the exports of the parent firms of the top twenty (excluding Petrobras and Natura due to lack of data) are added to the sales of their foreign affiliates, the total would be US$42 billion in 2006. By this calculation, international sales would represent 44% of total sales, a percentage in line with the 43% of the 100 largest MNEs from developing countries (UNCTAD 2007).

Increases in foreign sales point to a bigger and better capacity to respond to international customers and markets. They also reflect a better understanding of customers' needs, efficient responses to logistics and supply chains, and the adaptation to cultures and local values. Furthermore, Brazilian MNEs have experienced new roles as dominant players in some regions, resulting in greater bargaining power associated with more geographical options. As a matter of fact, some of the top twenty have stated that their most important competitive advantage is the ability to respond efficiently to the changing dynamics of customers' needs. Brazilian MNEs' ability to be responsive with regard to order processing and production has resulted in an increased capacity to serve different markets and varied demands.

7.6   Brazilian MNEs' Cross-Border Mergers and Acquisitions

Historically, the transnationalization process of Brazilian MNEs primarily involved establishing commercial offices abroad. These offices focused largely on supporting export activities. This trend has changed, as evidenced by the importance of cross-border mergers and acquisitions (M&As). Table 7.5 highlights the size and scope of the largest M&As in 2006.

Table 7.5 shows the high values of certain M&A transactions: Vale's acquisition of Inco for US$19 billion, AmBev's acquisition of Quilmes for US$1.2 billion, and Cia de Tecidos' merger with Springs, worth US$494 million. Notice that Brazilian MNEs are not focused solely on Latin America, resulting in a movement toward distant lands over the past few years. Regarding M&As, the predominant strategic drive for Brazilian MNEs has been diversification, although M&As have also enabled firms to add value to their production chains. In some sense, one can interpret these M&As as slowly decommoditizing, adding value to production chains historically built upon primary sectors and basic competitive advantages.

7.7   Tying the Pieces Together:
An Aggregated Analysis of Brazilian MNEs

CEOs and top executives from Brazilian MNEs describe their transnationalization efforts as if they were "playing alone." This feeling is the result of two factors: the relatively short period of time in which Brazilian MNEs have been competing globally, and the lack of basic institutional policies in place. The Brazilian government is trying to understand just how the transnationalization process works, in order to develop and implement polices and regulations that will benefit companies and their employees. Indeed, the transnationalization of many Brazilian MNEs has been the result of external market opportunities rather than a planned strategic transnational business model.

Table 7.5   The top three Brazilian cross-border M&A transactions, 2006

Date(s)	Acquiror name	Target company name	Target industry	Target country	% of shares acquired	Value of transaction (US$ millions)
November 2006– January 2007	Vale	Inco Ltd.	Metals and mining	Canada	89	19,466
August 2006	AmBev	Quilmes Industrial S.A. {Quinsa}	Food and beverage	Argentina	34	1,200
January 2006	Cia de Tecidos- Textile Bus	Springs Inds.	Textiles and apparel	United States	100	494

Source: Thomson Financial.

We began the discussion of the transnationalization process by looking at the broad picture of Brazil's total IFDI and OFDI flows. In 2006, for the first time since official statistics became available, OFDI flows (US$28 billion) exceeded IFDI flows (US$19 billion). After Hong Kong (China), Brazil was the most important outward investor among developing countries, in terms of OFDI in 2006, and the largest outward investor in Latin America. A large part of these flows took the form of M&As, but greenfield investments, primarily undertaken by Petrobras, were also quite important.

By the end of 2006, Brazil had accumulated an OFDI stock of US$114 billion, making it the third largest outward investor among developing countries after Hong Kong (China) and Singapore. In 2005, according to Brazil's Central Bank, the majority of this investment was in financial services (49%), followed by professional services (36%) and petrochemicals-energy (4%), with the lion's share located in Latin America and the Caribbean (56%), followed by Europe (36%) and North America (7%).

While the corporate headquarters of Brazilian MNEs are centrally located in the southeast of the country, the destinations of Brazilian MNEs are spread throughout the world. Looking beyond the top twenty Brazilian MNEs, Brazil's OFDI is undertaken by 885 MNEs, headquartered in Brazil. This number demonstrates that, apart from the firms captured in the ranking, there are many small and medium-sized Brazilian firms that are beginning their efforts to become competitive in foreign markets. In fact, certain medium-sized Brazilian companies are already born with a "transnationalization disposition," due to their international alliances and global mindsets. It is expected that, in the next few years, the number of Brazilian MNEs will match even that of certain developed countries.

Table 7.6 shows the three primary variables discussed in this chapter: foreign assets, sales, and employees. Using the ranking methodology discussed earlier, the Transnationality Index percentage and its subsequent ranking are displayed.

Table 7.6   Ranking of the top twenty Brazilian MNEs, 2006

Ranking based on Foreign assets	Trans-nationality Index (%)	Name	Industry	Foreign assets / Total (%)	Foreign sales / total (%)	Foreign employment / total (%)	Trans-nationality Index (%)	Number of host countries
1	2	Vale	Mining	46	18	24	29	10
2	18	Petrobras	Oil and gas	12	12	11	12	9
3	1	Grupo Gerdau	Steel	39	54	46	46	11
4	6	EMBRAER	Aviation	45	12	13	23	5
5	24	Grupo Votorantim	Diversified	5	9	4	6	12
6	13	CSN	Steel	18	28	3	16	2
7	9	Camargo Corrêa	Diversified	26	13	18	19	12
8	5	Grupo Odebrecht	Construction and petrochem	15	20	47	27	12
9	23	Aracruz	Pulp	19	n.a	1	7	5
10	7	WEG	Electro-mechanical	24	30	11	22	12
11	4	Marcopolo	Bus transport	30	30	22	27	7
12	11	Andrade Gutierrez	Diversified	4	7	41	17	8
13	8	Tigre	Construction	27	17	17	20	7
14	31	Usiminas	Steel	1	n.a	n.a	0.3	0
15	17	Natura	Cosmetics	22	3	15	14	7
16	15	Itautec	IT	19	20	6	15	8
17	19	America Latina Logistica	Logistics	2	11	23	12	1
18	26	Ultrapar/ Grupo Ultra	Diversified	2	2	3	2	2
19	3	Sabó	Automobile parts	16	43	27	29	11
20	22	Lupatech	Electro-mechanical	10	4	7	7	2

Source: FDC-CPII survey of Brazilian multinationals

A short analysis of the first two ranking columns reveals that a less-than-perfect correlation[5] exists between foreign assets and transnationality. Indeed, the fact that they are not statistically significant, given that foreign assets are a component of the Transnationality Index, is rather illuminating. This large divergence in the two rankings inspired further analysis of each of the three components of the Transnationality Index, as well as the number of countries in which the firms are present (table 7.7).

Naturally, we expected all four of these variables to be highly correlated. For example, if a firm invests its capital in a foreign operation, then it would employ individuals to work there and sell its products. When a firm invests in a greater number of countries, it is likely to have more foreign capital, employees, and sales. Indeed, the correlation would be expected to be significant.[6] Yet, while these variables are all positively correlated, none are statistically significant.

One correlation in particular stands out (in boldface): the correlation between the ratios of foreign to total assets and foreign to total employment.

Table 7.7 Correlation matrix of the three Transnationality Index variables, 2006

Variables		Foreign assets/ total assets	Foreign sales/ total sales	Foreign employment/ total employment	Number of host countries
Foreign assets / total assets	Pearson correlation				
	Sig. (2-tailed)				
	N				
Foreign sales / total sales	Pearson correlation	0.433			
	Sig. (2-tailed)	0.073			
	N	18			
Foreign employment / total employment	Pearson correlation	**0.184**	0.426		
	Sig. (2-tailed)	**0.451**	0.078		
	N	19	18		
Number of host countries	Pearson correlation	0.379	0.403	0.435	
	Sig. (2-tailed)	0.099	0.097	0.063	
	N	20	18	19	

Source: The authors calculations.

The coefficient correlation for these two variables was not significant,[7] suggesting two possibilities. First, even if a firm employs a high proportion of people abroad, this does not translate into a high proportion of assets abroad. Second, if a firm invests in a high proportion of assets abroad, it does not necessarily have to hire a high proportion of employees abroad. In the case of Brazilian MNEs, the latter explanation is more plausible, due to the high proportion of commodity-based firms in the top twenty Brazilian MNEs. This group of firms invests heavily in long-term resources, which require, proportionally, a smaller number of employees. Fortunately, it does appear that when a firm invests both capital and individuals, increased sales tend to result.

In summary, the transnationalization trend of Brazilian MNEs could be termed "dynamic," with some companies having taken the lead and becoming reference points for others. The examples of Vale, Petrobras, and Gerdau, together with other firms in the top twenty, have established that Brazilian firms have the courage to operate on the global stage. Brazilian MNEs have demonstrated that they can achieve competitive advantages not only within the domestic market, but also in a global environment. Even though the global environment is increasingly uncertain, the determination of Brazilian companies to operate in it is not.

Appendix I. Survey Items for OFDI Drivers

- Access to new markets.
- Looking for economies of scale.

- Opportunity to explore internationally the competitiveness of different products of the company.
- Search for greater knowledge of the needs of international consumers.
- Opportunity to explore internationally the technical capacity and management of the company.
- Learning and development of new competencies.
- Vision or desire of stockholders/owners/managers.
- Pressure of global competition.
- Saturation and/or growth rates of the domestic market.
- Reduction of business risk by geographical diversification and lower dependence on the domestic market.
- Opportunity to explore internationally the competitiveness of the company's costs.
- Positive effect for the image of the company in the country of origin.

Notes

1. We have based the analysis on 2004, 2005, and 2006 data for two primary reasons. First, now that we have three years of longitudinal data, we can look at recent *trends*. Second, although we were tempted to include 2007 data (or even wait until we have 2008 data), we believe that the analysis provided here offers the reader a rich examination of the *context* in which the company leaders had to base their internationalization decisions. Indeed, each year provides a new opportunity to study this topic.
2. The amount of US$17 billion was spent in 2006. The complete transaction was estimated at US$19 billion. See Vale's 2007 annual report.
3. See the appendix for actual survey items.
4. See *World Investment Report 2007.*
5. $rho = .36$, $p = .11$.
6. And to exceed $r = .50$, which incidentally would also provide a statistically significant hurdle of $p < .05$ (with $N = 20$). Yet while these variables are all positively correlated, none of them exceeds the .50 threshold.
7. At $r = .18$, $p = .45$ (*ns*).

References

Central Bank of Brazil (2008). "Balance of payments statistics," available at http://www.bcb.gov.br/?BALANCESPECIAL, last visited June 18, 2009.

Fundação Dom Cabral and Vale Columbia Center on Sustainable International Investment (2006). Ranking of Brazilian transnationals, available at http://www.vcc.columbia.edu/FDI_materials.php, last visited June 18, 2009.

House, R., M. Javidan, and P. Dorfman (2001). "Project GLOBE: an introduction," *Applied Psychology: An International Review* 50 (4), pp. 489–505.

Kumar, V. and N. Singh (2008). "Internationalization and performance of Indian pharmaceutical firms," *Thunderbird International Business Review* 50 (5), pp. 321–30.

Ramaswamy, K., K.G. Kroeck, and W. Renforth (1996). "Measuring the degree of internationalization of a firm: a comment," *Journal of International Business Studies* 27 (1), pp. 167–77.

Sullivan, D. (1994). "Measuring the degree of internationalization of a firm," *Journal of International Business Studies* 25 (2), pp. 325–42.
——— (1996). "Measuring the degree of internationalization of a firm: a reply," *Journal of International Business Studies* 27 (1), pp. 179–92.
UNCTAD (2007). *World Investment Report: Transnational Corporations, Extractive Industries and Development* (Geneva and New York: United Nations).
Vale (2008). *Vale's 2007 Annual Report*, available at http://www.vale.com/vale/cgi/cgilua.exe/sys/start.htm?tpl=home, last visited June 18, 2009.

Chapter 8

Takeoff and Turbulence in the Foreign Expansion of Russian Multinational Enterprises

*Kalman Kalotay**

Introduction: A Swift Takeoff

Over a historically brief period (a decade and a half), Russia has become a major outward-investing country on the global stage. According to data from the United Nations Conference on Trade and Development (UNCTAD), Russia's registered outward foreign direct investment (OFDI) stock increased from US\$2 billion in 1993, to US\$255 billion in 2007 (UNCTAD 2008), making it the fifteenth most important source economy of investments worldwide, and the second largest among emerging markets, behind Hong Kong (China) only and ahead of Brazil, China, India, and South Africa (figure 8.1). However, the onset of a major financial crisis in the second half of 2008, which affected Russia's economy significantly, raises questions about the immediate future, as well as the long-term sustainability, of those large outward investments.

This chapter explores the main features of OFDI by Russian corporations, their recent rise to global prominence, and questions surrounding their future. The analysis will focus more on the phase of "takeoff," as it is much better documented to date, and formulate mainly hypotheses about the turbulent period that started with the onset of the global crisis of 2008.

The most salient feature of this period of "takeoff" is that lower-middle-income Russia became, rather unexpectedly, a net capital exporter. A number of Russian firms, such as Gazprom, Lukoil, Norilsk Nickel, and Severstal, had already attained global status. In fact, it was emerging firms from the developing world, such as China, India, or West Asia, that were tipped to move rapidly onto the global scene. Firms from an economy in transition would seem to possess less experience in competing in global markets.

This chapter suggests that, while Russian firms that expand internationally constitute a mostly diverse group, in terms of ownership structures, motivations, and strategies, they do share at least three key attributes. The first is their leapfrogging onto the global stage, often through the leveraging

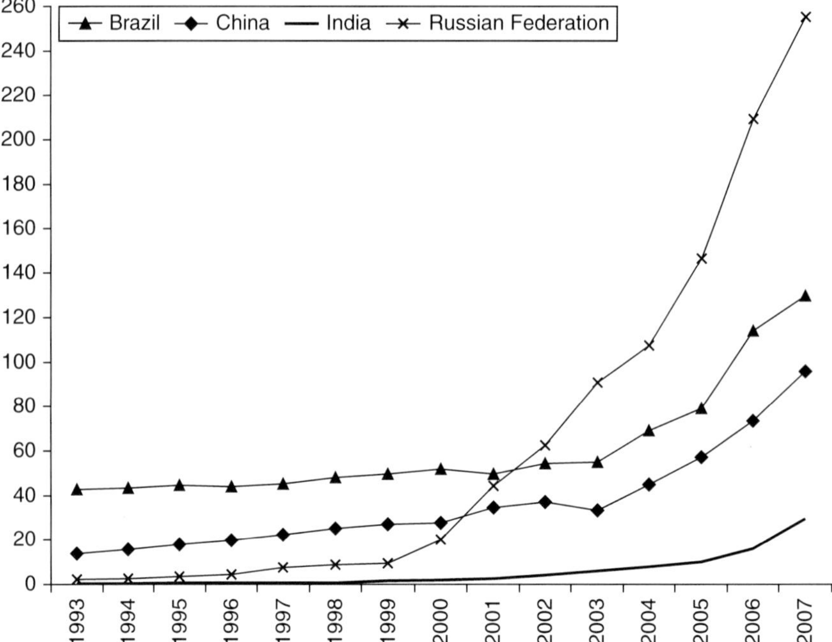

Figure 8.1　OFDI stock of Brazil, China, India, and Russia, 1993–2007 (US$ billions)

Source: UNCTAD, World Investment Report (2007): Transnational Corporations, Extractive Industries and Development.

of their natural-resource incomes. The second is their strong link with the natural resources of their home base, as until recently, most of them came from the oil and gas, metallurgy, and electricity generation and distribution industries. The third feature is the growing role of the Russian state (since 1999) in OFDI.

The remainder of the chapter analyses Russia's OFDI performance, from 1992 onward, including its geographical patterns, followed by a panorama of the largest Russian multinational enterprises (MNEs), their main characteristics, an analysis of the main drivers and motivations of Russian OFDI, a discussion on the role of government policies (including state ownership of MNEs), the impact of the current crisis of Russian OFDI, and general conclusions on the future of Russian OFDI.

8.1　The OFDI Performance of the Russian Federation

According to official statistics, the growth rate of Russia's OFDI stocks was the fastest of any emerging market, faster than other newly emerging source countries, such as India, or rapidly expanding offshore centers, such as the British Virgin Islands. However, the triple-digit growth rate of Russia's OFDI stock is partly a statistical artifact. It may well be that, in the 1990s, the outward investment position of the country was largely underreported. After

1999, the Bank of Russia began to receive increasingly accurate information, but was not fully in a position to revise its previous reporting (Kalotay 2008). That is partly confirmed by looking at the difference between outflows and outward stock data over the period 1999–2007: cumulative outflows reached US$117 billion, while OFDI stock rose by US$245 billion (table 8.1). Naturally, part of the discrepancy may be due to changing valuations, or the fact that not all private-sector outflows of that period were correctly recorded as OFDI. Nevertheless, the dynamic flow data also indicates rapid growth.

In general, the foreign direct investment (FDI) scoreboard of the Russian Federation indicates that, since the beginning of the transition, the country has been a major capital exporter, with FDI outflows sometimes exceeding inflows (and coming close to them in the rest of the period) (table 8.1). The ratio of OFDI to inward foreign direct investment (IFDI) remained close to one, despite the boom in the latter from 2002, and despite major improvements in Russia's business environment. Regarding OFDI stocks, at the beginning of transition, most OFDI was informal in nature; until 1999 the officially registered OFDI stock remained below US$10 billion (table 8.1).

The industry and geographical patterns of Russian OFDI must be estimated from data on cross-border mergers and acquisitions (M&As), given the lack of detailed FDI data available.[1] However, given that M&As are the preferred mode of foreign expansion for Russian MNEs, M&A data are indicative of the major trends, despite the methodological issue raised.[2] As a rough comparison of volumes, the cumulative cross-border M&A purchases of Russia (the equivalent of OFDI in the M&A terminology) totaled US$65 billion, as compared to cumulative FDI outflows of US$125 billion.

The dynamics of cross-border M&A purchases by Russian MNEs has closely followed the acceleration of OFDI flows. Given the high level of "lumpiness" of M&As, they are presented here in four-year periods (with the exception of the initial period of 1992–1996 and the final period of 2005–June 2008.) A period-by-period comparison reveals that cross-border M&A purchases tripled between 1992–1996 and 1997–2000, and between 1997–2000 and 2001–2004. In the final period, 2005–June 2008, they rose more than tenfold (table 8.2).

With regard to the geographical distribution of acquisitions abroad, data show that Russian firms have generally targeted developed country firms (table 8.2), especially in Europe and North America. This pattern is observed despite the fact that the expansion of Russian MNEs sometimes began in other member states of the Commonwealth of Independent States (CIS), especially when the MNE activity involved assets inherited from the breakup of the Union of Soviet Socialist Republics (USSR) (Kuznetsov 2008).[3] Over time, however, the CIS' share in cross-border M&As has increased, reaching a high of 28% in 2001–2004. (In 2005–June 2008, the CIS' share in cross-border M&As dropped to 16%, despite a sixfold increase in absolute values.) It is only since 2005 that Russian firms have made significant acquisitions in developing countries, focusing mainly on Asia but also Africa. These

Table 8.1 The foreign direct investment scoreboard of the Russian Federation, 1992–2007 (US$ millions and percentage)

Indicator	1992	1993	1994	1995	1996	1997	1998	1999	2000	2001	2002	2003	2004	2005	2006	2007
Inward FDI flows	1 161	1 211	690	2 066	2 579	4 865	2 761	3 309	2 714	2 748	3 461	7 958	15 444	12 886	32 387	52 475
Outward FDI flows	1 566	1 022	281	606	923	3 184	1 270	2 208	3 177	2 533	3 533	9 727	13 782	12 767	23 151	45 652
Ratio of outflows to inflows	1.3	0.8	0.4	0.3	0.4	0.7	0.5	0.7	1.2	0.9	1.0	1.2	0.9	1.0	0.7	0.9
Inward FDI stock	..	..	3 280	5 601	8 145	13 612	12 912	18 303	32 204	52 919	70 884	96 729	122 295	180 313	271 590	324 065
Outward FDI stock	..	..	2 588	3 346	4 390	7 633	8 866	9 553	20 141	44 219	62 350	90 873	107 291	146 679	209 559	255 211
Ratio of outward to inward stock	..	..	0.8	0.6	0.5	0.6	0.7	0.5	0.6	0.8	0.9	0.9	0.9	0.8	0.8	0.8
Inward FDI flows as a percentage of gross fixed capital formation	1.0	1.3	0.8	2.5	3.3	6.6	6.3	11.7	6.2	4.7	5.6	10.0	14.2	9.5	17.8	19.3
Outward FDI flows as a percentage of gross fixed capital formation	1.3	1.1	0.3	0.7	1.2	4.3	2.9	7.8	7.3	4.4	5.7	12.3	12.7	9.4	12.7	16.8
Inward FDI stock as a percentage of gross domestic product	..	..	0.8	1.4	2.1	3.4	4.8	9.3	12.4	17.3	20.5	22.4	20.7	23.6	27.6	25.1
Outward FDI stock as a percentage of gross domestic product	..	..	0.6	0.8	1.1	1.9	3.3	4.9	7.8	14.4	18.0	21.1	18.1	19.2	21.3	19.8

Source: UNCTAD, FDI/TNC database.

Table 8.2   Cross-border M&A purchases by Russian MNEs, by host country/region, 1992–June 2008 (US$ millions)

Country/region	1992–1996	1997–2000	2001–2004	2005–2008
World	511	2,211	5,498	56,794
Developed economies	511	2,151	3,962	44,287
Europe	311	1,749	2,766	30,575
European Union	311	1,749	2,566	30,160
Austria	–	–	4	1,662
Belgium	–	90	–	–
Bulgaria	–	816	37	–
Cyprus	–	–	–	511
Finland	45	45	–	276
Greece	–	–	–	806
Hungary	6	6	–	177
Italy	–	–	–	1,280
Luxembourg	–	–	–	1,660
Netherlands	245	245	–	–
Romania	–	300	121	–
Slovakia	–	–	72	–
Slovenia	–	–	–	50
Sweden	–	–	–	4,652
United Kingdom	–	211	2,273	19,016
North America	–	170	1,195	13,247
Canada	–	–	68	7,937
United States	–	170	1,127	5,310
Other developed countries	200	232	–	465
Australia	–	2	–	461
Japan	200	200	–	–
Developing economies	–	–	–	3,210
Africa	–	–	–	250
Nigeria	–	–	–	250
Asia and Oceania	–	–	–	2,945
Turkey	–	–	–	2,006
China	–	–	–	786
Malaysia	–	–	–	92
South-East Europe and the CIS	–	61	1,536	9,297
Southeast Europe	–	–	303	257
Bosnia and Herzegovina	–	–	–	157
Croatia	–	–	76	–
Serbia and Montenegro	–	–	225	59
Commonwealth of Independent States (CIS)	–	61	1,233	9,039
Armenia	–	–	27	423
Kyrgyzstan	–	–	–	150
Russian Federation	–	47	990	5,614
Ukraine	–	13	199	2,769

Source: UNCTAD, cross-border M&A database.

patterns are more in line with expectations: initially, Russian firms focused their foreign expansion on neighboring, relatively familiar regions (Europe and CIS), later moving farther afield.

The United Kingdom is the country with the largest M&A purchases from the Russian Federation. In 2001–2004, 41% of purchases took place in the United Kingdom, while in 2005–2008, the United Kingdom accounted for 33% of purchase. Canada and the United States were the second and third most important target countries. Geographical data also provide evidence of a high level of round tripping: in almost one-tenth of the cases, cross-border M&A purchases targeted firms abroad that ultimately invested in the Russian Federation (table 8.2). Round tripping is a phenomenon that exists in various emerging markets (in addition to Russia, it is also common in China). The main reasons for this strategy are related to tax benefits and foreign exchange controls (UNCTAD 1998).[4]

Regarding the sectoral composition of M&A purchases, most of the acquisitions of Russian firms were made in the primary sector (see table 8.3). On average, the primary sector accounted for 60% of investments in the last three subperiods. The share of the primary sector was low in 1992–1996 (9%). It has increased rapidly since then, especially in the case of the petroleum and gas industries, but also mining. In the early 1990s, most purchases took place in the manufacturing industry. However, by 1997–2001, its share fell to 8%, although this later increased, reaching 24% in 2005–2008. Within manufacturing, machinery, metallurgy, and motor vehicles were the three most important industries. A different pattern was followed by investments of Russian firms in the services sector. Their share in M&A purchases was

Table 8.3 Cross-border M&A purchases by Russian MNEs, by sector/industry, 1992–June 2008 (US$ millions)

Sector/industry	1992–1996	1997–2000[a]	2001–2004	2005–2008
All sectors/industries	511	1,700	5,498	56,794
Primary	45	1,098	2,980	33,485
Agriculture, forestry, and fishing	–	–	5	–
Mining, quarrying and petroleum	45	1,098	2,976	33,485
Mining and quarrying	–	–	1,546	15,742
Petroleum	45	1,098	1,430	17,743
Secondary	451	146	661	13,430
Food, beverages and tobacco	–	90	9	2
Wood and wood products	3	–	–	34
Oil and gas; petroleum refining	–	7	161	589
Chemicals and chemical products	–	–	164	113
Metal and metal products	–	31	306	2,914
Machinery	6	–	17	7,575
Electrical and electronic equipment	–	2	–	453
Electronic equipment	–	2	–	217
Communications equipment	–	–	–	143
Transportation equipment	442	15	–	1,537
Motor vehicles	200	15	–	1,537
Services	15	456	1,857	8,935
Electricity, gas, and water	–	177	60	1,042
Construction firms	–	–	100	1,637
Hotels and casinos	–	–	2	468
Trade	–	235	536	350

Continued

Table 8.3 Continued

Sector/industry	1992–1996	1997–2000[a]	2001–2004	2005–2008
Transport, storage and communications	15	13	1,106	3,880
Telecommunications	–	10	1,021	3,637
Finance	–	23	30	1,773
Business activities	–	2	23	116
Business services	–	2	19	250
Community, social and personal services	–	7	–	888

Source: UNCTAD, cross-border M&A database.

[a] Excluding unspecified.

very low in 1992–1996, but rose to 34% in 2001–2004. In the period from 2005 to June 2008, its share was 16%. Within services, telecommunications was the most important industry.

8.2 The Main Features of the Largest Russian MNEs: Dynamic and Natural-Resource-Based

There is no single methodology that would identify all large Russian out-ward-investing MNEs. One method is to use a list of the largest Russian MNEs, based on a survey (annex table 8.1; Skolkovo and VCC 2008). The main advantages of this survey method are that it measures foreign operations directly, and it covers firms that are not listed or are too small, in terms of total assets, to show up in a stock market list (e.g., OMZ). The disadvantages of this method are that it is based on declarations of firms that one cannot always verify, it may omit any firm that does not wish to participate in the survey (e.g., certain rare high-technology firms, such as the software firm Kaspersky Lab), and, for methodological reasons, it has to exclude banks. Another possibility is to draw upon the list of the largest Russian firms (annex table 8.2) by market capitalization, by eliminating the uninational firms. The advantages of this method are its relative reliability (as it builds on public reports submitted by firms to stock markets, including, in some cases, foreign markets), the fact that it is current (it is possible to compile data up to the end of 2008), and its capacity to capture all types of firms (including banks). The disadvantage of this method is that it ignores unlisted firms (e.g., the majority of shipping companies), MNEs that do not prepare consolidated reports (e.g., United Company Rusal),[5] and companies that have been restructured (such as the former state-owned electricity monopoly Unified Energy Systems, reor-ganized and dismantled in 2006–2008),[6] as well as the fact that it considers the full size of the firm and not just its foreign operations.

There are also descriptive studies that trace the foreign expansion of Russian firms through anecdotal evidence, but without any quantitative benchmark for the scale of the firm or its international activities. A recent study by Deloitte CIS (2008), for example, found twenty-five Russian

MNEs,[7] and even categorized them into three groups: a globally expanding "Big Six" (11–23), a "second tier" (24–27), consisting of nine firms, and a group of ten "regional players in the post-Soviet space" (28–32). These studies can provide valuable background information for further analysis, although the information cannot be directly used for the ranking of firms. Moreover, the Skolkovo-VCC list contains all "Big Six" and "second-tier" firms,[8] and three of the ten regional players.[9] A comparison with the quantitative rankings confirms that, despite its interesting insights, the anecdotal method may misinterpret the relative importance of certain firms.

A combination of the two quantitative methods mentioned above provides two distinct lists that complement each other and can be combined into a single list (table 8.4). They can be combined, as there are a number of important common points, such as the dominance of certain very large natural-resource-based firms (e.g., Gazprom, Lukoil, and Norilsk Nickel) in both lists (three of the "Big Six"). There are seven other firms that are identified by both methods: Evraz, Mobile TeleSystems, Norilsk Nickel, Novolipetsk Iron & Steel, Severstal, TNK-BP, and VimpelCom. The combined list also highlights the relative importance of state-owned MNEs (see table 8.4).

The universe of large Russian MNEs, by both measurements, is also dynamic in terms of new entries. In the first list, for example, Novolipetsk Iron & Steel became multinational between 2007[10] and 2008, following in the footsteps of other firms that became international almost overnight. There are also international firms such as the retail group X5 that entered the list thanks to its growing market capitalization (table 8.4; annex table 8.2). In turn, the restructured, former electricity monopoly, Unified Energy Systems, no longer features on the list of Russian firms with the largest market capitalization. However, one of its successors, InterRAO, appeared on the list of the largest MNEs ranked by foreign assets. The Skolkovo-VCC[11] list saw four new entrants between 2006 and 2007 (annex table 8.1).

A general caveat to both methods is that some of the firms that feature on the lists are not necessarily independent MNEs in the strict sense. Sibneft has become the affiliate of Gazprom and was renamed Gazpromneft. Sistema Holding owns the majority of Mobile TeleSystems, and Sitronics and the Industrial Metallurgical Holding Management Company (a nonlisted holding company) own OAO Koks. These affiliates are, however, separate legal entities, with a relatively important degree of autonomy of foreign operations, making it necessary to consider them also in the universe of major outward-investing firms.

We must also consider those cases in which foreign strategic investors have acquired more than 10% of voting rights in a company: BP controls 50% of the BP-TNK joint venture, Telenor controls more than 25% of VimpelCom, and ConocoPhillips owns 20% of Lukoil. In a very narrow sense, these foreign investors would be the ultimate parents, and these firms would not qualify as MNEs in their own right. However, if that ownership falls short of a majority, and the relationship with the foreign owner is closer to an equity-based strategic alliance than a control-hierarchy relationship, these firms can still be considered MNEs in a broader sense.

The group of thirty-four MNEs identified in table 8.4[12] at first sight appears fairly heterogeneous. These firms, however, share some common characteristics, as well as some salient features that apply to many, although not all, of them. The *first* and most important common characteristic is the relatively large absolute size of the majority of the firms. Among them, Gazprom, Lukoil, and Norilsk Nickel are particularly large in size (table 8.4; annex table 8.2). From this it can be inferred that Russian MNEs derive part of their competitive strengths ("ownership advantages") from their size at home. This feature in turn relates to the history of privatization in Russia in the 1990s, in which not only large industrial groups were created, but these firms immediately began the process of consolidating their industries,[13] first at home, and then abroad, with the latter being a logical expansion of domestic expansion. The firms that became Russian MNEs were created by a rushed privatization, under which "international investors were almost totally excluded from the mass privatization in 1992 and later from Loans for Shares in 1995 (which allowed the companies' capital to be transferred to a number of oligarchies at greatly reduced prices). Not until 1997 were the restrictions on their participation in Russian companies' capital lifted" (Locatelli 2006, 1081–82).[14] Once created, these large private oligopolies showed a desire for the further domestic consolidation of their respective industries, as corroborated by the frequency of merger talks and hostile take-over bids in Russia (Radygin 2002). These talks were sometimes called off, to be relaunched at a later date.[15]

In certain cases, large Russian groups combine horizontal and vertical integration of production capacities in their industries, and oligopolistic or monopolistic behavior in the home market, with conglomeration. Under conglomeration, such groups can also include not just production facilities, but also distribution networks and banking (separated from production during Soviet times). Alfa Bank, for example, is "banker" to the Alfa Group mentioned above. In this case, the bank acts as the coordinator of the group. In the case of the Gazprom Group, the roles are reversed, and the production company controls the Gazprombank.

A *second* major feature of large Russian MNEs, correlated with their large size, is the dominance of natural-resource-based firms in the sample, the result of technological and organizational reasons that drive natural-resource-based firms to increase their size. On the list of firms ranked by market capitalization (annex table 8.2) there are nine oil firms, five iron and steel companies, and two mining companies; the top four positions are occupied by oil firms. The list of the largest firms by foreign assets is slightly more diverse in terms of the number of firms, but not necessarily in terms of the amount of foreign assets (annex table 8.1). The latter top twenty-five include only three oil and gas firms (although they occupy the top two positions), six iron and steel companies, two mining companies, and one metals company. These firms together account for US$72 billion in foreign assets (figure 8.2), of which two companies (Lukoil and Gazprom) account for more than half (US$34 billion). This means that natural-resource-based firms account for four-fifths of the foreign assets of the top twenty-five.

Table 8.4 Consolidated list of the largest Russian MNEs, 2007/2008

Firm	Industry cluster	Skolkovo-VCC rank	Rank by market capitalization	Deloitte CIS category	Firm	Industry cluster	Skolkovo-VCC rank	Rank by market capitalization	Deloitte CIS category
State-owned MNEs					**Privately owned MNEs, with 10 to 50% foreign ownership**				
Gazprom[a]	Oil and gas	2	1	Big Six	Lukoil	Oil and gas	1	3	Big Six
Gazpromneft	Oil and gas	–	7	–	TNK-BP[b]	Oil and gas	12	9	–
Rosneft[a]	Oil and gas	–	2	–	VimpelCom	Telecom	9	12	Second tier
Alrosa	Metals and mining	22	–	Second tier					
InterRAO	Electricity	16	–	–					
Sovcomflot	Transport	6	–	–					
Sberbank	Banks	–	5	–					
VTB Bank[a]	Banks	–	11	–					
Privately owned MNEs, wholly local ownership									
Novatek	Oil and gas	–	13	–	Eurochem	Chemicals	15	–	–
Tatneft[c]	Oil and gas	–	15	–	Acron	Chemicals	21	–	–
Evraz	Iron and steel	4	16	Big Six	GAZ	Automotive and machinery	19	–	Regional player
Severstal	Iron and steel	5	17	Big Six	OMZ	Automotive and machinery	24	–	Second tier
Novolipetsk Iron & Steel	Iron and steel	10	10	Second tier	X5 Retail Group	Retail	–	19	Regional player

Industrial Metallurgical Holding Management Co.	Holding	–	–	–	*PriSCo*	Transport	11	–	–
				–	*FESCO*	Transport	13	–	–
OAO Koks	Iron and steel	14	–	–	*Sistema*	Holding	–	20	–
TMK	Iron and steel	17	–	Second tier	Mobile TeleSystems	Telecom	8	8	Second tier
ChTPZ	Iron and steel	20	–	Regional player	Sitronics	Other services	23	–	Second tier
Mechel	Iron and steel	–	23	Second tier	*Mirax*	Other services	18	–	–
Norilsk Nickel	Metals and mining	3	6	Big Six	*Ritzio Entertainment*	Other services	25	–	–
Rusal	Metals and mining	7	–	Big Six					

Source: Author, based on annex tables 8.1 and 8.2, and Deloitte CIS (2008).

Note: Ultimate parents are highlighted in *italics*

[a] Foreign investors own less than 10%.

[b] BP owns 50%.

[c] *Local public ownership (see annex table 8.2).*

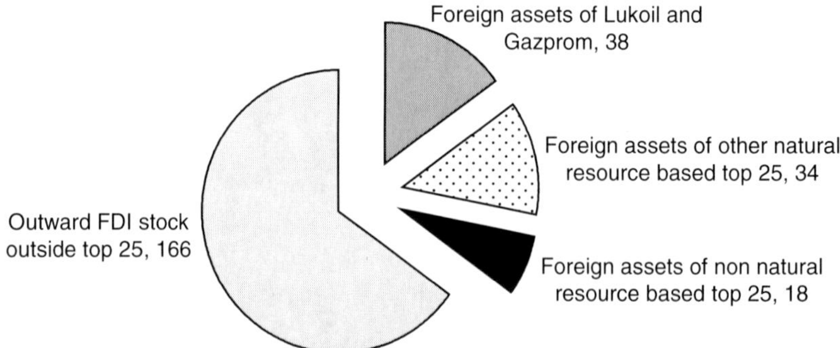

Figure 8.2   Foreign assets of the top twenty-five MNEs of the Skolkovo-VCC list and outward FDI stock of the Russian Federation, 2007 (US$ billions)

Source: Author's calculations, based on Skolkovo and VCC (2008) and UNCTAD (2008).

Setting aside the methodological differences between FDI and foreign asset data, a rough comparison of the foreign assets of the top twenty-five (US$72 billion) with the total OFDI stock of the Russian Federation, also for 2007 (US$255 billion), is possible. The former accounts for 35% of the latter and, given the fact that the top twenty-five list may exclude certain large, non-reporting firms, this ratio is an indication of a very high concentration of OFDI among a few firms.

A *third* general feature of Russian MNEs, derived from their size and their industry composition, is their high profitability[16] and rapid growth, at least up until the beginning of the 2008 crisis (annex table 8.2). Over the full year 2008, total sales of twenty-four of the twenty-five firms listed, showed double-digit growth; only Norilsk Nickel saw sales contract in 2008. This is explained by the fact that, over most of the period under observation, natural-resource prices evolved favorably from the point of view of Russian MNEs.

A *fourth* common feature is the uneven progress of Russian firms in foreign expansion. Certain firms, such a Lukoil, Gazprom, and Norilsk Nickel, are already giants abroad while others, although having a large domestic presence, have a relatively limited presence abroad.

A *fifth* feature is the recurrent presence of state-owned firms on the two lists: of the thirty-four firms monitored, at least nine are state owned, including Gazprom. In the list of the largest firms by absolute size (annex table 8.2), state-owned firms account for 55% of aggregate market capitalization. On the list of the largest MNEs by foreign presence (annex table 8.1), state-owned MNEs account for 26% of the sample's total foreign assets. These findings are generally in line with expectations that state-owned firms focus more on their home base, and internationalize more slowly than do their private-sector peers.

It should be underlined that, since 2001, state ownership appears to be on the rise in Russia, and with the advent of the financial crisis, it may further increase. One of the main indicators of this shift toward greater state owner-ship is the increased public participation in previously privatized Gazprom, from 38.4% to more than 50%, through the payment of US$7 billion in cash, in 2005 (Dittrick 2005, 28).[17] Furthermore, Gazprom, now majority state-owned, acquired privately owned assets, including Sibneft, in order to increase its share and influence in the natural-resources industry. The acquisition of various assets of the now-defunct Yukos by state-owned Rosneft, in 2004 and 2005, is another sign of rising state ownership.

State ownership can be both an advantage and a disadvantage: it can facilitate the expansion of Russian firms into locations where Russia enjoys good diplomatic relations, and it offers a form of guarantee in the case of engaging in more high-risk projects or in the case of a crisis. However, state ownership can be a handicap when international political conflicts occur, such as the Russian-Ukrainian gas conflicts and the war in Georgia. Moreover, the implementation of state policies, at the expense of business considerations, can prove harmful to profitability.

8.3 Drivers and Motivations of Russian MNEs: Exodus Versus Expansion

The data provided above indicate a fast and rather aggressive expansion of Russian firms abroad since the early 1990s. Russian firms have maximized the use of their natural-resource base as collateral to raise loans for investment abroad, especially during the years when prices for these resources were high. This leveraging of resources has produced major results since 2000, although the advent of the current financial crisis and recession, which have depressed export prices and seen foreign borrowings dry up, has created major indebtedness problems for some Russian firms, such as Norilsk Nickel (see below).

An explanation of Russian OFDI should take into consideration both home country factors that encourage firms to invest abroad (e.g., the impact of the home country environment—the so-called push factors) and the attractiveness of foreign locations for Russian firms, in terms of reaching their strategic goals (e.g., sources of enhanced competitiveness—pull factors). Russian MNEs have responded over time to both motivations. Using the terms of the literature, OFDI from Russia is both "exodus" and "expansion" (Liuhto 2005).

As for the push factor, over time it has undergone major changes. Early in the transition period, the Russia business environment was very difficult, prompting Russian firms to create safety nets abroad, protecting them from home country uncertainty. Some Russian MNEs still follow such "system-escape" motivations (Bulatov 1998). The advent of the global crisis and its negative fallout for Russia may resuscitate this motivation. The push factors also include an element of global strategy and the desire of Russian firms to maximize the advantage of the resource base in the global economy by expanding abroad. This motivation gained importance under the presidency of Vladimir Putin (1999–2008). Recent changes in the Russian business environment prove that the country is still midway between the two types of push factors. On the one hand, there have been a series of impressive measures to improve the Russian business climate, including the rationalization of taxation. On the other hand, there have been cases since 2001, such as the treatment of the Yukos, which have sent a contradictory message, where tax administration has been used to reach noneconomic, nonfiscal goals. In addition, in November 2004, when the tax authorities approached a joint venture with a foreign investor (TNK-BP) with a claim for taxes, it sent the message that a potential reversal of the improvement of the business climate could not be totally excluded (Ostrovsky 2004).

The pull factor of foreign locations is related closely to the motivations of Russian MNEs going abroad. Market-seeking MNEs are attracted to foreign markets that are either large in size or are growing fast. The first feature applies mainly to developed markets; the second characterizes some fast-growing emerging markets. As Russian OFDI has been always dominated by market-seeking motivations, it is no surprise that Russian MNEs have targeted mostly developed markets (and emerging markets since 2005; table 8.2). The most important Russian firms are natural-resource-based companies that operate upstream. They focus on integrating the supply chain downstream, to the level of the consumer (as evidenced by Gazprom's investment in European pipelines and Lukoil's purchase of Getty's gas stations in the United States).

Additionally, some of the projects in developed markets are strategic-asset seeking. In developing and transition economies, natural-resource-seeking motives also exist. The latter require further explanation. Why does a firm rich in natural resources at home invest in the same resources abroad? The reasons are mostly strategic: the firm gains greater control over upstream supply and prevents competitors from controlling those resources, especially in countries that Russian MNEs consider to be traditional partners (such as the CIS countries, or countries that previously maintained special relationships with the USSR).

In general, the motivations of exodus versus expansion have undergone various cycles: exodus was strong at the beginning of the transition (early 1990s), followed by less capital flight in the mid-1990s, followed by the crisis of 1998, which prompted a rise in capital flight, and normalization, especially under President Putin (Kalotay 2002). Most recently, the crisis of 2008 increased the motivation of exodus once again, as evidenced by dwindling central bank reserves (see below).

From the main characteristic of Russian MNEs, one can deduce that frequently these firms do not possess technology-related ownership advantages in the classical sense (Ot), although they possess some organizational advantages (Oa), as witnessed by their relative success in less-than-perfect business environments. The organizational advantages of Russian firms are, in part, linked to a peculiar Russian way of doing business and acquiring assets abroad, which enables them to overcome, in some cases, the reluctance of target countries to accept Russian investment. This method of investment abroad consists of transactions taking place through shadow (offshore) firms instead of the transparent purchase of shares in the MNEs' own names (Kalotay 2007). These strategies of proxy-based operations, however, can be double-edged in the longer term. In the short term, they increase OFDI.

In the longer term, however, they can reduce the readiness of host countries to accept Russian FDI. The strategy of using proxies, such as privately owned Western firms, to acquire assets abroad is usually seen as involving low-transparency transactions that raise concerns in host countries over a firm's intentions, although Russian experts insist that that the funds used for such transactions are of legal origin (Livshits 2001).

In most cases, the ownership advantages of Russian MNEs, although somewhat truncated, enable them to expand abroad smoothly. One can also hypothesize that, in certain cases, when ownership advantages are not yet complete, they are partly replaced by general home country factors (such as state-backing; see below), which enable them to invest abroad despite their apparent ownership handicap. Indeed, in such cases, state ownership and government policies play a major role in promoting OFDI.

8.4   The Growing Role of the State and Its Policies

The Russian Federation has always had OFDI policies, although not always in the sense understood by developed countries. First, Russia's policies were often less articulate and more implicit than in many other countries. Second, the Russian Federation has never had the same institutional setting to support the foreign expansion of its firms (e.g., separate investment insurance agencies). However, this does not mean that one cannot detect a clear trend from reluctant acceptance to endorsement over the years.

During the presidency of Boris Yeltsin, it was the Russian state that actively contributed to the creation of the large private monopolies that later gave birth to future MNEs. The Russian state, however, did not intend to promote actively OFDI at that time, and did not yet have a vision of using OFDI as a means of achieving international strategic goals. Capital account transactions were not liberalized (they required the permission of the central bank). However, restrictions on OFDI, instead of preventing it, resulted in the development of ways to bypass such controls (such as capital flight), as the domestic business environment was difficult and taxes were high. The state, having seen the prevalence of "exodus," directed most of its efforts toward regularizing unregistered outflows (Livshits 2001).

Under the presidency of Vladimir Putin, the Russian state has clearly shifted its objectives toward promoting OFDI, mostly in the service of national strategic goals.[18] That strategic shift was made possible by a major improvement in the domestic business environment, in the fiscal system, and in the growth record of the Russian economy in general, which together eased the pressure on economic actors to follow the motivations of "exodus." In this new context, Russian follows a "National Champions Policy" (Liuhto 2008, 5), consisting of the creation of Russian-owned corporations in key industries with the help of public finance or by using administrative measures.

The shift toward using OFDI for government-policy purposes is reflected most clearly in the strategy of Gazprom, which seeks to control its value chain, especially the downstream markets, in key developed economies, particularly in Europe. Compliance with national strategic goals has become straight-forward in the case of firms that maintained or regained majority state ownership (see above). However, state influence over the strategies of Russian MNEs that remained privately owned has also increased. The use of tax and other policies was the primary means of ensuring compliance with national strategic goals (Liuhto 2008). Another way was to use the growing financial strength of the state (e.g., growing international reserves, or the recently established sovereign wealth fund) to influence the actions of Russian firms. Indeed, currently the balance of influence between the state and the owners of privately owned MNEs (the so-called oligarchs) is changing in favor of the state, and may further accelerate as the crisis of 2008 shakes the fundamentals of privately owned firms. As a result, while capital account transactions have been in part liberalized, major transactions by Russian firms (whether on foreign projects or following the request of foreign partners to invest in Russian firms) still require the informal approval of the presidency.

The result of the growing state role is that the internationalization strategies of state-owned MNEs, such as Gazprom and Rosneft, are now largely driven by Russia's foreign policy.[19] In general, the Russian state considers these two firms to be examples of how publicly owned MNEs should be developed in the future. In the literature, they have been called "patriots" (Vahtra and Liuhto 2005) or "Kremlin universe" (Aton Capital 2004). In May 2008, when Dmitry Medvedev, a former chairperson of the board of Gazprom (2000–2001, 2002–2003), became President of the Russian Federation, and Igor Sechin, a former chairperson of the board of Rosneft (2004–2008), became Deputy Prime Minister (with supervisory control over natural resources), the relationship between the government and its state-owned MNEs became even closer. The distinction between government and business has become rather blurred, certainly more so than it has been at any time since the collapse of the Soviet Union in 1991 (UniCredit Aton Research 2008).[20]

As for institutional support, the State Corporation "Bank for Development and Foreign Economic Affairs" (Vnesheconombank) has traditionally focused on export support and export insurance, and not (yet) on support for foreign expansion directly, although it received officially such a mandate in 2007.[21] As a result, it can support FDI projects but only in the rare cases when their main foreign component is exports. The creation of a specialized agency for investment support, under the auspices of Vnesheconombank, was still a plan at the time of writing this chapter.

Another form of institutional support for investment relates to provision of information by the Ministry of Foreign Affairs of the Russian Federation to firms investing abroad. The Ministry has signed agreements with the Commercial and Industrial Chamber of Russia, the Russian Union of Industrials and Entrepreneurs, and certain other business associations. In 2006 and 2007, the Ministry also signed agreements of cooperation in matters related to information on OFDI with various large companies, including Vnesheconombank, the state-owned Russian Railways and Unified Energy System,[22] and the privately owned MNE, Lukoil.

8.5   The Crisis of 2008: Will It Stop Russian MNEs?

The general negative fallout of the economic crisis impacted FDI in 2008, with reduced access to finance; the gloomy assessment of prospects and risk aversion (UNCTAD 2009) affect the prospects of Russian MNEs as well. Indeed, the financial crisis of 2008 reached the Russian Federation quickly, and in many senses augurs badly for outward-investing Russian MNEs.

There are certain circumstances that render the impact of the crisis particularly harsh for Russian firms. For example, *greenfield investments* (new investments and expansion of existing facilities), which, to date, seem to be quite resilient to the crisis (UNCTAD 2009), represent a small portion of OFDI by Russian MNEs, as the latter have preferred M&As in their vision to leapfrog to global status. This is so because cross-border M&As are not only larger, in terms of the size of the project but, unlike greenfield investments, require a large upfront payment. In times of crisis, it is exactly those financial resources that become scarce.

Another problem has arisen from the industry structure of Russian OFDI. Natural-resource-based firms have played a dominant role in OFDI, and the prices of their export commodities—their principal source of revenue—declined sharply in 2008 (20% for steel, 54% for oil, and 63% for nickel; figure 8.3). This in turn has affected the market valuation of Russian firms: the

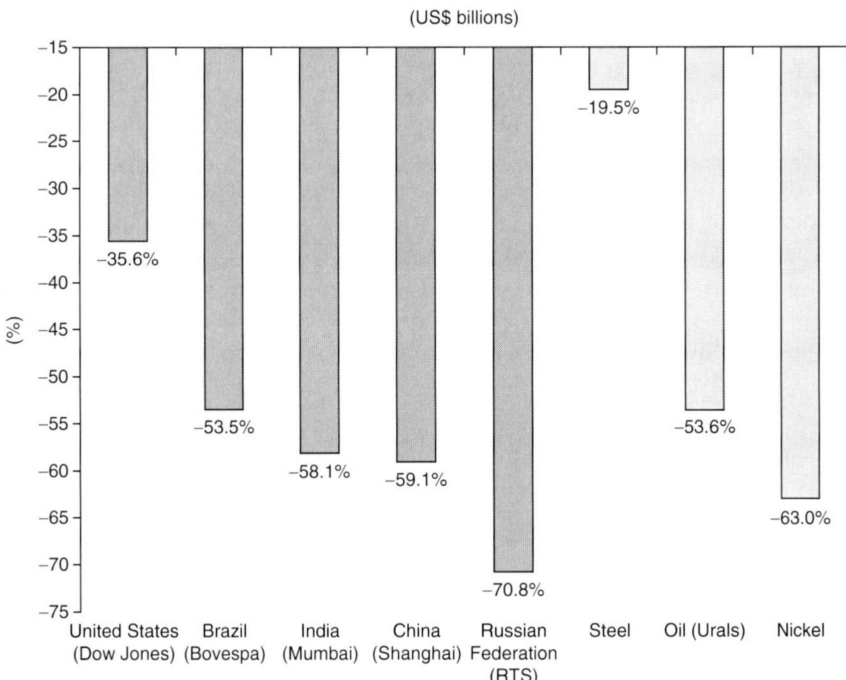

Figure 8.3   Year-to-year changes of selected stock market indices and commodity prices, 2008 (percentage)

Source: Author's calculations, based on raw data published in the *Russian & CIS Daily* of Unicredit Aton, Moscow.

Russian market index fell by 71% in 2008, a sharper fall than in Brazil, China, and India, and twice as much as the Dow Jones (figure 8.3). This is turn contributed to a dissimilar general economic performance between these large emerging economies, the BRIC countries,[23] (in terms of exchange rate stability and gross domestic product [GDP] growth), with Russia the weakest performer on all measures and China the strongest (table 8.5). Weak GDP growth and significant currency devaluation, in turn, contributed to the mounting difficulties of Russian MNEs in 2008.

Under such circumstances, one can question whether the BRIC group of countries still exists (in terms of general economic performance and in terms of OFDI), given the differences between the individual countries. The OFDI of Brazil, China, and India are much less dependent on the performance of a handful of large natural-resource-based firms, which makes Russian OFDI more vulnerable to the crisis. Therefore, the resistance of Brazilian, Chinese, and Indian MNEs to the downturn of 2008–2009 may be greater than that of Russian MNEs.

The ownership structure of Russian MNEs (a mix of oligarchs and the state) can also be a disadvantage, making it more difficult to raise capital form other sources. For example, in the past, some Russian MNEs have financed their expansion by leveraging their own resources; for instance, via initial public offerings (IPOs). With their export prices low, they can no longer engage in IPOs. Moreover, state ownership and influence has made raising capital abroad more difficult, as the onset of the crisis coincided with foreign policy problems (such as the war in Georgia and the gas transit crisis with Ukraine), which made foreign sources of financing even more reluctant to lend to companies associated with Russia as a home country.

While financing difficulties were increasing, the corporate debt of large Russian firms was rising (to an estimated US$110 billion to be paid in 2009)[24] as a result of past strategies of high leveraging. This is almost double the total owed in Brazil, India, and China combined. Since the changes in markets in 2008, this level of debt is no longer sustainable against the current valuation of Russian corporate assets. The list of Russian MNEs that have high levels of international debt (estimated to have tripled from

Table 8.5   Brazil, China, India, and Russia: change in the estimated GDP growth rate, 2009/2008, and change in the dollar exchange rate, February 2009/February 2008

Country	GDP growth, 2008	GDP growth, 2009	Change, 2009/2008	Change in US$ exchange rate
Brazil	5.3	1.6	−3.7	−29.3
China	9.0	6.0	−3.0	4.0
India	5.3	5.0	−0.3	−22.0
Russian Federation	6.0	1.0	−5.0	−33.1

Source: Author's calculations, based on data from the EIU (GDP growth) and from the FXConverter of OANDA.

2006 to 2008) include United Company Rusal, Norilsk Nickel, TMK, and Sistema. This inevitably leads to a need to find new sources of capital (e.g., in the form of state investment in troubled companies or foreign investments) or to a further consolidation of the universe of the largest Russian MNEs (with the healthier companies taking over the debt-ridden ones). Government assistance, in the case of Russian firms, can come from the state-owned Vnesheconombank, which is responsible for handling the bailout. In return for loans, Vnesheconombank places a representative in the company and has the right to veto any debt or major asset sale.

One further unfavorable development in Russia, in 2008, was the return of capital flight, which had largely disappeared after 1999. The Central Bank estimated that US$131 billion in foreign reserves were "lost" in the second half of 2008 alone (see http://www.cbr.ru/eng/). This capital flight, in turn, further reduces the ability of public authorities to bail out firms in trouble.

Despite these negative developments, in 2009 it was not yet certain to what degree Russian FDI would be affected during the crisis and beyond. In 2008, OFDI flows were still increasing, to a record level of US$56 billion (see http://www.cbr.ru/eng/). It was only from the last quarter of 2008 on that OFDI projects had to be put on hold and sometimes divested. For example, Lukoil attempted to acquire a 26% share in Spain's Repsol in November and December 2008, but did not find the necessary financing and was forced to suspend the deal. Other Russian firms, such as Norilsk Nickel, had to go even further and divest from existing foreign assets (in October 2008, Norilsk Nickel closed its Cawse plant in Western Australia, aiming to sell it; it sold its minority stakes in Canadian auto-parts producer, Magna, and German building company, Hochtief). In 2009, the OFDI flows of Russia declined to US$46 billion (an 18% drop) (see http://www.cbr.ru/eng/). Still, this was the second highest volume of outward FDI flows registered since 1992, when separate balance-of-payments reporting for Russia started.

The future of Russian OFDI hinges on the ability of Russian MNEs to withstand their current difficulties. One can construct three scenarios: an optimistic one, a base line ("muddle through"), and a pessimistic one. An optimistic scenario can build on a swift turnaround in the external environment, such as a recovery in oil and metals prices, coupled with a capacity of Russian MNEs to restructure quickly (perhaps through further industry consolidation). The probability of this scenario is further strengthened by Russia's experience with the previous major crisis (in 1998), when most outward-investing firms (especially Lukoil) managed to use foreign assets to shield their companies from the effects of the crisis (UNCTAD 1999). A baseline scenario would mean a more protracted crisis, with a slow recovery in domestic factors, such as GDP and stock markets, forcing MNEs to delay foreign expansion for a number of years. Finally, a catastrophe scenario would lead a series of bankruptcies in Russian business, wiping out a major part of past expansion by Russian MNEs. This scenario can, however, only take place if the global crisis turns out to be much severe than currently thought, and the Russian state no longer possesses the financial resource necessary to bail out large Russian firms (e.g., through accelerating capital flight). Overall, the probability of the first two scenarios is greater, although these two scenarios may lead to a situation whereby Russian OFDI grows more slowly than OFDI from China and India. Moreover, all scenarios can lead to greater state participation in Russian MNEs.

Conclusions

Russian OFDI has been a recent and fast-growing phenomenon. It is now moving from a phase of rapid expansion to a phase of consolidation of assets abroad. Consolidation is gathering speed as a result of the financial crisis of 2008, which has placed a strain on Russian MNEs. They have to select which foreign assets to maintain, where to continue to expand—on a more selective basis than before—and which assets to dispose of.

Nevertheless, over the longer term, OFDI from Russia is expected to stay with us, and Russian MNEs are likely to continue their global expansion. Some of their features may change, as Russian MNEs increasingly interact with their global peers. The high concentration of Russian OFDI in natural resources is also expected to be a long-term feature. It is, indeed, a major difference with OFDI from other emerging markets, which is more knowledge seeking. In the near future, Russian firms are expected to remain focused on controlling the upstream (exploration and extraction) and downstream (distribution) parts of their value chain, even if control of the firms may change hands.

Russian OFDI is also expected to remain closely related to state participation. The final form of the relationship between the state and large firms will have major implications for the future. On the one hand, if those firms are "washed back" to dependent status, they will become followers of the government's foreign policy, independently of their ownership. On the other hand, if the rise of the state's power is contained, one can expect more private interest and more diverse strategies from Russian MNEs. Future research must follow new developments in this respect and provide objective, scientific explanations for them.

For the study of OFDI, Russian MNEs raise questions about the applicability of our general analytical tools, such as the eclectic paradigm, to those firms. In general, it is less applicable to emerging market firms, as they have less obvious ownership advantages than their developed country peers, and are, in turn, more influenced by home country conditions, which are treated less than perfectly by the eclectic paradigm. Russia is probably an extreme case, in that the home country effect is the strongest. It is up to us to draw our own conclusions for FDI theory.

Annex: Profiles of Individual Russian MNEs

The discussion in this chapter is based on monitoring the profiles of thirty-four large Russian MNEs. Of these, nine appear on both the Skolkovo-VCC list (annex table 8.1) and the list of the largest Russian firms in terms of market capitalization (annex table 8.2). In addition, the former list contains a further sixteen MNEs, while the latter contains a further nine MNEs.

Annex Table 8.1   The Skolkovo-VCC ranking of Russian MNEs in terms of foreign assets, 2007 (US$ millions)

Rank	Previous rank	Firm	Industry	Foreign assets	State ownership[a] (%)
1	1	Lukoil	Oil and gas	20,805	–
2	2	Gazprom	Oil and gas	17,236	50.01
3	6	Norilsk Nickel	Metals and mining	12,843	–
4	11	Evraz	Iron and steel	6,221	–
5	3	Severstal	Iron and steel	5,130	–
6	5	Sovcomflot	Transport	4,874	100.00
7	4	Rusal	Metals and mining	4,533	
8	7	MobileTeleSystems (Sistema)	Telecom	3,812	–
9	8	VimpelCom	Telecom	3,572	–
10	14	Novolipetsk Iron & Steel[b]	Iron and steel	1,594	–
11	13	PriSCo	Transport	1,208	–
12	10	TNK-BP	Oil and gas	1,150	–
13	12	FESCO	Transport	1,055	–
14	–	OAO Koks	Iron and steel	978	–
15	17	Eurochem	Chemicals	901	–
16	15	InterRAO	Electricity	799	58.00
17	16	TMK	Iron and steel	606	–
18	–	Mirax	Real estate	470	–
19	18	GAZ	Automotive and machinery	384	–
20	21	ChTPZ	Iron and steel	262	–
21	23	Acron	Chemicals	261	–
22	20	Alrosa	Metals and mining	231	47.63% fed.+ 40% local
23	–	Sitronics (Sistema)	Other services	226	–
24	19	OMZ	Automotive and machinery	207	–
25	–	Ritzio Entertainment	Other services	200	–

Source: Based on Skolkovo and VCC (2008).

[a]A dash means the government does not have a major share in the company; it may hold small stakes through State-owned financial financial institutions
[b]Owned by the Industrial Metallurgical Holding Management Company

The list of the MNEs appearing on both lists includes:

(a) Oil and gas firms

1. *Gazprom*: It is not just the largest Russian firm (annex table 8.2) but also the second largest outward investor in terms of assets controlled abroad

Annex Table 8.2 The twenty-five largest Russian firms, ranked by market capitalization, end-2008

Rank	Firm	Industry	State ownership[a] (%)	Major foreign shareholder	Multinational?	Market value (US$ million)	EBITDA, 2008	Sales, 2008 (US$ million)	Growth of sales, 2008 (%)
1	Gazprom	Oil and gas	50.01	E.ON (6.5%)	Yes	91,663	55,303	123,567	31.8
2	Rosneft	Oil and gas	50.01	Petronas (5%), BP (4%), CNPC (2%)	Yes	41,333	14,627	73,176	48.7
3	Lukoil	Oil and gas	–	ConocoPhillips (20%)	Yes	30,195	20,508	114,098	38.7
4	Surgutneftegas	Oil and gas	–	–	Not[b]	22,850	9,168	26,895	25.5
5	Sberbank	Banks	60.25	–	Yes	17,184	11,912[c]	19,800	43.4
6	Norilsk Nickel[d]	Metals and mining	–	–	Yes	11,864	6,234	14,406	–15.8
7	Gazpromneft[e]	Oil and gas	38.83[c]	ENI (20%)	Yes	10,622	6,556	27,292	29.3
8	MobileTeleSystems[f]	Telecom	–	–	Yes	10,585	5,033	10,291	24.7
9	TNK-BP	Oil and gas	–	BP (50%)	Yes	10,433	11,074	31,709	28.1
10	Novolipetsk Iron & Steel	Iron and steel	–	–	Yes	7,791	4,731	11,781	52.6
11	VTB Bank	Banks	50.01	EADS (5%)	Yes	7,632	2,617[c]	5,451	28.0
12	VimpelCom	Telecom	–	Telenor (26.6%)	Yes	7,590	5,287	10,104	40.9
13	Novatek	Oil and gas	–	–	Yes	5,617	1,871	3,646	51.3
14	Polyus Gold[d]	Metals and mining	–	–	Not	5,014	459	1,124	29.6
15	Tatneft	Oil and gas	34.00[g]	–	Yes	4,677	3,105	17,309	36.1

16	Evraz	Iron and steel	–	–		Yes	3,482	6,335	21,119	64.9
17	Severstal	Iron and steel	–	–		Yes	2,993	5,180	20,961	37.5
18	Magnitogorsk Iron & Steel	Iron and steel	–	–		Not	2,794	2,482	10,004	22.0
19	X5 Retail Group	Retail	–	–		Yes	2,485	801	9,248	73.8
20	Sistema[f]	Holding	–	–		Yes	2,369	5,814	17,358	26.7
21	Transneft	Oil and gas	100.00	–		Not	2,337	5,602	10,395	19.8
22	Moscow Integrated DisCo	Electricity	..	..		..	2,303	860	2,462	91.1
23	Mechel	Iron and steel	–	–		Yes	2,006	3,333	9,621	43.9
24	Magnit	Retail	–	–		Not	1,958	375	5,360	45.8
25	OGK 5	Electricity	–		Enel (59.8%)	Not	1,402	74	1,406	25.3

Source: Author's calculations, based on company reports.

[a]A dash means the government does not have a major share in the company; it may hold small stakes through state-owned financial institutions.

[b]On 20 March 2009, agreed to buy a 21% stake in Hungary's MOL.

[c]Net interest income.

[d]Norilsk Nickel and Polyus Gold are part of the Interros Holding.

[e]Formerly called Sibneft; Gazprom acquired a 78% stake in September 2005, and renamed the company Gazpromneft.

[f]Sistema owns 52.8% of Mobile TeleSystems. It also owns other telecom companies (e.g., Comstar), a business service firm (Sitronics), an insurance company (Rosno), and so on.

[g]It is not the Federal Government but the Republic of Tatarstan that owns 34% of Tatneft.

(annex table 8.1), estimated to control more than 93% of Russia's natural gas production and about one-quarter of the world's gas reserves.[25] Its operations are spread globally: on the European continent alone, it has operations in at least nineteen countries, involving natural gas distribution and processing activities. The state regained majority control of the company in early 2000. Gazprom's international strategy has concentrated so far on acquiring and building gas transportation and distribution assets in Europe, with the aim of controlling the value chain in its export markets. Lately, the company has declared its intentions to enter into large-scale international projects to build gas infrastructures in South America and Northern Africa.

2. *Lukoil*: By foreign assets, it is the largest Russian outward-investing firm (annex table 8.1), and by market capitalization, it is the third biggest Russian corporation (annex table 8.2). It carries out international exploration and production in at least nine countries, refining in Bulgaria, Romania, and Ukraine, and downstream distribution in at least fifteen countries. Lukoil was one of the earliest internationalizers among Russian companies: its first large foreign acquisition (Getty Petroleum, United States) dates back to 2000.

3. *TNK-BP*: A joint venture between BP (United Kingdom) and Alfa group, it owns a petroleum refinery affiliate, as well as gas stations in Ukraine. TNK-BP operates a retail network of approximately 1,600 filling stations in Russia and Ukraine, working under the BP and TNK brands.[26]

(b) Metals and mining company
1. *Norilsk Nickel*: It is the largest Russian metallurgical MNE in terms of assets abroad, and is the third largest Russian MNE in terms of foreign presence (annex table 8.1). It is a world leader in the production of several strategic metals, in particular, palladium, platinum, nickel, cobalt, and copper. In 2003, it purchased the Stillwater Mining Company in the United States, followed by the acquisitions of OM Group's assets in Finland and LionOre (Canada) in 2007. Norilsk Nickel's international assets currently include mining operations and projects in Australia (in addition to the Cawse Plant divested in 2008, it owns three other nickel mines), Botswana (Tati Nickel), and South Africa (Nkomati).

(c) Iron and steel companies
1. *Evraz*: It is the second largest Russian corporation in metallurgy (annex table 8.2) and has large assets abroad (annex table 8.1), despite its late start in foreign expansion. It acquired Palini e Bertoli (Italy) and Vitkovice Steel (Czech Republic) in 2005, Oregon Steel Mills (United States) and Highveld Steel (South Africa) in 2007, and Claymont Steel (United States) in 2008. It also acquired Ipsco's (a wholly owned affiliate of Swedish steel company SSAB) Canadian plate and pipe business in 2008.

2. *Severstal*: It is the third largest Russian corporation in metallurgy (annex table 8.2), and is second in terms of foreign assets (annex table 8.1). It owns foreign production facilities in the United States, Italy, France, the United

Kingdom, and Ukraine. It has internationalized by acquiring assets in developed countries. It made its first foreign acquisition in the United States in 2003, taking over Rouge Industries, followed by Lucchini Industries (Italy) in 2005. It also entered into a coke-producing joint venture, and started to build greenfield steel plants in the United States and elsewhere.

3. *Novolipetsk Iron & Steel*: It is the largest Russian metallurgical corporation (annex table 8.2) but only third in terms of foreign assets (annex table 8.1). It is a specialist in cold rolled mill products and electric steel. The group acquired the Danish plant DanSteel in late 2006, and established a joint venture with Duferco Group (Switzerland) to co-own certain steel production and distribution facilities in Europe and the U.S. Novolipetsk Iron & Steel expanded further into the United States by acquiring Beta Steel in September 2008.

(d) Telecom firms

1. *Mobile TeleSystems*: It is Sistema Holding's largest company, and a market leader in wireless communication in various CIS countries. Mobile TeleSystems is one of the top three mobile phone operators in Russia and the CIS (Ukraine, Uzbekistan, Turkmenistan, Armenia, Belarus).

2. *VimpelCom*: It is the second largest telecom operator in Russia and the CIS (founded in 1992 and co-owned by Russia's Alfa Group and Norway's Telenor). It focuses on Kazakhstan, Tajikistan, and Ukraine. In addition, Alfa holds shares in a Ukrainian and a Kyrgyz operator and in 2005 purchased a 13% minority share in Turkish Turkcell, itself a major competitor in various CIS markets. The Group plans to expand into Vietnam and Cambodia.

The Skolkovo-VCC list of 2007 includes sixteen other companies that are missing from the list of largest companies by market capitalization for various reasons, including a lack of listing (e.g., the shipping companies) or a lack of consolidated reporting (e.g., United Company Rusal):[27]

(a) Metals and mining companies

1. *Rusal*: United Company Rusal is one of the world's largest producers of aluminium. It was established in March 2007, following the merger of three companies: Russian alumina and aluminium producers Rusal and Sual, and the alumina assets of Glencore (Switzerland). United Company Rusal's assets are spread over nineteen countries, including Guinea, Guyana, Jamaica, and Nigeria.

2. *Alrosa*: Majority state-owned Alrosa is Russia's largest diamond exploration, mining, manufacturing, and sales corporation, accounting for about one-quarter of the world's rough diamond supply and 97% of Russian production.[28] Alrosa operates two diamond mining joint ventures and participates in the construction of a related hydroelectric power station in Angola. It has representative offices in the main diamond trading centers (Belgium, Hong Kong [China], Israel, United Arab Emirates, the United Kingdom, the United States).

(b) Iron and steel companies
1. *IMH/Koks*: This holding consists of a number of metallurgical, coke chemical, and coal-mining enterprises. In 2007, the group, which had had no previous experience in cross-border acquisitions, bought the freshly privatized Slovenian Steel Group from the Slovenian government.

2. *TMK*: It is Russia's largest manufacturer and exporter of steel pipes, with production plants in Russia and Romania (a pipe plant and metallurgical works in the latter).

3. *ChTPZ*: Metallurgical producer ChTPZ is an integrated solution provider for the pipeline transportation industry. In 2006, it purchased MSA, a manufacturer of industrial valves in the Czech Republic. In the same year, it also acquired the Akzhal Ore Mining and Processing Mill in Kazakhstan. In June 2007, the Group bought Brock Metal, a United Kingdom producer of zinc and aluminium die-casting alloys.

(c) Transport companies
1. *Sovcomflot*: A 100% state-owned corporation, it is a born MNE, thanks to its maritime shipping activities. In 2008, it absorbed the assets of Novoship, another state-owned shipping company. The group owns Marpetrol, a Spanish-based company that operates a chemical tanker fleet.

2. *PriSCo*: The Primorsk Shipping Corporation specializes in marine transportation of bulk liquid cargo. It is based in Nakhodka, and has representative offices in Moscow, Vladivostok, and Singapore.

3. *FESCO*: This transportation group includes two shipping operators, a container company, the Vladivostok trade seaport, a railway container operator, and several other transportation-related firms. It offers intermodal transportation services, with a special focus on the Asia-Europe transit market.

(d) Chemical firms
1. *EuroChem*: It is the largest manufacturer of mineral fertilizers in Russia, also controlling mining and logistics companies, as well as a worldwide distribution network. In 2002, the company acquired Lifosa AB, a Lithuanian producer of fertilizers.

2. *Acron*: It is a major mineral fertilizer producer, and a major exporter to China, Latin America, Asia, and the CIS. In 2005, the company acquired a majority share in Shandong Chemical JSC Hongri Acron in China.

(e) Automotive and machinery firms
1. *GAZ Group*: Russia's largest automotive manufacturer owns eighteen automotive and machine-building plants in Russia and LDV Group in the United Kingdom.

2. *OMZ*: It specializes in engineering, production, sales, and maintenance of equipment and machines for the nuclear power, oil and gas, and mining industries. In 2003, it acquired Skoda Steel and Skoda JS, and in 2008, Cheteng Engineering, all in the Czech Republic.

(f) Services firms

1. *InterRAO*: It is one of the successor companies of the former electricity monopoly Unified Energy Systems, set up in 2008. It owns a number of generation and distribution assets in Russia and abroad (in a number of CIS countries).

2. *Mirax*: It is a real estate development corporation with projects in Russia, Montenegro, the United States, Turkey, Cambodia, and Switzerland.

3. *Sitronics*: It is a major provider of telecom, information technology (IT), and microelectronic solutions in Russia and the CIS, as well as in other countries in transition, West Asia and Africa. It maintains offices in thirty-two countries and exports its products and services to more than sixty countries. Telecom solutions operations are based in Prague, Czech Republic, and Athens, Greece, while the company's IT and microelectronic solutions divisions are based in Kiev, Ukraine, and Zelenograd, Russia, respectively. The company belongs to the Sistema Group.

4. *Ritzio Entertainment*: It is a gaming and entertainment services company. Most of the company's operations are located in Europe (Romania, Czech Republic, Italy, Germany, Croatia, Serbia, Russia, Ukraine, Belarus, Estonia, Latvia, and Lithuania), followed by Latin America (Bolivia, Peru, and Colombia).

The list of the largest Russian companies by market capitalization covers, in addition, seven uninational firms (according to the latest reports) and ten MNEs whose foreign assets are not reported in the Skolkovo-VCC list, either because they are banks, and therefore cannot be tracked by the same concept of "foreign assets," or their foreign assets are too limited, or because they are affiliates of other MNEs, although separate legal entities (e.g., Gazpromneft). These nine firms are:

(a) Oil and gas companies

1. *Rosneft*: This large majority state-owned oil MNE, which inherited a large part of the Russian assets of the bankrupted Yukos company, has relatively limited presence abroad, despite its size: exploration projects in Algeria and Kazakhstan,[29] of which the former is important in terms of the area covered (6,548 km²).[30]

2. *Gazpromneft*: In 2005, formerly independent Sibneft was acquired by, and became an affiliate of, Gazprom, and was renamed Gazpromneft. It had inherited Sibneft's foreign assets in Belarus and some foreign operations in Central Asia (Kazakhstan, Kyrgyzstan, and Tajikistan).

3.*Tatneft*: It is Russia's fifth largest oil producer (measured by reserves), and is present in the Ukrainian downstream market (141 gas stations).

4. *Novatek*: Privately owned gas producer Novatek registered its first two foreign (trading) affiliates in 2005 (Novatek Overseas AG and Runitek GmbH, both in Switzerland). In 2007, it acquired a working interest in a concession agreement in Egypt.[31]

(b) Banks
1. *Sberbank*: This majority state-owned bank has two major foreign affiliates: Sberbank Rossii (Kazakhstan) (formerly Texakabank), acquired in 2006, and Sberbank Rossii (Ukraine) (formerly NRB), acquired at the end of 2007. It also has cooperation agreements with several export credit agencies abroad, including Ex-Im Bank (United States), Eximbank Hungary, and the Israel Foreign Trade Risks Insurance Corporation.

2. *VTB Bank*: This foreign trade bank has major affiliates in London, Paris, Frankfurt, Zurich, and Limassol; it is also present in Singapore, Vienna, Luxemburg, Yerevan, Tbilisi, Kyiv, and Luanda.

(c) An iron and steel company
1. *Mechel*: Russia's fourth largest iron and steel company has opted for an internationalization strategy different from its peers, based on low-cost specialty steels and alloys. It owns coal operations in Kazakhstan, two steel mills in Romania, and a steel product manufacturer in Lithuania.

(d) A telecom firm
1. *Sistema*: While Mobile TeleSystems has so far concentrated on CIS markets, its parent company has recently acquired licenses in India, and plans to enter China and Bangladesh. These operations might eventually be integrated into Mobile TeleSystems.

(e) A retail company
X5 Retail Group: Russia's largest retail company has stores in twenty-two regions at home, as well as stores in Kazakhstan and Ukraine.

Notes

*United Nations Conference on Trade and Development, Geneva, Switzerland. The views in this analysis are those of the author and do not necessarily reflect the opinion of the United Nations. The author is grateful to Karl P. Sauvant for his comments on a previous version of this chapter, and to Alexei V. Kuznetsov for his detailed explanations on Russian government policies towards outward foreign direct investment.

1. The Bank of Russia does not provide a geographical or industry breakdown of FDI flows and stocks (with an exception of a differentiation between FDI with the CIS and other countries). As for the Federal State Statistics Service, it stopped reporting geographical data on FDI separated from portfolio investment and bank loans in the mid-2000s.
2. FDI and M&A data are collected through different methods and are thus not strictly comparable.
3. However, inherited assets do not show up in either FDI flow or in cross-border M&A data, which are both based on new transactions.
4. Additional indications of the existence of round tripping in Russia, especially before the financial crisis of 1998, included the fast parallel increase of inflows and outflows itself, and the persistently high proportion of offshore companies involved in both inflows and outflows based in Cyprus—a small island

that otherwise has no ownership advantages for its local firms (UNCTAD 2000; Pelto, Vahtra, and Liuhto 2004).

5. Rusal publishes the annual reports of individual companies in the group, but does not consolidate them.

6. For Unified Energy Systems, the first stage of its reorganization started in 2006, with the spinoff of two major generating companies. At the second stage, in 2007–2008, all other affiliates were spun off. On July 1, 2008 the company completed its reorganization and ceased to exist.

7. A note of caution about this list: it also covers Magnitogorsk Iron and Steel, which intended to purchase assets abroad but has failed so far. Despite that fact, the company is classified as part of the "second tier" (Deloitte CIS 2008).

8. Naturally with the notable exception of Magnitogorsk Iron and Steel.

9. In addition to the Skolkovo-VCC list, Deloitte CIS (2008) mentions Wimm Bill Damm, Nutritek Group (both food and beverages), Transmashholding (railway machines), Ristshelmash, Concern Tractor Plant (both agricultural machinery), and Euroset and Vester (both retail) as regional players. Of these firms, Euroset figured in the previous (2007) Skolkovo-VCC list.

10. For the list of 2007, see Kalotay (2008).

11. The Columbia Program on International Investment (CPII) became the Vale Columbia Center on Sustainable International Investment (VCC) on April 29, 2008. Materials produced before that date are published under the name of CPII.

12. Thirty-five, if OAO Koks and the Industrial Metallurgical Holding Management Company are counted separately.

13. In 2001, the Russian investment bank Troika Dialog calculated that around seventy large financial and industrial groups controlled 40% of the Russian GDP (Shekshnia 2001).

14. It was estimated that by 1998, 49% of former state properties had been privatized to insiders, compared to 3% in Hungary and 5% in the Czech Republic. Conversely, only 3% of former state properties had been sold to foreign buyers in Russia, compared to 48% in Hungary and 15% in the Czech Republic (Kalotay and Hunya 2000).

15. In the latest, and potentially the largest, bid, United Company Rusal bought 25% of Norilsk Nickel in May 2008, and aimed for a full takeover, which would result in the world's biggest metal company so far (Smirnov and Askerzade 2008).

16. As measured by EBITDA: Earnings Before Interest, Taxes, Depreciation, and Amortization.

17. Gazprom was created as a corporate entity (a then 100% state-owned joint stock company) in 1992 as a successor of a former Soviet gas monopoly. It was privatized in 1993, reducing the government's share to less than 40%. Foreign ownership was, however, restricted to 9% at that time, to be raised to 20% in the late 1990s. The return to majority state ownership in 2005 was followed by legislation passed by the State Duma (December 2005) which made state majority ownership mandatory in the Russian gas industry, but lifted the 20% limit on foreign ownership (Dittrick 2005, 27–29; UNCTAD 2006, 81).

18. See "Gosudarstvo podderzhit expansiyu rossiyksogo biznesa na zarubezhnykh rynkakh" [The State will support the expansion of Russian business on foreign markets], *Pravda.ru*, March 25, 2005, available at http://www.pravda.ru/

economics/2005/7/21/63/19414 expansion.html, last accessed on February 3, 2006.

19. See "Gosudarstvo podderzhit expansiyu rossiyksogo biznesa na zarubezh-nykh rynkakh" [The State will support the expansion of Russian business on foreign markets], *Pravda.ru*, March 25, 2005, available at http://www.pravda.ru/economics/2005/7/21/63/19414 expansion.html, last visited February 3, 2006.

20. See "Politics—Putin presents new cabinet, Rosneft chairman to control natural resources," *Russian & CIS Daily*, UniCredit Aton Research, Moscow, May 13, 2008, p. 2.

21. See "VEB gotov sozdat' Agenstvo po strakhovaniyu eksportnykh kreditov i investitsiy" [VEB ready to establish Export Credit and Investment Insurance Agency], *RBC Daily*, December 8, 2008, available at http://www.rcb.ru/news/17381, last visited March 19, 2009; and "VEBu trebuyetsya docherneye agensto" [VEB needs affiliate agency], *Vremya* online, December 9, 2008, available at http://www.vremya.ru/2008/228/8/218786.html, last visited March 19, 2009.

22. The latter ceased to exist in 2008. See note 7.

23. The hypothesis about the existence of an economic group called "BRIC," consisting of the large emerging economies of Brazil, Russia, India, and China (in that order) was first formulated by Goldman Sachs in 2001. The acronym and the hypothesis about a single group has since gained large popularity despite the dissimilarities of the economies in question in terms of economic structures such as natural resources endowments and major export products, demographic characteristics, and political systems ("Another BRIC in the Wall," *Economist*, April 21, 2008).

24. See "Oligarchs Seek $78 Billion as Credit Woes Help Putin (Update2)," *Bloomberg*, December 22, 2008.

25. See http://www.eia.doe.gov/cabs/Russia/NaturalGas.html.

26. See http://www.tnk-bp.com.ua/en.

27. These company snapshots are based on Skolkovo and VCC 2008.

28. See http://eng.alrosa.ru.

29. "Rosneft Inks US$23Bln Kazakh Deal," *Moscow Times*, July 7, 2005.

30. An alliance with Sonatrach (Algeria) and Stroytransgaz (Russia) was formed in 2001. It received the final approval for exploitation in 2009 only ("Algeria Approved Rosneft's Plans for Oil Fields Development," *Neftegaz.RU*, March 17, 2009, available at http://www.neftegaz.ru/en/news/view/87205, last visited March 23, 2009.

31. "Russia's Novatek Signs Concession Deal with Egypt," *Reuters*, September 27, 2007, available at http://uk.reuters.com/article/oilRpt/idUKL2781181320070927, last visited March 1, 2009.

References

Aton Capital (2004). *Russian Market 2005*, November 4 (Moscow: Aton Capital Group).

Bulatov, Alexander (1998). "Russian direct investment abroad: main motivations in the post-Soviet period," *Transnational Corporations* 7 (1), pp. 69–82.

Deloitte CIS (2008). *Russian Multinationals: New Players in the Global Economy* (Moscow: Deloitte CIS), available at http://www.deloitte.com/dtt/article/0,1002,cid%253D213485,00.html, last visited October 10, 2008.

Dittrick, Paula (2005). "Gazprom to sell additional stake to Russian government," *Oil & Gas Journal* 103 (24), pp. 27–29.

Kalotay, Kalman (2002). "Outward foreign direct investment and governments in central and Eastern Europe: the cases of the Russian Federation, Hungary and Slovenia," *Journal of World Investment* 3, pp. 267–87.

——— (2007). "The rise of Russian transnational corporations," *Journal of World Investment & Trade* 8 (1), pp. 125–48.

——— (2008). "How to explain the foreign expansion of Russian firms," *Journal of Financial Transformation* 24, pp. 53–61.

Kalotay, Kalman and Gábor Hunya (2000). "Privatization and foreign direct investment in Central and Eastern Europe," *Transnational Corporations* 9 (1), pp. 39–66.

Kuznetsov, Alexei V. (2008). "Pryamye inostrannye investitsii: 'effect sosedstva' " [Foreign direct investment: the "neighbourhood effect"] *Mirovaya ekonomika i mezhdunarodnye otnosheniya* 9, pp. 40–47.

Liuhto, Kari ed. (2005). *Expansion or Exodus: Why Do Russian Corporations Invest Abroad?* (Binghamton, NY: Haworth Press).

——— (2008). "Genesis of economic nationalism in Russia," Electronic Publications of Pan-European Institute 3/2008, Turku: Turku School of Economics, available at www.tse.fi/FI/yksikot/erillislaitokset/pei/Documents/Julkaisut/ Liuhto_32008.pdf, last visited March 5, 2009.

Livshits, Alexander (2001). " 'Vernis,' ya vse proshchu: Zametki ob utechke kapitala iz Rossii" [Return, I beg you. Remarks on the capital flight from Russia] *Izvestia* 21 (7), 258–59.

Locatelli, Catherine (2006). "The Russian oil industry between public and private governance: obstacles to international oil companies' investment strategies," *Energy Policy* 34 (9), pp. 1075–85.

Ostrovsky, A. (2004). "TNK–BP faces Dollars 87m back-tax bill," *Financial Times*, November 12, p. 16.

Pelto, Elina, Peeter Vahtra, and Kari Liuhto (2004). "Cyp-Rus investment flows to Central and Eastern Europe—Russia's direct and indirect investments via Cyprus to CEE," *Journal of Business Economics and Management* 5 (1), pp. 3–13.

Radygin, Alexander (2002). "Sliyaniya i pogloshcheniya v korporativnom sektore" [osnovnye podkhody i zadachi regulirovaniya] [Mergers and takeovers in the corporate sector (basic approaches and tasks of regulation)] *Voprosy economiki* 12, available at http://vopreco.ru/rus/archive.files/n12 2002.html, last visited January 10, 2006.

Shekshnia, Stanislav, V. (2001). "Troika Dialog founder Ruben Vardanian on building Russia's first investment bank," *Academy of Management Executive* 15 (4), pp. 16–23.

Skolkovo and VCC (2008). "Russian multinationals' foreign assets up 4 times in 3 years," Press release on the Skolkovo—VCC 2008 ranking of Russian multinational enterprises, Moscow and New York, November 11.

Smirnov, Dmitriy and Nailya Asker-zade (2008). " 'Rusal nachal agitatsiyu za svoyu vlast' sredi aktsionerov Nornickelya" [Rusal started campaigning for its take-over among Nornickel shareholders] *Komersant* 92 (3909), May 30, p. 12.

UNCTAD (1998). *World Investment Report 1998: Trends and Determinants* (New York and Geneva: United Nations).

——— (1999). *World Investment Report 1999: FDI and the Challenge of Development* (New York and Geneva: United Nations).

UNCTAD (2000). *World Investment Report 2000: Cross-Border M&As and Development* (New York and Geneva: United Nations).

——— (2006). *World Investment Report 2006. FDI from Developing and Transition Economies: Implications for Development* (New York and Geneva: United Nations).

——— (2008). *World Investment Report 2008: Transnational Corporations and the Infrastructure Challenge* (New York and Geneva: United Nations).

——— (2009). "Assessing the impact of the current financial and economic crisis on global FDI flows" (New York and Geneva: United Nations), available at www.unctad.org/en/docs/webdiaeia20091_en.pdf, last visited March 5, 2009.

Vahtra, Peeter and Kari Liuhto (2005). "Russian corporations abroad—seeking profits, leverage or refuge?" in Kari Liuhto and Zsuzsanna Vincze, eds., *Wider Europe* (Turku: Turku School of Economics and Business Administration), pp. 225–54.\

Chapter 9

Global Players from India: A Political Economy Perspective

Heather Taylor and Andreas Nölke

Introduction

Outward foreign direct investment (OFDI) from India has increased rapidly over the past two decades. In international terms, however, it remains negligible. The fact that Indian OFDI accounted for a mere 0.2% of global OFDI stocks at end-2007 (UNCTAD 2007a) only serves to underline this fact. In posing the question of why we should be concerned with Indian OFDI, the answer will not be found in macroeconomic data on trends and patterns in Indian OFDI. Rather, the need to study Indian OFDI arises from its idiosyncratic nature, particularly with regard to the substantial number of acquisitions undertaken by Indian firms in the Triad (United States, Western Europe, Japan-Australia) within the past decade. The need to focus on Indian OFDI from a microeconomic level of analysis becomes somewhat urgent given that Indian firms accounted for 60% of all mergers and acquisitions (M&As) undertaken by firms from Brazil, Russia, India, and China (the BRIC countries) in the Triad between 2000 and 2007 (Bertoni, Elia, and Rabbiosi 2007). Most acquisitions of Indian enterprises have received little media coverage, since most targets have been rather small. However, Tata Motors' takeover of Jaguar and Land Rover has significantly increased media coverage of Indian multinational enterprises (MNEs). This chapter seeks to complement and build upon macroeconomic analyses of Indian OFDI, which have given us a substantial overview of the trends and patterns of this phenomenon, by providing a microeconomic level of analysis that aims to "disentangle the strategies and characteristics" (2–3) of India's OFDI. Such an analysis can provide us with a comprehensive analysis of the drivers of and motivations behind Indian investments.

The global financial crisis and recession further warrant the need for microlevel analyses of Indian OFDI, as they allow for a more comprehensive examination of key actors, strategies, and motivations, as well as the impacts of OFDI. Of crucial concern, with regard to the impact of the global financial crisis on Indian OFDI, is the manner in which Indian firms have financed their foreign acquisitions. Since 2005, a growing proportion of

Indian acquisitions have been financed through debt from international capital markets.

The global financial crisis poses two significant challenges for the future of Indian OFDI. The first relates to the future of investments made by Indian firms, which between 2005 and 2008 financed almost 70% of the deal value of the top twenty outbound acquisitions through debt. The liquidity freeze has made it increasingly difficult for Indian firms to roll over their debt, and has subsequently led to a situation in which the acquirers are facing deteriorating market fundamentals. Tata Motors serves as the most recent example of an Indian firm facing difficulties in refinancing debt. In response to the credit crunch, Tata Motors has been forced to turn to offering public deposits as a means to refinance the US$2 billion bridge loan taken out for the acquisition of Jaguar and Land Rover.

The second challenge relates to the ability of Indian firms to continue to rapidly acquire firms in the Triad. The latest reports on Indian outbound acquisitions highlight the significant negative impact that the global financial crisis has had on Indian acquisitions: in January 2009, "cross-border M&A outflow totalled USD23 million, down 99 per cent from USD 1.8 billion in 2008" (*Financial Express,* February 23, 2009). Despite the rather harsh repercussions that the crisis has had on Indian OFDI, most observers expect Indian firms to continue to rise significantly in importance over the coming decades, particularly because of their distinguishing features.

Compared to other emerging market MNEs, most prominent among these features is their preference for M&As over greenfield investments with regard to their market entry mode. Moreover, Indian MNEs favor acquisitions in the Triad. Between 2005 and 2007, Indian M&As into the Triad increased almost sevenfold, from US$4.2 billion to US$27 billion. In comparison, over the same period, the value of purchases of Triad firms by Chinese, Hong Kong (China), and Russian MNEs all decreased. In 2007, the value of Chinese MNE acquisitions in the Triad totaled a mere US$2.4 billion; Hong Kong (China) MNE acquisitions US$2.6 billion; and Russian MNE acquisitions US$12 billion (UNCTAD 2008, 75). A third distinguishing feature of Indian MNEs is their focus on takeovers in high-technology, knowledge-intensive manufacturing industries, such as pharmaceuticals and information technology (IT) services.

These three distinct features not only make Indian MNEs unique, they also have the potential to arouse concerns in the countries of the Triad. Indeed, at first sight, the most obvious cause for concern would, perhaps, be related to the increase in acquisitions undertaken by Indian MNEs in the Triad. Notable in the significant rise in Indian acquisitions in the Triad is the lack of attention they have attracted—the result of the relatively small size of most acquisitions. Only a handful of Indian MNEs have been involved in mega-acquisitions, such as Tata's acquisition of Tetley Tea, Hindalco's acquisition of Novelis, or Dr. Reddy's acquisition of Betapharm. The majority of acquisitions performed by Indian MNEs in the past ten years have been microdeals, averaging less than US$100 million in volume and targeting smaller, "hidden" industry leaders. Moreover, their acquisitions have focused on those knowledge-intensive parts of the secondary and tertiary sectors that have been dominated by Triad economies. Will this lead to tensions with the management of acquired companies, labor unions, or local communities? Finally, given the traditional leadership role of the Indian government as speaker for the global South, will Indian MNEs adapt a similar role in global business fora and challenge the established leadership of Western MNEs?

Regarding the relationship between home and host economies, the public debate surrounding foreign takeovers of domestic firms is most often embedded in a steal-and-shutdown fear. This refers to the idea that, once the acquirer obtains and masters the target firm's knowledge and resources, the target will be closed, workers' contracts terminated, and either the target will be completely shut down or the location will be shut down, remaining a legal entity on paper but with production and resources moved to a country offering lower operating costs. Given that a majority of Indian MNEs have become global players because of lower-cost advantages, combined with their preference for attaining majority, if not full ownership, of their target firms, significant tensions may arise as Indian MNEs are forced to confront new situations in their Triad acquisitions, which prevent them from relying on such low-cost advantages. Betapharm, a wholly owned German subsidiary of Dr. Reddy's, serves as perhaps the most recent example, given that, one year after acquisition, Dr. Reddy's had officially moved over half of its production line to India and also laid off employees, due to alleged supply-chain bottlenecks and regulatory changes in the German market, resulting in Betapharm's operations becoming loss-making.[1]

On the subject of global economic regulation, MNEs are well known as key players on issues such as trade regulation, investment treaties, accounting standards, and corporate social responsibility (CSR). Until now, these activities have been dominated by MNEs from the Triad. The rise of Indian MNEs is too recent to have left its mark on global economic governance on a larger scale (Nölke and Taylor 2009a). Sooner or later, however, these companies will articulate their preferences on these issues. If they differ from those of Triad MNEs, we might envisage additional tensions, possibly even leading to a new North-South conflict (Nölke and Taylor 2009b). Given the traditional Indian leadership role in North-South negotiations, Indian MNEs will most likely be at the forefront of non-Triad inputs for global economic governance. Recent complaints over attempts by European Union (EU) MNEs to block generic pharmaceutical exports from India and Brazil into Africa (*Economic Times*, April 4, 2009), lodged with the World Trade Organization (WTO) by India and by Brazil, highlight the possibility for increased tensions.

However, limited knowledge of the origins and operations of Indian MNEs may be at the root of many of these concerns. In order to remedy this situation, our contribution will provide an overview of the salient features of Indian OFDI, with a particular focus on the growth of outbound M&As (section 9.1). Moreover, we will examine the factors that have made the recent success of Indian MNEs possible. In this context we will high-light both the driving forces behind the rise of individual enterprises, as well as the broader structural conditions that have enabled whole industries to expand globally (section 9.2). Based on a more nuanced picture of Indian MNEs, we will return to the issues raised above, identifying issues for policy makers and further research (section 9.3).

9.1   Salient Features of Indian OFDI: Where Is the Focus of Indian MNEs?

A simple observation of the trends in foreign direct investment (FDI), with specific regard to emerging markets, may cause one to question the need to discuss the salient features of Indian OFDI. As table 9.1 demonstrates, between 2005 and 2007, India was consistently among the poorest perform-ing emerging markets in terms of both OFDI and IFDI. Therefore, when it comes to judging on the basis of overall emerging market FDI trend com-parisons, a justification for selecting India as a relevant case study is lacking. Rather, the primary basis for justifying the study of Indian FDI patterns and trends comes precisely from its idiosyncratic features.

Among these peculiar features is the substantial geographical turnaround of OFDI flows, post-1991, from non-Triad to Triad economies. To be sure, substantial increases in Triad-destined OFDI in the past two decades have resulted in the total volume of FDI flows to the Triad region, from 1961 to 2007, exceeding those to non-Triad regions (Pradhan 2008c). Moreover, since 2000, there has been substantial growth in M&A activity by Indian firms. While Indian firms have undertaken M&As in both Triad and non-Triad regions, the Triad, as host region, has easily outranked the non-Triad as host region, both in the number of deals and in the total annual value of deals undertaken. Triad-destined M&As have been primarily focused on high-tech, knowledge-intensive manufacturing sectors.

Table 9.1   FDI inflows and outflows per selected economy, 2005–2007 (US$ millions)

	Outflows			Inflows		
Economy	2005	2006	2007	2005	2006	2007
Brazil	2,517	28,202	2,067	15,666	18,822	34,585
Chile	2,183	2,786	3,830	6,984	7,358	14,457
China	12,261	21,160	22,469	72,406	72,715	83,521
Hong Kong (China)	27,201	44,979	53,187	33,618	45,054	59,899
India	29,798	12,842	13,649	7,606	19,662	22,950
Mexico	6,474	5,758	8,256	20,945	19,291	24,686
Russia	12,767	28,151	45,652	12,886	32,387	52,745
Singapore	6,493	12,241	12,300	13,930	24,743	24,137
Republic of Korea	4,298	8,127	15,276	7,055	4,881	2,628
Taiwan Province of China	6,028	7,399	11,107	1,625	7,424	8,161

Source: UNCTAD, World Investment Report WIR (2007).

In the following we will give a more nuanced and systematic overview of these features, by looking at the following aspects:

- historical development
- mode of entry (M&As versus greenfield investments)
- most important OFDI country destinations
- most important OFDI industries.

The substantial growth in OFDI flows directed toward Triad versus non-Triad countries is one of the most striking features of Indian OFDI. With the liberalization of capital flows post-1991, Indian MNEs have been granted greater regulatory freedom in the type of outward investments they could pursue. While the development planning model was officially abandoned in 1991, the liberalization of the investment regime actually began in the 1980s. Prior to the first phase of liberalization, the lack of foreign-exchange reserves to promote OFDI growth, combined with an inward-looking industrial development plan, meant that the central government proactively sought to control and discourage OFDI through various regulatory controls—including the General Guidelines on Indian Joint Ventures Overseas, the Monopolies and Restrictive Trade Act, and the Foreign Exchange Regulation Act. Indeed, the restriction in capital outflows was in line with the goals of the multiple Five-Year Plans that had the overarching aim of attaining self-sufficiency and industrial development, through the production of capital goods. Thus, during this period OFDI was primarily seen as a tool for the promotion of South-South cooperation and development efforts.

Perhaps most interesting to note here is that, as a result of these plans, India took a substantially different trajectory toward development than did its non-Triad counterparts. Rather than attempting economic development through an industrial growth model that focuses primarily on growth through labor-intensive industries and subsequently capital-intensive (as was the case in China and Southeast Asia), the Indian development plan, from independence onward, focused on the development of capital-intensive industries. Nevertheless, restrictions in the trade and investment policy regime, as well as the substantial barriers to private sector growth in key industrial sectors, had only successfully managed to set in motion the "Hindu" rate of growth; that is, poor economic performance with decreasing productivity levels and increasing unemployment. "Starting in the 1980s, policy makers in India began to realize that efficiency, productivity, quality, and technological dynamism of domestic firms cannot be improved unless these firms are exposed to the competitive pressures of international markets" (Pradhan 2008c, 28). The liberalization of the OFDI regime was a vital part of seeking to improve global competitiveness. During the 1980s, this reform of the FDI regulatory regime focused primarily on easing import restrictions in order to allow industry upgrading and, subsequently, for improved export performance. In other words, a key focus was placed on liberalizing the import-export regime in capital goods. In doing so, numerous fiscal incentives were put in place to encourage export growth in the capital goods sector.

The in-depth reform of the OFDI regulatory regime, however, only began to take shape with the sweeping liberalization of the economy, beginning in 1991. Since then, regulatory changes have resulted in the lifting of restrictions regarding the type of investments pursued, the manner in which investments are financed, and the geographic orientation of investments.

Correspondingly, during the 1990s, a strong increase in the number of firms seeking approval to pursue foreign investments took place. The impact of liberalization on outward investment is evident: in 1983, only 228 OFDI projects had received approval from the government, whereas between 1997 and 2004, over 4,500 OFDI projects were approved (UNCTAD 2007a, 69). Moreover, from 1991 to 2000, there was about a twelvefold increase in the number of approvals granted for OFDI in the form of equity capital when compared to the period 1975–1990 (69).

In terms of geographic distribution, post-liberalization, there has been a clear shift in Indian OFDI flows toward the Triad regions (table 9.2). Indeed, this also signifies a shift in the general attitude shaping the FDI regulatory framework. In abandoning a regulatory framework that considers the utilization of OFDI primarily as a tool for improving South-South cooperation and development, the current framework has been constructed on the basis of improving the global competitiveness of Indian industry and firms. To be sure, the extent to which Indian firms have the capacity to become globally competitive hinges on their ability to obtain the assets—both tangible and intangible—that grant them the capacity to compete with Triad firms, as well as other non-Triad incumbents in the global market. Moreover, the focus of industrial policies in the pre-liberalization phase of development has significantly impacted OFDI industry distribution in favor of those industries that were the focus of industrial development pre-liberalization (tables 9.3 and 9.4). Similarly, the sectoral distribution of OFDI flows since liberalization has also impacted the geographical focus of Indian OFDI toward the Triad regions. In the post–World War II period, it is undeniable that the Triad possessed the tangible and intangible assets required by Indian firms to attain a competitive foothold in global markets in these industries.

Table 9.2 Indian OFDI flows per selected region, 1961–2007 (US$ millions)

Host country region	1961–1969	1970–1979	1980–1989	1990–1999	2000–2007
Triad	10	3	36	1,460	15,652
Non-Triad	22	84	116	1,890	8,788
European Union	2	3	18	1,021	12,061
North America	–	0.1	17	388	2,815
Africa	13	35	25	317	2,968
Latin America and the Caribbean	–	–	0.2	47	1,132
Asia and Oceania	9	46	61	1,445	3,407
Central and Southeast Europe	–	2	29	81	1,281

Sources: Pradhan (2008, 2008a).

Table 9.3 Total outward foreign direct investment, by investing sector, 2005–2006 (US$ millions)

	2005–2006	
Sector	US$ millions	% of total
Pharmaceuticals	1580	25
Banking	1180	18
IT and ITES	786	12
Metal	778	12
Energy	631	10
Automobile and automobile components	364	6
Telecommunications	308	5
Consumer durables	289	4
Food and beverage	266	4
Chemicals	235	4
Total	6,417	100

Source: CRISIL (2006, 33).

Table 9.4 Percentage share of industry sector in GDP output and employment of selected sectors, 1999–2000

Sector	Share in GDP	Share in employment
Agriculture	25	60.3
Mining and quarrying	2	1,1
Manufacturing	15	11.0
Electricity, gas and water supply	3	0
Construction	6	4.4
Trade, hotels, restaurants	14	10.3
Transport, storage, and communication	7	3.7
Finance, real estate, insurance and business services	13	1.2
Community, social and personal services	15	8
Total GDP	100	100

Source: Panagariya (2008, 284).

Equally significant is the shift toward M&As, particularly for projects for which Indian firms have obtained majority control of the target acquisition. Between 1991 and 2001, when grouped together, 70% of the total OFDI activities pursued by Indian MNEs, by value, could be classified as granting Indian firms a majority of 80% ownership or more in the foreign target firm (Pradhan 2007b, 13). The growth in OFDI through M&As corresponds to changes in the global economy that have reduced the ability of firms to remain competitive through a process of evolutionary internationalization alone. In a rapidly changing global economy, with ever-increasing competitive pressures (the result of increasing liberalization of capital and product market controls), firms have been forced to internationalize rapidly, in order to obtain the quintessential assets required to remain competitive—at home and abroad.

In addition to the growing preference for M&As, Indian MNEs have also been swift to take up a substantial portion of their acquisitions in the Triad (tables 9.5 and 9.6). Indeed, while the number of Indian acquisitions of firms from the non-Triad has increased, data on total OFDI clearly reveal that the geographic focus of acquisitions has increasingly been the Triad region.

This geographical focus is a strikingly salient feature when compared to the total amount spent on acquisitions of Triad firms by non-Triad firms. Indeed, from the data provided in table 9.7 we can identify two vitally important developments regarding the growth in Indian OFDI in the Triad region. First, it is obvious that, in 2007, the value of Indian purchases of Triad firms outranked every other Triad economy. Second, while the value of Chinese, Hong Kong (China), and Russian cross-border purchases in the Triad decreased between 2005 and 2007, there was an almost seven-fold increase in the value of Indian cross-border purchases in the same time period.

The geographic distribution of Indian OFDI (figure 9.1) shows the shift in favor of the Triad: the EU has become the preferred region for Indian direct investments. Within the EU, the primary destination for these investments has been the United Kingdom, followed by Germany. North America

Table 9.5 Triad-bound M&As by Indian MNEs, 2000–2008

Year	Value (US$ million)	Number of transactions	Aquiring firms	Triad host countries
2000	887	35	27	6
2002	118	19	14	5
2004	785	42	38	10
2006	5,976	151	114	23
2007	33,739	144	118	21
2008*	2,614	43	42	12

Source: Pradhan (2008, 14).

*First Quarter FY 2008 data.

Table 9.6 Non-Triad-bound acquisitions by Indian MNEs

Year	Value (US$ millions)	Number of transactions	Aquiring firms	Triad host countries
2000	21	4	2	4
2002	2,483	8	3	7
2004	2,228	19	15	14
2006	1,727	38	36	15
2007	3,271	44	37	19
2008*	1,019	7	7	6

Source: Pradhan (2008a, 31).

*First Quarter FY 2008 data.

Table 9.7 Total amount spent on purchases of Triad firms by selected non-Triad economies, 2005 and 2007 (US$ millions)

	Non-Triad purchases of Triad firms (US$ millions)	
	2005	2007
World	777,609	1,410,802
Triad economies	708,877	1,281,706
Non-Triad economies	57,692	101,594
Brazil	1,591	10,404
China	6,223	2,408
Hong Kong (China)	6,277	2,633
India	4,215	27,083
Mexico	2,136	17,321
Russia	19,031	12,479
Singapore	3,672	18,184

Source: UNCTAD (2008).

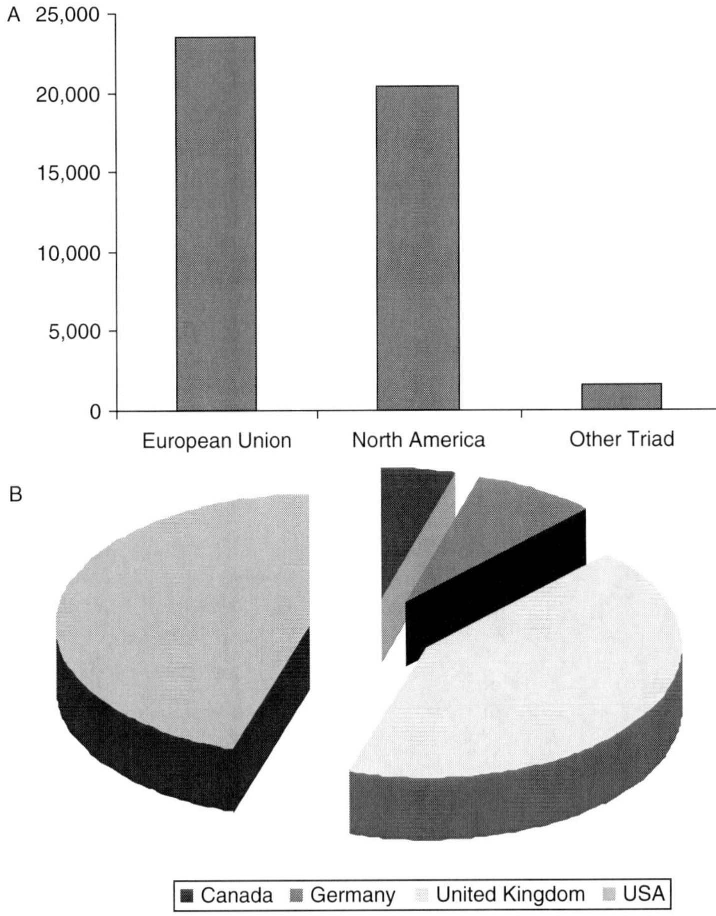

Figure 9.1 Value of Indian acquisitions per Triad host region, 2000–2008 (US$ millions)
Source: Pradhan (2008, 14–15).

is the next most favored investment region, with the United States the main recipient of Indian investment.

In terms of the sectoral focus of the M&A activity of Indian MNEs, the majority of M&As have been concentrated in the IT and business services industries, pharmaceuticals (including biotechnology and chemicals), and the automobile and automobile components industries; each of these industries has, typically, been dominated by Triad MNEs. Indeed, the manufacturing sector has clearly dominated OFDI projects in terms of value, volume, and contribution to gross domestic product (GDP) and employment growth.

In sum, the data presented in this section demonstrates the extent to which the salient features of OFDI projects pursued by Indian MNEs post-liberalization are related to the growth in Triad-bound OFDI projects focused on knowledge-intensive manufacturing industries. Table 9.8 provides data

Table 9.8 Selected Indian acquisitions in top Triad host countries, 2000–2008

Indian acquirer	Target	Sector	Host country	Year
Bharat Forge Ltd.	Carl Dan Peddinghaus GmbH	Automobile and automobile components	Germany	2003
Mahindra & Mahindra	Jeco Holding	Automobile and automobile components	Germany	2006
Sakthi Auto Component	Intermet	Automobile and automobile components	Germany	2007
Tata Motors	Jaguar & Landrover	Automobile and automobile components	United Kingdom	2008
Infosys Technologies Ltd.	Treasury Production division of Trade IQ	Banking and financial services	United States	2002
Nicholas Primal India Ltd.	BioSyntech Inc.	Biotechnology	Canada	2005
Biocon Ltd.	Nobex Corporation	Biotechnology	United States	2006
Kaashyap Technoloies Ltd	Consultancy Division of Logistics Solutions Inc.	Business advisory	United States	2007
Godrej Industries	Boston Analytics LLC	Business advisory	United States	2005
CRISIL	EconomoMatters Ltd. + subsidiaries	Business advisory	United Kingdom	2003
Tata Consultancy Services	Pheonix Global Solutioans	Business advisory	United States	2004
Tata Consultancy Services	Pearl Assurance	Business advisory	United Kingdom	
Sulzon Energy Ltd.	Repower	Electrical machinery	Germany	2007
Bharat Forge	Carl Dan Pettinghaus GmbH	Fabricated metal products	Germany	2003
Tata Tea	Tetley Tea	Food and beverage	United Kingdom	2001

Continued

Table 9.8 Continued

Indian acquirer	Target	Sector	Host country	Year
Tata Tea	Glaceu	Food and beverage	United States	2006
Tata Tea Ltd.	Energy Brands Inc.	Food and beverage	United States	2006
Gitanjali Gems Ltd.	Samuels Jewellers	Gems and jewellery	United States	2006
Shrenuj & Co. Ltd	Simon & Sons Inc.	Gems and jewellery	United States	2007
Wipro Technologies	Infocrossing Inc	IT and ITES	United States	2007
Saytam	Citisoft	IT and ITES	United Kingdom	2005
Firstsource Solutions	MedAssit Holdings	IT and ITES	United States	2007
Scandent Solutions Corporation Ltd.	Cambridge Integrated Services Group Inc.	IT and ITES	United States	2004
Hindalco Industries Ltd.	Novelis	Metal and metal products	United States	2007
Carborundum Universal Ltd.	Abrssives Enterprise	Non-metal mineral	Canada	2006
Grasim Industries	St Anne Nackawik Pulp Mill	Paper and pulp	Canada	2005
Dr. Reddy's	Betapharm Arzneimittel GmbH	Pharmaceuticals	Germany	2006
Reliance Industries Ltd.	Trevira GmbH	Plastic and plastic products	Germany	2004
Jindal Polyester Ltd.	Rexor, S.A.	Plastic and plastic products	France	2003
Tata Steel	Corus	Steel	United Kingdom	2007
Essar Steel	Algoma Steel Inc.	Steel	Canada	2007
Reliance Communication	FLAG Telecom	Telecommunications	United Kingdom	2004
Reliance Communication	Yipes Holding Inc.	Telecommunications	United States	2007
Skumar's	American Pacific	Textiles and apparels	United States	2006
Four Soft	DCS Transportation	Transport and communication	United Kingdom	2005

Sources: Pradhan (2007, 2007a, 2008b); CRISIL (2006); Goldstein (2007).

on 35 of the more than 500 acquisitions in the Triad since 2000, including information on the acquirer, industry, target firm, and host country.

Indeed, it becomes clear that Indian OFDI projects are not undertaken solely by large firms. While a large percentage of the firms are family conglomerate holdings, there are also a significant portion of small and medium-sized enterprises (SMEs) undertaking OFDI. The substantial growth in Indian FDI is a fairly broad phenomenon, one that involves both parent and target companies of varying sizes. Table 9.8 includes a number of parent SMEs, such as Grasim Industries, Carborundum Industries, Shrenuj and Company, and Skumars. Further evidence of the existence of SMEs on this list is the large number of SME targets that includes Betapharm, Rexor S.A., Trevira, St. Anne Nackawik, and Carl Dan Peddinghaus.

9.2 Driving Forces and Enabling Conditions: How Can We Explain OFDI from India?

How can we explain the specific pattern of Indian OFDI? Why do Indian MNEs specialize in specific industries and internationalize mainly by acquiring companies in the Triad, and all of this only during the past few years? In order to solve this puzzle, we will first turn to the established theories on the driving forces of OFDI, developed in business studies (section 9.2.1). Not all these developments, however, can be explained by examining company strategies and resources. In particular, the sharp and steady rise in OFDI since 2001 indicates changes in the policy landscape. In order to address these changes, we will look at the broader enabling conditions, with the assistance of a political economy perspective (section 9.2.2).

9.2.1 Driving Forces: Business Studies' Perspectives

In recent years, a substantial business literature on Indian MNEs and their success factors has emerged (e.g., Bergman 2006; Chadha 2005; CRISIL 2006; Das 2007; Gupta 2006; Kale 2008; Kumar 2007, 2008; Pradhan 2007a, 2007b; Sarathay 2006; Wyatt 2005). In terms of their analytical background, these studies do not develop specific theories on Indian MNEs or Indian OFDI; rather, they rely on existing theories of MNEs in general, and on emerging markets MNEs in particular. Perhaps the most influential of the theoretical studies on the expansion of OFDI from emerging markets over the past three decades has been John Dunning's ownership, location, and internalization (OLI) framework (Dunning 1977, 1981, 1986, 1988a, 1988b, 1995, 1998). Broadly speaking, the OLI framework outlines the conditions and motivational factors that drive MNE internationalization, particularly in the form of OFDI expansion. Five specific motivations for outward expansion are most commonly identified in the international business literature: (1) take advantage of the ownership advantages already internal to the firm; (2) enhance and/or acquire new ownership advantages; (3) seek out natural resources; (4) seek out and take advantage of (new) markets; and (5) "more effectively…coordinate and integrate existing cross-border operations" (Dunning, Kim, and Park 2008, 166). Both the first and the second motivational drivers are related to the ownership advantages summarized in the OLI framework, the third and fourth are related to locational advantages, and the fifth is related to internalization. The approach is focused on answering three main questions relating to outward expansion through OFDI: why does a firm internationalize; where does it internationalize; and how does it internationalize? To put it simply, the answers to these questions are as follows: (1) ownership advantages (why); (2) locational advantages (where); and (3) internalization advantages (how).

Ownership advantages are most typically associated with firm-specific advantages and intangible assets, such as proprietary technology, strong brand name, advertising, and marketing power. Locational advantages refer specifically to country-specific advantages, such as the quality of institutions, regulatory barriers, government restrictions, economic structure, and natural resources. Internalization advantages refer to the positive effects that a company would see from implementing the foreign business activity itself, rather than contracting it out to a local company. However, the cornerstone of the OLI framework is the focus on firm-specific ownership advantages. Given that internationalization is a costly process and carries with it significant risk of failure—upon entry into a foreign market the firm is always at an operational disadvantage when compared to local firms—ownership advantages are seen as crucial for successful OFDI. However, existing applications of the OLI framework for Indian MNEs have focused primarily on locational, country-specific factors, such as strategic asset seeking for acquiring technology and/or brands (i.e., the O-advantages that they simply do not possess yet); gaining global competitiveness; and avoiding home-country regulatory barriers and government restrictions. Undoubtedly, the most important locational, country-specific factor that enable substantial year-on-year increases in Indian OFDI flows has been the liberalization of investment policies post-1991.

There is now a broad consensus that the 1991 liberalization of the direct investment regime has been an important factor in the recent foreign expansion of Indian MNEs and their acquisitions in the Triad. Among the most relevant to mention here are the three amendments made to the "Guidelines for Indian Joint Ventures and Wholly Owned Subsidiaries Abroad," which essentially "provided for automatic approval of OFDI from US$2 million in 1992 to US$100 million in July 2002" (Kumar 2007, 3) and the eventual elimination of the cap by 2004. The elimination of the OFDI cap in 2004 virtually enabled firms to obtain automatic approval to undertake OFDI projects equivalent to 100% of the respective firms' net worth (3). These policy reforms had immediate effects on the type of investments pursued by Indian MNEs, most prominently the shift from greenfield investments to M&As (preferably with majority control). In the postreform era, "the share of minority ownership OFDI projects declined from 64 per cent to only 24 per cent, the share of majority ownership increased from 13 to 57 per cent" (UNCTAD 2007a, 71). Even though Indian MNEs had been undertaking OFDI activities prior to 1991, these were done by a very limited number of firms (mainly large family conglomerates), directed mainly toward other non-Triad markets, and were heavily regulated in terms of obtaining approval for outward investment as well as the type of investment allowed (i.e., joint ventures and minority ownerships). Administrative and bureaucratic barriers, as well as official policies, placed limits on who was allowed to undertake FDI, where such investment could be undertaken (IFDI was restricted to certain sectors; geographic constraints were placed on OFDI), and what type of activities firms were allowed to pursue. Shortly after the balance-of-payment crisis, which had been building up throughout the late-1980s, a series of structural market reforms was introduced, aimed at liberalizing the IFDI and OFDI regimes (covering both direct and portfolio investments), deregulating product and capital markets, and privatizing state-owned firms. These reforms enabled Indian MNEs to expand into Triad markets, in order to acquire technology and knowledge previously unobtainable.

The desire to reduce external debt was an important motivation in the liberalization of IFDI. This liberalization not only opened equity markets for portfolio investors, but also stimulated a surge in Triad MNEs setting up shop in India. The increase in Triad competitors in the Indian market directly threatened the viability of local firms, because they were confronted with competitors at a higher stage of technological development having marketing and branding techniques that were more sophisticated than those of Indian firms. As ODFI was also liberalized, Indian firms not only had to cope with fiercer domestic competition, but also had to focus on markets that would allow them to obtain comparatively easy profits, and, more importantly, new skills, products, brands, knowledge, and technology (CRISIL 2006; Das 2007; Gupta 2006; Kale 2008; Kumar and Pradhan 2003; Narlikar 2006; Pradhan and Alakshendra 2006; Pradhan 2007b; Ratnam 1998). Given that the government eased restrictions regulating the type of OFDI activities that could be pursued, and where they could be pursued, a significant portion of firms set their sights on Triad markets, considered to be the hub of global innovation. Moreover, the highly competitive domestic market also paved the way for Indian firms' to pursue international acquisitions. If, in order to access new resources and assets, an Indian firm invests time and financial resources in a target firm, it will likely choose the investment method that offers the greatest likelihood of resource internalization. This is to promote the accumulation of new competitive advantages that it can use in the competitive domestic market, especially in an environment with loosely enforced intellectual property rights (Gupta 2006; Pradhan 2007a, 2007b; Sarathy 2006).

Following the liberalization of the FDI regime, the initial players that emerged as leading OFDI investors were in industries that the government had closely protected in the pre-liberalization period, such as generic pharmaceuticals and IT software services (Kumar 2008, 12). In both industries, regulatory protectionism and supportive industrial and technological policies, from the 1950s onward, helped considerably in allowing firms to accumulate the technological capacity to expand abroad in the post-liberalization period (Pradhan 2008a). Government policies—in the restrictive, protectionist, and supportive sense—were reserved for specific industries that the government had earmarked as being the highest priority. Common among the earmarked industries were those related to science and technology. Indeed, one only needs to look at the formulation of each consecutive industrial policy, starting with that of Nehru and continuing to the most recent one, which seeks to promote industry growth in biotechnology. Government support, both pre- and post-liberalization, has been an extremely influential factor, shaping the industry structure at home and expansion abroad, particularly in the IT and information technology enterprise solutions (ITES) industries and the pharmaceutical, chemical, and biotechnology industries. During the protectionist period, Indian firms developed an undeniable strength in learning, absorbing, and adapting imported technology in the aforementioned industries. After the structural reforms, however, Indian companies were denied the full capacity to utilize this traditional strength. Given the abrupt market changes caused by foreign competition, Indian firms were pushed to leverage their core strengths abroad, in particular through the acquisition of established companies, thereby enabling Indian firms to take possession of strategic assets and become heavyweight competitors in both the global and the domestic markets (Kumar 2008, 12). The liberalization of the FDI regime provided the impetus for Indian MNEs to expand abroad; government policy in the pre-liberalization period played a significant role in demarcating the sectoral distribution of OFDI in the post-liberalization period, helping Indian MNEs gain competitive advantages, which they could then use when expanding abroad. The length of time that Indian MNEs have been involved in production has contributed significantly to their obtaining this advantage. As Nagesh Kumar remarked, the "(l)ong production experience in India gives to Indian companies not only skills and organizational capability to manage operations, but also experience of managing in multicultural settings, given the cultural diversity of the country" (17). The ownership and firm-specific competitive advantages of Indian MNES are, indeed, those that relate to the ability to operate in difficult markets and to integrate production under difficult conditions across large networks, together with engineering skills at low costs (Goldstein 2007; Hansen 2008; Kumar 2007, 2008; Kumar and Pradhan 2003; Milelli 2007; Pradhan 2004, 2007, 2008a; Pradhan and Alakshendra 2006; Ramamurti 2008; Ramamurti and Singh 2009a, 2009b).

9.2.2   Enabling Conditions: Comparative Capitalism Perspectives

To conclude, international business scholars have provided us with a wealth of information regarding the motivational drivers and explanatory variables behind the patterns of Indian OFDI growth in the past two decades. Nevertheless, an area that has perhaps been ignored in the literature is the institutional support behind specific firm and industry growth. Here, we refer specifically to factors that go beyond what is chiefly defined as institutional support in international business literature; that is, institutional quality and the foreign investment regime. Rather, we must pinpoint the interconnectedness between various dimensions of the socioeconomic environment of Indian MNEs, including the financial system, industrial relations, and the education system. In supplementing the substantial strides made in international business studies with a more institutional international political economy approach, we will be able to better understand exactly why it is that certain firms have internationalized in specific industries at specific moments in times.

For a more in-depth study of the institutional context of Indian MNEs we adopt a political science-political economy approach, an approach that allows us to examine the issue in terms of institutional categories. In particular, the "comparative capitalism" perspective[2] research program (Jackson and Deeg 2006) is well suited to serve as a heuristic framework for the study of the domestic institutional background of Indian MNEs, although it has only recently been extended to non-Triad economies (Schneider 2008; Nölke and Vliegenthart 2009). Comparative typologies of capitalism have become "canonical" among students of the political economy of Western societies (Blyth 2003, 215). Pioneered by scholars such as Andrew Shonfield (1965) and popularized by Michael Albert (1991), we can now choose from a large number of competing typologies within this research program (e.g., Crouch and Streeck 1997; Hollingsworth and Boyer 1997; Whitley 1999; Coates 2000; Hall and Soskice 2001b; Amable 2003; Schmidt 2003). Basic assumptions shared across the various strings of the comparative capitalism perspective include the following: "that capitalism is a socially embedded construction; that models of capitalism are distinguished one from the other by their underlying institutional configurations; and that modes of capitalist organisation are crucial in determining relative levels of economic performance" (Phillips 2004, 9).

For our purposes, the most important analytical contribution of the comparative capitalism perspective is the identification and elaboration of various core institutional domains within modern capitalism, including the financial system, corporate governance, industrial relations, skill creation, and the various mechanisms for the transfer of innovations throughout a specific capitalist formation (Jackson and Deeg 2006). At the core of our approach in this section is, therefore, an application of the comparative capitalism framework to Indian MNEs, in order to understand their domestic background. At the same time, our claim is not to replace existing studies on the business strategies of Indian MNEs, but rather to complement these studies with a political economy approach. The study of the reforms of the investment policy regime (section 9.2.1 above) may help to explain why Indian companies have developed a strong urge to pursue M&As in Triad economies over the past two decades, but it does not help us to understand why Indian companies were so successful in doing so. From our perspective, since the post-1991 reform era, a distinct socioeconomic system has been created in India, one that has strongly supported the transformation of domestic players into Indian MNEs. In what follows, we use the five spheres set out in the comparative capitalism framework to distinguish the unique characteristics of Indian MNEs and their institutional environment.

(1) The financial system. Most Indian MNEs are less dependent on (international) capital markets than are their Western counterparts (e.g., in the United States or the United Kingdom). Trading on Indian exchanges has remained extremely concentrated, which means that the bulk of shares in the most significant markets are rarely actively traded (Allen et al. 2006, 12–14). Furthermore, listings on foreign exchanges such as the New York Stock Exchange (NYSE), the London Stock Exchange (LSE), and Euronext are even more uncommon. Instead, companies rely primarily on family and friends for loans (start-up phase) and internally generated funds (later phases). Private bank lending to Indian MNEs has also remained comparatively limited. Start-up companies, therefore, have frequently turned to special financial institutions, such as the Small Industry Development Bank

(a wholly owned subsidiary of the state-owned Reserve Bank of India) or to a state financial institution (19–20). More generally, Indian MNEs frequently can make use of some kind of direct or indirect state financing, including fiscal incentives (e.g., tax credits), financial guarantees, and credits from state-owned banks. As more and more Indian MNEs begin to move into industries that require large investments in research and development (R&D), the supporting role of the state becomes crucial, as this offers Indian MNEs a means to overcome barriers to accessing risk capital (Khanna and Palepu 2006, 60–61). In summary, the role of kin-based finance, retained earnings, and state support effectively isolate many Indian MNEs from the volatility of international financial markets and, therefore, enable them to pursue long-term OFDI strategies.

(2) Corporate governance. There are strong complementarities between the systems of corporate governance and corporate finance of Indian MNEs. Indian MNEs typically are not dominated by dispersed shareholders and the organized forces of global capital markets (mutual funds, pension funds, investment banks, hedge funds, etc.), but instead are often family owned, kin based, or state controlled. In the majority of listed firms today, the largest blocks of equity typically remain in the hands of the founding family or controlling shareholder (Allen et al. 2006, 21). Family ownership might even be counted among the "distinguishing features" of Indian MNEs (31). Correspondingly, this corporate governance system not only allows for swift decisions to acquire foreign companies, but also allows for the pursuit of long-term strategies, without much interference from (Western) analysts, the financial press, or shareholder institutions.

(3) Industrial relations. Overall, four laws encompass the legal environment of the Indian labor market: The Factories Act, the Shops and Floors Establishments Act, the Trade Union Act, and the Industrial Disputes Act. The first two laws serve to regulate the safety and work conditions in manufacturing and services industries. Through the Trade Union Act, the right to form a union is established. The Industrial Disputes Act serves as a means to resolve disputes within the workplace, stipulating that the State will intervene in order to resolve matters between workers and employers (Nagaraj 2007, 5). However, the greatest amount of employment in India is found in informal and unorganized industries, thereby limiting the impact of these laws. In particular, in service industries there are significant deviations between what is written and what is actually enforced (Sharma 2006). Moreover, there is a significant correlation between the lack of enforcement of labor laws in service industries and the success of Indian IT and pharmaceuticals industries. Given that service industries are the primary driver of growth in the Indian economy, a blind eye has been turned to these regulations, in order to foster and ensure the growth of firms. However, most of the successful MNEs have invested significantly in improving the skill level of their workforce (Taylor and Nölke 2010).

(4) Skills creation. Generally, one of the most significant features of the Indian education and training system is its strong emphasis on higher education

compared with primary education (Milelli 2007). However, given the high population growth, combined with limited public funding, the focus is on quantity rather than on quality, as indicated, for example, by rather low salaries for university professors. Nevertheless, the high output of graduates (table 9.9), in particular of low-cost engineering labor, certainly has contributed to the expansion of Indian services MNEs.

We observe that, as more highly innovative industries develop in India, business is beginning to contribute to the educational system. It has done so largely in response to dissatisfaction with the current system, in terms of its inability to produce competent future employees. Looking at the example of the pharmaceutical industry, its attempts to attract Triad pharmaceutical MNEs in order to outsource clinical trial testing to India have been hindered severely by a lack of people trained to perform clinical trials, itself the result of a lack of university courses in this subject. The IT industry is also stepping up its involvement in the training of its future workforce: between January 2007 and March 2008 the top five firms in the industry spent approximately US$420 million on recruitment and training (David 2008). Many firms have also begun to establish their own university-like training and research centers, such as Saytam, which has built a campus adjacent to its headquarters in Hyderabad. Nevertheless, limits on the qualifications of Indian university graduates are among the factors that have led Indian MNEs to pursue M&As in the Triad.

(5) The transfer of innovations within the economy. The pursuit of certain public policies by the Indian Government has been crucial to the establishment of an institutional environment to support the transfer of innovation within the national economy, and to increase the possibility for technological upgrading. For example, a number of Indian firms have become MNEs largely because they were embedded in a policy environment that consisted of a "soft patent system to legalize reverse engineering" (Goldstein 2007, 95). Nevertheless, the later entrenchment of a strict(er) intellectual-property-rights (IPRs) regime at the national level has significantly altered the legislative scene in India. Given that Indian firms can no longer rely on a lax IPR regime to support their product portfolio and technological growth, many have increasingly utilized acquisitions (particularly in the Triad) as a means

Table 9.9 Number of universities and students, 1950s–2006 (millions)

Year	Universities	Students
1950–1951	45	0.6
1960–1961	93	2
1970–1971	123	2.8
1990–1991	184	4.4
2000–2001	272	8.8
2005–2006	335	10.5

Source: Panagariya (2008, 441).

to improve their innovative capacity in the new regulatory environment (Bartlett and Ghoshal 2000). Thus, the strict(er) IPR regime has, in effect, been one critical impetus spawning the increased intensity of Indian MNEs' aggressive pursuit of asset-seeking strategies in Triad markets. Indian MNEs have benefited substantially from inorganic growth in Triad markets because it has allowed them to increase profit margins rapidly, attain market presence, acquire brand names and technologies, and obtain intangibles assets, such as the ability to manage companies in a less-regulated environment, at a very rapid pace (Goldstein 2007, 63; Aykut and Goldstein 2006, 23–25).

9.3 Conclusions and Outlook:
What Are the Future Challenges for Research into Indian OFDI?

To summarize, support by the state and its public policies have been crucial factors in the rise of Indian MNEs, as evidenced by the government's financial support and innovation policies and its inward and outward investment regulations. Thus, the Indian state has been the major player in creating, shaping, and fostering the growth of Indian MNEs (Gupta and Dutta 2005; Gupta 2006). More specifically, the rise of Indian MNEs has been strongly supported by the network of public officials and upper management, in which many Indian firms are involved. Particularly in the aftermath of the post-FDI liberalization phase, these networks have become more active with regard to creating fora and partnerships (Confederation of Indian Industry; India Brand Equity Foundation; India Partnership Forum; Overseas Indian Facilitation Center; Tamil Nadu Technology Development & Promotion Centre, etc.). Overall, these ties have been very useful in providing firms with additional financial leverage, as well as the ability to shape domestic public policies in a manner that is conducive to the needs of each firm and the industry as a whole. Given these strong interconnections between Indian MNEs and the state, it is more and more difficult to demarcate clearly the dividing line between the role of the state and the role of the private sector, leading to the emergence of public private "hybrids" that have become the driving force behind the Indian national innovation and production system (Clifton, Comín, and Diaz- Fuentes 2007; Gupta and Dutta 2005). These findings raise a number of concerns for policy makers and further research. Two issues are of overriding importance: on the one side, the potential tensions between Indian MNE practices and host country institutions; and, on the other, the potential conflict between Indian MNEs and the established institutions of global economic governance.

In the past four decades, a vast amount of literature has appeared, dedicated to analyzing the extent to which MNEs import distinctive practices from their home countries into their host-country subsidiaries (Bae, Shyhjer, and Lawlwe 1998; Bruining and Boselie 2005; Dobbin 2005; Edwards, Colling, and Ferner 2007; Erramilli 1996; Ferner and Quintanilla 1998; Hamill 1984; Jain, Lawler, and Morishima 1998; Kahancová 2007; Muller 1998; Pulignano 2006). The most recent literature has drawn on new institutionalism in order to emphasize "the relationship between the organization and its institutional environment, and the way in which this relationship shapes the organization's internal structures" (Ferner and Quintanilla 1998, 712). This literature hypothesizes that, when entering a host country, either through greenfield investment or M&As, an MNE is confronted with a series of challenging isomorphic pulls that arise as a result of the differences between the MNE's home and host environment. In order to achieve consistency within the global organization as a whole, firms are often tempted to import certain practices, especially with regard to human resource management and employment practices, rather than to localize themselves.

Nevertheless, the degree of transferability of certain practices from the parent firm to a host country affiliate depends largely upon two factors. First, the coercive strength of the institutional settings (i.e., the laws and regulations) may leave no choice but for the organization to adapt (Dobbin 2005). Second, it is expected that the importability of practices will increase; for example, when a foreign affiliate is wholly owned rather than a joint venture. Moreover, firms face mimetic as well as normative pressures to isomorphize. The former refers to pressures to model behavior in order to be similar to other firms in the host country. Such pressures increase when there is a high degree of uncertainty in terms of management not knowing how to navigate the host environment. With regard to normative pressures, what is of specific interest is the ability that labor has to force the firm to localize. Labor, as a result of being embedded in a specific environment, may demand a certain behavior from their employers that would force the firm to adapt (Powell and DiMaggio 1991a, 1991b).

Unfortunately, on these issues there is an absence of empirical studies for the acquisitions of Indian MNEs. Therefore, we have to rely on a brief theoretical exposition, focused on labor markets, as the most sensible issue, in order to outline this research perspective. As a working hypothesis, we assume tensions with unions in the Organisation for Economic Co-operation and Development (OECD) area, when companies are taken over and local industrial relations models are not respected (Goldstein 2007, 139–40, 143–44). In particular, we assume that tensions arise as the low-cost production advantages enjoyed by Indian MNEs at home are often no longer available in Triad host countries. Moreover, we assume that the specific degree of these tensions depends heavily on the type of host country variety. Thus, we need to study the impact of the acquisition operations of Indian MNEs on industrial relations within liberal economies (e.g., the United States), coordinated economies (e.g., Germany), and state enhanced (e.g., France). Initial empirical studies on the subject indicate that Indian MNEs have tended to not take a conflictual approach toward labor in their expansion abroad. Indeed, Indian MNEs, for the most part, have been quite proactive, in terms of their willingness to listen and negotiate with labor. Perhaps the most problematic feature with regard to industrial relations, however, is related to the compensation schemes that Indian MNEs have favored establishing in their foreign affiliates. This is particularly acute in those subsidiaries that they have acquired in continental Europe. More specifically, they have systematically changed compensation schemes to performance-based compensation schemes in regions which, traditionally, are neither accustomed to, nor institutionally supportive of, such performance-based compensation or reward schemes. Given the recent character of these changes, however, little can be said in terms of the long-term consequences such change poses for the national system of industrial relations in these countries.

Regarding the second challenge outlined above, global expansion also entails confronting the international institutions and agreements governing the global economy. How are Indian MNEs mediating this confrontation? What preferences have Indian MNEs developed with regard to how the global economy should, optimally, be regulated? To what extent are current global economic governance institutions, arrangements, and mechanisms broadly in line with the needs and preferences of Indian MNEs? Again, no empirical research on these topics is available to date. Instead, we may extrapolate from our findings above on how the rise of Indian MNEs will affect global economic governance institutions. In the following we will sketch out a very first attempt to do so, by discussing how the existing global economic governance institutions have facilitated the rise of Indian MNEs, and by looking at the demands that they will have regarding the further evolution of these institutions and the potential conflicts with other stakeholders that may arise in this context.

Indian MNEs, typically, have grown based on a system of company finance that does not fully cater to the demands of global financial markets. Based on highly concentrated ownership structures, they have maintained a high degree of stability and an orientation toward the long term, thereby neglecting issues such as the protection of minority shareholders. Given the focus of most global institutions (such as the International Monetary Fund [IMF], the World Bank, and the OECD) on the further expansion of Anglo-Saxon standards in financial market regulation, we may expect increasing conflict over these issues, even if some of the more advanced Indian MNEs are moving progressively toward accommodating the needs of global financial markets.

Corporate governance issues are not regulated by a global regime such as the WTO, for example. Instead, these issues are rather loosely institutionalized. Most regulations are in the form of voluntary codes, such as those issued by the OECD, as well as by numerous private bodies. Similar to the issue of corporate finance, we expect a similar opposition against an overly forceful export of financial market-driven standards in corporate governance debates, as this might clash with the interests of strategic investors, the state, or the founding families that govern Indian MNEs. However, the debate may become more complex as a result of the recent wave of Western concerns over the increasing influence of non-Triad sovereign wealth funds (SWFs). Indian MNEs prefer less restrictive takeover regulations, given that they have increasingly relied on acquisitions in the Triad to acquire market access, higher profit margins, and brand recognition. Nevertheless, some Triad governments are becoming ever more wary of market-friendly standards and have begun to introduce institutions to protect against takeover by non-Triad state funds. Correspondingly, we expect increasing tensions and a growing importance of institutions such as the Committee on Foreign Investment in the United States (CFIUS).

In the field of industrial relations, we expect Indian MNEs to be unwilling to accept comprehensive global labor regulation by the International Labour Organization (ILO), because of the corresponding threat to the low (labor) cost strategy that has helped them to expand. Clearly evidencing the conflictual character of this issue is the opposing stance that the Indian government has taken with regard to the inclusion of a social clause in the free trade agreement it is currently negotiating with the EU. Finally, also in the field of CSR, MNEs from outside the Triad countries are normally less willing to accept stringent (self-)regulation (Goldstein 2007, 133). However, there is also the perspective that upgrading Indian MNE CSR activities in the medium term would be possible if more companies strongly participate in global value chains or are directly confronted with CSR-conscious Western consumers. Clearly this has been the case with Tata, as well as the implementation of "Triple Bottom Performance" across the board in many Indian MNEs. Moreover, pharmaceutical firms that have been expanding abroad have been particularly conscious of ensuring the development of a CSR policy oriented toward environmental protection and community healthcare awareness. Indeed, the successful integration of Betapharm (Germany) into Dr. Reddy's was precisely related to the expansive community development and awareness programs that Dr. Reddy's supports. Given that Betapharm, prior to the acquisition, had received numerous awards, in particular by the Bavarian government, it should be no surprise that a crucial element allowing for the smooth transition of ownership from German to Indian ownership was precisely due to Dr. Reddy's active CSR policy and its role in community development.

In contrast to many other capitalist institutions, the education and training systems are much less affected by comprehensive global regulation. Indian MNEs and their home countries are still somewhat unrestrained in their strategies. Concerning the level of production (or service) technology and how it is impacted by international regulation, the main issue is in the field of intellectual property rights, an issue that has been at the center of controversy in negotiations on a free trade agreement between India and the EU. Given that, originally, most Indian MNEs had been enabled to grow as a result of a less-than-strict intellectual-property-rights regime, a common assumption has been that they will push for the continued pursuit of more liberal IPR strategies. Nevertheless, when considering that there has not only been an increasing number of Indian MNEs involved in high-end R&D, but also the mere fact that the Indian government has chosen to make biotechnology its new "strategic industry" and aims to make it as successful as the pharmaceuticals and IT industries, these preferences may change in the future. Both of these matters stand in direct contradiction to the stance that the Indian Government has taken, generally, on the adoption and enforcement of a strict(er) IPR regime as demanded by the institutions and mechanisms of global economic governance. As such, the question is posed as to whether we are currently witnessing the beginning of a preference divergence among policy makers and industry leaders in India.

In sum, our extrapolation of how conflicts with Indian MNEs are being played out at the global economic governance level has not yet led to a clear picture. Even though we have noted numerous areas in which we expect intensified conflict in the near future, in other areas we assume that the preferences of Triad countries and Indian MNEs may gradually converge. However, we have also identified a number of areas in which Indian MNEs operate in closer collaboration with national governments than do Triad MNEs, indicating that the potential push for a more mercantilist form of global economic governance may be one of the most visible conflicts in future. Which of these trajectories gains the upper hand in the end is difficult to say at present—much more research on Indian MNEs and their position on global economic governance is needed.

Notes

1. Interview with a Dr. Reddy's executive wishing to remain anonymous: December 12, 2008.
2. For a more detailed account of these perspectives, see Taylor and Nölke (2010).

References

Albert, M. (1991). *Capitalism against Capitalism* (London: Whurr).

Allen, F., R. Chakrabarti, S. De, J. Qian, and M. Qian (2006). "Financing firms in India," *Working Paper 06-08* (Philadelphia: Wharton Financial Institutions Center, University of Pennsylvania), mimeo.

Amable, B. (2003). *The Diversity of Modern Capitalism* (Oxford: Oxford University Press).

Aykut, D., and A. Goldstein (2006). "Developing country multinationals: south-south investment comes of age," *OECD Working Paper 257* (Paris: OECD Development Centre), mimeo.

Bae, J., C. Shyh-jer, and J.J. Lawlwe (1998). "Variations in human resources management in Asian countries: MNC home-country and host-country effects," *International Journal of Human Resource Management* 9 (4), pp. 653–70.

Bartlett, C.A. and S. Ghoshal (2000). "Going global: lessons from late movers," *Harvard Business Review* 78 (2), pp. 132–42.

Bergman, A. (2006). "FDI and spillover effects in the Indian pharmaceutical industry," *RIS Discussion Papers 113* (New Delhi: Research and Information System for Developing Countries), mimeo.

Bertoni, F., S. Elia, and L. Rabbiosi (2008). "Drivers of acquisitions from BRICs to advanced countries: firm-level evidence," Paper presented at Emerging Multinationals from Emerging and Developing Countries, October 9–10 (Copenhagen: Copenhagen Business School), mimeo.

Blyth, M. (2003). "Same as it never was: Temporality and typology in the varieties of capitalism," *Comparative European Politics* 1 (2), pp. 215–25.

Bruining, H., and P. Boselie (2005). "The impact of business ownership change on employee relations: buy-outs in the UK and the Netherlands," *International Journal of Human Resource Management* 16 (3), pp. 345–65.

Chadha, A. (2005). "Trips and patenting activity: evidence from the Indian pharmaceutical industry," *Departmental Working Papers WP0512* (Singapore: Department of Economics National University of Singapore), mimeo.

Clifton, J., F. Comín, and D. Diaz- Fuentes (2007). *Transforming Public Enterprise in Europe and North America: Networks, Integration and Transnationalization* (Hampshire, England, and New York: Palgrave Macmillan), pp. 3–15.

Coates, D. (2000). *Models of Capitalism: Growth and Stagnation in the Modern Era*, (Cambridge: Polity Press).

CRISIL (2006). "Creating the Indian MNC," CRISIL Center for Economic Research, available at http://ibef.org/download/CII_Report_Outward_FDI_2006_270906.pdf, last visited September 10, 2009.

Crouch, C. and W. Streeck (1997). "Introduction," in C. Crouch and W. Streeck, eds., *Political Economy of Modern Capitalism: Mapping Convergence and Diversity*, (London: Thousand Oaks and New Delhi: Sage), pp.1–32.

Das, N. (2007). "The emergence of Indian multinationals in the new global order," *International Journal of Indian Culture and Business Management* 1 (1/2), pp. 136–50.

David, R. (2008). "Indian firms facing employee wage, quality pressures," *Forbes.com,*, February 15, available at http://www.forbes.com/2008/02/15/nasscom-software-convention-markets-equity-cx_rd_0215markets04.html, last visited February 16, 2008.

Dobbin, F. (2005). "Is globalization making us all the same?" *British Journal of Industrial Relations* 43 (4), pp. 569–76.

Dunning, J.H. (1977). "Trade, location of economic activity and the multinational enterprise: a search for an eclectic approach," in B.e. Ohlin, P.-O. Hesselborn, and P.M. Wijkman, eds., *The International Location of Economic Activity* (London: Macmillian), pp. 395–418.

——— (1981). "Explaining outward direct investment of developing countries: in support of the eclectic theory of international relations," in K. Kumar and M.G. McLeod, eds., *Multinationals from Developing Countries* (Lexington: Lexington Books and Washington, DC: Heath), pp. 1–22.

——— (1986). "The investment development and third world multinationals," in K.M. Khan, ed., *Multinationals of the South: New Actors in the International Economy* (New York: St. Martin's Press), pp. 15–47.

——— (1988a). "The eclectic paradigm of international production: a restatement and some possible extensions," *Journal of International Business Studies* 19 (1), pp. 1–25.

——— (1988b). "Trade, location of economic activity and the multinational enterprise: a search for an eclectic approach," in J.H. Dunning, *Explaining International Production* (London: Unwin Hyman), pp. 13–140.

——— (1995). "Reappraising the eclectic paradigm in an age of alliance capitalism," *Journal of International Business Studies* 26 (3), pp. 461–91.

——— (1998). "Location and the multinational enterprise: a neglected factor," *Journal of International Business Studies* 29 (1), pp. 45–66.

Dunning, J.H., C. Kim, and D. Park (2008). "Old wine in new bottles: a comparison of emerging-market TNCs today and developed country TNCs thirty years ago," in Karl. P. Sauvant with K. Mendoza, and I. Ince, eds., *The Rise of Translational Corporations from Emerging Markets: Threat of Opportunity?* (Cheltenham: Edward Elgar), pp. 158–82.

Edwards, T., T. Colling, and A. Ferner (2007). "Conceptual approaches to the transfer of employment practices in multinational companies: an integrated approach," *Human Resource Management Journal* 17 (3), pp. 201–17.

Erramilli, K.M. (1996). "Nationality and subsidiary ownership patterns in multinational corporations," *Journal of International Business Studies* 27 (2), pp. 225–48.

Ferner, A., and J. Quintanilla (1998). « Multinationals, national business systems and HRM: the enduring influence of national identity or a process of 'Anglo-Saxonization," *International Journal of Human Resource Management* 9 (4), pp. 710–31.

Financial Express (2009). "India focus M&A dips 49 pct in 2009," February 23, available at http://www.financialexpress.com/news/india-focus-m&a-dips-49-pct-in-2009/427073/, last visited May 10, 2010.

Goldstein, A. (2007). *Multinational Companies from Emerging Economies* (New York: Palgrave Macmillan).

Gupta, A. (2006). "Emergence of Indian multinationals," *Technology Exports* 8 (3). pp. 1–12.

Gupta, A. and P.K. Dutta (2005). "Indian innovation system," Paper prepared for the Asia-Pacific Forum on National Systems for High Level Policy Makers, mimeo.

Gupta, V.K. (2006). "'Inventor' productivity in a publicly funded R&D agency: the case of CSIR in India," *World Patent Information* 26, pp. 235–38.

Hall, P.A. and D. Soskice (2001a). "An introduction to varieties of capitalism," in P.A. Hall and D. Soskice, eds., *Varieties of Capitalism: The Institutional Foundations of Comparative Advantage* (Oxford: Oxford University Press), pp. 1–70.

———, eds. (2001b). *Varieties of Capitalism: The Institutional Foundations of Comparative Advantage* (Oxford: Oxford University Press).

Hamill, J. (1984). "Labour relations decision making within multinational corporations," *Industrial Relations Journal* 15, pp. 30–34.

Hansen, M. (2008). "Challenger firms from India: the rise of outward foreign direct investment from India," 12th European Association of Development Research and Training Institutes (EADI) General Conference Global Governance for Sustainable Development, June 2008, Geneva.

Hollingsworth, J. and R. Boyer (1997). *Contemporary Capitalism: The Embeddedness of Institutions* (Cambridge: Cambridge University Press).

Jackson, G., and R. Deeg (2006). "How many varieties of capitalism?: Comparing the comparative institutional analyses of capitalist diversity," *MPIfG Discussion Paper 06/02* (Cologne: Max Planck Institute for the Study of Societies), mimeo.

Jain, H.C., J.L. Lawler, and M. Morishima (1998). "Multinational corporations, human resource management and host-country nationals," *International Journal of Human Resource Management*, 9 (4), pp. 553–66.

Kahancová, M. (2007). "Corporate values in local contexts," *MpIfG Working Paper 07/01* (Cologne: Max Planck Institute for the Study of Societies), mimeo.

Kale, D. (2008). "Internationalisation strategies of Indian pharmaceutical firms," Paper presented at the conference on Emerging Multinationals from Emerging and Developing Countries, October 9–10 (Copenhagen: Copenhagen Business School), mimeo.

Khanna, T. and K. Palepu (2006). "Emerging giants: building world class companies in developing countries," *Harvard Business Review* 84 (10), pp. 60–69.

Kumar, N. (2007). "Emerging TNCs: trends, patterns and determinants of outward FDI by Indian enterprises," *Transnational Corporation* 16 (1), pp. 1–26.

——— (2008). "Internationalization of Indian enterprises: patterns, strategies, ownership advantages and implications" (New Delhi: Research and Information System for Developing Countries), mimeo.

Kumar, N. and J.P. Pradhan (2003). "Export competitiveness in the knowledge-based industries: a firm-level analysis of Indian manufacturing," *RIS Discussion Paper 43* (New Delhi: Research and Information System for Developing Countries), mimeo.

Kumra, Gautam and Kuldeep Jain (2009). "Corporate globalisation," in *Business Standard India 2009* (New Delhi: BS Books), pp. 113–25.

Milelli, C. (2007). "Outward expansion by Indian firms: the European route," *Working Paper 2007–25* (Paris: EconomiX), mimeo.

Muller, M. (1998). "Human resource and industrial relations practices of UK and US multinationals in Germany," *International Journal of Human Resource Management* 9 (4), pp. 732–49.

Nagaraj, R. (2007). "Labour market in India: current concerns and policy responses" (Mumbai: Indira Gandhi Institute of Development Research), mimeo.

Narlikar, A. (2006). "Peculiar chauvinism or strategic calculation?: Explaining the negotiating strategy of a rising India," *International Affairs* 82 (1), pp. 59–76.

Nölke, A. and A. Vliegenthart (2009). "Enlarging the varieties of capitalism: the emergence of dependent market economies in East Central Europe," *World Politics* 61 (4), October, pp. 670–702.

Nölke, A., and H. Taylor (2009a). "Non-Triad multinationals and global governance: still a North-South conflict?" in M. Ougaard, ed., *Business and Global Governance* (London: Routledge).

——— (2009b). "The rise of multinational firms from the non-Triad: implications for global governance" (Frankfurt: Goethe University Frankfurt am Main), mimeo.

Panagariya, A. (2008). *India: The Emerging Giant* (Oxford: Oxford University Press).

Phillips, N. (2004). "International political economy, comparative political economy and the study of contemporary development," paper presented at the annual meeting of the International Studies Association, March 8 (Montreal, Quebec, Canada).

Powell, W.W., and P. DiMaggio (1991a). "Introduction," in W.W. Powell and P. DiMaggio, eds., *The New Institutionalism in Organizational Analysis* (Chicago: University of Chicago), pp. 1–38.

——— (1991b). "The iron cage revisited: institutional isomorphism and collective rationality," in W.W. Powell and P. DiMaggio, eds., *The New Institutionalism in Organizational Analysis* (Chicago: University of Chicago), pp. 63–82.

Pradhan, J.P. (2004). "The determinants of outward foreign direct investment: a firm-level analysis of Indian manufacturing," *Oxford Development Studies* 23 (4), pp. 619–39.

——— (2007a). "Growth of Indian multinationals in the world economy: implications for development," *ISID Working Paper*, 2007/04 (New Delhi: Institute for Studies in Industrial Development), mimeo.

——— (2007b). 'Trends and pattern of overseas acquisitions by Indian multinationals," *ISID Working Paper, 2007/10* (New Delhi: Institute for Studies in Industrial Development), mimeo.

——— (2008a). "Indian direct investment in developed regions," Paper presented at the Emerging Multinationals from Emerging and Developing Countries Conference, October 9–10 (Copenhagen: Copenhagen Business School), mimeo.

——— (2008b). "Indian direct investment in developing countries," *ISID Working Paper, 2008/08* (New Dehli: Institute for Studies in Industrial Development).

——— (2008c). *Indian Multinationals in the World Economy* (New Dehli: Bookwell).

Pradhan, J.P. and A. Alakshendra (2006). "Overseas acquisitions versus greenfield foreign investment: which internationalization strategy is better for Indian pharmaceutical enterprises?" *GLOBELICS*, Trivandrum, India.

Pradhan, J.P. and R.P. Sahu (2007). *Transnationalization of Indian Pharmaceutical SMEs* (New Delhi: Bookwell).

Pulignano, V. (2006). "The diffusion of employment practices of US-based multinationals in Europe: a case study comparison of British- and Italian-based subsidiaries," *British Journal of Industrial Relations* 44 (3), pp. 497–518.

Ramamurti, R. (2008). "What have we learned about emerging market MNEs?: insights from a multi-country perspective," Paper presented at the Emerging Multinationals from Emerging and Developing Countries Conference, October 9–10 (Copenhagen: Copenhagen Business School), mimeo.

Ramamurti, R. and J.V. Singh, eds. (2009a). *Emerging Multinationals from Emerging Markets* (Cambridge: Cambridge University Press).

——— (2009b). "Indian multinationals: Generic internationalization strategies," in R. Ravi and J.V. Singh, eds., *Emerging Multinationals from Emerging Markets* (Cambridge: Cambridge University Press), pp. 110–66.

Ratnam, C.S.V. (1998). "Multinational Companies in India," *International Journal of Human Resource Management* 9 (4), pp. 567–89.

Sarathy, R. (2006). "Strategic evolution and partnering in the Indian pharmaceutical industry," in S.C. Jain, ed., *Emerging Economies and the Transformation of International Business* (Cheltenham: Edward Elgar), pp. 229–49.

Schmidt, V.A. (2003). "French capitalism transformed, yet still a third variety of capitalism," *Economy and Society* 32, pp. 526–54.

Schneider, B.R. (2008). "Comparing capitalisms: liberal, coordinated, network, and hierarchical varieties," draft, available at http://depot.northwestern.edu/school/wcas/poli-sci/schneider/recentpublications.html, last visited May 3, 2009.

Sharma, A. (2006). "Flexibility, employment and labour market reforms in India," *Economic and Political Weekly*, pp. 2078–85.

Shonfield, A. (1965). *Modern Capitalism* (London, New York: Oxford University Press).

Taylor, H. and A. Nölke (2010). "Indian multinationals and their institutional environment: a varieties of capitalism perspective," in H. Egbert and C. Esser, eds., *Aspects in Varieties of Capitalism: Dynamics, Economic Crisis, New Players*, vol. 3 (Saarbrücken: Lambert Academic Publishing (INFER Series in Applied Economics), 41–64.

UNCTAD (2006). *World Investment Report: FDI from Developing and Transition Economies—Implications for Development* (New York and Geneva: United Nations).

——— (2007a). *Global Players from Emerging Markets: Strengthening Enterprise Competitiveness through Outward Investment* (New York and Geneva: United Nations).

——— (2007b). *World Investment Report: Transnational Corporations, Extractive Industries and Development* (New York and Geneva: United Nations).

——— (2008). *World Investment Report: Transnational Corporations and the Infrastructure Challenge* (New York and Geneva: United Nations).

Whitley, R. (1999). *Divergent Capitalisms: The Social Structuring and Change of Business Systems* (Oxford: Oxford University Press).

Wyatt, A. (2005). "(Re)imagining the Indian (Inter)national economy," *New Political Economy* 10 (2), pp. 163–79.

Chapter 10

How Different Are Chinese Foreign Acquisitions? Adding an Indian Comparison

Huaichuan Rui, George S. Yip, and Shameen Prashantham

Introduction

China's outward foreign direct investment (OFDI) has developed extremely rapidly over the past few years, rising from US$2.5 billion[1] in 2002 to US$26.5 billion in 2007. Between 1978 and 2002, the accumulated value was US$30 billion, rising to US$57.2 billion by 2005, US$73.3 billion by 2006, and US$117.9 billion by 2007. By the end of 2007, a total of 7,000 Chinese firms had invested in 173 countries (MOC 2008). By 2008, China (including Hong Kong) had become the seventh largest source of OFDI worldwide, Chinese OFDI flows overtaking those of Japan (UNCTAD 2008). In addition to establishing new plants and subsidiaries overseas, Chinese firms have been rapidly acquiring well-known firms worldwide as a new form of transnational investment. Outward foreign acquisitions began in the late 1990s, logging US$344 million (nonfinance FDI) in 2000 and US$507 million in 2001. It jumped to US$2.8 billion in 2002, but subsequently fell to US$1.6 billion. However, since 2004 there has been an unprecedented rise, to US$3.9 billion in 2004 and US$6.5 billion in 2005, 53% of the total OFDI of the year (MOC and State Statistics Bureau 2006, 11). Outward acquisitions by Chinese nonfinance firms rose to US$15.8 billion during the first half year of 2008—61.6% of the total (MOC 2008). Table 10.1 lists the details of these acquisitions between 2004 and 2008.

It is widely acknowledged that China's economy has a number of rather unique characteristics. In certain respects, however, there are similarities with Brazil, India, and Russia. In terms of population, India comes close to China with 1.1 billion inhabitants. Also, since 1991, India has embarked on a series of liberalizing reforms—encouraging the country to emulate China's economic success. More importantly, in recent years there has been an equally dramatic rise in OFDI from India. The stock of Indian OFDI increased sixteenfold between 2000 and 2007, compared to an increase of approximately two-and-a-half times for developing economies as a whole (UNCTAD 2008). OFDI from India was insignificant from 1995 to 1999: it rose from

Table 10.1   Major Chinese foreign acquisitions (nonfinancial sector), 2004–2008

	Acquirer	Target	Sector	Year	Value (US$ millions)
1	Aluminum Corp. of China[a]	Rio Tinto (12%)	Mining	2008	14,280
2	COSL	Awilco Offshore	Drilling	2008	3,890
3	Huaneng Power	Tuas Power	Power	2008	3,070
4	Sinopec	Udmurneft	Petroleum	2006	3,500
5	CNOOC	South Atlantic Petroleum	Petroleum	2006	2,268
6	CNPC	PetroKazakhstan	Petroleum	2005	3,960
7	CNPC	Canadian Energy	Petroleum	2005	1,420
8	Nanjing Automobile, Shanghai Automobile	MG Rover	Automobile	2005	205
9	Lenovo Group Ltd.	IBM PC Business	IT	2004	1,760
10	Shanghai Automobile	Ssangyong Motors	Automobile	2004	509
11	CNPC	Pluspetrol Norte	Petroleum	2004	200
12	Ningbo Qingchun Clothing Factory	Younghwa Weaving and Dyeing Co.	Textile	2004	184
13	Cosco (China Ocean Shipping Co.)	Peninsular and Oriental Steam Navigation Co.	Shipping	2004	181
14	China Merchants Group	Ming Wah Universal	Transportation	2004	168
15	Sinopec	First International oil	Petroleum	2004	160

Source: Authors' research; Thomson Reuters (quoted from Miller 2008).

Note: Deals with the value of less than US$100 million have not been included.

[a] Joint deal with Alcoa.

US$119 million in 1995 to US$243 million in 1996, but declined to US$80 million in 1999 (Singh and Jain 2009). However, since 2004, the total has surged. Total OFDI from India increased from US$2.2 billion in 2004 to US$2.5 billion in 2005 and to US$9.7 billion in 2006. As a result, India's OFDI stock rose sharply to US$12.96 billion in 2006, up from a modest US$1.86 billion in 2000 (Exim India 2008).

More interestingly, in recent years, international acquisitions have also become a more important mode of OFDI for Indian firms. The value of cross-border mergers and acquisitions (M&As) undertaken by Indian firms from 2000 to 2008 totaled US$56 million, while the total sales of Indian firms was US$23 billion (UNCTAD 2008). Like Chinese firms, the overseas acquisitions made by Indian companies between 2005 and 2008 were substantially higher than in previous years. Table 10.2 lists the major acquisitions made by Indian firms between 2004 and 2008.

It is interesting to explore the extent to which the activity of Chinese firms can enrich the extant international business (IB) theories on multinational enterprises (MNEs), especially by comparing it with India's case. Contemporary IB theories on firms' internationalization has a long history of viewing MNEs as transferors of a bundle of resources and competences (Dunning and Lundan 2006) and of firms investing overseas as exploiting

Table 10.2 Major Indian foreign acquisitions (nonfinancial sector), 2004–2008

	Acquirer	Target	Sector	Year	Value (US$ million)
1	Wipro	Infocrossing	IT infrastructure	2008	600
2	Tata Steel	Corus Steel	Steel	2007	12,100
3	Hindalco	Novelis	Aluminium	2007	6,000
4	ONGC Videsh	Petrobas	Petroleum	2006	1,400
5	Tata Tea and Tata Sons	Glaceau	Health drinks	2006	677
6	Dr. Reddy's	Betapharm Arzneimittel GmbH	Pharmaceuticals and healthcare	2006	570.3
7	Suzlon Energy	Hansen Transmissions	Energy	2006	565
8	Kraft Foods Ltd	United biscuits	Food and beverages	2006	522
9	Ranbaxy Laboratories Ltd	Terapia SA	Pharmaceuticals and healthcare	2006	324
10	Tata Coffee	Eight O'clock Coffee Co.	Food and beverages	2006	220
11	Susken Communication Tech Ltd	Bornia Hightec	Information technology	2006	210
12	Ballarpur Industries Ltd.	Sabah Forest Industries	Pulp and paper	2006	209
13	Seagate Tech Ltd.	Evault Inc.	Information	2006	185
14	Ispat Industries Ltd.	Finmetal Holdings	Steel	2005	300
15	Videocon International	Thomson SA (CRT business)	Consumer goods	2005	289.2
16	VSNL Ltd	Teleglobe International Holdings Ltd.	Telecom	2005	254.3
16	Mtrix Laboratories	Docpharma NV	Pharmaceuticals and healthcare	2005	234.7
17	Tata Steel Ltd.	Millennium Steel	Steel	2005	175
18	ONGC Videsh	Greater Plutonio Project	Petroleum	2004	600
19	Opto Circuits India Ltd.	Eurocor GmbH	Medical equipment	2004	600
20	Tata Steel	NatSteel Asia Pte.	Steel	2004	283.7

Source: Nayyar (2008) own research.

their existing advantages, in a sequential and incremental way. However, a modern version of IB theory, based on latecomer MNEs, has long started to challenge this dominance by pointing to the possibility of the latecomers being motivated not by exploitation of advantages but by the desire to obtain them, and by being radical rather than incremental (see Mathews 2002; Yeung 1994 for reviews).

The springboard perspective on the internationalization of emerging market MNEs by Yadong Luo and Rosalie L. Tung (2007) made the even more specific claim that emerging market MNEs use international expansion as a springboard to acquire strategic resources and to reduce their institutional and market constraints at home. In so doing, they overcome their latecomer disadvantage in the global stage via a series of risk-taking measures by acquiring critical assets from mature MNEs to compensate for their competitive disadvantages. The rising research on China's OFDI (see, for example, Cai 1999; Deng 2004; Boisot 2004; Child and Rodrigues 2005; Buckley et al. 2007a; Morck, Yeung, and Zhao 2008) has discovered a number of features unique to Chinese MNEs regarding competitive advantage, entry mode, and other features.

The central issue we examine in this chapter is whether the overseas acquisitions by Chinese firms follow, or differ from, the current wisdom on internationalization established in international business literature. To do so, we will present a comprehensive literature review of both the old and new versions of IB theories on firms' internationalization in section 10.1. In section 10.2, we report on qualitative research that we have conducted at three Chinese firms that are among those prominent in foreign acquisitions. Specifically, we attempt to examine the features of Chinese foreign acquisitions by answering the following questions. First, do these firms possess ownership advantages? Second, is the exploitation of existing ownership advantages the motive for Chinese firms to invest abroad, or do they venture overseas in order to acquire such advantages? Third, why do they choose acquisition over other alternatives to full ownership? Fourth, what are the pull or push factors, if any, that affect their internationalization? Section 10.3 attempts to advance the above examination by comparing the foreign acquisitions of Chinese and Indian firms, in light of the dramatic rise in OFDI from India and the surprisingly lack of literature on Sino-Indian comparisons. In the final section, we conclude that the behavior of Chinese companies is very different from that suggested by conventional IB theories; rather, it has much more in common with emerging market MNEs as suggested by the modern version of MNE theories.

The research data on which this chapter is based are collected from both primary and secondary sources. Through December 2005 and January 2006, and again in June 2006, January 2007, and June 2008, we carried out an in-depth study of a small number of Chinese companies, namely Nanjing Automobile, Lenovo, and Huawei Technology, and conducted thirty interviews, including with Liu Chuanzhi, founder and former CEO of Lenovo. The selection of these three cases was based on our intention to choose companies from different industries and locations, and with different types of ownership. More importantly, they all made, or attempted to make, large acquisition deals in 2005. With both formal and informal connections, we were able to interview senior executives and officials at selected major Chinese companies and their rivals, government departments, and industrial associations, in order to gain a more detailed and unbiased picture of each case. With a view to furthering the understanding of the Chinese context, we present brief case findings—based on secondary research—of Indian counterpoints, which are particularly useful because much of the literature overlooks this potentially interesting comparison between the world's two largest nations. The brief cases pertain to automaker Maruti (counterpoint to Nanjing), information technology (IT) company Wipro (counterpoint to Lenovo), and IT company Infosys (counterpoint to Huawei).

10.1 Literature Review

This section will review the IB internationalization literature by focusing on the four categories that have not only aroused the most controversy between conventional and modern MNE theories, but are also the most relevant to our research concerning our Chinese cases; namely, prerequisites, process, entry mode, and impulses of latecomer MNE internationalization.

10.1.1 Prerequisites: Exploit or Explore Ownership Advantages?

For more than two decades, John H. Dunning's (1981) eclectic model has remained the most compelling explanation of the internationalization process of MNEs. According to him, a firm will engage in international production when three interrelated conditions are present: ownership-specific advantages, location-specific advantages, and internalization ability (OLI factors). Of the three conditions, possessing certain ownership advantages not possessed by competing firms of other nationalities is the first, and possibly the most important, prerequisite. Along with Dunning, early IB scholars typically based their MNE theories on evidence from developed countries (see, for example, Buckley and Casson 1985; Johanson and Vahlne 1977) and believed these MNEs to have particularly strong "intrinsic advantages, typically related to their technology or their brand recognition" (Bartlett et al. 2004, 4). Such views can be traced back to Stephen Hymer (1960) and Charles Kindleberger (1970), who envisaged that the prior existence of assets to be exploited abroad was the starting point for MNE activities.

This conventional view has been challenged by research based on MNEs from developing countries, the so called "modern version" of IB theories. This stream of research ranges from the earlier third-world MNE research (see, for example, Wells 1983; Lall 1984) to the latest research on "dragon multinationals" (Mathews 2002, 2006) and emerging market MNEs (Luo and Tung 2007). In contrast to the incumbents, latecomers and newcomers, since 1990s, have not been concerned with exploiting existing assets or resources, but with gaining access to resources through their international expansion. Their internationalization has been undertaken very much for the search for new resources that would otherwise be unavailable, thereby creating a global position for themselves.

Regarding how these newcomers can succeed without existing advantages to exploit, the explanation of the "LLL" framework (Mathews 2006) is that the newcomers are able to use resource "linkage, leverage, and learning" to close the gap with the incumbents and to win a position in global markets. This is similar to third-world MNE theories, in which partnerships and joint ventures are considered important for latecomers to expand internationally (see, for example, Wells 1983). Compared with the rather abstract LLL framework, the overarching "springboard" framework for emerging market MNEs (Luo and Tung 2007) presents the following factors as explanation: home government support for going global; the willingness of global players to share or sell strategic resources; offshore availability of standardized technology; a desire to enter key international markets; and entrepreneurial leadership.

In sum, modern MNE theory argues that latecomers tend to "explore" (or "voice") rather than to "exploit" (or "exit") their ownership advantages, by entering developed countries so as to catch up with "conventional" MNEs. Research on Chinese MNEs draws a very similar conclusion (see, for example, Child and Rodrigues 2005; Buckley et al. 2007a), concluding that Chinese firms go overseas in search of strategic assets and competencies that include market access, brands, and technology.

10.1.2   Process: Incremental or Accelerated Internationalization?

Among studies on the internationalization process, the best-known model in the academic literature is that of Jan Johanson and Jan-Erik Vahlne (1977), who developed a theory about the continuous incremental process that takes place in firms that enter foreign markets. Along with this, the conventional internationalization process logic suggests that firms enter new markets involving successively greater psychical distance, which is defined as differences in language, culture, political system, and so forth.

Modern theories on firms' internationalization, however, commonly claim that "accelerated internationalization" is the strategy often adopted by latecomer MNEs (see, for example, Mathews 2002). That they are "not path dependent nor evolutionary" is another feature of emerging market MNEs (Luo and Tung 2007, 2). A common explanation is that they are accelerating in search of advantages that they do not possess; the LLL model (Mathews 2006, 13) provides insights into how this could happen. In this view, latecomers make use of prior international connections, leveraging their own expansion through the use of such connections (such as contractors to existing MNEs), or being carried by a global customer into a new market.

10.1.3   Entry Mode: From Simple to Complicated?

Firms that internationalize have many choices of entry mode into the foreign market. The traditional path has been to move incrementally from low-commitment modes, such as exporting, to moderate-commitment modes, such as joint ventures, to reach high-commitment modes, such as greenfield entry or acquisitions.

International joint ventures (IJVs) have been suggested as a better choice over other modes, as they provide opportunities for each partner to gain access to existing knowledge and develop new knowledge (see, for example, Kogut 1988). Also, they are less risky when compared with acquisitions and greenfield investments. However, a striking problem is that of how to address the fact that many firms with superior technology are reluctant to transfer their superior technology to their partners. Paul W. Beamish and Iris Berdrow (2003) suggest that IJVs are not typically motivated by learning outcomes, because learning takes time, increases costs, and does not improve efficiency in the short term.

By contrast, acquisitions have many points in their favor. Firms' desires to realize synergies have been found to be the predominant explanation for cross-border acquisitions (see, for example, Seth, Song, and Pettit 2000). In other cases, firms make acquisitions to preempt their competitors. Compared with IJV and greenfield investment, an acquisition enables a firm to buy not only tangible, but also intangible, assets such as brands, local market knowledge, and relationships (see, for example, Eun, Kolodny, and Scheraga 1996). The research based on modern IB theory has discovered that many MNEs from developing countries directly invest in developed countries through acquisitions, in order to obtain advanced technologies and market access. They are characterized by a series of "aggressive, risk-taking measures by proactively acquiring or buying critical assets" (Luo and Tung 2007, 16) from mature MNEs to "catch up with incumbents" (16).

10.1.4   Impulses: Push or Pull?

Conventional MNEs pursue internationalization when their capabilities are "ready." Push or pull factors seem less relevant. However, modern MNE theories view the "first-wave" internationalization of latecomer MNEs, mainly from Japan, as driven more by push factors and "second-wave" firms, mainly from the Republic of Korea and Taiwan Province of China, more by pull factors. The springboard behavior of emerging markets MNEs is said to be fostered, or propelled, by several critical forces, including: (1) home government support for going global; (2) willingness of global players to share or sell strategic resources and offshore availability of standardized technology; (3) corporate entrepreneurship and strong motivation to enter key foreign markets; (4) increasing competitive pressure from global rivals; and (5) quick changes in technological and market landscapes and a heightened borderless world economy. The second force mentioned above is categorized as a pulling force, the fifth force can be both pull and push, and the remainder are push factors. In other words, there are both push and pull factors to drive current emerging market MNEs to internationalize differently from conventional MNEs.

10.2   Application of Chinese Company Findings to Theoretical Issues

In this section, we briefly describe three Chinese companies and their acquisitions, and then discuss the extent to which the Chinese experience can enrich the current MNE literature, relative to the four major points of disagreement between conventional and modern versions of MNE theories reviewed in the earlier section.

Nanjing Automobile (hereafter Nanjing), the first company we examined, is one of the oldest Chinese state-owned vehicle manufacturers. Nanjing was among the earliest Chinese automobile firms to receive foreign direct investment (FDI), in the form of technology transfer from Italy's Fiat Group, between 1986 and 1994. By 2004, Nanjing had an annual production capacity of 200,000 vehicles. It benefited from China's massive automobile market when its IJV with Iveco (Fiat's truck division) introduced a popular light-duty bus in 2000. However, with the increasingly open Chinese market and the entry of foreign MNEs, demand for Nanjing's models soon declined. Eventually, Nanjing was unable to produce at full capacity. In 2004, the Chinese automotive market was prospering, with total sales increasing by 15.5% per annum, whereas Nanjing showed a 5% decrease and a loss of over 300 million yuan (approximately US$37 million). It ranked eleventh in the domestic market in terms of revenues, far from its ambition to be among China's top five automobile producers and to be one of the most important passenger carmakers. According to a senior manager interviewed in 2005 and 2006, Nanjing needed a new strategy, if only for its survival.

Given this background, the opportunity to buy MG Rover in 2005 was very attractive. Despite MG Rover's financial difficulties, which had led to its bankruptcy, Nanjing believed MG Rover's technology was still world class. By paying GB£55 million, Nanjing obtained MG Rover's engine plant and other facilities, five Rover car brands, the opportunity to sell in Europe, and an existing network of procurement, selling, and service in Europe. Nanjing expected these assets to enable it to produce competitive cars, so as to obtain a stronger market position in China and to establish an exporting position in Europe. Nanjing's strategy to attract Chinese customers (particularly the newly rich middle class) was by "localizing" the brand; for example, by giving the new car the wonderful Chinese name "ming jue" with upper-class connotations and a similar pronunciation to MG Rover. European customers would be attracted by a high quality car, but at a much lower price than Rover had charged previously, the result of cost savings in car components and administration, as China was already one of the world's largest and cheapest car component makers.

The Lenovo Group was the second company, founded in 1984 by Liu Chuanzhi and eleven colleagues as a spinoff from the China Science Academy. It began by trading IT products, as most Chinese IT firms did at that time, when the domestic personal computer market was full of foreign brands. Gradually, and thanks to the fast growth and segmentation of the Chinese market and a wide range of products that met the demand of most Chinese customers, Lenovo became the number-one PC vendor in China, and remained in this position for nine consecutive years. In 2005, Lenovo still had about one-third of the market. In 2004, Lenovo announced that it would acquire IBM's global PC business for US$1.25 billion.

The important question was why Lenovo, with such a good position, needed to acquire IBM's PC business, which had been making losses for many years before the acquisition. According to our interviews, the primary explanation behind this was Lenovo's desire to pursue synergies between the two entities, to speed up its process, and to reduce the cost of entering foreign markets. This was to be achieved through leveraging Lenovo's strength in China and IBM PC's strength in advanced countries, developing procurement capabilities, optimizing supply relationships, and streamlining end-to-end processes from order through to fulfillment. By making use of such synergies, Lenovo expected to be able to "compete in more segments of all markets" (Lenovo 2005, 19).

A further question emerged as to why a company as strong as Lenovo needed to pay such a high price to acquire a foreign brand in order to expand into foreign markets, rather than settling for its most familiar and prospering home market. A crucial explanation emerging from our research was that the fast-growing domestic market had not only nurtured Lenovo's growth, but also attracted other global giants to enter China, which threatened Lenovo's sustainable competitive advantage. Despite Lenovo's large market share in China's PC market, the high-end segments had been mainly occupied by foreign firms such as IBM. Lenovo's key competitive advantage was its design and manufacturing niche, featuring PCs suitable for the Chinese. This advantage differentiated Lenovo from its competitors, Dell and HP, but was gradually diminishing as Dell and HP gained more knowledge of the local market and Chinese consumers. In global markets, even after acquiring IBM, Lenovo's market share was still far below that of its competitors. Such a situation clearly challenged Lenovo's strategy of focusing on low- and medium-end users and on the Chinese domestic market. According to Liu, by 2004 the company was at a crossroads and had to consider two options: globalization or diversification. Unfortunately, diversification had limited success because "almost every sector has been occupied by MNEs" (interview with Liu) and, also, because of the shortfall of internal management skills for diversification. Globalization became the only option for Lenovo.

Lenovo's acquisition of IBM's PC unit was, as shown above, not simply motivated by the desire to internationalize, but by other factors, such as the intense competition in its domestic market and the need to access new markets in order to leverage its own advantages, such as low costs. It was IBM's willingness to sell the brand and technology of its loss-making PC unit that eventually enabled Lenovo to internationalize. This supports the emerging market MNE springboard perspective.

The third company was Huawei Technologies, a telecom equipment vendor established as a private company in Shenzhen in 1988 with a seven-person investment of RMB20,000 (US$2,400). Huawei faced a market with great opportunities and challenges at the end of 1980s. On the one hand, the Chinese telecom equipment market was dominated by foreign companies with very high profits; on the other hand, many medium and low-end customers could not afford to buy the high-quality and expensive imported products (Xing 2005). Relying on an initial strategy of concentrating its overall capacity in R&D so as to make breakthroughs one product at a time in order to meet customer demand, Huawei succeeded in its expansion from rural to urban areas, from the lower to the higher end of the market, and from imitating foreign products and technology to independent innovation.

By the end of 2004, Huawei's products and solutions had been deployed by over 300 operators in over ninety countries. It had also set up eight regional headquarters and fifty-five branches around the world to provide services to its customers. By 2006, it had grown to be one of the largest telecommunications equipment manufacturers in China, with a revenue of 65.6 billion yuan (US$10 billion) in 2006, of which sales from overseas business accounted for 65%.

Having witnessed Huawei's rapid growth and internationalization, one could wonder why it launched a GB£600 million bid to acquire Marconi in 2005, the United Kingdom's last remaining telecommunication equipment provider, which was in severe financial difficulties. Furthermore, one could further wonder why this bid was topped by one of its competitors, Ericsson, which paid GB£1.2 billion for Marconi.

In a 2006 speech, Ren, chief executive officer (CEO) of Huawei, provided the two most convincing explanations: to get customers, wherever they are, and to obtain technology, wherever suitable. With regard to the first goal, Ren believed that the Chinese telecommunications market is the largest, and also one of the most open, markets in the world, which has attracted many global telecommunication giants into China. As a result, "the best food has all been eaten up by the global giants and what we can do is to have those leftovers" (Ren's interview). Huawei therefore understood early on that it must attack those markets in which global giants were unwilling or unable to succeed, such as rural markets in China and low-to-medium-end products in global markets. Internationalization has been one of the earliest strategies set up by Huawei (Ren 2006; Xing 2005). With regard to the second goal, Ren admitted that there were still large technology gaps between Huawei and its global competitors. Acquiring a company such as Marconi would have permitted Huawei to reduce such gaps and to fulfill its "truly global" ambition: first, Marconi possessed world-class technology that Huawei sought. Second, Marconi could have assisted Huawei in accessing European markets by providing both its long-held knowledge of local markets and its relationships with local giant carriers, such as BT. The acquisition became even more important when Huawei was selected as one of the suppliers of BT's twenty-first-century network.

10.2.1 Exploit Versus Explore

Do Chinese firms internationalize to exploit advantages (supporting traditional IB theory) or to explore and access advantages (supporting modern theory)? The descriptions above indicate that our findings are more in line with modern MNE theories and also consistent with much earlier research on Chinese MNEs, in that none of the three Chinese acquirers had "intrinsic" advantages (Bartlett et al. 2004, 4), such as original product invention, high-end product technology, and well-known brands. By contrast, all three acquisition efforts included the obvious intention to obtain advantages, such as "know-how" in producing the highest quality, well-known brands (such as IBM and Rover) and shortcuts to international markets.

At the same time, while modern MNE theories emphasize that latecomer MNEs internationalize mainly in order to explore competitive advantage, our findings provide substantial evidence that the Chinese MNEs do have various competitive advantages to exploit. This indicates that the application of the OLI model to Chinese firms is still valid. We determined that Chinese MNEs particularly enjoy the following competitive advantages:

Innovative products for niche markets. In the words of the former Lenovo CEO, Liu, "we do not have original product technology but applicable technology and niche market inventions" (2006). This is almost identical with Ren's claims regarding Huawei's technology strength. Such niche markets and applicable technology have proved to be in great demand by a large number of Chinese customers. For example, Lenovo's earlier success, in the 1980s and early 1990s, heavily relied on its innovative product "Legend Chinese System" (*Lixiang Hanka*), which enabled the PC products sold by Lenovo to be compatible with Chinese language systems. Again, in the late 1990s, Lenovo successfully manufactured basic, easy-to-use models: one model allowed the user to connect to the Internet and load a browser with the touch of a single key (Lin 2005). Similarly, Huawei's switch and Nanjing's light-duty bus reached the right markets at the right time. Such niche-market technologies proved to be important for these companies to win competitive advantages in not only Chinese markets, but also in other developing countries having similar demands.

Tremendous cost advantages in terms of manufacturing, labor, and overhead costs. Interviewees from all three companies confirmed that low-cost labor is a large advantage. For example, the manufacturing cost of a Lenovo PC is about one-third that of an IBM PC, according to two interviewees, in 2005. The cost for Huawei's research and development (R&D) employees is only one-fifth of that in Western telecommunication companies. Low-cost advantages might also help uncompetitive state-owned enterprises (SOEs), such as Nanjing Automobile, by allowing them to leverage their low-cost automobile components, available from China (e.g., to the acquired MG Rover technology). Moreover, low-cost advantages also ensure that these Chinese companies provide the most flexible and effective services to customers.

Established management system. Both Huawei and Lenovo have developed extremely innovative, unique management systems. Interviews and numerous internal speeches and documents have revealed that the two companies have shared some common management features. Besides the most noteworthy marketing strategy, which is dealt with in the next paragraph, here we would like to highlight three features. First, a highly centralized management system commanded by the entrepreneur leadership. Second, effective management systems that integrate both Western-style scientific management and innovative management styles specific to the respective companies. For example, both Lenovo and Huawei spent large sums to purchase and adopt world-class management systems. Lenovo adopted the ERP system from SAP, a Germany company, to ensure the most effective and efficient use of company resources (Lin 2005, 297–301), while Huawei applied IBM's IPD system to reform Huawei's product-development model, shorten the production time, reduce costs, and improve quality (Cheng and Liu 2006, 246). Meanwhile, both companies had many innovative systems, such as Lenovo's strict policy of being "on time" for conferences and appointments, and Huwei's policy that senior managers must have their mobile phones on twenty-four hours a day, to ensure that the most effective service was provided to its customers. Third, both had a corporate culture that advocates employees' loyalty and commitment to the mission and interests of the company. Extending working hours and sacrificing holidays to meet deadlines for customers are common in both companies. In Ren's words, "[w]e lag far behind the global competitors. We can only catch up by working every minute that our rivals are drinking tea and coffee."

Innovative and effective marketing and service. Lenovo and Huawei are excellent cases that integrate marketing strategies and techniques of both Western style and Chinese origin. For example, in 1999, Lenovo copied Hewlett Packard's dealer distribution system (see above), but, at the same time, this system was improved by combining it with fast, responsive, and nationwide customer service. Up to now, Lenovo has continued to enjoy this competitive advantage in the Chinese market, where other MNEs are unable to provide similar customer service. Huawei's marketing is regarded as one of the most effective in China (Tang 2004). On the one hand, it respects the "international rule," which regards international telecommunication exhibitions as the major channel for demonstrating and advertising telecom products. On the other hand, Huawei made the best use of a *guanxi* strategy: it has established representative offices across China in order to allow its marketing staff to be close to clients. Furthermore, it improved its marketing system by forming joint ventures with local telecommunication authorities that were, in fact, the major customers of Huawei. This enabled Huawei to secure a large local market share. Huawei's marketing system has been described as a net from which no potential customers can escape (ibid.).

Institutional advantages. Chinese companies also enjoy advantages arising from institutional factors. For example, the marketing capacity of Huawei and Lenovo benefits from their superior ability to cope with institutional barriers at home, and their deep understanding of *guanxi* and how to deal with Chinese institutions. One of the most important advantages Chinese MNEs enjoy is state support.

The three companies differ in ownership: one is state owned, one is private, and one is public, but all were supported by the state in their acquisition efforts, albeit in different ways. Huawei, a private company, has received billions of yuan in loans and bank guarantees from the State Development Bank and China's Import and Export Bank. Lenovo, a neither purely state owned nor private company, has benefited from its connection with China's Science Academy since its establishment (e.g., earning income by doing business with the Academy and receiving support to establish affiliates in Hong

Kong [China]). Many more examples have been described in the literature on Lenovo and Huawei (see, for example, Lin 2005; Cheng and Liu 2006).

Nanjing is the most instructive case. Compared with Huawei and Lenovo, Nanjing was the weakest firm in terms of its lack of technological innovation and its typical state-owned management style. However, with political and financial support from both the Jiangsu provincial authorities and the Nanjing City Government, Nanjing's Special Team for Negotiation with MG Rover in the United Kingdom "was confident and ready to bid whatever price," according to a senior manager involved in these negotiations. This case indicates that the institutional advantages that many Chinese companies enjoy could be as important as other ownership advantages in enabling MNEs from developing countries to succeed in their internationalization.

Chinese firms internationalize in order to acquire necessary competences, but they also own certain competences, which they can exploit and which help them to make major foreign acquisitions. This indicates that the OLI theory remains valid, even though its context and content may need to be revised. This is exactly what Dunning and Lundan (2006) have acknowledged.

10.2.2 Choice of Entry Mode

The Chinese cases also fit the modern MNE theory: in recent years they have increasingly favored acquisitions and other direct investments. However, we discovered some very different reasons for their choice of entry mode, which are closely related to their domestic environment.

A striking feature of recent Chinese acquisitions is that all these firms had previously formed IJVs. In particular, Nanjing Automobile already had a total of twelve IJVs, but still made every effort to acquire MG Rover with the stated purpose of using its brands and acquiring its technology. This phenomenon drew our attention because it obviously does not support the current wisdom, which views IJVs as a valuable vehicle for partners to learn from each other.

The answers we discovered from the three cases, particularly the Nanjing case, do not support the current wisdom that IJVs normally enable both partners to access existing knowledge. By stating this, we do not deny the spillover and demonstration effects of inward FDI in China in general (see, for example, Buckley et al. 2007b; Wei and Liu 2006). However, this does not prove that MNEs are willing to transfer their best technology to their Chinese partners. Technology diffusion may exist regardless of the owner's desire. In Nanjing's case, by 1995, and after ten years of technology transfer, Nanjing was unable to produce a light-duty bus based on the technology received ("not even able to understand the design maps fully," according to a senior manager in 2006). Also, the cooperation was difficult because of the different interests of the two partners. While the Chinese demanded the most up-to-date production line, so as to be stronger when facing increasingly competitive rivals in the market, the foreign partner did not agree to meet the demand because it had different purposes, according to the interviewees in Nanjing, namely: (1) maximizing profit from the existing production line and (2) not losing control to the

Chinese partner by risking the diffusion of its best technology. Such a situation was not limited to Nanjing. One interviewee, the former deputy minister of China's automobile industry, pointed out that many Chinese automobile firms suffered similar problems with their IJV partners.

Therefore, the revealed truth from Nanjing through interviews, in 2005, was that the Nanjing-Rover venture, followed by the acquisition of MG Rover, was expected, according to one interviewee, "to generate pressure on the current IJVs so as to stimulate the foreign partners to make more commitments to the IJVs such as upgrading new technology in time." Being asked how to generate pressure, the interviewee explained us that, if the current IJVs were still reluctant to provide key technologies, Nanjing would put more weight on the new venture with Rover, which, they believed, would certainly stimulate other foreign partners to increase inputs into their IJVs with Nanjing.

10.2.3 *Incremental Versus Accelerated Internationalization*

The foreign acquisitions by Chinese firms are typical examples of accelerated internationalization, a main theme of modern IB theories. Since the opening of China's economy in the early 1980s, the bulk of Chinese international activities have been limited to exporting. Furthermore, since 2000, a majority of this exporting activity has occurred via foreign MNEs that have entered China to source products (amounting to 57% of total exports in 2004) (MOC 2005). This export behavior fits well with conventional IB theory, in which China has been exploiting its factor cost advantage. But suddenly, after 2000 (and especially since 2004), many Chinese companies have begun to make overseas acquisitions. A significant aspect of this trend is that acquisitions made by the Chinese firms have increased dramatically. In our three cases, before acquiring foreign firms, all three had limited export but no overseas production experience. Moreover, they were more active in developing countries. What they acquired, or intended to acquire, were well-known firms in mainly developed countries such as the United States and the United Kingdom.

In order to have a better understanding of this accelerated internationalization, we must recognize how fiercely global MNEs are competing with Chinese firms in their backyard. This, together with the other factors as shown in the next section, is the most important driver pushing Chinese firms to expand overseas at a rapid pace.

10.2.4 *Push Versus Pull*

While the internationalization of first-wave MNEs is driven by push factors, and that of second-wave by pull factors, we think that Chinese MNEs are driven by both push and pull factors. Among numerous push and pull factors, the following are identified by interviewees to be the most relevant: already completed primary capital accumulation; government support; MNEs' willingness to sell no-longer-profitable businesses, and the huge market for low-cost and technology-intensive products in global markets. Among these, we found that the most common and important push factor for the three cases examined is the fierce competition these firms face in their domestic market. This feature is described as one common push factor for emerging market MNEs (Luo and Tung 2007), but we would argue that this feature is of even greater importance in the Chinese context. As widely recognized, "China is already a much more open market than Japan and South Korea were when they started to become IT powers, and its barriers to entry are still falling as it implements promises made as part of its 2001 accession to the World Trade Organization.... [P]articularly, the pace at which China is opening sectors gives local companies limited time to develop" (*Financial Times* 2005).

10.3 An Exploratory Comparison of Chinese and Indian OFDI

10.3.1 Selected Indian OFDI Transactions

In this section we briefly present findings on three Indian firms, with a view to furthering the understanding of the Chinese cases. The brief cases pertain to Maruti (counterpoint to Nanjing), Wipro (counterpoint to Lenovo), and Infosys (counterpoint to Huawei).

Maruti began as the automobile project of a prominent Indian politician (Indira Gandhi's younger son) in the late 1970s. The Government of India took it over, and eventually it became a joint venture with the Japanese company Suzuki. The partially state-owned Maruti-Suzuki was run by officers of the elite Indian Administrative Service, whose familiarity with dealing with the country's red tape served the company well (Pingle 1997). By the 1990s, Maruti was India's dominant car company, overtaking the extant Indian competition, including the ubiquitous Ambassador car produced by Hindustan Motors, the previous market leader.

In terms of internationalization, as its popularity within India grew, Maruti began exploring business opportunities overseas. Maruti has exported cars to a range of countries but, until very recently, the majority of its international markets were other Asian countries. In the period following the economic liberalization of the early 1990s, India began to witness growing levels of inward FDI from prominent international automakers. Korean companies, such as Hyundai, have enjoyed success in the Indian market, and Western MNEs, such as Ford, have consistently increased investment in the country. Moreover, the venerable conglomerate Tata entered the market as well. This competition has placed considerable pressure on Maruti's market share, which, in turn, has only intensified the company's domestic market focus. Retaining market share through a steady stream of new models at competitive prices seems the main goal. Consequently—and in contrast to Nanjing—OFDI does not seem to be a priority for Maruti. Instead, Maruti has gone through one of the most intense business-restructuring and cost-cutting exercise, and has successfully exported tens of thousands of cars a year to overseas markets, not only in Asia, but also in Europe. Currently, European countries account for 56% of Maruti's exports. Africa became its second largest export market. The company hopes to start exporting at least 200,000 cars per annum by 2011.

Wipro Technologies is an NYSE-listed company with over US$3 billion in revenues, generated from IT services, including software and business process outsourcing (BPO). Wipro is headed by a Stanford engineering graduate, Azim Premji, whose 80% stake in the company reputedly makes him India's richest man. Originally founded after World War II, Wipro began with non-IT interests in edible oils and detergents, but it is as an IT player that Wipro is best known. Having begun in the 1970s to exploit the void left by IBM's departure from India over policy differences, Wipro has grown beyond a hardware focus (e.g., PCs), aided by import-substitution policies, to emerge as one of the top-three Indian IT service companies, along with Tata Consulting Services and Infosys. Wipro was the partner of choice for the global conglomerate GE in areas such as medical systems.

Typically for an Indian IT company, international business is critical to Wipro's top- and bottom line. Notwithstanding this strong international focus, it was only in the twenty-first century that Wipro engaged in OFDI. Commenting in 2001, Premji intended to make international acquisitions with the following rationale: "what we would be looking to acquire are brand names—not projects, or technologies, or market access" (Ramamurti 2001, 17). Yet, when Wipro subsequently spent about US$300 million in a series of modest-sized deals, there were benefits in terms of capabilities and client relationships. To illustrate this, when Wipro acquired NerveWire in the United States, it also received a lucrative contract with General Motors. Premji has described this strategy as a "string-of-pearls" approach. The latest development in Wipro's foreign acquisitions indicates more clearly that the rationale for acquisitions is essentially that of strategic fit. In 2007, Wipro, armed with cash reserves of US$900 million, acquired U.S. infrastructure company Infocrossing, in an all-cash deal worth US$600 million. This was the single biggest acquisition undertaken by an Indian IT company. Wipro promised that all 900 employees of the acquired company would remain in the United States. Thus, rather than labor arbitration, Wipro seemed primarily interested in obtaining capabilities in infrastructure management and in the healthcare sector that Infocrossing specializes in. Additionally, Wipro benefits from a deeper presence in the United States, while the company can leverage its hosted and managed services to provide IT outsourcing solutions. Indeed, as the company claimed, the acquisition was a "perfect fit" (17) for its technology infrastructure services, and gives the company an "undisputed lead" (17) in remote infrastructure management services. This marked Wipro's twelfth IT acquisition, its ninth in the previous twenty-four months alone, as part of its "string-of-pearls" strategy. The indications are that Wipro's future acquisitions may not necessarily be as large as Lenovo's, but they must enhance strategic fit as in the case of Lenovo.

The third Indian firm we examined was Infosys Technologies Ltd. It was started in 1981 by seven people with only US$250, which was almost identical to Huawei's start. Today, like Wipro, Infosys is a global leader in IT and consulting with revenues of over US$4 billion. Infosys is arguably one of India's most respected companies and is routinely referred to as the bell-wether of Indian IT. In its early years, Infosys rapidly eschewed the domestic market, focusing instead on providing IT services to international markets. Furthermore, it boasts one reasonably successful software product (Finacle), which has been installed in many banks around the world. More generally, Infosys is widely feted in Indian corporate circles as exemplary in managing people and corporate governance, apart from its well-known technology skills. Indeed, a visit to the Infosys campus in Bangalore became part of the itinerary of visiting dignitaries to India, including Bill Clinton and Tony Blair.

Despite a strong reputation for excellence and a generally entrepreneurial posture, Infosys had been markedly coy in terms of making international acquisitions, until very recently. In 2003, it acquired an Australian company for approximately US$25 million and, more recently, in 2008, bought BPO facilities from Philips for a similar amount. Founder and CEO Narayan Murthi's explanation for this somewhat surprisingly timid track record is: "We don't believe in acquisitions to achieve top lines. We are more enamoured by bottom lines. Most acquisitions by companies are failures…Ownership of assets are not easy. Being an Indian company, it is difficult to take on people from countries outside India" (Padmanabhan 2006, 1). This remark illustrates that, notwithstanding considerable technological skill, the arena of international acquisitions represents a major challenge for latecomer MNEs.

However, Infosys offered a megadeal of US$753 million to acquire Axon in 2008. Axon, like Infosys, is among two dozen companies worldwide that implement back-office software systems. The company is based in the United Kingdom, but about half of Axon's revenue comes from the United States. It had a global presence in thirty countries, servicing clients that included BP and Microsoft. According to Gopalakrishnan, the CEO of Infosys, the acquisition would allow Infosys to compete more effectively with rivals such as Accenture, Oracle, and Cap Gemini on the international stage, and to enhance significantly its global reach, scale, and the ability to participate in large transformational deals (*Times* 2008). However, another Indian company, HCL Technologies, made a higher offer for Axon, which was favored by Axon's board. Following the downturn, Infosys did not make a counter-offer. This unexpected failure was similar to Huawei's in the Marconi case. At the same time, while Huawei has made several successful acquisitions after the Marconi case, Infosys is seeking acquisition opportunities in Germany, France, and Japan. Despite the slowdown in winning new outsourcing contracts, it is considering healthcare and energy and utilities as the two major areas for possible acquisitions (*Business Week* 2009).

10.3.2   *Comparing Chinese and Indian OFDI Transactions*

Despite the admittedly exploratory nature of our Sino-Indian comparison, we would argue that the experiences of Indian counterpoints strengthen the main argument in this chapter, which is that the internationalization process of Chinese firms is closely related to the special characteristics of the environment of emerging markets. Interestingly, our Sino-Indian comparison suggests that there are many similarities between the two. First, leading firms in India, like their counterparts in China, consider M&As as an important mode of acquiring strategic assets, especially in recent years. This can be evidenced by the dramatic rise of outward M&As by Indian firms, as shown in table 10.2. Wipro and Infosys have both been engaged actively in M&As. Maruti seems to favor exporting more than acquisitions at the moment, but this does not exclude the possibility of future acquisitions when the company needs them. Domestic rivals, such as Tata Motors, have already made such a move in acquiring foreign automobile firms. The possible indication, in our view, is that the difference between market environment and competitiveness of Nanjing and Maruti determines their different attitudes toward the choice of entry mode in their internationalization.

Second, it is widely acknowledged that, before 1990, India's MNEs were generally market seeking in low-technology areas, such as textiles and leather goods; but, since 2000, they have tended to be much more focused on strategic asset seeking, including more acquisitions in developed countries (Kumar 2004, 2006). Facing global competition, firms such as Wipro and Infosys are still seeking strategic assets to match the intense competition within the industry. Their intention to acquire strategic assets is obvious and remains a priority. With this comparison in mind, the Chinese companies' actions in pursuing radical acquisitions become more easily understandable.

Third, as regards the capability of internationalization and acquisition, these Indian firms possess strong ownership advantages. While India's IT and software companies, such as Wipro's and Infosys' core competences are apparent, leading firms in other industries also possess a certain level of competitive advantage. Although Maruti has not made any large acquisitions so far, its ability to make lower-cost cars for exportation is well known. Other carmakers from India are also exporting or operating in many developed markets, based on cost advantages and new models fitting these markets. Automotive designs in India cost US$60 per hour as opposed to US$800 per hour in European design houses. The Indian-developed Reva car costs less than half the price of the next cheapest electric car sold anywhere in the world (Srivastava 2009). This also means that India is set to emerge as the preferred R&D center. While China's labor cost advantages are prominent in manufacturing, and are strongly linked to acquisitive moves (e.g., Nanjing), India's cost advantages also facilitate Maruti's success in export and potential acquisitions.

Finally, whereas, arguably, the government plays a more active and explicit role in China, through diplomatic efforts and financial support, we must not underestimate the different, but crucially important, role played by the Indian government. It seems that India's OFDI pace is slower than that of China. The causes include, according to many researches, not only the later start of economic reform and the much smaller size of the domestic market in India, but also the different government policies of the two countries in promoting OFDI (Huang and Khanna 2003). In the earlier phase of Indian economic development (mainly before 2004), the Indian government implemented a more restrictive policy regime for OFDI, aimed at boosting domestic investment and enabling Indian enterprises to learn adaptive capabilities. Since 2004, the government has encouraged Indian companies to invest abroad in order to reduce the lack of strategic asset to sustain the domestic development processes. More importantly, the Indian government has implemented a liberal and innovative policy in encouraging the growth of entrepreneurship and private firms' internationalization (Singh and Jain 2009).

Even though the experiences of Indian counterpoints strengthen the observation that the internationalization of Chinese firms is closely related to the special characteristics of the environment of emerging markets, they do not suggest that all emerging market MNEs should pursue the same strategy of internationalization. Although China and India are both emerging markets, there are some interesting contrasts. First, whereas China's large domestic market drives acquisitions, in the Indian cases it was the attraction of a large international market (e.g., for Wipro) that was key. The possible explanation for this difference might be the difference in domestic market size and the intensity of competition between the two countries. The similarly populated India does not produce the same market demand and market size as does China. Consequently, the two markets have attracted different amount of IFDI, leading to different intensities of competition in many industries. Although India's car industry has become more competitive as a result of the entry of MNEs, this growing domestic market is not yet as competitive as China's. Maruti is still India's largest passenger car company, accounting for over 50% of the domestic car market. This may explain why Maruti is more focused on the domestic market, and relies more on exports (rather than on FDI).

Second, the government support policies are different, as discussed above, which may provide different incentives for indigenous firms and lead to different motivations and firm behaviors in the internationalization process. Tables 10.1 and 10.2 show that the large-scale foreign acquisitions made by Chinese MNEs were mainly made by large, resource-seeking, state-owned firms, while India's acquirers were mainly large private firms in manufacturing, IT, and the pharmaceutical sector. It remains to be seen whether such differences relate more to the different development stages of the two countries, or to the different government policies in shaping the internationalization process of their MNEs. Looking at the weaknesses of stated owned firms, and encouraged by successful private firms, Huang and Khanna (2003) speculated that India's policy may produce a more sustainable future for Indian firms' internationalization process, and also that India may overtake China in the future.

Conclusions

This research demonstrates how the overseas acquisitions of Chinese firms have not only provided evidence, but also enriched the content, of both conventional and modern MNE theories. First, Chinese MNEs' internationalization is more in line with modern MNE theories, especially the springboard perspective for emerging market MNEs (e.g., both explore advantages via internationalization; they do not follow the traditional pace and pattern of the foreign entry mode; and they tend to be imitators, fast followers or niche players). Such behavior is not only driven by the desire to acquire assets and opportunities, but also fostered by government support and impelled by intense competition.

At the same time, we cannot deny the validity of the OLI framework in terms of the ownership advantages that Chinese firms possess, although the context and content Dunning set for his OLI model might be very different from what Chinese firms now possess. Both Lenovo and Huawei had won their market position by being customer-focused applied-technology leaders before internationalizing. Even Nanjing possesses advantages, such as the full support of local government and its prospect of utilizing Rover technology in combination with low-cost components in China. This may also warn latecomer MNEs that there are still certain prerequisites to be met for firms in their internationalization process. This finding does not completely contradict modern MNE theories: the springboard perspective (Luo and Tung 2007) reminds us that emerging MNEs can exploit competitive advantages in other emerging markets; and the LLL model also considers how to leverage dragon multinationals' own competencies.

Second, MNEs in many developing countries "tend to rely more heavily on non-equity joint ventures" (Giddy and Young 1982, 55–78) rather than jump to the assumed final stage of the foreign entry mode to make aggressive acquisitions, as Chinese firms are doing. Japanese and Korean firms also acquired foreign firms when beginning their internationalization, as did some emerging market MNEs (Luo and Tung 2007); but Chinese firms have unique reasons to do so. Interviewees from all of our cases emphasized that the fact that China has one of the world's largest markets, as well as its World Trade Organization membership, has led many global firms to enter China, occupying the high-end market segment. Domestic companies had no choice but to "break out" (*tu wei*) to seek new market opportunities. At the same time, domestic firms are frustrated by the difficulty in accessing core technologies from their IJV partners, which further reinforced their intention to enter global markets and, through radical methods such as acquisitions, secure their global position. This was clearly reflected in Lenovo and Huawei's cases in which both learned from MNEs, by being the agents of global firms initially, then imitators, and finally contenders.

Third, the features of Chinese firms' internationalization are closely related to the special characteristics of the environment of Chinese firms, which include at least: (1) the very large scale of the domestic economy and market; (2) domestic market internationalization through the entry of foreign firms; (3) great cost advantages regarding labor, overhead, manufacturing, etc.; and (4) government support in many forms, from diplomacy to finance. These country characteristics appear in few countries other than the other three members of the BRIC group (Brazil, Russia, and India), each of which has some, but not all, of these features. While the experiences of Indian counterparts strengthens the argument that the internationalization processes of Chinese firms are closely related to the special characteristics of the environment of emerging markets, they do not suggest that all emerging market MNEs should pursue the same strategy of internationalization.

Note

1. In this chapter, OFDI figures refer to nonfinance FDI.

References

Bartlett, Christopher A., Sumantra Ghoshal, and Julian Birkinshaw (2004). *Transnational Management: Text, Cases, and Readings in Cross-Border Management* (London: McGraw Hill).

Beamish, Paul W. and Iris Berdrow (2003). "Learning from IJVs: the unintended outcome," *Long Range Planning* 36 (3), pp. 285–303.

Boisot, Max H. (2004). "Notes on the internationalization of Chinese firms" (Barcelona, Spain: Open University of Catalonia), mimeo.

Buckley, Peter J., Jeremy L. Clegg, Adam R. Cross, Xin Liu, Hinrich Voss, and Ping Zheng (2007a). "The determinants of Chinese outward foreign direct investment," *Journal of International Business Studies* 38, pp. 499–518.

Buckley, Peter J., Jeremy L. Clegg, and Chengqi Wang (2007b). "Is the relationship between inward FDI and spillover effects linear? An empirical examination of the case of china," *Journal of International Business Studies* 38 (3), pp. 447–59.

Buckley Peter J. and Mark Casson (1985). *The Economic Theory of the Multinational Enterprise: Selected Papers* (London: Macmillan).

Business Week (2009). "Infosys seeks acquisitions in Germany, France, Japan," March 5, available at http://investing.businessweek.com/research/stocks/snapshot/snapshot.asp?symbol=Infy, last visited March 12, 2009.

Cai, Kevin G. (1999). "Outward foreign direct investment: a novel dimension of China's integration into the regional and global economy," *China Quarterly* 160, pp. 856–80.

Cheng, Dongshen and Lili Liu (2006). *Huawei's Operation and Management* (Beijing: Contemporary China).

Child, John and Suzana B. Rodrigues (2005). "The internationalization of Chinese firms: a case for theoretical extension?" *Management and Organization Review* 1 (3), pp. 381–410.

Deng, Ping (2004). "Outward investment by Chinese MNEs: motivations and implications," *Business Horizons* 47, pp. 8–16.

Dunning, John H. (1981). *International Production and the Multinational Enterprises* (London: Allen & Unwin).

Dunning, John H. and Sarianna M. Lundan (2006). "The MNE as a creator, fashioner and respondent to institutional change," in Simon Collinson and Gleen Morgan, eds., *Images of the Multinational Firm* (Oxford: Blackwell), chapter 6.

Eun, Cheol S., Richard Kolodny, and Carl Scheraga (1996). "Cross-border acquisitions and shareholder wealth: test of the synergy and internalization hypothesis," *Journal of Banking and Finance* 20, pp. 1559–82.

Exim India (2008). *Developing Countries: Globalisation through Overseas Investment* (Mumbai: Export-Import Bank of India).

Financial Times (2005). "The myth behind China as a high-tech colossus," January 25, p. 17.

Giddy, Ian H. and Stephen Young (1982). "Conventional theory and unconventional multinationals: do new forms of multinational firms require new theories," in Alan Rugman, ed., *New Theories of the Multinational Enterprise* (London: Croom Helm), pp. 55–78.

Huang, Yasheng and Tarun Khanna (2003). "Can India overtake China?" *Foreign Policy*, July–August, available at http://www.foreignpolicy.com/story/story.php?storyID=13774, last visited September 20, 2007.

Hymer, Stephen H. (1960). *The International Operations of National Firms: A Study of Direct Foreign Investment* (Cambridge, MA: MIT Press).

Johanson, Jan and Jan-Erik Vahlne (1977). "The internationalization process of the firm: a model of knowledge development and increasing foreign market commitment," *Journal of International Business Studies* 8 (1), pp. 23–32.

Kindleberger, Charles P. (1970). *The International Corporation* (Cambridge, MA: MIT Press).

Kogut, Bruce (1988). "Joint ventures: theoretical and empirical perspectives," *Strategic Management Journal* 9, pp. 319–32.

Kumar, Nagesh (2004). "India," in Douglas H. Brooks and Hal Hill, eds., *Managing FDI in a Globalizing Economy: Asian Experiences* (New York: Palgrave Macmillan for ADB), pp. 119–52.

——— (2006). "Emerging multinationals: trends, patterns and determinants of outward investment by Indian enterprises" (New Delhi: Research and Information System for Developing Countries), mimeo.

Lall, Sanjaya (1984). *The New Multinationals* (New York: Wiley).

Lenovo (2005). *Lenovo Annual Report 2005* (Beijing: Lenovo Group).

Lin, Zhijun (2005). *Lenovo* (Beijing: CITIC).

Luo, Yadong and Rosalie L. Tung (2007). "International expansion of emerging market enterprises: a springboard perspective," *Journal of International Business Studies*, online version of April 19, pp. 1–18.

Mathews, John A. (2002). *Dragon Multinational: Towards a New Model for Global Growth* (New York: Oxford University Press).

——— (2006). "Dragon multinationals: new players in 21st century globalization," *Asian Pacific Journal of Management* 23, pp. 5–27.

Miller, Tom (2008). "Mainland firms triple deals abroad to $26USb; Beijing warns state-owned enterprises of investment risks," *South China Morning Post*, July 25, p.1.

Ministry of Commerce (2005). "Retrospect of China's foreign trade during the tenth Five Year Plan," available at http://gcs.mofcom.gov.cn/aarticle, last visited February 25, 2006.

Ministry of Commerce (2008). "Chinese outward FDI stock reached US$117.9 billion," Xinhua Net, September 8, available at http://news.xinhuanet.com/newscenter/2008–09/08/content_9857029.htm, last visited September 9, 2008.

Ministry of Commerce and State Statistics Bureau (2006). *Statistical Bulletin of China's Outward Foreign Direct Investment (non-Finance Part)* (Beijing: Ministry of Commerce).

Morck, Randall, Bernard Yeung, and Mingyuan Zhao (2008). "Perspectives on China's outward foreign direct investment," *Journal of International Business Studies* 39, pp. 337–50.

Nayyar, D. (2008). "Internationalization of firms from India: investment, mergers and acquisitions," *Trade and Globalization* (New Delhi: Oxford University Press).

Padmanabhan, Priya (2006). "Infosys silver jubilee special: Narayan Murthy interview," available at http://www.ciol.com/content/news/2006/106061305.asp, last visited September 15, 2007.

Pingle, Vibha (1997). "Managing state-owned enterprises: lessons from India," *International Journal of Sociology and Social Policy* 17 (7/8), pp. 179–219.

Ramamurti, Ravi (2001). "Wipro's chairman Azim Premji on building a world-class Indian company," *Academy of Management Executive* 15 (2), pp. 13–19.

Ren, Zhenfei (2006). "The practical R&D direction and our 20 years' endeavour: speech at a large scale project demonstrating conference," *Huwei People* 182, pp. 1–3.

Seth, Anju, Kean P. Song, and Richardson Pettit (2000). "Synergy, managerialism or hubris? An empirical examination of motives for foreign acquisitions of US firms," *Journal of International Business Studies* 31, pp. 387–405.

Singh, Lakhwinder and Varinder Jain (2009). "Emerging pattern of India's outward foreign direct investment under influence of state policy: A macro view," *MPRA Paper*, No. 13439, available at http://mpra.ub.uni-muenchen.de/13439, last visited March 15, 2009.

Srivastava, Siddharth (2009). "Indian automobiles making global inroads," available at http://www.dayafterindia.com/december2/auto.html, last visited March 12, 2009.

Times, August 26, 2008. "Infosys to buy UK consultancy Axon in £407m deal," available at http://business.timesonline.co.uk/tol/business/industry_sectors/technology/article4606620.ece, last visited May 7, 2010.

Tang, Shenping (2004). *Get Out of Huawei* (Beijing: China Social Science).

UNCTAD (2005). *Prospects for Foreign Direct Investment and the Strategies of Transnational Corporations, 2005–2008* (New York and Geneva: United Nations).

——— (2008). *World Investment Report: Transnational Corporations and the Infrastructure Challenge* (New York and Geneva: United Nations).

Wei, Yingqi and Xiamin Liu (2006). "Productivity spillovers from R&D, exports and FDI in China's manufacturing sector," *Journal of International Business Studies* 37 (4), pp. 544–57.

Wells, Louis T. (1983). *Third World Multinationals: The Rise of Foreign Direct Investment from Developing Countries* (Cambridge, MA: MIT Press).

Xing, Weixi (2005). "Globalization and catch-up in the Chinese telecommunications industry: the case of Huawei," unpublished Ph.D. Dissertation (Cambridge: University of Cambridge).

Yeung, Henry Wai-chung (1994). "Transnational corporations from Asian developing countries: their characteristics and competitive edge," *Journal of Asian Business* 10 (4), pp. 17–58.

Chapter 11

Unknown Multinational Enterprises: Top MNEs from Slovenia

Andreja Jaklič and Marjan Svetličič

Introduction

Even a decade ago, discussing Slovene multinational enterprises (MNEs) in Slovenia would have been akin to swearing. MNEs were perceived as the "bad guys," transferring profits abroad, hiding, and creating unbalanced development. MNEs were considered responsible for many of the country's economic problems and for leading to a culture of political dependency. MNEs were synonymous with large firms from Western industrialized countries, exploiting other (frequently less-developed) countries. Until very recently, Slovenia's own MNEs—that is, those originating in Slovenia and operating abroad—did not feature in public debates. Neoclassical thinking was also prevalent in academia during the 1990s: investing abroad was considered unpatriotic because capital was needed at home (Svetličič 1996, 4). As recently as 2008 (following the "Top 25 Slovene MNEs" press release by Vale Columbia Center on Sustainable International Investment (2008)), several major Slovene newspapers sought to interview the authors on whether Slovene firms were, in fact, MNEs, as the general belief has been that Slovenia does not have MNEs.

Such attitudinal barriers prevailed, despite the fact that Slovene MNEs greatly facilitated the transition that followed Slovenia's secession from the Socialist Federal Republic of Yugoslavia. Slovenia lost almost 50% of the domestic Yugoslav market following its declaration of independence in 1991. Strong export capabilities and an inherited network of foreign affiliates allowed firms to compensate for this loss of "domestic" sales, by increasing sales abroad—mostly to European Union (EU) markets, thus reducing the pain of economic transition. Early internationalization both facilitated the building of the new state and shortened the economic depression that accompanied the transition.

The improved infrastructure and legal framework that followed the liberalization of outward foreign direct investment (OFDI) in 1999, and EU accession in 2004, helped accelerate the internationalization of Slovene firms, and consequently also the (re-)creation of Slovene MNEs. Attitudinal barriers gradually disappeared. The limited size of the domestic market (two million inhabitants) has helped firms to view internationalization as a means of survival.

Systemic factors, which explained the majority of such operations before the transition, challenged what appeared to be a "reverse investment development path" model, meaning that OFDI occurred before inward foreign direct investment in Slovenia. Since many of these factors were system or transition related, they ceased to exist in parallel with the advancement of the transition, particularly after EU accession.

11.1 History

OFDI started in Slovenia in the late 1950s, when it was still part of Yugoslavia, and before joint ventures were allowed in 1967.[1] The process of outward internationalization was sequential rather than linear, and progress was irregular. OFDI liberalization occurred gradually from 1991 and was completed in 1999. Though initially OFDI exceeded inward FDI, and thus deviated from John H. Dunning's "investment development path," the latter developments confirmed the expected pattern (Jaklič and Svetličič 2003; Svetličič, Rojec, and Lebar 1994; Svetličič and Bellak, 2002; Svetličič and Rojec, 2003).

Until the 1990s, systemic factors, such as the sanctions imposed on Yugoslavia by Stalin in 1948 and the market-oriented reform of 1965, drove OFDI. The establishment of representative offices, branches, and affiliates abroad became a way of escaping the socialist system. It facilitated imports and, later, the promotion of exports. The existence of foreign affiliates enabled firms to increase their competitive edge through regular access to foreign currency, while benefiting from the margin that existed between market and official exchange rates. Such OFDI was not driven by genuine firm-specific advantages, but, rather, by stability-seeking motives (Svetličič et al. 1994, 365).

A small number of Slovene firms established their first foreign affiliates in the late 1950s. The first foreign affiliate was established by the trading company Intertrade in India in 1959. Gorenje, today the second-largest Slovene MNE, established its first affiliate in France in 1965. Iskra, then the largest Slovene firm, but today broken up into many different firms, established its first trading units in London and Stuttgart in 1967. Some of the early "prospective multinationals" no longer exist or have lost their importance. By 1988, Slovene enterprises were involved in eighty-seven firms abroad, which contributed to the accumulation of elementary internationalization knowledge and management skills.

Slovene MNEs are obviously not "transition babies." Only one of the top twenty-five Slovene MNEs was established during the transition, and became an MNE by leapfrogging stages, while the others followed a gradual internationalization path, in line with the Loustarinen-Uppsala school model—internationalizing trade functions initially, and much later production. The departure from the evolutionary Scandinavian model, at that time, was in terms of geographical dimension; in many cases the first affiliates abroad were not established in neighboring countries, but further afield, in developing or developed countries. This departure from the evolutionary model can be explained by institutional factors—the politics of nonalignment motivated firms to strengthen their economic cooperation in this way. Slovene authorities sought to facilitate this enhanced international economic cooperation through the establishment of joint representation offices abroad. In 1974, Ljubljanska banka,[2] the Slovene Chamber of Commerce and Industry, along with a number of firms, established a Special Fund to finance preinvestment studies and the establishment of affiliates in developing countries.

As the transition proceeded, OFDI accelerated despite several attitudinal barriers, including the perception that the export of capital was unpatriotic. The country's entrepreneurial spirit, suppressed during the socialist regime, asserted itself and contributed to the emergence of Slovene MNEs. At the same time, some investors were forced to close their foreign operations, either because these firms were dismantled or because the EU market could be efficiently served by exports—the "investment diversion effect." Large enterprises that were icons of socialism ceased to exist and only development-oriented parts survived. Spinoffs that were aimed abroad occurred as a side effect (details in Jaklič and Svetličič 2003, 46). This facilitated internationalization by means of knowledge spillovers and the early creation of international management experiences.

The emerging OFDI of Slovene firms, from the 1990s onward, can, therefore, be viewed as a phenomenon that is partly inherited and partly new. Nevertheless, early internationalization positively contributed to the development of the investing firms' capabilities, and has been instrumental in today's more organic internationalization. Today, most investors are, in fact, "leapfrogging globals," which multinationalize rapidly by leapfrogging certain stages of internationalization.

11.2 Drivers

Historically, the desire to escape the system constituted the most important push factor for OFDI. Later, as the economy developed, the country's strategy gradually became more outward oriented. The increasingly open economy and globalization became important drivers behind internationalization and pull factors for OFDI.

Among push factors, the most important nonsystemic determinant has been the small size of the domestic market. In order to survive in the face of ever-fiercer international competition, and to build economies of size and scope, firms had to export and to get closer to foreign customers by investing abroad. With the Transnationality Index[3] of the top twenty-five Slovene MNEs exceeding 45%, the case of Slovene MNEs demonstrates that firms from small countries must be more internationalized. Large emerging markets have a much lower transnationalization index (e.g., the top twenty-five Slovene MNEs have an index value that is 2.6 times higher than Brazil's top MNEs; see table 11.3). Small size has been a specific driver: the smaller the niche, the more internationalized a firm has to be in order to exploit it to gain economies of scale and scope. This has been followed, also, by small and medium-sized enterprises, which account for 75% of the total number of Slovene MNEs.

With the maturing of industries and the rather traditional product export structure, restructuring became an increasingly important factor, pushing firms to relocate parts of their labor-intensive processes abroad to maintain at least some of the more capital- or knowledge-intensive production processes at home. The incentive to "go international" arose from relatively rapid development, parallel with the progressing transition and increasing foreign competition in the domestic market, which pushed wages up and made several mature industries uncompetitive.

A particularly important push factor, also visible in other countries, but which has a relatively specific meaning in Slovenia, has been to gain first-mover advantages. Slovene firms have operated quite extensively in other parts of the former Yugoslavia, having (compared to other foreigners) gained a much better knowledge of these former domestic markets. This knowledge of doing business in the Balkan environment has been an important comparative advantage for Slovene firms; but it could be capitalized on only if exploited quickly, before competitors followed. Therefore, Slovene MNEs were pushed to move rapidly to exploit this first-mover advantage in the western Balkans.

Among the pull factors, two can be singled out as most important. First, ever-greater globalization (with a race to downsize) and the fragmentation of value chains invited firms to internationalize in order to exploit opportunities. The increasing share of intermediate products facilitates the internationalization of production for small firms that specialize in only one intermediate product. Second, firms that supply large MNEs with intermediate products have gradually been forced to follow their customers when they go abroad, relocating production. Several Slovene MNEs became MNEs to meet the requirements of their major clients, themselves large MNEs.

Tectonic changes in the world, particularly the recent, rapid growth of emerging markets, force firms to grasp emerging opportunities in growing markets with a rising share of middle-class consumers. Even small and medium-sized enterprises that supply large, western MNEs must follow their clients as they invest in China and other emerging markets, if they wish to continue their long-standing relationships.

Firms have realized that, without OFDI in emerging markets and its benefits in terms of cost reduction, access to new talent, and greater competitive advantage, they cannot maintain, let alone increase, their existing market share in Western markets. Therefore, it is not surprising that over 50% of the top twenty-five Slovene MNEs are global firms, present in key markets and increasing their investment in markets such as Russia, China, and India.

11.3 Slovene OFDI: General Trends and Developments

Macroeconomic data suggest that Slovenia is now between the second and third stage of the investment development path (Svetličič, Bellak, 2002), with

OFDI flows generally higher than inward FDI flows. This occurred for the first time in 2003 (figure 11.1); with the exception of 2004, this trend of net FDI outflows continued until 2008. Nevertheless, in 2007, the inward FDI stock was almost double the OFDI stock (Bank of Slovenia, 2007a). The rapid and constant growth of OFDI brought accumulated OFDI stock to EUR4.9 billion by the end of 2007 (Bank of Slovenia, 2007b). However, this lags behind the inward FDI stock, which totaled EUR9.7 billion (figure 11.2).

The role of the top MNEs in Slovene OFDI is crucial (figure 11.2). Their assets account for 86% of the country's total OFDI stock. The acceleration of OFDI since 2001 generally reflects the rising globalization trend as well as the need to restructure many Slovene firms that operate in mature industries. As noted previously, greater competition in the domestic market has also contributed to the internationalization of trading and manufacturing firms, as they seek to maintain and grow market share abroad by locating closer to customers.

Whereas greenfield investments were prevalent during the 1990s, mergers-and-acquisition (M&As) activity intensified after 2000 (Bank of Slovenia, 2007a, annex table 11.1).[4] This trend is explained in part by late privatization in a number of major host countries, such as Serbia and Montenegro. Larger acquisitions were undertaken in the financial industry,

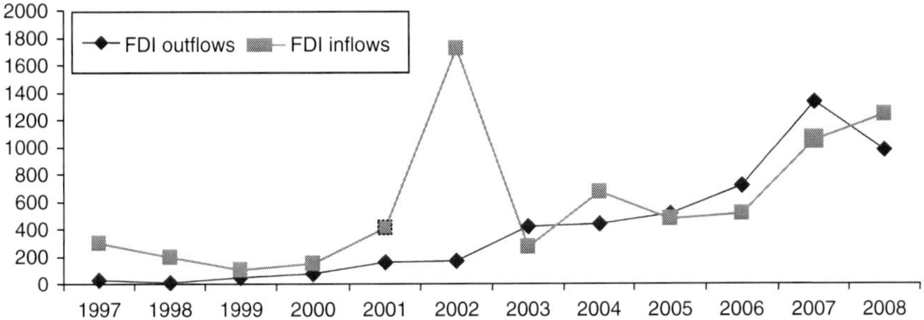

Figure 11.1   FDI outflows from, and inflows into, Slovenia, 1997–2006 (EUR millions)
Source: Bank of Slovenia.

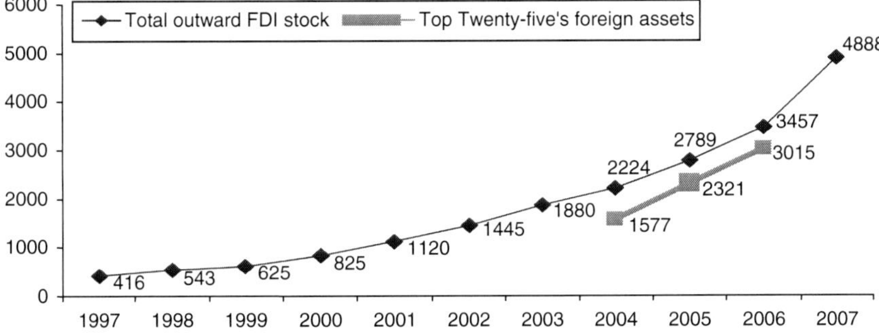

Figure 11.2   Stock of OFDI from Slovenia, 1997–2006 (EUR millions)
Source: Bank of Slovenia, CIR-VCC survey of Slovene MNEs (see www.vcc.columbia.edu).

the chemical industry (particularly pharmaceuticals), retail trade, the electrical appliances industry, and the food industry.

11.4 General Characteristics of the Top Twenty-Five Slovene MNEs

The survey of the top twenty-five Slovene MNEs covered only indigenous Slovene firms. Even if foreign-owned MNEs that are located in Slovenia and invest abroad (indirect investors) were included, only a few would qualify. Slovene MNEs are, therefore, more homegrown[5] than in other transition economies, where foreign-owned companies have played a greater role in outward investment.[6]

Slovenia's top twenty-five MNEs, valued by foreign assets, had almost US$4 billion[7] in assets abroad (table 11.1), almost US$4 billion in foreign sales (including exports), and employed 23,616 people abroad. Their foreign

Table 11.1 CIR-CPII ranking of the top twenty-five Slovene MNEs, in terms of foreign assets, 2006 (US$ millions)

Rank	Name	Industry	Foreign assets
1	Mercator	Retail trade	954
2	Gorenje	Electricity supply and manufacturing	668
3	Krka	Manufacturing	439
4	Droga Kolinska[a]	Manufacturing	352
5	Petrol	Oil supply	307
6	Merkur	Retail trade	203
7	Intereuropa	Transportation	127
8	Helios	Manufacturing	121
9	Iskra Avtoelektrika	Manufacturing	80
10	Elan	Manufacturing	75
11	Unior	Manufacturing	66
12	Lesnina	Retail trade	66
13	Kolektor Group	Manufacturing	59
14	Prevent	Manufacturing	50
15	Trimo	Manufacturing	46
16	Viator & Vektor	Transportation	40
17	HIT	Entertainment	37
18	JUB	Manufacturing	35
19	Hidria	Manufacturing	33
20	Perutnina Ptuj	Manufacturing	32
21	Kovintrade	Manufacturing	28
22	ERA	Retail trade	22
23	ETI Elektroelement	Manufacturing	21
24	Alpina	Manufacturing and retail trade	20
25	Kompas	Travel and related activities	20
TOTAL			3,903

Source: CIR-VCC survey of Slovene MNEs (see www.vcc.columbia.edu).

[a]Droga and Kolinska merged in 2004.

assets and employment each more than doubled between 2004 and 2006, while foreign sales increased by 60%. Foreign assets are concentrated in Europe. The top three MNEs account for more than half of the total assets of the top twenty-five, and the top five MNEs account for 68%. As a rule, they are private firms (with the exception of one public company, accounting for only about 2% of the aggregate foreign assets).

Slovene MNEs are small compared with their counterparts in emerging markets such as Brazil, India, China, and Russia[8] (the foreign assets of the top twenty-five are roughly 5% of the top twenty-five in Russia and the top twenty in Brazil). Nevertheless, they play a vital role in Slovenia's economy and a dominant role as outward investors. Today, more than 2% (approximately 970) of almost 50,000 corporations in Slovenia are involved in OFDI activity. However, the vast majority (almost 75%) of these 950 MNEs can be classified as small and medium-sized enterprises.

Obviously, Slovene MNEs are also much smaller than other international competitors. Not one of the Slovene top twenty-five makes it into the top fifty MNEs from developing countries (UNCTAD 2007). Their expansion has been rapid, however. Between 2004 and 2006, their aggregate foreign assets doubled, their foreign sales grew by more than 50% to US$7.3 billion (more than half of the top twenty-five's total sales), and foreign employment doubled to 23,616 people (table 11.2). Foreign expansion is the engine of growth of the top twenty-five. Their domestic sales dropped from 59% to only 48% of total sales in 2006. For the top two manufacturing firms, foreign sales amounted to 86% of their total sales, which demonstrates the extent to which trading companies and manufacturers of white goods are dependent on global markets.

A breakdown by industry reveals the predominance of manufacturing among the top MNEs. This can be explained by the structure of the

Table 11.2   A snapshot of Slovenia's twenty-five largest MNEs, 2004–2006 (US$ millions and number of employees)

Variable	2004	2005	2006	% change 2006/2005
Assets				
Foreign	2.068	2.680	3.903	31
Total	9.061	9.407	11.777	12
Share of foreign in total (%)	23	28	33	16
Employment				
Foreign	11.699	18.972	23.616	24
Total	69.655	77.027	81.349	6
Share of foreign in total (%)	17	25	29	18
Sales (including exports)				
Foreign	4.730	5.093	7.256	28
Total	11.497	11.045	13.885	13
Share of foreign in total (%)	41	46	52	13

Source: CIR-VCC 2008 survey of Slovene MNEs (see www.vcc.columbia.edu).

country's economy, wherein traditional mature industries, with strong cost competition and accelerating globalization, dominate. Firms in such sectors are under greater pressure to internationalize in order to reduce costs. Less-internationalized industries faced slower restructuring.

Manufacturing[9] is by far the most important industry of sixteen of the top twenty-five Slovene MNEs. It is followed by retail trade, with five MNEs. Other industries include transportation, electricity supply, oil supply, entertainment, travel, and related activities.

The top Slovene MNEs are also among the most respected companies in Slovenia, according to *DELO,* a major newspaper in Slovenia. Six of the ten most respected firms feature among the top twenty-five Slovene MNEs. The list of the sixty-three most successful firms in Slovenia, based on eighteen indicators, also includes fourteen of the top twenty-five Slovene MNEs (*DELO, FT,* November 26, 2007, 23). The largest Slovene MNEs are also among the 101 largest Slovene companies. Of the largest ten, five are top twenty-five MNEs, (see *Finance,* May 28, 2007, 30–34). Although big in Slovenia, these MNEs do not place highly in the ranking of the most profitable companies. They account for second, fourth, sixth, fourteenth, seventeenth, and nineteenth place among the twenty most profitable firms in Slovenia (*DELO,* May 21, 2007, 31) and consequently, they also fail to rank highly in terms of value-added per employee.[10] There are several reasons for this. First, these MNEs are mainly older companies, and many operate in medium-technology-intensive industries,[10] where cost competitiveness is essential and profit rates are, by definition, lower. Second, strategically they are long-term, and not short-term, profit-maximization oriented. They are generally not involved in rent-seeking financial operations or in selling or buying properties on the local market. Many of the most profitable Slovene companies are in highly capital-intensive sectors, in still-protected infrastructural operations.

The top twenty-five Slovene MNEs had 286 foreign affiliates across fifty-three countries in 2006; that is, eleven affiliates and a presence in nine countries, on average (annex table 11.2). The aggregate Transnationality Index of the top twenty-five Slovene MNEs increased between 2004 and 2006, from 36% to 45%, reflecting the rapid growth of international operations. These statistics show that Slovene MNEs do not lag far behind the largest firms in the world on this measure (UNCTAD, 2005). They are more multinational than firms from other transition economies. The most internationalized Slovene company is Droga Kolinska, a food manufacturer, with a Transnationality Index of 68%. For a small country of two million people, foreign growth through FDI means survival and is a vital engine of growth for Slovene firms.

Along with a small number of global players, such as Kolektor[11] and Iskravtoelektrika, many companies from the top twenty-five Slovene MNEs are regional MNEs. Slovene MNEs are generally regional market-seekers, with trade and production affiliates in the western Balkan countries. More than 80% of their foreign affiliates are located in Europe. Eight of the top twenty-five Slovene MNEs are established exclusively in Europe, as revealed by the Regionality Index (annex table 11.3), five operate on at least four different continents, and ten are present on at least three continents. Recently, Slovene firms have shown a growing interest in Russia, China, and other, more distant, Asian locations.

The top twenty-five Slovene MNEs include old and young MNEs. Seven MNEs have pretransition experience in OFDI. Gorenje, for example, undertook OFDI in the 1960s; Krka established a pharmaceutical firm near Nairobi in the mid-1970s, and Elan has produced skis in Sweden[13] since the 1970s. Nine Slovene MNEs made their first investment abroad in the mid-1990s, and nine others established their first foreign affiliate after 1999 (although the firms were established in the pretransition period).

The top twenty-five Slovene MNEs all use Slovenian as their official language, although fifteen MNEs also use foreign languages. Ten MNEs have Slovenian and English as official languages, two have three official languages (Slovenian, English, and German), and one has five official languages (Slovenian, English, German, Russian, and Croatian).

The internationalization level of management is relatively low, and, with the exception of one,[14] all CEOs are Slovene. Only eight out of the top twenty-five have more than 10% of foreign senior management.[15] In seventeen firms, senior management is entirely Slovenian.

11.5 Competitive Advantages

Some of the top twenty-five Slovene MNEs were previously included in a 2001 survey (Jaklič and Svetličič 2003, 125), allowing us to draw some broad conclusions about Slovene OFDI. Most Slovene outward investors claim that their competitive advantage lies in their superior technology, marketing, and/or management skills. Marketing know-how was considered the most important competitive advantage, followed by technological know-how and organizational knowledge (125). Companies have accumulated firm-specific advantages in their markets of penetration (differentiated products and services, etc.), which more than compensate for their weaknesses, when compared to large MNEs or local companies. Technological superiority results from the much larger research and development (R&D) expenditures of those firms investing abroad, compared to the average Slovene firm, as well as of the higher share of university-educated employees. Perhaps the primary managerial advantage is the knowledge and familiarity acquired from doing business in the western Balkans—generally treated as an unstable, opaque, and unpredictable environment. Some managers have developed a very specific management style based on personal contacts, which is highly adapted to the culture of the particular market in which they are undertaking OFDI. Previous experiences in the western Balkans, or other transition economies, demonstrate that a smaller cultural gap has facilitated such OFDI by Slovene MNEs. The management of companies has played a crucial role in OFDI. Without the clear and ambitious visions of the firms' managers, such successful internationalization would not have been possible. A realistic strategy, strong management with excellent training (many were trained abroad), adapted technology, and proprietary R&D have proved to be the key success factors in most cases.

Some of these advantages are temporary, and must be exploited rapidly, before other competitors enter the market.[16] The first-mover advantage (already mentioned) plays a much more important role than does, for example, experience acquired in industrial countries. The somewhat weaker ownership advantages, when compared to MNEs from large developed economies, drive Slovene MNEs to internationalize earlier than would otherwise be the case. This enables these firms to gain complementary advantages and to "buy time" before other MNEs enter the market.

Operating in medium- and even low-technology-intensive activities implies that soft factors, more than hard technological factors, constitute the decisive competitive advantages of Slovene MNEs. The relocation of labor-intensive activities from Slovenia to lower-labor-cost countries, following the Terutomo Ozawa theory (Ozawa 1992),[17] accelerated only after 2004 (Svetličič 2007, 67). Relocation occurred relatively later in Slovenia, the result of strong attitudinal barriers. Trade unions sought to retain jobs at home, rejecting arguments that such investments only complement local investment, local employment, and exports. As a result, managers, especially those in publicly owned firms, go international as a last resort, when wage levels becomes intolerable and they are faced with the dilemma of closing down the factory.[18]

Japec Jakopin, owner of the Slovene firm Seaway, a major designer of boats in Europe, argued that, by following the right strategy, small firms from small countries can turn their weaknesses into strengths. Their limited size forces the management of such firms to become well educated, to adapt, to learn from the experiences of others, and to seek to assimilate successfully the best practices of others. This is only possible, however, with excellent knowledge of foreign languages and with individuals with the ability to adapt to other cultures and assimilate knowledge. Jakopin explained that, by listening, one learns; by applying the best practices of many countries and firms in creating own solutions, one can outperform larger and stronger competitors; and by not claiming to be the best, small firms do not threaten the superiority complex of traditional, established, and large players: "We have thereby created, what we call a European sailing boat, which is appealing to the French, British, Swedes, and most other tastes" (Kavčič 2001, 7).

The case of Seaway demonstrates that a firm can become global and successful in a relatively small niche. It also appears that it is somewhat easier for a firm to become an important player if it specializes in an intermediate and not a final product, if it is a small or medium-sized enterprise, or if it comes from a small country. Final-product orientation and consumer goods production and marketing are more costly, more susceptible to changes in technology, and more brand and advertising intensive. Firms require an established global network in order to exploit their advantages in the shortest time possible. Supplying intermediate products brings safety, because one can become a major producer for many large MNEs and thus reduce dependence on any one purchaser or market. Such diversification also brings economies of scale and boosts competitiveness.

These competitive advantages have enhanced the international competitiveness of Slovenia. Investing firms, in general, perform better, and are more profitable, than noninvesting firms. Premiums in sales, profits, and productivity were highest among outward investors that established their first foreign affiliates between 1998 and 2000. The majority of managers also claimed that their competitiveness strongly improved thanks to OFDI (59%), which also enhanced the transformation of the economy (52%) (Svetličič 2007, 70; Jaklič and Svetličič 2003, 38, 67, 174).

11.6 Obstacles and Problems

Although most outward investors claim that their operations have been successful (Jaklič and Svetličič 2003, 165), the leading Slovene MNEs (and investors abroad in general) face several host-country, home-country, and firm-level barriers, weaknesses, and threats. Among the host-country barriers, political instability, high economic risk, the lack of a proper legal framework, and slow administrative procedures were considered major obstacles.

In terms of home-country barriers, firms considered the late liberalization of OFDI, the lack of governmental support and inadequate coverage of risks, the absence of intergovernmental agreements (because of the creation of new states), and a lack of information support the most challenging barriers. Unfriendly political and public opinion that regards OFDI as unpatriotic, entailing the export of jobs, or displacement of local investment also discouraged managers from embarking on the development of long-term OFDI plans. Stereotypes of FDI as a generally unwelcome activity, undermining national interests, have persisted since socialist times. The link between inward FDI and OFDI usually goes unrecognized. Inward FDI is frequently perceived by the general public and some academics (mostly based on national interests arguments) as unwelcome, whereas OFDI has recently been recognized as an activity that might help to enhance the competitiveness of firms and the national economy in general. A good example of the potential benefits of inward FDI is the enterprise Kolektor (see annex case box 11.1 and Svetličič 2008, 3–9). The Kolektor case illustrates how a firm can develop and enhance its capabilities by means of productive cooperation with foreign partners. The general public has begun to realize that investing abroad today is a survival strategy for several domestic firms. Having one's own MNEs seems to be more attractive to the general public than hosting foreign MNEs in Slovenia. The government has formally been enhancing its support for inward FDI, both in terms of regulations and in terms of official statements and policies. Nevertheless, whenever it comes to specific projects involving foreign acquisitions (which public opinion views as particularly unwelcome) and a heated public debate results, politicians tend to take a more defensive stance regarding inward FDI. Therefore, there is a persistent discrepancy between the official position of the government (welcoming inward FDI) and actual practice in making efforts to attract such investment. As the theoretical models and empirical evidence suggest, OFDI is a function of inward FDI; hence these barriers also influence internationalization.

Internal firm barriers were, in general (especially after the general business climate started to change in favor of outward investment), evaluated as being a greater hindrance than were external barriers. The greatest internal barriers to internationalization were a lack of experience, a lack of capacity to manage risks, and a lack of knowledge, including information on how to invest and operate abroad. Even the most internationalized and experienced firms claimed that they lack internationalization knowledge and more internationally experienced managers with internationalization-specific knowledge. Firms also claim that the galloping globalization squeezes the time for organic, gradual growth. Outward investment may begin without any substantial experience in international business, and the resulting risks may therefore increase.

The main reasons for problems and some failures were poor preparation, limited or inexperienced personnel (inadequate management of human resources), and limited or inadequate information. These factors all contributed to an internationalization that was sometimes carried out prematurely or unsuccessfully, often the result of poor choice in available investor capabilities or country location. Some firms also claimed that their mistakes stemmed from a gradual approach. Their plans to build a foreign network gradually were contradicted by experiences, which highlighted the need to begin at "full speed," establishing operations abroad quickly, without even considering the establishment of a small operation, which would then develop in line with the market. Rapid market changes and competition limit the time for gradualism.

Slovene firms face additional barriers when compared to other international investors, due to limited labor mobility. The relatively high quality of life in Slovenia makes it difficult to find experienced experts or managers willing to go abroad, despite substantial financial incentives. Limited mobility is compounded by high rates of female participation in the labor force, meaning that spouses may not wish to put their careers on hold to accompany their partner abroad, plus there may be children's schooling issues. Furthermore, case studies have revealed that the physical separation of families has led to divorces and, consequently, a high social cost of internationalization. In the long term, human capital seems to be the biggest barrier to firm internationalization (Jaklič and Svetličič, 2003, 150–51). Managers have identified limited labor mobility as the second most important factor in the success, or failure, of internationalization, stressing the lack of cross-cultural management knowledge as being an obstacle to expanding business beyond Europe (Jaklič and Svetličič 2008, 47).

11.7   Slovene MNEs in the International Context

There are many characteristics that distinguish Slovene MNEs from those from other countries. The major differences are as follows:

- they are much smaller, but relatively more internationalized;[19]
- foreign-owned firms are not important as outward investors from Slovenia;
- outward investors come predominantly from manufacturing industries;
- strategically, they are niche oriented, and manufacturing firms focus mainly on intermediate products;

- firms that undertake OFDI are generally older (established pretransition), private firms, but are "young MNEs."

Slovene MNEs are much smaller than MNEs from larger transition, or developing, economies. They find it difficult to compete on the basis of sophisticated technologies or know-how. The Balakrishnan (1975) hypothesis, which states that investment among developing countries comes at the fourth stage of the product life cycle (Vernon 1966), has proved relevant to both groups of countries. Generally, MNEs from transition economies build advantages in areas neglected by MNEs from developed economies, and pay more attention to assimilating or adapting their technologies. Simultaneously, they upgrade their specific advantages, which often consist of organization and design, rather than new products or brand names. The outward orientation of those firms that focused more on Western, than on socialist markets, also stimulated their capacity for internationalization.

The stronger involvement of small and medium-sized enterprises, in the case of Slovenia, is related to macrolocation-based factors and previously established networks in the common market of the now-disintegrated Yugoslavia. Several small and medium-sized MNEs were created by managers of former state monopoly firms who, upon the collapse of the state-owned firm, established their own firm, inheriting the experience and networks of the former. The new information technology (IT) infrastructure and increasingly integrated global production also makes it easier for small and medium-sized firms to internationalize today, particularly as suppliers to large MNEs (client-driven internationalization).

The ownership structure of affiliates abroad also differs: third-world MNEs have traditionally preferred joint ventures with local partners (Wells 1983, 115), whereas Slovene MNEs favor majority ownership of foreign affiliates. Firms seek to control their foreign operations partly out of weakness rather than strength (Svetličič and Jaklič 2003). The explanation is partly system specific: late privatization in host countries, nontransparent systemic conditions, and other instabilities that, in the case of shared ownership, would increase risk. Another explanation lies in the type of firm-specific advantages: similar to those a local partner would bring, there is no need to acquire them. Building partnerships is, thus, another weakness and limitation of Slovene MNEs.

Comparing the top Slovene MNEs with MNEs from three emerging markets[20] reveals significant differences and some similarities (table 11.3). The similarities are mostly in terms of regional orientation, dynamics (recent, rapid expansion), ownership (largely private), and the increasing degree of transnationality and development implications. The differences are mostly in terms of size, industry allocation, age, the role and geographical location of the MNE in the home country (headquarters location), and listing on the relevant stock exchange. As the countries compared are so different in size and other characteristics (Central Intelligence Agency, 2008), the differences are not surprising (see annex table 11.4).

Table 11.3   Profiles of the selected economies

Issue	Slovenia—top twenty-five	Brazil—top twenty	India—twenty large MNEs	Russia—top twenty-five
Size	Assets: US$ 4 billion. Small, largest US$ 0.96 billion. 23,616 employed abroad, 5% of assets of Russian or Brazilian MNEs, largest US$ 723 million, smallest US$ 15 million top 5 have 68% of assets abroad.	Assets: US$ 56 billion. Large dominate, 2, CVRD and Petrobras, more than US$ 10 billion, each, 77,000 employed abroad (all 20), but smaller also growing fast.	Assets: US$ 3.56 billion. Large dominate, Tata Group over US$ 2.091 billion. (59%), Satyam computer services over US$521 million, 13 companies over US$ 20 billion, 53,000 employees abroad, several companies have a low level of foreign employment, 4 less than 1% (offshoring, IT specific).	Assets: US$ 59 billion. The largest, Lukoil US$ 18 billion, the smallest US$ 116 mil, 130,345 employed abroad The smallest would be seventh among Slovenia's top twenty-five MNEs.
Average size 2006 **- assets** **- sales** **- employees**	US$ 0.47 billion US$ 0.55 billion 3.24 thousand	US$ 13.85 billion US$ 9.5 billion 20.3 thousand	US$ 2.8 billion US$ 2.2 billion 17.6 thousand	US$ 18.5 billion US$ 84.3 billion 12.6 thousand
Sectors	54% manufacturing (by number of firms)	66% of for. assets by natural resource firms, manufacturing 19%	IT services (52%) pharmaceuticals (16%) automotive (10%)	53% resources, 25% metal mining, 1% manufacturing, telecom., etc.
Importance	86% of Slovenia's OFDI stocks	na	21% OFDI stocks	38% OFDI stocks
Ownership	Private, only 1 state owned	Private, only Petrobras state owned	Mostly state owned, only one private	5 state owned, others private (27% of assets)
Regional orientation	80% Europe (by number of affiliates), 9 MNEs only in Europe, now alsoglobally	50% Latin America (by number of affiliates)	Global orientation; Europe predominates (35% of affiliates), followed by North America (20%), and South Asia (14%)	63% Europe (by foreign assets), now more globally
Transnationality Index	45%, up from 36% in 2004	17.5% (arithmetic mean)	Rapid increase	30%

Shares of (2006)				
- assets abroad	33%	20%	9%	13%
- employment	29%	19%	16%	6%
- sales	52%	16%	12%	63%
Age	Old pretransition established firms, 7 invested already during socialism, But young as MNEs	Young 4 (of 18) began internationalizing. between 1990 and 1996	Mostly young, 13 invested abroad before 1994, 15 after 3 established since 1945	Young, 18 after 1999
Location of headquarters	19 out of the capital city	50% Sao Paulo	52% Mumbai, 26% Bangalore	17 from the capital city
Dynamics	Foreign assets and employment more than doubled 2004–2006.	Recent fast expansion, more than doubled assets	Recent fast expansion (2006), assets (259%) and sales (158%) abroad—considerably more than employment abroad (40%)	Recent, fast, faster than Slovene MNEs, Foreign assets more than doubled (2005–2006)
Inward/outward ratio	For 3 years outward flows larger than inward	In 2006 outward larger than inward for the first time	Outflows lower than inflows, inward stock significantly lower	Balanced, but in 2006 inward was higher
Impact on domestic investment, growth, employment	Not impeding, rather they complement	na	na	Not impeding
Listing at the Stock exchanges (SE)	10 Ljubljana SE	na	2 London Stock Exchange3 New York Stock Exchange and Luxembourg Stock Exchange	9 London Stock Exchange 2 New York Stock Exchange

Source: Authors' calculations, based on reports for the four countries, available at http://www.vcc.columbia.edu.

Note: OFDI does not come at the expense of existing home country employment, investment and/or sales, but is complementary. Domestic sales and employment have both remained stable. The top twenty-five remain among the most important domestic employers, while their home country assets of the top twenty-five grew by around 15% between 2004 and 2006.

In line with expectations, Slovene MNEs are much smaller than those from Russia, Brazil, and India, yet the company differences are less than the country-size differences would indicate.[21] Slovene MNEs are comparatively large, given the country size, and have higher relative importance for the home country, which demonstrates the small-country effect of internationalization. Firms from small economies are confronted by a much weaker starting position than are firms in larger economies, and have to grow internationally in order to survive. Consequently, they are also more internationalized, as the Transnationality Index differences in table 11.4 confirm. The strong regional foothold of all countries' top MNEs is unsurprising. Slovene, Russian, and Indian MNEs are mostly Europe oriented, while Brazilian MNEs are Latin America oriented. Indian MNEs have, by far, the most global orientation. The dominant Slovene MNEs are manufacturing and trading companies while, as expected, Russian and Brazilian MNEs are strong in the natural-resources industries, particularly oil and minerals (Brazil). The top Indian MNEs work, predominantly, in IT.

More surprising is the age of these top MNEs. While major MNEs from emerging markets (Russia, India, and Brazil) are generally young firms, Slovene MNEs are generally older firms, established under socialism, but younger in terms of becoming MNEs. Although Slovenia and Russia are former socialist economies, their major MNEs are privately owned. While Russian and Indian MNEs are listed internationally, some Slovene MNEs are not listed, even on the domestic Ljubljana Stock Market.

Differences were found in the location of the leading MNEs. In Slovenia, they are mainly located outside the capital city; in Russia, India, and Brazil, they are mostly located in the capital or main city of the country. This is the result of the different development strategy of each country. Slovenia has had a more decentralized development strategy, instituted in socialist times, but also the result of the country's size, where the distance from the center is small, and hence the disadvantages of being a "regional outsider" are weaker. The experiences of managers revealed that, even in the socialist system, firms located outside the center had to rely much more on their own capabilities, while those in the center strengthened their competitiveness by networking with politicians and banks (crony socialism).

Another explanation is the commitment of management and those employed in such firms: they are more committed to the company and its international growth because it is often the lifeblood of the place where they live. Frequently, the MNE in question is the only firm, or, at the very least, a significant firm in the region. This brings greater employment stability and improved management, which has been demonstrated to be a key success factor (Jaklič and Svetličič 2003, 183).

11.8 Strategy and Policy Matter

Policy implications, dating from the time of Yugoslavia, suggest one important conclusion: outward-looking strategies matter, and the export promotion strategy that began in 1970 has facilitated inward FDI and OFDI.

Gradually, firms have realized that maintaining market share abroad, in certain locations, is not possible without a direct presence and close connection with customers. Similarly, purchases become more efficient with internationalization.[22] An early start was even more important given the slow changes observed in the general perception of, and attitude to, internationalization.

In addition, a decentralized development strategy has facilitated OFDI, stimulating the growth of a number of firms from outside Ljubljana, the capital city. During socialism, these firms were forced to rely on their real competitive advantages rather than on advantages based on relations with politicians or bankers. When globalization forced these firms to go international, these competitive advantages formed the material basis for further internationalization. It is not surprising that, due in part to such decentralized development strategies, as many as 76% of the leading Slovene MNEs are located outside of Ljubljana.

Slovenia's policy framework for OFDI has evolved over time (Svetličič 2007, 76–78): from a restricted policy environment, to specific promotional programs, and now to the creation of infrastructural preconditions without specific promotional measures. The policy of the Slovene government toward OFDI has developed from an initially passive, reactive policy to the active promotion of internationalization. This is explained in part by firms' demands for liberalization, later induced also by the signing of the Association Agreement with the European Union and by EU membership. The most recent programs, however, place greater emphasis on inward FDI.

The country's legal framework for OFDI has been adjusted in line with EU regulations; investments are regulated by the Foreign Exchange Act of October 2, 2003. The Act on Attracting FDI and the Internationalization of Companies of 2004 further demonstrated a shift in policy toward promoting such forms of international cooperation. In 1999, a new concept of industrial policy—enterprise and competitiveness development—was introduced. The Ministry of the Economy sought to strengthen competitive capacity, thereby expanding exports and enhancing the internationalization of small and medium-sized firms, and to attract strategic foreign investment and promote OFDI by Slovene companies (Ministry of the Economy, 2005b). In 2002, a special promotional program for OFDI was launched[23] as part of the entrepreneurship promotion and competitiveness strategy.[24] The OFDI program was conceived largely as the promotion of the internationalization of small and medium-sized firms—still at an early stage of internationalization.

Nevertheless, in value terms, the FDI promotion program initially played a relatively marginal role in state aid programs, implemented by the Ministry of the Economy. According to a survey for the 2001–2003 period, based on a sample of firms that had received state aid[25] in 2003, the promotion of inward FDI, surprisingly, received less funding than did OFDI (Andrič 2003). Five percent of all funds was allocated to the promotion of OFDI (12% including the program for stimulating the internationalization of small and medium-sized firms) and 4% for stimulating inward FDI. The analysis also concluded that more than two-thirds of OFDI projects would have been realized even without government supportApplicants' financial participation in these projects was almost twenty times higher than the contribution of the Ministry. Obviously, bottom-up incentives for internationalization are much stronger, whereas government stimulation only plays a supportive role (Deloitte and the Faculty of Economics of the University of Ljubljana 2004, 15). These findings resulted in a policy change, from providing direct financial incentives promoting outward internationalization, to mostly indirect support such as training, consultancy, and infrastructural support. This was the purpose of the Public Agency for Entrepreneurship and Foreign Investment (JAPTI), established in 2006 as a one-stop agency providing institutional facilities primarily for the promotion of inward FDI, but also to support the outward internationalization of Slovene firms. It provides information support, consultancy services, support for promotional activities, training, and capacity-building activities. The new policy places greater emphasis on the aggressive marketing of Slovenia as a destination for FDI. The key task of JAPTI is to promote inward FDI, although it also embraces internationalization in general, with the aim of:

- increasing the annual inflow of greenfield FDI (excluding acquisitions and privatization-related FDI) from 1% to 1.5% of GDP;
- creating 1,000 to 1,500 new jobs annually;
- attracting at least one new high-tech FDI project and at least three FDI projects in export services. (Ministry of Economy 2005a, 7)

In 2008, JAPTI's inward FDI "Cost-Sharing Grant Scheme" allocated EUR5.9 million to various projects. The purpose of the scheme is to lower the entry (startup) costs for investors whose activities will have a positive impact on new employment, knowledge and technology transfers, and the facilitation of balanced regional development, and will foster alliances between foreign investors and Slovene companies. Despite this supportive official policy, inward FDI has for many years been a matter of highly sensitive political debate in the context of the national interest. A comprehensive inward FDI strategy was adopted at the end of 2006; the law on inward FDI was adopted in 2004 and amended by a law promoting FDI in 2006. This new strategy includes also the promotion of the outward internationalization of Slovene firms.

Consequently, OFDI promotion services have become a minor activity of the Public Agency for Entrepreneurship and Foreign Investment, even though the total infrastructure costs of the agency are relatively high, particularly those costs related to their offices abroad, which should provide support for outward internationalization. Cost allocation does not offer an insight into the allocation of funds for outward and inward internationalization, but rather into priorities, such as small and medium-sized firms, their first foreign market entry, and for larger, established investors venturing into new markets. There are also market priorities; namely, increasing market share in traditional markets and new markets. The central role of the new program is to provide support for internationalization through the establishment of representative offices abroad[26] and other consultancy and information services, rather than through special financial incentives. In the medium term, the network is expected to include fifteen to twenty foreign offices (Ministry of the Economy 2005c, 8, 17). Thus far, seven offices have been established—in Milan, Düsseldorf, Bucharest, Istanbul, Shanghai, Sao Paolo, and Kazan (Russia). Their role is to provide support for the internationalization of small and medium-sized firms through enhanced competitiveness in the context of the increasing oligopolization and concentration of global markets. The response of firms to this challenge has been a selective strengthening of their own capabilities through the enhancement of management and organizational skills, R&D efforts, innovation and creativity, and a focus on core capabilities. Firms are becoming aware that, in the future, longer-term strategic or equity-inward cooperation with foreign partners can be a strategic response to the growing challenges of globalization. Such orientation has proved to be necessary, particularly in view of the increasing vulnerability and turbulence of the global environment. Another strategy is diversification. In some cases, firms adhere to their core business niche when going international, but diversify at home. Others try to diversify internationally. The prime dilemma here involves the tradeoffs between the benefits of specialization and the costs of diversification compared to the reduced risks.

Conclusions and Way Forward

Over time, even the most skeptical policy makers and managers have realized that, in the era of globalization, outward internationalization has became a precondition for growth and enhanced competitiveness. Fortunately, Slovene MNEs came into existence before the disintegration of Yugoslavia. They facilitated the development of this new, small state that faced the loss of almost half of its former domestic market. Slovene firms that exported and invested abroad were in a much stronger position to gain market share to replace that lost with independence. Due to its small size and openness, it is expected that the Slovenia economy will be dominated by highly internationalized firms, both domestic and foreign owned. Local firms, operating mainly in the local market, will eventually be in the minority. Slovene MNEs, therefore, became an important development instrument, which was not the case some fifteen years earlier, when attitudinal barriers actually restricted outward internationalization. Not all such attitudinal barriers have been eliminated. The first policy objective of eliminating such negative perceptions and stereotypes regarding OFDI, therefore, remains.

The second policy priority is to overcome the notion that inward FDI and OFDI are different animals: they are, in fact, two sides of the same coin. There is still a tendency to look upon OFDI more favorably than inward FDI. However, it is becoming apparent that the Slovene economy requires more inward FDI if it is to enhance added-value in its industries and services.

The third priority is to overcome the lack of human resources, which has proved to be a major barrier to internationalization, particularly for small and medium-sized firms. Managers emphasize the lack of soft skills, relating to negotiations, conflict management, and cross-cultural and diversity management. Existing education and training programs are overly specialized, and the development of specialists is a poor basis for the development of international managers capable of addressing a wide range of problems. There is a need for holistic education that provides a complex, though not detailed, knowledge of many areas of international business—from law and economics to business and human-resource management, and even international relations.

Along with management training, the fourth priority is to develop supportive education programs for accompanying persons and/or families. The lack of family support has proved to be a substantial impediment to mobility. Programs that help expatriates to become integrated into their new location must be developed. Furthermore, many expatriates have complained about the lack of opportunity upon their return to their home country, which further decreases the motivation to accept management posts abroad.

Finally, the global financial crisis and recession have influenced the outward internationalization strategies of firms, but has not halted their long-term orientation. Firms still plan to internationalize, but have been forced to modify such programs in the short term due to financial constraints. At the same time, firms also view outward internationalization as a response to this crisis. Firms realize that, by going abroad, they can maintain customers and market share more easily than through exports. The reaction to the crises may be recognized by changes in the regional orientation of their foreign activities; cooperation with still-growing (large) emerging markets and innovation has increased, but accompanied by cost-cutting measures and the internal reorganization of companies.

Annex Table 11.1 The top ten Slovene outward mergers and acquisitions, 2005–January 2008 (US$ millions)

Date	Acquirer name	Target name	Target industry	Target economy	% of shares acquired	Value of transaction
2006	Mercator	Rodić Trgovina	Retail	Serbia and Montenegro	100.00	198.00
July 6, 2005	Nova Ljubljanska Banka dd	Continental Banka	Banking	Serbia and Montenegro	98.43	59.08
2007	Mercator	Presoflex, d.o.o	Retail	Croatia	100.00	50,79
April 24, 2007	Telekom Slovenije dd	Gibtelecom	Telecommunications	Gibraltar	50.00	49.97
August 28, 2007	Holding Slovenske Elektrarne	Toplofikatzia Ruse EAD	Electricity and heating	Bulgaria	100.00	46.70
November 7, 2007	Adria Mobil doo	Sun Roller SA	Mobile homes	Spain	80.00	13.75
October 19, 2006	Pozavarovalnica Sava dd	Polis Osiguranje	Life insurance	Serbia and Montenegro	100.00	13.58
March 27, 2006	Investor Group	MAIB	Banking	Moldova	19.66	9.80
January 5, 2007	Pozavarovalnica Sava dd	Tabak Osiguranje	Life insurance	Macedonia	53.65	9.08
March 20, 2006	Telekom Slovenije dd	On.net	Internet service provider	Macedonia	76.00	5.71
October 3, 2007	Telekom Slovenije dd	ANEKS doo	Telecommunications	Bosnia	70.00	4.69
February 20, 2006	Nova Ljubljanska Banka dd	Klas dd Sarajevo	Groceries	Bosnia	5.54	1.57

Sources: Thomson Financial and SEO net.

Annex Table 11.2 CIR-CPII ranking of the top twenty-five Slovene MNEs, by key variables, 2006 (US$ millions and number of employees)

Ranking				Assets		Sales		Employment				
Foreign assets	Transnationality Index	Name	Industry	Foreign	Total	Foreign	Total	Foreign	Total	Transnationality Index (%)	Number of foreign affiliates	Number of host countries
1	20	Mercator	Retail trade	954	2,456	585	2,725	5,892	19,539	30	5	5
2	6	Gorenje	Electricity supply and manufacturing	668	1,194	1,254	1,466	2,109	10,556	54	41	26
3	7	Krka	Manufacturing	439	1,160	759	881	2,113	5,759	54	14	12
4	2	Droga110 Kolinska	Manufacturing	352	577	315	446	2,605	3,577	68	11	6
5	24	Petrol	Oil supply	307	1,112	354	2,561	363	2,768	18	6	5
6	23	Merkur	Retail trade	203	1,153	464	1,318	661	4,075	23	8	7
7	13	Intereuropa	Transportation	127	383	194	290	1,018	2,310	48	12	10
8	3	Helios	Manufacturing	121	340	416	342	920	2,211	66	21	13
9	17	Iskra Avtoelektrika	Manufacturing	80	223	199	261	443	2,534	43	12	11
10	4	Elan	Manufacturing	75	161	145	162	337	1,267	54	7	6
11	19	Unior	Manufacturing	66	513	255	376	645	3,796	33	21	17
12	12	Lesnina	Retail trade	66	129	94	182	303	683	49	6	2
13	10	Kolektor Group	Manufacturing	59	235	302	327	1,110	2,879	52	10	9
14	11	Prevent	Manufacturing	50	285	468	435	1,143	3,817	52	5	5
15	5	Trimo	Manufacturing	46	162	231	222	278	979	54	12	12

16	15	Viator & Vektor	Transportation	40	289	322	315	549	2,554	46	11	9
17	25	HIT	Entertainment	37	400	25	300	236	2,548	9	3	3
18	1	JUB	Manufacturing	35	68	84	116	136	342	55	9	9
19	18	Hidria	Manufacturing	33	238	182	243	330	2,400	34	21	17
20	21	Perutnina Ptuj	Manufacturing	32	249	98	219	625	2,289	28	5	3
21	16	Kovintrade	Manufacturing	28	146	166	235	134	294	45	10	9
22	22	ERA	Retail trade	22	91	12	107	163	371	27	2	2
23	14	ETI Elektroelement	Manufacturing	21	83	84	94	431	1,745	47	10	10
24	8	Alpina	Manufacturing and retail trade	20	80	62	75	866	1,625	54	8	7
25	3	Kompas	Travel and related activities	20	51	152	216	206	431	52	16	16
TOTAL				3,903	11,777	7,256	13,885	23,616	81,349		286	53

Source: CIR-VCC survey of Slovene MNEs (see www.vcc.columbia.edu).

Annex Table 11.3 The top twenty-five Slovene MNEs: Regionality Index, 2006

Name	Europe	CIS	Middle East	Africa	North America	Latin America	Southeast Asia	Australia
Mercator	100	–	–	–	–	–	–	–
Gorenje	98	–	2	–	–	–	–	–
Krka	79	14	–	–	7	–	–	–
Droga Kolinska	100	9	–	–	–	–	–	–
Petrol	100	–	–	–	–	–	–	–
Merkur	100	–	–	–	–	–	–	–
Intereuropa	83	17	–	–	–	–	–	–
Helios	81	19	–	–	–	–	–	–
Iskra Avtoelektrika	42	17	8	–	8	8	17	–
Elan	71	–	–	–	14	–	14	–
Unior	71	–	–	–	5	–	19	5
Lesnina	100	–	–	–	–	–	–	–
Kolektor Group	50	–	–	–	20	10	20	–
Prevent	40	–	–	–	–	20	20	–
Trimo	75	25	–	20	–	–	–	–
Viator & Vektor	91	9	–	–	–	–	–	–
HIT	100	–	–	–	–	–	–	–
JUB	89	11	–	–	–	–	–	–
Hidria	67	5	–	–	5	14	10	–
Perutnina Ptuj	100	–	–	–	–	–	–	–
Kovintrade	100	–	–	–	–	–	–	–
ERA	100	–	–	–	–	–	–	–
ETI Elektroelement	80	–	–	–	–	–	20	–
Alpina	63	13	–	–	13	–	13	–
Kompas	88	6	–	–	6	–	–	–

Source: CIR–VCC survey of Slovene MNEs (see www.vcc.columbia.edu).

Note: The Regionality Index is calculated by dividing the number of a firm's foreign affiliates in a particular region of the world by its total number of foreign affiliates and multiplying the result by 100.

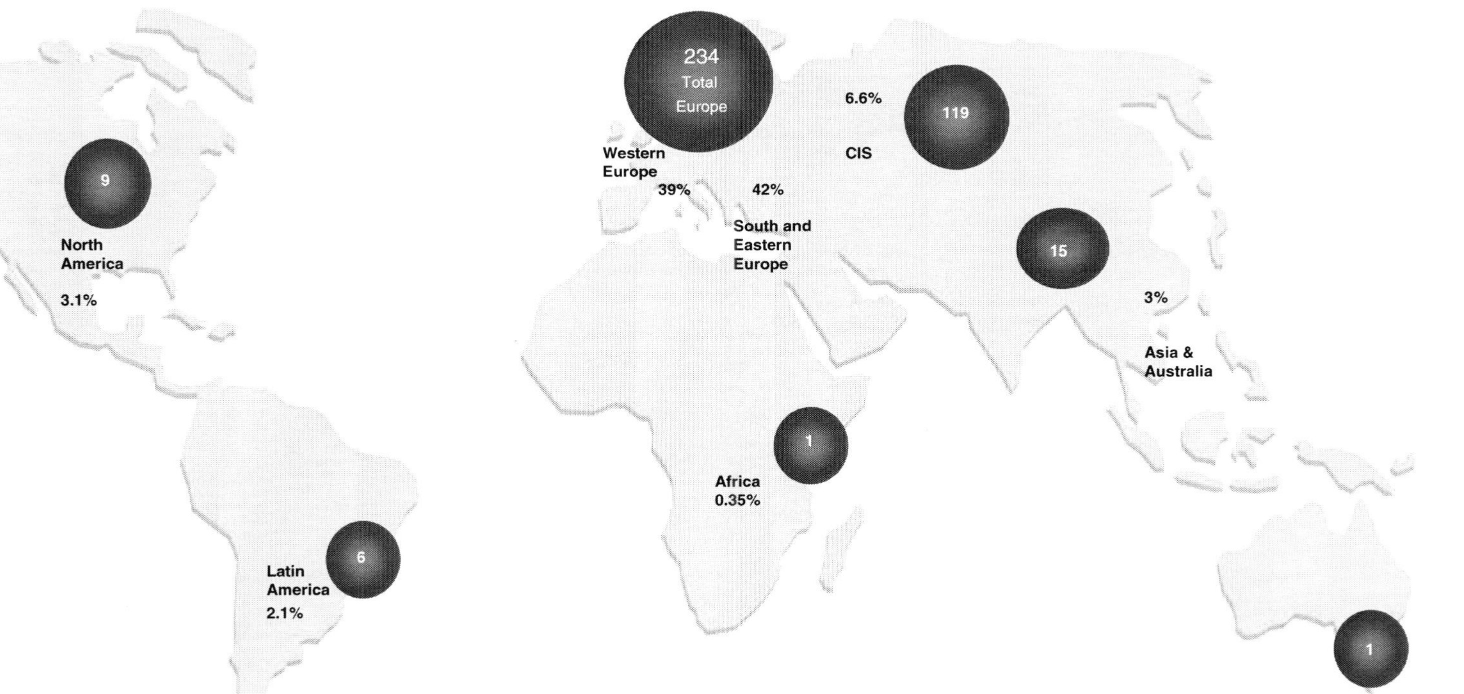

Annex Figure 11.1 Foreign affiliates of the top twenty-five Slovene MNEs, by region, 2006 (number of foreign affiliates and percentage of foreign assets)

Source: CIR-VCC survey of Slovene MNEs (see www.vcc.columbia.edu).

Annex Table 11.4 Profiles of the selected economies

Item	Slovenia	Russia	Brazil	India
Population est. millions	2	141	190	1.147
GDP in US$ billions, est.	55	2.076	1.838	2.965
GDP pc in US$ PPP, est.	27.300	14.600	9.700	2.700
Foreign assets by top MNEs	US$3.9 billion	US$58 billion	n.a.	US$3.56 billion.

Source: CIA World Factbook, 2008, and CIR-VCC survey of Slovene MNEs (see www.vcc.columbia.edu.)

Annex Case Box 11.1   Kolektor: from local to foreign ownership to a Slovene MNE

Kolektor, now a leading producer of commutators in the world (20% of worldwide demand and over 50% of European demand), started as a small Slovene company in 1963. It entered into a joint venture agreement with the German firm Kautt & Bux (K&B) in 1968. In 2002, Kolektor bought out its parent firm and acquired the K&B factory in Germany, becoming a Slovene MNE. It began to transnationalize production in 2000. Today, it produces commutators in a number of major markets: Germany, the United States, China (one greenfield investment, one joint venture), the Republic of Korea, Brazil, and Iran. Cost considerations have also motivated the relocation of production to Bosnia and Herzegovina.

Source: CIR-VCC Survey of Slovene MNEs; see http://www.vcc.columbia.edu.

Annex Case Box 11.2   NLB group among the largest Slovene MNEs

If banks were included in the ranking list, the second-largest MNE in terms of employees abroad and the third in terms of invested capital abroad (probably the first, if investments by its firms abroad were included) would be Slovenia's largest bank, NLB Group. NLB is partially owned by KBC (Belgium) (34%) and the European Bank for Reconstruction and Development (EBRD) (5%). NLB Group's total assets (2006) were US$25 billion, and it had 3,000 (38%) employees abroad—out of a total of 8,000 employees. Its transnationalization began in the 1970s when it was 100% Slovene owned. It now has forty affiliates in sixteen countries. Sixteen of the forty affiliates are banks in which US$624 million was invested by the parent firm, mostly through acquisitions from 2003 to 2007. Most of the affiliates are located in South-East Europe and other Central and Eastern European countries, but also in the European Union. NLB aims to become one of the leading financial groups in its target markets.

Notes

1. Interestingly, the type of joint venture first permitted in Slovenia later served as the model for China.
2. Now NLB; see annex case box 11.2.
3. The Transnationality Index is a composite ratio calculated by averaging the relative shares of foreign assets, foreign employees, and foreign sales as a percentage of their respective totals. See UNCTAD (2007).
4. The data on the top Slovene multinationals are the result of a joint project between the Centre of International Relations, Faculty of Social Sciences, University of Ljubljana, and the Vale Columbia Center on Sustainable International Investment, reassessed on March 18, 2008.
5. Only 11% of companies investing abroad were foreign owned during the early 2000s (Jaklič and Svetličič 2003, 59).
6. The only substantial foreign-owned investor abroad would be Lek, a pharmaceutical company acquired by Novartis in November 2002. Even Lek developed its internationalization strategy as a Slovene firm, becoming an acquisition target for that reason. It was acquired already having twenty-seven affiliates abroad. An opposite example is that of Kolektor, which started as a Slovene firm, later entered into a joint venture with a foreign partner, and in 2004 took over the foreign partner's share and bought its factory in Germany as well, once again becaming a Slovene firm and now an MNE (see annex box 11.2).
7. The following EUR/USD exchange rates, based on XE.com Universal Currency Converter (http://www.xe.com/ucc/), were used throughout: 1.31954 (2006); 1.18395 (2005); 1.35338 (2004).
8. See the ranking lists at http://www.vcc.columbia.edu.
9. This includes food and beverages, chemical and pharmaceutical products, machinery and equipment, electrical equipment, and sport apparel.
10. Calculated as the difference between total sales revenues plus other revenues and stock differences minus total costs of goods, material, services, and other costs per employee (the average annual number of employees is taken).
11. Out of sixteen firms in manufacturing, only one is in a high-tech industry, nine are in medium-technology-intensive industries (mostly medium-high), and five in low-technology-intensive industries.
12. See annex case box 11.2.
13. Ingemar Stenmark, the famous Swedish skier, used Elan skies for racing.
14. The CEO of Droga Kolinska, Slobodan Vucicevic, is Serbian.
15. In these eight MNEs the breakdown is as follows: 40% or more of top management that is foreign: three MNEs; 30% or more of top management that is foreign: two MNEs; 20% or more of top management that is foreign: two MNEs; 10% or more of top management that is foreign: one MNE.
16. For instance, many products and brand names are known to the older generation that lived in Yugoslavia, but not to today's younger generation.
17. Ozawa explained trade- and development-promoting FDI as a result of country's development, own R&D effort, and outward-oriented strategy that altogether attract foreign investors.
18. A very good example is ISKRAEMECO, one of the most internationalized Slovene MNEs, which faced the challenge of technological modernization several years ago. The firm was not able to introduce digital electric meters

into its production program by its own efforts, but refused to go into a strategic partnership or cooperation with a foreign investor, fearing foreign ownership. It has also not properly internationalized its production, only slowly relocating low-end phases to a low-cost country, although the firm does have operations in Malaysia, for instance. Two years ago, the company was faced with closing. With government support, it partially closed and needed to reduce the number of employees substantially. In 2007, it was finally acquired by an Egyptian partner with poor prospects for survival, as the foreign partner is not among the leading ones in the world in electric meters, the major product of ISKRAEMECO.

19. The Transnationality Index of 45 comes close to the 55.8% of the world's 100 largest MNEs (UNCTAD 2005, 17–19).

20. Based on VCC surveys in 2008; see http://www.vcc.columbia.edu.

21. The average top Slovene MNE is thirty-nine times smaller than the average top Russian MNE in terms of assets, and 153 times in terms of sales. The top Brazilian and Indian MNEs also lag well behind the Russian average (8.8 and 38.3 times, respectively, table 11.3). Russian MNEs have the largest average assets and sales, while Brazilian and Indian MNEs are larger in terms of number of employees. Brazilian MNEs have the highest average number of employees, exceeding 20,000. In terms of population, Slovenia is seventy times smaller than Russia, ninety-five times smaller than Brazil, and 573 times smaller than India. The difference in gross domestic product (GDP) is less pronounced, but still ranges from thirty-three to fifty-three times less. Slovenia's GDP per capita, calculated on the basis of purchasing power parity, is almost twice as high as that of Russia, almost three times higher than that of Brazil, and ten times that of India. However, in terms of total assets abroad, the top Slovene MNEs lag behind Russian MNEs by slightly less than fifteen times.

22. In some instances, investing abroad was a means of securing imports of required raw materials from less-developed countries, or intermediate resources from OECD countries.

23. Companies could receive support for (1) the preparation of projects up until the registration of an affiliate abroad (feasibility studies, training) and (2) startup operations abroad and strengthening development work in the parent company (the financing of mentors, production startup costs, material investments, etc.).

24. All together, seventeen programs were introduced. Of these, two were for stimulating exports by SMEs (one for startup activities of microfirms in international markets) and one for stimulating inward FDI. There was obviously a shift from initially restricting outward investment to promoting it. Promoting inward FDI became less important in such a restructuring/enhancing competitiveness strategy context. Promoting inward FDI was nevertheless still considered important, but part of a special program.

25. The survey included projects constituting approximately 49% of all funds allocated in these programs. Hence, the survey can be considered as quite representative (Deloitte and the Faculty of Economics of the University of Ljubljana 2004, 31).

26. Several organizational forms of these offices are foreseen. They can be representative offices of the JAPTI, of Slovene companies or their groups, which receive support in public-tendering procedures, and the internal units at the embassies and consulates of Slovenia abroad.

References

Andrič, V. (2003). "Evaluation of the public biddings for the promotion of entrepreneurship and competitiveness of the Ministry for the Economy," Ljubljana, October.

Balakrishnan, K. (1975). "Indian joint ventures abroad: a case study of foreign investment from the developing countries: a research proposal," mimeo.

Bank of Slovenia (2007a). *Direct Investment 2006* (Ljubljana: Bank of Slovenia), December.

——— (2007b). *Monthly Bulletin* February–March (Ljubljana: Bank of Slovenia).

Central Intelligence Agency (2008). *The World Fact Book 2008* (Washington, DC: Central Intelligence Agency).

DELO, FT (2007). "Največja slovenska podjetja" (The Largest Slovenian Enterprises) May 21, p. 31 (Ljubljana: *DELO*).

———(2007). "Najboljša slovenska podjetja" (Best Slovenian Enterprises) November 26, p. 23 (Ljubljana: *DELO*).

Deloitte and the Faculty of Economics (2004). *Evaluation of Public Biddings on Enhancing Entrepreneurship and Competitiveness 2001–2003* (Ljubljana: University of Ljubljana) (Zaključno poročilo, "Evalvacija razpisov področja za spodbujanje podjetništva in konkurenčnosti v letih 2001–2003").

Finance (2007). May 28, Appendix Top 101, pp. 30–34 (Ljubljana: *Finance).*

Jaklič A., A. Burger, and M. Rojec (2005). *Dinamika in makroekonomske posledice izhodne internacionalizacije v Sloveniji*, CMO-FDV September (Ljubljana: University of Ljubljana), mimeo.

Jaklič, A. and Marjan Svetličič (2003). "Enhanced transition through outward internationalization: outward FDI by Slovenian firms," *Transition and Development* (Burlington, Vermont: Ashgate).

——— (2008). "Največje slovenske multinacionalke—majhnost presegajo v večjo internacionalizacijo" (The largest Slovenian multinationals fighting smallness by internationalization), *IB Review* 42 (2), pp. 40–49.

JAPTI (2008). *Poročilo Javne agencije za podjetništvo in tuje investicije (JAPTI) za leto 2007*, Ljubljana, maj., available at http://www.japti.si/resources/files/doc/dokumenti-pravne-podlage/porocilo-javne-agencije-rs-za-podjetnistvo-in-tuje-investicije-za-leto-2007.pdf , last visited on February 5, 2009.

Kavčič, P. (2001). Editorial, *Podjetnik (Enterpreneur)* (Ljubljana: *Podjetnik*) 17, December.

Ministry of the Economy (2005a). "Programme for the Internationalisation of Firms 2005–2009," draft, July 11 (Ljubljana: Ministry of the Economy).

——— (2005b). "Programme of the Government of the Republic of Slovenia for the promotion of FDI 2005–2009," draft, July (Ljubljana: Ministry of the Economy).

——— (2005c). "Representative Offices of the Slovenian Economy," draft, July 11 (Ljubljana: Ministry of the Economy).

Ozawa, Terutumo (1992). "Foreign direct investment and economic development," *Transnational Corporations* 1, pp. 27–54.

Svetličič, M. (1996). "Outward foreign direct investment and restructuring," *Naše gospodarstvo* 5/6, Letnik 42 (Naše gospodarstvo: Maribor), pp. 3–18.

——— (2007). "Slovenian outward FDI," *Transnational Corporations* 16 (1), pp. 55–81.

——— (2008). "Reversed internationalization path; the case of Slovenia," *AIB Insights* 8 (1), pp. 3–9.

Svetličič, M. and A. Jaklič (2003). "Outward FDI by transition economies: basic features, trends and development implications," in M. Svetličič and M. Rojec, eds., *Facilitating Transition by Internationalization: Outward Direct Investment from Central European Economies in Transition* (Transition and Development Series) (Burlington, Vermont: Ashgate).

Svetličič, M. and C. Bellak (2002). "Investment development path of small transition countries: comparative evaluation of Austria and Slovenia," in M. Svetličič and M. Rojec, eds., *Facilitating Transition by Internationalization: Outward Direct Investment from Central European Economies in Transition* (Transition and Development Series) (Burlington, Vermont: Ashgate), pp. 17–28.

Svetličič, M. and M. Rojec, eds. (2003). *Facilitating Transition by Internationalization: Outward Direct Investment From Central European Economies in Transition* (Transition and Development Series) (Burlington, Vermont: Ashgate).

Svetličič, M., M. Rojec, and S. Lebar (1994). "Internationalisation strategies of Slovenian firms: the German market case," in K. Obloj, ed., *High Speed Competition in a New Europe, Proceedings of the 20th Conference of EIBA,* Warsaw, December 11–13.

UNCTAD (2005).*World Investment Report: Transnational Corporations and the Internationalization of R&D* (New York and Geneva: United Nations).

——— (2007). *World Investment Report: Transnational Corporations, Extractive Industries and Development* (New York and Geneva: United Nations).

Vale Columbia Center on Sustainable International Investment (2008). "Slovenian multinationals—small but growing rapidly,"February 18, available at http://www.vcc.columbia.edu/projects/documents/CIR-CPIIPressReleaseSlovenianMNEs-18March2008.pdf, last visited September 12, 2009.

Vernon, R. (1966). "International investment and international trade in the product cycle," *Quarterly Journal of Economics* 80, pp. 190–207.

Wells, L. Jr. (1983). *Third World Multinationals: The Rise of Foreign Investment From Developing Countries* (Cambridge, MA; London; England: MIT Press).

Chapter 12

South-South Foreign Direct Investment and Political Risk Insurance: Challenges and Opportunities

Multilateral Investment Guarantee Agency,
*World Bank Group**

Introduction: FDI Trends and the Rise of Political Risk

According to the United Nations Conference on Trade and Development (UNCTAD), South-South foreign direct investment (FDI) has been growing rapidly, from an estimated US$6.5 billion in 1990 to some US$60 billion as of 2004 (UNCTAD 2006). UNCTAD estimates that there are over 20,000 multinational enterprises (MNEs) headquartered in emerging markets; many with significant potential to expand further their overseas presence. With global FDI flows estimated at US$1.5 trillion in 2007, and flows from emerging markets an estimated US$210 billion in 2006 (figure 12.1), South-South FDI is poised to increase further.

The latest boom in FDI is taking place as MNEs everywhere are becoming more conscious of the presence of political (noncommercial) risk. This includes government actions that have a direct impact on the conduct of business in a foreign country, such as expropriation, breach of contract, or currency transfer restrictions, as well as war and civil disturbance, including terrorism. According to a global survey of 602 executives carried out by the Economist Intelligence Unit (EIU), there is a growing perception in the MNE world that political risk is on the rise (EIU and CPII 2007). More importantly, over the next five years, political risks, and the threat of production disruption arising from such risks, are expected to increase. Another important finding of the EIU survey was that political risk is perceived to be more significant than economic risk, particularly for investments in developing countries, where political risk was identified as the main constraint by nearly half of the respondents to the survey.

Another survey on the presence and management of different types of risk was carried out in 2007, through some 900 interviews conducted around the world. Ernst & Young interviewed 435 large MNEs with headquarters in twelve developed countries, having links with emerging market companies

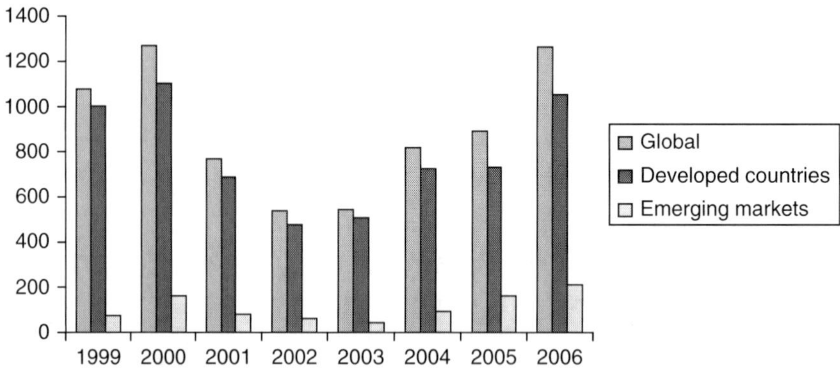

Figure 12.1   FDI outflows, 1999–2006 (US$ millions)
Source: EIU and CPII (2007).

in the form of affiliates, joint ventures, customers, suppliers, and third-party intermediaries. They also interviewed 501 companies in emerging markets (mainly in Brazil, China, India, Russia, and Turkey), which were affiliates of companies in industrialized countries, joint ventures, intermediaries, sizeable customers, or suppliers. A key finding of that survey was that companies based in industrialized countries placed a much greater emphasis on political, operational, and supply chain risk than companies based in emerging markets, which were more concerned with market and currency (exchange rate) risks. This underscores the asymmetry between the importance of political risk in the perception of parent companies on the one hand, and foreign affiliates and related companies on the other.

Perceptions of political risk for South-based MNEs depend on a variety of factors:

- *The industry of investment.* FDI in natural-resource extraction is viewed as riskier than other industries, with mining, oil and gas contract renegotiations, nationalizations, and rising domestic ownership ceilings on the rise. Illustrating this is the experience of Petrobras, Bolivia's largest foreign investor with assets worth US$1.5 billion. Bolivia ordered all oil and gas companies operating in the country to enter into new contracts with the state company, Yacimientos Petrolíferos Fiscales Bolivianos (YPFB), within 180 days. In June 2007, Petrobras transferred all the shares of Petrobras Bolivia Refinancion S.A. to YPFB for US$112 million as the buy-back price. Infrastructure investments are also considered riskier because they are usually large and operate in state-regulated industries, and companies deal directly with governments.
- *The mode of investing.* Greenfield investments, as well as public-private partnerships, are seen as riskier than joint ventures or cross-border mergers and acquisitions. The presence of a domestic partner tends to reduce risk perceptions.
- *The location of investment.* Investments in countries with close cultural affinity or geographical proximity are perceived to be less risky than

investments in far-flung locations with less cultural affinity. Examples of the former include Indian investments in South Asia, Chinese investments in Southeast Asia, and Middle East and North African investments in the Arab world.

- *The home country environment.* A company's experience at home with political and regulatory processes influences its tolerance of political risk when investing abroad. Thus, MNEs based in countries in which there is a perception of high political risk tend to be less sensitive to political risk when investing abroad. Indian MNEs that were interviewed, for example, mentioned that their higher risk tolerance arises from having to operate in a domestic environment characterized by greater political (and economic) uncertainty with frequently changing regulations.
- *The size of the investor/investment.* Large MNEs are more likely to be aware of political risk and to consider mitigating risk, especially for large investments. Smaller companies are less likely to do so, in part because they are less likely to be able to afford political risk insurance.
- *History and experience in investing overseas.* Investors tend to discount the importance of political risk when projects run successfully over a relatively long period of time.

In early 2008, the Multilateral Investment Guarantee Agency (MIGA) presented a special online feature entitled "South-South FDI and PRI: Challenges and Opportunities." The feature addressed the perception of political risk; the demand for, and use of, political risk insurance among South-based MNEs; and the availability of political risk insurance through national public providers. In the context of this feature, MIGA surveyed two large investor countries, India and China, on the availability of political risk insurance by national providers. This research was complemented by inputs from two regional export credit agencies offering investment insurance, the African Trade and Insurance Agency and Islamic Corporation for Insurance of Investments and Export Credits (ICIEC 2007). The surveys sought to gauge South-based investor perceptions of political risk and their demand for PRI, while the inputs (case studies) focused on the availability (supply) of political risk insurance to South-based investors through export credit agencies. The main findings of the surveys and case studies are presented in this chapter.

12.1　South-Based Investors Are Becoming More Aware of Country Risk

In December 2007, MIGA carried out a survey of South-based private companies registered with its online investment information services. The purpose of the survey was twofold: to shed light on the perceptions of, and attitudes toward, political risk by South-based private companies; and to assess the extent to which these companies use investment insurance to mitigate political risks.

The survey was sent to 832 private firms that had specified a developing country as their headquarters or residence. The response rate was just over

4%. While respondents were geographically diverse and represented many sectors, most were based in Africa (North and sub-Saharan) and Central Asia, and were in agribusiness, oil, gas, and mining. The majority were either small or medium-sized enterprises with less than 100 employees, or significantly larger with over 300 employees. In terms of the respondents' investment plans, more than 90% expected their overseas investments to increase over the next five years and more than 80% planned to invest in emerging markets over the next year.

The main findings of the MIGA survey regarding South-based investor perceptions were as follows:

- Political risk is rising in the world today, and it is higher in emerging markets than in industrialized countries. The expected trend is that political risk in emerging markets will stay the same or increase over the next five years.
- Political risk matters a great deal when investing in emerging markets, and virtually all companies that considered it important carried out some type of risk assessment. Such assessments were based primarily on published reports and market intelligence, but also on own experiences and informal discussions with other investors.
- Respondents that did not assess political risk said that they felt comfortable with the country in question on the basis of their own positive past experiences, or because of a good relationship with the country's government.

The case studies that complemented the survey present an additional dimension to the findings. MNEs based in India do seem to have a lower perception of political risk when investing abroad (box 12.1). Interviews of three top MNEs in India carried out in the context of this case study—Tata Steel, NIIT (a global IT solutions corporation), and pharmaceutical company Ranbaxy Laboratories Ltd., as well as two fairly new outward investors, SRF (technical textiles, refrigerant gases) and DCM Sriram Consolidated Limited (DSCL) (chlorovinyl and agribusiness)—all considered investing in the developing world to be relatively safe for foreign investors. The main argument used to support that perception was that host country governments are unlikely to act arbitrarily against foreign investors, because such investment is now globally recognized as an important vehicle for economic development. Says Rajendra Prasad, Chief Financial Officer of SRF, "Developing countries develop not only economically but politically as well. They are unlikely to act arbitrarily against foreign investments, now globally accepted as a force for development," (cited in Nazareth 2007). Some of these companies also cited their ability to operate in a domestic environment with frequently changing regulations as their reason for greater tolerance of political risk abroad.

Firms based in the Middle East and North Africa (MENA) region also appear to have a higher tolerance for risk compared with other investors, as the case study of ICIEC illustrates (box 12.2). Historically, MENA-based investors have not been active users of political risk insurance, feeling

Box 12.1   India: A new investor with a long history of political risk insurance

Indian companies began to set their sights overseas after the liberalization of outward investment in the 1990s removed restrictions on equity investments abroad and increased automatic approval ceilings. However, it was not until the early part of this decade that India began to emerge as an important outward investor, with FDI outflows reaching around US$11 billion in 2006–2007.

Indian investment is flowing to a diverse range of countries across all continents, but increasingly Indian companies are favoring destinations in the industrialized world (Australia and European countries), where political risk is negligible. The bulk of Tata Steel's overseas investment, for instance, has been the US$12 billion purchase of the British-Dutch steel giant, Corus. Ranbaxy and NIIT are investing mostly in the United States, but are also locating in other developed and emerging markets with relatively low perceived political risk.

By industry, two-thirds of India's total outward investment in 2006–2007 was in nonfinancial services. Further, Indian companies are investing overseas primarily through the takeover of existing firms, rather than through greenfield investments. Of the over 300 overseas investments that Indian companies have made since 2000, mergers and acquisitions have almost quintupled—from 37 in 2001 to 170 in 2006. But even those companies that are putting their money into developing countries—such as SRF, with a chemical manufacturing joint venture in China, and DSCL with hybrid seeds operations in the Philippines, Vietnam, and Thailand—do not feel a strong need to insure themselves. As the executives interviewed explained, given that these overseas acquisitions have operated successfully for years, they perceived them to be sufficiently risk tested and not requiring further political risk insurance.

Apart from Tata Steel, none of the companies interviewed have purchased political risk insurance. Tata Steel is currently in the process of implementing a US$100 million ferro-chrome project in South Africa, for which it has been required—as are all foreign direct investors in the country—to buy the civil disturbance and terror coverage provided by the South African Special Risks Insurance Association.

Political risk mitigation in India for outward investment is carried out solely by the Export Credit Guarantee Corporation of India (ECGC), which set up its Overseas Investment Insurance program in 1980, to support Indian companies venturing abroad. Like many other export credit agencies based in emerging markets, investment insurance is a small part of its business. Over the past couple of years, it accounted for about 1% of its premium income. ECGC's Overseas Investment Insurance Program has been restricted by its limited capital base, the amount of reinsurance it raises from the state-run General Insurance Company, and difficulties in raising additional reinsurance from the international market. India has also set up the National Export Insurance Account (US$452 million), with the aim of providing export credit risk covering project exports (for example, related to construction projects) and other large export transactions, thus boosting India's overseas projects.

ECGC protects companies against risks related to expropriation, war, and restrictions on remittances, as well as other political risks as approved by the government. Coverage is up to fifteen years, and only new investments funded by equity or loans are eligible. Coverage is offered for investments in more than 230 countries for which the agency has political risk assessments. While ECGC's concentration of investment guarantees has been in emerging markets in Southeast Asia (especially Indonesia) and a few countries in sub-Saharan Africa (Nigeria and Kenya), more recently it has issued guarantees for investments in the Middle East, emerging Europe, and China. ECGC has only paid out one claim to date—in the former Yugoslavia.

Exim Bank of India, though actively supporting Indian outward investment through a range of products and services, including through direct equity participation, does not provide investment insurance, but does require it as a precondition for lending. However, ECGC and Exim Bank of India are working together to familiarize Indian investors with the concept of political risk insurance.

Source: Nazareth (2007) and Exim Bank of India (2007).

Box 12.2   ICIEC: Thriving on specialized product offerings

Capital flows from the Middle East and North Africa have been increasing substantially over the past few years, with Islamic nations representing a natural path for growth for MNEs based in that region. FDI flows from the Middle East are estimated by UNCTAD to have increased to US$14 billion in 2006, with companies investing increasingly in sub-Saharan Africa, Central and South Asia, and Southeast Asia.

Founded in 1994, the Islamic Corporation for the Insurance of Investment and Export Credit (ICIEC), a member of the Islamic Development Bank Group, provides export credit and insurance to its member states across the Middle East, North and sub-Saharan Africa, and Asia. In addition to export credits and investment guarantees, ICIEC provides reinsurance facilities to member export credit agencies.

A special feature of ICIEC is that it provides insurance facilities to exporters and investors in accordance with *shariah* principles. These principles mean that ICIEC: (1) endeavors to achieve mutual cooperation of policyholders through their collective sharing of losses that any one policyholder may suffer; (2) distributes the surplus that may accrue from the insurance and any reinsurance operations to policyholders after meeting statutory reserve obligations; (3) excludes cover of contracts for the sale of goods prohibited under *shariah*, as well as interest accruing from export credit or investment loans; and (4) invests its own funds in accordance with Islamic principles.

Unlike most other political risk insurance providers, ICIEC specializes in the provision of *shariah*-compliant products to investors. Even though investment insurance is still a small share of its total volume of business, it has been increasing rapidly, with new insurance commitments rising by 73% in the past year. Breach of contract and war and civil disturbance coverage have been particularly popular. Like other political risk insurance providers, ICIEC has engaged in partnerships with other organizations leveraging them to increase capacity constraints in its investment insurance and reinsurance activities. Recently ICIEC collaborated with MIGA to insure a container terminal project in Djibouti under an Islamic financing structure.

Source: ICIEC (2007).

comfortable with their investments mainly in the same region. However, as more of these investors evolve from small, family-owned businesses to sizable international firms with global investment plans, they become more conscious of political risk and the need for risk management.

As South-based firms become more-active investors overseas, their perception of political risk is gradually changing, which is translating into increased demand for political risk insurance. This is evident, for example, in the case of Chinese MNEs in sub-Saharan Africa, which are increasingly exposed to labor unrest, civil strife, and terrorist attacks and are seriously considering such risks as potential threats to their investments there. While these firms are mostly state owned, and may be able to discount such risks in lieu of the perceived long-term benefits their investments will bring to the country, their demand for investment insurance is increasing. This is best exemplified in the portfolio of Sinosure (2007), China's national export credit agency, for which the share of outward investment insurance has jumped from 0.7% in 2004 to 8.7% in 2006. While demand for political risk insurance goes hand in hand with the growing exposure of Chinese MNEs in other emerging markets, the government's policy of encouraging such investment, including through the provision of political risk insurance, helps considerably in mitigating risk, as the case of Sinosure illustrates (box 12.3).

South-based firms also see the specific risk of terrorism, war, and civil disturbance as intensifying over the next few years. For example, Indian MNEs, while discounting risks associated with expropriation or transfer restrictions, do view the specific risk of terrorism as a growing concern.

12.2 Political Risk Mitigation Gaining Ground

The MIGA survey of South-based companies also investigated ways in which these firms mitigate political risk. More than half of the respondents claimed to have either an in-house risk-assessment team or a process in place. One-third claimed that they did not devote any resources to assessing or managing political risk. The main findings of the MIGA survey regarding risk-mitigation tools and political risk insurance were as follows:

- Some 70% of respondents mitigate political risk in some way, and about half do so by purchasing political risk insurance.

Box 12.3   China: Sinosure complements a coordinated outward investment drive

With over 10,000 operations abroad to date and over US$16 billion in outward FDI in 2006 alone, China is emerging as a premier overseas investor. In 2000, China launched a "Going Global" strategy, which entailed, among other things, accessing foreign markets and natural resources via FDI. Various measures were introduced across government ministries and agencies to support this strategy, including new regulations, fiscal incentives, information sharing, and financial assistance.

Sinosure, China's investment insurance agency for both inward FDI (IFDI) and outward FDI (OFDI), was set up in 2001 to support the "Going Global" strategy. The use of political risk insurance expanded quickly in tandem with the growth of OFDI. In 2004, Sinosure set up a separate investment insurance department to address political risk concerns of Chinese companies venturing abroad. As a result, the share of investment insurance in Sinosure's overall business portfolio increased from 0.7% in 2004 to 8.7% in 2006. Sinosure's political risk products are designed to support and encourage Chinese firms to invest abroad by providing coverage for expropriation, war and political violence, transfer restrictions, and breach of contract by the government. As a government-backed agency, Sinosure is active in promoting political risk insurance as a tool for managing cross-border investments.

Sinosure's investment portfolio is heavily skewed in favor of oil and gas, which accounts for 83% of the total by liability. By number of projects, Sinosure's portfolio is more evenly distributed across the principal sectors, with oil and gas accounting for 31%, followed by power and mining. By region, Africa accounts for 84% of the agency's portfolio by number of projects, but only for 20% by liability. To date, Sinosure's portfolio is dominated by state-owned firms. The agency has also concluded cooperation agreements with other political risk insurance providers, as well as reinsurance agencies. Sinosure also offers advisory services and mobilizes financial resources.

Source: Sinosure (2007).

- About 50% of the respondents that purchase political risk insurance do so only sometimes; another 30% does so always.
- For those respondents that do not purchase insurance, the principal reason cited for not doing so was lack of knowledge on how to go about purchasing political risk insurance, followed by cost considerations (insurance being too expensive) and being comfortable with the risk profile of the country in question.
- Over two-thirds of respondents that do purchase political risk insurance do so for projects under US$20 million, especially projects under US$5 million. In terms of industry, the respondents sought political risk insurance coverage largely for manufacturing projects, followed by oil, gas and mining, infrastructure, and agribusiness.

- In terms of region where investment projects are located, sub-Saharan Africa occupied the top spot, followed by North Africa, South Asia, and Central Asia.
- Breach of contract topped the list of type of risk, followed by war, civil disturbance, and terrorism.

Most industrialized countries offer investment insurance to their companies investing overseas via public export credit or investment insurance agencies; the availability of political risk insurance to South-based MNEs is not as widespread. Brazil, for example, a country whose firms invested US$28 billion abroad in 2006,[1] does not have a national agency insuring the overseas investments of Brazilian firms. Other emerging markets, however, have taken steps in offering insurance to their homegrown MNEs mostly through their established export credit agencies.

The structure and products/services of such agencies go hand in hand with the country's history of outward investment, but in many cases the investment insurance dimension has been added to the existing export insurance products. Many of the national agencies, such as the Export Credit Guarantee Corporation of India (ECGC) and the People's Insurance Company of China Group (PICC Group)—the predecessor of Sinosure—were set up initially to issue just export credit insurance. With ECGC established in 1957 and the PICC Group in 1949, these agencies have acquired considerable experience on export credit risk over time. However, only when India and China began to emerge as outward investors did they expand their products and services to offer overseas investment insurance. In the case of China, an altogether new agency (Sinosure) had to be set up in 2001 to specifically address risks associated with cross-border investments.

In addition to national agencies, there are several multilateral organizations that provide political risk insurance, such as the Multilateral Investment Guarantee Agency, the Asian Development Bank, ICIEC, and the African Trade Insurance Agency (ATI 2007). These agencies provide investment insurance to companies investing in their member countries, including South-based MNEs. Apart from private insurers, these agencies may be the sole providers of political risk insurance for some developing country firms that lack such support from their own governments. Pulling resources together into regional agencies, such as ATI, has allowed smaller countries to reap economies of scale in issuance when the small volume of business does not justify the establishment of national agencies.

Like their counterparts in the industrialized world, the structure and governance of the national and regional investment insurers based in emerging markets varies. India's ECGC, for example, is a government-owned agency. Likewise, Sinosure is a state-owned, nonprofit entity whose purpose is to support China's outward investment policies. ATI was funded by its member countries using concessional loans from the World Bank's International Development Association to facilitate trade and investment flows to the region. ICIEC was established by the members of the Organization of the Islamic Conference to promote the use of *shariah*-compatible trade and investment risk-mitigation instruments. All of these agencies have established partnerships with other institutions worldwide (other private or public insurers), multilateral agencies, as well as reinsurers, to increase capacity.

It is important to keep in mind that trade, not investment, is the focus of all of these agencies. For India's Export Credit Guarantee Corporation, its investment insurance portfolio is miniscule, accounting for only 1% of its premium income in the past couple of years, despite the growth of outward investment by Indian firms. ECGC believes that, as Indian companies invest more in emerging markets, there will be a need to raise awareness about the existence of political risk insurance products and to build adequate corporate capacity to address such risk. ICIEC's investment insurance portfolio has also been increasing, but still accounts for only 4% of its business volume. The African Trade Insurance Agency is the exception, with investment insurance accounting for 47% of its portfolio to date (box 12.4).

In the case of emerging markets, when national export credit agencies or other entities offer investment insurance, their product/service range may vary from what is offered by their counterparts in the industrialized world. For example, India's ECGC does not explicitly offer coverage for breach of

---

Box 12.4   African trade insurance agency: born out of multilateral development initiatives

With oil prices at an all-time high and commodity prices at historically high levels, FDI flows into sub-Saharan Africa have been increasing rapidly. Interest in the region by investors from all regions has been rising, with China, India, and Middle Eastern countries making new forays there. South African MNEs are becoming top investors in the region, drawing upon their experience in doing business there.

The African Trade Insurance Agency (ATI), the continent's only multilateral credit insurance agency, was set up in 2001 to provide political risk coverage for trade and investment projects in its member countries. It originated from a World Bank International Development Agency regional initiative, which provided US$100 million in concessional loans to the founding member countries to set up the agency. ATI is registered as an international organization. Despite its development orientation in deciding upon eligible projects, ATI's business is very similar to that of other public political risk insurance providers. However, ATI makes a special effort to support private-sector participation in the economies of its members through a variety of political risk insurance products. With a membership of twelve African states to date, as well as other organizations, ATI has been active in leveraging partnerships with public- and private-sector agencies to insure investments in its members. ATI has also been seeking to expand its membership to other states in North Africa, as well as to countries in other regions, especially India and China. South-based investors from sub-Saharan Africa and Asia have been active users of ATI's products and services.

Source: Africa Investor (2007).

contract, although it allows for such coverage if specifically approved by the government. Related to that are issues of capacity, pricing, and access to reinsurance, as well as products tailored to the needs of small and medium-sized firms, which are often the core of outward investment from emerging markets. In general, the products and services offered by political risk insurance providers based in emerging markets tend to be more rudimentary, less sophisticated, and not as extensive as those in the developed world.

Some products offered by South-based investment insurers are better tailored to the needs of investors. One such example is *shariah*-compliant investment insurance offered by ICIEC to foreign investors, including those from its own member countries. Another example is Sinosure, with services that go beyond political risk insurance as it seeks to facilitate access to financing for Chinese companies by mobilizing financial resources. It also helps companies develop effective solutions for expanding overseas by providing information regarding laws and regulations and investment approval procedures. This similar to products of export credit agencies and investment insurance providers in industrialized countries, which often offer advisory services to potential investors, including country-specific information, to help companies assess risks before deciding on a particular location.

To assess risk-mitigation tools available to South-based investors, MIGA conducted a survey of political risk insurance providers during November–December 2007 with the purpose of (1) gauging their perceptions of the presence of political risk and (2) taking stock of their investment risk-mitigation products, with particular focus on South-South instruments. MIGA surveyed sixty-eight political risk insurance providers that are (1) members (public and private) of the Berne Union's Investment Committee and the Prague Club; (2) members of the Lloyd's syndicate; and/or (3) multilateral institutions. The response rate was 35% (over 50% for Berne Union members alone and more than 80% for multilateral institutions). For nearly 71% of the responding agencies, revenue from investment insurance constituted less than half of total revenues, and for 60% of them, investment insurance operations employed less than ten people. Projects in emerging markets feature large in their portfolios, with one-third of the responding agencies claiming that such projects account for all investment insurance issued in the last year of operation. Apart from investment insurance, trade insurance and finance are the principal services offered in general by these agencies, while some also offer consultancy services.

The main findings of this survey were as follows:

- For 40% of the responding agencies, demand for political risk insurance had remained steady, and for 47% it had increased over the past five years.
- The total number of investment insurance contracts issued by relevant respondents increased from 362 in 2002 to 502 in 2006.
- Almost two-thirds of respondents felt that demand for political risk insurance was likely to grow over the next five years; less than one-third felt that it would stay the same. Some 80% of the responding agencies expected

demand for political risk insurance by South-based investors to increase over the next five years.

- By type of political risk and in terms of contracts issued, expropriation and war, civil disturbance, and terrorism were in the highest demand, followed by breach of contract. Demand for transfer restrictions was ranked as "medium."
- By industry of investment and in terms of contracts issued, finance was in top place, followed by infrastructure and manufacturing. East Asia and the Pacific, followed by Latin America, were the biggest investment destinations.
- Most investment contracts for the last available year had been issued for projects in the value range of US$5–20 million. There were very few projects over US$80 million. Premiums charged were between 30 and 100 basis points. Companies purchasing investment insurance from the responding agencies employed between 100 and 300 people.
- The two top factors hindering the purchase of investment insurance by South-based investors were lack of perceived need and lack of awareness of investment insurance as a risk-mitigation instrument. Cost was also cited as a relatively important consideration.

The survey findings, coupled with case studies for India, China, ICIEC, and ATI, suggest that the increase in South-based FDI and growing awareness on the part of South-based companies about the availability of risk-mitigation instruments is translating into a sustained increased demand for political risk insurance. However, for most providers, investment insurance is still a small, but growing, part of their overall business volume. South-based political risk insurance providers are responding to this demand to varying extents, but some are facing constraints in terms of capacity. There are concerted efforts to overcome these by leveraging partnerships with other providers and reinsurers. At the same time, providers are seeking to further boost general investor awareness of political risk insurance, and to develop products suited to their specific requirements.

Conclusions

As the world becomes a riskier place for investors, it is in the interest of governments to ensure that their companies are protected against political risk when investing abroad. Many countries actively promote OFDI, and political risk mitigation could become an integral part of such programs. Initiatives may include expanding the services offered by existing export credit insurance agencies to include investment insurance; awareness raising of the different political risk insurance products available; and campaigns to increase awareness about the presence of political risk and appropriate mitigation tools.

Notes

*This chapter is based on research undertaken by the Multilateral Investment Guarantee Agency (MIGA) of the World Bank Group for an online feature that appeared on PRI-Center (http://www.PRI-Center.com) in 2008 on "South-South FDI and Political Risk." It was first presented by Persephone Economou at the Five-Diamond International Conference on "Thinking Outward: Global Players from Emerging Markets," held at Columbia University, April 28–29, 2008.

1. Much of that was due to the purchase of Inco (Canada) by Vale for US$17 billion.

References

ATI (2007). *Regional Trends in FDI and PRI: The Case of the African Trade Insurance Agency* (Nairobi: ATI), mimeo.

Economist Intelligence Unit (EIU) and Columbia Program on International Investment (CPII) (2007). *World Investment Prospects to 2011: Foreign Direct Investment and the Challenge of Political Risk* (London and New York: Economist Intelligence Unit).

Ernst & Young (2007). *Risk Management in Emerging Markets* (London: Ernst & Young).

EXIM Bank of India (2007). *Developing Countries—Globalizing through Overseas Investment* (Washington, DC: EXIM Bank of India), mimeo.

ICIEC (2007). *Regional Developments in FDI and PRI: The Case of the Islamic Corporation for the Insurance of Investment and Export Credit* (Jeddah, Saudi Arabia: ICIEC), mimeo.

Nazareth, Premila (2007). *India's Political Risk Insurance Industry* (New Delhi), mimeo, available at http://www.pri-center.com/documents/south_south/India.pdf, last visited May 11, 2010.

Sinosure (2007). *The Business of Investment Insurance* (Beijing, China: Sinosure), mimeo.

UNCTAD (2006). World Investment Report 2006: FDI from Developing and Transition Economies: Implications for Development (New York and Geneva: United Nations).

Part Three

The Policy Landscape—Outward FDI from Emerging Markets

Chapter 13

What Can Emerging Markets Learn from the Outward Direct Investment Policies of Advanced Countries?

Peter J. Buckley, Jeremy L. Clegg, Adam R. Cross, and Hinrich Voss

Introduction

In scholarly and political circles, the economic gains to a country of attracting inward foreign direct investment (IFDI) are now largely uncontested. Such investments are generally perceived to bring a number of benefits to a host economy, not least in relation to employment, productivity levels, organizational and managerial practices, backward and forward linkages, technology, and greater participation in the international division of labor (Buckley and Casson 1998). In recognition of these benefits, much of the policy debate concerning foreign direct investment (FDI) has revolved around IFDI policies and international investment agreements (IIAs), with capital exporting countries usually seeking greater market access, nondiscriminatory treatment, and investment protection in host countries that improves the competitiveness of their own multinational enterprises (MNEs), and developing countries offering increasingly attractive investment policy regimes (UNCTAD 1995). One outcome is that policies toward IFDI have now become relatively well established, wide ranging, and transparent among both developed and developing countries. At the same time, our understanding of the relationship between policy and inward investing firm behavior is reasonably well advanced (Rugman and Brewer 2001).[1]

The same cannot be said, however, for outward foreign direct investment (OFDI). It is common for the home countries of MNEs to experience distinctive phases of OFDI policy, often linked to their level of economic development. This has given rise to a policy continuum that ranges from regimes that are highly liberalized and FDI promoting, to those that are neutral and permissive (where market forces largely dictate firm behavior), through to those that are, for the most part, regulatory and restrictive in nature, with outright prohibition at the extreme (Moran 2008). The position of a home country along this policy spectrum depends, more often than not, on whether OFDI is considered to strengthen or weaken its economy, with key influences being, in addition to the level of national economic development, their perceived dependence on international financial flows and, typically, concerns over total factor productivity growth, domestic investment levels, export intensity (Kokko 2006), and the balance of payments, especially in times of foreign exchange shortfalls (UNCTAD 1995, 2006b). Other factors, such as the effect of OFDI on other policy priorities, such as those relating to research and development (R&D) activities, education and training, migration of talent, and technology transfers, may also come into play (Moran 2008). In general, more advanced economies have come to adopt a liberalized approach to OFDI, albeit with FDI promotion policies sometimes subsumed within those that promote exports or downplayed amid societal concerns that MNEs export jobs. In contrast, many developing and transition economies have historically adopted a policy orientation that is either neutral (because low magnitudes render it irrelevant, for example) or, more commonly, is restrictive in character (UNCTAD 1995). The latter orientation typically derives from the imposition of exchange controls such as, among other things, capital export restrictions (to keep investments at home), controls on capital flight, and limitations on the repatriation of foreign-owned capital (to encourage reinvestment), with OFDI restriction a policy objective or, at times, an unintended consequence (UNCTAD 2006b). At the same time, OFDI policy, in both developed and developing countries, is generally much more amorphous, diffused, and less clearly delineated in comparison with policies toward export promotion, inbound FDI, and IIAs. Moreover, much less analytical attention has been given to the policy and regulatory stance of developed countries toward OFDI, either in terms of the overall effectiveness of policy (i.e., value for money) and of the government agencies that administer them, or the concomitant effect on, for example, the volume, industry composition, and direction of OFDI (Te Velde 2007; UNCTAD 2006b; but see Moran 2008; Solis 2003).

Over the past decade, the rise of FDI from emerging markets (developing countries and transition economies), and from large emerging markets in particular, has dramatically altered the policy landscape (Sauvant 2005; Sauvant, Mendoza, and Ince 2008; UNCTAD 2006b). This can be attributed to, among other things, the response of private firms from developing countries to heightened international competition (especially in domestic markets) and a desire to improve foreign market access. However, it also reflects a more liberal policy stance toward OFDI. Recognition is growing among many developing countries that OFDI can bolster the competitiveness of indigenous firms, or bring other benefits to the domestic economy, such as greater integration into the global economy—the means to overcome domestic supply constraints in areas such as raw materials, energy, skilled labor, and proprietary assets. Singapore, for example, has introduced a range of measures to facilitate the international expansion of both public and private enterprises under its 2004 "year of internationalization" initiative; China has done the same under its "Go Global" policy, which was formally adopted in 2000 (see chapter 15), and, in 2005, the Indian government announced its intention to remove barriers to the growth and internationalization of Indian companies (see chapter 9). In some cases, this is being financed by sovereign wealth funds (SWFs). However, despite this broad shift in outlook among developing countries at the national level, policies that provide practical support and assistance to firms in a proactive manner are generally absent or in a nascent state (UNCTAD 2006b).

Given this backdrop, the purpose of this chapter is to assess the policy framework of developed countries toward OFDI and to draw lessons from this for policy formulation in developing countries. For the purposes of this study, we follow John Kline (2003) who conceptualized this framework as being implemented through the introduction of home country measures (HCMs), which comprise those laws, regulations, policies, and programs that affect outflows of FDI.[2]

To understand better the process of OFDI and to infer lessons for emerging markets, especially for those that are becoming increasingly important as sources of FDI, we assess the evolution of the policy environment on OFDI in developed countries from the late nineteenth century until today. Our assessment draws on the neoclassical static theoretical models of FDI and brings the analysis up-to-date using modern theory. These earlier models have been remarkably tenacious in some quarters of intellectual thinking, particularly in policy decision making, especially up to the late 1960s, and even beyond (Dunning and Lundan 2008). And yet, as we show in this chapter, the premises of neoclassical theory are frequently irrelevant or misleading in the modern context. With the shift in academic focus from the viewpoint of capital flows being an aggregate toward concentrating on the agent, namely the MNE, our understanding of the consequences and impact of OFDI has become more refined. We have seen the outcome of this in the form of more positive home country policies toward OFDI.

The remainder of the chapter first presents a theory of OFDI and discusses some potential effects on the home economy. Following the establishment of the theoretical foundation for our study, we discuss and assess OFDI policies in developed countries from two perspectives: (1) restrictive policy and (2) promotional policy. The first is important for policy formulation in developing countries for understanding the appropriate timing of OFDI liberalization, and the second for understanding how governments may encourage the development and growth of domestic MNEs. Our focus is on the principal source countries for FDI, namely, the United States, Japan, and the United Kingdom (UNCTAD 2007). We then use our analysis to propose development policy lessons for emerging markets. The last section concludes the chapter and outlines recommendations for further research.

13.1 The Neoclassical Theory of Outward Investment

The neoclassical theory of outward investment assumes that capital is homogeneous between different locations and firms (MacDougall 1960). It is further assumed that perfect competition, full-labor employment, and diminishing returns on investment exist and that no barriers impede international capital transfer (Hood and Young 1979). Based on these assumptions, the neoclassical theory focuses on investment flows only and analyzes the effects of OFDI on the level of investment in the home and host economies. Following these preconditions, a firm allocates its investments to the location where it can achieve the highest returns. Hence, and as the Feldstein-Horioka model shows, capital is reallocated from capital-rich, low-interest-rate countries to countries with higher interest rates and a lower capital stock. This process continues until the interest rates and capital stock of the countries in approximation have reached equilibrium (Feldstein and Horioka 1980). If investors were constrained to invest only locally, then capital-rich countries would limit domestic investors to lower rates of return, and a globally inefficient allocation of capital would result.

Under these classic static conditions, three scenarios (table 13.1) concerning the effects of OFDI on the home economy are theoretically possible (Hood and Young 1979).

13.1.1 Classical Assumption

Under the classical assumption, OFDI substitutes for domestic investment in the home country and increases the level of investment in the host economy by the same amount. This "Penrosian" view of the constraints on firm growth assumes that the firm is effectively capital rationed because of managerial constraints on business expansion, so investment abroad substitutes for investment at home (a firm-level argument).

13.1.2 Reverse Classical Assumption

Under the reverse classical assumption, foreign investment substitutes for host country investment and leaves the home country level of investment unchanged. This might occur, for example, if OFDI is directed toward retaining lost market share and defending existing shares, or when capital markets are segmented, and outward investment is financed by local host country borrowings.

Table 13.1   Effects of OFDI on the total level of investment in the host and home economy

Assumption	Economy	
	Home economy	Host economy
Classical	–	+
Reverse classical	None	–
Anticlassical	None	+

Source: Based on Hood and Young (1979).

13.1.3 Anticlassical Assumption

Under the anticlassical assumption, an increase in world investment through FDI is stipulated. FDI adds to host country investment with no decline in investment levels in the home economy. This might be caused, for example, by a switch from consumption to investment as expected future returns encourage investment over consumption.

The justification for restrictions on OFDI is premised upon the existence of distortions (a divergence between private and social values) in some parts of the home country economy.

OFDI restrictions can take the form of:

- Specific restrictions or requirements for approval to purchase foreign exchange for the purpose of acquiring assets abroad
- Limits on the amount of foreign exchange that can be transferred for the purpose of investment abroad
- Requirements, authorizations, or restrictions on the repatriation of capital or foreign exchange holding
- Multiple currency practices that apply to the purchase or surrender of foreign exchange-related capital transfers. (Johnston and Ryan 1994)

One could add to this list OFDI project approval processes and requirements to declare, report, notify, or register investment intentions and activities (UNCTAD 2006b). Based on the three assumptions provided above, the rationale for restricting outward investment in these ways can be derived. First, when domestic savings are scarce, they should be used for domestic investments only, as the country's economy gains little (if at all) from investments abroad (the classical assumption). Second, it is important for the home country to maintain a stable and sustainable tax base in order to generate a sufficient income to fulfill the political and social spending objectives of government. Outward investment would reduce domestic investment and therefore the tax base (the classical assumption) (Mathieson and Rojas-Suarez 1992; Hood and Young 1979). Third, and as James S. Duesenberry (1966) argued, free international capital flows are undesirable because (1) the effectiveness of domestic monetary policy decreases and (2) internationally uniform interest rates are required to diminish the likelihood of investment distortion. Hence, Duesenberry argued that private outward investment has to be "... 'made good' by corresponding volumes of exports or imports or offset by other financial transactions" (Duesenberry 1966, 348). An export surplus large enough to offset the outflow of capital and its effects on the balance of payments has to be generated. Therefore, Duesenberry suggested the following: (1) the restriction of outward investment through taxation or regulation; (2) the counterbalance of capital outflow through long-term borrowing; or (3) the maintenance of higher interest rates.

From a similar balance-of-payments perspective, Stephen G. Triantis (1952) argued, with reference to the *Report of Advisory Committee on Overseas Investment* (1950), that some countries (such as Canada, for example) may have limited capability to invest abroad when a large current account surplus is absent. He qualified this finding as being short-term oriented, however, and argued that, in the long term, outward investment may help to improve the balance-of-payments situation of a country. However, capital controls can "create inefficiencies in the domestic financial system and inhibit risk diversification" (Mathieson and Rojas-Suarez 1992, 26). Capital controls can also reduce productivity and performance gains for local companies, as higher returns on investments abroad are placed beyond their reach. This weakens the competitiveness of local producers.

One shortcoming of the classical assumption is that it does not take into account second- and third-order effects of outward investment on the home economy (table 13.2), nor does it place much importance on the strategic considerations of the firms involved, their investment motives, and the kind of investment projects they undertake. In other words, the classical assumption does not consider the firm as the unit of analysis or the way by which the creation of internal markets that help the firm to overcome market imperfections changes the rationale underpinning policy on international investment (Buckley and Casson 1976). Neither does it consider how the pursuit of market power might impact on policy toward outward investment.

The neoclassical model of OFDI has influenced strongly policy decision making, as we show below when we introduce the case studies of selected developed countries. Before doing so, however, we revisit post-neoclassical thinking on OFDI. Intellectual change set in with the Hymerian revolution

Table 13.2 Balance-of-payments effects of OFDI

Effect	Type of transaction	Susceptibility to quantitative measure	Balance of payments effect
Immediate effects	OFDI flows	Balance of payments data	–
	Related merchandise exports	Breakout from balance of payments data and special surveys	+
Secondary (second order) effects	Export of materials and spare parts	Survey data on OFDI operations	+
	Exports of services, including management and patent rights	Balance of payments data and special survey	+
	Earnings remitted	Balance of payments data and special survey	+
Tertiary (third order) effects	Export promotion through overseas affiliates	Data on operation of direct investments	+
	Export displacement by production of overseas affiliates	Data on operation of direct investments	–
	Import competition	Data on operation of direct investments	–

Source: Bruck and Lees (1968, 27).

and the age of the modern theory of OFDI, but policy making did not change.

13.2 Toward a Modern Understanding of OFDI

Neil Hood and Stephen Young argue that the "theoretical case for restricting outward direct investment is by no means strong, particularly once some of the other restrictive assumptions of the [neoclassical] models, e.g., perfect competition, diminishing marginal productivity of capital, etc., are abandoned.... Not all... divergence [between social and private interest] provide arguments for limiting outward direct investment" (1979, 287). Indeed, there are efficiency gains to be reaped from greater capital account liberalization. On a global scale (and assuming no significant market distortions), savings are allocated in the most productive location, which brings benefits to everyone. On a national and subnational level, the opening of capital accounts for OFDI increases the competitive pressure on indigenous firms, which can lead to efforts to increase their productivity (Mathieson and Rojas-Suarez 1992). Theoretical advances in the understanding of the raison d'être of the MNE inform this analysis, as we now show.

Stephen Hymer (1960) argued that firms internationalize because they develop a dominant position in their home economy and therefore possess advantages over other domestic firms. These advantages can then be exploited in a monopolistic fashion in the host country. The monopolistic rents that the company gains during this period must be large enough to compensate for the risks associated with investing in a new and unfamiliar business, political, and cultural environment or, in other words, to compensate for the liability of foreignness (ibid.). International expansion through FDI is undertaken to gain or exploit an advantage over (local) competitors in a host country by replacing imperfect external markets in intermediate products and services with their organizational, hierarchical corporate structure and by appropriating the returns that this may generate (ibid.; Buckley and Casson 1976; Buckley 1988). By internalizing the market, companies can benefit from lower transaction costs (such as communication and contracting costs), improved protection of intangible assets, increased bargaining power, improved buyer-seller certainty, and expanded transfer pricing possibilities (Agarwal 1980). They can also fully appropriate the returns on their investment. All this alludes to the fact that the allocation of capital and its employment is heterogeneous across both firms and locations, as some firms achieve a more efficient allocation of capital, especially when they can create an internal international capital market.

Internalization theory and the gains of monopolistic advantage are incorporated in the Ownership-Location-Internalization (OLI) paradigm proposed by John H. Dunning (1977, 2001; see also Dunning and Lundan 2008). Besides considering ownership advantages (O) and internalization advantages (I), Dunning added locational advantages (L) to create a triumvirate of factors that determines FDI. Locational advantages normally take the form of immobile factor endowments that are combined with the ownership advantages of a firm. Related to the OLI paradigm are the firm's inherent motives to invest abroad; that is, for market-, resource- or efficiency-seeking purposes. Whatever the precise motive for FDI, its purpose is to increase profit (and market capitalization). For this reason, we need to compare the (marginal) returns on FDI (overseas assets) with the (marginal) returns on domestic investment (assets). With these firm-centered approaches, we can also take into account global changes in demand and technology. In this respect, FDI and exports may be complements, not substitutes.

Following the modern understanding of the MNE and the determinants of OFDI, a wider spectrum of welfare effects on the home country's economy can be analyzed (table 13.3). Possible negative welfare effects stimulate a discussion of outward investment restrictions. The welfare effects are discussed here under the assumption that a country is only a source for FDI but does not receive any IFDI. This qualification is lifted in the concluding discussions of this chapter. In welfare terms, remitted profits, as a return on FDI, represent one type of benefit to the home country. These remitted profits are taxed by the home country's government and provide it with social benefits (Casson 2007). Secondary effects arise from increases in exports, which can benefit a wider range of domestic businesses (Visser 2006). Further effects derive from a redistribution of wealth from labor to capital and a substitution of skilled labor for unskilled labor (Hood and Young 1979). The latter describes a relocation of "blue-collar" employment to foreign affiliates, while efforts in R&D, marketing, and general headquarters management are increased at home, leading to greater employment, especially of "white-collar" workers.

Table 13.3　Effects of OFDI on the home economy

Effect	Type of transaction	Effect on the home economy
Immediate firm effects		
	Employment	?
	Sales	+
Mid-term economy effects		
	Wealth distribution from labor to capital	?
	Imports	−
	Exports	+
	Skilled labor demand	+
	Unskilled labor demand	−
	Remittance of profits	+
Long-term economy effects		
	Technology export	−
	Imports	+
	Exports	−

Sources: Casson (2007); Hood and Young (1979).

Analyzing the social and private outcomes of OFDI, Anthony E. de Jasay (1960) concluded that it is not possible to determine when private FDI is too large or too small to impact negatively on the home country. General recommendations for public policy, he therefore continued, are not possible. This is because there is no domestic loss from OFDI (e.g., in the case of resources or market-seeking investment) when domestic investments are not feasible. Market-seeking FDI, for instance, is a means of circumventing trade barriers; and, in certain cases, such as global oligopolies, the nature of international competition requires direct investment in markets abroad to preserve market share.

Under modern theoretical reasoning, it is appropriate to consider whether there is a case for subsidizing or supporting OFDI by nonfinancial means. The argument here must rest on the existence of positive externalities from OFDI. Those spillovers (to the home country), or nonpriced effects, must provide dynamic benefits or welfare gains at home. The argument for the creation of "national champions" relies on such effects, for example. A subsidy for leading firms enables them to overcome barriers to internationalization (possibly host-government imposed) so that economies of scale and scope can be reaped, which enables profitability to be increased. Another version of this argument is to support "asset seeking" abroad, which enables home country firms to acquire foreign assets to combine synergistically with their existing internal assets, again to enhance long-term profitability. Such assets may relate to immobile factor endowments such as natural resources (resource-seeking FDI) and technology, brands, and other types of intellectual capital (strategic asset-seeking FDI). An analogous argument is derived from the so-called "global war for talent," which implies that OFDI is necessary to tap into immobile pools of skilled (knowledge) workers. A more intangible argument is nationalistic in nature and proposes that "our" firms need to locate in foreign R&D clusters to gain benefits. All these arguments assume that the asset sought is immobile and can best be accessed through undertaking OFDI. A weaker version of the support for the OFDI argument is an informational one, in that the provision of information (rather than financial subsidies) by government institutions is necessary to assist firms with OFDI. Again, this argument depends on externalities being internalized that ultimately will reap benefits for the home country in the form of (future) profits, and that these can then be taxed for the social good. We return to these discussions later in this chapter.

A further argument to be derived from the modern theory of the MNE is that policies need to be nuanced to account for different investment *types*, as FDI is not an undifferentiated phenomenon. Examples of differentiated policies might be by entry mode (so that mergers and acquisitions are treated differently from greenfield entry and wholly owned subsidiaries from joint ventures, for instance), or by motive (market-seeking versus resources-seeking versus efficiency-seeking). It also raises the argument that policies should be differentiated over time, according to whether future FDI is to be conducted by small firms, emerging MNEs, or established MNEs. This suggests a sequencing of policy stances as the country's OFDI develops. Indeed, policies could be tailored to be destination specific, industry specific, volume specific, or mode and motive specific. The problem with highly differentiated policies is that governments simply do not have the knowledge and information that are of a sufficiently timely nature to implement policies strategically. One area where this is essential, however, is in the distinction between legitimate capital outflows and illegitimate ones. Any well-designed policy to encourage OFDI must identify and discriminate against money laundering, capital flight, "round tripping," and tax evasion, for example. It is often difficult to make this distinction with any precision, and this is a major discouragement to policies that support OFDI. All these issues are of particular concern to policy formulation in emerging markets.

We can conclude from this brief discussion that the motives of firms investing abroad are crucial to the design of policies on OFDI. It follows that, in order to be effective, such policies should take account of the nature and extent of the ownership advantages of those domestic firms that are already internationally active or have the capabilities and capacities to become so.

13.3 Historic Development of Capital Controls in Developed Countries

Capital controls are a subclass of capital restrictions in the capital account of the balance of payments that involve quantitative restrictions (as opposed to unlimited restrictions at a penalty price) (Cooper 1999). OFDI is recorded under the capital accounts and can, therefore, be affected by capital controls (table 13.4). This section discusses capital controls and other measures historically employed by home countries to restrict the outflow of long-term capital. We discuss the OFDI controls of some selected developed countries with an emphasis placed on the United States as a major source of FDI.

In the modern era, it was commonplace for countries to introduce capital restrictions during World War I to secure a financial base to conduct the war. To achieve this, capital outflows for the purchase of foreign assets were generally prohibited. Such controls tended to disappear after World War I, only to be reintroduced following the economic crisis of the 1930s, in order to achieve greater monetary policy freedom and exchange rate stability (Neely 1999). Later, in the immediate post–World War II period, it was again argued that OFDI should be restricted on the basis that it was detrimental to the objective of achieving full employment (Balogh 1945). Hence, the International Monetary Fund (IMF) Article of Agreements from the mid-1940s (Article VI, section 3) explicitly allowed member countries to implement capital controls to restrict such outflow (Neely 1999). However, some commentators, such as Arthur I. Bloomfield (1946), placed an emphasis in their analysis on raising "good" long-term investment (i.e., OFDI) and on better control of short-term investments only. Capital controls were widely applied in developed countries after World War II (Johnston and Ryan 1994), and this limited net foreign assets acquisition during much of the 1950s and 1960s (Mathieson and Rojas-Suarez 1992; Johnston and Ryan 1994). Capital controls were maintained throughout most of the 1960s

Table 13.4 Purposes of OFDI-focused capital controls

Purpose of control	Rationale	Example
Generate revenue/ finance war efforts	Controls on capital outflows permit a country to run higher inflation with a given fixed-exchange rate and also hold down domestic interest rates	During World War I and World War II
Financial repression/ credit allocation	Governments that use the financial system to reward favored industries or to raise revenue may use capital controls to prevent capital from going abroad to seek higher returns	Historically common in developing countries
Correct balance-of-payments deficit	Controls on outflows reduce demand for foreign assets without contractionary monetary policy or devaluation. This allows a higher rate of inflation than otherwise would be possible	U.S. Interest Equalization Tax 1963–1974
Preserve savings for domestic use	The benefits of investing in the domestic economy may not fully accrue to savers so the economy, as a whole, can be made better off by restricting the outflow of capital	
Protect domestic financial firms	Controls that temporarily segregate domestic financial sectors from the rest of the world may permit domestic firms to attain economics of scale to compete in world markets	

Source: Neely (1999).

and 1970s but were eased with regard to OFDI in a growing number of developed countries from the 1950s and 1960s onward (Areskoug 1976), to be phased out by many in the 1970s. Key drivers of liberalization in the developed countries were the deepening integration of global capital markets (which meant that governments were less concerned about the detrimental effects on balance of payments), the liberalization codes of the Organisation for Economic Co-operation and Development (OECD) and the economic deepening of the European Community, with one fundamental tenet of this being the free movement of capital (UNCTAD 1995). By the end of the 1970s, most OECD countries had introduced more liberal policies toward OFDI (OECD 1979). However, the pace of liberalization was uneven across countries. France and Italy abandoned major capital controls in the late 1980s and, by 1994, of the OECD countries, only Japan, Portugal, and Turkey continued to have some measure of outward investment control in place, albeit with a focus on financial institutions and benefits to the home country (UNCTAD 1995; Mathieson and Rojas-Suarez 1992). The liberalization of capital accounts was typically accompanied by extensive economic stabilization and reform programs (Mathieson and Rojas-Suarez 1992).

13.3.1   United States

The U.S. government intervened in capital exports for much of the first two decades of the twentieth century and exhibited a tendency toward nationalism in policy formulation (Edwards 1924). By 1946, however, the United States had removed the majority of war-related capital controls and restored unrestricted freedom on outward capital movements (Bloomfield 1946). Writing on this period, Bernard Goodman states that "it is a widely accepted premise…that the United States Government should pursue policies to encourage a substantial increase in outflow of [private] capital" (Goodman 1957, 263), primarily to support economic development in underdeveloped foreign areas, to support the reconstruction of war-affected countries, and to raise the competitiveness of its firms. To this end, private investment was preferred over government-led investment, and state guarantees were introduced in 1950 to reduce investment risk for companies. This included the "guarantees of convertibility and freedom of expropriation" (Wu 1950, 61). Further measures included the appointment by the U.S. government of consultants to advise on ways of stimulating OFDI, the identification by consular staff of overseas investment opportunities for U.S. companies and the organization of events to promote investments in particular regions, such as Latin America (Goodman 1957). The political perception of OFDI in the United States at this time was that it served national interests because it helped to spread democracy, stabilize countries, and bring peace (ibid.). In the 1960s, however, capital controls were incrementally reintroduced to improve a weakening balance-of-payments position caused by overvaluation of the U.S. dollar and a sharp rise in U.S. OFDI (Bruck and Lees 1968; Johnston and Ryan 1994; Eichengreen 2000; Wright and Moloy 1974; Lancaster 1969). The U.S. Treasury's stance toward OFDI was based on the perception that the payback period was too long (Lindert 1971). In 1963, the U.S. government introduced the Interest Equalization Tax to raise the prices of foreign bonds and reduce foreign lending. This did not reduce net outflows as such but altered the direction of flows, as Canada and the developing countries were exempted from the regulation and so was OFDI (Hewson and Sakakibara 1975; Eichengreen 2000; Neely 1999). In 1965, the U.S. government attempted to reduce the capital account deficit and requested companies to reduce voluntarily their OFDI activities. To encourage the scheme, OFDI ceilings were introduced the following year. The voluntary scheme allowed participating companies to contribute to the balance of payments in the areas of (1) OFDI to developed countries; (2) receipts from fees, royalties, and income on OFDI from developed countries; and (3) receipts from exports to all countries (Bruck and Lees 1968). In 1966, specific OFDI reduction targets were introduced, and companies were requested to limit their OFDI in the years 1965–1966 to no more than 135% of the average for the years 1962–1964, a threshold that was gradually reduced to 120% for the period 1966–1967 and 100% for 1967–1968 (Bruck and Lees 1968). By the end of 1966, 900 companies participated in the voluntary scheme (Areskoug 1976). In 1968, this scheme was replaced by a mandatory Foreign Direct Investment Program administered by the Office of Foreign Direct Investment within the Department of Commerce (Areskoug 1976; Eichengreen 2000; Neely 1999). This program introduced both a ceiling on capital flows from U.S. parent companies to their foreign affiliates and minimum standards of remittances from the U.S. affiliates abroad to their U.S. parent firms (Areskoug 1976). The effect of this regulation varied, depending on the category of host country concerned, which ranged from (1) mildly restricted countries (developing countries); (2) intermediately restricted countries (Ireland, Japan, New Zealand, Spain, the United Kingdom, oil-producing countries); and (3) severely restricted countries (the rest of Western Europe and South Africa) (ibid.). Canada was exempted from the regulation because of its dependence on U.S. investments (Wright and Molot 1974; Lancaster 1969).

The voluntary and mandatory programs had a number of effects, with the latter having a stronger negative effect on OFDI than the former, especially in nonmanufacturing industries (Scaperlanda and Mauer 1973). The programs inhibited OFDI by newly investing firms because such firms struggled to comply with obligations concerning their contribution to the balance of payments, unlike established U.S. MNEs, which found these obligations much easier to fulfill (Areskoug 1976). The capital control programs were largely ineffective. While the constitution of some parts of the balance of payments improved, others deteriorated, and this turned the whole attempt into a zero-sum game (Hewson and Sakakibara 1975). The programs affected the international operations of U.S. MNEs by restricting the supply of working capital to foreign affiliates and by restricting the access of foreign affiliates to U.S. capital markets (Areskoug 1976). The regulations were ill-defined and ill-implemented, with some discretionary power for special cases. These factors, together with the neutral-to-negative effect of controls on the balance of payments, spoke against the imposition of outward investment barriers (Behrman 1969). Because of the restrictions, firms either postponed their investments or relied more heavily on foreign borrowings (Eichengreen 2000). Firms also established financial centers outside of the United States (Areskoug 1976). Capital controls were relaxed from 1969 onward, and in 1974 the U.S. government ended its controls on capital outflows, in line with a general reduction of intervention in private business transactions (Hewson and Sakakibara 1975). There were attempts to return to a more inward-looking policy, illustrated by the proposed Hartke-Burke Bill (also known as the Foreign Trade and Investment Act of 1972), which sought to limit technology transfers and OFDI, especially offshore manufacturing (with employment effects a major criterion) through presidential licensing but which did not pass Congress (Canto 1983; Solis 2003). But the momentum for further liberalization had been established: by the end of the

1970s, no OFDI-restricting regulations were in place in the United States (OECD 1979).

13.3.2 Japan

In 1949, Japan passed the Foreign Exchange and Foreign Trade Control Law, which prohibited any foreign exchange transactions and allowed only selected transactions in accordance with ministerial exemption (Mathieson and Rojas-Suarez 1992). Restrictions remained in place until the late 1960s. Ceilings were imposed on overseas assets held by Japanese firms, and a formal approval process was implemented. Prior to 1967, all OFDI projects were screened on a case-by-case basis, though approval criteria were not published by Japan's Ministry of International Trade and Industry (MITI). The Ministry of Finance granted permission to undertake OFDI only after MITI approval and confirmation that job relocations were not involved (Bailey, Harte, and Sugden 1994). In October 1969, the Foreign Exchange and Foreign Trade Control Law was relaxed to allow automatic approval for investments of up to US$200,000 in specific industries, such as banking and securities. The ceiling was increased to US$1 million in 1970 and abolished in 1971 (Litvak and Maule 1973), as was formal case-by-case screening (Bailey, Harte, and Sugden 1994). Government attitudes toward OFDI became more liberal and facilitating during the 1970s (Stone 1998). In 1972, OFDI monitoring and foreign exchange restrictions were eased to reduce the large foreign exchange reserves and to prevent a revaluation of the yen (Bailey, Harte, and Sugden 1994). Despite liberalization, the Japanese government retained a mandate to guide OFDI in a manner that supported national industrial policy objectives. Firms were generally expected to respect this guidance. In addition to the economic evaluation of an OFDI project, the potential political impact became an assessment criterion because of unease in some host countries concerning high levels of inward Japanese FDI. Investment project refusals were mainly made on political grounds. Approved OFDI was supported through tax and insurance schemes (ibid.). In the mid-1970s, the deterioration of the Japanese balance of payments, caused by the oil crisis and domestic recession, saw the active promotion of OFDI come to an end, and MITI once more strengthened its control over OFDI (ibid.). In 1978, a system of prior notification replaced the approval system (ibid.). However, Bank of Japan authorization was still required for projects in particular industries (such as banking and finance, pharmaceuticals, fishing, and pearl cultivation) and regions (e.g., South Africa, Namibia, Zimbabwe) (OECD 1979). Japan passed a new Foreign Exchange and Foreign Trade Control Law in 1980 and, if not stated specifically otherwise, this allowed any foreign exchange transactions. The new law meant the *de jure* elimination of OFDI approvals. In practice, however, prenotification of an OFDI project was still required, and investment project applications could be altered or suspended by the relevant ministries. Particular OFDI projects that faced problems in the informal prenotification stage were normally not put forward for formal approval, and this reduced the number of formal rejections (Bailey, Harte, and Sugden 1994; Mathieson and Rojas-Suarez 1992). Capital controls were directed toward ensuring that savings were used domestically. Japan started to dismantle these controls in the 1980s (Johnston and Ryan 1994); in 1995 it abolished the OFDI approval period for most industries and reintroduced measures to encourage OFDI (Miniane 2004).

13.3.3   *United Kingdom*

Before World War I, there was no statute on the basis of which the British Government influenced OFDI (Laves 1931, 704). There was no need for such a policy because, arguably, business and politics were closely aligned and pursued similar objectives (ibid.). The United Kingdom avoided formal capital controls during World War I (Cooper 1999). In the interwar period, capital controls on overseas lending were introduced, but this did not affect British OFDI (Moggridge 1971). In 1947, the United Kingdom introduced the Exchange Control Act to *de jure* control OFDI and discourage investments outside the sterling area. British MNEs invested heavily outside of the United Kingdom, and investment proposals were seldom rejected by the government (Bailey, Harte, and Sugden 1994). However, OFDI regulations were tightened during the 1960s because of balance-of-payments concerns. Restrictions on investments outside the sterling area were introduced in 1965, and a voluntary OFDI restriction policy on investments in nondeveloping countries within the sterling area was introduced in 1966 (ibid.). Applications had to be made to the Bank of England, except for large transactions, which required approval from the Treasury and other relevant government agencies (OECD 1979). Restrictions on the use of sterling were eased in 1979 and by 1980, capital controls had been completely abolished (OECD 1979; Johnston and Ryan 1994). As a result, the financing of OFDI shifted from foreign currency to sterling-denominated borrowings (Mathieson and Rojas-Suarez 1992).

13.3.4   *European State-Owned Enterprises*

A special case for outward investment regulation relates to European state-owned enterprises (SOEs). They were required to obtain outward investment approval from the relevant government bodies (ranging from a designated agency to national parliament) for each investment project. They were not allowed to invest freely, as they had a mandate to support the domestic economy and, if necessary, to create employment when and where the private economy failed to do so. This was most evident during the 1970s, when European "countries with balance of payments and employment problems have…adopted measures…to spur exports and limit foreign direct investment. Yet, such measures are only partially effective: private firms which see a real advantage in going abroad do so anyway" (Mazzolini 1979, 19). This placed a particular burden on government-controlled enterprises, as the pressure to support the domestic economy tended to fall on them.

One conclusion to draw from this account is that developed countries have been able to experiment and implement OFDI liberalization measures for a number of decades, and could do so when foreign equity participation in the domestic economic was less intense than it is today. This is not the case for developing countries, which have a considerable "policy-distance" to travel over a much shorter time than did the developed countries, and at a time when global economic volatility is much more prevalent. Arguably, this makes the careful design of appropriate policy much more problematic than it was for the developed countries.

13.4   Developed Countries OFDI Policy: Some Lessons for Developing Countries

As we have seen, in the 1980s and 1990s, after a period of restricting OFDI, a significant number of industrialized country governments began to dismantle capital controls and other barriers to OFDI, and to proactively support the international investments of firms domiciled in their territory. Table 13.5 summarizes the key institutions currently involved in Germany, Japan, the United Kingdom, and the United States and their scope of activity. In effect, unilateral HCMs have been adopted to enhance firm competitiveness and promote national interests (e.g., in respect of natural-resources supply, industrial restructuring, and foreign market access) (UNCTAD 1999, 2001; Solis 2003). For some, such as New Zealand, the internationalization of domestic firms is considered to be a key element of the national economic agenda (Mallard and Goff 2007); for others, such as the United Kingdom, unilateral support is more equivocal, because the investing firm and the recipient country are perceived as major beneficiaries (House of Commons 2007). Nonetheless, countries have considerable autonomy and scope to influence OFDI flows, not least because corporate decision making is affected by the legal framework governing international capital flows and because there is no international regime comparable to the OECD agreement on export credits that restricts the subsidization of FDI (Solis 2003).

What can developing countries learn from the HCM policies of developed countries? This is a difficult question to answer, for three reasons. First, the proactive and facilitating HCMs that have been adopted by developed countries vary widely in terms of structure and scope, and are often directed toward particular types of home country firms, or target particular host regions and country types. There is no "one-size-fits-all" approach to policy formulation in this area, so it cannot be assumed that what works for a developed country will work for a developing country (UNCTAD 2006b; Moran 2008). Prescriptive policy recommendations would be inappropriate without due consideration of, for example, a country's stage of development, its sources of comparative advantage, its industrial structure, the overall development objectives of the country, and the absorptive capacity and capabilities (i.e., the international competitiveness) of its indigenous firms (UNCTAD 2006b). Second is the relative dearth of formal, systematic analyses on the effects of HCMs on OFDI in both industrialized country

Table 13.5 Key OFDI supporting organizations in leading developed countries

Country	Institution	Mandate	Information and technical assistance	Financing	Insurance
Germany	Germany Trade & Investment[a]	Provision of information about foreign markets	X		
	Kreditanstalt fuer Wiederaufbau (KfW)	Supporting financially international investment and trade	X	X[b]	X
	Foreign Trade and Investment Promotion Scheme	Supporting financially international investment and trade		X	X
	Deutsche Auslandshandelskammern (AHKs; German Chambers of Industry and Commerce)	Represents and supports German businesses globally	X		
Japan	Japan Bank for International Cooperation (JBIC)[c]	Maintaining and improving the international competitiveness of Japanese industries and the Japanese economy		X	
	JETRO	Increase inward FDI, support international trade, and expansion of Japanese firms (focus on small and medium-sized enterprises)	X		
United Kingdom	UK Trade & Investment (UKTI)	Supports British firms globally	X		
	Export Credits Guarantee Department (ECGD)	Provision of insurance and guarantees for bank loans		X	X
	CDC (Commonwealth Development Corporation)	A UK government-owned fund of funds that invests private equity funds mainly in emerging markets		X	
	China-Britain Business Council (CBBC)[d]	Supports British firms in trading with and investing in China	X		
United States	International Trade Administration	To strengthen the competitiveness of U.S. industry, promote trade and investment, and ensure fair trade and compliance with trade laws and agreements	X		

Continued

Table 13.5 Continued

Country	Institution	Mandate	Information and technical assistance	Financing	Insurance
	Overseas Private Investment Corporation (OPIC)	To mobilize and facilitate the participation of U.S. private capital and skills in the economic and social development of less developed countries and countries in transition from nonmarket to market economies		X	
	International Trade Commission (USITC)	To provide the President, Trade Representative, and Congress with independent analysis, information, and support on matters of tariffs, international trade, and national competitiveness	X		
	Office of the U. S. Trade Representative (USTR)	To develop and coordinate U.S. trade, commodity, and direct investment policy, and oversee negotiations (Connected with OPIC)	X		
	Export-Import Bank of the United States (Ex-Im Bank)	To help finance the export of U.S. goods and services and enhance the international competitiveness of U.S. firms		X	X

Source: Organization homepages.

[a]Established on January 1, 2009 through the merger of Bundesagentur für Außenwirtschaft (Bfai) and Invest in Germany GmbH.

[b]Export credits through its subsidiary KfW IPEX-Bank GmbH (http://www.kfw-ipex-bank.de/EN_Home/index.jsp); support of investments in developing countries through its subsidiary DEG (http://www.deginvest.de/EN_Home/index.jsp).

[c]Formerly known as The Export and Import Bank of Japan (JEXIM). JEXIM was merged with the Overseas Economic Cooperation Fund (OECF) to form JBIC in 1999. On October 29, 2008, JBIC merged with the International Financial Operations (IFOs); the National Life Finance Corporation (NLFC),); the Agriculture, Forestry and Fisheries Finance Corporation (AFC); and the Japan Finance Corporation for Small and Medium Enterprise (JASME) to form the Japan Finance Corporation (JFC). The established brand name JBIC retains its international mandate (http://www.jbic.go.jp). JBIC provides export loans, and investment loans, engages in equity participation, and provides guarantees.

[d]Private organization.

and developing country contexts (ibid.; Te Velde 2007). Much analysis in this policy area focuses primarily on (1) the effectiveness of industrialized country HCMs at promoting growth and development and reducing poverty in developing host countries (e.g., CUTS 2003; Te Velde 2007; UNCTAD 2001; Krut and Moretz 1999); (2) how the transfer of technology to developing countries can be facilitated (UNCTAD 2004); or (3) an assessment of the impact of HCMs on home country competitiveness (e.g., Kokko 2006; Meijer 2006). Little formal empirical research has been done to assess what policy options are most appropriate for adoption by developing countries. The present contribution represents a step in this direction. Third, research and theory building on HCMs are hampered by the counterfactual problem: how would companies (and economies) have performed without the intervention of government, and how can the benefits (costs) of intervention be assessed when the direct consequences of nonintervention are not easily measurable?

One approach to answering the question of what developing countries can learn from the HCM policies of developed countries is to consider how successful proactive HCMs have been in industrialized countries, in terms of fulfilling the mandate of the administering agency, and the cost-effectiveness and value for money received by domestic taxpayers. A small number of national-level audits and impact studies provide some insights for this type of analysis, which we discuss below.

At the outset, it seems reasonable to suggest that HCM policies should be targeted to where the greatest gains can be reaped in the shortest period of time. However, governments also confront a number of challenges in achieving this. First, although a small but growing number of developing countries are now actively promoting OFDI, relatively few have explicit and transparent policy frameworks in place (UNCTAD 2004). This is a new policy area for many governments, and experience is limited. Second, many developing countries do not have the income levels necessary to provide a sufficiently sound "safety blanket" for rapid liberalization (although this constraint will slowly ameliorate with domestic economic growth). Third, many developing countries are particularly vulnerable to national, regional, and international economic shocks (such as, for example, the Asian financial crisis of 1997 and the global financial crisis of 2007 and proceeding years). Perhaps inevitably, this often results in a cautious approach to policy formulation. Finally, many countries suffer institutional constraints, and these can give rise to adverse selection problems and the risk of regulatory capture, among other things. Government agencies and institutions in developing countries may lack the competences or resources needed to implement appropriate administrative systems or to pick appropriate industries and firms to support, and they may be vulnerable to lobbying, corruption, cronyism, or other types of regulatory capture from larger private firms, national champions, or government-controlled and government-owned firms (many of which do not invest abroad on purely commercial grounds). Such effects may lead to an inappropriate or suboptimal allocation of resources as a result of government policy. With these provisos in mind, we now consider the types of HCMs employed by developed countries and consider their applicability to developing country contexts.

Although no standard classification of HCMs exists (Te Velde 2007), a number of broad categories identify the major types of HCMs used in the industrialized countries to promote or otherwise influence FDI outflows (UNCTAD 2001). First, it is important to recognize that OFDI-related policies can be either indirect or direct in their effect. Indirect (or general) policy relates to industrial policy and other policies aimed at improving the international competitiveness, productivity, and performance of domestic firms; direct policies are those that specifically interact with the foreign investment intentions of domestic firms. Seven broad categories of direct HCMs can be identified: (1) the provision of information and technical support; (2) financial support; (3) fiscal incentives; (4) investment insurance and guarantees; (5) support of national champions (Moran 2008); (6) international investment-related concordats and agreements (UNCTAD 2001); and (7) official development assistance (ODA) programs. Most developed country governments are active in at least one of these categories. The distinction between indirect and direct OFDI policy is an important one: for many developing countries, it may be more appropriate for the government to direct resources and support to the creation of a more competitive and favorable business environment at home (e.g., by investing in the promotion of innovative and entrepreneurial activities or in human capital development and technological infrastructure), or that attract IFDI (which often brings positive spillover effects, competition effects, and demonstration effects) (see Buckley et al. [2002] in the case of China). This is because the resultant gains to individual domestic firms and overall industrial competitiveness of indirect measures may generate greater economic returns to the economy than the promotion of OFDI using direct HCMs (UNCTAD 2006b). Notwithstanding this, we now briefly consider each of the direct HCMs employed by developed countries and assess their relevance to developing countries.

13.4.1 *Information and Technical-Assistance Schemes*

Information and technical-assistance schemes provide economic and market-related information about potential host economies, their political and legal frameworks, sectoral and market conditions, business practices, investment incentives, and other factors that contribute to the country's investment climate. A variety of dissemination mechanisms are used, such as conferences, investment missions, trade fairs, seminars, bespoke consultancy services, "matchmaking" services, and sector-specific investment opportunities databases. The underlying rationale for governments to provide information and technical-assistance services is that they address market failure in private-sector provision and economize on the need for firms to generate this type of information for themselves (which could lead to unnecessary duplication across firms and a wasteful allocation of resources from a societal perspective—the public-good argument for information provision). This type of information can be important in assisting an investing firm in choosing between competing locations (both nationally and at subnational levels). Improved information about investment opportunities may reduce uncertainty for investing firms and therefore mitigate economic risk (that is, the uncertainties associated with the costs and benefits of investment projects) (Te Velde 2007). Such uncertainty can be high, especially in situations that involve large sunk or irreversible costs. Informational shortcomings may therefore see investment decisions delayed or forgone until further information becomes available (ibid.).

Because the risk of internationalization increases with lack of familiarity, this type of HCM is particularly relevant for smaller or less-experienced firms. It is also particularly relevant for those firms that are considering investing in countries about which little information is readily available (i.e., to close an information gap), or that are small or psychically or physically distant from the home country and might otherwise be overlooked for consideration. Such information is generally provided by foreign ministries, consular offices, and trade-promotion agencies. The relevant agencies in the United States, Japan, and the United Kingdom are, respectively, the Overseas Private Investment Corporation (OPIC, an independent government agency that sells investment protection services to U.S. companies), the Japan External Trade Organization (JETRO, a Japanese government-related organization that seeks to promote "mutually beneficial" trade and investment relations), and UK Trade and Investment (UKTI, a government department under the remit of the Minister of State for Trade and Investment).

Evidence on the effectiveness of this type of HCM in the industrialized countries can be drawn from national evaluations of agency performance and value for money assessments. For example, a recent cost-benefit analysis of government support for international trade (and, by implication, OFDI) in the United Kingdom found that net additional benefits in the region of GB£17 million are generated per GB£1million of total costs across the range of services provided by UKTI (DTI 2006). The study also found that substantial qualitative benefits accrued to firms supported in terms of increased skills and improvements to products and practices. The authors infer from this that the capabilities and absorptive capacity of firms using UKTI services were increased, an effect that was found to be especially strong among innovative firms. In addition to the provision of information and advice, the DTI study highlighted the important role of government in facilitating the development of social and business networks by serving as a trusted intermediary between businesses and potential partners or sources of knowledge, using its established network of key contacts, consulates, and embassies at relatively low additional cost to current diplomatic functions. It also found that services provided by UKTI strengthen the internationalization capabilities of innovative businesses, especially in relation to addressing deficiencies in internationalization skills, which may lead to suboptimal market research and marketing strategies that are wasteful on firm resources. At present, developing countries generally rely on information-related services provided by supranational organizations operating at a regional or national level. Information-related market failures are likely to be especially prevalent in developing countries, and so information-related HCMs would seem to be one area that could be implemented in a relatively straightforward and cost-effective manner by developing countries. In contrast, it is possible to argue that the rapid dissemination (and take-up) of information and communication technologies (ICT), especially Internet-based tools (such as email, search engines, business-to-business marketplaces [e.g., the China-based Alibaba], and online auction websites) have dramatically reduced the information costs and transaction costs of identifying markets (especially in the developed world, about which considerable amounts of economic information are available online at relatively low cost). This suggests that developing countries need to provide more nuanced and tailored information-related services to their firms. Indeed, the governments of Malaysia, Mexico, Singapore, and Thailand now provide matchmaking services (including official missions to potential target countries), and Singapore and Mexico have established dedicated industrial parks with points of contact with home government institutions in key host country markets (such as China, the United Kingdom, and the United States) to facilitate the entry process (UNCTAD 2006a). When combined with careful selection of client companies to target, it is possible to argue that innovations such as these will generate greater returns for developing country governments and the home economy than will efforts to collate and disseminate generic international business information to firms.

13.4.2 Financial Support, Fiscal Incentives, and Insurance and Investment Guarantees

Although it is normal to distinguish between financial support, fiscal incentives, and insurance and investment guarantees as three separate types of HCM, we consider them together here, on the basis that the implications of these policies for developing countries' governments are more or less equivalent.

Direct financial support generally takes the form of preferential overseas investment-related loans, grants (e.g., to fund feasibility studies and project development), equity participation in FDI projects, and export support to foreign affiliates. Developed country governments also offer fiscal incentives to overseas investing firms (in the form of tax exemptions, deferrals, credits for taxation of foreign income, and general tax-saving provisions), often in relation to FDI in developing countries. Insurance and investment guarantee schemes are designed to cover political and noncommercial risks in the host country, such as risks of expropriation, war, restrictions on remittances, currency inconvertibility and breach of host-government undertakings, which are not available in conventional private insurance schemes. Such schemes help to protect investing firms from risk (especially political risks) and therefore promote FDI, especially in the case of developing country investment destinations (where governments may be weak and may be forced to breach their contractual terms), and in industries in which investments involve substantial sunk costs, such as infrastructure and natural-resources exploitation (Te Velde 2007). Export credit agencies (ECAs) offer export finance and

FDI-related lending and insurance, as well as overseas development assistance. OPIC has a narrow focus on OFDI promotion (so long as it does not damage U.S. employment or exports or impinge negatively upon the environment or host country workers' rights), mainly through finance (loans and loan guarantees) and by providing credits to private investment funds that invest equity in firms in less-developed countries (Moran and Bergsten 2003). It also links its risk insurance of an FDI project with economic growth in developing countries and insures U.S. investors against political risk (expropriation, currency inconvertibility, political violence) (ibid.). The Japan Bank for International Cooperation (JBIC) has a much broader remit (including export, import, FDI finance, untied loans, and foreign aid) (Solis 2003). The JBIC is also not constrained in terms of the support of particular firm types (e.g., small and medium-sized enterprises), and it does not need to prove that financed projects do harm to domestic employment, exports, or the environment (ibid.). JBIC is highly dependent on public funds, however, while OPIC finances its operations mainly from retained earnings and bond issues. Such financial, fiscal, and insurance schemes are often either linked to national economic development goals or international development objectives (and therefore may be specific to certain industries or host countries and regions) (UNCTAD 2001).

Financial support lowers the economic risks of the firm involved and can be used to leverage investments from other private sources that might otherwise be reluctant to participate (Te Velde 2007). Germany and Japan are cases in point: the German government supports investments of small and medium-sized enterprises in developing countries through preferential loans and consulting, and Japan has a range of government agencies among which the Export-Import Bank of Japan has been one of the largest institutional sponsors of OFDI. Mireya Solis (2003) argued that home government policy toward OFDI exhibits greatest heterogeneity in the role that states play as financiers of MNEs. Some organizations, however, may only financially support activities if the supported activity is not potentially harmful to the home economy. The Export-Import Bank of the United States (Ex-Im Bank), for example, can refuse support when the supported activity leads to the establishment of production facilities for products that could have been exported from the United States instead. Solis argues that public credit is an important instrument of industrial policy because it permits the targeting of individual industries and projects as opposed to the traditional instruments of OFDI policy (such as exchange controls, insurance, tax treaties), which generally apply uniformly to all industries.

In an evaluation of the rationale for OPIC's existence, Theodore H. Moran and C. Fred Bergsten (2003) report that it has supported more than US$145 billion of U.S. OFDI, and that, by 2002, this generated US$65 billion of exports and created more than 254,000 jobs in the United States since its inception in 1969. Between 1998 and 2003, the authors estimate that OPIC's loans and insurance schemes have involved an average of forty-five projects per year, with a total value of US$2.5 billion, and investments in seventy countries. They assert that OPIC has had an "indispensable role to play" (Moran and Bergsten 2003, 2) in overcoming market failures associated with private finance and insurance provision, and that this has led to positive externalities for both recipient countries and the U.S. economy (in the form of higher exports, higher domestic wages, greater stability in domestic markets, and positive externalities for U.S. firms, workers, and communities in the locations in which MNEs are based). One important aspect is that OPIC's activities are backed by IIAs and the clout of the U.S. government, and this helps to mitigate the threat of opportunistic behavior of host country governments (for instance, in situations when domestic pressure to change, tighten, or revoke an investment agreement heightens) and facilitates dispute resolution. However, Moran and Bergsten also highlight a number of areas in which OPIC could be reformed to help broaden the scope of its overseas investment portfolio and the benefits it derives for domestic employment. These include the adoption of measures that would enable it to identify more accurately those OFDI projects to be supported (that is, to shift the emphasis of evaluation criteria away from an assessment of the impact of an OFDI project on absolute domestic job losses toward consideration of whether or not a project has an overall net positive effect on domestic workers, firms, and communities); to extend access of OPIC services to a larger pool of client firms (especially small and medium-sized enterprises looking to expand from servicing overseas markets through exporting to developing foreign-based marketing and assembly operations, as well as to foreign firms based in the United States); and to improve the way that OPIC markets its services. In a cost-benefit analysis by NERA (2003) of the subsidies provided by the United Kingdom's Export Credits Guarantee Department, the authors noted that the organization is demand driven and, in this respect, does not play an active role in determining the composition of its portfolio. This suggests that better marketing of services would represent an important step in diversifying the investment portfolio of institutions that provide this type of HCM. Furthermore, Moran and Bergsten (2003) also drew attention to complaints about the slow service and onerous reporting requirements imposed by OPIC that have been addressed through the streamlining of its operations, although they did point out that moves to expand disclosure and external observation of conformity to its own standards may serve to discourage investors from using its services. This discussion suggests that developing country governments should seek to establish a coherent framework and transparent set of criteria for administering the provision of finance- and insurance-related HCMs and for selecting firms to support. Attention should also be given to how services are marketed to current and future investing firms and to institutional efficiency issues.

In a review of the financial support available to British companies, Dirk Willem Te Velde (2007) observed industry variations in the companies that seek and obtain this type of government assistance. He argued that power industry and financial services firms, in particular, tended to benefit from equity positions provided by the Commonwealth Development Corporation (CDC), whereas minerals, oil, and gas industry firms (major investors in non-OECD countries) tend not to, preferring instead to obtain financing from larger, multilateral, development-related financial institutions, such as the European Investment Bank and the International Finance Corporation of the World Bank. Similar variation is observed in the use of risk insurance provided by the Export Credits Guarantee Department, with firms in the power and water industries (which involve considerable sunk and exit costs and a long payback period) being the principle users, whereas manufacturing and service sector companies (whose activities often involve much smaller sunk costs) are not, probably because they are exposed to fewer political risks and require less insurance. One anomaly is oil and gas industry firms, which are also low users of risk insurance. Te Velde (2007) argued that this is because they have alternative political risk mitigation strategies established through lengthy experience of operating internationally. This suggests that the effectiveness of finance-related HCMs will vary depending on the industry concerned, which developing country governments should be cognizant of when designing and targeting this type of measure for home country firms.

All these issues highlight some of the potential challenges associated with the introduction of developing country institutions to support OFDI through the provision of financial and fiscal incentives to outward investing firms. Clearly, those developing countries that enjoy a balance-of-payments surplus, such as China, might find it easier to provide this type of support than might countries with balance-of-payments deficits. In addition to the direct costs (which might be prohibitively high, in relative terms, in times of balance-of-payments shortfalls), there are a number of institution-related constraints that developing countries must address in order for this type of HCM to be effective. In particular, such institutions need to adopt policies that mitigate the adverse selection problem and have clear and effective procedures in place concerning, for example, the targeting of client firms, the criteria on which cost-benefit analyses are undertaken, and the marketing of services to local firms. They will also need to take care to manage the expectations of client firms, especially with regard to the timeliness of their processes and decision making, in order to encourage the continued take-up of their services. It should also be pointed out that one of the reasons why OPIC has been successful is the backing it receives from the U.S. government and the effect that this has on the behavior of host country governments. For many major trading and FDI-exporting developing countries, such as China, India, and Russia, the involvement and support of national government in the negotiation and administration of finance and insurance packages for its MNEs may have a similar effect on host countries. However, for other countries, whose economic influence is not as great, the involvement and support of government may do little to negate the possibility of opportunistic behavior (such as reneging on their contractual commitments) of host countries.

13.4.3 National Champions

Some governments focus their industrial policy on the development and support of selected companies. Companies are chosen on the basis that they provide either a service that is deemed of national importance or are able to rise to become dominant global players in their industry. Examples of the latter can be identified in the Republic of Korea and China, and also in Europe (e.g., Airbus). It can, however, be problematic for governments to identify successfully those domestic companies with the dynamism and innovativeness required to compete successfully internationally while enjoying subsidies and tariff- and market-protection advantages at home. Moreover, it is not always certain that government-supported companies will conform to government preferences concerning, for example, the international production or marketing strategy they choose to pursue (Solis 2003; Moran 2008; Euh and Rhee 2007; Seabright 2005). In his analysis of studies on industrialized country national champions, Moran (2008) argued that to have an efficient national champion scheme in place governments need to have the tools and long-term insights to pick and nurture the right companies in the right industries, and the knowledge that markets would have failed to achieve the same objectives. This may work if there are "clear market failures that prevent the emergence of national firms and/or clear externalities that are derived from their operations" (289). Arguably, this is sound from a theoretical standpoint, but may be unfeasible in reality. It is not possible to have a clear-cut definition of an industry that might justify national champion treatment. The common national security theme can be extended to virtually any industry; for example, agriculture (food), media (information and propaganda), and construction (military bases and infrastructure). Evidence from Europe and Asia points to the fact that, under national champion schemes, resources are often directed toward declining industries as a lifeline, and firms outside the system can become more powerful international players than domestic counterparts that enjoy this type of government support (e.g., Toyota and Honda versus Isuzu and Mitsubishi in the case of Japan). Further, national champions that internationalize may start to treat their home country as just another country in which they operate and may become more responsive to international competitive forces as well as more appreciative of protective policies in host countries for their own sake (cf. Mittal Steel's corporate behavior prior to and after its acquisition of U.S. Steel). The analysis by Moran implies that home country governments should, if at all, direct their support to firms that increase productivity and wealth regardless of their nationality and whether or not they are parent companies or foreign affiliates.

13.4.4 International Investment Agreements

Despite the range of possible support activities and governmental endorsement of OFDI outlined above, host country economic fundamentals, such as, among other things, market size and the competitive situation may influence investment decision making more than any direct domestic government support (UNCTAD 1995). Home country governments can help their MNEs to gain access to host country markets through the negotiation of bilateral investment treaties (BITs). This may be further facilitated through membership of multilateral investment agreements, such as those administered under the umbrella of institutions that include the World Trade Organization (WTO), the North America Free Trade Agreement (NAFTA), and the Association of Southeast Asian Nations (ASEAN). Double taxation treaties (DTTs) may provide investing firms with fiscal-related and concomitant risk-reducing benefits. These types of international agreements offer developing home countries with a relatively cost-effective and tested framework for improving the competitiveness of indigenous firms in foreign markets (UNCTAD 2001). In a report by UNCTAD (2001), the argument was made that IIA negotiations provide an opportunity for developed and developing countries to adopt a coordinated approach to the design, development, and implementation of HCMs in order to improve the quality and quantity of FDI from the former to the latter, and this argument can be extended to the case of agreements between developing countries. In the past, this was often subject to the relative bargaining position of the countries concerned, with many early agreements between developed and developing countries being oriented toward improving market access and investment security of MNEs from the former countries in the latter, and with policy pronouncements concerning host country development often being generalized and hortatory in the developed countries (ibid.). UNCTAD (2001) argued for more substantive policy and programmatic commitments to development assistance through the use of HCMs among developed countries. By extension, these observations suggest that developing countries should do the same when looking to conclude IIAs, especially with other developing countries. As developing country governments increasingly view the promotion of OFDI as a key policy objective, the negotiation (or renegotiation) of IIAs should see the scope of such agreements broadened to address the needs of their MNEs, especially with respect to clarity in obligations regarding FDI treatment in host countries and the articulation of specific items or procedures to be implemented that will translate policy into practice (ibid.).

13.4.5 *Official Development Assistance*

Official development assistance (ODA) programs can help to improve the economic fundamentals of a country and, in turn, therefore, its investment climate. As such, they constitute an HCM. In developed countries, it is not uncommon for investment support to be linked to development-related government objectives. For example, OPIC is mandated to link financial support for U.S. firms to the social and economic impact of their investments in developing countries. It is also important in the context of aid agreements between South-South countries (UNCTAD 2006b). Many such agreements include conditions that obligate recipient host countries to grant market access (e.g., in the form of government contracts and mineral rights) to donor country firms. Examples include China's aid program in Africa and its links to the internationalization of Chinese firms. In a survey on the effectiveness of HCMs adopted by the United Kingdom, Te Velde (2007) reported a positive correlation between aid flows and changes to UK FDI stocks in non-OECD countries for the period 1997–2001. As with IIAs, one policy recommendation that arises is for developing country governments to include market-access provisions in the negotiation of ODA packages with other developing countries.

In addition to these specific observations concerning the relevance of particular developed country HCMs to developing country OFDI policy, we can also make the following general observations. For many of the HCMs we outline above, the case for support of OFDI depends on the ability and willingness of governments to identify and correct market failures by acting as a substitute for absent or inefficient private institutions. Most developing country governments limit themselves to information provision, on the grounds that there is significant failure in the market for information, particularly about foreign opportunities. However, many emerging markets, such as China, could claim that deficiencies in their domestic capital markets mean that significant opportunities abroad would be missed if state funds did not compensate for missing private funding; for example, in the absence of domestic venture capitalist and private equity funds. This suggests that developing country governments should consider the full range of HCMs available to them (taking into account home country conditions, particularly the character of private-sector provision) and not confine themselves to the provision of information-related services alone. Home country governments also need to have institutional checks in place to prevent rent seeking (e.g., the subsidization of inefficient economic sectors) and to address adverse selection issues (Solis 2003).

The macrotheory of OFDI we outline above suggests that the one unequivocal private benefit that arises for the source country is the remittance of profits and the corresponding social benefit is the taxation (and potential redistribution) of these profits. Generally, this has been considered as a narrow basis on which to establish a general policy of OFDI encouragement. Correspondingly, the costs have not been felt to be sufficient to justify a policy of OFDI retraction except in times of financial (or political) crises or actual or perceived capital shortages at home. The nonsubstitutability of home for foreign investment is often evident at the level of the firm, where modern analysis places most emphasis (as we show above), and the view has generally been taken in industrialized countries that firms are the best judges of their own investment decisions.

Emerging markets are often perceived to be capital deficient and their firms to be capital rationed, so there may be a presumption that OFDI should not be encouraged. However, when we consider industry-specific capital and the motives behind emerging market firms' investment abroad (asset, market, and resource-seeking), it becomes equally difficult to argue a general case for OFDI restrictions. In many cases, there exist in resource-rich and low-cost labor-rich economies (e.g., the oil-exporting nations and China), massive balance-of-payments surpluses, and the need for effective recycling often calls for OFDI. The danger is, however, that capital abundance at home will mean wasteful FDI, where capital rationing does not improve efficient investment. For example, there is much evidence (some of it anecdotal) that developing country firms do not extract the same quality of minerals in extractive industries as could be done on the technical frontier, that their management skills are not adequate, and that information barriers reduce the effectiveness of OFDI from emerging markets. In many respects, the lessons for emerging markets are thus less in terms of policy and more in terms of management and other types of human capital augmentation at home. This might also include a focus on indirect (or general) policy aimed at improving the international competitiveness, productivity, and performance of domestic firms (e.g., IFDI policy). Moreover, our analysis suggests that developing country governments must be careful to balance the package of HCMs offered (information, finance, insurance, FDI-related provisions in IIAs and ODAs) against the ownership advantages and characteristics (e.g., the international competitiveness, managerial capabilities, size) of the firms concerned, the industry (large sunk costs, high exit costs versus low sunk cost, low exit costs), the investment motive (market-seeking versus resources-seeking versus efficiency-seeking), and the locational advantages of the host country. This may necessitate considerable investment in domestic institutions involved in the administration of HCMs to improve their capabilities, efficiency, and decision-making processes. Another observation concerns the organization of the delivery of HCMs to outward investing firms. In their discussion of the effectiveness of OPIC, Moran and Bergsten (2003) observed that, in addition to its support of small and medium-sized enterprises, such firms can also solicit support from the U.S. Foreign Commercial Service, the U.S. Export Assistance Centers, and the U.S. Ex-Im Bank, the Small Business Administration, and various other state and municipal business support services. This list alludes to the multifarious nature of HCM support provision in the industrialized countries, and this may give rise to a lack of explicit coordination at operational and strategic levels, an observation made in the specific case of the United Kingdom by Te Velde (2007). In turn, this may be confusing to outward investing firms. Developing countries have the opportunity to create new OFDI-supporting infrastructures without the institutional heritage found in developed countries, perhaps through the establishment of "one-stop shops" (similar to inward investment promotion agencies) to centralize and coordinate the provision of HCMs (Te Velde 2003).

Conclusions

The statement that "if uncertainty were taken into account, the conclusion might be that the United States should subsidize rather than restrain its capital outflows" (Fieleke 1971, 20) encapsulates the classic argument for government provision of subsidies and information in support of OFDI. It may be that information gathering helps to overcome risk, but in the absence of proven externalities that actually accrue to the home country, little can be said, in general, to support an overall subsidy of OFDI. However, in certain specific cases there may be a case for subsidies. For instance, in situations in which MNEs have monopsony power in a host economy, they can reap all the profits from their operations and remit them to their home countries where they will be taxed. The home country thus gains all the benefits from the foreign operation (Casson 2007).

We should remember that OFDI is not a goal in itself but is a means to an end. That end is development. Although building competitive firms may be a way of achieving this, it needs to be weighed against all other alternative means. Government policy sets the macrocontext within which micro–decision making takes place. An optimal strategy will only be achieved when optimum theoretical reasoning is used.

This chapter has shown that, in developed countries, the development of policies toward OFDI has had a somewhat tortuous history. In fact, it has often been the result of policies directed toward other objectives (e.g., balance-of-payments issues) rather than toward OFDI per se. The fact that there is no long-term consistency in policies reflects governments' attitude that OFDI is not a major policy focus and, lately, that the market solution represents the best outcome. This somewhat complacent stance is currently challenged by the ramifications of the current global financial crises (or "credit crunch") in which government intervention is now firmly on the agenda and OFDI is once again regarded as highly uncertain. The lessons for emerging markets are, therefore, very specific in both time and external circumstances. A prudent policy must be linked to the current and expected financial and economic situations of countries at both the micro and macro levels. We are a long way from having a notion of optimal policy toward outward investment. Pragmatic caution is probably the best council.

The key difficulty that all governments face in designing OFDI policies is to evaluate the efficacy of foreign investment in terms of domestic policy objectives. A clear definition of such policy objectives could, in principle, be fed back into a refined policy stance on OFDI. This could be supported by a systematic analysis of the costs and benefits of HCMs and the effectiveness of the institutions and agencies that administer them. Such a formal analysis is currently lacking (Te Velde 2007). This is one important gap that the academic community could do more to address. It is difficult to estimate the efficiency of government promotion or restraint on OFDI, but such modeling would be the second stage of the construction of a rational policy for OFDI. The final element would be the integration of OFDI policy with other domestic policies. In this chapter, we have provided pointers to the elements that make up such an integrated policy. We have not yet been able to present a holistic policy framework—but then, neither, so far, has any government.

Notes

1. One notable exception, arguably, relates to international mergers and acquisitions, on which policy development, even among the industrialized countries, can often be ambiguous and lackluster.
2. This is a broader definition of "home country measures" (HCM) and allows for both restrictive (regulatory) and promotional (liberalizing) measures to be included. Some studies confine the term "HCM" to FDI-promoting measures only.

References

Agarwal, Jamuna P. (1980). "Determinants of foreign direct investment: a survey," *Review of World Economics* (Weltwirtschaftliches Archiv) 116 (4), pp. 739–73.

Areskoug, Kaj (1976). "The liberalization of U.S. capital outflows: international financial consequences," *New York University, Graduate School of Business Administration Bulletin* 1976-2 (New York: New York University).

Bailey, David, George Harte, and Roger Sugden (1994). *Transnationals and Governments: Recent Policies in Japan, France, Germany, the United States and Britain* (London and New York: Routledge).

Balogh, Thomas. (1945). "Some theoretical problems of post-war foreign investment policy," *Oxford Economic Papers* 7, pp. 93–110.

Behrman, Jack N. (1969). "Assessing the foreign investment controls," *Law and Contemporary Problems* 34 (1), pp. 84–94.

Bloomfield, Arthur I. (1946). "Postwar control of international capital movements," *American Economic Review* 36 (2), pp. 687–709.

Bruck, Nicholas K. and Francis A. Lees (1968). "Foreign investment, capital controls and the balance of payments," *New York University, Graduate School of Business Administration Bulletin* No. 48–49 (New York: New York University).

Buckley, Peter J. (1988). "The limits of explanation: testing the internalization theory of the multinational enterprise," *Journal of International Business Studies* 19 (2), pp. 181–93.

Buckley, Peter J., Jeremy L. Clegg, and Chengqi Wang (2002). "The impact of inward FDI on the performance of Chinese manufacturing firms," *Journal of International Business Studies* 33 (4), pp. 637–56.

Buckley, Peter J. and Mark C. Casson (1976). *The Future of the Multinational Enterprise* (Houndsmill: Palgrave).

——— (1998). "Models of the multinational enterprise," *Journal of International Business Studies* 29 (1), pp. 21–44.

Canto, Victor A. (1983). "U.S. trade policy: history and evidence," *Cato Journal* 3 (3), pp. 679–703.

Casson, Mark C. (2007). "Multinational enterprises: their private and social benefits and costs," *World Economy* 30 (2), pp. 308–28.

Cooper, Richard N. (1999). "Should capital controls be banished?" *Brookings Papers on Economic Activity* 1, pp. 89–141.

CUTS (2003). "Home country measures and FDI: implications for host country development," Centre for Competition, Investment and Economic Regulation, Monograph on Investment and Competition Policy No. 13 (Jaipur: Consumer Unity & Trust Society), mimeo.

DTI (2006). "International trade and investment—the economic rationale for government support," Department of Trade and Industry (DTI) Economics Paper Nr. 18 (London: DTI), mimeo.

Dooley, Michael P. (1996). "A survey of literature on controls over international capital transactions," *Staff Papers—International Monetary Fund* 43 (4), pp. 639–87.

Duesenberry, James (1966). "Domestic policy objectives and the balance of payments," *Journal of Finance* 21 (2), pp. 345–53.

Dunning, John H. (1977). "Trade, location of economic activity and the MNE: a search for an eclectic approach," in B. Ohlin, P.O. Hesselborn, and P.M. Wijkmon, eds., *The International Location of Economic Activity* (London: Macmillan), pp. 395–418.

Dunning, John H. (2001). "The eclectic (OLI) paradigm of international production: past, present and future," *International Journal of the Economics of Business* 8 (2), pp. 173–90.

Dunning, John H. and S.M. Lundan (2008). *Multinational Enterprises and the Global Economy,* 2nd ed. (Cheltenham: Edward Elgar).

Edwards, George W. (1924). "American policy with reference to foreign investment," *American Economic Review* 14 (1), pp. 26–35.

Eichengreen, Barry (2000). "From benign neglect to malignant preoccupation: U.S. balance-of-payments policy in the 1960s," *NBER Working Paper Series 7630,* Cambridge, MA.

Euh, Yoon-Dae and Jay Hyuk Rhee (2007). "Lessons from the Korean crisis: policy and managerial implications," *Long Range Planning* 40, pp. 431–45.

Feldstein, Martin and Charles Horioka (1980). "Domestic savings and international capital flows," *Economic Journal* 90, pp. 314–29.

Fieleke, Norman. S. (1971). "The welfare effects of controls over capital exports from the United States," *Essays in International Finance No. 82,* Department of Economics (Princeton: Princeton University).

Goodman, Bernard (1957). "The political economy of private investment," *Economic Development and Cultural Change* 5 (3), pp. 263–76.

Hewson, John and Eisuke Sakakibara (1975). "The impact of U.S. control on capital outflows on the U.S. balance of payments: an exploratory study," *IMF Staff Papers* 22 (1), pp. 37–60.

Hood, Neil and Stephen Young (1979). *The Economics of Multinational Enterprise* (London and New York: Longman).

House of Commons (2007). *Trade and Industry: Sixth Report,* available at http://www. publications.parliament.uk/pa/cm200607/cmselect/cmtrdind/557/55702. htm, last visited April 18, 2008.

Hymer, Stephen (1960). *The International Operations of National Firms: A Study of Direct Investment* (Cambridge, MA: MIT Press).

Jasay, Anthony E. de (1960). "The social choice between home and overseas investment," *Economic Journal* 70 (277), pp. 105–13.

Johnston, Barry and Chris Ryan (1994). "The impact of control of capital movements on the private capital accounts of countries' balance of payments: empirical estimates and policy implications," *IMF Working Paper* WP/94/78 (Washington, DC: IMF).

Kline, John M. (2003). "Enhancing the development dimension of home country measures," in UNCTAD, ed., *The Development Dimension of FDI: Policy and Rule Making Perspectives* (New York and Geneva: UNCTAD).

Kokko, Ari (2006). "The home country effects of FDI in developed economies," Working Paper No. 225, European Institute of Japanese Studies, Stockholm School of Economics.

Krut, Riva and Ashley Moretz (1999). "Home country measures for encouraging sustainable FDI," Occasional Paper No. 8, report as part of the UNCTAD/CBS (Copenhagen Business School) project: Cross Border Environment Management in Transnational Corporations (Copenhagen: CBS), mimeo.

Lancaster, W.W. Jr. (1969). "The foreign direct investment regulations: a look at ad hoc rulemaking," *Virginia Law Review* 55 (1), pp. 83–137.

Laves, W.H.C. (1931). "National and international control of foreign investment," *American Political Science Review* 25 (3), pp. 704–13.

Lindert, Peter H. (1971). "The payments impact of foreign investment controls," *Journal of Finance* 26 (5), pp. 1083–99.

Litvak, Isaiah A. and Christopher J. Maule (1973). "Japan's overseas investments," *Pacific Affairs* 46 (2), pp. 254–68.

MacDougall, G.D.A. (1960). "The benefits and costs of private investment from abroad: a theoretical approach," *Economic Record* 36, pp. 16–35.

Mallard, Trevor and Phil Goff (2007). *Internationalisation and Investment: Cabinet Paper*, originally published on August 30, 2007 to the Chair of the Cabinet Economic Development Committee, New Zealand, available at http://www. med.govt.nz/upload/50276/cabinet-paper.pdf, last visited April 18, 2008.

Mathieson, Donald J. and Liliana Rojas-Suarez (1992). "Liberalization of the capital account: experiences and issues," *IMF Working Paper* WP/92/46 (Washington, DC: IMF).

Mazzolini, Renato (1979). "European government-controlled enterprises: explaining international strategic and policy decisions," *Journal of International Business Studies* 10 (3), pp. 16–26.

MacDougall, G.D.A. (1960). "The benefits and costs of private investment from abroad: a theoretical approach," *Economic Record*, 36, pp. 16–35.

Miniane, Jacques (2004). "A new set of measures on capital account restrictions," *IMF Staff Papers* 51 (2), pp. 276–308.

Moggridge, Donald E. (1971). "British controls on long term capital movements, 1924–1931," in D.N. McCloskey, ed., *Essays on a Mature Economy: Britain after 1840* (London: Methuen), pp. 113–38.

Moran, Theodore H. (2008). "What policies should developing countries adopt towards outward FDI? Lessons from the experiences of developed countries," in Karl P. Sauvant, ed., with Kristin Mendoza and Irmak Ince, *The Rise of Transnational Corporations from Emerging Markets: Threat or Opportunity?* (Cheltenham: Edward Elgar), pp. 272–98.

Moran, Theodore H. and C. Fred Bergsten (2003). *Reforming OPIC for the 21st Century*, Policy Analyses in International Economics 69 (Washington, DC: Institute for International Economics).

Neely, Christopher J. (1999). "An introduction to capital controls," *Federal Reserve Bank of St Louis Review* November/December, pp. 13–30.

NERA (2003). "Estimating the economic costs and benefits of ECGD: a report for the Export Credit Guarantee Department" (London: NERA Economic Consulting).

OECD (1979). *International Direct Investment: Policies, Procedures and Practices in OECD Member Countries* (Paris: OECD).

Rugman, Alan M. and Thomas L. Brewer, eds. (2001). *The Oxford Handbook of International Business* (New York: Oxford University Press).

Sauvant, Karl P. (2005). "New sources of FDI: the BRICs. Outward FDI from Brazil, Russia, India, and China," *Journal of World Investment and Trade* 6 (5), pp. 639–710.

———(2008). "New sources of FDI: the BRICs. Outward FDI from Brazil, Russia, India, and China," *Journal of World Investment and Trade* 6, pp. 639–709.

Sauvant, Karl P. with Kristin Mendoza and Irmak Ince (2008). *The Rise of Transnational Corporations from Emerging Markets: Threat or Opportunity* (Cheltenham: Edward Elgar).

Scaperlanda, A.E. and L.J. Mauer (1973). "The impact of controls on United States direct foreign investment in the European Economic Community," *Southern Economic Journal* 39 (3), pp. 419–23.

Seabright, Paul (2005). "National and European champions: burden or blessing?" *CESifo Forum* 2, pp. 52–55.

Solis, Mireya (2003). "The politics of self-restraint: FDI subsidies and Japanese mercantilism," *World Economy* 26 (2), pp. 153–80.

Stone, Ian (1998). "East Asian FDI and the UK periphery," *Asia Pacific Business Review* 5 (2), pp. 59–94.

Te Velde, Dirk W. (2007). "Understanding developed country efforts to promote foreign direct investment to developing countries: the example of the United Kingdom," *Transnational Corporations* 16 (3), pp. 83–104.

Triantis, Stephen G. (1952). "Obstacles to Canadian investment overseas," *Canadian Journal of Economics and Political Science/ Revue canadienne d'Economique et de Science politique* 18 (1), pp. 92–95.

UNCTAD (1995). *World Investment Report 1995: Transnational Corporations and Competitiveness* (New York and Geneva: United Nations).

——— (2001) *Home Country Measures*, IIA Issues Paper Series, UNCTAD/ITE/IIT/24 (New York and Geneva: United Nations).

——— (2004). *Facilitating Transfer of Technologies to Developing Countries: A Survey of Home-Country Measures*, UNCTAD Series on Technology Transfer and Development, UNCTAD/ITE/IPC/2004/5 (New York and Geneva: United Nations).

——— (2006a). "Developing countries are beginning to promote outward FDI," UNCTAD Investment Brief No. 4 (New York and Geneva: United Nations).

——— (2006b). *World Investment Report: FDI from Developing and Transition Economies: Implications for Development* (New York and Geneva: United Nations).

——— (2007). *World Investment Report: Transnational Corporations, Extractive Industries and Development* (New York and Geneva: United Nations).

Visser, Hans (2006). "Outward foreign direct investment: is it a good thing?" in Gerrit Meijer, Wim J.M.Heijman, Johan A.C.van Ophem, and Bernard H.J.Verstegen, eds., *Heterodox Views on Economics and the Economy of the Global Society* (Wageningen: Wageningen Academic), pp. 343–58.

Wright, Gerald and Maureen A. Molot (1974). "Capital movements and government control," *International Organization* 28 (4), pp. 671–88.

Wu, Yuan-li (1950). "Government guarantees and private foreign investment," *American Economic Review* 40 (1), pp. 61–73.

Chapter 14

Changing Policy Regimes in Outward Foreign Direct Investment: From Control to Promotion

Filip De Beule and Daniël Van Den Bulcke

Introduction

Following in the footsteps of the developed countries, more and more firms from emerging markets have gradually accumulated sufficient technological and other capabilities—also known as firm-specific advantages—to allow them to expand their operations to other countries and can consequently be labeled multinational enterprises (MNEs) (van Agtmael 2007). As a result, flows of outward foreign direct investment (OFDI) from emerging markets have increased significantly over the past thirty years (chapter 1; Gammeltoft 2008).

Patterns of OFDI reflect the particular institutional and policy context in which the investing firms have evolved and developed their ownership advantages. Corporate decisions are affected by the legal framework governing international capital flows, as well as by proactive policy measures to assist companies in their internationalization process (UNCTAD 2006).

This chapter will first look at the evidence on the impact of OFDI on home countries through a short empirical literature review. After discussing in some detail the changes in the OFDI policies of individual emerging markets, an historical analysis of the changes in the policy stance of developed countries is made. These policies will be compared subsequently to more recent policies by newly developed and emerging markets. Next, an overview of specific policy measures to promote OFDI is presented, before drawing some conclusions on the sequencing of control and promotion policies.

14.1 Effects of OFDI on the Countries of Origin: The Evidence

Outward investment has been opposed in home countries as substituting for exports, reducing domestic capital investment, and causing the loss of jobs, but it has been defended as being necessary for the growth and prosperity of home-based firms in the contest for worldwide markets and for the competitiveness of firms from the countries of origin.

Previous research regarding the effect of OFDI on domestic investments has been inconclusive. Some studies concluded that a positive relationship exists between investment at home and abroad (Noorzoy 1980; Borensztein, Gregorio, and Lee 1998). Other studies have shown a negative relationship between foreign direct investment (FDI) and home country investment (Belderbos 1992; Stevens and Lipsey 1992). The latter studies argue that a firm's capital constraints would result in OFDI crowding out domestic investment. Pontus Braunerhjelm, Lars Oxelheim, and Per Thulin (2006) found that a complementary relationship can be expected in vertically integrated industries, whereas a substitution relationship can be expected in the context of horizontally organized production. Empirical analysis confirmed a significant difference between these two categories of industries with regard to the impact of OFDI on domestic investment for Sweden.

Studies on home country employment effects have also obtained mixed results. A first group of studies, on the employment effect of OFDI, found a substitution effect between a foreign affiliate's activity and its parent's employment (Kravis and Lipsey 1988; Brainard and Riker 1997; Braconier and Ekholm 2001; Konings and Murphy 2001; Cuyvers et al. 2005). Several studies have concluded that substitution occurs between countries with comparable factor endowments (Brainard and Riker 1997; Slaughter 2000; Braconier and Ekholm 2001; Konings and Murphy 2003; Hansson 2005). Other studies have shown that U.S. MNEs, using the vertical FDI model, appear to reduce employment at home, relative to production, by allocating labor-intensive stages of their production to their affiliates in developing countries (Brainard and Riker 1997; Slaughter 2000; Blomström, Fors, and Lipsey 1997). Jozef Konings and Alan P. Murphy (2003) also concluded that labor substitution is more likely to take place if factor proportions are different in various locations and vertical FDI dominates.

Other empirical studies concluded that complementary effects are achieved, meaning that a positive employment effect from a foreign affiliate's activity was detected (Lopez-de-Silanes, Markusen, and Rutherford 1996; Feenstra and Hanson 1996; Lipsey, Ramstetter, and Blomström 2000; Masso, Varblane, and Vahter 2007). The logic behind this is that the opportunity to invest in a low-cost host country could increase a firm's competitiveness, promote its use of economies of scale, and reduce its costs, which may lead to an increase in home country employment. Research on Japanese firms showed that home country employment grew by investing abroad (Lipsey, Ramstetter, and Blomström 2000). This was explained as the result of allocating labor-intensive production to developing countries, which allows increasing supervisory and ancillary employment at home to service foreign operations. Peter M. Debaere, Hongshik Lee, and Joonhyung Lee (2006) found that, on the one hand, moving to less advanced countries (as an initial foreign investment or as a redirection of previous investment) decreases a company's employment growth rate. On the other hand, moving to a more advanced country does not affect employment growth in any significant way.

The existing empirical evidence on the impact of outward investment on exports is similarly mixed. Some research, especially using cross-sectional data, concluded that FDI had a complementary positive net effect on domestic exports (Lipsey and Weiss 1984; Head and Ries 2001), but other studies found a significant negative impact on home country exports (Horst 1972; Pain and Wakelin 1997; Blonigen 2001). Roger Svensson (1996), for instance, obtained evidence for a substitution effect using Swedish data, with exports to third parties from the foreign affiliates of Swedish companies being at the expense of exports from the parent firm. Other studies suggest that the time-series relationship between outward investment and exports may vary across countries and across time (Johnson 2006). Any initial stimulus to exports of intermediate goods may fade over time. On balance the evidence from cross-sectional studies and panel studies with a limited time dimension suggests that the two are complements, whereas studies with a greater time dimension obtain stronger evidence that the two are substitutes (Pain and Wakelin 1997).

Despite the many studies on the impact of OFDI on domestic investment, employment, and exports, it seems impossible to come to a one-for-all and once-and-for-all conclusion. Increasingly, moreover, attention seems to be shifting from macroeconomic impact toward microeconomic significance. In a rapidly globalizing world, companies can no longer merely count on their home markets as a relatively secure source of profits (UNCTAD 2007). Competition from foreign firms is everywhere—through imports, inward FDI (IFDI), and nonequity forms of participation. These conditions make it all the more important for firms to pay attention to their competitiveness (Sauvant 2005). OFDI is an important aspect of this consideration and a vehicle for integrating developing country firms into the global economy. The benefits of internationalization for increasing firm competitiveness are demonstrated by the fact that more firms are investing abroad and more countries are encouraging their firms to do so. In particular, OFDI can help firms increase their revenues, assets, profitability, market reach, and exports (UNCTAD 2007) and avoid the one-sided globalization of a country.

14.2 OFDI Policies of Emerging Markets: Country Case Studies

The reduction of barriers to capital outflows has been paralleled by increased outward flows from many economies, such as Taiwan Province of China and the Republic of Korea. Singapore declared 2004 to be the "year of internationalization," whereby the government implemented a range of measures to facilitate the international expansion of its public and private companies. China's "Going Global" strategy, outlined in 2000, is among the most explicit policy initiatives taken by an emerging market to boost FDI overseas (see chapter 15). The Indian government also wants to remove all barriers to growth and encourage Indian companies to go global (see chapters 9 and 10). The global expansion of South African firms is supposed to benefit significantly the home economy: expanded market access, increased exports, and improved competitiveness. In 2003, Brazil set a target of having ten fully transnational companies by the end of President Lula da Silva's second term of office in 2011.

14.2.1 Taiwan Province of China

As early as 1962, Taiwan Province of China published a policy statement on the screening and handling of outward investment and outward technical cooperation projects. Even after several revisions, this remained the mainstay of OFDI regulations. Although Taiwan Province of China was among the first emerging markets to dismantle investment restrictions, only a few hundred OFDI projects were approved by 1978.

From 1979 onward, the economy began to promote OFDI, in order to secure access to natural resources and confront the first major energy crisis of that year. Despite this, the number of projects remained low. The promotional program received a boost from the expanded efforts launched in 1984. Between 1984 and 1986, incentives to take advantage of the "Caribbean Basin Initiative" were introduced, aimed at small and medium-sized enterprises that were interested in investing in Latin America and the Caribbean. Tax incentives were offered to FDI projects that engaged in processing activities abroad, the distribution of agricultural and raw materials products and the transfer of specific technologies. The Export-Import Bank initiated investment insurance for OFDI and was allowed to extend grants to Taiwanese entrepreneurs with foreign investment projects.

In 1987, foreign exchange controls were finally relaxed and there was a further revision of outward investment regulations. Projects could be approved if they met certain, rather broad, criteria that were considered to be advantageous to the economy, such as acquiring resources, maintaining market shares, acquiring management and production know-how, promoting international economic cooperation, as well as restructuring and upgrading domestic industries (UNCTAD 1995, 326).

Today, Taiwanese overseas direct investors require approval from the competent authority only when the investment exceeds US$50 million over one year. For a capital flow of less than that amount, only a postinvestment report is required within six months, except for investments in mainland China, where an advance application is required (UNCTAD 2006, 338–39). At the beginning of 2008, this condition was relaxed for Taiwanese banks, when it was acknowledged that the slowness of the administrative process damaged their competitive position on the mainland (*Financial Times* 2008).

14.2.2 The Republic of Korea

Until 1987, the Republic of Korea applied extensive controls even though OFDI had been permitted since 1968. The Republic of Korea's move toward a more open OFDI policy was based on the favorable balance-of-payments development and the increasing domestic wage level, which was hindering its competitive position. The new attitude toward OFDI was part of a more general liberalization trend, which also included a more open policy toward

IFDI, with the added intention of balancing investment flows. Apart from a simplification of the application procedure for offshore investors, which began in 1981, the government introduced threshold values for projects: small investments required only certification from exchange banks, mid-sized projects had to follow a notification procedure, and large projects had to undergo an approval and screening procedure.

In 1994, a "negative" list was adopted, in which only a few sensitive business areas were included, meaning that OFDI was permitted for all other firms (UNCTAD 1995, 324). At the end of the 1990s, the sole remaining requirement consisted of prior notification and approval by a foreign exchange bank, regardless of the size of the project (UNCTAD 2006, 208). The government has not only become an active promoter of OFDI, it has also adopted certain measures to counter the risk of the hollowing out of its industries by focusing on the development of new technologies in high-growth industries, and supporting domestic industries that produce materials and components for companies that have shifted part, or all, of their production abroad, thereby stimulating intrafirm trade (218).

14.2.3 *Singapore*

Crucial periods in the OFDI policy of Singapore are the mid-1980s and the first half of the 1990s. Yet, by the end of the 1960s, Singapore was already an early promoter of OFDI. Partly inspired by an enviable balance-of-payments situation and a plan to develop a regional financial center, in 1986, the Singaporean government published a report entitled "The Singapore Economy: New Directions," in which OFDI was one of the strategic options. In 1992, the mandate of the Economic Development Board (EDB) was extended to include OFDI promotion, particularly in the Asian region ("Regionalization 2000" program). Between 1987 and 1993, the total value of incentives (consisting of different types of loans), grants, and fiscal advantages for domestic enterprises with investments abroad doubled from US$155 million to US$326 million (UNCTAD 1995, 337). In 1993, new fiscal measures included a ten-year income tax exemption for outward investors, a double-tax deduction for expenses made for the development of OFDI opportunities, and incentives to repatriate foreign income.

The Singaporean government has a strong influence on the economy as a whole and also on OFDI. Its government linked companies (GLCs) are former state-owned enterprises (SOEs) in which the government retains an important influence on decision making and strategic orientation via state-owned holding companies (UNCTAD 2005c, 16–17). Singapore has established a large number of agencies to enhance the competitiveness of its domestic enterprises, also with regard to the regional and global markets. These agencies include IE Singapore (the former Trade Development Board), which administers the numerous tax incentives; the EDB, which participates in equity financing for overseas expansion that matches half of the funds raised from third-party interests; and SPRING Singapore. The Local Industry Upgrading Program (LIUP) supports local suppliers that upgrade their activities through collaboration with foreign firms. The Regionalization Finance Scheme (RFS) helps small and medium-sized enterprises to set up foreign activities. The Overseas Investment Incentive (OIT) supports, over three years, local companies that set up foreign affiliates that generate spinoffs to Singapore through increased exports of goods or services. (For a complete overview see the list of measures in UNCTAD 2005c, 22–24.)

In addition to tax incentives and subsidies to stimulate OFDI, Singapore has established a complete institutional framework to prepare and strengthen its enterprises as they confront regional and global competitors in an increasingly competitive arena. Such a framework is likely to be more effective in supporting OFDI than other measures, while at the same time avoiding a hollowing out of the domestic industry.

14.2.4   India

In his extensive analyses of Indian OFDI,[1] Jaya Prakash Pradhan (2007a, 2007b) distinguished two waves in the country's outward investment. The first wave ran until 1990 and was mainly oriented toward manufacturing industries in developing countries. This was done largely through minority participations, in order to acquire new markets or resources or to escape India's restrictive government policies. During the second wave, OFDI spread to all sectors, even though service industries dominated (e.g., information technology and communications [ITC] sector). Furthermore, Indian investors entered more countries on the basis of majority or complete ownership and entered developed countries to acquire strategic assets such as technology, marketing know-how, brand names, and existing distribution systems.

In terms of the different stages in the Indian OFDI policy regime, 1992 marked the turning point (Pradhan 2007b, 176; UNCTAD 2005b). This seems to indicate that OFDI liberalization was carried out shortly after Indian internationally oriented firms had already accelerated and extended their process of multinationalization. Between 1969 and 1992, India sought to use OFDI as an instrument of South-South cooperation, possibly following the example of developed countries. At the same time, the government attempted to limit the foreign exchange cost of OFDI by insisting on the capitalization of Indian know-how and capital goods (but excluding second-hand machinery) and minority joint ventures. Foreign joint ventures were only allowed in the same line of business as the parent company, and they had to be approved by an interministerial committee.

When India changed its OFDI priorities in 1992, it focused on promoting the global competitiveness of its companies, completely removing restrictions on the types of equity participation and ownership, and extending this liberalization to all business activities. Moreover, when certain thresholds were respected, automatic approval by the Reserve Bank of India became possible. These thresholds were gradually increased to US$2 million, US$15 million, and US$100 million in 1992, 1995, and 1999, respectively. In 2005, it was decided that any amount up to 200% of the net worth of the

India entity could be accepted. India has included a regional dimension to its OFDI policy by allowing higher threshold ceilings for investments in Nepal and Bhutan, as well as for Myanmar, Bangladesh, the Maldives, Sri Lanka, and the countries of the South Asian Association for Regional Cooperation (SAARC). Between 2001 and 2004, no less than twenty-nine changes in the OFDI policy regime were carried out (Pradhan 2007a, 183–85).

Although UNCTAD recognized that OFDI has become a distinguishing feature of the Indian economy, it stressed that "[t]he need for capacity building and strengthening Indian technological capability deserves closer attention by the Government, the private sector and research institutions" (UNCTAD 2005b, 14).

14.2.5 China

China's attitude toward the internationalization of its companies has changed dramatically over time.[2] It is certainly surprising that, from the very beginning of its economic liberalization program, which started in 1978 and dealt with FDI in policy decrees signed in 1979, China allowed OFDI (Zhang 2003). Yet, the Chinese government had approved only fifty overseas nontrade subsidiaries by 1982. In the early 1980s, the screening of OFDI by the Ministry of Foreign Trade and Cooperation (MOFTEC) was highly centralized and restrictive, albeit less strenuous for smaller projects (UNCTAD 1995, 329–30). In fact, until 1985, the Chinese authorities devoted little attention to the development potential abroad and the implications for its economy. At this time, practically all foreign affiliates were still established by state-owned foreign trade companies, which mainly established commercial activities abroad.

After 1985, the rapid growth of a number of overseas investment projects carried out by industrial firms convinced the government that it was necessary to integrate these offshore activities into their overall economic development strategy. On the one hand, a set of regulations governing the approvals process, foreign exchange controls, accounting systems, and other aspects were introduced. On the other hand, a number of large SOEs were granted greater decision-making authority and autonomy over the management of their foreign operations. By the second half of the 1980s and early 1990s, Chinese SOEs attracted worldwide attention with the acquisition of raw-material-producing companies in Australia, Peru, and the United States (Zhang and Van Den Bulcke, 1996).

The gradual liberalization process of Chinese OFDI continued with steps taken in 1985, 1989, and 1995, which decentralized authority to lower levels of government based on ceilings expressed in value. OFDI procedures were temporarily tightened in 1993, after some irregularities were found in investments in Hong Kong (China). Projects valued at US$30 million and above required the "blessing" of the State Council; those below US$1 million came under the supervision of the Commission of Foreign Trade and Economic Cooperation. Those in between were controlled by the State Planning Commission and MOFTEC for a more detailed follow-up. The policy switch toward promotion is important. This occurred in the late

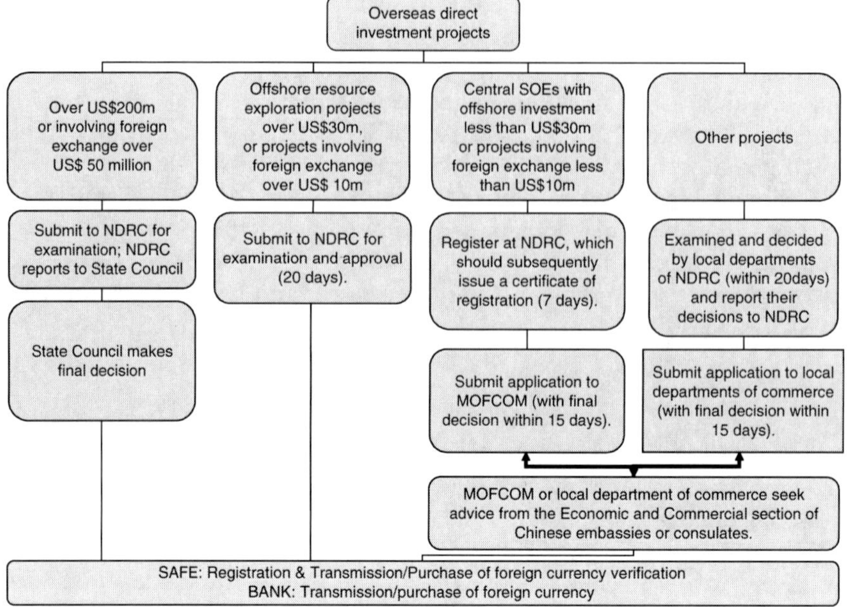

Figure 14.1 China's outward investment approval procedures

Source: Adapted from Zhang (2005) and Pamlin and Long (2007).

1980s, when it was decided to exempt foreign affiliates from taxes for the first five years of their existence. In addition, OFDI projects with specific objectives (e.g., for acquiring technology raw materials, foreign exchange earnings, and for strengthening ties with neighboring countries) became eligible for incentives. From 1991, links were developed between Chinese development assistance and OFDI in Africa, although on a much smaller scale than in the first half of the twenty-first century. It is worth mentioning that China not only promotes traditional OFDI, but also includes overseas construction contracting and international service promotion.

The launch, in 2000, of its "Go Global" or "Go Out" policy and membership in the World Trade Organization (WTO) in 2001, heralded China's entry into the twenty-first century and into the merger and acquisition (M&A) major league, with acquisitions of well-known MNEs in developed countries. China's OFDI regime gradually abandoned the approval method in favor of a system of supervision, even though the institutional setup may well be too complicated for the country's stage of development (figure 14.1). Since then, the African focus of Chinese OFDI has moved to a higher gear, illustrated by the much publicized visits of its leaders to a number of resource-rich African countries and the establishment of a special China-Africa Development Fund.

14.2.6 South Africa

A key driver of South African OFDI was, undoubtedly, the relaxation of sanctions in 1990 and the subsequent end of its political isolation. Although a small number of foreign affiliates existed before the end of the apartheid regime, South African companies had concentrated on the domestic market, in some instances expanding through the takeover of affiliates disinvested by Western MNEs. After 1994, and due to exchange restrictions, twenty-seven South African companies listed their shares on the London Stock Exchange, thereby contributing to the rapid growth of South African FDI stock in Europe, which amounted to approximately three-quarters of its total outward investment in 2003 (UNCTAD 2005d, 4). Listings in London provided access to more and cheaper sources of capital and were instrumental in establishing a global presence (8).

While South Africa became a platform for foreign investors seeking to invest in other African countries, the government's support for the New Partnership for African Development (NEPAD) (Thomas 2006) encouraged its "parastatals," or state-owned companies, to focus on other African countries, especially after 2000. Privatization allowed South African firms to seize investment opportunities in neighboring and other African countries, as they were quite familiar with the culture and business environment. Consequently, South Africa has become the major foreign investor on the continent (Games 2004; South Africa Foundation 2004). From the mid-1990s onward, South Africa gradually eased restrictions on OFDI, until controls were abolished in 2004 (UNCTAD 2006).

14.3 OFDI Control and Promotion

14.3.1 Waves of OFDI Policies

To evaluate the OFDI policies of emerging markets, it is extremely important to look back to the measures adopted by developed countries during the 1960s and 1970s; that is, during the period of emergence of U.S. and European MNEs, to find out in which sequence this occurred. This analysis will be based on the historic policies of thirteen developed countries (Australia, Belgium, Canada, Denmark, France, Germany, Japan, the Netherlands, Norway, Sweden, Switzerland, the United Kingdom, and the United States) (Van Den Bulcke 1979).

After World War II, most developed countries attached much less importance to FDI than to exports. OFDI was not regarded as positive and was even explicitly controlled. In this latter case, priority was given to domestic investment, and scarce foreign exchange was protected through exchange regulations (such as in France and Germany). In order to secure necessary supplies of raw materials, restrictive policies were applied in a flexible way (e.g., in Japan). When the United Kingdom suffered from balance-of-payments deficits during the 1960s, it also moved toward a more restrictive regime. In 1961, on the basis of its foreign exchange regulations, UK companies were obliged to obtain authorization to invest in non-sterling countries and, later, even for projects in other sterling countries.

The United States, however, began to promote the foreign activities of its enterprises rather early on. Other countries, which originally were opposed to the investments of their firms abroad, mainly because of the scarcity of foreign exchange and shortages in the internal capital market, gradually took a more positive stance toward OFDI. Yet, the promotional measures were mainly or exclusively oriented toward FDI in developing countries. This meant that investment abroad was supported, not only for commercial purposes, but also as an instrument of development policy.

The first measures taken by the United States to incentivize its companies to invest abroad were fiscally oriented. Some measures, such as the "Exports Trade Assets Corporations" for Latin America, made it possible to avoid taxes on export profits if those profits were not repatriated to the United States. After World War II, international investments were regarded as an integral part of U.S. foreign policy, which initially was aimed at the reconstruction of war-ravaged Europe. However, already in 1948, the "Point Four" program, launched by President Truman, began to focus on developing countries.

At the beginning of the 1960s, the mood of U.S. policy makers toward OFDI became less positive, and measures were taken to make investment abroad less attractive. In 1961, the Kennedy administration decided to tax immediately the proceeds of FDI that were transferred to tax havens; previously, these profits were only taxed when repatriated to the United States. The continuing balance-of-payments problems of the United States during the first half of the 1960s resulted in the "Voluntary Restraint Program" (1965) which, in 1968, became compulsory and only ended fully in 1974. However, those restrictions were not, or were less, applicable to developing countries. If the so-called Hartke-Burke law (1971) had been approved by the U.S. Congress, FDI would have been severely curtailed. That enthusiasm for U.S. OFDI remained at a low level was illustrated by the vehement opposition to a proposed extension of the activities of the "Overseas Private Investment Corporation" (OPIC) until 1981.

Stefan H. Robock and Kenneth Simmonds wrote: "Control programs over multinational enterprises are still in an incipient stage. Certain traditional control programs adopted for national security reasons, for balance-of-payments considerations, and in support of domestic antitrust philosophy have been applied to international business operations and other types of international economic relations. But control programs inspired by the international business phenomenon per se are only in an early stage of evolution" (1977, 214–15). Contrary to these expectations, there was a movement not only toward the liberalization of OFDI during the 1970s, but also toward the promotion of such investments by fiscal, financial, and other measures taken by developed home countries.

In 1960, only the United States, Germany, and Japan had established a system of insuring their companies against the political risks of long-term investments abroad. A decade later, ten countries had introduced such an insurance system for their MNEs. This illustrates clearly the gradual move toward a positive attitude regarding OFDI on the part of developed country governments. Such a move occurred in France. After World War II, the French government was opposed or neutral to OFDI. However, in the Fifth Plan, and especially in the Sixth Plan (1970–75), when the advantages of investment abroad were stressed from the point of view of the supply of raw materials, export promotion, and the necessity for companies to acquire international investment and management experience (essential ingredients in the development of a strong competitive position), the French position shifted. Although foreign exchange controls and compulsory notification remained in place, France ceased to use those instruments in a restrictive way (Van Den Bulcke 1979).

As the United States changed course and became more restrictive, Germany and Japan started to explicitly promote direct investment abroad, especially after 1969, as an alternative to revaluing their respective currencies. Japan liberalized its OFDI regulations in 1969 and 1971. Germany targeted its OFDI promotion efforts exclusively at developing countries, even though an exception was made for the provision of the necessary raw materials. Since 2000, China's support for OFDI has also been taken place in connection with its balance-of-payments surplus and an appreciating currency.

To use the example of a small country, it was not until the beginning of the 1970s that Belgium took measures to stimulate investment abroad. In 1966, the Minister of Foreign Trade continued to react negatively to demands by the Federation of Belgian Industries to allow for the insurance of political and catastrophic risks of its companies' FDI. The minister feared that this would result in capital flight. It was suggested that, instead, bilateral investment agreements should be used to stimulate investment abroad. In 1971, Belgium was one of the last developed countries to introduce risk investment insurance for its companies. Although Belgium was eleventh out of the thirteen developed countries to launch such a system, and only preceded France and the United Kingdom, these latter countries had already introduced certain guarantee modalities previously.

Measures to restrict OFDI were driven largely by the balance-of-payments situation, as well as by concerns over the value of the exchange rate. For these reasons, the United States restricted outward investment between 1965 and 1974, while the United Kingdom transformed its voluntary registration of OFDI in countries of the sterling zone into compulsory regulation. At one time, Sweden decided to require its MNEs to submit their foreign expansion plans to an evaluation of the associated employment effects. Until 1967, France required its companies to request preliminary authorization to invest abroad. Later, France moved to compulsory notification, which still left the possibility for the government to intervene if it was judged to be necessary. However, already from 1972 onward, a maximum level of French OFDI could benefit from automatic authorization. During this period, French restrictions did not apply to countries in the "zone franc," where French firms could invest freely.

The adoption of flexible and floating exchange rates and the increasing availability of capital as a result of the globalization of financial markets allowed capital control restrictions to be lifted. Membership of international organizations, such as the Organisation for Economic Co-operation and Development (OECD) and the European Union, contributed to this process, as it also implied the liberalization of capital movements among member countries.

In 2006, only a few OECD countries retained certain (limited) controls for specific reasons or on specific industries. Portugal and Japan maintained certain restrictions on their financial institutions during the 1990s

(UNCTAD 1995, 310); others excluded sensitive industries (e.g., arms) or countries to which there were objections for political reasons (e.g., Cuba for the United States), or concerns over the respect for human rights (e.g., Myanmar for Germany) (UNCTAD 2006, 204).

14.3.2 Promotional OFDI Policies

Typically, the following categories are distinguished in promotional OFDI policies:

1. Guarantee systems for political and other noncommercial investment risks
2. Loans and participations in the equity capital by the government or public organizations
3. Fiscal allowances and advantages with regard to the profits earned or used abroad
4. Information and technical support for firms considering investing abroad and financing or cofinancing of preinvestment and feasibility studies
5. Bilateral investment agreements for investment protection.

The following section will deal with four promotional policies: insurance of noncommercial investment risks, financial participation, fiscal incentives, and informational assistance to foreign investors. Bilateral investment agreements will not be dealt with. The topic of OFDI promotion by international organizations will not be taken into account, nor will the recent expansion of sovereign wealth funds (SWFs) be included in the analysis. Figure 14.2 shows the different forms and stages that are applied by home countries to promote OFDI.

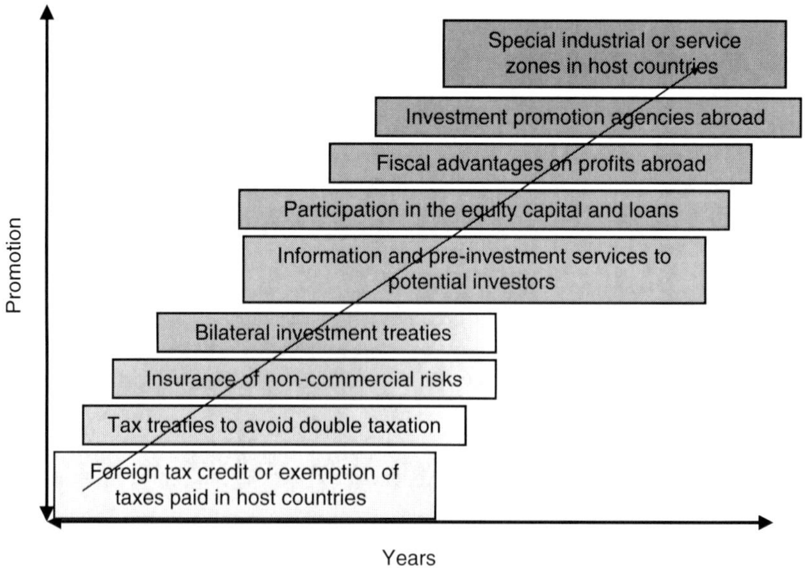

Figure 14.2 Types and stages in OFDI promotional policies
Source: The Authors.

14.3.2.1   Insurance of Noncommercial Investment Risks

By the mid-1970s, many developed countries had established an insurance and guarantee system for noncommercial risks of FDI projects. In five of the thirteen industrial countries surveyed (Australia, Belgium, Canada, Denmark, France, Germany, Japan, the Netherlands, Norway, Sweden, Switzerland, the United Kingdom, the United States), the guarantee system was applicable to all those countries where their MNEs were located (Van Den Bulcke 1979). The majority of developed countries limited their insurance and guarantee system to all, or to a restricted number of, developing countries. Some of those countries only allowed their system to be used when a bilateral investment agreement had been signed. Yet, countries such as France and Germany could extend their risk insurance to host countries that provided sufficient investment guarantees.

With regard to the nature of the insured political and catastrophic risks, there were few differences among the countries of origin. Nine of the thirteen developed countries studied insured equity capital and the repatriation of the profits, loans extended by the parent company, and royalties to be received for licensing agreements. Interestingly, eight of the countries put forward the condition that the insured investments should contribute to the economic development of the host country. In practice, this meant that the country in which an affiliate was located had to authorize the investment project. That home countries did not neglect their own interests is indicated by the export expansion condition imposed by five of the developed countries included in the survey. With respect to the amount covered by insurance, a distinction was made between equity capital, reinvested earnings, and repatriated profits. The period of insurance varied between a maximum of five and twenty years.

In most developed countries during the 1970s, the insurance of investment risks was carried out by institutions that were already responsible for insuring exports for political and catastrophic risk. In some countries, these were not public institutions, but, for instance, in Germany and the Netherlands, private enterprises. However, the government gave final authorization or took care of the reinsurance of risks. During this period the United States examined the possibility of privatizing OPIC and limiting its role to reinsurance.

Evaluating the impact of these guarantee systems on the development of FDI is rather complicated. Investors do not necessarily rely on these provisions when they estimate that the risks are not sufficiently important, or the premiums that have to be paid are considered to be too high. According to Michael Emerson (1970), about two-thirds of the U.S. investments abroad that could be covered by those arrangements were insured. The amounts that had to be paid out as a result of incurred risks represented only 0.1% of the total insured sums. An earlier study by the World Bank (1962) had shown that two-fifths of the surveyed companies considered the guarantee systems efficient, while about half of the companies surveyed considered them as essential. Hearings in the German Parliament, at that time, indicated that most of the intervening company representatives stressed the need to insure OFDI risks and that it had a positive impact on the decision to invest abroad.

For developing countries, the insurance of noncommercial risks was not a priority initially, mainly because of the scarcity of potential investors. Also, the fact that MNEs from developing countries are more familiar with the often unfavorable economic conditions in other developing countries, have greater experience of operating in an unstable political environment, and cope with unclear and corrupt bureaucracies, may help explain this situation. To the extent that MNEs from developing countries are investing in developed countries, the need for such investment insurance might be perceived as less relevant than it is for investors from developed countries with investment plans in less developed nations. Even when political risk insurance services have been developed, the capacity to underwrite is limited in developing countries. Of course, the establishment of the Multilateral Investment and Guarantee Agency (MIGA), in 1985, reduced the need for the establishment of national insurance institutions. The proliferation of foreign private companies to provide political risk insurance to potential investors from developing countries also makes this less of a priority, given the many urgent development needs of these countries. Yet, according to UNCTAD (2006, 211–12), at the end of 2005, seventeen Export Credit Agencies (ECAs) had become full members of the Berne Convention, an international organization that groups most of these agencies, and a similar number were part of a less stringent group. As happened before in developed countries during the 1970s, many developing countries entered into investment insurance through an extension of the activities of their institutions responsible for export credit insurance.

14.3.2.2   Financial Institutions to Participate in Foreign Investment Projects

At the end of the 1970s, eight of the thirteen developed countries surveyed (Van Den Bulcke 1979) had established an institution to stimulate OFDI through financial incentives, such as participations in the equity capital or loans to affiliates abroad or through state guarantees. The oldest of these institutions were the British "CDC" (1948) (originally the Colonial and later the Commonwealth Development Corporation) and the French "CCCE" (originally the "Caisse Centrale de la France d'Outremer" and later the "Caisse Centrale de la Coopération Economique"). The German "DEG" (Deutsche Entwicklungsgesellschaft) (1962) was used as the model for the establishment of similar organizations in Denmark and the Netherlands. For most developed countries, the operations of these financial institutions were limited to developing countries. Some countries (e.g., the Netherlands) even restricted their activity to the least developed countries; others (e.g., Germany) insisted on a minimum level of development to ensure that the absorptive capacity would be high enough to benefit from the German direct investment projects.

The government financial institutions that stimulated OFDI only intended to play a catalyzing role, as their capital participation in affiliates

could not exceed a certain level (e.g., 25% for the Dutch FMO—
"Financieringsmaatschappij voor Ontwikkelingslanden"). Also they
intended to withdraw their participation and sell it to private partners after
a period of, for example, five years, when the affiliate had reached a satisfactory and profitable stage.

Most developed country governments' that had set up such institutions
before the end of the 1970s had two major aims. On the one hand, the project had to be development oriented, which meant that the host country had
to accept it. On the other hand, the objectives had to be in accordance with
the goals of the country of origin, although this was not the case for the
Netherlands or the United Kingdom.

Although private firms that benefit from such financial support are profit
oriented, this is not necessarily the first priority for government-owned institutions. A number of the financial institutions had also acquired shares in
development banks in the host countries, which allowed them to influence
the management strategy and have a seat on the board that could be useful
to the industries of the home country. That these financial institutions were
quite large is illustrated by the fact that, for example, by the late 1970s the
British CDC and the French CCCE each employed about 1,000 people. Also,
the CDC had representatives in a large number of host countries and could
even take the lead in new projects, whereas in most other countries it was
only possible to intervene at the initiative of the private firms. The German
DEG often relied on special missions to investigate investment opportunities
in the potential host countries (Van Den Bulcke 1979).

Already by the mid-1980s, a number of emerging markets granted direct
financial support to their companies that ventured abroad. While UNCTAD
wondered why capital exports should be subsidized, it concluded that "the
measures were an indication of the importance these countries attach to
facilitating the internationalization of their firms" (1995, 336). Examples of
such initiatives are the Export-Import Bank of Korea, which provides information services and overseas investment credits; the Indian Export-Import
Bank, which provides equity financing for joint ventures and wholly owned
foreign affiliates; the Export-Import Bank of Thailand, which can participate in the equity capital and grant loans; and the Export-Import Bank of
Taiwan, which provides outward investment insurance and grants.

14.3.2.3 *Fiscal Incentives to Stimulate OFDI*

In the 1970s, practically all developed countries applied the so-called "resi-
dential tax principle." This meant that the entire income of their companies was taxed, including income generated by foreign affiliates. Differences
in the application of their systems, as well as variations in the interpretations by the countries that applied this principle, resulted in much complexity. Countries such as Belgium, Germany, the Netherlands, the United
Kingdom, and the United States taxed their enterprises on the basis of their
global income; countries such as France and Italy (until 1974) relied on the
"territorial principle" and only took into consideration that income realized on their national territory. Evidently, those countries that taxed profits

earned abroad caused double taxation, because such income had already been taxed by the fiscal authorities of the host country. Most countries that taxed the income from their residents in other countries allowed the deduction of the corporate income tax paid abroad by using the "foreign tax credit" (Japan, the United Kingdom, the United States), or the "method of exemption" (France, the Netherlands). Because these systems are not completely fail-safe, double taxation treaties (DTTs) were concluded to avoid this problem.

The measures taken by home countries to avoid the negative effects of double taxation are often regarded as incentives to invest abroad, even if they are intended to do away with the potential discrimination between domestic and international investments. The panic that struck U.S. MNEs in the early 1970s, when the Hartke-Burke proposal sought to eliminate the foreign tax credit and the tax deferral in order to protect domestic jobs, clearly illustrated the importance of such general fiscal arrangements for OFDI.

Next to their existing global fiscal system, developed countries took special measures to stimulate investment abroad, especially in developing countries. Already in 1963, the German Parliament approved a law (systematically extended until 1978) that allowed German MNEs to create a reserve, on the basis of realized profits exempted from taxes, that could be used in the least developed countries or in countries that were explicitly referred to in the law. Germany also introduced other advantages for its internationalizing firms (Van Den Bulcke 1979, 74). In 1964, Japan made it possible for its MNEs to place half of the losses realized by their foreign affiliates in a special reserve and to deduct them from the taxes to be paid in the home country. The upheaval caused by a proposal to end this advantage earlier than planned caused much commotion in Japan and indirectly shows how important it was for Japanese outward investors.

The tax incentives used by developing countries during the 1980s present similarities to the systems introduced previously by developed countries. The Republic of Korea grants a foreign tax credit and includes loss-reserve provisions among its tax incentives for OFDI, which reduce the corporate income tax for the parent company under certain conditions, as well as tax exemption on dividends for resource-development projects in host countries. Singapore combines financial and tax incentives to stimulate OFDI. In 1988, it allowed a write-off for overseas investment losses and eliminated certain taxes on overseas income, such as dividends, royalties, and management fees. A rather unique measure taken by the Singaporean government is the tax advantage offered to domestic and foreign companies to set up regional headquarters in its territory. Whereas Singapore relies heavily on fiscal incentives for its promotion of outward investment, Thailand, until 1993, did not use a favorable tax regime to help its outward investors. Malaysia granted tax incentives for projects that met criteria such as supplying inputs required by domestic companies, improving foreign market access and using Malaysian raw materials or components. Also, projects that contributed to South-South cooperation could benefit from an advantageous tax incentive in Malaysia. In 1995, the government even decided to abolish the tax on remitted profits altogether, in order to promote OFDI and encourage profit repatriation (UNCTAD 1995, 338).

14.3.2.4 Information and Assistance to Potential Foreign Investors

On the one hand, establishing a foreign affiliate, even for developed country firms, is an important strategic step, especially when a firm is still in the early stages of the internationalization process. On the other hand, companies may not be sufficiently aware of the potential advantages of investing abroad and may be hesitant, even after they have considered such opportunities. Developed home countries, therefore, took initiatives to provide valuable information on investment conditions and incentives abroad to eliminate the possible inertia that may exist in the minds of potential outward investors. Several countries also finance preinvestment studies, when a company wants to know if a foreign venture is a realistic option. Canada reimbursed half the expenses of the necessary surveys and technical-economic studies as well as the first foreign-travel expenses up to a certain limit. In the United States, OPIC carried out so-called "fifty-fifty surveys," in which firms were reimbursed for only half of the incurred expenses, when the project could not be carried out. Other countries insisted on reimbursement of the government's support when the project was successful, however. Supporting the establishment of commercial offices abroad was another way in which developed countries stimulated OFDI in the 1970s, as they often were the first step in an ongoing internationalization process, aptly described and praised by the so-called "Uppsala" or "Scandinavian" school. The approach of stimulating commercial outposts that might consequently develop into production activities does not seem to be relied on by emerging markets.

For small and medium-sized enterprises from emerging markets, in particular, the need for specific information on foreign markets, as well as technical and other assistance, is quite high. Even Hong Kong (China), which has pursued a noninterventionist policy with regard to OFDI, launched some promotional activities in 1989. The Ministry of Industry in Hong Kong (China) established training facilities and technical services to support firms investing abroad. Around the same time, Singapore used overseas offices to establish a database to identify overseas investment opportunities. The main "engine" for stimulating Singapore's OFDI is the EDB. Its mandate to promote OFDI was extended several times during the 1990s, following the "Regionalization 2000" program. Over the years, Singapore has developed a whole battery of institutions to foster international entrepreneurship and to stimulate its companies to invest abroad (UNCTAD 2005d). A far-reaching initiative that was pioneered by Singapore was the China-Singapore Suzhou Industrial Park, which tries to create a "full-proof" environment, adapted to the preferences of investors from the country of origin. Having experienced this approach as a host county, China is introducing the concept of industrial parks into its African investment forays. Meanwhile, Singapore established similar parks in India and Indonesia. The Republic of Korea followed this example in a narrower and industry-specific way, by establishing "iParks" (i.e, overseas information technology [IT] support centers), which offer legal, marketing, financial, and other services. At the end of 2005, the Republic of Korea had eight iParks in China, Japan, Singapore, the United Kingdom, and United States, which hosted a total of sixty-seven resident firms (UNCTAD 2006, 211).

Thailand's Overseas Investment Unit, which is part of the Board of Investment, helps its companies with the identification of foreign investment opportunities and provides services, such as conducting feasibility studies, organizing missions, and establishing contacts with agencies in the host countries.

Home country organizations, established to help domestic companies to venture abroad, may also engage in matchmaking services; for example, to identify potential joint-venture partners. According to UNCTAD (2006, 210), Malaysia, Mexico, the Republic of Korea, Singapore, and Thailand provide services that include inviting investors to participate in official missions to discover investment opportunities via meetings with government officials and businessmen in targeted countries.

Several countries have not established separate institutions for policy measures, such as the insurance of noncommercial risks, financial support via equity participations, and loans or specialized services to potential and existing investors abroad. Their export-import (EX-IM) banks, or other financial institutions, often take care of these different functions. In other cases, either export promotion agencies have been upgraded and given a mandate to promote OFDI, or the responsibilities of the inward investment promotion agencies (IPAs) were extended to include outward investments. There is little or no evidence as to which might be the most effective administrative approach. To conclude, "Relatively little is known about the effectiveness of individual policy instruments, as there have been few serious evaluations. However, all promotional measures involve costs of some kind. Every country therefore needs to determine the optimal level and form of support to OFDI in the context of its particular situation" (UNCTAD 2006, 215).

14.4   Sequencing of OFDI Control and Promotion

Although countries have various foreign exchange arrangements and/or restrictions with regard to OFDI, these vary extensively across countries and across time. On the one hand, some countries prohibit OFDI as part of a package of investment measures to ensure balance-of-payments equilibrium. On the other hand, as countries liberalize their FDI policies, outward policies seem to lag behind their inward counterparts. To some extent, this is a reflection of the "investment development path" (Dunning 1986; Dunning and Narula 1996), in which governments not only follow the strategic decisions of their firms, but may also orient them. As globalization has led to a tremendous increase in competition for firms, this in turn has led to the increased importance of OFDI for these firms. As a result, most countries seem to move to a policy in which they increasingly liberalize OFDI, which implies a switch, from incrementally reducing the financial and operational requirements, to incrementally enhancing the financial and operational incentives.

14.4.1 *Sequencing of OFDI Control and Restrictions*

After World War II, when developed countries had to cope with the demands of some of their companies to invest abroad, they only gradually allowed this because of the looming uncertainty about their future balance-of-payments developments and the shortages of foreign exchange. Balancing the need to control cross-border capital outflows with the pressure from firms to internationalize was therefore of paramount importance. Once the macroeconomic skies had cleared at the beginning of the 1970s, most developed countries rather quickly relaxed these restrictions, even though employment concerns almost caused a revival of OFDI controls in a country such as the United States.

Twenty years later, when the balance-of-payments situations of the Southeast Asian economies started to improve, they also discontinued most of their control measures, although in a much more gradual way than occurred in the developed countries. For developing countries it remains a challenge to use foreign exchange controls in such a way that OFDI is possible, but "capital flight" is made more difficult.

Even as some developed countries have kept only a few restrictions from the 1980s (UNCTAD 1995), changes in global economic conditions and the evolving nature and expansion of MNEs also transformed the policies of the governments of emerging markets toward OFDI. The globalization of financial markets and the integration of value-added activities across national borders heightened international competition. These mounting competitive pressures convinced a number of developing countries that OFDI had become a necessary strategic option in order to acquire resources such as raw materials, energy, labor, skills, and technology and know-how. The so-called "Asian Tigers" from Southeast Asia were among the first economies to liberalize and to start promoting OFDI. Improvements in the balance of payments of countries and the buildup of foreign exchange reserves were often necessary, but not sufficient conditions, to reevaluate OFDI policy.

Of the 155 developing countries surveyed by the International Monetary Fund (IMF), 78 economies (40 in Africa, 23 in Asia, and 15 in Latin America and the Caribbean) had restrictive measures. Forty countries applied approval requirements combined with various kinds of restrictions, such as quantitative, sectoral, and/or an obligation to declare, report, notify, or register the intended investment abroad. Approval is sometimes based on subjective criteria, such as national interests. In other countries approval depends on more objective measures, such as the value of the project. In most countries, restrictions on OFDI apply to all sectors and industries without discrimination. Some countries have, however, tried to enhance the competitiveness of certain industries by targeting specific investment projects (UNCTAD 2006).

As of 2005, just over 60% of developing countries applied some form of OFDI controls, with a lower incidence in Latin America, the Caribbean, and Asia and Oceania than in Africa (figure 14.3). Developing countries with considerable FDI outflows, despite the existence of controls, include Brazil, China, Malaysia, the Philippines, the Republic of Korea, and South Africa. A number of economies in Latin America (Chile, Costa Rica, and Mexico)

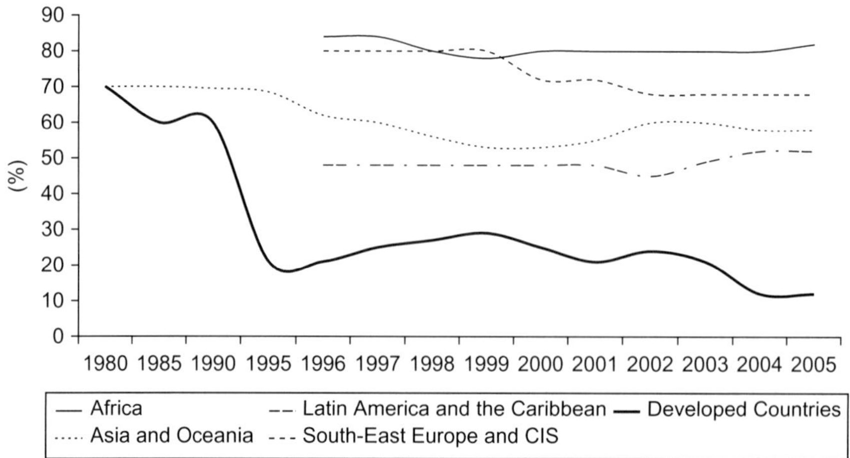

Figure 14.3 Share of countries with control or notification requirements on OFDI, by region (1980–2005)

Source: Adapted by the authors, based on WIR (1995, 1996).

Note: Until 1995, Asia is limited to Southeast Asia, while afterwards it consists of Asia and Oceania.

and Asia (Hong Kong [China], Singapore, and the United Arab Emirates) have completely liberalized FDI outflows. Several African countries have also removed their restrictions on OFDI. Other examples of gradual OFDI liberalization include Singapore, which today has no restrictions on OFDI, and the Republic of Korea, which still retains some controls.

14.4.2   Sequencing of OFDI Promotion

During the 1960s and 1970s, developed countries used a number of direct or indirect measures to stimulate their enterprises to venture abroad via OFDI. Essentially, emerging markets during the 1990s and the first decade of the new millennium relied on the same measures, although there were differences in the intensity with which they were applied. Also, the direct links between the government and business in some countries (such as China and Singapore) gives the promotional programs of many emerging markets a special dimension, in which it is difficult to disentangle the real influence that is exerted on their OFDI policy (see, for China, Morck, Yeung, and Zhao 2008).

Even though the loss of employment was a very serious concern in developed countries during the 1970s, it is somewhat surprising that this issue is not very prominent in the discussion about the attitudes of developing countries toward OFDI. This may be the result of several reasons. First, this might be explained by the absence of strong trade unions in developing countries. During the 1970s, especially in the United States, but also in the European countries with high rates of trade union membership, the opposition to outward investment was based on fear of permanent job losses and deindustrialization of the economy. Meanwhile, it has been accepted that OFDI does not necessarily lead to unemployment when the core activities are retained at the

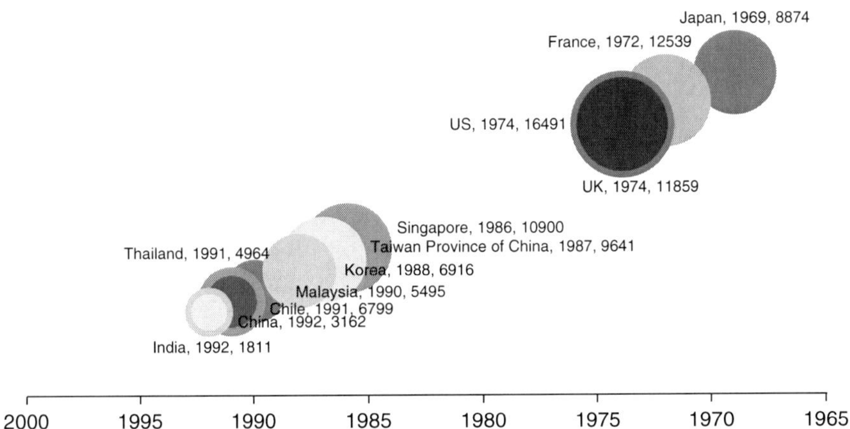

Figure 14.4   Timing of introduction of promotional OFDI policy

Source: Authors' calculation from Groningen Growth and Development Centre.

parent company in the country of origin, or when exporting is not sufficient to maintain foreign market shares. Second, to the extent that outward investment from developing countries is resource seeking and strategic asset seeking, the employment effects may be negligible. Third, as developing countries still find themselves relatively cost competitive when compared to developed countries, there is less risk of relocating divestment. This is so because developing countries are increasingly joining the ranks of outward investors at an earlier stage of development. Figure 14.4 shows some selected countries at a time when they implemented a policy of OFDI promotion.

Although it is not always possible to choose a particular year for the introduction of a promotional policy, figure 14.4 indicates when these selected countries started to promote OFDI. For the economies of Southeast Asia, this took place in the second half of the 1980s and early 1990s; that is, Singapore in 1986, Taiwan Province of China and the Republic of Korea in 1987, and Malaysia and Thailand in 1991. China and India gave a new impetus to their OFDI policy from 1992, Chile eliminated most of its restrictions on outward investment in 1991, and South African firms could engage more easily in OFDI after the relaxation of the sanctions imposed by the rest of the world at the end of the apartheid policy in 1990.

Conclusion: Some Policy Dilemmas

Most developing countries have not yet reached a stage at which a proactive approach to OFDI is feasible or desirable. Many low-income countries should instead focus on the enhancement of their domestic firms' capabilities. Specific policies on OFDI should be positioned within a national strategy aimed at enhancing international competitiveness. Whether active or proactive promotion of OFDI is warranted still deserves careful consideration. Also, the criteria applied by governments to discriminate (e.g., size, industry, host country) among companies that benefit from promotional policies, based on incentives or subsidies, should be studied carefully before being applied.

The liberalization of OFDI and the introduction of promotional measures in many developing countries were stretched out over a relatively long period of ten years or more. According to UNCTAD (1995, 323), this was due to the experience of early liberalizers, such as Argentina and Chile, which undertook a rapid internal and external liberalization in the late 1970s and were obliged to reintroduce restrictions, when their economies suffered from a financial crisis and capital flight associated with the external debt crisis at the beginning of the 1980s. Whereas it is preferable to loosen the controls rather quickly, it is understandable that developing countries want to continue to monitor their capital flows to allow for a timely intervention should this become necessary. Perhaps it is worthwhile to consider promoting OFDI without loosening controls altogether. More and more emerging markets are joining the ranks of outward investors at an earlier stage of development, making some form of capital control still necessary. Therefore, most developed countries reduced controls before implementing promotion, if at all; while more developing countries started actively promoting direct investment abroad before abolishing controls on OFDI. Figure 14.5 indicates two possible paths for OFDI policies. Increasingly, developing countries are taking a different approach to outward investment than did the earlier round of countries.

When the conditions are ripe for relaxing restrictions on OFDI, given the improvements in the macroeconomic situation and the economic environment, countries should not necessarily carry out this process in an overly gradual manner, as they run the risk of unnecessarily postponing, or even canceling, worthwhile overseas investments by their firms. In particular, this is the case for countries that are latecomers to outward investment. Their companies no longer have the time to proceed on the basis of the learning approach or the "establishment chain," previously urged by proponents of the Scandinavian school for internationalizing firms. Still, approval procedures and reporting requirements should be adapted to the internationalization needs and "readiness" of the companies. Formulating a schedule of the intended stages and relevant criteria of the promotional measures beforehand may allow for better planning of future investment decisions on the part of companies.

With regard to small and medium-sized enterprises, it is often true that they are confronted with structural rigidities to investing abroad, and that stimulating measures might be defended on the basis of this argument. However, overstimulation of OFDI, in particular for small and medium-sized enterprises, should be avoided, as the failure of an affiliate abroad may cause the whole company to collapse. Large established MNEs and business groups should not be the main beneficiaries of a government's promotional efforts, although it may be necessary to ensure that there is a "level playing field."

In developing countries, little is known about public opinion to the promotion of outward investment. Even in developed countries, during the 1970s, little attention was given to the policy reorientation toward

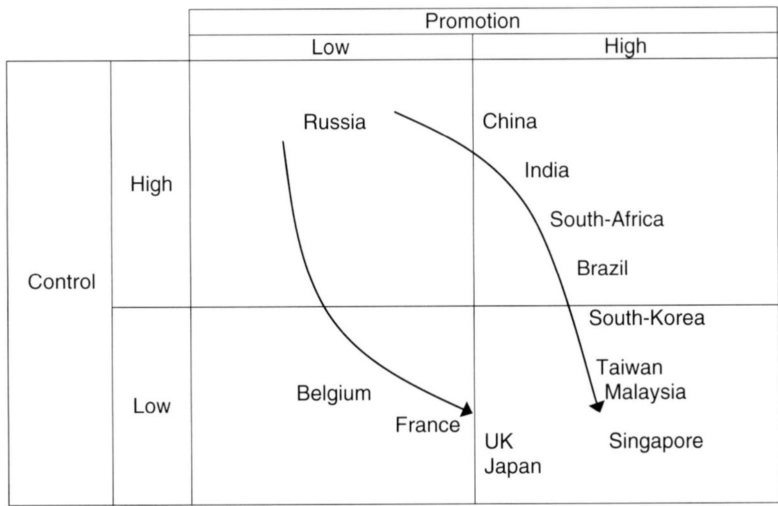

Figure 14.5 Various positions and paths of the OFDI policy regimes of selected developed and developing countries

Source: Authors.

promoting OFDI and the discrete decisions that were taken in this respect, possibly because of the unpopularity of MNEs at that time. Yet, according to Yongjin Zhang (1993), there was rather significant ideological opposition to OFDI in China during the 1990s. To extend OFDI incentives to foreign affiliates in the home country, which use it as a platform for investments in neighboring countries or the surrounding region, is probably not an immediate concern for those countries. In the United States, to benefit from OPIC's insurance system or other incentives, it is not required that the foreign affiliate is wholly owned or controlled by U.S. investors. However, in the case of joint ventures, only the portion controlled by the U.S. company is insurable (UNCTAD 1995, 314). Likewise, Singapore does not discriminate between domestic and foreign-owned firms when they request support for their initiatives to establish foreign affiliates controlled from Singapore. For Singapore, this attitude fits into its policy of convincing domestic and foreign MNEs to establish regional headquarters within its borders.

Even though the advantages linked to the activities of MNEs have become more and more appreciated by host and home countries alike, the fact remains that a high proportion of FDI goes to a relatively limited number of countries. If successful emerging markets would succeed in targeting lesser developing countries, it may be possible to spread the benefits of FDI more broadly and in a more sustainable way. To the extent that the activities of third-world MNEs would be better adapted to the level of development of those countries and the absorptive capacity of their firms, one might wonder if multilateral organizations such as the International Finance Corporation (IFC) and MIGA should not play a more active role in stimulating OFDI, or if regional organizations, such as the Association of Southeast Asian Nations (ASEAN), South African Development Community (SADC), SAARC, and others should not try to activate OFDI in their respective regions.

China has been criticized for using overseas development aid to obtain permission to launch resource-seeking FDI projects in Africa. The link between overseas development aid and OFDI should not necessarily be rejected, as it may allow—using a Chinese expression—"double happiness" for the least developed of the developing countries. Yet, overseas development aid should be relied upon in such a way that it procures tangible benefits for the host countries and does not interfere with the competitive process among the potential investors. Most importantly, overseas development aid contributions should be transparent.

In 2005, UNCTAD (2005e), more specifically its Trade and Development Board, organized a special meeting of experts during which OFDI was praised for its positive effects on enterprise competitiveness. Based on case studies commissioned for this meeting (UNCTAD 2005a, 2005b, 2005c, 2005d), it is suggested that emerging markets should concentrate their promotional policies on small and medium-sized enterprises. Yet, except for the study on Singapore that refers to a survey, these reports present little hard evidence on the issue of improved competitiveness as a result of outward investment or its promotional policies. In a sample of almost 200 Singaporean MNEs, two-thirds answered that the impact on their competitive advantage was positive. When specifying the nature of this advantage, half of those firms refer to "greater familiarity and experience," while two-fifths mention a "better reputation." Around one-quarter of the responding companies found that the advantages consisted of better managerial experience and better product quality and services; one-fifth mentioned special contacts and connections and specialized resources and materials (UNCTAD 2005d, 14). It would seem that the link between competitiveness and OFDI is an underresearched area and merits greater attention, both from academics and policy makers.

To conclude, it must be stressed that the above considerations are based on the implicit assumption of the continued growth of the world economy and emerging markets. It is evident that the global financial and economic crisis of 2008–2009 has put a halt to this. Yet, it is far from certain that these traumatic events will bring about important changes in the OFDI policies of emerging markets. Much will depend on the longer term objectives of their governments, the sectors, and the type of FDI. Although it is likely that market-seeking FDI, which is mainly oriented toward developed countries, will suffer, and it is difficult to assess how efficiency-seeking investments will develop, there are indications that resource-seeking FDI from certain emerging countries (e.g., China) is continuing. In more general terms, while discussing the more positive driving forces of FDI during a financial crisis and challenging economic period, UNCTAD wrote that such situations "… also offer opportunities to companies to buy assets at 'bargain prices' and take advantage of large-scale industry consolidation in some activities. For aggressive, cash-rich TNCs—or those from cash-rich countries—the acquisition of undervalued assets may boost their investment in both developed and developing countries, depending on the circumstance and opportunities" (2009, 13).

Notes

1. See also chapters 9 and 10 in this volume.
2. See also chapters 10 and 15 in this volume.

References

Belderbos, Rene (1992). "Large multinational enterprises based in a small economy: effect on domestic investments," *Weltwirtschaftliches Archiv* 128, pp. 543–83.

Blomström, Magnus, Gunnar Fors, and Robert E. Lipsey (1997). "Foreign direct investment and employment: home country experience in the United States and Sweden," *Economic Journal* 107, pp. 1987–97.

Blonigen, Bruce (2001). "In search of substitution between foreign production and exports," *Journal of International Economics* 53 (1), pp. 81–104.

Borensztein, Eduardo, Jose De Gregorio, and Jong-Wha Lee J.W. (1998). "How does foreign direct investment affect economic growth?" *Journal of International Economics* 45, pp. 115–35.

Braconier, Henrik and Karolina Ekholm (2001). "Foreign direct investment in Central and Eastern Europe: employment effects in the EU," *CEPR Working Paper* No. 3052.

Brainard, S. Lael and David A. Riker (1997). "Are U.S. multinationals exporting U.S. jobs?" *NBER Working Paper* No. 5958.

Braunerhjelm, Pontus, Lars Oxelheim, and Per Thulin (2006). "The relationship between domestic and outward foreign direct investment: the role of industry-specific effects," *International Business Review* 14 (6), pp. 677–94.

Commission on Capital Flows to Africa (2003). "A ten-year strategy for increasing capital flows to Africa," June (Washington, DC: Commission on Capital Flows to Africa), available at http://www.iie.com/publications/papers/africa-report.pdf, last visited October 11, 2009.

Cuervo-Cazurra, Alvaro (2007). "Sequence of value added activities in a multi-nationalization process of developing country firms," *Journal of International Management* 13, pp. 258–77.

Cuyvers, Ludo, Michel Dumont, Glenn Rayp, and Katrien Stevens (2005). "Home employment effects of EU firms' activities in Central and Eastern European countries," *Open Economies Review* 16 (2), pp. 153–74.

Daniels, John D., Jeffrey A. Krugand, and Lee Trivino (2006). "Foreign direct investment from Latin America and the Caribbean," *Transnational Corporations* 16 (1) April, pp. 27–53.

Debaere, Peter Marcel, Hongshik Lee, and Joonhyung Lee (2006). "Does where you go matter? The impact of outward foreign direct investment on multination-als' employment at home," *CEPR Discussion Paper* (July) No. 5737.

Dunning, John. H. (1986). "The investment development cycle and Third World multinationals," in K.M.e. Khan, ed., *Multinationals of the South: New Actors in the International Economy* (New York: St. Martin's Press), pp. 15–47.

Dunning, John H. and Rajneesh Narula (1996). "The investment development path revisited: some emerging issues," in J.H. Dunning and R. Narula, eds., *Foreign*

Direct Investment and Governments: Catalysts for Economic Restructuring (London and New York: Routlegde), pp. 1–41.

Emerson, Michael (1970). "Les investissements au Tiers Monde," *L'Observateur de l'OCDE* August (Paris: OECD), pp. 6–7.

Feenstra, Robert C. and Gordon H. Hanson (1996). "Globalization, outsourcing, and wage inequality," *American Economic Review* 86, pp. 240–45.

Games, Dianna (2004). *The Experience of South African Firms Doing Business in Africa. A Preliminary Survey and Analysis* (Pretoria: South African Institute of International Affairs).

Gammeltoft, Peter (2008). "Emerging multinationals: outward FDI from the BRICs countries," *International Journal of Technology and Globalization* 4 (1), pp. 5–22.

Hansson, P. (2005). "Skill upgrading and production transfer within Swedish multinationals in the 1990s," *Scandinavian Journal of Economics* 107 (4), pp. 673–92.

Head, Keith and John Ries (2001). "Overseas investment and firm exports," *Review of International Economics* 9 (1), pp. 108–22.

Horst, Thomas (1972). "The industrial composition of U.S. exports and subsidiary sales to the Canadian market," *American Economic Review* 62 (1), pp. 37–45.

Johnson, Andreas (2006). "FDI and exports: The case of the high performing East Asian Economies," *Working Paper Series in Economics and Institutions of Innovation* 57, Royal Institute of Technology, CESIS—Centre of Excellence for Science and Innovation Studies.

Konings, J. and A. Murphy (2003). "Do multinational enterprises relocate employ-ment to low wage regions? Evidence from European multinationals," *LICOS Centre of Institutions and Economics Performance Paper* No. 131.

Kravis, I.B. and R.E. Lipsey (1988). "The effects of multinational firms' foreign operations on their domestic employment," *NBER Working Paper* No. 2760.

Lipsey, R.E., E. Ramstetter, and M. Blomström (2000). "Outward FDI and parent exports and employment: Japan, the United States and Sweden," *Global Economy Quarterly* 1, pp. 285–302.

Lipsey, R.E. and M.Y. Weiss (1984). "Foreign production and exports of individual firms," *Review of Economics and Statistics* 66, pp. 304–8.

Lopez-de-Silanes, F., J.R. Markusen, and T. Rutherford (1996). "Trade policy subtle-ties with multinational firms," *European Economic Review* 40 (8), pp. 1605–27.

Masso, Jaan, Urmas Varblane, and Priit Vahter (2007). "The impact of outward FDI on home-country employment in a low-cost transition economy," *University of Tartu Faculty of Economics and Business Administration Working Paper No. 52-2007; William Davidson Institute Working Paper* No. 873.

Morck, Randall, Bernard Yeung, and Minyan Zhao (2008). "Perspectives on China's outward direct investment," *Journal of International Business Studies* 39, pp. 337–50.

Noorzoy, S. (1980). "Flows of direct investment and their effects on U.S. domestic investment," *Economics Letters,* 5, pp. 311–17.

OECD (1975). *Investir dans le Tiers Monde* (Paris: OECD)

Oman, Charles (1989). *New Forms of Investment in Developing Countries: Mining, Petrochemicals, Automobiles, Textiles, Food* (Paris: OECD).

Pain, Nigel and Katharine Wakelin (1997). "Export performance and the role of foreign direct investment," Discussion Paper 131, National Institute of Economic and Social Research, *http://www.niesr.ac.uk/pubs/dps/dp131.pdf.*

Pamlin, Dennis and Baijin Long (2007). *Rethink China's Outward Investment Flows* (Gland: WWF).

Pradhan, Jaya Prakash (2007a). *Growth of Indian Multinationals in the World Economy* (New Delhi: Institute for Studies of Industrial Development), Working Paper, March.

——— (2007b). *Indian Multinationals in the World Economy. Implications for Development* (New Delhi: Institute for Studies in Industrial Development).

Robock, Stephen and Kenneth Simmonds (1977). *International Business and Multinational Enterprises* (New York: R. Irwin)

Sauvant, Karl. P. (2005). "New sources of FDI: the BRICs: outward FDI from Brazil, Russia, India, and China," *Journal of World Investment and Trade* 6 (5), pp. 639–709.

Slaughter, M. (2000). "Production transfer within multinational enterprises and American wages," *Journal of International Economics*, 50, pp. 449–72.

Stevens, G.V.G. and R.E. Lipsey (1992). "Interactions between domestic and foreign investment," *Journal of International Money and Finance* 11, pp. 40–62.

Svensson, R. (1996) "Effects of overseas production on home country exports: Evidence based on Swedish multinationals," *Weltwirtschaftliches Archiv* 132, pp. 304–29.

Thomas, Wolfgang (2006). "South African direct investments in Africa: catalytic kingpin in the NEPAD process?" *Africa Institute of South Africa Occasional Paper Series* (Pretoria: Africa Institute of South Africa). .

UNCTAD (1995). *World Investment Report: Transnational Corporations and Competitiveness* (New York and Geneva: United Nations).

——— (2005a). "Case study on outward direct investment by Russian firms," *Trade and Development Board*, November (Geneva: UNCTAD Secretariat).

——— (2005b). "Case study on outward foreign direct investment by Indian small and medium sized enterprises," *Trade and Development Board*, October (Geneva: UNCTAD Secretariat).

——— (2005c). "Case study on foreign direct investment by Singaporean firms: Enterprise competitiveness and development," *Trade and Development Board*, December (Geneva: UNCTAD Secretariat).

——— (2005d). "Case study on outward foreign direct investment by South African enterprises," *Trade and Development Board*, November (Geneva: UNCTAD Secretariat).

——— (2005e). *Internationalization of Developing-Country Enterprises through Outward Direct Investment*, Issues Note, November (Geneva: UNCTAD-Secretariat).

——— (2005f). "Report of the expert meeting on enhancing productive capacity of developing countries through internationalization," *Trade and Development Board*, December (New York and Geneva: United Nations).

——— (2005g). *South-South Cooperation in International Investment Arrangements, Series on International Investment Policies for Development* (New York and Geneva: United Nations).

——— (2005h). *World Investment Report: Transnational Corporations and the Internationalization of R&D* (New York and Geneva: United Nations).

——— (2006). *World Investment Report: FDI from Developing and Transition Economies—Implications for Development* (New York and Geneva: United Nations).

——— (2007). *World Investment Report: Transnational Corporations in the Extractive Industries and Development* (New York and Geneva: United Nations).

UNCTAD (2009). *Assessing the Impact of the Current Financial and Economic Crisis on Global FDI Flows* (New York and Geneva: United Nations).

United Nations (2008). "Mobilizing international resources for development: foreign direct investment and other private flows," General Assembly, Informal review session on chapter 2 of the Monterrey Consensus, February 15 (New York), p. 9.

Van Agtmael, Antoine (2007). *The Emerging Markets Century. How a New Breed of World Class Companies Is Overtaking the World* (London: Simon and Schuster).

Van Den Bulcke Daniël (1979). *Investeren in het Buitenland* (Antwerpen: Vlaams Economisch Verbond).

Wee, Kee Hwee (2006). "The outward foreign direct investment by enterprises from Thailand," *Transnational Corporations* 16 (1), pp. 89–116.

Zhang, Haiyan and Daniël Van den Bulcke (1994). "International management strategies of Chinese multinational firms," in John Child and Yuan Lu, eds., *Management Issues in China: Volume 2* (London: Routledge), pp. 141–64.

——— (1996). "China: rapid changes in the investment development path," in John. H. Dunning and Rajneesh Narula, eds., *Foreign Direct Investment and Governments: Catalysts for Economic Restructuring* (London: Routledge), pp. 380–422.

Zhang, Kenny (2005). *Going Global: The Why, When and How of Chinese Companies' Outward Investment Intentions*, Canada in Asia, 5 (Vancouver: Asia Pacific Foundation of Canada).

Zhang, Yongjin (2003). *China's Emerging Global Businesses, Political Economy and Institutional Investigations* (Basingstoke: Palgrave).

Chapter 15

The Role of Government Policies in Promoting Outward Foreign Direct Investment from Emerging Markets: China's Experience

Qiuzhi Xue and Bingjie Han

Introduction

What role do government policies play in the process of enterprises' outward foreign direct investment (OFDI), especially enterprises from emerging markets? As emerging market OFDI retains the momentum of stable and rapid development, more and more scholars (Deng 2004; Peng, Wang and Jiang 2007; Witt and Lewin 2007; Yamakawa, Peng, and Deeds 2008) are paying attention to the institutional factors, in addition to the strategic motivations (Luo 2007) that drive enterprises abroad. However, the main thrust of this scholarly research is to assess the normative and cognitive pillars (Scott 1995, 33) of institutions; few studies explicitly focus on the role of OFDI regulation. We proceed, instead, with a pragmatic elaboration of the important role of governmental policies of encouragement, illustrated by several examples from China, relevant to the international business (IB) field.

The purpose of this chapter is to contribute to OFDI research through the analysis of China's complex regulatory and political system—thought to be associated with the increase in OFDI from Chinese multinational enterprises (MNEs). The Chinese example represents an ideal lens through which we can examine the relationship between regulatory institutions and OFDI, because the Chinese economy was a planned and closed system until the end of the 1970s, grew into a "Socialism with Chinese characteristics" arrangement through the 1980s and until the mid-1990s, and then into a much more market-based and internationalized economy in its present state. From the instigation of the "Open-Door" policies in 1978, to the implementation of the "Going Abroad" policies in 2000, China has evolved from being of marginal OFDI relevance to becoming an important source country among developing countries in the past thirty years. During the 1980s, Chinese OFDI flows, although rising at a rapid pace, did not exceed US$1 billion. In the 1990s, OFDI flows almost tripled, but still amounted to only a small proportion of global OFDI flows. Since 2002, however, Chinese OFDI flows have reached approximately US$16 billion. The same trend can be found in the development of China's OFDI stock. Several "blowouts" (e.g., in 1992, 1993, and 2001) suggest that, in addition to mere economic motivators, other factors are driving OFDI. It seems likely that the reforms of the regulatory and political system have contributed to these increases.

The contribution of this research is twofold. First, it contributes to a better theoretical understanding of institutional business by relating institutional changes to OFDI flows. We argue that IB research, especially its recent focus on emerging markets, provides an opportunity to shed light on questions regarding the regulatory framework for OFDI. Second, we provide a comprehensive framework for policy makers and practitioners to understand how policies affect the character, scope, motivation, and mode of Chinese OFDI activities. This research will serve as a useful reference for policy makers in other emerging markets, who can use it to learn from the Chinese example to offset their own policy weaknesses. Practitioners, Chinese or otherwise, will benefit from having a clearer understanding of the Chinese regulatory landscape.

This chapter is organized as follows: Part one depicts the relationship between departments regulating OFDI in China and explains the main functions of these departments. Part two reviews Chinese policies relating to OFDI since the 1980s and examines the logic behind these policies. The evolution of, and changes in, OFDI regulation over the past thirty years are also discussed. Part three assesses the extent to which the Chinese OFDI policy system contains policies of encouragement, policies of approval, and policies of supervision. We will also present details of different applicable policy catalogs. Finally, we summarize and conclude this chapter.

15.1   OFDI Regulators in China

15.1.1   The Approval Process for OFDI Projects

Before introducing the relevant regulators, we first turn to the OFDI approval process, to help us better understand the relationship between regulators and OFDI policies in China. The basic OFDI approval procedure remains the same today, although modified several times, and with many steps eliminated in recent years. All state-owned enterprises (SOEs) that are subject to the State-owned Assets Supervision and Administration Commission (SASAC) must apply for approval from the Ministry of Commerce (MOC). OFDI projects from privately owned enterprises (POEs) that invest in one of 135 designated countries or regions are approved by local Foreign Economic Relation & Trade (FERT) committees (which provide a record to the MOC); OFDI projects from POEs investing in other countries or regions are approved by the MOC itself. If the destination of the OFDI project involves Hong Kong (China) or Macao (China), MOC approval is required.

It is clear that the MOC has delegated considerable approval authority to the FERT, which is very convenient for firms investing abroad. A firm first applies to the State Administration of Foreign Exchange (SAFE) to use foreign exchange earnings abroad and, then applies to the MOC or FERT for the approval of the project business cases (Deschandol and Luckock 2005). After the application materials are accepted, the decision will usually be made within fifteen working days. If the approval also requires MOC determination, a further five working days are required, meaning that the approval process should be cleared within twenty working days.

Enterprises wishing to undertake OFDI should prepare application material that includes (1) the application (name of new company, registered capital, amount of investment, business scope, operate duration, organizational form, ownership structure, etc.); (2) the statutes of the new company or cooperation contracts; (3) reviewed comments from SAFE; (4) all related licenses or certifications; and (5) other forms in special situations.

15.1.2   The OFDI Responsibilities of Each Regulator

There are a number of key political and administrative actors in China who exercise considerable influence over Chinese OFDI, by setting the laws and regulations applicable to outward investment and through their control of the investment approval process. The main actors are the State Council, the MOC, the People's Bank of China (PBC), SAFE, SASAC, and the State Development and Reform Commission. Figure 15.1 outlines the interaction between these entities, the antecedents of each actor, and how the regulatory systems regarding OFDI have evolved over time.

15.1.2.1. State Council

All actors are subordinate to the State Council, which is responsible for drafting and developing laws and regulations, as well as coordinating national economic development. Besides economic development, the State Council also deals with political, cultural, and military affairs. The State Council decides upon major economic policies and liberalization measures, although the policy initiatives for these steps may come from subordinate authorities such as the MOC.

15.1.2.2. The People's Bank of China

The PBC was established as China's central bank in 1983, and is directly supervised by the State Council (Zhang 2004). It can impact outward investment through monetary policies or through the supervision and management of foreign exchange reserves. By increasing or decreasing the issuance of Renminbi (RMB), interest rates, and the reserve ratio, it can influence the inflation rate. Prior to 2005, the PBC pursued a fixed exchange rate regime. These policies determine the appreciation or depreciation of the RMB and, thus, encourage or discourage outward investment. For example, the appreciation of RMB makes investment abroad more attractive. The PBC also supervises and manages China's foreign exchange reserves. With respect to this function, the PBC imposed significant changes on China's foreign exchange regime in 1994, which provided for a tightening of foreign exchange controls.

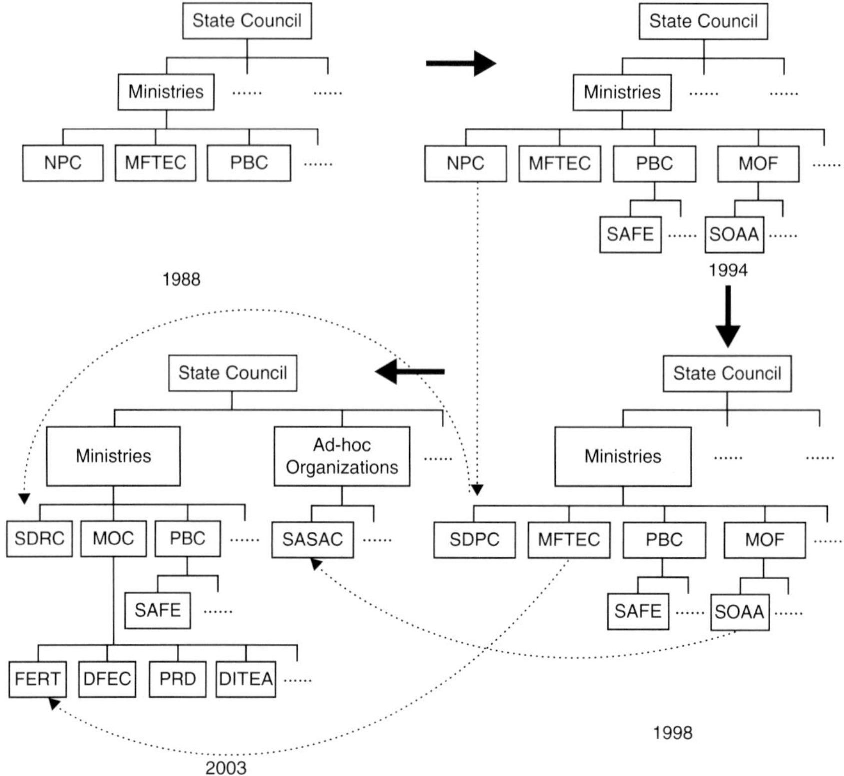

Figure 15.1   The evolution of China's OFDI regulation departments, 1998–2003

Source: http://www.china.org.cn; http://www.mofcom.gov.cn

Notes: NPC (National Planning Commission); MFTEC (Ministry of Foreign Trade and Economic Cooperation); PBC (People's Bank of China); MOF (Ministry of Finance); SOAA (State-owned Assets Authority); SAFE (State Administration of Foreign Exchange); SDPC (State Development Planning Commission); MOC (Ministry of Commerce); SDRC (State Development and Reform Commission); SASAC (State-owned Assets Supervision and Administration Commission); DFEC (Department of Foreign Economic Cooperation); PRD (Policy Research Department); DITEA (Department of International Trade and Economic Affairs); FERT (Foreign Economic Relation & Trade).

15.1.2.3. *State Administration of Foreign Exchange*

The State Administration of Foreign Exchange (SAFE) was established in 1979, under the PBC, and was subsequently shifted to the newly created central bank, the PBC. Its responsibility is to administer the usage and flow of foreign exchange. It carries out its OFDI-related mandate in the following ways: (1) it reports balance-of-payment data to the State Council and the International Monetary Fund (IMF); (2) it recommends foreign exchange policies to the PBC; (3) it oversees the transfer of foreign exchange into and out of China under the capital account of the balance of payments; and (4) it manages China's foreign exchange reserves (Zhang 2004).

15.1.2.4. *Ministry of Commerce*

The MOC was set up in its current form and function in 2003. The major responsibilities of the MOC with regard to Chinese OFDI relate to (1) the supervision of Chinese OFDI by drafting and implementing policies and regulations and considering nonfinancial OFDI projects for approval; (2) bilateral and multilateral negotiations on investment and trade treaties and representing China in the World Trade Organization and other international economic organizations; (3) ensuring the alignment of China's economic and trade laws with international treaties and agreements; and (4) coordinating China's foreign aid policy and relevant funding and loan schemes (Munro and Yan 2003).

The MOC combines numerous functions from other departments that existed before its establishment. One example is the Foreign Economic Relation and Trade (FERT). FERT's antecedent is the Ministry of Foreign Trade and Economic Cooperation (MFTEC), which, hierarchically, was once directly under State Council. Furthermore, MFTEC was the main department dealing with OFDI affairs before the MOC assumed responsibility (figure 15.1). Now each local government has a FERT, and the authority to approve POEs' OFDI projects has been delegated to them.

Other examples of merging functions include the Policy Research Department (PRD), the Department of International Trade and Economic Affairs (DITEA), and the Department of Foreign Economic Cooperation (DFEC) (figure 15.1). PRD facilitates OFDI from Chinese enterprises by providing analyses of international economic development trends, interpreting investment attraction policies of other countries, and preparing a "Country Trade and Investment Environment Report" to guide the direction of Chinese outward investment. One of DITEA's important duties is to deal with international economic organizations such as the Organisation for Economic Co-operation and Development (OECD) and the United Nations Conference on Trade and Development (UNCTAD). DFEC is the main department that approves or rejects OFDI projects.

15.1.2.5. *State Development and Reform Commission*

The State Development and Reform Commission (SDRC), formerly known as the State Development Planning Commission (SDPC), emerged from the institutional structure of the National Planning Commission (NPC). Currently, the SDRC is one of the predominant ministries in China. It designs, regulates, and coordinates the economic development and industrial policy of China. With regard to OFDI, and in cooperation with the MOC, the SDRC has published a host country catalog that lists the countries for which the government of China subsidizes OFDI projects (Zweig and Bi 2005). Large-scale OFDI projects in natural resources that involve a significant investment (over US$30 million for resource-oriented investments and over US$10 million for all others) require prior approval from the SDRC. This authority stems from its responsibility for maintaining equilibrium in the balance of payments (Munro and Yan 2003).

15.1.2.6. *State-Owned Assets Supervision and Administration Commission*

The State-owned Assets Supervision and Administration Commission's (SASAC) predecessor was the State-owned Assets Authority (SOAA), which was subordinated to the Ministry of Finance (MOF). After the integration of scattered functions into a number of ministries, SASAC was established by the State Council in 2003 as an "ad hoc organization." As the representative of the government of China, which is the ultimate investor in and owner of nonfinancial SOEs, SASAC has wide-reaching responsibilities and power and directly controls 170 national SOEs (Naughton 2007). All OFDI projects undertaken by SOEs under the supervision of SASAC must have its explicit approval.

15.2   A Review of the Evolution of Chinese OFDI Policies

In this section we discuss the evolution of the Chinese OFDI policy system and explore the logic behind changes introduced over time. Chinese OFDI policies are generally regarded as having developed in five distinctive phases (Wong and Chan 2003; Ye 1992), although some scholars (Buckley et al. 2010) consider three phrases. In this study, we develop the argument in three phases. Our principal focus is the amount of OFDI flows, rather than symbolic changes in Chinese OFDI policies. In China, policy changes usually precede a rise in OFDI flows. In figure 15.2 (table 15.1 lists the related regulations) we see two major spikes (1992–1993 and 2001) in Chinese OFDI flows. In light of these two abnormal increases, we will assess the following three periods: 1984–1990, 1991–2000, and 2001–2007.

15.2.1   Phase 1 (1984–1990): "Fresh Flowers" or "Poisonous Grass"?

Our discussion begins with 1984, the year in which the first OFDI regulation was adopted. After a decade of Cultural Revolution, China's economy was on the brink of collapse, so much so that economic reform was absolutely necessary. In the context of implementing Deng Xiaoping's "Open-Door"

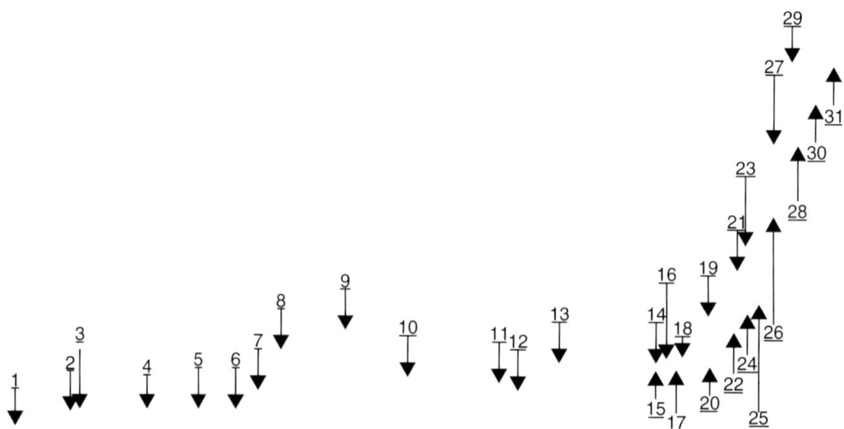

Figure 15.2   Correlation between Chinese OFDI trends and corresponding regulations

Source: The Authors.

Notes: 1. The numbers in this figure correspond to the regulations in table 15.1. Through this figure we want to show the correlation between various regulations and their impact on Chinese OFDI.

2. Because we have OFDI data up to 2006, regulations promulgated after 2007 are not included in this figure.

Table 15.1 China's key OFDI regulations

Number	Regulation	Enunciator	Month of issuance	Key points
1	Circular concerning the approval authorities and principles for opening nontrade joint venture overseas as well as in Hong Kong (China) and Macao (China)	MFTEC	May 1984	The first regulation on Chinese OFDI.
2	Circular on the approval procedures for international economic and technical cooperation corporation to set up overseas subsidiaries	MFTEC	July 1985	1. Lay out the principal for the regulation of OFDI. 2. Opened OFDI for all economic entities with financial resources, foreign joint venture partner and relevant capabilities.
3	Provisional regulation governing the control and the approval procedure for opening nontrade enterprises overseas	MFTEC	July 1985	Ceiling for investments at $ 10 million.
4	Measures for foreign exchange control relating to overseas investment	SAFE	March 1989	1. SAFE evaluates the source of fund of investing abroad and the foreign exchange risk. 2. 5% of the OFDI sum had to be deposited in a special count. 3. Profit earned abroad should be remitted back to China.
5	Rule for the implementation of administrative measures for the investment of foreign exchange overseas	SAFE	June 1990	Detailed regulations enumerated in the "Measures for foreign exchange control relating to overseas investment."
6	Opinion of the State Planning Commission on the strengthening of the administration of overseas investment projects	NPC	March 1991	1. A core document throughout the 1990s and give out the direction of Chinese OFDI. 2. Point out that Chinese OFDI should focus on using overseas' technologies, resources, and markets. 3. OFDI projects should have a feasible report in the process of going abroad. 4. Projects which sum exceeding 1 million should be approved by NPC; sum exceeding 30mn should be approved by State Council. 5. Projects concerning state-owned assets should be approved by State Council.
7	Regulations on examination and approval of project proposal and feasibility report on FDI projects	NPC	August 1991	1. Detailed the content of feasible report. 2. Specified that the approval result should be given in sixty days.
8	Regulations of MOFCOM on the administration of the approval and examination of nontrading overseas enterprises (trial draft)	MFTEC	March 1992	Synthesized and detailed all earlier regulations concerning OFDI.

Continued

Table 15.1 Continued

Number	Regulation	Enunciator	Month of issuance	Key points
9	Examination and approval standards on foreign exchange risk and fund source examinations for outbound investments	SAFE	September 1993	1. Specified that the responsibility of SAFE is to review the certification of investor, foreign exchange risk, and source of investment fund. 2. Firstly detailed the management of foreign exchange after the approval of OFDI projects.
10	Notice on supplemental provisions to the administration measures on foreign exchange for overseas investment	SAFE	September 1995	Chinese investors are allowed to purchase foreign exchange for an OFDI project; prior to this, a Chinese investor had to earn the foreign exchange needed.
11	Credit for the Support of Overseas Processing and Assembling Business Using Materials from China Guidance Opinion	SAFE PBC	June 1999	1. Purpose is to encourage exports. 2. Provide a loan to enterprises that use mature technology and equipment to invest abroad; most of these enterprises are concentrated in light industries, textile industries, or home appliance industries. 3. Going with the industry restructuring within China.
12	Certain Items Exempted from Paying Security Deposits for Remittance of Profits from Overseas Investment Circular	SAFE	September 1999	Constituted a degree of liberalization: Affected OFDI projects with foreign processing or assembly operations, noncash investments and foreign aid: these projects could present a letter of undertaking rather than the security deposit required previously.
13	Measures for the Administration of International Market Developing Funds of Small-and Medium-Sized Enterprises (for Trail Implementation)	MFTEC MOF	October 2000	1. These Measures are formulated to support the development of small-and medium-sized enterprises, to encourage small- and medium-sized enterprises to join in the competition of international markets. 2. Set up "international market developing funds of small- and medium-sized enterprises."
14	Comprehensive external investment results evaluation procedures	MFTEC	October 2002	Clarification of standards and procedures for evaluating OFDI projects that have been operating overseas.
15	Joint annual inspection of overseas investment tentative procedure	MFTEC SAFE	October 2002	Postinvestment evaluation of OFDI projects.

16	Statistic system of overseas investments	MFTEC	Dec. 2002	1. The purpose is to master first-hand data about investing overseas. 2. Provide training for enterprises going abroad to report correctly. 3. Only after this document, the real facets just like the mode of entrance, performance of OFDI, and situations of operation became known. 4. It is a very meaningful step for either regulators or scholars.
17	Notice on certain issues relating to simplify foreign exchange fund source examination for overseas investment	SAFE	March 2003	1. SAFE is only investigating domestic foreign exchange sources. 2. Foreign exchange obtained from a source outside of mainland China no longer examined.
18	Providing Credit Supports to the Key Overseas Investment Projects Encouraged by the State	SDRC	May 2003	OFDI projects fulfilling one of the following requirements will be provide with a lower lending rate credit fund: 1. natural resources which are lacking China is short; 2. manufacturing promote export of technologies, products, and equipments; 3. R&D projects that could bring in advanced technologies, managerial experience and specialized talents. 4. M&As to increase international competitiveness and market exploration of firms.
19	Circular of the State Administration of Foreign Exchange on Relevant Issues Concerning Deepening the Reform of Foreign Exchange Administration on Overseas Investment	SAFE	November 2003	1. Simplification of approval procedures concerning foreign exchange. 2. Establishment of pilot areas for SAFE eased and extended local authority.
20	Circular of the General Office of the Ministry of Commerce on Setting up An Information Bank of Overseas Investment Intention of Enterprises	MOC	November 2003	To set up an information bank of overseas investment intentions of enterprises for guidance and coordination, requirements for application enterprises: 1. The registered capital of the enterprise is more than RMB 10 million Yuan, and the enterprise has made profits in three consecutive years. 2. The amount of overseas intention investment of a single project is more than US$ one million.
21	Decision on Reforming Investment System	State Council	July 2004	1. A major reform of the approval but not limited to OFDI. 2. Provide the basis for the subsequent reforms.

Continued

Table 15.1 Continued

Number	Regulation	Enunciator	Month of issuance	Key points
22	Countries and Industries for Overseas Investment Guidance Catalogue	MOC	July 2004	1. Lists more than seven supported industries and sixty-seven approved countries. 2. Companies complying with requirements have preferential treatment concerning funding, tax collection, foreign exchange, customs, and others.
23	Verification and Approval of Overseas Investment Projects Tentative Administrative Procedures	SDRC	October 2004	1. All kinds of companies are allowed to invest abroad 2. Set up the threshold values for examination at national level and clarifies the approval process. 3. This measure replaces the policy from August 1991.
24	Provisions on the Examination and Approval of Investment to Run Enterprises Abroad	MOC	October 2004	1. Threshold of sum of OFDI projects needing approval degraded. 2. Approval process simplified and some authorities been delegated. 3. Time span of the process should not exceed twenty working days. 4. Feasible report not included in the application materials.
25	Obstacle Report Rules on the Investment to Different Countries	MOC	November 2004	Using annual reports from enterprises investing abroad, MOC collects information on all kinds of obstacles and problems confronted by companies undertaking OFDI. These reports form the basis of "Foreign Market Access Reports." The reports, prepared by the enterprises abroad, should include the following information: 1. Overall situation of the investment and operations of the enterprise. 2. Information about the investment environment such as laws or rules that have a negative effect on operation in host country. 3. Investment barriers set up by host governments. 4. Possible measures corresponding to these situations.
26	Regulation on Report before Enterprises' Overseas Mergers and Acquisitions	MOC SAFE	March 2005	1. Requires enterprises intending to undertake M&As abroad to report to MOC. 2. Improving the supervision of M&As.

27	Circular of the State Administration of Foreign Exchange on Enlarging the Reform Pilots regarding the Administration of Foreign Exchange for Overseas Investment	SAFE	May 2005	1. Reform of the exchange approval regime is extended to the whole country. 2. Further decentralization: local SAFE decide about a higher threshold (from US$3 million to US$10 million). 3. Total foreign exchange available for all investors increased from US$3.3billion to US$5 billion.
28	Detailed rules for the examination and approval of investments to open and operate enterprises abroad	MOC	October 2005	Specifies and clarifies the 2004 regulation on requirements, risk avoidance, and project feasibility.
29	Notice of the Ministry of Finance and the Ministry of Commerce on Printing and Distributing the Measures for the Administration of Special Funds for Foreign Economic and Technical Cooperation	MOC MOF	December 2005	Set up a special fund to encourage Chinese enterprises to invest abroad. Special funds may be used to support foreign economic cooperation as follows: 1. Subsidies for pre-operational fees. 2. Interest discounts for medium and long-termed loans. 3. Subsidies for operational fees.
30	Soliciting Opinions on Several Opinions of Encouraging and Supporting the "Go-global" of Individually-Run Enterprises (Draft)	MOC	February 2006	The first regulation that explicitly treats private-owned enterprises as the principal object and sets out an outline for future refinement.
31	Notice on the adjustment of certain foreign exchange control policies for overseas investment	SAFE	June 2006	1. The branches (foreign exchange management departments) of SAFE will not verify the quota for purchasing foreign exchange for overseas investments. 2. The necessary foreign exchange for a domestic investor to invest abroad may include self-owned foreign exchange, foreign exchange purchased by RMB or domestic and overseas foreign exchange loans.
32	Notice on the statistical system of direct overseas investment	MOC	January 2007	Incorporate quarterly information on the signing of overseas investment projects and round-tripping investment via tax havens and to better track and account for investments by private enterprise.
33	Adjusting the Relevant Matters on the Examination and Approval of Overseas Investment	MOC	December 2007	Enlarges the number of countries where local enterprises may establish branches that are examined and approved by local authorities.

Source: www.mofcom.gov.cn; www.fdi.com.cn

Notes: Although some regulations are updated annually, the principal provisions do not change. Therefore, in table 15.1, we give only the first edition.

policy, the extent to which OFDI benefited the Chinese economy or signaled a departure from socialist ideology, was heavily discussed among policy makers during the 1980s. This discussion reflected the classic dispute over the potential (diversionary) impact of OFDI on domestic investments and economic development (Zhang 2003). The sobering fact was that Chinese enterprises were not experienced in operating abroad, with the result that a liberal approach to OFDI was not considered favorably (Buckley et al. 2010).

Rather, the objective of China's OFDI regulation during this period was to accumulate foreign exchange. Only companies that had been granted an export license had the right to retain a share of foreign exchange earnings. Thus, regulations regarding foreign exchange limited the capability of Chinese enterprises to pursue OFDI projects (e.g., "measures for foreign exchange control relating to overseas investment"). SAFE evaluated the sources of funding of planned investments abroad and the related foreign exchange risk, and 5% of the OFDI sum had to be deposited into a special account with SAFE. The application process was very strict, and all OFDI projects required approval from the NPC or State Council. OFDI project values could not exceed US$10 million, and all related profits earned abroad had to be remitted back to China. As a consequence, China's OFDI amount in this phase stayed at a relatively low level, not exceeding US$10 billion.

15.2.2 *Phase 2 (1991–2000): "Finding the Stepping Stone"*

The debate over "whether the road is capitalist or socialist" (*Xing zi hai shi xing she*) was brought to an end with Deng Xiaoping's journey to the south of China in 1992. This landmark journey strengthened the liberal politicians in the Communist Party (CCP) and bureaucrats in government agencies (Buckley et al. 2010). As a consequence of this newly gained liberalization momentum, Chinese OFDI officially became part of China's national economic development plan and was publicly endorsed by the then-chairperson of the CCP, and later president of China, Jiang Zemin (Zhang 2003). A good understanding of this period's *de jure* and *de facto* change of Chinese OFDI policies can be gleaned from two key policy developments.

On the one hand, the government of China worried about the loss of state assets through the establishment of questionable international ventures. In combination with the Asian financial crisis in 1997, several policy changes occurred: approval procedures were tightened, and the strict screening and monitoring of each OFDI project was enforced (Wong and Chan 2003). After containing inflation at the beginning of the 1990s, the government of China dealt with the very difficult problem of how to implement the reform of SOEs, regarded as symbols of the Communist regime. The guidelines for SOEs' reforms, set down by Zhu Rongji, Premier from 1998 to 2002, were "to seize the big and free the small" (i.e., to maintain close oversight of the large SOEs and subject smaller SOEs to market competition). As a result, a group of national monopolistic enterprises emerged, such as China National Offshore Oil Corporation (CNOOC), China National Cereals, Oils & Foodstuffs Import & Export Corporation (COFCO), and China

Minmetals Corporation, each of which rank among the top 100 developing country MNEs as published by UNCTAD (2006). The effects of these guidelines appeared only several years later: SOEs with national monopolies *de facto* became the mainstream Chinese outward foreign direct investors. Lacking strict limitations, firms in light industries (e.g., textiles, machinery, electrical equipment), in particular, were encouraged to "go international" (Wong and Chan 2003).

On the other hand, regulations regarding foreign exchange were adopted. With the liberalization measures taken in 1995 (i.e., "Notice on Supplemental Provisions to the Administration Measures on Foreign Exchange for Overseas Investment"), the government of China moved from an "earn-to-use" to a "buy-to-use" foreign exchange policy regime (Buckley et al. 2010). This meant that foreign exchange could be bought from SAFE to finance OFDI projects, regardless of whether the applicant firm had earned foreign exchange.

At the beginning of the 1990s, the "Opinion of the State Planning Commission on the Strengthening of the Administration of Overseas Investment Projects" was promulgated by the NPC. It provided the fundamental document with regard to OFDI and the direction that Chinese OFDI should take to acquire overseas' technologies, resources, and markets. It announced that OFDI projects exceeding US\$1 million should be approved by the NPC, projects exceeding US\$30 million should be approved by the State Council, and projects concerning state-owned assets should also be approved by the State Council. Applicant OFDI enterprises in this phase were also required to prepare feasibility reports ("Regulations on Examination and Approval of Project Proposal and Feasibility Report on FDI Projects"). Another important document is "Measures for the Administration of International Market Developing Funds of Small- and Medium-Sized Enterprises" (2000), which outlines the policy to encourage small and medium-sized enterprises to join the competition for international markets through the establishment of "international market developing funds of small- and medium-sized enterprises."

15.2.3   Phase 3 (2001–2007): "Going Abroad"

In 2000, during the Fifth Plenary of the 15th Central Committee of the Communist Party of China, the government of China formally launched the "Going Abroad" policy. As a national policy, it provided a strong public endorsement for an institutional environment that fosters OFDI. Based on this principal strategy, a series of regulations were promulgated in the years after 2000, and a series of policies of encouragement, approval, and supervision was established. The government of China also completed the transformation from regulator to guide or supporter, from a regime that directly intervenes in business decisions and commands business outcomes to a regime that influences and directs the market at arm's length, through rules and a broader set of administrative bodies (Bach, Newman, and Weber 2006).

Assessing the regulations issued in this period, we can see that a new policy system had been arranged by the government of China. First, OFDI rules concerning foreign exchange, which were once the main capital-control tools of the government, were changed through a series of regulations. These included the "Notice on Certain Issues Concerning the Simplification of Examination of the Source of Foreign Exchange for Overseas Investment" (2003), the "Circular of the State Administration of Foreign Exchange on Enlarging the Reform Pilots regarding the Administration of Foreign Exchange for Overseas Investment" (2005), and the "Notice on the Adjustment of Certain Foreign Exchange Control Policies for Overseas Investment" (2006). In this last regulation, the quota for purchasing foreign exchange for overseas investments was dropped, meaning that the foreign exchange required for an OFDI project could come from self-owned foreign exchange, foreign exchange purchased in RMB from SAFE, or domestic and overseas foreign exchange loans.

Second, in line with a change in policy focus from OFDI amounts to OFDI performance, the government of China outlined a series of regulations regarding monitoring of the performance of OFDI. To this end, standards and procedures for the annual evaluation of OFDI projects were adopted. (See "Comprehensive External Investment Results Evaluation Procedures" [2002] [table 15.1, regulation 14] and the "Joint Annual Inspection of Overseas Investment Tentative Procedure" [2002] [table 15.1, regulation 15].) To master firsthand data on overseas investment opportunities, statistical systems for overseas investment were established. (See "Statistic System of Overseas Investments" [2002] and "Notice on the Statistical System of Direct Overseas Investment" [2007].)

Finally, the government of China changed its role from that of regulator, or controller, to that of guide, or supporter, of OFDI. These changes are reflected in a number of ways: (1) OFDI approval processes were simplified and thresholds for OFDI projects reduced; (2) for the purposes of guidance and coordination, an information source concerning the overseas investment intentions of enterprises was established; (3) a guidance catalog was issued by the MOC, with companies complying with requirements enjoying preferential treatment in funding, tax collection, foreign exchange, customs, and others factors; and (4) using the annual reports of enterprises investing abroad, MOC collects data on all types of obstacles and problems encountered abroad.

Despite liberalization and decentralization measures and political assurances, criticism of the current OFDI policy regime persists (Buckley et al. 2010). The division of approval responsibilities between the SDRC and the MOC[1] is often unclear for potential Chinese investors and local government agencies. However, this problem occurs during the transition of Chinese OFDI policy systems following a China-typical trial-and-error path.

15.3 Overview of the Extant Chinese OFDI Policy Regime

We have discussed the evolution of China's OFDI policy regime, but so far only from a longitudinal perspective. What about the landscape of the Chinese OFDI policy system from a cross-sectional perspective? In the following section, we discuss the characteristics of the Chinese OFDI policy regime. We believe that the *raison d'être* for OFDI policies is to provide support to enterprises seeking to undertake OFDI. Following this approach, policies can be classified into three categories: approval policies, encouragement policies, and supervision policies (figure 15.3).

15.3.1   Approval Policies

In order to support OFDI, the government of China does its best to simplify the approval process. The approval of projects with low investment values (below US$30 million for resource-oriented investments and below US$10 million for others) has been delegated to the FERT in each province or municipality. The approval process should not take longer than twenty working days (five working days for confirming the application materials and fifteen working days for making the approval decision). More importantly, companies no longer need to prepare feasibility reports. These rules show that the government of China endeavors to improve the efficiency of services and does not seek to block enterprises from going abroad.

15.3.2   Encouragement Policies

First, the government of China provides financial support to enterprises investing abroad. General corporate income tax principles are used to avoid double taxation, and a double-taxation treaty network has been set up to cover Chinese OFDI (as of March 2007, eighty-nine international or bilateral agreements had been signed for this purpose). The Export-Import Bank of China provides funds to support key OFDI projects. These funds have low lending rates, fast approval processes, and flexible terms. Also, enterprises investing abroad can obtain discount bank loans in China. If the currency of the loan is RMB, the discount rate should not be higher than the effective interest rate and will be capped by the benchmark interest rate offered by the PCB; if the loan is in foreign currency, the discount rate should not be higher than the effective interest rate and will be capped at 3%.

The government of China also provides subsidies for enterprises that are in the process of "going abroad." For example, the "International Market Developing Funds of Small- and Medium-Sized Enterprises" was set up by the MOF. The government offers, for instance, subsidies (not over 20%) for carriage costs if the investment is resource oriented and will transport resources back to China. Other costs in the OFDI planning phase, such as consulting costs or information gathering, can also be cofinanced by the government. With regard to foreign exchange policy, the maximum threshold of foreign currency spent on FDI has been increased to US$5 billion. At the time of writing this chapter, the government was considering to drop this quantitative limitation completely.

Second, the government of China maintains a risk-safeguard mechanism with regard to OFDI. On a macro level, the government has concluded OFDI promotion and mutual protection agreements with many countries (currently

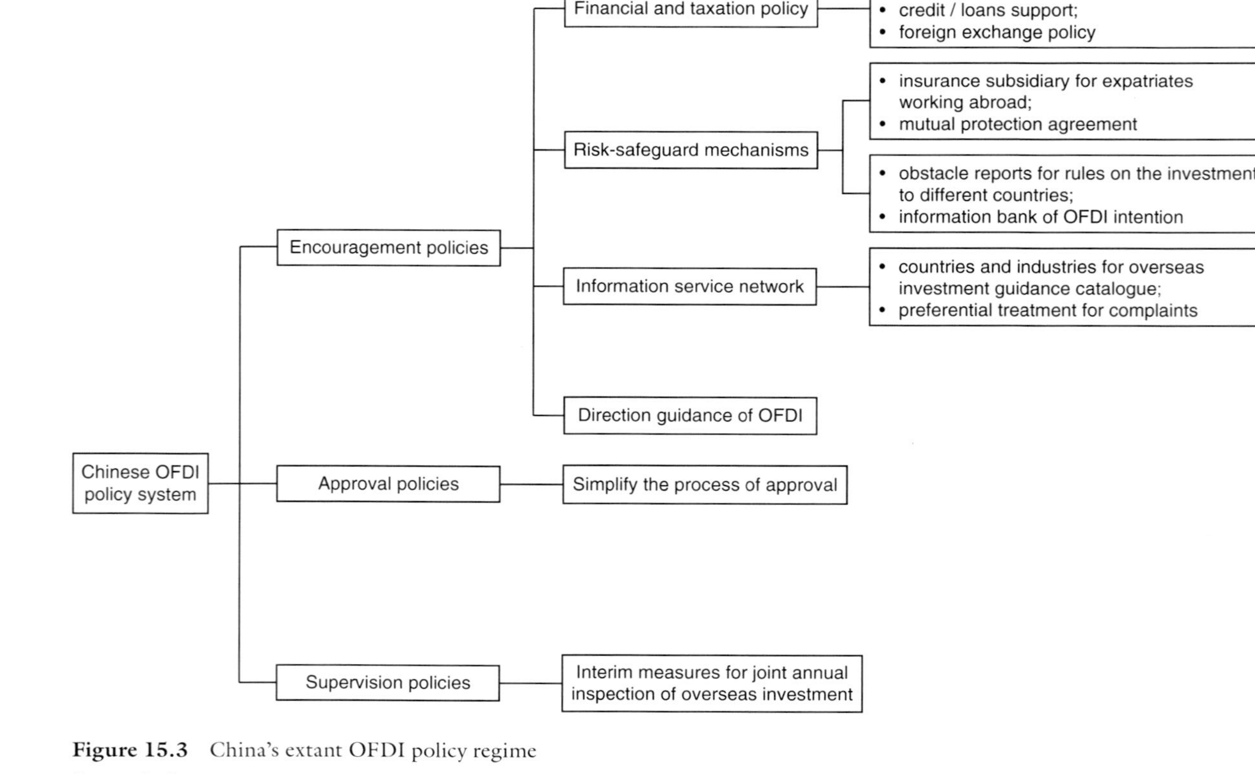

Figure 15.3 China's extant OFDI policy regime

Source: Authors.

115 countries have signed such agreements with China). On a micro level, the government provides personal accident insurance subsidies for expatriates working abroad (each premium should not be higher than RMB500,000, and the ratio of subsidy should not exceed 50% of the premium).

Third, to help enterprises to overcome investment obstacles in host countries, the government of China makes a significant effort to establish an information service network. Through "Obstacle Report Rules on the Investment to Different Countries," information on problems encountered by enterprises during the investment phase and while operating abroad is collected. The government then edits this and issues an annual "Report on the Trade and Investment Environment in Different Countries." In order to provide a platform for companies to communicate with each other, the government has developed an information system in which the investment intentions of Chinese enterprises are published. In addition, diversified associations, such as the "China Council for International Investment Promotion," have been established to help companies that wish to compete in global markets.

Finally, the government of China also guides the direction of OFDI as a whole. Particularly, the "Countries and Industries for Overseas Investment Guidance Catalogue" (a reference list for foreign economic cooperation departments in offering guidance and assessment of overseas investment by Chinese companies) was issued in connection with several supporting policy measures. All investments complying with this list may enjoy favorable financial support, exchange rate, taxation, and other preferential treatment. This guidance document is adapted to different regions and industries (e.g., the "Guiding Catalogue on Investment in Processing Trade of Textiles and Clothing in Some Latin-America Countries").

15.3.3 Supervision Policies

There are not only policies of promotion, but also policies of supervision. The "Interim Measures for Joint Annual Inspection of Overseas Investment" and the "Measures for Overseas Investment Comprehensive Performance Evaluation (Trial)" list details rules regarding the operations of corporations undertaking FDI. From these supervision policies, it can be derived that the key focus of Chinese OFDI policies has changed from encouraging OFDI projects in general to a more qualitative approach.

Conclusions

Can governmental policies provide a panacea for solving problems in the process of OFDI? The answer is an emphatic "no." The changes in Chinese OFDI regulations mirror the economic development and different governmental purposes at different periods of times. Functional overlaps among the different departments involved in China's OFDI approval and regulatory process persist, and the policy system is not "cutting edge." Nevertheless, the government of China has set up a comprehensive policy framework, composed of various encouragement policies, approval policies, and supervision policies that will positively stimulate China's OFDI in the future.

This chapter can serve as a basis for further research and for the further development of OFDI theory. It provides a strong foundation for further research from a political economy perspective. We laid out the evolution of the structure of Chinese OFDI regulation and the complicated relationships between regulators. Further research needs to assess the exact relationships between economic development and political structures. There is a range of other research questions that should be addressed in order to improve further our understanding of the effects of policies on OFDI. Some of the more interesting future directions could include the following research questions: is the composition of OFDI (e.g., enterprises in the textile or oil industries) coming from emerging markets the result of policy stimulation or economic factors? Do encouragement policies or preferential rules for OFDI benefit enterprises' competitive advantage?

In addition, previous studies on emerging market OFDI have typically adopted either a resource-based methodology or relied on a single lens to answer related questions in escapism perspectives. Both approaches have limitations. On the one hand, some emerging market firms are strongly internationalized, but still lack core competencies. The cohesive force behind these firms is home country support. On the other hand, an escapism view cannot explain the fact that, by now, most emerging market governments do not show a negative attitude toward OFDI and usually create an enhancing OFDI climate for domestic enterprises. Instead, we untangle this puzzle in an attempt to examine positive institutional effects on the internationalization of enterprises. Regulatory institutions, we argue, directly influence the amount and the performance of OFDI. This study fills a gap in research focused on institutional theory that is limited to host country institutions.

To conclude, this review is far from complete, and the discussions presented here have some limitations. We did not catalog policies encouraging OFDI in different industries. The question of how the government of China's policies deal with different kinds of OFDI enterprises (SOEs or POEs) is not answered either. Finally, we use only descriptive statistics to depict the correlation between changes in OFDI amounts and the issuance of OFDI policies, which may, in fact, not represent a causal relationship.

Note

1. For example, on almost the same date in October 2004, SDRC and MOC issued near-identical regulations (table 15.1, regulation 23 ["Verification and Approval of Overseas Investment Projects Tentative Administrative Procedures"] and regulation 24 ["Provisions on the Examination and Approval of Investment to Run Enterprises Abroad"]).

References

Bach, David., Abraham L. Newman, and Steven Weber (2006). "The international implications of China's fledgling regulatory state: from product maker to rule maker," *New Political Economy* 11 (4), pp. 499–518.

Buckley, Peter J., Jeremy L. Clegg, Adam R. Cross, and Hinrich Voss (2010). "What can emerging markets learn from the outward direct investment policies of advanced countries?" in Karl P. Sauvant, Wolfgang A. Maschek, and Geraldine McAllister, eds., *Foreign Direct Investment from Emerging Markets: The Challenges Ahead* (New York: Palgrave Macmillan), chapter 13.

Deng, Ping (2004). "Outward investment by Chinese MNCs: motivations and implications," *Business Horizons* 47 (3), pp. 8–16.

Deschandol, Jean-Marc and Tom Luckock (2005). "Tips for foreign vendors in Chinese M&A," *International Financial Law Review* 24 (1), pp. 31–32.

Luo, Yadong and Rosalie Tung (2007). "International expansion f emerging market

enterprises: A springboard perspective," *Journal of International Business Studies* 38 (4), pp. 481–98.

Michael A. Witt and Arie Y. Lewin (2008). "Outward foreign direct investment as escape response to home country institutional constraints," *Journal of International Business Studies* 38, pp. 579–94.

Mike W. Peng, Denis Y.L. Wang, and Yi Jiang (2007). "An institution-based view of international business strategy: a focus on emerging economies," *Journal of International Business Studies*, April 3, 2008, pp. 1–17.

Munro, Susan and Sherry Yan (2003). "Recent government reorganization in China," *China Law &Policy—Newsflash*. O'Melveny & Myers LLP.

Naughton, Barry (2007). *The Chinese Economy: Transitions and Growth* (Cambridge, MA: MIT Press).

Scott, W. Richard (1995). *Institutions and Organization* (Thousand Oaks, CA: Sage).

UNCTAD (2006). *World Investment Report: FDI from Developing and Transition Economies: Implications for development* (New York and Geneva: United Nations).

Witt, Michael A. and Arie Y. Lewin (2007). "Outward foreign direct investment as escape response to home country institutional constraints," *Journal of International Business Studies* 38 (4): 579–94.

Wong, John and Sarah Chan (2003). "China's outward direct investment: expanding worldwide," *China: An International Journal* 1 (2), pp. 273–301.

Yamakawa, Yamakawa, Mike W. Peng, and David L. Deeds (2008). "What drives new ventures to internationalize from emerging to developed economies?" *Entrepreneurship Theory and Practice* 32 (1), pp. 59–82.

Zhang, Peter G. (2004). *Chinese Yuan (Renminbi) Derivative Products* (Singapore: World Scientific).

Zhang, Yongjin (2003). *China's Emerging Global Businesses: Political Economy and Institutional Investigations* (Basingstoke: Palgrave Macmillan).

Zweig, David and Jianhai Bi (2005). "China's global hunt for energy," *Foreign Affairs* 84 (5), pp. 25–38.

Chapter 16

Multinational Enterprises from Emerging Markets: Implications for the North and the South

Harry G. Broadman

Introduction

Not too long ago, the topic of multinational enterprises (MNEs) from developing countries was something of a novelty. In the mid-1980s, when I first began to teach a graduate course on the economics of the MNE, I would always devote one of thirteen classes to the topic (in part, selfishly, because in addition to industrial organization, my other field is development and, therefore, I found the topic fascinating). I recall just how thin the literature on this issue was then, both empirical studies and conceptual work. It was a struggle to put together interesting—and rigorous—material for the students. Today, as reflected by this conference volume, the flows of outward foreign direct investment (OFDI) from emerging markets have become substantial, both in volume and in breadth, although certainly they are much smaller than are flows from the advanced countries, where MNEs have a very long history. Settling on a course reading list now would be something of a challenge.

To be sure, as with the phenomenon itself that is under examination, the literature on OFDI from developing countries is still in a nascent phase compared to the literature on OFDI from advanced countries. As time passes and MNEs from emerging markets (presumably) become more extensive and more research on them is carried out, the corresponding literature will enlarge. No doubt it will also strengthen.

It is a given that facilitating the latter was one of the objectives of the conference at which most of the chapters in this volume were presented. This is the spirit in which this essay is written. It summarizes a presentation made at the 2008 Five-Diamond International Conference that draws, in part, on a review of four of the papers the conference organizers asked me to focus on and that now appear in this volume: the chapters by the Multilateral Investment Guaranty Agency (chapter 12); Peter J. Buckley, Jeremy Clegg, Adam Cross, and Hinrich Voss (chapter 13); and Filip De Beule and Daniël Van Den Bulcke (chapter 14).

All of these chapters have a global focus: their unit of analysis is not OFDI from any specific country or region or OFDI flows between any particular country or region. As a contributor to this literature myself—most recently at the country and regional level—based on empirical research on Chinese and Indian businesses investing and operating on the sub-Saharan African continent (Broadman 2007, 2008), the essay also draws on insights from that work.

16.1   A New Theory for MNEs from Emerging Markets?

As is well known to academic experts in this field, the received theory—actually there are theo*ries*—of the archetypal modern MNE is predicated on the notion that the home market of an MNE is an advanced country. At the risk of oversimplification, this is generally taken to mean a country that, in comparative terms, for instance, has a prosperous population, mature manufacturing and/or services sectors, well-educated and highly skilled workers, technological prowess, well-developed infrastructure (including finance, transport, and communications), and substantial openness to international trade.

Needless to say, there are differences among these traditional theories as to just how fundamental to the construct of each is the nature of the MNE's home market. But in virtually every case the theory is conditional on the underlying nature of the firm's home market, as well as how that market compares to a potential host market (which may well be another advanced country or a developing country).

In this context, it seems reasonable to posit that those who argue for a *wholly different theory* for MNEs emanating from developing countries bear a special burden. If a *new* theory is required to explain this phenomenon it should be predicated on fundamental differences between emerging and advanced countries as *home markets*. But the bulk of this new literature—as illustrated by most of the chapters in this volume—tends to focus primarily on the extent to which *the firms* from these two types of markets differ, with little regard to how the firms' attributes may—or may not be—rooted in organic differences at the underlying, country level.[1]

Of course, the most obvious differences between an advanced country home market and a developing country home market are that the latter has much smaller purchasing power, less skilled labor, poorer developed infrastructure, and weaker market institutions than the former. If a "new" theory is in fact needed to explain the advent of MNEs from emerging markets, then it would seem obligatory that it be based on these attributes and indicate how they specifically shape the emergence, structure, conduct, and performance of such MNEs in a logically consistent different manner than MNEs from advanced countries.

In the face of broad empirical evidence this would seem to be a tall order. One obvious difference between emerging market MNEs and advanced country MNEs is that MNEs from developing countries generally are emerging much earlier in the development cycle of these countries than did their advanced country counterparts. On the surface, this facet certainly looks substantially different from what received theories of the MNE could support. However, a different conclusion emerges after a more detailed assessment. Let us unbundle this phenomenon into two parts.

First, the typical MNEs from emerging markets are those that enjoy competitive advantages at home. In this case, they happen to be enjoying those advantages in emerging market economies rather than in advanced economies. The chapters in this volume give many examples of such firms from a wide variety of emerging markets. To take the specific case of Chinese and Indian investors on the African continent, the vast majority of them—whether one considers state-owned enterprises from China or privately owned firms from India—are generally some of the best performing firms in their respective home countries. What are the implications of these findings? The notion that "success at home breeds success abroad" is a central tenet of one of the earliest of the orthodox explanations for the rise of the MNE (see, for example, Hymer 1976). At least from this perspective, the need to resort to a wholly new theory of MNEs from emerging markets seems inconsistent with empirical evidence.

Now let us turn to the "early" launch cycle of developing country MNEs itself. The crucial point is that the time scale of the emergence of these MNEs is not necessarily artificially compressed. Rather, the timing likely reflects a rational response by businesses in these countries to evolving market incentives in both their home markets and in host countries. Indeed, this evolution in incentives is responsible for the significant rise of South-South FDI and trade flows that have been occurring over the past few decades: MNEs domiciled in developing countries almost always penetrate other developing countries as their initial host markets, and tend to make such countries their principal permanent host markets—although this does not rule out investments by developing country MNEs in advanced countries.

Why is this seemingly compressed launch cycle occurring? Is it inconsistent with received theories of MNEs? Firms from developing countries have incentives to engage in OFDI earlier than did their advanced country counterparts precisely because the host markets they are producing and selling in are also developing countries—that is, much like these firms' home markets, their host countries have markets characterized by demand that is both relatively less mature and heterogeneous compared to advanced countries. Still, there is differentiation between developing country home and host markets. These differentials rise to complementarities. These complementarities create the incentives for cross-country OFDI among the countries in the South.

Taken together, it is arguable that the overall evolution of OFDI flows among Southern countries and the "shortened" time cycle of emerging market MNEs are consistent with the traditional "product life cycle" theory of MNEs, as developed by Raymond Vernon (1966, 1979). There is empirical evidence that seems to confirm this.

Although South-South FDI flows are occurring on a global basis, they are perhaps epitomized by the explosion in commerce between the developing countries in Asia, especially China and India, and in Africa (Broadman

2008). Such commerce is driven by the burgeoning middle classes in Asia's emerging economic giants, whose appetite for Africa's natural resources is growing, and by rising economic growth in sub-Saharan Africa, which is increasing the demand for Chinese and Indian manufactured goods and machinery. In many respects, this pattern of interregional FDI flows—at present—is not too dissimilar from Africa's earlier North-South commercial relations: Chinese and Indian FDI is generally concentrated in Africa's raw material sectors, while most African countries import value-added products from China and India.

Even so, this pattern is beginning to change, and in some cases, rapidly. New firm-level data on the business operations of Chinese and Indian MNEs in Africa indicate that these investments are starting to diversify into other sectors beyond oil and natural resources, such as telecommunications, financial services, food processing, infrastructure, and tourism.[2] At the same time, some of these MNEs are engaged in comparatively sophisticated production processes, sometimes linked to global trade networks. The result is that semi- to fully processed goods are sometimes now being exported from the African continent, embodied with a relatively high value-added content. This is contrast to the raw materials that traditionally have characterized Africa's exports.

16.2   Are Advanced Country MNEs Under Threat?

The rise of some of the largest MNEs from emerging markets—especially those from the BRIC countries (Brazil, Russia, India, China)—are increasingly being seen as beginning to pose a threat to advanced country MNEs. Some of the threats are occurring in emerging markets. This is a result of advanced country MNEs being challenged in third countries in which South-South investment is taking place. But these threats are less potent than when MNEs from emerging markets penetrate the home markets of advanced country MNEs.

Indeed, emerging market MNEs are not exclusively engaged in OFDI in their neighboring regions. They are also targeting host markets in the advanced countries in the North, although at a much smaller scale and pace than in the South. There are an increasing number of these initiatives taking place from a wide variety of countries. Some of the investments have been consummated, others have not. Continuing with the examples of China and India is instructive.

As part of China's "Go Out" strategy,[3] the Industrial and Commercial Bank of China (ICBC) successfully purchased a 20% stake in London-headquartered Standard Chartered Bank. The Aluminum Corp of China (Chinalco) teamed up with the U.S. firm Alcoa to purchase 12% of the Anglo-Australian mining firm Rio Tinto. The China National Offshore Oil Corporation (CNOOC) attempted to acquire the U.S. oil firm Unocal, and Huawei Technologies sought to purchase the U.S. computer and telecommunications firm 3Com. The former investment was not concluded when CNOOC backed away from the transaction following a counterbid from a rival U.S. suitor for Unocal amid criticism (and legislation) from the

U.S. Congress about the national security threat posed by the proposed investment. Huawei's investment was formally blocked on national security grounds within the executive branch.

India's Tata Group has made an increasing number of investments in advanced countries. In the United Kingdom, Tata Steel acquired 100% of Corus Steel, and Tata Tea acquired 100% of the Tetley Group. In the United States, the Indian metals firm, Hindalco, purchased 100% of the aluminum firm Novelis, and Reliance Infocomm acquired 100% of Flag Telecom. The German pharmaceutical company Betapharm Arzneimittel GmbH was fully acquired by the Indian firm Dr. Reddy's. In Belgium, Suzlon Energy purchased 100% of Hansen Transmissions.

Some authors in this volume suggest that the new threats posed in advanced country markets may become so strong that MNEs domiciled there will no longer be able to count on even those home markets as being safe. Indeed, the argument runs, the rise of emerging market MNEs means that now *all* markets are contested.[4]

There are two problems with this argument. First, MNEs from advanced countries have long been threatened on their home turf—indeed by other advanced country MNEs (see, for example, E.M. Graham [1978] and Frederick T. Knickerbocker [1973]); that is, not only is rivalry at home not new for advanced country MNEs, but it has come from firms of equivalent "pedigree."

Second, the notion that competition from emerging market MNEs means that advanced country MNEs now face threats in host as well as in home markets begs the question: is the distinction between a firm's "home" and "host" market still a useful one? In a truly globalized marketplace in which MNEs have nominal national headquarters locations and engage in cross-border network trade—either on an intrafirm or an arms-length basis—such that it is virtually impossible to determine the "country of origin" of the final product, it is becoming more and more difficult to make the case. Importantly, like above, this is not a new phenomenon linked only to the rise of MNEs from emerging markets. Indeed, this issue has been at the center of the generic debate on globalization and MNEs for more than fifteen years, at one point posed as the question: "Who Is Us?" (Reich 1990).

Overall, while MNEs from emerging markets clearly are posing new competitive threats to traditional MNEs—both in their advanced and developing country market operations—it is important not to overstate these threats. They are not particularly novel or relatively large compared to competitive threats from advanced country MNEs. At the same time, because the rise of these new MNEs conflate an already weakened distinction between "home" and "host" markets, it is increasingly difficult to discern meaningfully where these threats are actually being played out.

16.3 Implications for Emerging Market MNEs and Their Constituencies in the South

The new literature on the implications of South-South flows of FDI rightfully focuses on the costs and benefits of these flows, just as the traditional literature did on North-South FDI flows. There are several major challenges that confront the new assessments. One, as pointed out in the chapters in this volume, is the lack of data on public perceptions of OFDI, both in the recipient and source countries. Gathering these data is resource intensive and will take time. By definition, the countries in question do not have well-developed infrastructure systems to facilitate the gathering of data, so the information-collection process will be a laborious one, if the results are to be representative and credible.

Moreover, there are numerous countries involved, and there are great variations among them. The continent of Africa—often talked about even in academic circles as a monolithic, analytical unit—of course comprises fifty-three heterogeneous countries. Again, if the goal is unbiased views, careful sampling techniques will be required.

A more fundamental challenge is unbundling the heterogeneity *within* countries. In every country worldwide there are varying degrees of separation between the interests of the state, the business community, and civil society (including labor unions). In assessing the benefits and the costs of OFDI in emerging markets, where arguably the gulf between the interests of the state and business elites and those of civil society are widest, the analysis must tread quite carefully. To take the concrete—yet highly charged—example of Chinese investment in sub-Saharan Africa, public opinion on both sides of the equation (recipient markets and source market) varies appreciably among different constituencies. At the risk of oversimplification, while some African government and business leaders believe there is much to be gained with Chinese investment on the continent, many African workers and university students, for example, hold negative attitudes toward inward Chinese FDI flows.[5] At the same time, workers in China, for example, resent OFDI by their native firms in Africa, voicing a preference for these firms to invest more in poor regions in the domestic economy.[6]

The issue of assessing the costs and benefits of large flows of FDI when there is significant disjuncture between the interests of the state and those of civil society is, of course, not just an academic one—especially in developing countries, where rules-based institutions are either nascent or nonexistent. Rather it is one of assessing real problems arising from weak governance, such as corruption. In this regard, the stakes are high in ensuring credibility and accuracy in measuring the costs and benefits so that any policy reforms based on such assessments have a fighting chance of popular support and thus succeeding.

16.4　OFDI and the Development Objectives of Emerging Market Economies

To be sure, like much of the traditional literature on MNEs, there is much to be commended in the nascent work on MNEs from emerging markets. The conceptual discussions are becoming increasingly rich, the research designs are becoming more ambitious as better data become available and, as a result, the analytics are becoming more rigorous. This is not surprising given the historical foundation on which this literature is being built.

But there is a critical aspect on which this new literature has yet to place sufficient emphasis that is unique to emerging markets: the role that OFDI plays in the overall development process. In particular, OFDI is not—or should not be—seen by policy makers as a goal in and of itself. Rather, OFDI is just one part of a country's overall strategy of economic development. It is a means to an end, not the goal itself. Indeed, the goals are a competitive enterprise sector, flexible labor markets, the protection of property rights, economic growth, and reduction of poverty.

Notes

1. In this context, the chapters in this volume by Yair Aharoni (chapter 3), Rob van Tulder (chapter 4), Alan M. Rugman (chapter 5), and Art Durnev (chapter 6) discuss the question whether the existing theoretical framework needs to be amended or renewed in order to explain emerging market OFDI.
2. These data are presented in detail in Broadman (2007).
3. See, for instance, Qiuzhi Xue and Bingjie Han (chapter 15).
4. See, for instance, Filip De Beule and Daniël Van Den Bulcke (chapter 13).
5. Based on the author's interviews in more than eight African countries during 2007–2008.
6. The author did a call-in television show in China on the "China-Africa" issue. Of the seventeen callers, fifteen complained, saying that Chinese state-owned enterprises (SOEs) investing in Africa should stay home and invest more in China's poorest regions.

References

Broadman, Harry G. (2007). *Africa's Silk Road: China and India's New Economic Frontier* (Washington, DC: World Bank).

———(2008). "China and India go to Africa," *Foreign Affairs* March/April, pp. 95–109.

Graham, E.M. (1978). "Transatlantic investment by multinational firms: a rivalistic phenomenon?" *Journal of Post-Keynesian Economics* (1) Fall, pp. 82–99.

Hymer, Stephen H. (1976). "'A comparison of direct and portfolio investment' and 'The theory of international operations,'" *International Operations of National Firms* (Cambridge, MA: MIT Press).

Knickerbocker, Frederick T. (1973). *Oligopolistic Reaction and Multinational Enterprise* (Cambridge, MA: Harvard University Press).

Reich, R.B. (1990). "Who is us?" *Harvard Business Review* January–February, pp. 53–64.

Vernon, Raymond (1966). "International investment and international trade in the product life cycle," *Quarterly Journal of Economics* 80, pp. 190–207.

———(1979). "The product cycle hypothesis in a new international environment," *Oxford Bulletin of Economics and Statistics* 41 (4), pp. 255–67.

Part Four

The Policy Landscape—Inward FDI from Emerging Markets

Chapter 17

Is the European Union Ready for Foreign Direct Investment from Emerging Markets?*

Judith Clifton and Daniel Díaz-Fuentes

Introduction

The European Union (EU) boasts one of the world's most liberal foreign direct investment (FDI) regimes (OECD 2007). EU member states are hosts to MNEs in most sectors, from virtually every corner of the globe, and many of the new FDI players from emerging markets opt for the EU as host. In the context of increased FDI flows from 2004, peaking at an historic US$1.9 billion in 2007, the EU—like most countries—was rightly criticized for increasing the implementation of restrictive policies and practices with an aim to limit inward FDI (IFDI) as and when governments thought barriers necessary or desirable (UNCTAD 2008). The EU has been criticized by various business executives from emerging markets for raising protectionist barriers to their firms, including Gazprom (Traynor 2007) and Mittal (as chronicled by Bouquet and Ousey 2008). The financial crisis and economic recession triggered by the collapse of the sub-prime market in the United States since 2007 changed the international context for FDI policy significantly. UNCTAD (2009) estimated that IFDI and cross-border mergers and acquisitions (M&As) to the EU declined by around one third in 2008: this represents the largest decline in any part of the world. Even larger declines are predicted for 2009. Governments in the EU are divided over needing short-term capital investment to guarantee jobs and economic growth, and the requirement that they satisfy medium- to long-term political and economic concerns, which fueled the rise of FDI restrictions in the first place. These concerns could escalate if the temptation toward protectionism is not firmly resisted.

In order to understand the dynamics of the international investment climate in the EU, particularly from the perspective of emerging markets, three levels of analysis are required. First, individual member states' behavior must be examined, given that national governments establish FDI policy, satisfy political economy demands, and protect welfare at the national level. Second,

European authorities, principally the European Commission, require analysis as the main institution responsible for forging the Single European Market and ensuring the "four freedoms," meaning movement of goods, services, capital, and people. Third, the changing international context must be analyzed; in particular, the ways in which FDI from emerging markets has challenged the *status quo* of the traditional investment climate, as well as the unfolding financial crisis and economic recession. In this light, this chapter argues that the EU remains one of the most open locations for investment in international comparative terms. As elsewhere, this openness is far from complete, and multiple barriers to investment continue to exist. Much of the controversy around FDI in European circles, in the recent period, has crystallized around the notion of IFDI as a potential threat to "strategic industries." Since the 1990s in particular, the EU has been engaged in an advanced process of market integration, which involves the liberalization, deregulation, and privatization of many former publicly owned monopolies in sectors such as energy, communications, transportation, water and sanitation, and multiple social services, as well as banking and financial services. It is these reforms which, implemented in many countries around the world, have generated a huge increase in FDI flows to these service industries (UNCTAD 2008). In addition, though there was massive privatization and liberalization of industrial sectors from the 1980s, some governments retained partial control over "national champions," enterprises that were historically associated with the nation and also regarded as "strategic." As integration advances, pressure from the Commission increases to liberalize these national "crown jewels." However, there is suspicion at the national level that open FDI regimes may mean foreign takeovers of these "strategic" national assets, many of which were used for decades to satisfy political economy and welfare demands. In this regard, there is legal grey area between the Commission, responsible for liberalizing markets, and national governments, responsible, in the last resort, for defining and guaranteeing national security. The coming of age of emerging market MNEs (Goldstein 2007) coincides with these internal tensions. There have been several highly publicized cases, some of which are discussed in this chapter, in which potential M&As, originating in emerging markets, have been blocked in the EU. However, there have also been multiple cases where potential M&As by other EU member states were blocked; so IFDI restrictions are, by no means, applicable only to non-EU investors.

With the aim of evaluating how ready the EU is for FDI from emerging markets in a fast-changing environment, the remainder of this chapter is organized as follows. First, the EU IFDI regime is put in international context, to demonstrate that it is still one of the most open regimes in the world, though its openness is uneven; certain member states offer greater protection for IFDI into particular sectors than into others. Second, the evolution of recent policy reform that directly or indirectly impinges on IFDI is analyzed, and the role of the Commission, as "neutralizer" of potential or real restrictive attitudes toward IFDI at the national level, is considered. Third, a number of recent cases studies on frustrated M&As are discussed, with a view to understanding what is at issue in the protection of "strategic" industries in the EU. The conclusions follow.

17.1 The Changing EU FDI Regime in the International Context

When comparing the openness of the EU FDI regime at the international level using OECD (2007) methodology, it is apparent that the EU can be classified, on average, as being one of the most open regimes in the world, comparable to the United States, and more open than Australia, Canada, Mexico, and New Zealand. The EU is also much more open than most emerging markets: of the BRICs countries (Brazil, Russia, India, China), Brazil is the most open, which helps to explain why OFDI from the EU is largely concentrated there. That said, openness is uneven, as there are important differences in the extent to which individual member states protect diverse sectors. Generally speaking, the most open regimes are the United Kingdom, Ireland, the Netherlands, Germany, Belgium, and Italy, while Finland and Spain pose the greatest restrictions. With regard to sectoral openness, manufacturing is generally much more open than utilities and services in the EU (140).

Most of the tension in the EU over IFDI revolves around a concern to protect "strategic" industries, which are defined differently at the national level (Schulz 2008). While, traditionally, much concern was focused on military-related sectors, of late, increased attention is being placed on infrastructure, such as energy, communications, transportation, and water, as well as on financial and banking sectors. Though the EU is as open as the United States, in general, both its electricity and telecommunications sectors are more protected than their U.S. counterparts. It has to be remembered that, historically, these sectors, along with other network industries, were organized as state-owned monopolies for most of the twentieth century, managed according to particular social welfare principles and heavily unionized. Even at the beginning of the twenty-first century, they are still broadly perceived as being "public services," associated with the welfare state requiring special regulation (Clifton and Díaz-Fuentes 2010). Beyond this, the telecommunications industry is much more open to IFDI than is the electricity industry. Explanations can be found in geopolitics or political economy. In particular, the smaller EU member states located close to Russia's borders have put in place the greatest restrictions on IFDI in electricity. These countries are concerned about the foreign takeover of their energy industries, a concern exacerbated by their small size or their Russian neighbor (Klinova 2007). France, too, maintains above-average protection of its electricity industry, which has a political economy explanation. The most liberal electricity regimes are found in Belgium and Spain (which have historically had regionally based companies, with limited competition, and significant private sector involvement) and the United Kingdom (which implemented market-oriented reforms early on). In contrast, the telecommunications sector in the EU, which is often described as a "strategic" sector in many countries, is on average as open to IFDI as any other industry sector in the EU.[1]

In terms of the direction of recent IFDI flows into EU member states, almost two-thirds were intra-EU flows, though in some countries, such as

Table 17.1 FDI inflows main EU receptors by country and group of countries, 2004–2006 (EUR millions average for the EU 27 and percentages)

	European Union 27	United Kingdom	Ireland	Germany	Nether-lands	France	Sweden	Luxembourg	Spain	Poland	Austria	Hungary	Czech Republic	Italy
Million EUR (percentage by country or group)	311,142	55,357	32,074	30,704	23,210	17,065	14,097	11,613	10,711	8,500	6,044	5,759	5,547	4,842
Intra European Union 27	65.2	43.9	51.4	74.7	55.6	81.6	58.3	89.1	85.5	85.5	59.8	79.4	94.8	68.1
Extra European Union 27	34.8	56.1	48.6	25.3	44.4	18.4	41.7	10.9	14.5	14.5	40.2	20.6	5.2	31.9
Offshore financial centers	4.9	3.6	17.8	2.7	8.8	3.2	0.7	2.4	1.6	2.5	1.1	−0.7	0.5	1.5
U.S.	19.1	37.6	22.0	10.0	18.7	5.7	11.7	−6.3	7.8	8.9	16.2	5.9	4.1	12.0
Japan	1.2	3.2	−0.3	1.3	1.5	2.7	0.0	1.7	0.0	0.1	0.2	0.3	−1.6	1.7
BRICs	0.7	0.2	0.0	0.8	0.1	0.1	0.0	0.6	0.0	0.8	4.3	2.2	0.1	0.1
Brazil	0.3	0.0	0.0	0.0	0.1	0.0	0.0	0.2	0.0	0.0	0.1	2.1	0.0	0.1
Russia	0.3	0.0	0.0	0.6	0.0	0.1	0.0	0.2	0.0	0.7	1.0	0.1	0.1	0.0

Source: Elaborated by the authors, based on UNCTAD (2008).

France, Germany, Spain, Poland, Luxembourg, Hungary, and the Czech Republic, this ratio was even higher (table 17.1). IFDI from emerging markets has grown rapidly in recent years, even if it remains marginal in volume terms. The BRIC countries account for the larger part of these IFDI flows, which represented 0.7% of total IFDI into the EU. Brazil and Russia each account for 0.3%. While Russian inflows have been mainly directed toward Austria, Poland, and Germany, Brazilian inflows have focused on Hungary.[2]

With regard to the M&A track record, the EU regime is also relatively open when compared internationally. The entry of MNEs from emerging markets into both northern and southern markets has increasingly attracted the attention of scholars.[3] In recent years, dozens of MNEs from emerging markets have entered the EU, including Tata, Mittal, Nanjing, Marcopolo, Cemex, Weg, Orascom, Lukoil, Gazprom, PEMEX, Hyundai, Sungwoo, Samsung, Sabó, Sonatrach, Orascom, and Grupo Bimbo, some taking over flagship European firms (see, for example, Antkiewicz and Whalley 2006; El País 2007; Lapper and Wheatley 2008). Of course, a considerable number of the attempts by MNEs from emerging markets to enter the European energy and telecommunications infrastructure have been frustrated, such as recent failures experienced by Russia's Gazprom and Mexico's Grupo Carso. However, just as emerging market MNEs have been frustrated, so have many MNEs based within the EU. To illustrate this briefly: Catalan's Gas Natural and German's E.On energy firms were frustrated in their attempts to take over Spanish Endesa; in 2006, Spanish Abertis was blocked when it tried to merge with Italian Autostrade, even though the European Commission later ruled that Italy had violated EU law. While it is possible to catalog a list of M&A failures and success stories, it is difficult to draw clear and definitive conclusions about how ready the EU is for emerging market MNEs, because patterns of declared and revealed preferences are not always coherent (Goldstein 2008. One way to better evaluate the current climate for IFDI in the EU, especially from emerging markets, is to follow the evolution of policy—which, directly or indirectly, affects the FDI regime of the EU and its member states. We do this in the next section.

17.2 FDI Policy in the EU: Recent Developments

Because of its "multilevel" governance structure, the EU offers an interesting arena for the analysis of FDI policy. With different remits and objectives, policy developments in the Commission and at the national level do not necessarily move in the same direction. The EU's liberal FDI regime, both with regard to other EU states and third parties, can be traced back to the Treaty of Rome (1957), in which the "four freedoms" were outlined: free circulation of goods, services, people, and capital, as well as the right of establishment. However, implementation of the four freedoms, in the first decades of the EU, was irregular and uneven. Though the main beneficiaries in these processes were member states, increased liberalization at the international level occurred as a "spill-over effect": as nonmember state capital entered

the EU, it became increasingly difficult to discriminate against these capital flows. The Commission is, therefore, legally responsible for overseeing
member states' application of treaty law with regard to the free movement
of capital.[4] The freedom of capital movement also applies to third countries,
even though Articles 57, 59, and 60 of the treaty allow for specific exceptions, sanctions, and safeguard measures. The Commission also establishes
and supervises European law regarding cartels, antitrust, mergers, state aid,
and takeovers. All of these rules must be implemented by national governments, and failure to do so can result in infringement cases brought against
individual governments.[5] One of the Treaty of Lisbon's aims is to increase
the Commission's competence in investment policy, and this development is
still ongoing.

In contrast, the FDI regime of each member state is decided at the
national level and is usually implemented via bilateral agreements. It addition, it falls to individual governments to protect citizens by guaranteeing
national security and welfare. This "multilayered" governance can generate tensions. To illustrate this, on the one hand, it is the national government that defines those industries deemed to be of "strategic" importance,
as well as the degree of protection from IFDI that those industries would
enjoy. The Commission, on the other hand, has to ensure liberalized markets, unless this would threaten national security. In practice, this is a grey
area in legal and political terms. There are many recent examples that illustrate this point. Perhaps most dramatically, the terrorist attacks that have
occurred since September 11, 2001, have had infrastructure as their central
target, and have often used infrastructure services to orchestrate attacks.[6]
Debate has been renewed on how "critical infrastructure" can be protected,
including aspects of its ownership and regulation. For many Europeans, the
cold month of January 2009 was accompanied by the threat or actual lack
of gas, the result of a standoff between Russia and Ukraine, discussed in
the third section. Certainly, if there is a blackout, an energy or water failure, or paralysis of the urban transportation system, European citizens hold
their national government accountable, regardless of who owns and runs
the network (Clifton, Comín, and Díaz-Fuentes 2007; Costas 2007). The
same perception characterizes the current financial crisis: national governments are held accountable by their citizens. There is some evidence that
this belief in national accountability is getting stronger: according to special
Eurobarometer surveys regarding energy issues, in 2006, 57% of Europeans
stated that energy challenges should be managed at the local or national level,
and not at the European level, up from 45% in 2005 (European Commission
2006). Unsurprisingly, this change was particularly strong in countries near
the Russian border (Estonia, Latvia), near Ukraine (Romania, Hungary), as
well as in smaller countries, such as Austria, Cyprus, Greece, and Ireland.

Another reason for the tensions between member states and the
Commission is the need for the former to satisfy political economy interests. A number have opted to protect business in certain industries by using
"national champion" policies. In particular, former monopoly incumbents
in energy, water, and communications have enjoyed a temporary "respite"

from European liberalization directives, by delaying opening up at home while aggressively pursuing expansion opportunities abroad. For instance, with virtual monopoly privileges at home, the Spanish MNE Telefonica expanded early into the Latin American telecommunications markets, which were privatized from the early 1990s onward, following the region's debt crisis. EDF, Telecom Italia, Deutsche Telekom, and Suez are just some of the enterprises that have used "asymmetrical" behavior to emerge as MNE world players (Clifton, Díaz-Fuentes and Revuelta 2010).

17.2.1 Recent Trends in Policies and Practices Affecting FDI

Since the current financial crisis spread to most other areas of economic life, there have been many threats and declarations by governments and trade unions from various EU countries over the need to purchase nationally produced goods. In the United Kingdom, strikes have taken place to protest firms' hiring of nonnational (Italian) workers. Protectionism, it would seem, could spiral out of control if left unchecked. At the same time, most of these threats have been countered by reminders as to the cause of the Great Depression and the futility of isolation. Declared and revealed preferences are often contradictory, however. This section focuses on the way in which the EU, following global patterns, has implemented an increased number of policies and practices that have negatively affected IFDI in the past few years.

The most common, formal instruments to restrict FDI are ownership restrictions, obligatory screening and approval procedures, and other formal restrictions, such as rules on the composition of the board and restrictions on the employment of foreign nationals. All of these instruments have been used by one EU member state or another in recent years. There are, of course, numerous other policies that do not necessarily focus directly on IFDI, but work in other ways to restrict it. These mechanisms may be more subtle, such as the existence of complex regulatory frameworks or systems of corporate control. In addition, informal practices, such as the publication of opinions by policy makers or members of the business community in order to steer an "unfriendly" investment climate, are also likely to affect the climate for IFDI. An evaluation of the importance of these formal and informal instruments on FDI must be made carefully. Just as the World Trade Organization (WTO) prefers "transparent" tariffs to other forms of protectionism, because they are easier to quantify and, therefore, compare, formal instruments relating to FDI, such as laws, regulations, and screening mechanisms, are easier to quantify than are their informal counterparts. However, even though an analysis of formal FDI rules provides a useful—if impressionistic—picture of an economy's position vis-à-vis IFDI, of greater importance is the *use made* of the FDI framework. For instance, there have been some important cases of restricting FDI in EU member states using *existing* FDI regulations. To complicate matters further, it is not always easy to know the facts about why one deal is blocked and another is accepted, and the real role of IFDI restrictions in the process. With these caveats in mind, this section analyzes policy responses, first by member states and then by the Commission. Two main areas are covered: the policy responses based on concerns about security, however defined, and EU member states' responses to the rise of sovereign wealth funds (SWFs).

At the individual member state level, Germany has perhaps gone furthest in the introduction of new policies that restrict IFDI. In September 2008, the German Cabinet approved a new bill that will allow prospective IFDI, involving 25% or more of a company's stake by non-European firms, to be screened for approval. According to German officials, one of the triggers for this reform was in 2003, when a U.S. private equity investment firm acquired a German submarine manufacturer (Government Accountability Office 2008, 61). Alarm was raised about the lack of legal clarity in the protection of German military and strategic interests and, the following year, section 7 of the German Foreign Trade and Payments Act was enacted, which established limits to the free movement of capital into Germany on the grounds of "security." IFDI would be subject to review if it involved acquisition of a domestic company producing or developing weapons or other military equipment. German Chancellor Angela Merkel claimed that Germany needed a "light CFIUS" (Benoit 2007) and, even though the German government has downplayed the importance of this new bill, many local businesses have expressed concern over the negative signals that this may send to international markets. The stated concern behind this bill was the need to clarify German law in order to ensure "strategic" industries were protected, and officials stress that Germany is only adapting its policy framework to the U.S. or UK model. As shown in table 17.1, Germany is relatively more exposed to Russian IFDI than are most other EU member states, which could partly explain their concerns. In addition, Germany has been more open to IFDI in the electricity and telecommunications industries than are EU member states on average. This confirms the understanding that the new bill could be interpreted as a move away from relative openness toward the EU average, though it remains to be seen how the Commission will respond. This is already the second version of the bill; the first version was rejected by the Commission (Walker 2008).[7]

France has also attracted much attention for its recent IFDI reforms. Facing the prospect of a hostile takeover of Danone, a food company, then Prime Minister Dominique de Villepin celebrated "*patriotisme économique*" (*Le Monde* 2005). In 2005, the French government compiled a list of "strategic" and "sensitive" industries in which foreign investors would be subject to government screening (UNCTAD 2006; OECD 2007).[8] The Commission criticized Decree 2005–1739, which stated that it did not respect the principle of "proportionality," was unnecessarily unfavorable to IFDI, included "casinos" (which were already protected by another French law), and discriminated between EU and non-EU investors, because potential investors from non-EU countries would be required to provide more data to the review process board. In the face of criticism, the French government appealed to the principle of subsidiarity, claiming that it has the ultimate duty to defend the "national interest, as well as the legal responsibility to define what constitutes a "strategic" industry. The Commission formally requested France to modify the decree in October 2006. At the same time, in French policy circles, concerns have grown over the security of the country's energy infrastructure and supply. Since winning the presidential elections in 2007, President Sarkozy has publicly declared his preference for an active industrial policy approach. In June 2007, inspired by developments in Germany, the French parliament produced a report suggesting that the energy sector should be added to the list of protected industries. This debate has been "uploaded" to the European level, as we shall see later in this section. Finally, with the onset of recession in 2008 and, in response to a concern that distressed assets in the EU could be bought up cheaply by foreigners, Sarkozy proposed the creation of a European SWF, in order to protect Europe's "strategic" industries, though nothing has come of this initiative to date. Appealing to populist sentiment, Sarkozy was quoted as saying "I don't want European citizens to wake up in several months time and find that European companies belong to non-European capital, which bought at the share prices' lowest point" (*International Herald Tribune*, October 21, 2008).

There are several other developments at the national level. Hungary has earned the disapproval of the Commission, which issued a formal letter of concern to its government over its new company law on FDI, passed in 2007. The Commission perceives this law as incompatible with European law. While Hungarian authorities claim this law aims to secure the public supply of services such as energy and water, the Commission argues that it has two main and undesirable effects: first, the Hungarian government will have the right to place politicians on the boards of energy firms; and second, that it will slow down and publicize potential M&As, which could eliminate the element of surprise, thus increasing prices, and opening up further opportunities to block operations (European Commission 2007).[9] In 2006, Hungary was also asked by the Commission to modify its privatization law, which, the Commission claimed, confers golden shares to firms in industries including food, pharmaceuticals, financial services, telecommunications, energy, and defense.

The retention of "golden shares" in privatized industries has been an area in which the EU has been active vis-à-vis national governments. Infringement procedures have been initiated with regard to various countries, but firms and the Commission state that special rights are still conferred on privileged investors, preventing capital from flowing freely. In January 2008, the Commission referred Portugal to the European Court of Justice over its alleged special rights in Portugal Telecom (European Commission 2008d) and Energias de Portugal (European Commission 2008c), and in July 2008, the European Court of Justice found the requirement that potential acquisitions of Spanish energy firms had to be approved by the National Energy Commission to violate Community law (European Commission 2008a).

Member states' behavior has thus been subject to review by the Commission in the areas in which it has competence. In general, the Commission functions as the "liberalizing machine," correcting national economic policies if they violate the free movement of capital. Two important developments, however, have emerged at the supranational level which concern—directly or indirectly—IFDI flows: energy policy and responses to SWFs.

European energy policy can be traced back to the Treaty of Rome, particularly with regard to the European Coal and Steel Community Treaty and the Euratom Treaty on civil use of nuclear energy. However, until the 1990s, little was done to forge an internal market in energy and other infrastructure, and providers were usually organized as national or local state-owned monopolies. From the late 1990s onward, market-oriented reforms began, particularly in telecommunications, electricity, and gas. Though belated, these reforms caused great expectations and, between 1993 and 2000, the worldwide race for FDI was dominated by investment in telecommunications and energy utilities. Nearly two-thirds of world FDI during this period took place within the EU, and the utilities industries were responsible for nearly three-quarters of privatization proceeds (Clifton, Comín, and Díaz-Fuentes 2003). As world FDI flows dropped by approximately half between 2000 and 2003, in the EU, delays dogged the implementation of European liberalization directives on electricity and gas, while the reforms already implemented did not always deliver what had been promised, in terms of competition, price reductions, and market power. A second round of reforms was launched in 2003 (European Directives on Electricity 2003/54/EC and Gas 2003/55/EC) with the stated aims of providing more competition (highest priority), improving service quality and universal services, and ensuring the security of supply. Despite the rhetoric, the main focus of the Commission was economically driven: market competition was sought above all, at the expense of the other two objectives. One year later, the Commission found that eighteen member states had not implemented the new directives adequately. In 2005, the Commission took Estonia, Greece, Ireland, Luxembourg, and Spain to court for failing to adapt national laws to the directives. The following year, the Commission took action against seventeen countries for failing to implement legislation. After several years of attempted reform, the largest generator in the electricity market in EU member states often enjoys huge market shares. Stephen Thomas (2003) predicted that these liberalization reforms would lead to monopolistic competition between the "seven brothers," though there were arguably only five or six by 2009. While some member states liberalized quite deeply (the United Kingdom, Spain, Belgium), other member states were much more reluctant. Some electricity firms aggressively exploited opportunities presented by liberalization programs abroad, while they enjoyed restricted or delayed liberalization at home (table 17.2). Smaller economies, particularly those bordering Russia, avoided M&As in their electricity markets based on "security" concerns. Many governments and their firms were simply flouting European legislation in terms of unbundling and liberalization. In 2006, a further Directive (2005/89/EC) was passed concerning measures to safeguard the security of the electricity supply and infrastructure investment.

In 2007, the new energy policy was launched by the EU, which includes issues beyond purely economically driven concerns, such as increased attention to the promotion of new or diverse energy sources, climate change,

Table 17.2 Market share of the largest generator in the electricity market of each country, 1999–2001, 2004–2006

Country	1999–2001	2004–2006	Change
United Kingdom	21.5	20.9	−0.6
Finland	24.1	24.0	−0.1
Germany	30.4	28.4	−2.0
Spain	46.0	34.0	−12.0
Italy	54.3	38.9	−15.4
Sweden	50.3	46.3	−4.0
Ireland	96.9	68.4	−28.5
Portugal	59.3	54.5	−4.8
Denmark	37.3	41.0	3.7
Belgium	92.0	85.9	−6.1
France	91.3	89.3	−2.0
Greece	97.7	96.2	−1.5
Poland	20.0	18.1	−1.9
Hungary	39.9	38.6	−1.3
Slovenia	50.7	51.5	0.8
Lithuania	74.5	72.9	−1.6
Slovakia	84.4	79.1	−5.3
Czech Republic	70.0	72.9	2.9
Estonia	91.3	92.0	0.7
Latvia	95.8	92.9	−2.9

Source: Elaborated by authors, based on EUROSTAT (2008).

and the coordination of energy "security of supply." Security of supply is understood as an emphasis on diversity of energy types and sources, dialogue and agreements with trading partners, and preparation for an energy crisis (European Council 2006). In the face of maverick firms and member states delaying or refusing to unbundle, the Commission has relaxed its policy stance somewhat, opting for "competition for the market" rather than "competition in the market." Some European politicians claim that Russia's decision to cut off energy supplies to Ukraine in 2006 triggered this shift in European energy policy. One development is that the Commission is seeking to impose a "reciprocity" clause (sometimes called the "Gazprom clause"), so that companies buying EU energy transmission assets would have to abide by similar rules to those of the EU with regard to liberalizing markets. A further clause stipulates that "third-country individuals and countries cannot acquire control over a Community transmission system or transmission system operator, unless this is permitted by an agreement between the EU and the third country." The clause, once adopted as law, would remove national competence in the area and require that any bilateral energy agreements with third countries are dealt with exclusively at the Community level. The current Energy Commissioner, Andris Piebalgs, justified the reciprocity clause on the grounds that it would give third-country suppliers "clear rules" for investment in the European market (*Euractiv* 2007; Wolf 2007). Discussions are ongoing, and the Council adopted the development as part of the internal energy market package in February 2009.

The second area in which significant developments have occurred is with regard to SWFs. Already controversial before the current financial crisis and recession, falling asset values in the EU have made this topic even more contentious. The main thrust of the development has been to work on guidelines for both the recipient country and the agent behind the fund in order to increase the transparency and predictability of this type of investment. Here, the ongoing work of the OECD (2009) has been helpful for EU policy makers in drawing up key principles and a common EU code was drafted at the end of 2008 (European Commission 2008b).

Thus, the Commission has been active in reversing "golden shares," rejecting or diluting national government's lists of "strategic industries," and enforcing the free movement of capital, both within the EU and with regard to third countries. Yet, there remains a grey area between market liberalization and nationally defined "security interests" into which the majority of disputes fall. Moreover, there are delays in the liberalization process of some industries, such as energy, where, for instance, unbundling policies will not be easy to enforce.

17.3 FDI and Europe's "Strategic" Industries

There have been several highly publicized, controversial cases recently, in which attempts by investors to enter EU energy and other infrastructure markets have failed. This section selects two cases for in-depth analysis with a view to understanding the central issues and informal dynamics around FDI in "strategic" industries. The first case analyzes what is probably the most controversial instance of IFDI from an emerging market: Gazprom, making explicit the concerns over this MNE from an EU perspective. The second case discusses the controversy around the so-called "Endesa saga." Here, three levels of protectionism can be seen: first, a leading emerging market MNE, América Móvil of the Grupo Carso, was frustrated in its efforts to enter the EU; second, protectionism among members of the EU; and third, protectionism at the national level and between rival political-economic groups.

17.3.1 Gazprom

No other global player from an emerging market has aroused as much controversy in the EU as has Gazprom. Though the vast majority of Russian MNEs are privately owned, Gazprom constitutes an important exception. The over-riding concern in the EU is that its business may be politically motivated. As Åslund (2006, 1) notes, "the fundamental question is to what extent [Gazprom] represents the state and business interests, respectively," while, according to the OECD (2002, 106), "it can at times be difficult even to identify where the state budget ends and Gazprom's begins." However, the *Financial Times* (February 13, 2008) harbors no such doubts: "all decisions are taken in the Kremlin. Both psychologically and practically, Gazprom is not a commercial enterprise."

Strong ties have bound Gazprom and the Russian state since 1993, when the company was formed out of the Russian part of the Ministry of Gas Industry, by the last Soviet Minister, Viktor Chernomyrdin (who would become Prime Minister of Russia under Yeltsin in 1992–1998). Its governance remained opaque and, in the early 2000s, under pressure from international investors,[10] the new president Vladimir Putin removed Gazprom management and appointed a duo of trusted advisors. Other sources of power consist of KGB staff from St. Petersburg and old Gazprom hands. For Putin, who took a very active interest in management issues and relied on Gazprom to solidify his broad popular support, this split into three groups resulted in great leeway to balance them (Åslund 2006).

Under Dmitry Medvedev, who was also head of the presidential administration, and CEO Alexei Miller, who had worked with Putin in the mayor's office in St. Petersburg, Gazprom has gained in assertiveness, and completed its ascendancy as Russia's preeminent economic institution and a central player in domestic politics.[11] Gazprom—in which the government controls 50.002% of shares through the Russian Federal Agency for Federal Property Management (Rosimushchestvo), Rosneftegaz, and Rosgazifikatsiya— generates 8% of national tax revenue and employs over 430,000 staff (*Economist*, October 8, 2005). The main objective of the new management has been to boost its stock price, which has increased more than tenfold in the past three years. Although Gazprom is one of the world's most valuable companies, it also had one of the lowest returns on assets in the energy sector (Ostrovsky 2006).

Initially, the new management focused on recovering assets that had been sold off cheaply to other companies, when not "lost." Another important step was to homogenize its prices of natural gas on the Russian border. While Gazprom's Western European customers paid negotiated market prices (which include large transportation costs in pipelines and substantial taxes), former Soviet republics paid highly differentiated prices.[12] This offensive has led to a number of incidents, including with allies such as Belarus. The struggle between Russia and Ukraine, and to a lesser extent Moldova, during the last week of 2005 and the beginning of 2006, renewed anxieties regarding European gas import dependence.[13] Problems reoccurred in February 2008, when Gazprom again threatened to reduce gas supplies to Ukraine to force repayment of what it claims is a debt of a US$1.5 billion. Yet again, in the coldest days of the year, in January 2009, Gazprom cut off its gas supply to Ukraine over price disputes, though Gazprom firmly blamed Ukraine for closing down the export pipelines. Despite the claims and counterclaims, thousands of European citizens were denied basic access to gas provision.

The major grievance expressed by the EU (and by the United States) is that politics played a major role in these dramas. It is fair to say that Gazprom's strategy of raising prices relatively quickly makes business sense in the current energy market environment. The next key task is to raise the domestic Russian gas price. In fact, a partial deregulation of the domestic gas market is also in the interest of the Unified Energy System, which despairs at the shortage of gas in Russia. At present, the pretax wholesale price for gas is around US$42 per 1,000 cubic meters.[14]

Gazprom's strategy has been to use excess profits to acquire downstream assets, mainly access to distribution networks, in a bid to reach the final consumer. Whether through debt-for-share agreements, or upstream-downstream swaps (UDS), Gazprom has been quite successful in solidifying its presence in the EU. It is particularly active in Eastern Europe (in Bulgaria, for instance, its 50% joint venture with Overgas, a Bulgarian-Russian company, has twenty-seven urban distribution licenses, including in Sofia) but also, and increasingly, in the West. In the United Kingdom, for instance, it controls Pennine, the largest privately owned gas supplier. There was a mooted (but never confirmed) intention of buying a stake in Centrica, Britain's largest gas supplier, in 2006 (Williamson 2006).[15] In addition, Gazprom launched a bid to take control of Petroleum Industries of Serbia (NIS) at what seemed a bargain price—so much so that many saw this as a *quid pro quo* for Russian support for Serbia over Kosovo. Elsewhere, Gazprom has announced multibillion exploration and production investment projects in Bolivia and Nigeria—both difficult countries where Western investors were, until recently, dominant (MacDonald 2008; Schipani 2008).

Meanwhile, Gazprom has invested little in the development of new major gas finds. New prospects, such as the Yamal peninsula and the offshore Shtokman field, are years from coming on stream. European gas demand will rise from presently 540 billion cubic meters (bcm) to around 800 bcm in 2030. Thus, a potential supply gap is appearing that may take time and money to close (Goldthau 2008; Mandil 2006). Åslund (2006) argued that Gazprom does not invest more because the domestic gas price is still too low to cover the associated costs, but other analysts claim that management is concentrating its efforts in protecting its monopoly position. Gazprom has acquired various assets within Russia quite cheaply because of its combination of monopoly power over pipelines, pricing, exports, and state regulation. Small independent gas producers have been squeezed out and forced to sell their assets cheaply to Gazprom, which, in 2005, also bought Sibneft and became Russia's fifth-largest oil producer. In the Sakhalin II project, the Kremlin exercised pressure on Shell Royal Dutch until the company agreed to renegotiate its product-sharing agreement and to give a large share of its investment to Gazprom. TNK-BP, half-owned by BP, is currently going through similar difficulties, arguably in order for Gazprom to acquire eventually a stake in the giant Kovykta gas field in East Siberia. Gazprom's long-term industrial strategy is to produce more coal and increase its use in electricity generating and home heating in Russia, freeing more gas for export. Gazprom had been buying electricity-generating companies from the state electricity company, which is being split up. In February 2008, Gazprom acquired control of the Siberian Coal and Energy Company, Russia's largest coal producer by volume.[16] The joint venture will retain Siberian's name but be controlled by Gazprom, while Gazprom has also diversified into other business such as nuclear power (100% of *Atomstroïexport*) and media (NTV, *Izvestia,* and *Tribuna*).

Gazprom is also very active in transmission investments. The bulk of exports currently go to Europe, via a pipeline through Ukraine, with the remaining 20% traveling through Belarus and Poland. Two approaches are being tried to get around this unsatisfactory situation. First, to build the Baltic pipeline (Northstream) directly from Russia to Germany through the Baltic Sea, as well as a second one to Italy (Southstream). Second, in 2006, Putin decided that Gazprom will build one or two gas pipelines to China, rather than invest in a liquefied natural gas plant designed for exports to the United States. Gazprom has also derided as "unrealistic" the construction of a Trans-Caspian gas pipeline from Kazakhstan to Turkey and into Europe that could greatly enhance Europe's energy security (Catan 2006).

The EU has so far failed to present a unified position vis-à-vis Gazprom. Germany, for instance, has preferred to develop a special energy relationship with Russia, although the Merkel government has been more cautious than its predecessor.[17] Italy has also negotiated the entry of Gazprom into the domestic downstream market in exchange for space to its energy giants ENI and ENEL in Russia.[18] What is certain is that, to date, Russia has commonly refused to come to terms with European requests. Moscow has consistently refused to sign up to any kind of political agreements, such as the Energy Charter (EC) Treaty and its Transit Protocol under the EU-Russia Partnership and Cooperation Agreement.[19] The EU now insists on a liberalization of the Russian (and European) gas market, free and nondiscriminatory access to pipeline systems throughout Europe, including Russia, commitments to uninterrupted supplies, and mutually equal conditions for investment in the energy sector.

In summary, Gazprom and the EU are stuck in an imbroglio that is largely explained by their mutual dependence (Grigoryev 2008). Eirik Lund Sagen and Marina Tsygankova (2008) used both theoretical and numerical tools to study the potential effects of different Russian domestic gas prices and production capacities in 2015 on Russian gas exports. Their main findings suggest that both increased domestic gas prices and sufficient production capacities are vital to maintaining Gazprom's market share in Europe over the next decade. In fact, Russia may struggle to carry out its current long-term export commitments if domestic prices are sufficiently low. At the same time, if Russian prices approach European levels, Gazprom may reduce exports in favor of a relatively more profitable domestic market.

The objectives of the EU as importer would be best served by deregulation and liberalization, lifting restrictions on foreign or independent investors wishing to gain access to Russian reserves, and unhindered access to the pipeline infrastructure and export markets. At the same time, alternative sources are either more expensive or politically unfeasible. In the current political context, it is doubtful whether the Russian Federation would consider higher domestic Russian gas prices, enhanced energy efficiency and increases in non-Gazprom production as its supreme objectives. Gazprom, however, cannot realistically expect to diversify significantly its customer base toward China and other Asian countries, or to make any significant progress in downstream markets, unless it is ready to give way in its home market.

17.3.2 Endesa

The Endesa "saga" has been one of the most controversial deals in the EU to date. The saga involved Gas Natural (from Catalunya, Spain) and two leading electricity incumbents, German E.On and Italian ENEL. The Commission intervened repeatedly, making eight "decisions" concerning mergers and the free movement of capital in the light of unfolding events. From the 1980s onward, Endesa transformed itself from a local, state-owned enterprise to the world's fourth-largest electricity MNE. From 2006 onward, it participated in the generation, transportation, and distribution systems in France, Italy, Germany, Poland, Portugal, South America, and North Africa. Nevertheless, its core activities remained in Spain, where it is the largest domestic power supplier, providing 45% of power generation and 40% of distribution (Clifton, Comín, and Díaz-Fuentes 2007).

In September 2005, Gas Natural (whose major shareholders were La Caixa of Catalonia and Repsol) launched a hostile takeover bid (EUR22.5 billion) for Endesa. The aim was to create a national champion large enough to compete with the other EU firms, such as EdF, E.On,[20] RWE, and Enel. This bid did not advance as the Spanish and Catalonian governments had anticipated, however, due to the managerial opposition of Endesa chairperson, Manuel Pizarro. Party politics played a role: whereas Pizarro was associated with the conservative Partido Popular, La Caixa was associated with the Socialist Party. The acquisition of Endesa by La Caixa could create a Socialist economic block, so Pizarro sought a "white knight" in the shape of E.On to avoid this: FDI from Germany was preferable to national capital representing Catalonian Socialists.

Accordingly, in February 2006, E.On launched a bid to acquire Endesa (EUR29 billion). The Commission approved the bid, not regarding it as one that would impede effective competition. The Spanish government, led by President Zapatero and his Socialist party, however, objected. Several days later, the government extended the power of the electricity and gas regulator (CNE), giving it responsibility to authorize any acquisition over 10% (Decree-Law 04/2006). The Commission stepped in, considering this restricted the free movement of capital and the right of establishment, as enshrined in EU Treaty rules (Articles 56 and 43, respectively).

Though the Spanish government was asked to rectify this legislation, the government went further: it introduced additional restrictions in November 2006, when the conditions for the takeover were modified, requiring E.On to respect the following decisions: (1) Endesa would maintain its brand for a five-year period; (2) the companies owning electricity assets outside mainland Spain would be kept within the Endesa Group for five years; (3) Endesa's power plants that used domestic coal would continue to use this energy source as foreseen in the national mining plans; and (4) E.On would not adopt strategic decisions with regard to Endesa and the security of supply in violation of Spanish law. All of these newly imposed conditions were deemed incompatible with the EC Treaty's rules on free movement of capital (Article 56) and on the freedom of establishment (Article 43). The condition about the use of domestic coal was also incompatible with the EC Treaty's rules on free movement of goods (Article 28).

A few months later, a third bid to control Endesa was launched, this time by Enel[21] and Acciona.[22] The Commission approved the operation in March 2007. Given the EU policy of avoiding market concentration, Enel and E.On agreed that E.On would buy most of Enel's assets in Spain (electricity generation, distribution, supply) including Viesgo. In addition, Endesa Europe (including assets in Italy, France, Poland, Portugal, and Turkey) had to be sold off. However, Endesa's market concentration in Latin America was reinforced.

Again, the Commission condemned Spain for the conditions imposed by the Spanish regulator on Enel and Acciona in the takeover process, which were, fundamentally, similar to those which had been imposed on E.On: (1) to allow Endesa to remain independent, including keeping its own brand, and its decision-making center in Spain; (2) to limit the firm's debt-service ratio; (3) to limit the firm's dividends distribution policy; (4) to ensure certain amounts of national coal were used in Endesa's generation assets; and (5) to keep the assets of nonmainland electricity systems within the Endesa Group. Not surprisingly, the Commission found these conditions restricted FDI and violated the treaty's rules on the free movement of capital and the freedom of establishment, even as the obligation to acquire domestic coal also violated the rules on the free movement of goods.

It is believed that President Zapatero and Prime Minister Prodi came to an agreement during February 2007, whereby Enel (in which the Italian state still had 30% ownership) would take over Endesa. Interestingly, three weeks after this deal was closed, Telefónica acquired an indirect 10% stake of Telecom Italia. A few weeks earlier, an interest in Telecom Italia had been shown by a consortium composed of AT&T and Mexican MNE América Móvil. América Móvil, a spin-off of Telmex, is one of the leading telecommunications MNEs from emerging markets. The potential acquisition of Telecom Italia by this consortium raised eyebrows in Italy: Prodi stated that he wished Telecom Italia to remain in Italian hands, and called on Italian bankers to make counteroffers for the shares. The Italian government even threatened regulatory changes that would reduce Telecom Italia's network advantages. Within a few days, AT&T pulled out, citing regulatory uncertainty, leaving Carlos Slim's América Móvil alone in the bid. Slim reluctantly withdrew, making room for the acquisition by "archrival" Telefonica, along with a consortium of Italian banks (Burnett and Kiefer 2007). Telefonica paid 40% over the market value to join the winning consortium. Politically, this was a winning "European" formula: Prodi obtained his "Italian solution" in exchange for the Spanish concession into its energy market. The efforts of the non-EU investors including those of Carlos Slim were, however, frustrated. Interestingly, the Italian government did not introduce new policies to restrict IFDI, though Prodi made clear that Italian capital was his priority. This case does not necessarily indicate there was a clear preference for EU investment, but that business, of mutual interest, between Italy and Spain was the priority.

Conclusions

The EU has one of the most liberal FDI regimes in the world, and is increasingly a host for IFDI and MNEs from emerging markets. At the same time, the EU is not immune to a general increase in concern over IFDI by governments around the world, which has been complicated considerably by the financial crisis and economic recession. Member states have, in recent years, introduced new measures that aim to restrict IFDI, particularly from third countries (Clifton, Díaz-Fuentes and Revuelta, 2010). Informal practices have also proved unfavorable to IFDI. The main justifications given by EU and national policy makers for any increase in FDI restrictions revolve around questions of "national security" and "strategic industries." Behind these concerns lies a diverse, contradictory set of interests, including bitter experiences with Europe's dependency on Russia gas, demands of incumbent business groups to protect national champions, economic nationalism sentiment, and (perhaps most importantly) knee-jerk protectionist impulses, based on fears over job losses and firm closure in the face of recession. The rise of MNEs from emerging markets is a newly emerging issue for EU leaders, and this comes at a difficult time, when the Single Market is mature though still blocked in complex sectors. These internal tensions are only compounded and intensified as new global players from emerging markets strive to enter at a time of financial crisis and economic recession, which may render distressed EU assets attractive to international investors. From a purely economic point of view, this is to be welcomed, though when the other, wider dimensions (such as long-term national interests) are considered, the picture is much less clear. The leading light in this period of relative darkness is the maturity of institutions repeatedly insisting on rational, thought-out collective action, an element missing in the 1930s.

Notes

*The first version of this chapter was presented at the Five-Diamond International Conference on "Thinking Outward: Global Players from Emerging Markets," Columbia University, April 28–29, 2008. The authors would like to thank Karl P. Sauvant, the other organizers, and Andrea Goldstein.

1. However, there are above-average levels of protectionism in Austria, Hungary, Poland, and Spain. In the case of Spain, the telecommunications sector was organized as a private monopoly, and its main players were treated as "national champions."
2. This is largely due to the investment of Sabó, a car component manufacturer, founded by a Hungarian immigrant in the 1950s, and a global supplier to Volkswagen.
3. See, for instance, Amsden (2001); International Finance Corporation (2006); Goldstein (2007); Lall (1983); Ramamurti and Singh (2009); Sauvant (2008); and UNCTAD (2006).
4. As a general rule, and according to the principles of subsidiarity and proportionality, policy should be, by "default," conducted at the national level, with European-level policy only occurring when the EU enjoys legal competence to act, and where subsidiarity and proportionality are respected.

5. An ongoing list of infringement cases is available at http://ec.europa.eu/internal_market/capital/analysis/index_en.htm.

6. Mobile telephony has been used to organize the logistics of the attacks as well as to time bomb explosions; public infrastructure (trains, metros, buses, and airplanes) has been specifically targeted for explosions; commercial airplanes were used as weapons of mass destruction; and the postal system was used for sending dangerous substances.

7. Also in September 2008, the Commission handed the German government a "final warning" on the so-called "VW law," which was found in 2007 to violate EU rules on the free flow of capital. This law prevents the car company from being taken over, as the Lower Saxony state government owns 20% of Volkswagen (Schäfer 2008).

8. The decree protects gambling and casinos, private security, research and development in substances of potential interest to terrorists, equipment designed to intercept communication, testing of information technology systems, products for information systems security, cryptology equipment, activities carried out by firms entrusted with defense secrets, research or production of arms or war materials, and activities carried out by firms for the design or supply of equipment for the Ministry of Defence.

9. Ongoing developments in the completion of the Single Market are found at http://ec.europa.eu/internal_market/capital/analysis/index_en.htm.

10. In the mid-1990s, a large minority share of Gazprom was privatized to managers and employees, but share sales were restricted. As a result, a considerable price differentiation evolved between domestic, restricted shares, and the few internationally tradable shares. Another consequence was that all Gazprom shares were extremely cheap relative to the purported asset values. Managers were shifting corporate assets to entities controlled by friends and relatives. In late 2000, journalists at the *Wall Street Journal*, the *Financial Times*, and *Business Week* began to write stories about corporate governance problems at Gazprom, based on research by Bill Browder, manager of The Hermitage Fund, a hedge fund focused on Russian investments. Eventually the CEO was fired and corporate reforms were enacted. Since late 2006, Browder has been impeded from entering Russia. Corporate governance problems resurfaced again in connection with the true nature of RosUkrEnergo, the secretive energy trader that dominates gas supplies from Central Asia to Europe. See *Financial Times* (2006).

11. In the run-up to the 2008 elections, there were rumors that Putin might succeed Medvedev as Gazprom chairperson. As it turned out, Prime Minister Viktor Zubkov took over and Putin became Prime Minister.

12. In Russia's WTO accession negotiations, some WTO members, among them Europe, argued that dual pricing acted as a trade barrier by providing unfair advantages to Russian energy-intensive companies and, therefore, that gas prices should be unified. Aldo Spanjer (2007) argued that the perceived advantages of unified Russian gas pricing to Russia, as well as Europe, are, in fact, overstated and that EU security of supply might worsen under unified gas prices.

13. On New Year's Day, following a disagreement concerning subsidized gas prices paid by Ukraine for Russian gas, Gazprom decided to reduce gas supply to this country. The Ukrainian pipeline system, however, is pivotal in supplying gas to the EU and as a consequence, the EU gas supply was affected: from January 1–3, Gazprom's gas supply to France decreased by

25–30%; supply to Austria decreased by 33%; and Italy received approximately 25% less gas than normal. Dependency on Russian supply of natural gas among large EU economies is spread between roughly one-quarter in France (where gas accounts for a relatively small share of the energy mix) and Italy to almost one-half in Germany and more than that in Poland. Across Europe, import dependence is expected to grow from roughly 50% today to more than 80%.

14. In the context of Russia's WTO accession, the EU signed its bilateral protocol in May 2004. The conflict over domestic price of natural gas (of particular relevance to producers of mineral fertilizers) was settled on conditions favorable to Russia. Although competitors are now complaining anew that the Russian domestic gas price has failed to keep pace with the increases on the world market, Gazprom is now worried that the low cost has encouraged wasteful domestic use.

15. The *Financial Times*, which originally carried the story of British opposition to any Gazprom takeover of Centrica, later backtracked.

16. Russia generates 43% of its electricity from natural gas and 23% from coal. By comparison, in the United States, 49% of the electricity is generated from coal, according to the Energy Information Administration. Gazprom has a surplus of carbon emissions credits under the terms of the Kyoto Protocol because of Russia's industrial contraction in the 1990s, and thus has spare capacity to burn more coal under the agreement, which Moscow signed. See Kramer (2008).

17. BASF, which has a 24.5% stake in the North-European Gas Pipeline Company and whose subsidiary Wintershall owns 51% of Wingas, the joint venture with Gazprom that trades Russian gas in Western Europe, has gained access rights to the Ioujno-Rousskoe fields. See the *Economist* (May 6, 2006).

18. In addition to the possibility of investing in one of the local utilities, Gazprom would like to buy a stake in SNAM, the ENI subsidiary that controls the gas transmission network. See *Corriere Economia* (2006, 2008).

19. The Energy Charter was negotiated in 1991, before Russia's new energy interests had been formed. The United States and Canada never signed the charter because of legal concerns, and Norway had other legal concerns, so it did not ratify the charter.

20. E.On is the product of the merger of former state-owned enterprises Veba and Viag electricity utilities (PreussenElektra and Bayernwerk) in 2000. It is now one of the largest energy MNEs in the world. From the outset, E.On had participations in the Czech Republic, Denmark, Italy, Latvia, the Netherlands, Poland, Russia, and Sweden. Since then, E.On acquired companies in Bulgaria, Finland, Hungary, Germany, Romania, Slovakia, Switzerland, the United Kingdom, and the United States. E.On is, however, not active in France, Portugal, Ireland, or Spain.

21. Enel is the main Italian electricity company for generation, distribution, and supply of electricity to both domestic and industrial users, and is active in Spain, Bulgaria, Romania, the Slovak Republic, Russia, France, and the Americas. Enel is also active in the purchase and sale of natural gas for domestic electricity generation and gas operations in Italy.

22. Acciona is a Spanish business corporation, whose main activities are the development and management of infrastructure and real estate projects, the provision of transport, urban, and environmental services, as well as the development and operation of renewable energies.

References

Amsden, Alice (2001). *The Rise of the Rest: Challenges to the West from Late-Industrializing Economies* (Oxford: Oxford University Press).

Antkiewicz, Agata and John Whalley (2006). "Recent Chinese buyout activity and the implications for global architecture," NBER working paper series, 12072, National Bureau of Economic Research, MA, mimeo.

Åslund, Anders (2006). "Gazprom's Strategy." Testimony before Hearing on EU Economic and Trade Relations with Russia, Committee on International Trade, European Parliament, Brussels, November 21.

Benoit, Bertrand (2007). "Germany plans for own CFIUS deal watchdog," *Financial Times* September 27.

Bouquet, Tim and Bryon Ousey (2008). *Cold Steel: the Multi-billion Dollar Battle for a Global Industry* (New York: Little Brown).

Burnett, Victoria and Peter Kiefer (2007). "Italian banks win control of Telecom Italia," *International Herald Tribune*, April 29.

Business Week (2006). "Why Russians love Gazprom—no matter what the world thinks," *Business Week*, July 31.

Catan, Thomas (2006). "Interview: Alexander Medvedev of gazprom," *Financial Times*, May 29.

Clifton, Judith, Francisco Comín, and Daniel Díaz-Fuentes (2003). *Privatization in the European Union* (Dordrecht: Kluwer).

——— (2007). *Transforming Public Enterprise in Europe and the Americas: Networks, Integration and Transnationalisation* (Houndsmill: Palgrave).

——— (2008). "The rise of the new public service transnationals," in Harm Schroeter, ed., *The European Enterprise: Historical Investigation in a Future Species* (Dordrecht: Springer), pp. 209–22.

Clifton, Judith and Daniel Díaz-Fuentes (2010). "Evaluating EU policies on Public Services: A Citizens' Perspective," *Annals of Public and Cooperative Economics* 81 (2) pp. 281–311.

Clifton, Judith, Daniel Díaz-Fuentes, and Julio Revuelta (forthcoming). "The political economy of telecoms and electricity internationalization in the single market," *Journal of European Public Policy* 17 (7).

Corriere Economia (2006). "C'è Hera nel mirino di Gazprom," *Corriere Economia*, March 27.

——— (2008). "Gazprom preme su Eni," *Corriere Economia*, February 25.

Costas, Antón (2007). "De consumidor a ciudadano. El papel de la calidad del servicio de los mercados de servicios públicos," *Información comercial española* 836, pp. 35–50.

Economist (2005). "Russia's energetic enigma," *Economist*, October 8.

——— (2006). "Divided and panicky: the EU and Gazprom," *Economist*, May 6.

Economist Intelligence Unit and Columbia Program on International Investment (2007). *World Investment Prospects to 2011: Boom or Backlash?* (Economist Intelligence Unit and Columbia Program on International Investment).

El País (2007). "Vuelven los dineros con acento árabe," *El País*, September 30, p. 7.

Euractiv (2007) "'Gazprom clause' issues Russia ultimatum for energy co-operation," September 20, www.euractiv.com, last visited March 31, 2008.

European Commission (2006). "Energy Policy," Special Eurobarometer, available at http://ec.europa.eu/public_opinion/archives/ebs/ebs_258_en.pdf, last visited November 10, 2008.

——— (2007). "Free movement of capital: Commission scrutinizes amendments in Hungarian company law," Brussels: EC, available at http://europa.eu/rapid/

pressReleasesAction.do?reference=IP/07/1681&format=HTML&aged=0&language=EN&guiLanguage=en, last visited November 10, 2008.

European Commission (2008a). "Commission v. Spain: judgment of the Court of Justice in Case C-207/07," available at http://curia.europa.eu/en/actu/communiques/cp08/aff/cp080054en.pdf, last visited November 10, 2008.

——— (2008b). "A common European approach to sovereign wealth funds," COM(2008) 115 final (Brussels: Commission of the European Communities), available at http://ec.europa.eu/commission_barroso/president/pdf/COM2008_115_en.pdf, last visited June 14, 2008.

——— (2008c). "Free movement of capital: Commission refers Portugal to European Court of Justice over special rights held by State in EDP," available at http://europa.eu/rapid/pressReleasesAction.do?reference=IP/08/1357&format=HTML&aged=0&language=EN&guiLanguage=en, last visited November 10, 2008.

——— (2008d). "Free movement of capital: Commission refers Portugal to European Court of Justice over special rights held by State in Portugal Telecom," available at http://europa.eu/rapid/pressReleasesAction.do?reference=IP/08/120&type=HTML&aged=0&language=EN&guiLanguage=en, last visited November 10, 2008.

——— (2008e). "Standard Eurobarometer 69," available at http://ec.europa.eu/public_opinion/archives/eb/eb69/eb_69_first_en.pdf, last visited November 10, 2008.

European Council (2006). "Presidency Conclusions," available at http://ue.eu.int/ueDocs/cms_Data/docs/pressData/en/ec/89013.pdf, last visited November 10, 2008.

Financial Times (2006). "Gazprom's secretive Ukrainian partner tells of lone struggle to build business," *Financial Times*, April 23.

——— (2008). "Kremlin celebrates Gazprom's power," *Financial Times*, February 13.

Goldstein, Andrea (2007). *Multinational Companies from Emerging Economies* (Houndsmill: Palgrave).

——— (2008). "Who's afraid of the emerging-market TNCs? Or: are developing countries missing something in the globalization debate?" in Karl P. Sauvant with Kristin Mendoza and Irmak Ince, ed., *The Rise of Transnational Corporations from Emerging Markets: Threat or Opportunity?* (Cheltenham: Edward Elgar), pp. 183–203.

Goldthau, Andreas (2008). "Rhetoric versus reality: Russian threats to European energy supply," *Energy Policy* 36 (2), pp. 686–92.

Government Accountability Office (2008). *Foreign Investment: Law and Policies Regulating Foreign Investment in Ten Countries* (Washington: GAO), available at http://www.gao.gov/new.items/d08320.pdf, last visited November 10, 2008.

Grigoryev, Yuli (2007). "Today or not today: deregulating the Russian gas sector," *Energy Policy* 35 (5), pp. 3036–45.

International Finance Corporation (2006). *Southern Multinationals: A Rising Force in the World Economy* (Washington, DC: International Finance Corporation and *Financial Times*).

Klinova, Marina (2007). "Privatization and transnationalisation of Russian enterprises," in Judith Clifton, Francisco Comín, and Daniel Díaz-Fuentes, eds., *Transforming Public* Enterprise (Houndsmill: Palgrave), pp. 157–71.

Kramer, Andrew (2008). "Gazprom moves into coal as a way to increase gas exports," *New York Times*, February 27.

Lall, Sanjaya (1983). *The Multinational Corporation* (London: Macmillan).

Lapper, Richard and Jonathan Wheatley (2008). "Higher ground: Vale signals the rise of the multilatina," *Financial Times*, March 10.

Lund Sagen, Eirik and Marina Tsygankova (2008). "Russian natural gas exports: will Russian gas price reforms improve the European security of supply," *Energy Policy* 36 (2), pp. 867–80.

MacDonald, Neil (2008). "Gazprom raises offer for Serbia oil and gas group," *Financial Times*, January 16.

Mandil, Claude (2006). "Russia must act to avert a gas supply crisis," *Financial Times*, March 22.

Le Monde (2005). "Dominique de Villepin en appelle au patriotisme économique," *Le Monde*, July 29.

OECD (2002). *OECD Economic Surveys: The Russian Federation* (Paris: OECD).

—— (2003). *Experiences from the Regional Corporate Governance Roundtables* (Paris: OECD), available at http://www.oecd.org/dataoecd/19/26/23742340.pdf, last visited April 16, 2008.

—— (2007). *International Investment Perspectives 2007* (Paris: OECD).

—— (2009). "Foreign government-controlled investors and recipient country investment policies: a scoping paper" (Paris: OECD), mimeo.

Ostrovsky, Arkady (2006). "Energy of the state: how Gazprom acts as lever in Putin's power play," *Financial Times*, March 13.

Ramamurti, Ravi and Jitendra Singh (2009). *Emerging Multinationals in Emerging Markets* (Cambridge: Cambridge University Press).

Renaissance Capital (2008). *Economic and Political Update: 7 April 2008*, available at http://www.rencap.com/eng/, last visited April 14, 2008.

Sauvant, Karl P., with Kristin Mendoza and Irmak Ince, eds. (2008). *The Rise of Transnational Corporations from Emerging Markets: Threat or Opportunity* (Cheltenham: Edward Elgar).

Schäfer, Daniel (2008). "Germany handed final warning over VW law," *Financial Times*, September 10.

Schipani, Andres (2008). "Bolivia signs gas deal with Gazprom," *Financial Times*, March 18.

Schulz, Martin (2008). "A return of protectionism? Internal deregulation and external investment restrictions in the EU," *Discussion Paper 08–04* (Tokyo: Fujitsu Research Institute, Economic Research Centre), mimeo.

Spanjer, Aldo (2007). "Russian gas price reform and the EU–Russia gas relationship: incentives, consequences and European security of supply," *Energy Policy* 35 (5), pp. 2889–98.

Thomas, Stephen (2003). "The seven brothers," *Energy Policy* 31 (5), pp. 393–403.

Traynor, Ian (2007). "Gazprom told to slim to compete in Europe," *Guardian*, September 20.

UNCTAD (2006). *World Investment Report: FDI from Developing and Transition Economies: Implications for Development* (New York and Geneva: United Nations).

—— (2007). *World Investment Report: Transnational Corporations, Extractive Industries and Development* (New York and Geneva: United Nations).

—— (2008). *World Investment Report: Transnational Corporations and the Infrastructure Challenge* (New York and Geneva: United Nations).

—— (2009) *World Investment Report: Transnational Corporations, Agricultural Production and Development* (New York and Geneva: United Nations).

Walker, Marcus (2008). "Germany tinkers with foreign takeovers plan," *Wall Street Journal*, January 14.

Williamson, Hugh (2006). "Putin hits out at European investment 'double standards'" *Financial Times*, April 28.

Wolf, Martin (2007). "Why plutocracy endangers emerging markets," *Financial Times*, November 7.

Chapter 18

Is the United States Ready for Foreign Direct Investment from Emerging Markets? The Case of China*

Karl P. Sauvant

Introduction

Among emerging market multinational enterprises (MNEs), none have received more attention than those headquartered in China. Within the span of fewer than ten years (2000–2007), they invested an estimated US$68 billion abroad, for a total stock of US$96 billion at the end of 2007 (figures 18.1 and 18.2), catapulting China into the ranks of the leading outward investors among emerging markets. This investment takes place in all sectors (and especially services) (table 18.1) and regions of the world (table 18.2), "through more than 5,000 Chinese investment entities [having] established nearly 10,000 overseas enterprises through direct investment across 172 countries and/or economies" (OECD 2008, 71).[1]

Although there are many firms that undertake outward foreign direct investment (OFDI), the great majority of the largest Chinese MNEs consists of state-owned enterprises (SOEs), administered by the central government. They accounted for 83% of OFDI flows in 2005; by the end of 2005, their share of OFDI stock was 84% (Cheng and Ma 2007, 15).[2] Eighteen among the largest had, in 2006, US$79 billion of foreign assets, employed over 120,000 persons abroad, and had US$79 billion in sales by their foreign affiliates (table 18.3). Like their competitors from developed countries (and, for that matter, also increasingly from other emerging markets), Chinese firms rely more and more on mergers and acquisitions (M&As) rather than greenfield investment when entering foreign markets (tables 18.4 and 18.5).

Even though China's OFDI position may not look that impressive when compared with that of other, especially developed, countries, what needs to be taken into account is that Chinese firms only recently have begun their outward expansion and that it is only since the beginning of 2001 that the government supports this trend through its "Go Global" policy.[3] Moreover, outflows may well grow considerably in the coming years. During 2008,

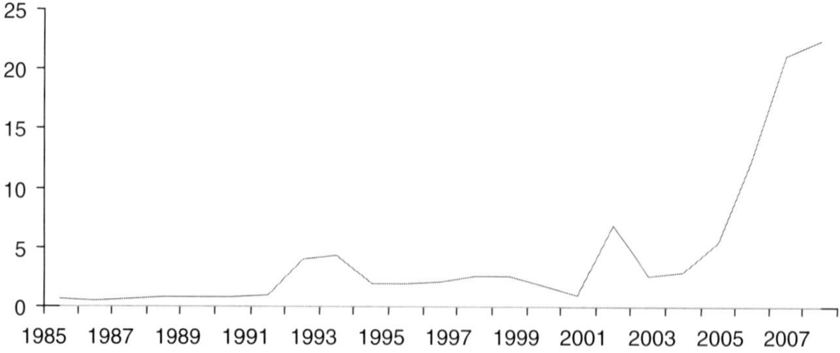

Figure 18.1 China's outward FDI flows, 1985–2007 (US$ billions)
Source: UNCTAD, http://stats.unctad.org/FDI/.

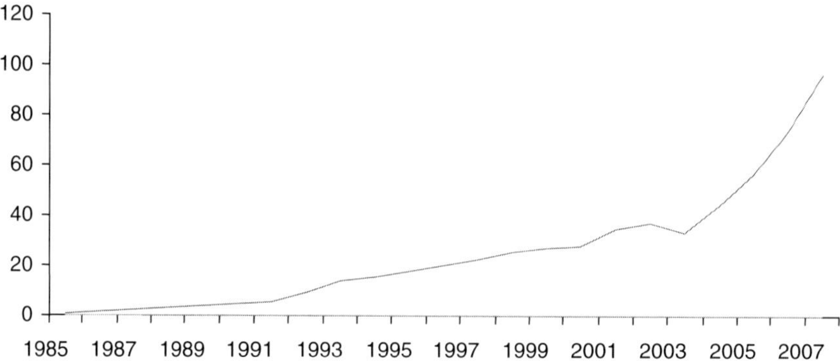

Figure 18.2 China's outward FDI stock, 1985–2007 (US$ billions)

nonfinancial Chinese MNEs invested roughly twice at much abroad (over US$50 billion) than during 2007 (US$22 billion); during 2009—when world FDI flows dropped by some 40%—outflows from China appeared to have remained about the same as in the year before. If China's sovereign wealth fund (SWF), the China Investment Corporation, should become more active in the FDI market, this figure could rapidly become higher, although the financial crisis and recession may well temporarily slow down outward FDI (OFDI) flows.

These developments raise an important question: is the world ready for FDI—and especially M&As—from emerging markets? To put it differently: can emerging market MNEs be integrated smoothly into the world FDI market, as part of a broader integration of these economies into the world economy? It is a question that needs to be asked because there are some indications that some countries have difficulties accepting "the new kids on the block" (Sauvant 2009). And it is a question to be asked especially for MNEs based in China, as their outward expansion—from Africa to the United States—is receiving considerable attention from the media and from policy makers.

Table **18.1** Sectoral distribution of China's OFDI stock, 2006 (US$ millions)

Primary sector	18.718 (25%)
Agriculture, forestry, husbandry and fishery	807 (1%)
Mining, quarrying and petroleum	17.902 (24%)
Secondary sector (manufacturing)	7.530 (10%)
Tertiary sector	48.778 (65%)
Lease and business services	19.464 (26%)
Wholesale and retail	12.955 (17%)
Transport and storage	7.568 (10%)
Others	8.791 (12%)
Total	75.026 (100%)

Source: OECD, *OECD Investment Policy Reviews: China 2008* (2008, 136).

Table **18.2** Regional distribution of OFDI stock from China, 2006 (US$ millions)

Asia	47,978 (64%)
Hong Kong, China (as a share of Asia)	42,270 (88%)
Latin America (LA)	19,694 (26%)
3 offshore financial centers (as a share of LA)	18,977 (96%)
Europe	2,270 (3%)
Western Europe (as a share of Europe)	1,050 (46%)
Central and Eastern Europe (as a share of Europe)	1,220 (54%)
Africa	2,557 (3%)
North America	1,584 (2%)
Oceania	939 (1%)
Total	75,026 (100%)

Source: OECD (2008, 135).

Table **18.3** FUDAN-VCC ranking of eighteen large Chinese multinational enterprises in terms of foreign assets, 2006 (US$ millions)

Rank	Name	Industry	Foreign assets	Foreign sales	Foreign employment
1	CITIC Group	Diversified	17,623	2,482	18,305
2	China Ocean Shipping (Group) Co.	Transport and storage	10,397	8,777	4,432
3	China State Construction Engineering Corp.	Construction and real estate	6,831	4,376	5,820
4	China National Petroleum Corp.	Petroleum (exploration / refining / distribution)	6,374	3,036	22,000
5	Sinochem Corp.	Petroleum and fertilizer	5,326	19,374	220
6	China Poly Group Corp.	Trade, real estate	5,113	1,750	na
7	China National Offshore Oil Corp.	Petroleum and natural gas	4,984	3,719	984

Continued

Table 18.3 Continued

Rank	Name	Industry	Foreign assets	Foreign sales	Foreign employment
8	Shougang Group	Diversified	4,875	2,250	n.a.
9	China Shipping (Group) Co.	Diversified	4,600	4,324	2,433
10	TCL Corp.	Electrical and electronic equipment	3,875	3,366	32,078
11	Lenovo Group	Computer and related activities	3,147	9,002	6,200
12	China Minmetals Corp.	Metals and metal products	1,266	2,527	630
13	China Communications Construction Corp.	Construction	1,162	2,855	1,078
14	Shum Yip Holdings Company Ltd.	Real estate	972	123	28
15	Baosteel Group Corp.	Diversified	968	4,231	170
16	Shanghai Automotive Industry Corporation (Group)	Automotives	442	4,133	7,175
17	China Metallurgical Group Corp.	Diversified	439	314	745
18	Haier Group	Manufacturing, telecommunications, IT	394	1,870	6,800
TOTAL			78,788	78,509	123,670

Source: School of Management at Fudan University—Vale Columbia Center on Sustainable International Investment (FUDAN-VCC) survey of Chinese MNEs.

Note: NA—Not available.

Table 18.4 M&As vs. China's OFDI, 1988–2006

	1988–1989 (average)	1990–1991 (average)	2000–2002 (average)	2003	2004	2005	2006
China's deals (US$ millions)	109	430	3,561	1,647	1,125	5,279	14,904
As a ratio of total OFDI flow (%)	13.9	16.7	43.6	57.7	20.5	43.1	84.5

Source: OECD (2008, 75).

This chapter focuses on one subset of this question, namely: Is the *United States* ready for FDI—and especially M&As—from China? The question is all the more important as Chinese FDI in the United States, while still small (table 18.6 and figure 18.3), is bound to rise. After all, the United States is the single biggest and most attractive market in the world, and most firms think they need to establish themselves there, to include the country in their portfolios of locational assets. This applies also to Chinese firms.

Table 18.5 Major OFDI deals by Chinese enterprises, 2004–2007

Chinese Enterprises	Invested project / acquired asset	Host country	Estimated investment amount (US$ billions)	Year	Comment	Major motivation
Wuhan Iron and Steel and other three stell mill companies	Wheelara joint-venture with BHP Billiton for mining iron ore	Australia	9.3	2004	Agreement signed	(1) Iron ore
CNPC	Petrokazakhstan	Canada / Kazakhstan	4.18	2005	Acquired	(1) Oil
China Minmetals	CODELCO	Chile	0.55	2005	Agreement signed	(1) Copper
Sinopec	99.49% stake in Udmurtneft OAO	Russia	3.65	2006	Acquired	(1) Oil
CITIC	Kazakh oil assets of Nations Energy Company	Canada / Kazakhstan	1.91	2006	Acquired	(1) Oil and (4)
China Metallurgical Group	Aynak copper field and related infrastructure project	Afghanistan	2.8	2007	Agreement signed	(1) Copper
Shanghai Baosteel	Joint-venture with Companhia Vale do Rio Doce for a steel slab plant	Brazil	3–4	2007	Letter of intent signed	(1) Steel
Sinopec	Development of Yadavaran onshore oil field	Iran	2	2007	Agreement signed	(1) Oil
Industrial and Commercial Bank of China	20% stake in Standard Bank	South Africa	5.49	2007	Completed	(2) and (4)
Bank of China	669 branches including a recent opening at London	28 countries	40% of its net profits from overseas	By 2007	By 2007	(2) and (4)
Lenovo	IBM (PC hardware division)	United States	1.75	2004	Completed	(3) Computer
Nanjing Auto	MG Rover	United Kingdom	N/A	2005	Completed	(3) Automobile

Continued

Table 18.5 Continued

Chinese Enterprises	Invested project / acquired asset	Host country	Estimated investment amount (US$ billions)	Year	Comment	Major motivation
China Mobile	China Resources Peoples Telephone	Hong Kong (China)	0.43	2005	Completed	(4)
Bank of China	Singapore Aircraft Leasing Enterprise	Singapore	3.43	2006	Completed	(4)
State Grid Corporation	Consortium led bu the Philippines' Monte Ore Grid Resources for grid operation privatisation	Philippines	3.95	2007	Bid awarded	(4)
Failed Deals						
China Minmetals	Noranda	Canada	5	2004	Aborted	(1) Copper and zinc
CNOOC	Unocal	United States	19.5	2005	Aborted	Oil
Haier	Maytag	United States	1.28	2005	Aborted	Washing machine
China Mobile	Millicom International Cellular	Luxembourg	5.3	2007	Aborted	(3)

Source: OECD (2008, 95).

Note: Major motivations include (1) resource seeking; (2) market seeking; (3) strategic asset seeking; (4) diversification seeking; and (5) efficiency seeking

NA-Not Available

Table **18.6** China's foreign direct investment into the U.S., 2002–2007

Year	(US$ millions)
2002	385
2003	284
2004	435
2005	574
2006	973
2007	1091

Source: U.S. Bureau of Economic Analysis, http://www.bea.gov.

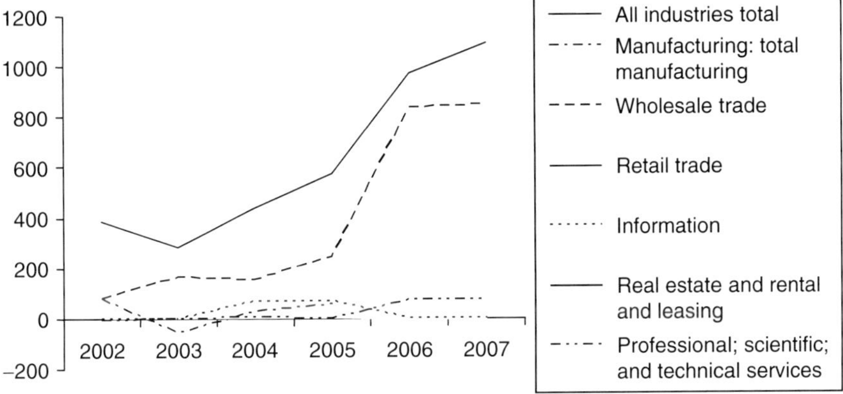

Figure 18.3 Chinese FDI in the United States, by industry, 2002–2007ª (US$ billions)

Source: U.S. Bureau of Economic Analysis data, www.bea.gov.

ªForeign direct investment position in the U.S. on a historical-cost basis.

The short answer to that question is "yes." Indeed, the United States has one of the most open investment frameworks in the world, and its states and many municipalities actively seek to attract FDI. The long answer is still "yes," but with a number of qualifications attached to it, as there are all sorts of tricky and difficult issues that need to be taken into account by emerging market MNEs in general, and by Chinese MNEs wishing to enter the U.S. market in particular. The focus of this chapter is these tricky and difficult issues and how foreign firms can deal with them in terms of entering, operating in, and prospering in the U.S. market.

18.1 Entering the U.S. Market

18.1.1 *Mergers and Acquisitions vs. Greenfield FDI*

For many firms, the typical way to establish themselves in a foreign country is through mergers and acquisitions (M&As), as opposed to greenfield investments (i.e., the establishment of new production facilities). In fact, in developed countries, the bulk of FDI takes place through this mode of entry. In 2007, there were 10,145 cross-border M&As globally, valued at US$1.6 trillion; of these, 78% of the M&As and 89% of the total value involved developed countries (UNCTAD 2008). This compares with FDI inflows to developed countries of US$1.2 trillion in the same year.[4] The United States is no exception to this pattern. In 2007, there were 2,040 M&As undertaken in this country by foreign firms, at a value of US$380 billion; in the same year, FDI inflows amounted to US$230 billion (ibid.).

M&As and greenfield investments both have a number of advantages and disadvantages for firms and host countries (Globerman and Shapiro 2010; UNCTAD 2000). For firms, M&As have the advantage of allowing them to enter a market rapidly—and in today's globalizing world economy, in which competition is everywhere, speed is often of the essence. Moreover, if the acquired firm controls an extensive distribution network, state-of-the-art research and development (R&D) facilities, and valuable brand names, the acquiring firm obtains a portfolio of locational and proprietary assets that are key to international competitiveness. Deep market penetration can be achieved quickly in this manner, which is also useful if the acquiring firm already exports to the foreign market. If experienced staff can be retained in the acquired firm, the acquiring firm minimizes learning costs associated with operating in a new market; in fact, it obtains local knowledge and skills, as well as a network of relationships that can be important for prospering in a new environment.

However, cross-border M&As also involve a number of difficulties and risks. To begin with, the proper target needs to be identified, and a deal needs to be negotiated. If the corporate cultures of the acquiring and acquired firms differ substantially—and this is likely to be the case if the acquiring firm is from China (or, for that matter, any other emerging market) and the acquired firm is in the United States—there is the additional challenge of meshing different cultures. At the same time, the new unit needs to be incorporated into the international production network of the parent firm. This, in turn, may involve a restructuring of the acquired assets, including the closing down of existing production lines, the relocation of R&D facilities, and layoffs—all actions that may encounter the resistance of labor unions; local, regional, or national authorities; and other stakeholders. In fact, resistance may already start earlier, especially if stakeholders—rightly or wrongly—anticipate some of these actions (and others, such as increase in concentration and therefore a possible decrease in competition) once an M&A is consummated. Resistance in the host country can be particularly high if the target is in a sector that is considered of great economic or strategic importance or involves a national champion, or if the acquirer is an SOE, especially from an emerging market (which would typically be the case for Chinese MNEs, as most of the important ones have some percentage of state ownership).

Given all these difficulties and risks, it is not surprising that many M&As have not lived up to their expectations and that a number have even been unwound. Even long-established MNEs may not succeed—witness the acquisition of Chrysler by Daimler Benz, a move that was undone after a few years. However, many M&As do succeed. The secret is careful planning, experience, and having the skills and patience to navigate the difficulties and risks that are inherent in cross-border M&As.

Greenfield investments allow a firm to start from scratch, beginning with the choice of the location; they are unencumbered by various legacy costs and practices that are established in an acquisition target.[5] However, it takes time to establish a greenfield investment and to develop a network of relationships, and it requires more learning in terms of operating in a new environment.

Moreover, greenfield investments are uniformly welcomed by host countries (and typically even benefit from various incentives) as they create new production capacity, whereas M&As represent only a change in ownership and the shifting of control of a domestic entity to a parent firm headquartered abroad. Greenfield investments also mean new jobs, and they may bring new technologies, skills, competition, and exports. Exceptional circumstances aside (like a rescue operation of a firm in danger of failing), governments prefer greenfield investments to M&As. This preference holds even though the positive economic effects of greenfield investments and M&As converge over time and, hence, do not support discrimination between these two forms of market entry (UNCTAD 2000).

18.1.2 *The Regulatory Environment*

These different perceptions of M&As and greenfield investments by host countries find their expression in the regulatory framework that governs FDI in the United States, with the former investments potentially facing scrutiny, whereas the latter are uniformly welcome. In fact, the United States has one of the most open investment frameworks in the world, reaffirmed in May 2007 in a statement on "Open economies" by President George W. Bush and the establishment of "Invest in America" within the Department of Commerce.[6] Moreover, virtually all states of the Union fiercely compete for FDI. Many of them have established investment promotion offices abroad. Hence the short answer of "yes" to the question: "is the United States ready for FDI from China?"

But, the "rise of the rest" (Zakaria 2008)—meaning especially FDI from emerging markets—is creating adjustment problems that are also visible in U.S.-China relations. As former U.S. Secretary of the Treasury, Henry M. Paulson, remarked: "Economic nationalism…has been a growing concern in the United States in recent years….Foreign investment into the United States, especially by SWFs and SOEs, is also increasingly viewed with suspicion by some U.S. companies, various members of the national security community, and the American public at large, despite regulations by the Committee on Foreign Investment in the United States that provide sufficient protections in sensitive sectors" (Paulson 2008, 72).

In the aftermath of September 11, 2001, in particular, national security concerns have entered the realm of the FDI field, mixed with apprehension about the rise of emerging market MNEs, especially from countries that are considered to be potentially unfriendly or strategic competitors. The importance of SOEs in the OFDI of a number of emerging markets and the growing role of government-controlled SWFs add to this apprehension. Among emerging markets, China receives particular attention, precisely because it is seen as an important strategic competitor and because the bilateral balance-of-payments deficit of the United States with China, combined with what is regarded an undervalued Chinese currency, are held responsible for some of the difficulties that the U.S. economy is experiencing.

The result has been the strengthening of the established screening mechanism for FDI, the Committee on Foreign Investment in the United States (CFIUS). Originally provided with formal authority to review foreign investments with a nexus on U.S. national security interests in the late 1980s, the Committee's role in screening certain FDI was further enhanced through the Foreign Investment and National Security Act of 2007 (FINSA), and the subsequent President's Executive Order of January 2008, and the final regulations issued by the Treasury Department (which entered into force on November 21, 2008) (see Fagan 2010).

In brief, the precise legal and institutional framework for any given investment in the United States depends largely on the facts and circumstances relating to any particular investment, including the nature of the transaction, the location of an investment (which may determine what local laws or institutions can impact prospects for success), the sector of an investment, the size of the investment, and specific facts of a particular transaction (such as the legal compliance reputation of the acquirer and U.S. target and the potential broader legal liabilities of the U.S. target). In the case of M&As, furthermore, U.S. antitrust legislation may well come into play. All this makes the U.S. FDI framework less predictable than it was in the past.

Foreign investors undertaking M&As in the United States must pay special attention to the security review conducted by CFIUS. (Greenfield investments are exempted by statute and regulation from review by CFIUS.) In particular, there is a presumption that M&As by state-controlled entities are subject to additional scrutiny in the form of an "investigation," which follows an initial thirty-day review, unless certain statutory triggers (related to senior-level sign-off within the CFIUS process and the absence of any remaining national security issues) for terminating the review at thirty days are met. Figure 18.4 presents, succinctly, the principal aspects of this process. The critical threshold questions for a CFIUS review are whether there is foreign control over a U.S. business; if there is control, whether a transaction presents any significant national security concerns; and if there are such concerns, whether they can be mitigated through contractual commitments from the parties involved ("mitigation agreements"). Importantly, "national security" is not defined.

The CFIUS process can be crucial for Chinese MNEs, as most of the biggest are state-controlled entities. This creates special challenges for Chinese MNEs (as well as for state-controlled entities of other countries) to obtain regulatory approval and manage the potential for a particular transaction becoming an object of political debate (e.g., the aborted takeover attempt of UNOCAL by CNOOC and the acquisition by Dubai Ports World of the Peninsular and Oriental Steam Navigation Company, which operated terminals at six major U.S. ports).

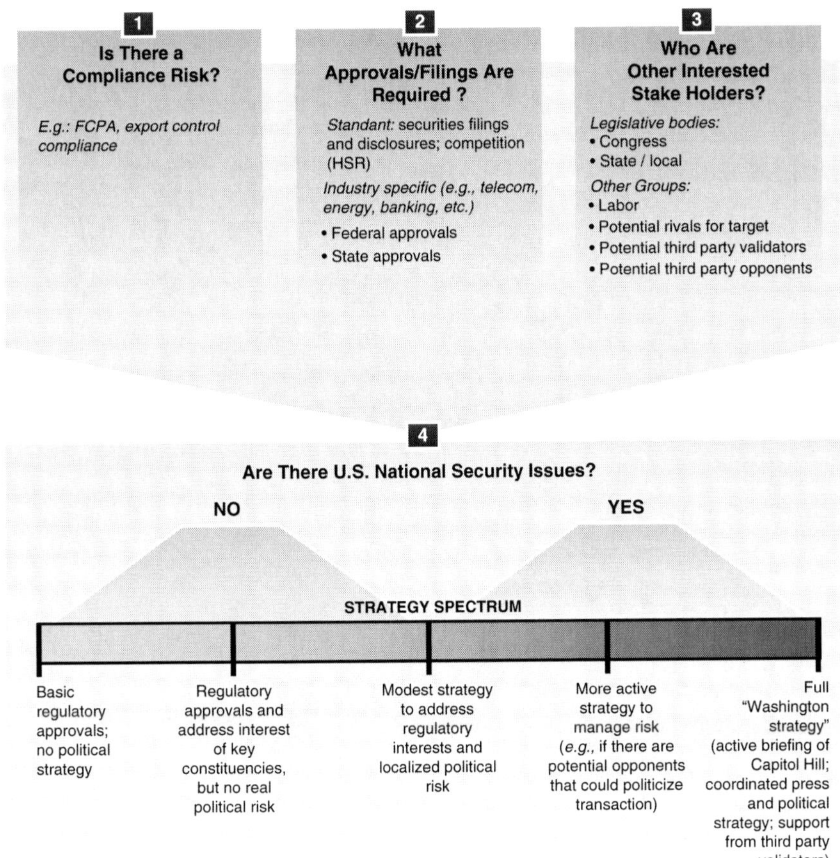

Figure 18.4 The U.S. regulatory and strategic due diligence flowchart for cross-border M&As

Source: David N. Fagan, "The U.S. regulatory and institutional framework for FDI" (copyright Covington & Burling LLP) in Karl P. Sauvant, ed., *Investing in the United States: Is the US Ready for FDI from China?*, op. cit., chapter 2.

Notifications to CFIUS were up considerably in 2007 and 2008 (figure 18.5), reflecting the changed investment climate in the United States. Even though no deals were blocked, six were subject to investigation in 2007 and twenty-two in 2008. In February 2008, a filing involving a minority Chinese investment in a U.S. telecoms firm was withdrawn in the face of national security concerns. While the data certainly shows a substantial increase in scrutiny, the numbers involved are small compared to the total number of cross-border M&As in the United States. Still, the growing number of CFIUS notifications and investigations signal that the regulatory framework for FDI in the United States is changing.

Developing an appropriate regulatory and political strategy is particularly important for MNEs entering the United States through M&As and prospering in that country, as it is not only the various agencies that make up CFIUS that decide on a specific deal, but Congress itself and the entire

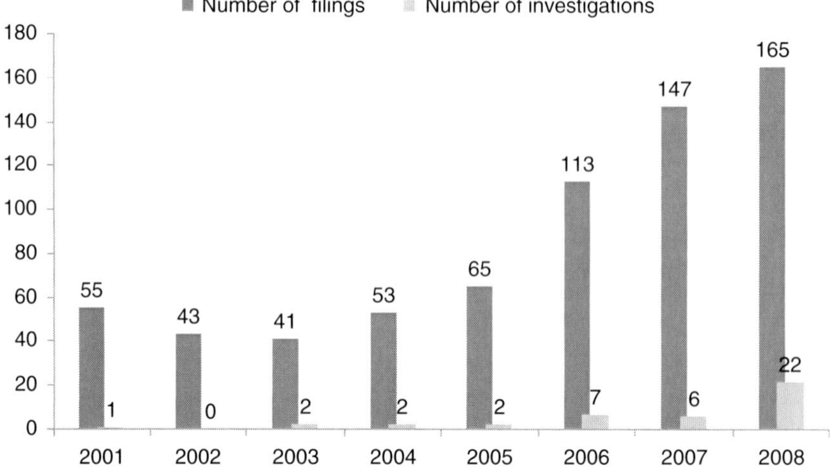

Figure 18.5   CFIUS filings and investigations, 2001–2008
Source: U.S. Treasury Department.

political establishment can get involved. This is especially true when high-profile transactions are contemplated—and any large M&A by a Chinese firm potentially falls into this category. Navigating the U.S. political land-scape for FDI is, indeed, a real challenge for foreign investors, not only inves-tors from China (Frye and Pinto 2010).

The dynamics in this landscape are complex. U.S. presidents, respon-sible for the country as a whole, have generally been supportive of a liberal investment framework, although they also need to take national security concerns into account (see the statement of President Bush mentioned earlier). Within the executive branch, the cross-pressures between open-ness and national security are balanced in CFIUS in the context of specific M&As, as its members represent a wide range of approaches and interests. But for individual members of Congress, the situation is different, because they represent individual districts. As a result, members of Congress need to deliver benefits to their own districts if they want to be reelected by their constituents, especially if representatives hold marginal seats. Depending on how members of Congress see themselves affected by China in gen-eral and the country's FDI in particular, they will seek to shape policies accordingly.

Members of Congress interested in China have organized themselves into political groups, most important among them the Congressional China Caucus and the U.S.-China Working Group. The former focuses on the strategic and political concerns associated with China (and is typically critical of China); the latter focuses on the economic opportunities that result from engaging China (and therefore is typically pro-China). The saliency of these groups can be illustrated in reference to the vote in the House of Representatives in June 2005 on a resolution that called upon the president to "initiate imme-diately a thorough review of the proposed acquisition, merger or takeover" if

UNOCAL accepted CNOOC's bid. The resolution was passed by a vote of 398 to 15. Tellingly, eight of the fifteen representatives who voted against the resolution were from the U.S.-China Working Group, while not one member of the Congressional China Caucus opposed it. In addition, six of the fifteen "no" votes came from representatives of districts in the state of Washington, a state that has substantial exports to China.

Moreover, beyond the executive branch and Congress, there are many other stakeholders that have an interest in the China-U.S. relationship in general and FDI from China in particular. Figure 18.6 lists a number of them and their overall orientation and attitude.

What this underlines is that M&As by Chinese firms in the United States are not only an economic issue—they are, especially when it comes to larger acquisitions in sensitive sectors, as much or more a political issue, even if they make economic sense. Hence, to smooth the entry process, it is important to understand Washington's political landscape, know what the interests of key

		General attitude	
		Relatively pro-China	Relatively anti-China
Motivation	Economic	Financial firms (private equity, M&A players) Business associations (Business Roundtable, Financial Services Forum) Liberal think tanks (IIE; OFFI) Congress: U.S.-China Working Group U.S. states actively seeking foreign investment The public: richer, more educated people who value cosmopolitanism	Labor leaders and unions Conservative think tanks (American Enterprise Inst.; Heritage Foundation) Labor-affiliated think tanks Congress: Congressional China Caucus House membership The public: antiglobalization and concerned about trade with China and "U.S. jobs"; human rights advocates
	Nationalistic/ strategic	"Panda huggers" in defense community (none identified)	U.S. military; security community Congress: Congressional China Caucus The public: slight tendency to be wary of China for people concerned about U.S. military superiority

Figure 18.6   U.S. stakeholders' position on economic liberalization toward China

Source: Timothy Frye and Pablo M. Pinto, "The politics of Chinese investment in the US", in Karl P. Sauvant, ed., *Investing in the United States: Is the US Ready for FDI from China?*, op. cit.

players are, learn to navigate the committee network in Congress, and build alliances from the local level upward.

18.2　Operating

Once the mode of entry (M&A vs. greenfield investment) has been chosen and regulatory barriers have been navigated, the challenge for foreign investors—and Chinese ones in particular—is to operate successfully in the highly competitive, sophisticated, and litigious U.S. market and prosper in it. To do that, foreign investors need to overcome the "liability of foreignness" (Eden and Miller 2010). As observed by one of the leading academics in the FDI field many years ago: "Alien status always imposes some penalty on managerial effectiveness" (Caves 1971, 6). "Liability of foreignness," therefore, is the liability of being a stranger in a strange land. It revolves around a number of costs that foreign firms—but not domestic ones—incur by operating abroad. These involve, most notably, unfamiliarity costs arising from a lack of knowledge about the host country; the potential (and sometimes subtle) differential treatment of foreign affiliates by host country organizations and institutions; costs arising out of the need to manage relations between the parent firm and its foreign affiliate; and the relations of foreign affiliates and local partners and stakeholders from a distance. These costs can be particularly high if the gap between the regulatory, normative, and cognitive situations in the home country (e.g., China) and the host country (e.g., the United States) is high. The challenge to handle such costs is accentuated for firms from a country with weaker institutions that need to operate in countries with stronger institutions.

Chinese MNEs certainly face the entire range of liability-of-foreignness costs when establishing themselves in the United States. On the regulatory side, they need to operate in a country with a highly developed legal system and a strong legal culture. Naturally, the entire set of laws and regulations governing enterprises applies to Chinese foreign affiliates. Some regulatory instruments that are particularly relevant relate to corrupt practices, corporate governance, financial practices, foreign trade, transfer pricing, occupational health, labor safety, civil rights, age discrimination, and employees with disabilities. In addition, a number of industries are subject to sector-specific federal and state regulatory regimes (e.g., banking, telecommunications). All this adds up to a complex regulatory framework that is typically enforced at the federal or state level or both. Foreign affiliates are well advised to observe these laws and regulations scrupulously, lest their operations risk legal difficulties. This is a particular challenge for Chinese firms as they typically have little experience with operating foreign affiliates, including in the United States.

At the same time, Chinese firms established in the United States (like those of other countries) benefit from various protections against unwarranted action by the authorities, contained in U.S. national and international investment laws (Kantor 2010), the latter even though there is no investment treaty between the United States and China.[7] Most important are the World

Trade Organization (WTO) General Agreement on Trade in Services (the GATS Agreement, which, in "Mode 3," provides a number of protections to service businesses conducted through a "commercial presence" [akin to FDI] in the United States) and the WTO Agreement on Trade-Related Investment Measures (the TRIMs Agreement) (prohibiting certain performance requirements). The enforcement of both these agreements occurs via the state-to-state dispute settlement mechanism in the WTO Dispute Settlement Understanding. The normal remedy for breach of the GATS or TRIMs agreements is withdrawal of trade benefits, a remedy that is not necessarily valuable to injured investors.

But Chinese investors can obtain the protection of a bilateral investment treaty—and, for that matter, also a double taxation treaty—between the United States and a third country by means of "treaty shopping"; that is, by investing in the United States via a company they have established in that third country, provided that company has "substantial business activities" in that country. Once they do that, all the protections of that third country's bilateral investment treaty with the United States apply. As of 2008, the United States had bilateral investment treaties with forty-seven economies[8] and various types of tax treaties with sixty-five.[9] A similar approach may be taken with respect to establishing an investment vehicle in a third country that has a free trade agreement with the United States (including the North American Free Trade Agreement [NAFTA]), as long as it has applicable investment provisions.

Such protection involves, among other things, payment of fair market value compensation in the case of expropriation, including indirect expropriation. Applicable international investment agreements (IIAs) also provide protection against U.S. legislative, regulatory, or judicial treatment contrary to the international investment law principle of "fair and equitable treatment." Subject to specific exceptions, they guarantee nondiscrimination on the basis of nationality ("most-favored-nation treatment" and "national treatment"). They guarantee the free repatriation of dividends, the free distribution of the proceeds of the sale of an investment, and the free transfer of other payments. They prohibit restrictions on the nationality of senior managers. Finally, they prohibit certain performance requirements (often beyond those already prohibited by the TRIMs Agreement). In contrast to the GATS and TRIMs agreements, applicable IIAs also allow foreign investors to initiate investor-state arbitration proceedings. The normal remedy in investor-state arbitration for the breach of an IIA is the payment of damages to compensate for injury.[10]

However, U.S. IIAs (like the WTO agreements) contain an "essential security" exception under which the United States is entitled, notwithstanding other provisions of such treaties, to take measures to protect its essential security interests. Furthermore, recent U.S. treaties expressly state that the exception is "self-judging"; that is, the U.S. government alone decides whether or not a given measure is necessary in a particular situation. Still, despite this and other limitations, the protections offered to foreign investors in the United States are among the strongest in the world.

18.3 Prospering

How to deal with the liability of foreignness? What, in particular, can Chinese firms do to prosper in the United States? The answer to this question has many facets—and it can draw on the experience of firms from Japan that were in a situation similar to that of Chinese firms today when they entered the United States in the 1980s (Milhaupt 2010).

During the 1980s, the macroclimate of U.S.-Japanese relations was characterized by trade frictions, exchange-rate controversies, concerns about the nature of the Japanese economy ("Japan Inc."), fears about Japan's economic ascendance, and cultural misperceptions. The media and politicians had a field day with "Japan bashing."

Despite this climate, Japanese FDI in the United States rose from less than US$1 billion annually during the 1970s, to a peak of nearly US$20 billion in 1988–1990.[11] It received special attention and faced resistance, exacerbated at times by the relative inexperience of Japanese firms: they (like their Chinese counterparts today) had just embarked on an accelerated internationalization process through FDI and hence had not yet accumulated the experience that comes with operating abroad for decades. During the second half of the 1980s, in particular, when M&As became the principal mode of entry for Japanese firms, a number of high-profile acquisitions (e.g., that of the Rockefeller Center) received considerable publicity. One attempted acquisition—Fujitsu's bid for Fairchild Semiconductor (already foreign owned)—actually contributed to the adoption of the Exon-Florio Amendment, which is the original statute governing the CFIUS national security review process. Moreover, a number of Japanese affiliates in the United States faced legal difficulties in the employment area, with one suit reaching the Supreme Court.[12] All in all, Japanese FDI in the United States had a rough time.

The parallels in the macroclimate between the United States and Japan then and the United States and China now are indeed striking.[13] Some of the reactions to Chinese FDI in the United States are also strikingly similar, even as far as the reaction by the media and politicians is concerned, and the strengthening of CFIUS through FINSA. Yet, in the case of Japanese FDI in the United States, the controversies died down during the 1990s. Today, Japanese firms are firmly implanted in the United States; they have become an integral and valuable part of the country's economic and social fabric, and Japan remains an important source of FDI.

What can we learn from the Japanese experience and, broader, how can Chinese foreign affiliates in the United States prosper in the U.S. market? (Milhaupt 2010; Eden and Miller 2010). The basic approach is clear: Chinese firms—like those from other countries before them—need to become insiders, and they need to build up a positive company brand name, to be accepted in the United States. Various strategies can be pursued to that effect.

Where Chinese firms have a choice between entering the U.S. market through an M&A or a greenfield investment, the safer route (politically speaking) is the latter. And even in the case of M&As, follow-on greenfield investments can be important to increase the acceptability of a given invest-ment. Greenfield investments, as was pointed out earlier, are universally wel-come, as they create new production capacities and employment and are not subject to a potential CFIUS review. For Chinese firms exporting to the United States, perhaps the best way is to establish assembly facilities and eventually move on to full-production capacities (thereby reducing the trade deficit). A number of Japanese firms successfully followed this path, espe-cially in the automotive industry.

In the case of M&As, mention has already been made of the need for an appropriate political strategy, avoiding, if possible, high-profile takeovers, especially hostile ones. Part of such a strategy is to examine carefully who is affected by a planned acquisition and to understand the interests of the principal stakeholders involved. Stakeholder management and learning how to navigate the political process and institutional system at the U.S. federal level is very important, either individually or together with other non-U.S. MNEs;[14] discrete lobbying may be an important part of this process. The objective needs to be to reduce, to the greatest extent possible, negative publicity and hence to avoid starting out on the wrong foot. If this can-not be done, an attempted acquisition may not come to fruition or may be vetoed.

Once established, foreign affiliates need to observe local laws and regula-tions scrupulously—this goes without saying.[15] This requires a thorough understanding of the country's regulatory framework and its functioning. Compliance training and working with local partners who understand U.S. regulations can be important here.

More than that, foreign affiliates need to integrate themselves as tightly as possible in the communities in which they are established. This means, among other things, growing roots by creating backward linkages with local enterprises, giving them a stake in the well-being of the affiliate. It also means recruiting high-level U.S. citizens for management positions, the board of directors, and especially positions in an affiliate that involve an interface with public and private U.S. organizations. Finally, integration involves cultivating the local community which, in turn, has its own links to the state and federal governments. All politics (including in Washington, D.C.) is, in the end, local. Organizations that foster communications among business people have a role to play as well; the U.S.-China Business Council is important in this regard, and eventually its degree of penetration may be as deep as that of the U.S.-Japan Business Council.

Another important means to advance integration is corporate social responsibility (CSR). It is a concept that has great saliency in the United States—firms are expected to pay full heed to it, at the local, state, and fed-eral levels. Japanese firms became fully cognizant of the importance of CSR as part of their efforts to become accepted and integrated. Donations to local charities have a role to play here, as has the establishment of foundations in support of education and the endowment of chairs at major universities.[16]

Pursuing these strategies allows foreign affiliates to create a dense net-work of economic, social, and cultural interactions and ties that embed them and their reputation in their communities and, eventually, make them insiders with a good corporate brand name.

Naturally, this requires considerable learning on the part of the managers of foreign affiliates and their parent firms. Building that human capacity is one of the key challenges facing Chinese MNEs. This begins with training when it comes to M&As (and seeking advice where this is needed), learning the ropes of the political system, knowing how to become a good corporate citizen, and demonstrating the contribution that foreign affiliates make to the local and national economy. It also requires that the government of the home country of foreign affiliates (in this case, China) encourages foreign affiliates to become insiders in the host country and acquire a good corporate brand name. It also requires that the media, the public, and the political establishment of the host country (in this case, the United States) recognize the value of Chinese FDI and respect the principle of nondiscrimination in the treatment of such investment; a bilateral investment treaty can help in this respect.

Summary and Conclusions[17]

There are indications worldwide that the climate for FDI is becoming less welcoming, just as Chinese enterprises are appearing on the global stage. In particular, a number of developed countries, including the United States, Japan, and Germany, are taking a more cautious approach to cross-border M&As, by far the most important mode of entry into foreign markets by MNEs and, increasingly, for Chinese enterprises as well. Particularly since CNOOC withdrew its bid for Unocal in mid-2005, cross-border M&As by Chinese firms have attracted special attention, and there is ample indication they will continue to do so for the foreseeable future.

The reasons for this nervous reaction to Chinese OFDI are mixed, but they are largely political in nature. Questions are raised about the governance of Chinese firms and the fear that Chinese acquirers, especially when they are state owned, may enjoy financing advantages. This is less an issue for the shareholders of acquisition targets than for rival firms competing for the same assets. There is also some concern, especially in Europe, about the ability of Chinese firms to manage cross-border M&As successfully and that any failures would have implications for host countries, especially in terms of unemployment and the business of suppliers. Most importantly, there is the suspicion that cross-border acquisitions by SOEs are not necessarily driven by commercial motives alone, but are rather the result of political or strategic calculations determined (or at least influenced) by the government that controls them. The formal launch in September 2007 of the China Investment Corporation, China's new SWF with US$200 billion in foreign exchange reserves at its disposal, has only fueled speculation about the link between Chinese OFDI and the country's wider geopolitical goals.

If this were not enough, Chinese enterprises are seeking to enter the global FDI market at a time when economic tensions between China and its major trade partners are at an all-time high. In the United States, currency valuation has emerged as a lightning rod, while fast-growing trade imbalances with the United States, Europe, and, more recently, Japan, have deepened frictions as well. In fact, some observers trace a direct link between China's trade surplus and the rapid growth of Chinese OFDI, especially its state-financed portion.[18] Other issues unrelated to Chinese FDI have helped sour public perceptions of Chinese business, especially product recalls involving Chinese-made goods. To the average U.S. or European citizen, unfamiliar with even the largest Chinese companies, it becomes quite easy to allow negative associations to fill the void, with very predictable consequences in the political arena.

Given the speed at which Chinese firms are going global, and the fact that SOEs account for a substantial portion of China's FDI, Chinese firms are encountering a rapidly evolving political environment in the United States and other developed markets. In July 2007, the United States revised the Exon-Florio Amendment, including a presumption that filings relating to acquisitions by state-controlled foreign entities will require investigation by CFIUS. Notification to, and investigation by, CFIUS have risen substantially. In a number of European countries, as well as Australia and Canada, investment reviews are now being strengthened, including through the introduction of a CFIUS-like screening process in Russia and Germany. With Japan and Canada recently strengthening their oversight of cross-border M&As, the global investment environment seems to be tightening just as Chinese enterprises are poised to enter the world FDI market.

What to do in light of the vulnerability of Chinese OFDI? It is only natural that, with the reemergence of China as a major economy, its firms spread their wings and become major players in the world FDI market (Sachs 2008). The world needs to accept that Chinese MNEs are here to stay, and that OFDI is another aspect of the country's integration into the world economy. The issue for all stakeholders is how to handle this process smoothly.

At the most basic level, it is essential that the nondiscrimination principle—which is central to the international laws governing cross-border investment—is applied by the United States to Chinese OFDI as it is applied to the investments of other countries; if a BIT should, indeed, be negotiated, nondiscrimination would presumably feature prominently in it.

Chinese companies, too, need to be mindful of managing their international growth in light of the sensitivities that exist—rightly or wrongly—about the transnationalization of Chinese business. This begins with the training of executives not only in matters related to the management of their firms, but also in those related to the political economy and culture of the United States and other major host countries. Stakeholder management is particularly important here vis-à-vis policy makers, labor, investors, local communities, and the public. Furthermore, any acquisition by an SOE and/or investments with a potential impact on national security will need particularly careful preparation. The same goes for acquisitions in sectors that are perceived to be off-limits to foreign investors from China. On the public relations side, it needs to be shown that Chinese FDI is fundamentally no different from that of other countries—and hence contributes to the economic growth and development of its host countries. Naturally, this message will be better received if Chinese companies behave as scrupulously good corporate citizens when operating abroad, by observing the laws and regulations of their host countries and by exercising exemplary corporate social responsibility.

Whatever the overall impact and perception of Chinese OFDI, Chinese firms may want to draw on the experience of Japanese firms in the United States. When Japanese companies burst onto the world FDI market in the 1980s (partly through high-profile M&As), there was widespread fear that they would come to dominate the world economy; attitudes in the United States in particular were defensive. Some of these fears began to dissipate as Japan entered a period of stagnation in the 1990s. Yet, perhaps more importantly, Japanese firms began to change their basic approach to investing in the United States. Their understanding of the U.S. market and the ability to build key relationships with governments and communities grew. In addition to M&As, Japanese companies began to establish assembly facilities in the United States and, later, full-production units. As their readiness to address U.S. market entry challenges increased, they found that the receptivity of the U.S. business environment rose as well, in a virtuous cycle. Under the best of circumstances, Chinese firms and other stakeholders in the U.S.-Chinese investment relationship will embark on a similar trajectory in a more compressed time frame. Chinese firms, together with their counterparts in other emerging markets, can then look forward to a normalization of their investment relationships with the United States.

Notes

*This text is adapted from "Is the United States Ready for FDI from China? Overview," in Karl P. Sauvant, ed., *Investing in the United States: Is the US Ready for FDI from China?* (Cheltenham: Edward Elgar, 2010). Very helpful comments on the earlier text were received from Lorraine Eden, David N. Fagan, Timothy Frye, Steven Globerman, Mark Kantor, Curtis J. Milhaupt, Stewart R. Miller, Pablo M. Pinto, and Daniel Shapiro. They are gratefully acknowledged. Special thanks go to Lisa Sachs for helping finalize this chapter.

1. At the same time, the concentration ratio is high (as in the case of other countries), as the top five economies accounted for 86% of total outflows and 85% of total outward stock, especially Hong Kong (China) and tax havens (Cheng and Ma 2007, 15).
2. These figures do not include SOEs administered by regional governments. According to the same source, the share of state-owned enterprises in the total number of outward investing entities had dropped from 43% in 2003 to 29% in 2005.
3. See chapter 15 by Qiuzhi Xue and Bingjie Han in this volume.
4. Since M&As can be financed from sources other than FDI, it is very difficult to determine the exact share of FDI accounted for by M&As.
5. It is notable that Japanese automotive firms, when entering the U.S. market, deliberately established themselves in areas in which there had not been an automotive industry previously.
6. Invest in America, http://www.investamerica.gov/index.asp, last visited May 6, 2010.

7. However, the beginning of negotiations of a bilateral investment treaty was announced in June 2008.

8. As of December 2008, the United States had signed a bilateral investment treaty with Albania, Argentina, Armenia, Azerbaijan, Bahrain, Bangladesh, Belarus, Bolivia, Bulgaria, Cameroon, Democratic Republic of the Congo, Republic of the Congo (Brazzaville), Croatia, Czech Republic, Ecuador, Egypt, El Salvador, Estonia, Georgia, Grenada, Haiti, Honduras, Jamaica, Jordan, Kazakhstan, Kyrgyzstan, Latvia, Lithuania, Moldova, Mongolia, Morocco, Mozambique, Nicaragua, Panama, Poland, Romania, Russia, Rwanda, Senegal, Slovakia, Sri Lanka, Trinidad & Tobago, Tunisia, Turkey, Ukraine, Uruguay, and Uzbekistan (U.S. State Department, http://www.unctad.org/sections/dite_pcbb/docs/bits_us.pdf (last visited June 14, 2010).

9. As of December 2008, the United States had signed a tax treaty with Australia, Austria, Bangladesh, Barbados, Belgium, Bulgaria, Canada, People's Republic of China, Commonwealth of Independent States (Armenia, Azerbaijan, Belarus, Georgia, Kyrgyzstan, Moldova, Tajikistan, Turkmenistan, and Uzbekistan), Cyprus, Czech Republic, Denmark, Egypt, Estonia, Finland, France, Germany, Greece, Hungary, Iceland, India, Indonesia, Ireland, Israel, Italy, Jamaica, Japan, Kazakhstan, Republic of Korea, Latvia, Lithuania, Luxembourg, Mexico, Morocco, Netherlands, New Zealand, Norway, Pakistan, Philippines, Poland, Portugal, Romania, Russia, Slovak Republic, Slovenia, South Africa, Spain, Sri Lanka, Sweden, Switzerland, Thailand, Trinidad and Tobago, Tunisia, Turkey, Ukraine, United Kingdom, and Venezuela (U.S. Department of the Treasury, http://www.irs.gov/pub/irs-pdf/p901.pdf and http://www.ustreas.gov/offices/tax-policy/treaties.shtml, last visited June 14, 2010).

10. Virtually all of these protections, though, are also found in the U.S. Constitution and U.S. statutory enactments—and U.S. domestic protections are often even stronger than those contained in U.S. treaties. (The principal difference is that the protections of a U.S. IIA can be enforced before a neutral international arbitral panel, while U.S. constitutional and statutory rights are enforced before U.S. courts and administrative agencies.)

11. Flows declined thereafter, when Japan entered a decade of economic difficulties. They only surpassed the 1990 peak in 2007.

12. *Sumitomo Shoji America, Inc. v. Avagliano,* 457 U.S. 176 (1982)

13. There is, however, one major difference: China is seen as a strategic competitor in the United States in the political and military areas,.

14. The Organization for International Investment, grouping a number of foreign affiliates, is an example.

15. As we know from the experience of Japanese affiliates in the United States, employment practices are a particularly sensitive matter.

16. For example, the Fuyo Professorship at Columbia Law School was established in 1980 by the Fuyo Group (one of the six major *Keiretsu* corporate groups then in existence).

17. This section draws on Clarence Kwan and Karl P. Sauvant, "Chinese Direct Investment in the United States: The Challenges Ahead" (*Location USA 2008*, 39–46).

18. It should be noted that, while a substantial revaluation of the RMB would reduce the trade surplus, it would further encourage outward FDI from China, as it would make U.S. and other foreign assets cheaper in terms of that currency.

References

Caves, R. (1971). "International corporations: the industrial economics of foreign investment," *Economica* 38, p. 6.

Eden, Lorraine and Stewart R. Miller (2010). "Revisiting liability of foreignness: socio-political costs facing Chinese multinationals in the United States," in Karl P. Sauvant, ed., *Investing in the United States: Is the US Ready for FDI from China?* (Cheltenham: Edward Elgar).

Fagan, David N. (2010). "The U.S. regulatory and institutional framework for FDI," in Karl P. Sauvant, ed., *Investing in the United States: Is the US Ready for FDI from China?* (Cheltenham: Edward Elgar).

Frye, Timothy and Pablo M. Pinto (2010). "The politics of Chinese investment in the U.S.," in Karl P. Sauvant, ed., *Investing in the United States: Is the US Ready for FDI from China?* (Cheltenham: Edward Elgar).

Globerman, Steven and Daniel Shapiro (2010). "Modes of entry by Chinese firms in the United States: economic and political issues," in Karl P. Sauvant, ed., *Investing in the United States: Is the US Ready for FDI from China?* (Cheltenham: Edward Elgar).

Kantor, Mark (2010). "International investment law protections for Chinese investment into the U.S.," in Karl P. Sauvant, ed., *Investing in the United States: Is the US Ready for FDI from China?* (Cheltenham: Edward Elgar).

Kwan, Clarence and Karl P. Sauvant (2008). "Chinese direct investment in the United States: the challenges ahead," *Location USA*, pp. 39–46.

Leonard K. Cheng and Z. Ma (July 2007). "China's outward FDI: past and future," available online at http://www.nber.org/books_in_progress/china07/cwt07/cheng.pdf, last visited June 24, 2009.

Milhaupt, Curtis J. (2010). "Is the U.S. Ready for FDI from China?: lessons from Japan's experience in the 1980s," in Karl P. Sauvant, ed., *Investing in the United States: Is the US Ready for FDI from China?* (Cheltenham: Edward Elgar).

OECD (2008). *OECD Investment Policy Reviews: China 2008* (Paris: OECD).

Paulson, Jr. Henry M. (2008). "A strategic economic engagement: strengthening U.S.-Chinese ties," *Foreign Affairs* 87 (September/October), pp. 59–77.

"President Bush's Statement on Open Economies," May 10, 2007, available at http://www.whitehouse.gov/news/releases/2007/05/20070510-3.html, last visited June 23, 2007.

Sachs, Jeffrey D. (2008). "The rise of TNCs from emerging markets: the global context," in Karl P. Sauvant with Kristin Mendoza and Irmak Ince, eds., *The Rise of Transnational Corporations from Emerging Markets: Threat or Opportunity?* (London: Edward Elgar), pp. 15–22.

Sauvant, Karl P. (2009). "Driving and countervailing forces: a rebalancing of national FDI policies," in Karl P. Sauvant, ed., *Yearbook on International Investment Law and Policy 2008/2009* (Oxford: Oxford University Press), pp. 215–72.

UNCTAD (2000). *World Investment Report 2000: Cross-Border Mergers and Acquisitions and Development* (Geneva: UNCTAD).

——— (2008). *World Investment Report 2008: Transnational Corporations and the Infrastructure Challenge* (Geneva: UNCTAD).

White House Press Release (2007). "President Bush's Statement on Open Economies," May 10, available at http://www.whitehouse.gov/news/releases/2007/05/20070510-3.html, last visited May 30, 2007.

Zakaria, Fareed (2008). *The Post-American World* (New York: W.W. Norton).

Chapter 19

Bringing Trust Back to the International Investment Regime

Anthony O'Sullivan

Introduction

International investment is an important driver behind sustainable economic growth, contributing to higher employment, spillovers of technology and skills, and greater productivity. The Organisation for Economic Co-operation and Development (OECD) has a rich tradition of facilitating international cooperation, policy analysis, and advice to governments on how best to enhance the positive contribution of investment in their economies.[1] Given the interlinked nature of the global economy—which brings both enormous benefits and potential drawbacks—a challenge for the OECD in the coming years will be to engage both members and nonmembers to continue promoting open, stable, transparent, and predictable investment regimes. Following a brief review of current OECD investment instruments and trends in the openness to international investment, this chapter argues that the OECD can contribute to maintaining and building trust in the international investment regime by adapting existing tools to nonmember states, expanding the number of countries that adhere to the investment instruments, and involving selected emerging markets and developing countries in the next revision of these instruments.

In its efforts to promote open, transparent, stable, and predictable investment regimes, the OECD takes a two-pronged approach. The first focuses on establishing and promoting binding disciplines and legal instruments. The key OECD investment instruments are the OECD Code of Liberalisation of Capital Movements, adopted in 1961, and the OECD Declaration on International Investment and Multinational Enterprises of 1976 (and revised as of 2000). These instruments contain procedures for notification and multilateral surveillance under the broad oversight of the OECD's governing council to ensure their observance. The instruments were designed to embody principles of nondiscrimination, transparency, progressive liberalization, "standstill," and unilateral liberalization (box 19.1). The second approach involves working closely with OECD countries—and increasingly, nonmember states—to support the implementation of the instruments through peer review, dialogue, and policy recommendations. Examples of implementation

---

Box 19.1   Key OECD principles

Nondiscrimination. Foreign investors are to be treated not less favorably than domestic investors in like situations. While the OECD instruments protect directly investors established in OECD member countries, they also commit members to using their best endeavors to extend the benefits of liberalization to all members of the International Monetary Fund.

Transparency. Information on restrictions on foreign investment should be comprehensive and accessible to everyone.

Progressive liberalization. Members commit to the gradual elimination of restrictions on capital movements across their countries.

"Standstill." Members commit to not introducing new restrictions.

Unilateral liberalization. Members commit to allowing all other members to benefit from the liberalization measures they take and not to condition them on liberalization measures taken by other countries. Avoidance of reciprocity is an important OECD policy tradition. The OECD instruments are based on the philosophy that liberalization is beneficial to all, especially the country which undertakes the liberalization.

Source: Excerpt from Progress Report by the OECD Investment Committee, 7th Roundtable on Freedom of Investment, National Security and "Strategic" Industries, which took place in Paris on March 26, 2008.

---

support for nonmember states include the Middle East and North Africa (MENA) Investment Programme, the Eurasia Competitiveness Programme, and the Investment Compact for South East Europe.[2]

19.1   A Growing Hesitancy Toward Foreign Investment

Global foreign direct investment (FDI) inflows reached record levels in 2007 at US$1.9 trillion, surpassing the previous peak reached in 2000. However, over the past few years, many host countries have been more careful about opening their markets to FDI. Some of the observed restrictions to FDI could be justified through legitimate national security concerns.[3] But in other cases the "national security" rationale was less compelling—witness the failed attempt by Dubai Port Authority in 2006 to acquire six U.S. ports (*New York Times* 2006). Other drivers behind increasing restrictions to investment are the growing number of acquisitions made by state-owned companies that lack transparency and can be suspected of having noncommercial motives. For example, when, in 2005, the state-owned China National Offshore Oil Corporation (CNOOC) attempted an US$18.5 billion purchase of U.S. oil company Unocal, questions were raised surrounding the business interests of CNOOC and whether a national security threat existed (*New York Times*, August 4–5, 2005). Another example is the failed attempt by Children's Investment Fund, a British hedge fund, to increase its holding from 9.9% to 20% in Japan's Electric Power Development Company (or J-Power) (*New York Times*, January 23, 2008).

The growing number of acquisitions made by foreign companies—in particular from companies based in emerging markets—also ignited a public fear of countries being "sold off." The specter of selling prized economic assets to foreigners has been further inflamed by the press: for instance, the January 2009 cover of Paris-based *Le Figaro Magazine* had the following headline: "Who Is Buying France: Why (Our Companies Interest Foreign Investors and How We are Counter-attacking (*Figaro Magazine* 2009, 1, translation by author)." The subtitles on the menacing dark cover suggested who the culprits to be blamed were: "Kings of Oil, Russian Billionaires, Chinese Capitalists, Indian Tycoons, and Sovereign Wealth Funds" (ibid).

With the onset of the global financial crisis, the risk to freedom of investment is becoming more acute and has started to spread to emerging markets (as host countries). A number of emerging markets—which in the past ten years have initiated significant reforms to promote an attractive investment environment—are sending signals of protectionism, at a time when they need investment more than ever to help sustain growth and employment. For example, investors in the United Arab Emirates (UAE) are concerned by a proposal to regulate the dismissal of nationals working in the private sector, making it harder for businesses to trim local staff in the face of an economic downturn (*Financial Times* 2009). In Algeria, a series of government announcements aim to restrict the participation of foreign investors to a minority stake in the companies in which they invest, and to review existing rules on the repatriation of capital by foreign companies (MEED 2008).

The crisis has sparked dramatic falls in world trade and investment flows. The OECD projects that FDI inflows will continue to decline sharply in 2009, given the speed with which the crisis deepened in the third and fourth quarters of 2008 (OECD 2008). On current trends, international merger and acquisition (M&A) activity (which constitutes a significant portion of FDI) will decline by 29% from record levels reached in 2007. Two primary factors contribute to the grim outlook for FDI: first, the freezing of credit markets in combination with sharp declines in equity markets are forcing firms to rely on cash reserves to finance investment; and, second, global gross domestic product (GDP) is forecast to grow by 2.2% for 2009 (compared to 5% in 2008) while growth in OECD countries is expected to fall to 0.3%. In such a context of low growth, investment in new capacity is considerably reduced.

Emerging markets are no longer immune to a crisis that has now become global. Consider the Middle East. FDI in this region fell by 21% in 2008, with multinational enterprises (MNEs) investing US$56.3 billion in 2008 compared to US$71.5 billion in 2007 (MEED 2009). The financial crisis has hit existing investment projects: for example, Rio Tinto has canceled plans to finance a 49% stake in an aluminium smelter in Saudi Arabia (EIU 2009d). Investment in the real estate sector in the Middle East and North Africa will likely be hit hard, as the global project finance market has almost dried up (EIU 2009e). In the UAE nearly every major real estate scheme in Dubai has slowed or stopped, including signature projects like the Dubai Waterfront and the Trump International Hotel and Tower. The downturn of FDI in the Middle East and North Africa region is happening despite the fact that three of the world's largest investment funds are located in the Gulf: the Abu Dhabi Investment Authority (with assets of US$875 billion), the Kuwait Investment Authority (assets of US$264 billion), and the Qatar Investment Authority (US$60 billion).

The effects of the crisis are also being felt in the Balkans. In the third quarter of 2008, FDI in Croatia fell to EUR107 million, representing a reduction of 59% from the previous year. Romania's auto industry is suffering, with automaker Dacia (a subsidiary of Renault) announcing work closures: initial figures indicate car production and assembly declined by 78.6% on a year-on-year basis in December 2008 (EIU 2009b, 2009c).

Resource-rich countries in Central Asia and the South Caucasus are experiencing the pain of the financial crisis by way of lower prices for oil and gas exports and reduced investment in extractive industries. In Azerbaijan, for example, gross annual FDI inflows of US$3 billion are expected to fall significantly. Commercial banks in Azerbaijan are finding it more difficult to raise capital abroad and dampened growth is expected in the non-oil economy. Securing additional investment for the Nabucco pipeline will be difficult, owing both to the credit squeeze and doubts about commercial viability (EIU 2009a).

In this frightening context, the last thing that market economies should want is to exacerbate the effects of the crisis by making their markets less attractive to investment. How can freedom of investment be maintained in a context of crisis?

19.2. The OECD's "Freedom of Investment, National Security and 'Strategic Industries'" Project

To help maintain markets that are transparent and open to investment, the OECD Investment Committee initiated the Freedom of Investment (FOI) project in early 2006 (box 19.2). The FOI project provides a forum for intergovernmental dialogue on reconciling the need to preserve and expand an open international investment environment with the duty to safeguard essential security interests.[4] Dialogue has taken place involving the thirty OECD members, the eleven nonmember adherents[5] to the Declaration on International Investment, and other major nonmember countries (such as Russia, China, India, Indonesia, and South Africa). The FOI project continues a tradition of OECD dialogue on investment issues that has been framed by the two OECD investment instruments.

Box 19.2 The OECD investment committee's freedom of investment project

The FOI discussions take the form of "Roundtable" discussions and include peer-monitoring sessions through *tours d'horizon* of national developments, in-depth policy discussion of selected national security topics, and identification of good investment policy practices.

To date nine roundtable discussions have been held, and summaries are publicly available on the OECD website in addition to background reports by the OECD's Investment Division.

Source: http://www.oecd.org/document/25/0,3343,en_2649_34887_42105753_1_1_1_1,00.html, last visited October 11, 2009.

19.3. Possible Policy Responses to Help Maintain Global Markets Open to Investment

In order to help maintain markets open to investment, the following directions should be considered.

19.3.1 Adapt the FOI Process to Emerging Markets

The importance of keeping the FOI process open to emerging markets is paramount. This gives them a firmer stake in working with OECD countries and keeping their investment policies on a path of reform. Adapting the FOI process to emerging markets could be done in consultation with the stakeholders and under the umbrella of existing OECD regional programs that support business climate development in emerging markets. Additional areas that could be attached to the FOI process for emerging markets include encouraging better corporate governance, responsible business conduct, and increased transparency of emerging market MNEs (all covered by the *OECD Guidelines for Multinational Enterprises*). In this regard, it could also be beneficial for some emerging markets to set up National Contact Points modeled along those of the OECD, which would communicate the benefits of the OECD guidelines and help resolve problems arising from their implementation.[6]

19.3.2 Encourage Government Policies to Increase the Quality of Investment

The more foreign investment generates value added and employment, the more it will be accepted by all constituencies even in difficult times. Active government policies such as linkage programs between foreign and local companies or competitive clusters that put an emphasis on innovation would contribute in this regard. In order to maximize the benefits of foreign investment, some emerging markets (such as Kazakhstan, Uzbekistan, Azerbaijan, Algeria, and the United Arab Emirates) must place a particular emphasis on diversifying sources of foreign investment outside of hydrocarbon and hydrocarbon-related products.

19.3.3 Leverage Regional Programs to Promote Dialogue and Peer Review between Emerging Markets in the Area of Investment Policy

Existing regional programs, such as the MENA Investment Programme, the Eurasia Competiveness Programme, and the Investment Compact for South East Europe, offer a forum in which to transfer OECD tools and policy recommendations to emerging markets. OECD tools, such as the FOI project, can be adapted to the needs and context of emerging markets under the umbrella of these programs. They can also offer a platform for dialogue between the public and private sectors at the regional level.

19.3.4   Reaffirm Reforms at the Political Level

Emerging markets should reconfirm at the highest political level their commitment to maintain reforms that enable open, transparent, predictable, and stable business environments. By reaffirming their commitment to openness, leaders of developing countries simultaneously send positive signals to the international business community and reinvigorate their officials in proceeding with implementation of important policy reforms. Such commitments can have an even greater impact on investor perceptions if they are also made at the regional level.

Notes

1. http://www.oecd.org/investment and http://www.oecd.org/department/0,3355,en_2649_40340912_1_1_1_1_1,00.html, last visited October 11, 2009.
2. http://www.oecd.org/department/0,3355,en_2649_40340912_1_1_1_1_1,00.html, last visited October 11, 2009.
3. The final elements of the *OECD Guidelines for Recipient Country Investment Policies Relating to National Security* were agreed at the 8th Roundtable on Freedom of Investment (http://www.oecd.org/dataoecd/0/23/41456730.pdf, last visited October 11, 2009).
4. http://www.oecd.org/daf/investment/foi, last visited October 11, 2009.
5. Argentina, Brazil, Chile, Egypt, Estonia, Israel, Latvia, Lithuania, Peru, Romania, Slovenia.
6. National Contact Points for the *OECD Guidelines for Multinational Enterprises*: http://www.oecd.org/document/60/0,3343,en_2649_34889_1933116_1_1_1_1,00.html, last visited October 11, 2009.

References

BBC (2008). "Japan shuns UK power investment," BBC, April 16, available at http://news.bbc.co.uk/2/hi/business/7350481.stm, last visited September 8, 2009.

EIU (2009a). *Country Report Azerbaijan* 2009 (London: Economist Intelligence Unit).

——— (2009b). *Country Report Croatia* 2009 (London: Economist Intelligence Unit).

——— (2009c). *Country Report Romania* 2009 (London: Economist Intelligence Unit).

——— (2009d). *Country Report Saudi Arabia 2009* (London: Economist Intelligence Unit).

——— (2009e). *Country Report Tunisia 2009* (London: Economist Intelligence Unit).

Financial Times (2009). "UAE to safeguard jobs of nationals," February 18.

MEED (2008). "Algiers reigns in foreign ownership," September 14.

——— (2009). "Gulf suffers significant fall in foreign direct investment," February 15.

OECD (2008). "Grim outlook for FDI and shifting global investment patterns," *OECD Investment News*, Investment Division, November (Paris: OECD), available at http://www.oecd.org/dataoecd/56/43/41671320.pdf, last visited September 8, 2009.

Part Five

The Path Ahead

Chapter 20

The Rise of Emerging Market Multinationals: Investment Promotion Challenges Ahead

Henry Loewendahl

Introduction

Attracting foreign direct investment (FDI) has become an indispensable economic development tool for countries, regions, and cities. Worldwide, there are estimated to be over 10,000 government agencies at the national and subnational levels with a remit for attracting inward investment. Many of these agencies are large, well funded, and professionally staffed organizations with overseas office networks and significant influence over policy making.

The inward investment attraction budgets of these investment promotion agencies (IPAs) are typically around US$3–5 million per annum. For larger countries, including emerging markets, budgets of US$50–150 million per annum are not uncommon.

Given the critical need to attract FDI as a key lever for economic development and, as indicated above, the extensive resources being committed to this task, understanding how current trends in the market are likely to influence how governments should attract FDI is of key importance for policy makers around the world.

This chapter provides the latest research on trends in the FDI market, focusing on the growth of investment from emerging markets, and explores the implications for how governments can attract foreign investment to their jurisdictions. The impact of the current global recession on FDI and government policies to attract investment is also examined.

20.1 Research Methods

Most studies of FDI rely on FDI capital flow data.[1] FDI is defined by the International Monetary Fund (IMF) as any capital invested by a foreign entity in a new or existing enterprise when the investor holds 10% or more of the equity. This definition covers many types of investment, including mergers & acquisitions (M&As), greenfield investment, joint ventures, privatization investment, and long-term loans.

In practice, official FDI flow data is heavily eschewed by the M&A and privatization deals that took place, by the sequencing of companies' cross-border capital transfers and by different tax and regulatory regimes, which encourage companies to transfer capital to and from the most efficient locations.

Other than encourage policies to change the overall regulatory regime in a country, there is little an IPA can do to influence much of the FDI flows going into its location. In particular, very few IPAs have historically had the remit to promote M&As, which has been the primary driver of the global FDI market, as not only does this involve a potentially politically risky strategy of selling local companies to foreign buyers, but government agencies, for the most part, lack the expertise to be able to set up, negotiate, and implement M&A deals.

Instead, IPAs have been focused on attracting new greenfield investment projects and expanding the operations of existing foreign affiliates. Greenfield investment is "real" investment—productive investment in the manufacturing plants, offices, hotels, logistics, et cetera—of foreign companies that directly creates jobs in the local economy and stimulates economic development.

Official data on FDI do not segment FDI flows by type of FDI, limiting its relevance for investment promotion. To understand the trends and implications of greenfield investment, this chapter draws on the FDI database of the fDi Intelligence division of the Financial Times Ltd, called fDi Markets, and the author's own experience of working with over seventy IPAs in some thirty countries.[2]

20.2   Global Investment Trends

International production, undertaken by multinational enterprises (MNEs), is the productive core of the globalizing world economy. Table 20.1 shows that FDI inflows have grown from just US$58 million in 1982 to nearly US$1 trillion in 2005 and over US$1.9 trillion in 2007, with a global estimated stock of over US$15 trillion. Employment of foreign affiliates increased from 63.8 million to 81.6 million over the same period. Table 20.1 shows that cross-border M&As have been the key driver for FDI flows, and employment by foreign companies.

Greenfield investment has also grown rapidly, with a 50% growth in projects and a doubling of capital investment from 2005 to 2008. In 2008, the estimated new capital investment companies announced in their foreign affiliates reached a record US$1.5 trillion. The number of new jobs created by greenfield investment projects also reached a record four million in 2008.

20.3   The Evolution Of Investment Promotion

20.3.1   Growth of IPAs

The growth in the number of IPAs has gone hand in hand with the rapid growth of the global FDI market. The first IPAs to respond to growing

Table 20.1 Indicators of FDI and international production, 1982–2008

Indicator	1982	1990	2005	2007	2008
Greenfield FDI projects	–	–	10,481	11,928	15,454
Greenfield FDI capital investment ($bn)	–	–	741	989	1,512
Greenfield FDI new jobs (million)	–	–	2.34	2.95	4.0
FDI inflows ($bn)	58	207	946	1,833	1,449
Inward FDI stock ($bn)	789	1,941	10,048	15,211	–
Income on inward FDI ($bn)	44	74	759	1,128	–
Cross-border M&As ($bn)	–	200	716	1,637	–
Sales of foreign affiliates ($bn)	2,741	6,126	21,394	31,197	–
Gross product of foreign affiliates ($bn)	676	1,501	4,184	6,029	–
Total assets of foreign affiliates ($bn)	2,206	6,036	42,637	68,716	–
Exports of foreign affiliates ($bn)	688	1523	4,197	5,714	–
Employment of foreign affiliates (millions)	21.5	25.1	63.8	81.6	–

Sources: UNCTAD (2007, 2008, 2009); fDi Markets database, Financial Times Ltd., http://www.fdimarkets.com.

Note: There are more than 80,000 MNEs in the world today, and they hold ownership stakes in more than 800,000 foreign affiliates all over the world. These are important actors in today's world, employing around eighty-two million people in their affiliates overseas, and with total assets of US$69 trillion, sales of some US$31 trillion and exports of around US$6 trillion as of 2007. MNEs account for about half of the world's total research and development (R&D) expenditure and more than two-thirds of the world's business R&D. They are responsible for much of the world's trade, about one-third of which takes place within their international corporate networks.

opportunities for FDI were established in the 1970s, with the Irish Development Agency (IDA), Invest in Britain Bureau (now known as UK Trade & Investment), and Singapore Economic Development Board (SEDB) among the earliest—and most successful—examples.

During the 1980s, the number of IPAs multiplied. By the mid-1990s, most developed economies had established national IPAs—dedicated, well-funded and resourced agencies with the specific remit of attracting greenfield inward investment to their countries.

At the same time, regional development agencies (RDAs) have been established in most developed countries, and almost all have specific investment promotion divisions. The larger cities have also established IPAs, with well-known examples including Think London, MIDAS Manchester, Copenhagen Capacity, Stockholm Business Region, Montreal International, and Cincinnati USA Partnership.

The first countries and regions to establish IPAs were those that had a weak base of globally competitive indigenous business, had high unemployment, or were small, export-based economies, dependent on international business. Attracting FDI was seen as the number-one policy tool for stimulating economic development and creating much-needed new jobs.

For large economies with a very strong base of indigenous industry, like Germany, Japan, and the United States, it was only in the post-2000 period that investment promotion to attract FDI started to be taken seriously. The United States was among the last developed economies to establish a national IPA—Invest in America, in 2007.

Setting up dedicated IPAs or divisions was by no means unique to developed economies. Developing countries were also establishing national IPAs—often with the encouragement and technical and financial support of the European Union (especially in Eastern Europe), United Nations Conference on Trade and Development (UNCTAD), the World Bank, and major national aid agencies, such as the United States Agency for International Development (USAID) and the United Kingdom's Department for International Development (DFID). The Costa Rican Investment Board (CINDE) has stood out as one of the most successful IPAs in a developing country to be established.

With the focus of MNEs rapidly shifting to developing countries in the past decade and with the emergence of MNEs from developing countries themselves—demonstrating the value of being part of the globalizing world economy—during the first decade of the twenty-first century, most developing countries also established national IPAs. In the wealthier emerging markets, these are large, well-funded, and increasingly sophisticated organizations, with the Brazilian Trade and Investment Promotion Agency, APEX Brazil, a high-profile recent example, which hosted the World Association of Investment Promotion Agencies annual conference in December 2008.

The most recent trend is for regions and cities in developing countries to establish IPAs. For example, regions and cities in Colombia and Brazil are establishing IPAs, some with the support of the World Bank's Foreign Investment Advisory Service (FIAS). Cities in Africa are getting support from the Millennium Cities Initiative of Columbia University to build the capability for investment promotion.[3]

20.3.2   *Approaches to Target Manufacturing Investment*

While the growth in the number of IPAs, especially in developing countries in recent years, has reflected the growing opportunities for attracting inward investment, the strategy and activities of IPAs has also evolved.

The typical IPA in the 1970s and 1980s was focused on attracting greenfield manufacturing projects. Manufacturing FDI boomed in developed economies, in part to circumvent trade barriers, but also with the rapid emergence of Japanese companies as new global players, which needed to expand their operations worldwide. The agencies put together a package of incentives, infrastructure improvements, training and skills programs, and supplier linkage programs to attract manufacturing projects (Loewendahl 2001). As the opportunities—and competition—to attract investment grew, IPAs became more proactive and started to target directly decision makers in potential investors to put their location "on the map" of the investor, before their competitors, so that, when the company had a project, their location would be a front contender.

The targeting of manufacturing companies was relatively straightforward. An IPA would identify the industries it was competitive in (e.g., based on size and performance of the industry in its location) and the industries in which there was a strong FDI market, and then would identify the major companies within that sector, based typically on turnover, employment, growth metrics, and whether or not the company already had a presence in the region or country. Before making an approach to a company, the IPA would first need to identify within the companies the appropriate divisions and decision makers to contact, which is time consuming, and many IPAs purchased databases from companies such as Dun & Bradstreet and many other corporate intelligence providers, as well as conducting their own desk and telephone research.

As inward investment increased, the IPAs realized it was becoming equally important to embed the foreign investors into the local economy to ensure that investment would not relocate to another location, to increase the spillover benefits to the local economy, and to further expand the initial investment over time. By the mid-1990s, many agencies had established "aftercare" and "supplier development" programs, with agencies in the United Kingdom, such as the Welsh Development Agency (now called International Business Wales) and Northern Development Company (now called ONE North East), among the first to establish comprehensive programs (Loewendahl 2001).

The more sophisticated IPAs, as exemplified by regions in the United Kingdom and the SEDB, used their aftercare and supplier development programs to target FDI intelligently. They conducted detailed supply chain analysis of the main manufacturing sectors in their locations and then targeted specific foreign investors to fill supply chain gaps.

The most advanced agencies from regional manufacturing hubs, such as IDA Ireland and CINDE Costa Rica, examined the cycles of industries and individual company product life cycles to see when there would be a need for new global capacity, and then targeted these industries and companies. Key examples included tracking the U.S. Food and Drug Administration's (FDA) patent approvals in pharmaceuticals or chip cycles in the semiconductor sector, which helped secure huge new investments in both Ireland and Costa Rica.

As IPAs become more proactive in targeting investors, many established overseas offices in the key source markets for investment, to be closer to the key decision makers in new and existing customers and to promote the location on the ground. This led to rapidly growing budgets for investment promotion, with a typical overseas office costing around US$500,000–$1 million per annum to run. The larger and well-funded agencies often established more than ten offices around the world.

20.3.3 The Shift to Services

By the early 1990s, it was becoming apparent that the type of inward investment was rapidly shifting from manufacturing to services. The boom in manufacturing investment was coming to an end in the developed economies[4] and was being replaced by companies looking to establish "front and back office" service functions. Advances in information and communications technology (ICT), and the growing international networks of MNEs, meant that considerable cost savings could be achieved from consolidating service function in one or more locations around the world. In some cases, companies such as Oracle cited costs savings as high as US$1 billion by centralizing service functions.

Ireland and regions in the United Kingdom, Spain, Portugal, and Canada were highly successful in attracting front office operations (customer support centers) and back office operations (shared service centers). In "near-shore" locations, such as Dublin, Manchester, and New Brunswick, tens of thousands of new jobs were created.

The boom in services had significant implications for the activities of IPAs. The standard formula of providing a package of capital investment incentives, infrastructure development, training programs, and supplier development initiatives was not as relevant for these service functions.

The service activities being targeted by IPAs were labor intensive, not capital intensive. Front and back office operations were drawn to locations that offered turnkey solutions of high-quality, affordable office space and large pools of educated, multilingual, and reasonably low-cost labor. Human resources become the key location determinant, rather than access to markets, infrastructure, and incentives. Service functions were truly mobile—they could be located anywhere on the planet where there was the appropriate ICT infrastructure.

To offer a competitive solution to these highly mobile investors, IPAs had to reconsider their incentives packages. Capital investment incentives—which were typically worth 20%–30% of the investment value—were no longer relevant for operations that could create hundreds of jobs but for only a few million dollars capital investment outlay. Tax incentives were also not as relevant for operations that were often cost centers, not profit centers. The incentives offered by IPAs become linked to job creation and, in some cases, to the wage levels paid by investors. IPAs also developed "soft" incentives packages that included subsidized or ready-made office space and specialized skills and training programs.

Attracting these rapidly growing service functions was not only a challenge in terms of developing a new package of benefits to the investor, but also in terms of how IPAs targeted investors. While the targeting of manufacturing investors, as discussed in the section above, was relatively straightforward, the service functions being targeted were so new that industry and company classification had not yet realigned to these new activities—and have only in part done so today. How could an IPA identify which company and which individual within a company to target for a customer support center or shared services centers? There was no database listing of these companies, no division within the company responsible yet for these service functions.

The shift to services (UNCTAD 2004)[5] required a more sophisticated approach to identifying companies. As table 20.2 shows, the top three industries for FDI projects from 2003 to 2008 were all services industries. IPAs put a renewed focus on their aftercare programs. As well as trying to grow manufacturing investment and supply-chain linkages, IPAs were now in

Table 20.2 Top twenty industries for greenfield FDI projects, 2003–2008

Sector	2003	2004	2005	2006	2007	2008	Total
Financial services	636	642	789	1,138	1,137	1,568	6,010
Software and IT services	938	1,192	1,201	1,333	1,430	1,476	7,656
Business services	415	551	572	770	801	1,158	4,370
Real estate	238	228	269	509	598	880	2,762
Industrial machinery, equipment, and tools	319	399	426	520	590	781	3,098
Textiles	423	589	411	515	522	757	3,256
Food and tobacco	541	599	592	621	533	708	3,661
Consumer products	395	431	404	587	458	592	2,919
Communications	339	365	527	564	442	582	2,852
Metals	433	372	539	444	458	581	2,858
Coal, oil, and natural gas	443	258	327	281	291	556	2,213
Hotels and tourism	306	287	266	296	298	553	2,059
Transportation	176	265	367	412	457	548	2,272
Electronic components	266	316	357	359	335	463	2,123
Automotive components	381	406	348	375	358	437	2,327
Alternative/renewable energy	48	41	75	178	291	406	1,084
Chemicals	438	416	316	373	370	378	2,307
Automotive OEM	354	338	311	309	307	346	1,981
Plastics	225	230	232	265	204	257	1,423
Pharmaceuticals	208	205	200	197	197	240	1,260
Other sectors	1,929	2,093	1,952	2,129	1,851	2,284	12,366

Source: http://www.fdimarkets.com.

contact with existing investors to understand the strategy of the company for service functions, and to use the existing investors to find the right contacts in the company. With manufacturing investment starting to relocate eastward to lower-cost locations, IPAs also worked with existing investors to maintain employment levels in the local economy by establishing service operations, even if manufacturing jobs were being relocated.

While most large industrial companies had manufacturing operations worldwide, which they benchmarked in terms of plant performance, and had in-house experts in logistics, supply chains, and so forth to help make their site selection decisions, the new service functions often required specialist outside skills. The role of corporate-location or site-selection consultants was particularly pronounced in advising major companies on where to locate front and back office operations around the world. The more proactive IPAs quickly recognized this, and they started to target actively the site-selection consultants to demonstrate their location advantages for service functions.

In the second half of the 1990s, another boom in services investment started to take place—that of the software and information technology (IT) sector. Within a decade, software and IT became the leading industry for

FDI worldwide, as measured by the number of inward investment projects.[6] Table 20.2 shows that, over the period 2003–2008, software and IT services were the leading industry for FDI projects, although in 2008, financial services became the leading industry. With much of this investment involving "knowledge-based" design and development activities, the skills and availability of the labor force became even more important as the key location determinant for site-selection decisions. Such was the importance governments gave to supporting IT and software investment that, in many countries, government policies changed to allow for fast-track immigration for skilled IT staff—even in countries historically cautious about immigration, such as Germany—and in some cases significant income tax reductions were given for IT professionals.

Skills availability became the key selling message that IPAs took to potential investors. The most sophisticated IPAs conducted full IT skills audits for their locations, quantifying skills availability among the existing workforce and in universities in specific computer languages. Invest Northern Ireland was among the first IPAs in the world to conduct such an audit—and the region has been the leader in the developed world for software development FDI projects for the past few years.

Many IPAs started to package their offer in terms of the advanced, knowledge-based "clusters," which would give investor access to specialized skills, technology, know-how, and partners. Universities and research institutes, and the skills and expertise of these organizations, were at the core of these clusters and became key assets that IPAs used to attract software development and other knowledge-based R&D activities to their locations. The World Association of Investment Promotion Agencies offered dedicated training programs for IPAs in how to link cluster development to FDI promotion,[7] reflecting the rapid growth in technology-based FDI.

20.3.4 The Shift to Emerging Markets

By 2000, manufacturing FDI had grown rapidly in many emerging markets. In Europe, a huge relocation of manufacturing activities from Western Europe to the low-cost, high-skill countries of Central and Eastern Europe was in full swing, and Mexico had become a major offshore manufacturing hub for the North American market. In the years after 2000, the shift of manufacturing investment to the East continued, as more and more emerging markets became attractive for investment to lower costs and access large, and rapidly growing, markets. Whereas China has been the number one location for manufacturing FDI worldwide, table 20.3 shows that, while still dominant, the global shift to the developing world is now fueled by other emerging markets. Manufacturing investment in India, Thailand, Russia, and Vietnam skyrocketed and, in 2008, India overtook the United States as the second leading location in the world for manufacturing FDI projects, after China. In 2008, only two of the ten leading locations for manufacturing investment were in developed countries—the United States and France. In Europe, in the decade following 2000, another wave of manufacturing relocation to the Balkans countries took place, with Romania, in particular, attracting record levels of manufacturing investment, overtaking the much larger economies of Germany, the United Kingdom, and Spain.

As early as 2000, front and back office service functions also began to be relocated eastward, as labor pools became tighter and costs increased. In Europe, companies responded by shifting their focus to Central and Eastern Europe (in particular, Prague and Budapest). In North America, the focus shifted to smaller, lower cost cities in Canada and the United States. Latin America and the Caribbean (in particular, Costa Rica, Chile, Jamaica) started to attract investment. In Japan, language barriers meant that much of the relocation of investment was internal, to lower cost cities in Japan. However, in the past few years, specialized language training has resulted in China attracting Japanese services investment.

By the early 2000s, what began as relocation to lower cost near-shore locations became a full-scale relocation to offshore locations in Asia, and to other countries in Central and Latin America. Table 20.4 shows the leading countries in greenfield FDI, ranked by number of direct jobs created in front and back operations. India was the top location, closely followed by the Philippines, which has seen rapid year-on-year growth in investment in these service functions, with companies drawn by the quality and clarity of the English language skills, the very low cost levels, lower labor turnover than in India, and less political backlash when compared to outsourcing to India.

Table 20.3 Top twenty countries for greenfield FDI projects in manufacturing, 2003–2008

Destination Country	2003	2004	2005	2006	2007	2008	Total
China	672	686	473	530	435	532	3,346
India	93	133	128	232	188	289	1,077
United States	250	201	199	249	251	231	1,402
Thailand	87	75	60	52	68	190	545
Russia	179	135	156	126	133	147	881
Vietnam	68	71	68	89	116	143	558
France	37	63	137	154	117	142	672
Mexico	71	68	53	96	88	135	520
Poland	65	116	138	140	121	123	705
Brazil	164	151	78	55	48	93	592
Romania	44	68	97	104	104	87	509
Spain	67	68	45	80	87	84	434
Germany	67	76	59	67	71	73	416
United Kingdom	74	88	71	71	55	71	440
Malaysia	62	46	30	34	36	64	276
Hungary	102	84	81	89	97	53	509
Czech Republic	73	68	74	76	50	42	383
Indonesia	29	31	26	43	43	42	215
Serbia	10	22	17	9	27	42	129
Slovakia	41	51	61	51	50	39	295
Bulgaria	32	51	34	56	40	37	251
Other countries	914	828	802	711	804	969	5,089

Source: http://www.fdimarkets.com.

Table 20.4 Top twenty countries for greenfield FDI—jobs created in front and back offices, 2003–2008

Destination country	2003	2004	2005	2006	2007	2008	Total
India	34,380	37,817	30,764	39,277	28,214	20,859	191,637
United States	2,578	2,158	3,832	4,363	22,196[a]	18,917[a]	56,309
Philippines	4,082	13,943	13,718	13,898	10,496	18,080	74,711
China	5,388	2,712	7,289	6,066	7,379	11,550	40,384
Poland	1,861	651	4,829	8,048	4,206	4,700	24,725
Romania		417	1,708	6,096	2,167	3,589	13,977
Brazil	279	3,655	3,422	7,185	363	2,617	17,521
Australia	1,708	880	671	901	1,663	2,539	8,362
United Kingdom	7,002	3,731	4,972	6,056	4,619	2,508	28,888
Mexico	375	7	1,627		1,180	2,197	5,487
Malaysia	3,992	2,002	1,134	3,463	2,604	2,090	15,465
Colombia			832	1,600	6,000	1,834	10,266
Singapore	1,413	2,426	1,331	2,847	548	1,802	10,367
Spain	1,038	2,304	2,190	2,769	1,792	1,756	11,849
El Salvador	587	660			200	1,533	2,980
Guatemala					1,400	1,360	2,760
Thailand	1,172	314		400		1,281	3,167
Argentina		250	682	2,330	2,893	1,280	7,435
Uruguay		262	458		850	1,207	2,777
Nicaragua						1,150	1,150

Source: http://www.fdimarkets.com.

[a]Includes interstate projects within the United States.

The United States is still a relatively small player for foreign investors, but data for 2007 and 2008, which also include interstate investment within the United States, show that U.S. companies continue to create thousands of jobs in front and back offices domestically. However, in 2008, U.S. companies created over 50,000 front and back office jobs overseas, many more than the 17,000 interstate jobs created.

Table 20.4 also shows that China, Poland, and Romania, together with many countries in Central and Latin America, became more attractive for companies to invest in. The massive importance of the Chinese market has led many companies, in the past few years, to establish Asia-Pacific technical support and shared service operations in China, as well as customer support centers covering the Chinese market. In Central and Latin America, sustained economic growth, rising education levels, and a comparative cost advantage are leading to very strong growth in services investment, not only to serve the U.S. market, but increasingly as pan-regional operations to serve Latin America, which has become one of the most important growth markets in the world.

20.4   The Growing Role of Emerging Market Investment

20.4.1   Latest Trends in Developing Country Investment

At the same time as developing countries have become key locations for FDI, companies from developing countries are rapidly internationalizing and becoming MNEs. Table 20.5 shows that FDI outflows from developing countries rose nearly tenfold from 2003 to 2007, reaching nearly US$253 billion in 2007, while FDI outflows from developed economies increased threefold. The number of greenfield FDI projects from developing countries nearly doubled in the period 2003–2008.

The value of M&As by developing countries increased fivefold from 2003 to 2007, reaching US$180 billion in 2007. M&As from developed economies also increased fivefold over the period—the primary growth engine for developing country FDI has been through greenfield investment rather than M&A.

While FDI from developing countries is growing rapidly, and much faster than FDI from developed economies, developed economies remain the main

Table 20.5 FDI from developed and developing countries, 2003–2008

Indicator	2003	2004	2005	2006	2007	2008
World FDI outflows (US$ billions)	**617**	**877**	**881**	**1,323**	**1,997**	**1,858**
Developed countries	577	746	749	1,087	1,692	1,507
Developing countries	29	117	118	212	253	293
Africa	1	2	2	8	6	9
Latin America and Caribbean	11	28	36	63	52	63
Asia and Oceania	17	88	80	141	195	220
West Asia	−4	8	12	23	44	34
South, East, and Southeast Asia	21	79	67	118	151	186
Transition economies	11	14	14	24	51	59
World outward FDI projects (number)	**9,446**	**10,221**	**10,481**	**12,166**	**11,914**	**15,454**
Developed countries	7,824	8,707	8,943	10,110	10,005	12,557
Developing countries	1,449	1,323	1,337	1,830	1,698	2,572
Africa	65	49	70	83	60	191
Latin America and Caribbean	154	176	103	180	252	270
Asia and Oceania	1,230	1,098	1,164	1,567	1,386	2,111
West Asia	209	179	240	432	288	577
South, East, and Southeast Asia	1,021	919	924	1,135	1,098	1,534
Transition economies	173	191	201	226	211	325
World cross-border M&As (purchases in (US$ billions))	**297**	**381**	**929**	**1118**	**1637**	**na**
Developed countries	257	341	778	930	1411	na
Developing countries	31	38	100	157	180	na
Africa	1	3	19	24	6	na
Latin America and Caribbean	12	15	12	34	42	na
Asia and Oceania	19	21	70	99	133	na
West Asia	2	1	20	42	43	na
South, East, and Southeast Asia	17	19	49	57	89	na
Transition economies	9	1	23	11	18	na

Sources: UNCTAD (2007, 2008, 2009); fDi Markets database, Financial Times Ltd., http://www.fdimarkets.com.

Note: Na—Not available.

source of global FDI. In 2007, developing economies accounted for just 13% of global FDI flows, 11% of cross-border M&As, and 14% of global greenfield investment projects.

Within developing countries, the key OFDI actors are companies from Asia and Oceania. Companies from this region—which are primarily based in China, India, Hong Kong (China), and Singapore—accounted for over 75% of OFDI from developing countries in 2007 and over 80% of OFDI projects.

The most recent 2008 data for greenfield investment show a significant growth in FDI from developing countries. The number of projects from developing countries grew by 50% in 2008, compared to a 25% increase in investment from developed economies. Africa was the fastest growing region, with a tripling of OFDI projects, followed by West Asia (Middle East and Turkey), with a doubling of investment projects. Asia and Oceania and the transition economies recorded 50% growth in outward projects. The market share of developing countries in global greenfield FDI projects increased from 14% in 2007 to 17% in 2008. The "FT Top 500 Companies List," which ranks companies by market capitalization in 2008, also showed that developing countries accounted for 17% of the world's leading companies. In terms of banks, which in 2008 became the leading sector for FDI worldwide, more than two-fifths of the "FT Top 1000 Banks," and more than one-third of the top twenty banks were from developing countries.

Table 20.6 shows the fastest growing countries for OFDI projects in 2008 in greater detail. All but one of the twenty fastest growing countries for OFDI were developing countries in 2008. Many of these countries had a

Table 20.6 Fastest growing source economies for greenfield FDI projects in 2008

Rank	Fastest growing	Rank	Fastest growing, with >50 projects
1	Kenya	1	Qatar
2	Serbia	2	Kuwait
3	Tunisia	3	Portugal
4	Qatar	4	South Africa
5	Nigeria	5	Turkey
6	Kazakhstan	6	Bermuda
7	Kuwait	7	UAE
8	Bahrain	8	Singapore
9	Portugal	9	Israel
10	Vietnam	10	Malaysia
11	Jordan	11	Czech Rep
12	Egypt	12	Norway
13	Croatia	13	India
14	South Africa	14	Japan
15	Azerbaijan	15	Brazil
16	Turkey	16	Italy
17	Bermuda	17	Switzerland
18	Pakistan	18	Russia
19	UAE	19	Hong Kong (China)
20	Singapore	20	Australia

Source: http://www.fdimarkets.com.

very low level of OFDI in 2007, so a small increase in the number of projects led to large growth rates. The right side of the table, therefore, shows the fastest growing countries, but only those with more than fifty OFDI projects in 2008. We can see that twelve (60%) of the top twenty fastest growth countries were developing countries, with four of the top seven from West Asia. These trends clearly show the rapidly growing role of developing countries in OFDI.

20.4.2 Nature of Developing Country Investment

Table 20.7 examines the proportion of FDI that is intraregional. We can see that nearly two-thirds of African greenfield investment projects were from one African country to another in 2008. Africa has the highest level of intraregional investment, and intraregional investment has been the key driver for the growth of inward FDI and OFDI in Africa. African companies also have the highest proportion of investment projects in developing countries—over 80% of projects in 2008. In South, East, and Southeast Asia, over half of FDI is intraregional, but as this region is the dominant region for OFDI, in absolute terms there is significant investment in the rest of the world. In 2008, over 70% of FDI projects from this region were in other developing countries, compared to 60% of projects from developed economies being in developing countries. This shows that companies from emerging markets are more likely to invest in other emerging markets than companies from developed economies—although the difference is perhaps not as marked as one would expect—which shows the growth of greenfield OFDI from Asia to developed economies.

Latin America and Caribbean have a relatively low level of intraregional investment and investment in developing countries compared to other developing country regions. This could be in part explained by close proximity to the huge U.S. market—companies from Latin America and Caribbean have invested twice the proportion of projects in the United States compared to companies from South, East, and Southeast Asia. West Asia has the lowest proportion of intraregional projects—fewer than one-third went to other countries in West Asia, reflecting the small overall market size of the region.

Table 20.7 Greenfield FDI projects by destination region, 2008

Region	% intraregional	% in developing countries
Africa	65	81
South, East, and Southeast Asia	54	71
Latin America and Caribbean	43	63
West Asia	32	75
Developed economies	41	59

Source: Derived from http://www.fdimarkets.com.

However, West Asian companies had the second highest proportion of projects in other developing countries.

The main industries for investment from developing countries can be seen in table 20.8. The leading industry is financial services, accounting for 14% of OFDI projects from developing countries over the period. For developed countries, financial services accounted for only 7% of OFDI projects, indicating the rapid growth and globalization of financial services companies from developing countries.

Software and IT services and real estate are the second and third industries for FDI from developing countries. Some 7% of FDI was in software and IT services (compared to 12% from developed economies) and 7% in real estate (4% for developed economies). Developing countries are less specialized in software and IT than developed economies (reflecting the lower level of technological development), but are more specialized in real estate, which is eschewed by the huge level of real estate investment from the oil-rich Middle East. In terms of motives that drive companies from developing countries to invest overseas, figure 20.1 shows that, from a sample of over 1,500 projects, over 50% invested overseas for reasons of host market growth potential and proximity to markets or customers.

The regulations/business climate, infrastructure and logistics, and skilled workforce available were also important location determinants for 10% of projects. The investment motives of firms from developing countries are broadly similar to those of developed countries, with the principal exception that skilled workforce availability is more important for companies from developed economies—cited by 16% of projects, compared to 10% for developing countries. Again, this reflects the higher level of overall technological development and therefore technology-related FDI from developed

Table 20.8 Greenfield FDI projects from developing countries, by leading sectors, 2003–2008

Sector	2003	2004	2005	2006	2007	2008	Total	Average Annual Growth
Financial services	171	142	156	253	223	439	1,420	28.0%
Software and IT services	95	112	106	114	140	170	747	12.9%
Real estate	70	44	73	148	137	234	716	39.0%
Communications	80	74	94	115	73	99	544	8.2%
Metals	52	35	50	79	106	148	475	28.4%
Food and tobacco	75	73	60	71	54	102	439	12.6%
Coal, oil, and natural gas	71	53	56	60	60	118	433	16.8%
Transportation	32	40	77	117	70	81	423	29.0%
Textiles	79	63	43	67	78	74	408	3.0%
Business services	31	39	42	76	72	129	395	37.7%
Other sectors	693	648	580	730	685	1,004	4,403	9.8%
Overall total	1,449	1,323	1,337	1,830	1,698	2,598	10,235	15.0%

Source: http://www.fdimarkets.com.

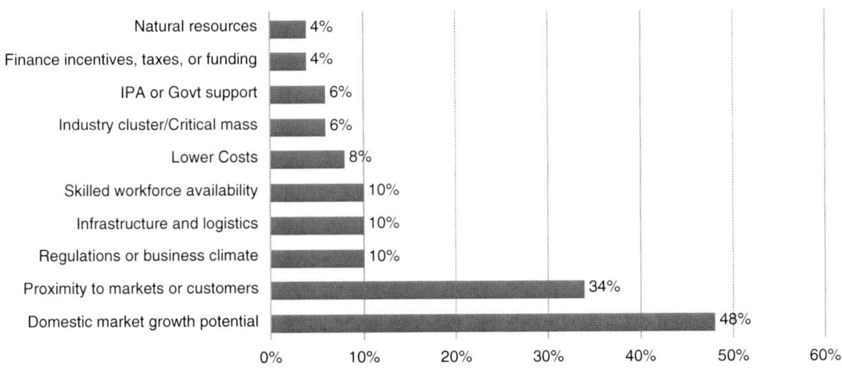

Figure 20.1 FDI from developing countries: proportion of companies citing location factor

Source: Derived from http://www.fdimarkets.com.

Note: Based on 1,577 projects recorded 2003–2008, with more than one response possible.

economies. Figure 20.1 shows that companies from developing countries are primarily driven by market-seeking motives.

20.4.3 Future Growth of Investment from Emerging Markets

OFDI from developing countries is expected to continue to grow faster than OFDI from developed economies, as developing countries achieve much higher levels of economic growth (especially China and India), and as their already large base of companies has the resources, know-how, and critical mass to expand overseas. Table 20.9 shows the number of companies in major emerging markets and developed countries for three key industries for FDI. We can see that, for all the industries, emerging markets have built up a critical mass of companies that is at least as big as many of the largest developed economies.

In software and IT services, Russia is second only to the United States in terms of the number of companies, and is set to become a major player in the sector, while Brazil and India are ahead of France, Spain, and Canada. In automotive components, China is number one, with double the number of companies of the United States, indicating the potential for China to become a leading global player in this industry. India, Brazil, Russia, and Turkey all have more companies in automotive components than Germany and other major developed economies, bar the United States and Japan, and Mexico is ahead of Spain, Canada, and France. In chemicals, China is again number one. Russia, India, and Brazil have more chemicals companies than Japan and all the major developed countries, apart from the United States. Turkey has more chemical companies than the United Kingdom, Spain, and France, and Mexico has more than Canada.

In addition to FDI from traditional players, the past few years have seen several new, nontraditional entities engaging significantly in FDI. These

Table 20.9 Number of companies in major developed and emerging markets, by industry, 2009

Country	Software and IT services	Automotive components	Chemicals
Brazil	73,480	6,270	20,635
Canada	19,207	869	3,489
China	27,840	24,488	82,532
France	35,508	829	5,452
Germany	97,127	3,325	10,128
India	39,190	8,763	28,282
Italy	65,604	2,863	9,815
Japan	101,039	11,155	17,969
Mexico	4,590	1,715	4,839
Russia	215,722	5,356	29,952
Spain	27,155	1,580	6,084
Turkey	892	5,083	8,145
United Kingdom	140,310	2,150	6,987
United States	415,101	11,248	43,324

Source: http://www.fdibenchmark.com.

include private equity funds and venture capital funds, the diaspora, and sovereign wealth funds (SWFs).

- **Private equity/venture funds:** Investments by venture funds are in the form of equity capital and tend to be concentrated in certain sectors, typically those involving advanced technologies.
- **Diaspora FDI:** investment from immigrants back into their country of origin is being courted actively, especially in the case of China and India, the countries with the largest diasporas, but also in developed economies, such as regions in France and the United Kingdom. For India, there are more than 200,000 millionaires of Indian origin in the United States, and the Indian community has the highest average family income group. Remittances from migrant workers are fast outpacing official aid flows and even FDI, with remittances to India rising from an estimated US$12.3 billion in 1996–1997 to approximately US$27 billion in 2007 (*Indian Express Finance,* January 4, 2009).
- **SWFs:** growing in size and diversifying their investment portfolios to include not only real estate and troubled financial institutions but also private companies, SWFs are a new player in the FDI arena whose impact has yet to be felt and assessed fully. According to the Sovereign Wealth Fund Institute, the value of all SWFs has edged up to nearly US$4 trillion, a figure that may well more than double in the next five years. Their size is now larger than that of hedge funds and private equity funds combined, and new funds are being created.

20.5 The Impact of the Global Recession and Financial Crisis

With the turmoil that followed the global recession and financial crisis continuing into 2009, the current rate of FDI expansion will slow down and,

Table 20.10 Latest trends and forecasts for foreign direct investment, 2007–2009

Indicator	2007	2008[a]	2009[b]
FDI inflows (US$ billions)	1833	1449	735
Greenfield FDI projects[c]	11,916	15,454	13,300

Sources: UNCTAD (2009); fDi markets databasehttp://www.fdimarkets. com; EIU forecasts.

[a]Preliminary estimates.
[b]Forecasts as of January 2009.
[c]Barometer of trends in greenfield FDI. Data capture the major but not all projects. Jobs data include estimates.

as table 20.10 shows, it is already in decline. FDI flows declined by 21% in 2008, to US$1.45 trillion, and the Economist Intelligence Unit forecasts a further 49% decline in FDI flows in 2009.

The decline in FDI flows is driven primarily by the fall in cross-border M&As. The financial crisis is restricting the ability of companies to finance M&As. Furthermore, the value of M&As fell 27% in 2009 compared with 2008 (mergermarket 2010, 2), as share prices, and hence the values of companies, have declined, depressing the value of FDI flows. Similarly, as companies in the technology industry find it more difficult to raise financing for initial public offerings, the level of M&As and greenfield investment will drop.

Greenfield FDI projects, which peaked in 2008 at nearly 15,500 projects recorded, are also forecast to decline in 2009, by 13%. Job creation through greenfield investment is forecast to fall from a peak of 4 million in 2008 to 3.1 million in 2009. Greenfield investment in developed countries is expected to fall significantly more than this, while investment in developing countries is expected to achieve similar levels to 2008.

The global recession is hastening the shift of focus toward developing countries, as they remain the sole source of growth in the world economy. Even as developed economies recover from recession, developing countries are expected to grow much faster, and Africa in particular is expected to become a much more important player in FDI, a trend we are already beginning to see.

Economic growth in the developing world will accelerate as urbanization grows. China will add at least 342 million people to its cities by 2030; India, 271 million, and Latin America, 169 million people. In sub-Saharan Africa, the urban population will grow by 395 million people over the same period, over double its current population, and a larger absolute increment than China will experience.[8] Urbanization will offer huge opportunities for accelerating economic development and for inward FDI and OFDI.

Even though the global recession and financial crisis will reduce the levels of FDI flows and cross-border investment projects, the future of the FDI market is increasingly determined by the developing world. The structural changes taking places in the global political economy will lead to a rapid rebalancing, not only of the location of FDI, but also the source of investment in the coming decade.

20.6   Investment Promotion Challenges Ahead

IPAs around the world, no matter their level of maturity and sophistication, are grappling with how best to adapt to the rapidly changing and increasingly multipolar global economy. The immediate issue facing IPAs is the impact of the global recession and financial crisis on FDI. The preceding sections have shown that developed countries are bearing the brunt of the crisis; FDI in developing countries has yet to experience a significant decline.

IPAs from developed countries inevitably face a declining market for FDI projects. As a result, budgets have to be tightened and resources channeled into activities that can achieve "quick wins" for the local economy while, at the same time, developing a strategy for sustainable investment in the long term.

IPAs from developing countries face, at best, static FDI market conditions. Most developing country IPAs should expect to maintain the level of investment projects secured before the global economic crisis; in particular, playing on their cost advantages (which have become ever more important to MNEs) and underlying growth prospects.

However, while budgets and targets must adapt to changing market conditions, a more fundamental shift in the structure and activities of IPAs is starting to take place, reflecting the structural changes in the global political economy. Five key challenges include:

- How to promote and facilitate non-greenfield FDI?
- How to attract FDI from emerging markets?
- How to focus efforts on growth sectors in a declining market?
- How to benefit from the growth of sovereign wealth funds?
- How to attract investment from the diaspora?

Each of these challenges is discussed in greater detail below.

20.6.1   How to Promote and Facilitate Non-greenfield FDI?

Attracting greenfield FDI has been the main activity of IPAs worldwide. Whereas the core focus on greenfield FDI is unlikely to change, as greenfield FDI directly creates new jobs and expanded output in the local economy, IPAs have began to examine if and how they should attract other types of FDI.

The above analysis of global investment trends showed that M&As have been the key driver of FDI flows. Most IPAs found it extremely difficult to promote M&As, not just because of political and legal sensitivities, but because of a lack of capability. However, the attitude to M&As is beginning to change. In light of the economic recession, finding overseas buyers for struggling domestic companies has become essential to sustaining jobs and output. With the economic recession, IPAs are becoming focused as much on protecting existing investment as attracting new investors. The latter increasingly involves bringing in foreign investors and capital, especially from the rapidly growing emerging markets, and specifically China and India.

At the same time, whereas joint ventures, alliances, and partnerships have been for many years a key globalization strategy for companies, especially those in technology industries or in emerging markets, IPAs have traditionally avoided promoting and facilitating them, not only because of the uncertain and hard-to-quantify economic benefits, but also because of lack of capability. The global economic recession has put a heightened emphasis on such arrangements to enable companies to globalize, as it is a more cost-effective strategy and often a quicker route to access new markets and capabilities, compared to greenfield investment or M&As. Companies from developing countries, which are the fastest growing source of FDI projects, are more likely to engage in joint ventures, alliances, and partnership-type investments, as they lack the experience of international investment and knowledge of overseas markets, and so often look for a local partner to help their initial investment.

As IPAs recognize the benefits of M&As and other types of inward FDI, and as they struggle to attract the same volumes of greenfield FDI, more and more IPAs are grappling with the challenge of how to promote these types of FDI.

One key shift we are seeing, in part as a response to this challenge, is a growing integration of trade and investment agencies. With the trade side being responsible for the business expansion of domestic companies and investment side responsible for attracting foreign investors, combining trade and investment under one umbrella should, in principle, increase the capability of the agencies to promote and facilitate M&As and other types of investment—which essentially is a matchmaking process. By pooling market intelligence and overseas offices, significant cost savings should also be achieved, particularly important in today's fiscal climate.

We are already seeing ambitious moves by some of the largest countries to combine trade and investment. One of the first major agencies to make this change was Scottish Development International (formerly Locate in Scotland), shortly followed by UK Trade & Investment (formerly Invest UK). In 2009, Germany announced it was bringing trade and investment under the same umbrella. Some agencies are now developing websites that explicitly or implicitly promote M&As and joint ventures, alliances, and partnerships, and other agencies are building specialist units for this type of investment.

Much more research is needed on how best to bring trade and investment together, what the impact is on inward FDI results, and what the best practices are for promoting, facilitating, monitoring, and evaluating the effectiveness in attracting M&As and other types of investment.

20.6.2 How to Attract FDI from Emerging Markets?

While most global cross-border investment still comes from large developed economies, growth is being fueled by emerging markets. The evidence indicates that they will rapidly become a major player in OFDI.

Even though the FDI opportunity from emerging markets is still small relative to countries such as the United States, the United Kingdom, Germany, or Japan, the structural changes in the world economy will rapidly change the sources of global investment. The fastest growing sources of greenfield investment are almost all from developing countries. China (and India) will inevitably become major outward investors—and not just in terms of lower level activities. China will become an intellectual property powerhouse. In the next few years, Chinese-based technology will start to make a global impact—already Western companies are being successfully sued for infringing on Chinese patents (*Economist,* April 25–May 1, 2009). Intraregional investment is also growing rapidly. For many IPAs from emerging markets, attracting investment from neighboring and other emerging markets will become increasingly important.

Therefore, IPAs from around the world are reorienting their focus and service offer toward emerging markets. IPAs are establishing overseas offices in the major emerging markets, in particular China, where many IPAs from the West have multiple offices, but also in the other large emerging markets. Where resources, and the current size of the opportunity, do not justify an office, IPAs are recruiting consultants to conduct lead generation programs in the major emerging markets.

However, attracting emerging market investment is not only about increasing resources for lead generation in these countries. Attracting their investment is often more challenging than attracting inward FDI from the more transparent and private-sector-driven developed countries.

First of all, the role of the government in business is typically much more pronounced in developing countries. To attract major companies to invest often requires high-level political access and negotiations. An IPA on its own may not have the political clout and will need to partner with government ministers and even heads of state to gain the required access and influence.

Second, emerging market companies are, in most cases, new to international investment. They require, therefore, a much more consultative approach in terms of providing more detailed information on everything from market conditions, to how to invest, to how to navigate the political system of the host country.

Third, business and personal networks are generally even more important in emerging markets than elsewhere. The business community is often closely connected to certain families or schools where the future industry leaders meet, and these networks continue into business life. The IPA needs to be able to tap into these networks; making the right recruitment is often critical for success.

Fourthly, the indigenous technology sectors in emerging markets are largely embryonic, making it hard to identify the future investors.

IPAs therefore face new challenges in trying to attract investment from emerging markets, and may need to employ a different set of capabilities and resources to be successful in attracting this investment.

20.6.3. How to Focus Efforts on Growth Sectors in a Declining Market?

In tough market conditions it is essential that IPAs focus on high-growth sectors. Research by the fDi Intelligence unit of the Financial Times Ltd. has identified some of the key sectors, which will offer continued FDI growth despite the global recession and financial crisis.[9] Topping the list is environmental technology, which, with continued government funding, is experiencing rapid growth in FDI, in particular in wind and solar power-related areas. IPAs from Spain and Germany in particular have successfully penetrated this sector, achieving very high levels of FDI. Government policies in both countries have strongly supported inward FDI, with Germany, for example, offering 50% capital investment grants in areas such as solar energy. Other sectors that are generally resilient to recession include healthcare, food and beverages, infrastructure, and defense.

IPAs around the world need to ensure they have the intelligence resources to be able to identify in a fast-changing market the new growth sectors, and to identify the key investors to target in these sectors.[10] They also need to be able to influence government policy to incentivize investors to invest in these areas, as the examples of Spain and Germany above in environmental technology show. Especially in a recession, IPAs must forge joint strategies with other government departments to ensure that government legislation and funding is aligned to supporting IFDI in the growth sectors—or face losing investment to competitor locations. It will be a major challenge for IPAs to change their historic sector-targeting strategies, to understand the new growth industries, and to influence government policy to support them—and act fast!

20.6.4 How to Benefit from the Growth of Private Equity, Venture Capital Funds, and SWFs?

The growth of private equity and venture capital funds and, in particular, SWFs is challenging the traditional remit and activities of IPAs. Some of the best lessons in how to attract this new type of investor come from emerging markets, in particular in the Middle East, which has been most exposed to these new types of investors. The Jordan Investment Board, for example, recently developed a new two-pronged strategy for attracting FDI. For attracting traditional investors (i.e., corporate entities establishing productive greenfield operations under their ownership, management, and control) the board has developed sector propositions outlining the comparative advantages of investing in Jordan for each sector. For attracting new types of investors the board has taken a very different approach: it has identified and developed concrete business cases with financials for specific projects that

SWFs and other private-equity-type investors (including rich individuals) can invest in. These projects could include a construction project, investing in a local company, or establishing a new operation to meet a particular need or gap in the market. The IPA is seeking to attract foreign capital, rather a subsidiary of a company, to invest in specific opportunities in the host country—significantly broadening the type of FDI IPAs target.

As SWFs become a more important source of global investment, IPAs from other regions of the world are expected to respond and adapt the way in which they promote their locations for FDI. This will be a major challenge for IPAs—they need to change their traditional marketing approach, from one of selling location features and benefits, to one of defining and promoting specific, profitable projects that these funds can invest in. The IPAs that get this right could generate very significant volumes of inward capital flows for their location.

20.6.5 How to Attract Investment from the Diaspora?

The diaspora, as we saw in previous sections, has become a valuable source of inward capital flows, most pronounced in India and China, but also of critical importance in smaller economies such as Lebanon. However, developing a specific investment-promotion strategy to attract diaspora investment has only recently been experimented with by IPAs. Examples include certain regions in France, which have developed a comprehensive strategy for attracting successful French citizens back to their regions, targeting, in particular, French business people in the technology industry, who had migrated to California and London. More recently, IPAs from the United Kingdom have started to look at this area—with the Scottish agency developing a specific website to encourage Scots overseas to move back and establish businesses in Scotland (see http://www.scotsin.com/).

The key challenges of developing a strategy to attract diaspora investment include (1) establishing a reliable database of diaspora from the location; (2) facilitating conditions for inward investment by the diaspora, including incentives and soft support services (such as provision of contacts, matchmaking); and (3) improving information provision to the diaspora, such as through a website, newsletters, or embassy contacts.

Conclusions

Entering the second decade of the twenty-first century, IPAs are likely to have a significantly greater remit and international operations than is currently the case. Increasingly, IPAs will be promoting FDI from different types of business entities from a much wider range of source markets. IPAs are likely to become more active in promoting cross-border M&As, partnerships, and capital investments, as well as traditional greenfield investment projects. To make this shift will require growing linkages with other government agencies, in particular on the trade side, as well as new capabilities to attract investment from emerging market companies and new types of investors. IPAs will need greater political influence and support to penetrate emerging markets and to align regulations and incentives to growth sectors for investment. Greater overseas networks and relationships will be required. Intelligence gathering and dissemination will become even more important—but now involving intelligence not just on foreign companies, but on local businesses seeking international partnerships or capital, and on the diaspora in key business hubs around the world. The use of technology, especially websites and business intelligence databases, will become even more essential to the activities of IPAs—where most business is generated through inbound enquiries and where the quality and speed of response to these enquiries is critical to winning new business.

Even as previous shifts in investment promotion, such as aftercare, supplier development, and the promotion of services have been led by a relatively small number of IPAs from the rich countries, the new shift toward promoting all types of investment with a much greater emphasis on emerging markets will be more widespread in initial adoption. Indeed, given their first-mover experience, IPA best practices in this new phase of investment promotion are likely to come from developing country IPAs as much as those from developed countries. As the marketplace and opportunities for FDI become more global, so will the competition.

Notes

1. See UNCTAD for the most authoritative source of data on FDI flows.
2. fDi Markets (http://www.fdiintelligence.com/index.cfm?page_name=markets) is a database that tracks greenfield investment projects worldwide in real time. Quantitative and qualitative information is captured for every project, and the database is accessed online. It is a unique tool for conducting up-to-date analysis of the FDI market. It is especially relevant for the study of IPAs, whose primary role is to attract greenfield investment projects to their jurisdictions.
3. See http://www.vcc.columbia.edu.
4. The main exception was in the United States, where the southern states still experienced strong inflows of manufacturing investment as much inward investment in the United States has been interstate rather than foreign investment. Eastern Germany also experienced a strong growth in FDI in the 1990s.
5. The rapidly growing importance of FDI in services and policy implications was the main feature in the UNCTAD *World Investment Report* of 2004; the author of this chapter contributed to that volume.
6. See http://www.fdimarkets.com and www.eyeim.com for trends in greenfield investment.
7. See http://www.undp.lv/files/waipa.pdf for the first such workshop.
8. Source: http://www.citiesalliance.org/ca/sites/citiesalliance.org/files/CA_Docs/resources/cds/cds-guidelines/role_of_cities.pdf
9. Financial Times Ltd. (2009). The Future of FDI," presentation to the World Bank, March 3, in Washington, DC.
10. A key resource is http://www.fdimarkets.com.

References

Economist (2009). "Intellectual property in China," *Economist* April 25–May 1.

fDi Markets database, from the Financial Times Ltd., see http://www.fdimarkets. com/, last visited April 24, 2009.

Loewendahl, H.L (2001). *Bargaining with Multinationals* (Houndmills, Basingstoke, Hampshire: Palgrave Macmillan).

Mergermarket (2010). "Press release mergermarket global m&a round-up for year end 2009," available at http://www.mergermarket.com/pdf/Press-Release-for-Financial-Advisers-Year-End-2009.pdf, last visited May 19, 2010.

UNCTAD (2004). *World Investment Report 2004: The Shift towards Services* (New York and Geneva: United Nations).

——— (2007). *World Investment Report 2007: Transnational Corporations, Extractive Industries and Development* (New York and Geneva: United Nations).

——— (2008). *World Investment Report 2008: Transnational Corporations and the Challenge of Infrastructure* (New York and Geneva: United Nations).

——— (2009). "Assessing the impact of the current financial and economic crisis on global FDI flows," January (New York and Geneva: United Nations), mimeo.

Chapter 21

The Rise of Emerging Market Multinationals: Economic and Business Challenges Ahead

Gary Clyde Hufbauer and Matthew B. Adler

Introduction

Foreign direct investment (FDI) has expanded at a rapid pace. In 2007, the outward stock of world FDI totaled over US$15.5 trillion, up roughly US$12 trillion from the 1997 stock of US$3.7 trillion (UNCTAD 2009). Much of this growth has come from multinational enterprises (MNEs) based in developed countries members of the Organisation for Economic Co-operation and Development (OECD). But FDI from developed countries is no longer the only significant source of FDI. Emerging market MNEs (any corporation with headquarters located in an emerging market and affiliates elsewhere) have contributed a rising share to world outward FDI (OFDI). In 2007, FDI flows from Brazil, China, India, Mexico, and Russia made up roughly 5% of the world's OFDI flows. In 1997, the same figure was only 2% (ibid.).[1] By 2017, we might see this share rise above 10%, and perhaps reach 15%.

Operating with greater visibility in this new landscape, MNEs based in emerging markets will face new challenges, as will the host countries for their FDI. MNEs based in developed countries will also face fresh challenges, mainly the onslaught of new competitors; but these challenges are similar to new competition that MNEs have confronted in the past. In this chapter, we do not focus on challenges to developed country MNEs.

Some of the new challenges that are the subject of inquiry in this chapter have already surfaced. Two illustrations are the public outcry, in the United States, over the security and geopolitical aspects of takeover proposals by Dubai Ports World and China National Offshore Oil Corporation (CNOOC). Other challenges are still on the horizon. In this chapter we try to identify the challenges ahead. Our ideas, for the most part, are not new. Many of the challenges we discuss were once lively issues when OFDI from the OECD countries boomed in the 1980s. Our contribution is to turn familiar debates around and view them in the context of an outward thrust by MNEs based in emerging markets.

In this chapter, when we refer to emerging market MNEs, we are, in fact, talking about corporations based in very few countries. There are roughly 190 countries in the world today. Excluding some twenty-three highly developed members of the OECD,[2] that leaves approximately 165 emerging markets: countries that are developing or are economies in transition. However, in this chapter we have geared our comments toward only some of these emerging markets. The Boston Consulting Group's 2008 list of "Global Challengers" (corporations based in emerging markets that could become market powers) has corporations from only fourteen countries: Argentina (one); Brazil (thirteen); Chile (one); China (forty-one); Egypt (one); Hungary (one); India (twenty); Indonesia (one); Malaysia (two); Mexico (seven); Poland (one); Russia (six); Thailand (two); and Turkey (three) (BCG 2007). Even on this short list, there is a clear domination by China, India, and Brazil. This list certainly does not represent the total number of emerging market MNEs, but it does indicate where the dominant emerging market MNEs are likely to come from.

The Republic of Korea is also a large source of OFDI, and its larger companies are firmly established (such as Hyundai, Samsung, Kia) on a world scale. The Republic of Korea (like Mexico) is an OECD member, and will soon cross the border to join the club of developed countries. For our work here we do not take into consideration FDI from the Republic of Korea, Hong Kong (China), Singapore, Taiwan Province of China, the British Virgin Islands, Bermuda, or the Cayman Islands. A recent United Nations report on FDI from emerging markets and a recent comprehensive volume on rising emerging market MNEs covered these countries (UNCTAD 2006; Sauvant 2008). We do not include these countries because their circumstances identify them as highly open and near developed (Republic of Korea, Taiwan Province of China), as already developed (Hong Kong [China], Singapore), or as tax havens (British Virgin Islands, Bermuda, Cayman Islands). The circumstances make the mentioned countries more like Japan, the United States, the European Union (EU), or Switzerland with respect to the economic issues we discuss, than emerging markets. In addition to the Boston Consulting Group's list of countries with "Global Challenger" corporations, we also consider Bahrain, Colombia, Kuwait, Nigeria, Panama, South Africa, the United Arab Emirates, and Venezuela as relevant countries for a discussion of emerging market MNEs and OFDI.[3]

21.1 Challenges to All Developing Countries and Transition Economies as Hosts for MNEs from Major Emerging Markets

MNEs from major emerging markets present few new challenges for host emerging markets as a whole. For years, developing countries have welcomed FDI from developed country MNEs. Hence the issues raised by accepting FDI from a somewhat different source are not new. Possibly the biggest difference is that nationalistic voices that enjoy demonizing MNEs will find their task somewhat harder when an MNE is based in India than when it is based in the United Kingdom.

In response to the huge flows of FDI from developed countries to developing countries and economies in transition, a large literature investigates the role of FDI in promoting development. The main takeaway is that FDI often promotes development, but with many caveats.[4] This message implies that host developing countries face multiple questions on the type of FDI they want, how to attract or deter FDI, and how to maximize their own benefits from FDI once attracted. Since host developing countries have a long experience in dealing with these issues, the rising importance of emerging market FDI only underscores a preexisting challenge. Most developing countries have long since decided to welcome almost any FDI, despite the litany of caveats in the academic literature. Their stance is not likely to change when the newest MNE is based in Brazil or China. Similarly, countries that have an established practice of screening inward FDI (IFDI) are likely to apply the same bureaucratic sieve to investors from India or Mexico.

Host countries want technology to be transferred from arriving MNEs to the local economy. Spreading the technologies of an MNE throughout a host country is a major avenue through which FDI promotes development. Emerging market MNEs that invest in other emerging markets were, at one time, likely to have benefited from technology transfer.[5] Prior history may or may not make them more apt and willing to share their own technology with host-market companies. The technology gap in South-South relationships is not as large as North-South, so the potential gain for developing country hosts from emerging market FDI may not be as great as from developed country FDI. In efforts to promote IFDI from emerging markets, developing countries should recognize that, in terms of technology transfer, they might find more willing partners in emerging market MNEs, but they may not be able to extract as much from those partners.

Tax competition has always been a salient feature of FDI promotion and could become even fiercer with the rise of emerging market MNEs. Hosts for FDI often offer tax incentives to attract MNEs, and they use low taxes as a selling point. Typically, developing countries have lower statutory and effective corporate tax rates than developed countries (see table 21.1). The rise of emerging market MNEs will increase the population of firms that face relatively low home country tax rates. One implication is that developing countries will lose some of their competitive edge in the tax arena. For example, Turkey has a 20% statutory corporate tax rate. For companies looking to invest abroad partly for tax reasons, Turkey (even without additional tax incentives) looks attractive for companies based in the United States (statutory rate of 39%) or Italy (statutory rate of 33%). However, for a company based in Russia (statutory rate of 20%), Turkey looks no different than its home environment. Turkey might have to enrich its tax incentives to attract Russian firms. The growing prominence of emerging market MNEs, could, at the margin, intensify the tax competition that is already a prominent feature of the FDI world.

A frequently cited benefit of FDI for host countries is job creation. When entering a foreign market there are two avenues open to an MNE: mergers and acquisitions (M&As) or greenfield investment. M&As account for the

Table 21.1 Statutory corporate tax rates in various locales

Destination	2008 Tax Rate	Destination	2008 Tax Rate
Jamaica	33.3	USA, Colorado	38.0
Japan	41.0	USA, Connecticut	39.9
Jordan	25.0	USA, Delaware	40.7
Kazakhstan	30.0	USA, Florida	38.6
Korea	27.5	USA, Georgia	38.9
Latvia	15.0	USA, Hawaii	39.2
Lithuania	20.0	USA, Idaho	39.9
Luxembourg	30.4	USA, Illinois	39.7
Macau	12.0	USA, Indiana	40.5
Malaysia	25.0	USA, Iowa	41.6
Malta	35.0	USA, Kansas	39.8
Mauritius	3.0	USA, Kentucky	38.9
Mexico	28.0	USA, Louisiana	38.5
Montenegro	9.0	USA, Maine	40.8
Netherlands	25.5	USA, Maryland	39.6
New Zealand	33.0	USA, Massachusetts	41.2
Norway	28.0	USA, Michigan	38.9
Oman	12.0	USA, Minnesota	41.4
Pakistan	35.0	USA, Mississippi	38.3
Panama	30.0	USA, Missouri	38.4
Peru	30.0	USA, Montana	39.4
Philippines	30.0	USA, Nebraska	40.1
Poland	19.0	USA, Nevada	35.0
Portugal	26.5	USA, New Hampshire	40.5
Puerto Rico	20.0	USA, New Jersey	41.1
Qatar	35.0	USA, New Mexico	39.9
Romania	16.0	USA, New York	39.9
Russia	20.0	USA, North Carolina	39.5
Saudi Arabia	20.0	USA, North Dakota	39.6
Serbia	10.0	USA, Not Specified	39.3
Singapore	18.0	USA, Ohio	38.3
Slovak Republic	19.0	USA, Oklahoma	38.9
Slovakia	19.0	USA, Oregon	39.3
Slovenia	21.0	USA, Pennsylvania	41.5
South Africa	34.5	USA, Rhode Island	40.9
South Korea	24.5	USA, South Carolina	38.3
Spain	32.5	USA, South Dakota	35.0
Sri Lanka	35.0	USA, Tennessee	39.2
St. Lucia	30.0	USA, Texas	36.0
Sweden	28.0	USA, Utah	38.3
Switzerland	21.3	USA, Vermont	40.8
Taiwan	25.0	USA, Virginia	38.9
Tanzania	30.0	USA, Washington	39.2
Thailand	30.0	USA, West Virginia	40.9
Trinidad and Tobago	25.0	USA, Wisconsin	40.1
Turkey	20.0	USA, Wyoming	35.0
UK	30.0	USA, U.S. Virgin Islands	0.0
Ukraine	25.0	Uzbekistan	44.0
UAE	0.0	Venezuela	34.0
Uruguay	25.0	Vietnam	25.0
USA, Alabama	37.8		
USA, Alaska	41.1		
USA, Arizona	39.5		
USA, Arkansas	39.2		
USA, California	40.7		

Source: KPMG (2009a, 2009b); Hodge (2008)

larger share of FDI flows by far—at a maximum around 75%.[6] However, more new jobs are associated with greenfield investment because green-field investment either creates an entirely new entity or expands an existing enterprise. By contrast, M&A can even spell job losses if an existing firm is downsized following the takeover. As with FDI generally, the dominant form of entry for emerging market MNEs are M&As—for the twenty-two countries we identified, at a maximum, M&A could account for around 75% of FDI outflows as well.[7] The implication is that, for host markets, the job-creation selling point will not be any easier as emerging market MNEs become more prominent. In fact, given the reputation of emerging markets as "hard taskmasters"—China, Mexico, and Russia are prominent in this respect—the fear of job losses and slender pay packets might be greater than for MNEs based in Japan or Germany.

Finally, developing country hosts must recognize that emerging market MNEs are often seeking to acquire natural resources. Chinese and Indian MNEs are particularly prominent in this area (UNCTAD 2006). This type of FDI is risky for developing host countries. Foreign MNEs may be more productive than domestic firms at extracting natural resources, but they might also care less about sustainability than domestic firms do. Developing countries must recognize when they are being "plundered" by foreign MNEs and respond accordingly. They must also monitor and inform public opinion on this issue; people may believe that all foreign MNEs are robbing their country of its natural resources, and this could lead to a widespread backlash that does not differentiate between types of foreign FDI.

21.2 Challenges to Developed Countries as Hosts for MNEs from Major Emerging Markets

For developed countries that host MNEs from major emerging markets, tax competition will remain fierce, and potential job destruction could become a hot political issue. The technology-transfer debate, so familiar in develop-ing countries, could be turned on its head: some developed countries may criticize emerging market MNEs for "slurping up" valuable know-how only to improve the competitive position of the home country. The national secu-rity and geopolitical dimensions of FDI from emerging market MNEs are likely to attract close scrutiny. Few of these countries are traditional allies of the United States, the EU, or Japan; and the most prominent are potential adversaries—here we are thinking of China, India, and Russia.

A large challenge facing developed country hosts with the rise of emerg-ing market MNEs will be to manage security and geopolitical concerns in a constructive way. We have already seen examples of the "wrong way" to deal with security concerns. In the Dubai Ports World and CNOOC episodes, the United States blocked otherwise sound investments on hazy grounds, tarnishing the U.S. reputation as "open for business."[8] By contrast, Lenovo's takeover of IBM's personal computer division is a good example of how security concerns can be properly addressed.[9]

To be clear, we do not advocate that security issues should be dismissed with regard to IFDI in the United States or elsewhere, but there should be an objective process for dealing with security issues. In the United States, the Committee on Foreign Investment in the United States (CFIUS) process is intended to handle security-related FDI questions, but in the cited cases it was run over by a Congressional uproar.[10] We see two challenges for developed country hosts in future cases. First, to ensure that broad "economic interests" are not allowed to masquerade as security concerns. Second, to manage the fallout when genuine security concerns lead to the rejection of a takeover. The verdict is still out whether the United States and the EU will rise to these challenges. As for Japan, the country has a proven record of obstructing inward foreign investment, no matter the source, so there is no reason to expect that emerging market MNEs will fare better than MNEs based in the United States or Europe.

Security and geopolitical concerns are likely to flare up with natural-resource-related FDI from emerging markets. The Russian giants Lukoil and Gazprom have made inroads into EU energy markets, and this has alarmed many European policy makers. CNOOC's proposed takeover of Unocal, a small part of China's quest to secure growing quantities of oil, was simply unpalatable in the U.S. political arena. Recognizing when a legitimate security risk is at play, or when threats have been overblown, will be a repeated challenge for developed countries in the years to come.

Finallly, the state ownership or state funding of many emerging market MNEs will create an array of new challenges. This issue is most pressing in M&As, as some emerging market MNEs have, as of late, successfully outbid developed country firms in takeover attempts, partly because of the large war chests provided by their government—or "M&A subsidies" in blunt parlance. Sovereign wealth funds (SWFs)—government-owned and -operated investment funds—are often the culprits of subsidized M&As, and public trepidation of SWFs has grown in recent times (see Truman 2008 for discussion). Some subsidy cases are more objectionable than others, and these are the cases that should be targeted if developed countries seek to curtail subsidies in the M&A context. Rejecting all M&As tinged with government subsidies would impede a significant amount of capital flows and be painful for developed countries and emerging countries alike. An international agreement should be negotiated on proper limits for M&A subsidies (see Hufbauer, Moll, and Ribini 2008 for discussion), although reaching such an agreement will be a difficult undertaking.

21.3 Emerging Market Challenges in Their Role as Home Countries

With the rise of emerging market MNEs, home countries will face challenges that mirror those currently faced by developed countries with their own MNEs. Whereas there are many benefits to serving as a base country for MNEs—contrasted with purely domestic firms, MNEs often pay higher wages, conduct more trade, and finance greater research—there are also costs, which we discuss in a moment. For emerging markets, balancing the benefits with the costs will be the prime challenge.

OFDI will prompt some home countries to fear the loss of tax revenue. Income earned on OFDI can be taxed in one of three ways by home countries: they can treat the income the same as domestic income and tax it accordingly, they can exempt it completely, or they can recognize host country taxes when applying their own imposts. In practice, countries choose between the second and third alternatives.

The first option would severely constrict OFDI because MNEs would have to pay taxes on the same income both to the host country and home country—in other words, double taxation. For that obvious reason, the first option has never migrated beyond the academic literature. The second option may encourage OFDI because MNEs have the choice of avoiding home country taxation by locating production in lower tax destinations. This can cost the home country tax revenue that might otherwise be earned. However, positive externalities from OFDI can make the "territorial approach," as it is called, a worthwhile strategy. The third option, espoused in the United States but never fully practiced, attempts to take taxes out of the location decisions of MNEs. Under an idealized form of this approach, MNEs make foreign investments when their competitive advantages dictate it, not to reduce tax burdens, because the tax will be the same whether they invest at home or abroad. Choosing a tax approach that is politically tenable and economically advantageous will be an important policy challenge for emerging countries as their MNEs grow.

A common but fallacious concern in developed countries (particularly the United States) regarding OFDI is that it sacrifices jobs and reduces wages. This does not actually occur (see, for example, Desai, Foley, and Hines 2009) but it remains a political sentiment that grips public opinion. Emerging markets will, at some point, face the same popular fears. The sooner they conduct objective research on links between OFDI and employment and wages at home, the better prepared they will be. To address genuine concerns, social safety nets should be created to help those workers who are actually displaced by OFDI.

In a widely cited article, Alan S. Blinder (2007) investigated the number of jobs in the United States that are offshorable, and calculated that anywhere from 22% to 29% of all U.S. jobs potentially fall in this category. Bradford J. Jensen and Lori G. Kletzer (2008) calculated that anywhere from 11% to 15% of all U.S. jobs are potentially offshorable to low-wage, labor-abundant countries. However, Jensen and Kletzer also forecast that job gains from "inshoring" will outweigh job losses and that jobs gained will typically be high-wage, high-skill positions. Similar or higher rates of "offshorability" might be found for most emerging markets, and gains in terms of high-wage, high-skill jobs might be nonexistent. Losing jobs is not yet an issue for emerging market countries because they have found a winning combination of low labor costs and moderate skills. Eventually, however, as the labor markets in other developing countries improve, emerging market jobs could be "outsourced" to more competitive developing countries working their way up the ladder. Indeed, we have already seen the beginning of this process: Indian information technology (IT) firms have begun offshoring jobs to China and other countries. Social safety nets for affected workers could be one way to cope with this challenge; objective studies will be another.

In the lore of strategic trade policy, certain large firms are called "national champions" and given special attention by government policies. According to Theodore H. Moran there are three reasons why countries strive to assist national champions: (1) "to ensure that there are national firms participating in sectors…that are considered particularly valuable" (2008, 283); (2) to ensure that there is a "presence in sectors in which economies of scale are especially large, barriers to entry especially high and rents and externalities especially abundant" (283); and, (3) for national security reasons. Emerging market countries have their own national champions. These include: Mexico's CEMEX, Brazil's Petrobras, China's China Steel and China Telecom, India's Tata Group, and Russia's Gazprom and Lukoil (UNCTAD 2006). In the years ahead, emerging market governments will need to determine how much assistance they will continue to give their national champions, especially as these companies spread their wings beyond national borders.

Among developed or near-developed countries, Europe, Japan, and the Republic of Korea have been the dominant advocates of national champions. Moran found that "the record of both Europe and Asia shows national champions losing their ability—and willingness—to respond to home country economic and political needs if such actions run contrary to their own corporate self-interest" (2008, 290). Breaking away from the demands of governments is an inevitable consequence as national champions grow up. Emerging markets will likely experience the same "breaking-away" phenomenon in the coming years, just as Europe and Asia already have. However, in emerging market countries the "coming of age" process may be more painful than in Europe or Asia because many emerging market MNEs are partially state run. Emerging market governments will be faced with an explicit policy choice: constrain national champions to ensure that they continue to expand at home, or let them blossom on the world stage. Both choices have costs as well as benefits.

21.4   Challenges For MNEs from Major Emerging Markets

Emerging market MNEs are often venturing into more competitive markets than they know at home, and will have to adjust rapidly to succeed. Because the coming competitive challenges are predominantly industry and company specific, we will focus instead on the systemic challenges that emerging market MNEs will create by their own rise to prominence.

The financial crisis of 2008 has heightened existing fears of globalization. Despite the outbreak of smoldering protectionism in 2008 and 2009, new barriers to trade and investment were not, on the whole, severe. But threats of worse are lurking. The Dubai Ports World controversy in the United States illustrated that a single sensitive investment can inflame public attitudes toward FDI. As emerging market MNEs become prominent and powerful, similar episodes may recur. Emerging market MNEs are well advised to prepare the ground. Because greenfield investment is usually associated with job creation, it might be a good idea to announce expansion plans in conjunction with M&A bids.

Emerging market MNEs will also face political pressures at home as they grow abroad. Many emerging market MNEs are national champions, often dependent upon and indebted to their home country's governments. To thrive in the global marketplace, those MNEs must eventually move away from such ties. But historic transitions must be managed with care, because fears of runaway plants, lost jobs, and lower tax revenue are as likely to erupt in emerging countries as in developed nations.

As emerging market MNEs expand abroad they will face stricter regulatory scrutiny than they may be accustomed at home. A look at 2008 Environmental Performance Index (EPI), which ranks countries on the environmental impact of its policies, shows that emerging markets are typically lower ranked (i.e., less environmentally friendly) than developed countries. In the rankings, whereas Russia (twenty-eighth) and Brazil (thirty-fifth) occupy relatively high spots (higher than the United States [thirty-ninth], in fact), China (105th) and India (120th) are much lower ranked. Other developed countries, mostly in Europe, occupy the top spots in the ranking (EPI 2008). If rankings were available for labor standards and plant safety, it seems likely that emerging market countries would usually rank lower than developed countries.

What do these characteristics mean for emerging market MNEs? As they move into developed countries, they may be at a disadvantage because their technical know-how is geared toward more lenient standards. However, their know-how may be well suited to operations in developing countries. Emerging market MNEs might choose to concentrate on countries with fewer regulatory barriers, but this strategy could slow down their ascent on the technology ladder. For example, Switzerland is the top-ranked country on the 2009 Environmental Performance Index, and the Swiss labor force is highly skilled. An MNE that avoids Switzerland will probably lose out both in terms of acquiring the best environmental techniques and in terms of mastering a high degree of labor productivity.

Emerging market MNEs will also be somewhat handicapped by the higher trade barriers surrounding their home markets. The average U.S. and EU most-favored-nation (MFN) applied tariffs are 3.5% and 5.2%, respectively, while average MFN applied tariffs are 10.0% in China, 14.5% in India, and 12.2% in Brazil (WTO 2008). Kei-Mu Yi (2003) found that a great deal of trade growth over the past few decades can be explained by vertical trade within a single company. Because of higher trade barriers in their home markets, emerging markets MNEs that expand abroad will not be able to source intermediate inputs as efficiently as MNEs headquartered in countries with lower trade barriers. As they come to appreciate this disadvantage, emerging market MNEs could become more vocal advocates for lowering their home country barriers.

Finally, there is the overriding issue of human resources. Corporate cultures are different from Detroit to Dallas or from Rome to Milan, let alone Beijing to Morrisville, North Carolina (the site of Lenovo's U.S. headquarters). As emerging market MNEs move into different locales they will be forced to deal with attitudes toward business operations that are far different from those they are accustomed to. Established developed country MNEs have already dealt with this hurdle and have factored it into their business models; emerging market MNEs will initially be at a disadvantage in this respect.

Conclusions

While our discussion is speculative, the challenges we list are not entirely new. Emerging market MNEs are based in home markets that are in the "teen years" of development. There will be bumps in the road. Home governments may at times be reluctant to let their national champions wander the globe; at other times they may send them on a controversial quest for natural resources, sensitive markets, or prized technologies. Host countries may worry about undue influence by the MNE's home country. These are difficult issues, but no more difficult than the issues raised by the postwar explosion of MNEs on the world stage.

Perhaps the greatest challenge over the next decade will be sustaining public support for economic globalization. Emerging market MNEs are a modest force that can add to public skepticism of globalization; other forces, starting with the financial collapse, are far more important. But as they stand taller on the world stage, emerging market MNEs must recognize that the stage itself badly needs support.

Notes

1. FDI outflows from the listed countries in 1997 totaled US$8 billion; in 2007 they totaled US$97 billion. World FDI outflows in 1997 were US$476 billion; in 2007 they were US$1,997 billion.
2. Of the thirty OECD members, we do not consider Mexico, Turkey, Poland, Hungary, Czech Republic, Slovakia, and the Republic of Korea to be highly developed.
3. These countries represent all those developing countries without a "Global Challenger" according to the Boston Consulting Group or a special caveat (like the Republic of Korea or Bermuda) but with more than US$5 billion in outward FDI in 2005 (UNCTAD 2006). The list of countries we are considering here, which we refer to as "major emerging markets," is therefore: Argentina, Bahrain, Brazil, Chile, China, Colombia, Egypt, Hungary, India, Indonesia, Kuwait, Malaysia, Mexico, Nigeria, Panama, Poland, Russia, South Africa, Thailand, Turkey, the United Arab Emirates, and Venezuela.
4. See Moran, Graham, and Blomstrom (2005) for a survey.
5. In China, for example, up until 2001, the only permissible form of foreign entry for MNEs was through joint ventures (Long 2005).
6. The value of cross-border M&As is not directly comparable to FDI flows because funds for M&A do not always come from FDI. *If* all cross-border

M&A funds were FDI based, then, in 2006, the latest year with available data, total world M&A purchases (US$880 million) would be roughly 67% of world OFDI flows (US$1,323 million). In 2005, *if* all M&A funds were FDI based, total world M&A purchases (US$716 million) would be roughly 81% of world OFDI flows (US$881 million) (UNCTAD 2009).

7. If all cross-border M&A purchases from the twenty-two emerging market countries we identified were FDI based, then, in 2005 M&A purchases would have made up 90% of all outward FDI flows from the twenty-two countries—US$66 billion in M&A purchases and US$72 billion in FDI outflows. In 2006, M&A purchases were roughly 60% of total OFDI flows from the twenty-two countries—US$93 billion M&A purchases and US$152 billion FDI outflows (UNCTAD 2009).

8. See "Company's Takeover of U.S. Ports Raises Security Concerns," *NPR: Morning Edition,* February 14, 2006 (retrieved via http://factiva.com, April 27, 2009). Also see "Analysts Question U.S. Security Concerns over CNOOC," *Reuters News,* June 27, 2005 (retrieved via http://factiva.com, April 27, 2009). The Dubai Ports World case was particularly egregious, because Dubai is in fact a U.S. military ally.

9. See Steve Lohr, "Sale of IBM Unit to China Passes U.S. Security Muster," *New York Times,* March 10, 2005, http://query.nytimes.com/gst/fullpage.html? res=9D05E7D9163CF933A25750C0A9639C8B63&n=Top/Reference/Times%20Topics/Subjects/F/Finances (last visited on April 29, 2009).

10. CFIUS is chaired by the U.S. Treasury and has as members all the relevant executive branch departments.

References

Blinder, Alan S. (2007). "How many US jobs might be offshorable?" CEPS Working Paper No. 142. March 2007, available at http://www.princeton.edu/~blinder/papers/07ceps142.pdf, last visited April 29, 2009.

The Boston Consulting Group (BCG) (2007). *The 2008 BCG 100 New Global Challengers,* December, Report, Boston.

Desai, Mihir A., C. Fritz Foley, and James R. Hines (2009). "Domestic effects of the foreign activities of US multinationals," *American Economic Journal: Economic Policy* 1 (1), pp. 181–203.

Environmental Performance Index (EPI) (2008). *Country Scores,* available at http://epi.yale.edu /CountryScores, last visited April 29, 2009.

Hodge, Scott A. (2008). *US States Lead the World in High Corporate Taxes.* Table 1. Fiscal Facts, March 18, 2008, available at Tax Foundation. http://www.taxfoundation.org/publications/show/22917.html, last visited April 29, 20089.

Hufbauer, Gary, Thomas Moll, and Luca Ribini (2008). "Investment subsidies for cross-border M&A: trends and policy implications," United States Council Foundation, Occasional Paper No. 2, April.

Jensen, J. Bradford and Lori G. Kletzer (2008). "Fear and offshoring: the scope and potential impact of imports and exports of services," Peterson Institute for International Economics Policy Brief, Number PB08-1, Washington, DC.

Karl P. Sauvant, with Kristin Mendoza and Irmak Ince , eds. (2008). *The Rise of Transnational Corporations from Emerging Markets: Threat or Opportunity?* (Cheltenham: Edward Elgar)

KPMG (2009a). *2006 and 2007 Federal Income Tax Rates for Income Earned by a Non-Canadian Controlled Private Corporation,* available at http://www.kpmg.

ca/en/services/tax/documents/2006%202007%20CCPC%20June06.pdf, last
visited April 29, 2009.

KPMG (2009b). *KPMG's Corporate and Indirect Tax Rate Survey 2008*, available
at http://www.kpmg.com /SiteCollectionDocuments/Corporate-and-Indirect-
Tax-Rate-Survey-2008v2.pdf, last visited April 29, 2009.

Long, Guoqiang (2005). "China's policies on FDI: review and evaluation?" in
Theodore H. Moran, Edward M. Graham, and Magnus Blomström, eds., *Does
Foreign Direct Investment Promote Economic Development?* (Washington: Institute
for International Economics and Center for Global Development), pp. 315–36.

Moran, Theodore H. (2008). "What policies should developing country governments
adopt toward outward FDI? Lessons from the experience of developed countries," in Karl P. Sauvant, with Kristin Mendoza and Irmak Ince, eds., *The Rise
of Transnational Corporations from Emerging Markets: Threat or Opportunity?*
(Cheltenham: Edward Elgar), pp. 272–98.

Truman, Edwin M. (2008). "A blueprint for sovereign wealth fund best practices,"
Peterson Institute for International Economics Policy Brief. Number PB 08-3,
Washington.

UNCTAD (2006). *World Investment Report 2006: FDI from Developing and
Transition Economics: Implications for Development* (New York and Geneva:
United Nations).

———— (2009). "Foreign direct investment statistics, interactive database," available
at http://www.unctad.org/Templates/Page.asp?intItemID=3199&lang=1, last
visited April 29, 2009.

World Trade Organization (WTO) (2008). *World Tariff Profiles 2008*, Geneva,
available at http://www.wto.org/english/res_e/booksp_e/tariff_profiles08_e.
pdf, last visited April 29, 2009.

Yi, Kei-Mu (2003). "Can vertical specialization explain growth of world trade?"
Journal of Political Economy 111 (1), pp. 52–102.

Chapter 22

The Rise of Emerging Market Multinationals: Legal Challenges Ahead*

José E. Alvarez

Introduction

Lawyers are interlopers when the discussion concerns the business challenges that multinational enterprises (MNEs) from emerging markets face today, and are likely to face in the future. As many readers might know from their own (perhaps not entirely pleasant) encounters with lawyers, lawyers ask a lot of questions before they offer advice to their clients. They are notoriously cautious and curious. Accordingly, in this chapter, I would like to raise some of the questions a lawyer would want those running emerging market MNEs to answer, before beginning to suggest the legal ways forward. In doing so, I will begin by outlining some of the background realities that inspire these questions.

22.1   Background Realities

Lawyers attempting to give advice as to the future would keep at least the following five issues in mind.

22.1.1   Differences between Emerging Market MNEs and Traditional MNEs

First, it appears that emerging market MNEs, including those emerging from the BRIC countries, differ from their developed country rivals in a number of ways. The data seem to suggest that emerging market MNEs have tended to internationalize their operations at an earlier stage in their development than MNEs from richer states. It has also been suggested that although they may be smaller in size, emerging market MNEs may be ready to take greater risks, at least by operating in international environments that pose a higher set of economic or political risks. Finally, it has been suggested that many emerging market MNEs are not as overly "lawyered" in their operations, including with respect to their decisions on whether to internationalize or where to do so, as their wealthy country counterparts. This may stem from the fact that their home countries tend not to be as heavily "lawyered" as say, the United States. As I will argue below, these differences suggest the need for some caution with respect to the ways in which emerging market MNEs may respond to the inevitable legal challenges ahead. We cannot presume that they will respond in the same way as MNEs from wealthy countries would (or have in the past).

22.1.2   Rising Political Risk

Second, it appears that firms choosing to internationalize today are doing so at a time of rising political risk. Political risk today takes various forms. The most prominent is highlighted by the "war" on terror. Terrorist violence frequently targets, intentionally or not, economic globalization. The risk of such violence threatens to derail the overseas expansion plans of even the most risk-taking MNEs. But political risk is not limited to instability and uncertainty prompted by the threat of terrorist attacks. It has emerged recently in a number of countries in Latin America, as evidenced by Bolivia's May 2007 notice to the International Centre for Settlement of Investment Disputes (ICSID) announcing its withdrawal from the ICSID Convention, the most prominent multilateral arrangement authorizing the arbitration of investment disputes. It clearly is evident in Hugo Chavez's Venezuela, whose actions, particularly in the energy sector, including its own threats to limits ICSID's jurisdiction, are likely to produce streams of foreign investment complaints for years to come. It is also evident in Ecuador's recent denunciation of nine of its own bilateral investment treaties (BITs), and indications that it will no longer recognize ICSID's jurisdiction over investment disputes in the oil, gas, and mining sectors.

This is a period in which—despite the fact that much of the world has decisively turned to the free market, privatization, and liberalized capital flows—many countries are experiencing various forms of "foreign investment backlash." For a lawyer, the evidence of backlash appears as straws in the wind that are a little less obvious than some of the cases in Latin America. Recent United Nations Conference on Trade and Development (UNCTAD) reports indicate, for example, that while the network of investment treaties continues to expand, the numbers of successful ratifications of these conventions, which have successfully greased the wheels of cross-country capital flows for decades, have slowed down (UNCTAD 2005).

22.1.3   Rising Regulatory Risk

A third background fact is closely related to the second: the growing political risks faced by foreign investors are now buttressed by what Karl P. Sauvant calls growing "regulatory risks" (Sauvant 2006, 75) of various kinds. Foreign investment flows do not rely solely on BITs; they need an encouraging regulatory framework that supports nondiscriminatory treatment on entry and postentry, provides assurances against expropriation or other forms of proprietary government takings of property, and generally permits companies to have ready access to courts to resolve ordinary disputes with contractors or suppliers. UNCTAD, which for some years has kept track of national regulatory changes that affect foreign investment, is now reporting a disturbing trend: while most changes in national investment laws continue to be made in the direction of encouraging incoming foreign investment (as they have over recent decades), for the first time, a significant percentage of those changes in national law is now in the other direction (ibid.).

What is most disturbing is that, far from resisting this trend, some of the erstwhile leaders of free trade, including the United States and Western Europe, appear to be leading the charge. There are now highly public debates, reminiscent of those in more protectionist times, in the United States and Europe when it comes to the wisdom of foreign mergers and acquisitions (M&As), particularly, but not only, in sensitive sectors such as banking, and the risk that foreign investors will be more ready than other companies to engage in "offshore" hiring. In the United States, the politically charged attempt by Dubai Ports World to acquire P&O Steam Navigation Company (owned by a UK firm)—which was only successful after Dubai Ports World agreed to divest itself of its U.S. assets—has lead to a reinvigorated process permitting the U.S. government to screen incoming foreign investment which could affect the "national security" of the United States. An inter-agency committee, the Committee on Foreign Investment in the United States (CFIUS), chaired by the U.S. Secretary of the Treasury, is charged with examining especially (but not only) would-be acquirers of U.S. companies if these are controlled or are acting on behalf of foreign governments. CFIUS can block any proposed merger or acquisition. Since the Dubai Ports fiasco, filings to seek advance (CFIUS) approval have become ubiquitous, and that committee's investigations have become more frequent and stringent (see White and Case 2007; U.S. Senate 2005; Mostaghel 2007; Weisman 2008).[1] Further, there are signs that other leading capital importers, such as Germany, Hungary, and China, are considering emulating the CFIUS model or making their already existing review mechanisms more stringent (Sauvant 2006, 2009). Because few countries, including the United States, define with any precision what they mean by possible threats to their national or essential security, it is possible that such mechanisms could return us to a world in which governments routinely exclude foreign investment based on perceived threats to their "economic security." This is certainly suggested by the revival of claims among European politicians, particularly in France, that governments need to protect certain "national champions." Increased government screening of incoming investment is also likely given ongoing debates, including in the European Union, about potential economic or security threats posed by investments by sovereign wealth funds (Council of European Union 2008).

Developed countries' second thoughts about the international investment regime that they, more than any other group of states, helped to fashion, is also clearly emerging in the form of some of the new model BITs these countries are now concluding. Consider three provisions of the U.S.-Uruguay

BIT of 2004, a treaty that reflects the new 2004 U.S. model that will henceforth be the prototype for future investment treaties by that country. If one compares the text of the 2004 U.S. model dealing with the rights of foreign investors to "fair and equitable treatment," to compensation upon expropriation, and to permit host countries to take measures to protect their "essential security," to those dealing with the same three subjects in the original U.S. model BIT of 1984 (see supplemental chart), it is clear that the United States, the country that once led the world in promoting international legal protections for foreign investors, is now backing away from that stance.

The 1984 U.S. BIT was a broad statement that foreign investors were entitled to be treated "fairly and equitably" and were, *in addition*, entitled to treatment as required by international law (see Article II(2), 1984 model BIT). This language licenses arbitrators to engage in a broad inquiry as to whether any government action, whether in the form of an administrative regulation, a law, or a court action, results in unfair or inequitable treatment. It further suggests that when such treatment emerges from any violation of international law by a host country, including, for example, a violation of its commitments under the General Agreement on Tariffs and Trade (GATT), the investor can claim a violation of the BIT and seek investor-state dispute settlement.[2] The 2004 version of the "fair and equitable treatment" rights of foreign investors now makes such claims untenable. It limits the meaning of "fair and equitable treatment" to rights under the "customary international law minimum standard of treatment of aliens" (Article 5(1), (2), and Annex, U.S.-Uruguay BIT). As suggested in the Annex to Article 5 of the new 2004 U.S. model BIT, the intent seems to be to restrict the right of investors to only those customary rights that are clearly established. The new limited definition of "fair and equitable treatment" expressly does not include rights that may emerge from the violation of any other treaties. If the Annex is taken at face value, investors under the 2004 treaty appear to be restricted to making claims based on ill-treatment that they receive in a host country's courts that are so beneath the standards of civilized treatment that it violates the international minimum standard of treatment (as articulated in very old cases before the modern investment regime at the turn of the twentieth century [Gantz 2003, 937–50]).[3] If this is what foreign investors need to prove to win under this provision, the "fair and equitable treatment" standard, which until now has been the guarantee that has been most relied upon by foreign investors, may become an almost empty right.

The United States' attempt to narrow foreign investors' rights to compensation for government takings of their property is even more obvious. Whereas in 1984, the United States agreed to reciprocal assurances that all investors would be fairly compensated for any "direct" or "indirect" expropriation of their property, the new language in the 2004 model BIT defers to old (narrower) customary law on point. It clearly indicates that "direct takings" are restricted to takings in which the host country seizes property outright, especially through a formal transfer of property.[4] Given that formal nationalizations of this kind are largely a thing of the past, foreign investors today are far more likely to need to rely on guarantees of compensation for "indirect takings," as where government regulation makes continued business operations untenable. But this possibility is also limited in the 2004 treaty, which provides that indirect takings require a fact-based inquiry that considers the economic impact of the governments' actions, the degree of interference with the investors' "distinct, reasonable investment-backed expectations," and the "character" of the government action (Annex B, U.S.-Uruguay BIT). The 2004 treaty makes a claim for an indirect taking of property all the harder because the treaty provides that the fact that the government's action has an adverse effect on the economic value of an investment does not alone make the investors' case. The 2004 treaty also creates a presumption in favor of the legality of government action taken to protect the government's "legitimate public welfare objectives" (Annex B, U.S.-Uruguay BIT).

While these new preconditions to making a claim for an indirect taking might appear reasonable, it is important to bear in mind their origins. The preconditions imposed under Annex B, Paragraph 4 of the 2004 model BIT, are drawn almost verbatim from the leading U.S. Supreme Court case on government takings of property, interpreting what constitutes a compensable taking under the U.S. Constitution.[5] The United States' new Annex B language, therefore, turns what was once an absolute guarantee, to be determined by international arbitrators without concern for national law, into a closely conditioned right that attempts to limit foreign investors' rights to those that U.S. investors receive under U.S. law. By adopting this language for its investment agreements after 2004, the United States appears to be responding to the demands of many U.S. politicians, including the U.S. Congress, that foreign investors be treated "no better" than U.S. investors (Gantz 2003–2004). There is, of course, a profound irony in the United States adopting such a position today. For decades, the United States waged a largely successful war against Latin American states' insistence on the "Calvo Clause," a principle established by an Argentinean jurist that insisted that foreign investors are entitled to no better treatment than that accorded by a country to its own investors. The "Calvo Clause," once incorporated in laws and constitutions throughout the region, had been eclipsed by the rise of BITs, including the widespread influence of the United States' 1984 model BIT. The new U.S. model BIT appears to give Calvo new life.

But the final change in U.S. BIT policy is potentially the most ominous of all for foreign investors. The language in the U.S. 1984 model BIT appears in a number of old BITs of the United States still in effect (as between the United States and Argentina). Under that original text, the state parties to the U.S. BIT were each permitted to take certain measures that it proved were "necessary" to maintain public order or to protect its essential security interests.[6] As Argentina has learned to its regret in a number of recent arbitral awards directed against it, this text makes it difficult, if not impossible, for a state such as Argentina to proclaim a national emergency and use that excuse to breach its commitments to foreign investors. In those cases, the arbitrators decided (in my view, correctly), that the language of the original U.S. BIT requires a host country attempting to excuse actions in violation of a BIT to prove not only that the crisis that it faced was extremely serious and was not caused by its own actions, but that its responses to that crisis were the "only way" to address the crisis. Three of the four tribunals that have considered the claims of U.S. investors under the U.S.-Argentina BIT determined that Argentina (which had proclaimed national emergencies repeatedly over the past century with adverse consequences to investors) did not satisfy this high standard, and that protecting investors in the midst of such crises was what BITs (or at least the U.S. BIT) was all about.[7]

In the United States' 2004 treaty, the old "essential security" clause has been replaced by one that permits either state party to take any measures "that it considers necessary" to protect its essential security interests (see Article 18, U.S.-Uruguay BIT). Under this provision, it appears that any state willing to claim that what it did to any investor was needed to protect its "essential security interest" would prevail. The new "which it considers" language is presumably intended to make this provision of U.S. BITs "self-judging" so that no arbitrator can examine, much less disagree with, a state's self-interested proclamation under that clause. While some have tried to make this provision a bit narrower in scope by suggesting that arbitrators could still examine whether a state that makes an essential security claim did so in "good faith," at least one recent U.S. investment agreement, with Peru, indicates that this even minimal basis of independent third-party scrutiny would not be possible. The U.S.-Peru Trade Promotion Agreement states that invocation by either state of the essential security provision would render an investor's claim inadmissible.[8] If this is what the new essential security clause in U.S. BITs does, it would appear that the principal benefit of such treaties—to provide foreign investors with a forum capable of enforcing their claims and thereby secure a binding judgment against a host state—has been eviscerated.

It is also worth noting that the 2004 U.S.-Uruguay BIT provides, in addition, a provision (taken from the NAFTA) permitting the state parties, when acting in concert, to issue binding interpretations of their treaty whenever they wish (see Article 30(3), U.S.-Uruguay BIT). This provision also undercuts the guarantee of objective, third-party investor-state dispute settlement in U.S. BITs, as it apparently permits the state parties when they act jointly to change the meaning of the treaty even in the midst of litigation or in the face of pending claims by investors. This provision undercuts the notion that BITs intend to provide their third-party beneficiaries, namely foreign investors, with assurances of stable investment rules. Like the self-judging language in Article 18, this too violates the wise principle in international law that parties ought not to be permitted to serve as judges in their own cause. Finally, the new U.S. BIT permits yet another vaguely defined excuse for host country actions that violate the rights of foreign investors engaged in or affected by financial services; the state parties are now permitted to take any measures relating to financial services for "prudential reasons" (see Article 20(1), U.S.-Uruguay BIT).

What makes these changes in recent U.S. BITs particularly astonishing is, of course, that they emerged from the United States and an otherwise strongly pro-free trade Bush Administration. Given the United States' historic leadership role in the international investment regime, the changes to U.S. BITs are likely to be emulated by others. Indeed, the text of the latest Canadian model investment treaty suggests that this nation, no less than its neighbor to the south, has become considerably less enamored of foreign investors' rights since 1994 when it joined the NAFTA's Chapter Eleven.[9]

22.1.4 The Rise of International Investment Disputes

A fourth background fact to bear in mind is that the number of investor-state investment disputes is at an all-time high. By the end of 2006, UNCTAD reported that 258 international treaty-based arbitration cases had been initiated, of which some two-thirds were being heard before ICSID.[10] Some 47% of these claims arose in the past three years. Whether this reflects a more confrontational state of affairs between MNEs and host countries, or merely greater awareness (or comfort with) international arbitral mechanisms or some combination of both, remains conjectural (Salacuse 2008). What is not debatable is that, largely as a consequence of such disputes and resulting arbitral decisions, international investment law is developing at a rapid pace. The issues involved in such disputes cover the full spectrum of the typical guarantees contained in the nearly 3,000 international investment agreements now in existence. They include many arbitral decisions interpreting the meaning of "fair and equitable treatment" and underlying customary international law standards, of nondiscriminatory and "most-favored-nation" treatment (and especially of "in like circumstances" with respect to such guarantees), and of umbrella clauses (which protect investors' contracts with host states). Dozens of arbitral decisions now offer guidance to states and foreign investors on what "investment" actually means—and whether, for example, some or all investment agreements extend their protections to minority shareholders, to licensees of the principal investor, or to intangible interests (such as for intellectual property). As the Argentina cases indicate, we now know more than we did before about the interplay between investment agreements and traditional customary legal defenses to liability, such as necessity, force majeure, or distress. Although investor-state arbitrations, which can occur under institutional auspices such as ICSID, or merely through recourse to rules such as those promulgated by the United Nations Commission on International Trade Law (UNCITRAL), are not subject to a common law doctrine of formal precedent and not all investment decisions are made public, the arbitral decisions that are available indicate that investor-state arbitrators, who are usually drawn from a relatively small number of specialists in commercial or international law, are very much aware of each others' decisions. Cross-citations and informal reliance on precedent are common. Investor-state arbitrators usually attempt to render decisions that are, at least in terms of legal reasoning if not always the result, consistent with one another. Indeed, the rare instance in which arbitrators do not make such an effort typically earns a rebuke—at least from a growing academy of scholars focusing on this rapidly developing body of law.

For these reasons, although the international legal regulation of investment is not subject to a single multilateral agreement setting out global standards, or a single institutionalized dispute settlement system, complete with panels of arbitrators from approved lists and an appellate body—as under the World Trade Organization (WTO)—it is not entirely wrong to describe investment law as a single regime, even though it is largely based on bilateral agreements that, as is clear with respect to the United States, may evolve over time. The rise of international investment law is also aided by strong pressures, particularly in Canada and the United States, insisting that investor-state dispute settlement be subject to the same degree of transparency that citizens have come to expect of other government efforts. Such pressures help explain why even the briefs filed in NAFTA cases, and not only the resulting awards, are readily available on the Internet and why some investor-state proceedings (as in the World Bank in Washington, DC) have been opened to the general public. All this means that international investment law is becoming a rapidly changing and sophisticated body of law, no less than general corporate law, competition law, or labor law.

22.1.5 *Rising Resistance to International Investment Law*

My final background comment emerges from the fourth: at least some of the backlash against the foreign investment regime, discussed above, stems not from political developments or concerns over security. Critical reactions to the investment regime now stem, in part, from adverse reaction to investment law itself. The increased availability of arbitral decisions and the prominence of at least some of the most high-profile disputes (such as those involving Argentina) have engaged ever-higher numbers of government officials and civil servants, academics, and nongovernmental organizations (NGOs). The investment regime, and specifically NAFTA disputes, now occupies the time of the second largest office within the Office of the Legal Adviser of the U.S. State Department. It has generated a subspecialty within the U.S. international legal academy, such that Columbia Law School alone now regularly offers three courses on the subject. It takes up a substantial portion of the time of activists in NGOs such as the United States' Public Citizen or Canada's International Institute for Sustainable Development.

All of this attention does not always generate positive reactions. Indeed, the adverse reaction of government lawyers in the United States and Canada, charged with responding to a number of high-profile NAFTA claims against their respective governments, probably helps to explain the "sovereignty-protective" changes in those countries' respective BIT policies (Gagné and Morin 2006). A growing tide of critical commentary on the emerging investment case law, by academics, NGOs, and the media, has also helped to fan investment backlash in developed countries (Moyers 2002).

22.2 Questions

Based on these five background realities, discussed above, I will now discuss five questions with regard to emerging market MNEs.

22.2.1 *Do Emerging Market MNEs Care About National Laws Relating to the Treatment of Their Investment?*

Some representatives of emerging market MNEs have suggested that they really do not want anything from their own governments, and presumably from the governments of the countries in which they invest. They seek no government handouts and no special favors. They simply want government to stay out of their way, so that they can internationalize in peace. At the risk of offending those who really believe this Chicago School rhetoric, I am curious about whether those who say this really mean it. Although it may be true that emerging market MNEs are high-risk takers when it comes to decisions to invest abroad, is it not the case that even such MNEs would prefer to invest in enabling environments that permit and encourage such investments?

Property rights, whether on the national or international level, do not enforce themselves. It takes laws and administrative agencies to recognize them, courts and arbitral bodies to enforce them, and properly trained lawyers to assist in all of this. I consider it wrong to suggest that governments spend money only on so-called "positive" rights, such as the guarantees to health care or social security in old age. If it is true, as has been suggested by many, that foreign investment generally does not flow in the absence of infrastructure to support it, and often an educated local workforce, why is it not any less true that absent special circumstances, it does not ordinarily flow or flow as smoothly unless governments spend considerable capital on providing the legal infrastructure that enables capitalism to function and transnational investment to flow?

The World Bank spends considerable energy on ranking countries with respect to their relative efficiencies when it comes to starting a business, dealing with licenses, employing and firing workers, registering property, securing credit, protecting investors, paying taxes, trading across borders, enforcing contracts, and closing a business (World Bank 2007). It attempts to calculate the speed with which governments deal with all of these regulatory matters, such as the time it takes for governments to handle traders' attempts to export their goods, including time needed to prepare the necessary government documents and to go through customs and inspections (ibid., Figure 1.3 at 2). The World Bank even attempts to rank governments by the extent to which they have successfully reformed or improved in all of these areas, the implication being that such information is valuable to those considering investing in particular locales.

Is it really the case that emerging market MNEs pay no attention to such data, that they choose to invest in countries that rank low on the World Bank's doing business ratings? Or that they do not really care whether their own governments set good examples on such issues? It has been suggested that because emerging market MNEs operate (and have succeeded) in national environments that do not rank highly in these respects, they are accustomed to operating under similar chaotic conditions elsewhere. I wonder whether this is really the case: are the most successful emerging market

MNEs really from countries that score relatively low on the World Bank's "doing business" scorecard? Further, I wonder whether, even if that were the case, such companies would not rather operate in more business-friendly places, all else being equal.

My own suspicion is that, over time, emerging market MNEs will increasingly take national law into account in choosing where and how to invest. This is especially true to the extent that national laws are changing in less investor-friendly directions. Emerging market MNEs, like all MNEs, would appear to need to stay abreast of adverse legal developments. Although it is true, for example, that the United States blocks relatively few foreign mergers or acquisitions through its reinvigorated CFIUS process, that process has subtle as well as obvious chilling effects on certain transactions, and even those transactions that are permitted to take place may be subject to government-imposed "mitigation" agreements that might condition entry on, for example, selling off of a subsidiary. The more knowledge MNEs have of what has happened to others, as under the United States' CFIUS process, the better—especially given the likelihood that other countries will emulate the United States' efforts to engage in "national security screening" of incoming investment.

22.2.2   *What Kind of International Investment Regime Do Emerging Market MNEs Want?*

As my background facts suggest, this is a time of active ferment in the international investment regime. Yet there is insufficient discussion as to whether BITs or other investment agreements influence investment decisions and, if so, how. This is to be expected. Surveys of developed country MNEs do not suggest that such questions rank at the very top in terms of corporate decisions to internationalize. Far more important, depending on the industry, are such practical factors as access to raw materials or consumers, political stability, or the ease to export or import materials or products. Nonetheless, given the changes afoot in the investment regime, this may not be the best time to ignore it. The last time the investment regime was on the brink of massive change—when the OECD was engaged in the ultimately unsuccessful negotiations to conclude a Multilateral Agreement on Investment (MAI)—it appears that even MNEs from the developed world were not actively involved in showing their (presumed) strong support for the proposed MAI. Some commentators suggest that the MAI failed in part because the business community did not step up to the plate (Graham 2000, 49). Inaction has consequences.

Investment agreements come in all shapes and sizes. Even though there are many reasons to think emerging market MNEs would prefer, all things being equal, a strongly investor-protective agreement, such as the 1984 U.S. model BIT, over its much weaker 2004 sibling, there may be special reasons, unique to some MNEs, that may make them more inclined to favor investment agreements that seek to "balance" the rights of foreign investors and the state (as does the 2004 U.S. BIT).

It is also important to recognize that the changes made in the 2004 U.S. BIT may be only the tip of the iceberg. A recent paper by UNCTAD (2000) considers a number of possibilities whereby investment agreements might be changed to provide greater "national policy space" and enhanced "sovereign rights to regulate," in order to provide what that organization calls "flexibility for development." UNCTAD's report enumerates various ways investment agreements might be changed to provide such flexibility. These include preambular statements that make it clear that the treaty ought to be interpreted, not only to enhance the protections of investors, but to enable governments to engage in sustainable development, differential treatment for developing country treaty partners depending on their level of development, or exclusions from BIT protections or from dispute settlement for certain types of investments. Others have suggested the introduction of investor responsibilities into BITs, as through the incorporation of the OECD's Guidelines for Multinational Corporations, or through provisions that would indicate that investors who fail to live up to their commitments to abide by certain environmental, anticorruption, or labor standards would be precluded from filing investor-state claims or face the prospect of counterclaims with respect to such issues by host states (Muchlinski 2008). The International Institute for Sustainable Development's proposed model agreement "on investment for sustainable development" even includes an extraordinary provision, undoubtedly inspired by the Bhopal litigation in the United States, that would subject foreign investors to civil actions for liability *in their home state courts* for "acts or decisions taken" in the host state that lead to "significant damage, personal injuries, or loss of life in the host state" (Model International Agreement on Investment for Sustainable Development, Article 17, http://www.iisd.org/investment/model/).

Given the reciprocal nature of BITs and their most-favored-nation clauses, emerging market MNEs would appear to have some interest in the kind of investment agreements presently favored by their own home governments. It may also be the case, given the trend toward less investor-friendly BITs, that some MNEs may favor the approach apparently favored by Brazil, namely, not to engage in BIT negotiations. But to the extent their home states engage in BITs, as do most governments, the corporate world must ask itself what it wants from such agreements or from the investment regime generally. Apart from agreements that would better protect their own rights as investors, one could imagine some MNEs desiring treaties that would stabilize their own domestic environments (as would a BIT with the United States, perhaps). Alternatively, a BIT between an MNE's home state of Chile and a place where it seeks to invest, such as Ethiopia, for example, might be desirable to the extent it helps to stabilize investment conditions in Ethiopia. But particular MNEs might seek an investment agreement with environmental or corporate responsibility provisions to enhance their own public image at home or abroad or, in the case where such provisions merely replicate those in an MNE's national law, to level the playing field with competitors abroad (Abbott 2001, 275–96).[11]

To the extent that multilateral reforms are being urged for the investment regime, it would appear that emerging market MNEs would have at least as much of a stake in these proposals as do other companies. Would, for example, emerging market MNEs favor a new effort to attempt a multilateral agreement on investment, perhaps in an organization other than the OECD? Or would emerging market MNEs from particular regions favor a more regional effort instead (such as the proposed investment chapter for the Free Trade Agreement for the Americas)? Would emerging market MNEs favor ICSID's recent proposal to establish an appellate body to hear investor-state disputes or greater involvement by ICSID staff in these cases (as now occurs in the WTO with respect to WTO dispute settlement)? Even though these changes to investor-state dispute settlement could result in greater consistency of the resulting case law, MNEs are likely to bear some of the attending costs, as through more expensive and more time-consuming efforts to resolve their disputes.

22.2.3   What Is the Attitude of Emerging Market MNEs toward Arbitrating Their Investment Disputes?

As noted above, although there was a time when ICSID was a sleepy institution facing little or no work, this is no longer the case. Investors are now lining up at its door in large numbers. Are emerging market MNEs likely to be among them? There are some reasons to think that such MNEs are less likely to appear as claimants in investment disputes. If it is true that emerging market MNEs are generally less "lawyered" than developed state MNEs, it stands to reason that international litigation may not be their favored option. Moreover, to the extent that emerging market MNEs turn to local law firms or their own general counsels for their legal needs, it is not clear that such lawyers are likely to be as aware of (or comfortable with) international investment law as are the prominent New York, London, and Paris firms that now dominate investor-state dispute settlement and increasingly claim to specialize in such litigation.

Investment lawyers are increasingly skeptical of the premise that investor-state dispute settlement has "leveled the playing field" as between developed nations (and their MNEs) and less developed states (and their MNEs). It is true that international arbitration is an improvement on this score compared to the old way such disputes were handled; namely, by having states "espousing" the claims of their injured investors at the diplomatic (interstate) level. Diplomatic espousal—backed by gunboat diplomacy—elevated the claims of powerful states' investors at the expense of others. But investor-state arbitration, although in theory open to any injured investor, no matter how small the company or from which home country, remains subject to other resource and knowledge constraints. It took smaller, less powerful GATT members some years before they were comfortable filing complaints before the WTO, and it would not be surprising if the same holds true for investor-state dispute settlement—even though the latter is open to any investor and is not dependent on their government's action. These concerns have prompted some to propose an investor-state counseling service for developing states faced with investor-state claims but few have suggested a comparable need for assistance for investors from less developed states and particularly for small investors for whom the prospect of international arbitration would appear especially daunting. The negotiators of the NAFTA took one modest step in this direction by permitting the consolidation of claims. The intent was to permit a number of small investors, all of whom have been injured by the same government's action, to consolidate their respective claims, thereby encouraging the bringing of a case that perhaps no single small investor would have the capacity or the will to undertake. Perhaps this is the kind of special provision that some emerging market MNEs might want to see in their home country's BITs?

However, it is possible that many emerging market MNEs may be less likely to arbitrate any claims that they may have against their host state(s) for other reasons, including cultural ones, having little to do with access to legal counsel or lack of information about international arbitration. It may be that if they are internationalizing at an earlier stage in their own development, they have all the more reasons not to disrupt host country relationships that are still fragile; such companies may have all the more reason not to offend their hosts by filing a formal complaint. If so, it may be that emerging market MNEs could lead the way toward reforming the investment regime in a direction that some are now urging; namely, toward mediation or other forms of informal dispute settlement less likely to prompt adversarial relations between host states and investors (Salacuse 2007, 138–84).

22.2.4 *What Kind of Relationships Do Emerging Market MNEs Have or Want to Have with Civil Society?*

As my background facts suggest, current debates over the legitimacy of the investment regime, particularly in the West, reflect a somewhat acrimonious relationship between prominent members of civil society and defenders of the investment regime, including members of the business community. Some prominent NGOs, particularly those engaged in issues involving the environment, labor, and human rights, active at both the national or international levels, have taken the position that investment agreements, and the investment regime as a whole, need recalibrating, to strike a better balance between protecting investors and the needs of sovereign states. NGOs, which are assuming prominent places at the table before national lawmaking processes and international organizations, contend that the investment regime and the arbitral decisions produced under it create needless tensions between a state's social contract with its citizens, the state's commercial contracts with investors, and state's sovereign arrangements with its sovereign equals.

The critical rhetoric deployed by NGOs and their academic fellow travelers can be quite provocative. It has been suggested that recourse to investor-state arbitration, whether in BITs or Chapter Eleven of the NAFTA, constitutes an undemocratic delegation of authority to unaccountable bodies, thereby trumping the freedom of action of national lawmaking authorities (Public

Citizen 2005; Atik 2004, 215–34); that investor-state arbitration is displacing the gunboat diplomacy of old with "gunboat-arbitration" (Montt 2007, 80) or that such arbitral tribunals are "businessmen's courts" (Van Harten 2007, 153); that international investment law threatens to become "privilege law for foreigners" (Montt 2007, 80); that many arbitral outcomes (such as those involving Argentina that I have mentioned) are affronts to sovereignty and states' right to self-preservation (Bottini 2008, 145–64); that what investment treaties compel governments to do threatens their ability to protect their citizens' rights to equality, life, liberty, and security of the person (Forcese 2006, 321–22; Office of the High Commissioner of Human Rights 2003, 17); or that investment treaties, far from promoting the rule of law and democratic governance, create legal enclaves that *discourage* generalized rule of law reforms in developing countries and in fact "retard the development" of certain regulatory initiatives that are the hallmarks of the mature social welfare state (Newcombe 2007, 394; Ginsburg 2005, 107–23).

As Nestlé learned, to its regret, when it was subject to a highly public lobbying campaign (and consumer boycotts), prompted by the public health consequences of its attempts to market powdered breast milk for use in less developed countries, highly charged accusations from NGOs or academics may resonate deeply and come to affect the corporate bottom line (Sikkink 1986, 815–40). MNEs ignore such accusations, true or not, at their peril. It seems evident that recent statements of U.S. members of Congress and even of U.S. presidential candidates on the continued merits of the NAFTA or other free trade and investment agreements have been influenced by such contentions (Veroneau 2007).[12]

The views of NGOs are now undoubtedly being considered by arbitrators deciding investor-state disputes. The recent Methanex Case, involving an unsuccessful NAFTA challenge by a Canadian investor to California's attempts to prohibit the sale of a gasoline additive on environmental grounds, is particularly instructive. Numerous environmental NGOs sought to participate in that dispute by submitting "amicus briefs" (literally "friend of the court" submissions), a practice common to U.S. courts whereby nonparties are permitted to submit their views to judges hearing a case. The Methanex tribunal ultimately decided to accept such briefs, thereby establishing a clear precedent, at least under the NAFTA, that this practice will continue in other investor-state cases.[13] As their decision acknowledged, the Methanex arbitrators had to overcome a number of hurdles to permit NGOs to file amicus briefs. The investor in that case argued (predictably) that accepting such amicus briefs would add considerably to its litigation burdens and would impact on the confidentiality of the hearings in the case. Mexico, as one of the NAFTA parties likely to be affected by any decision even though it was not a party to the Methanex dispute itself, suggested that a decision to accept such participation would exceed the powers expressly given to the tribunal. There was, in addition, nothing in the UNCITRAL Arbitration Rules governing that dispute or in the NAFTA itself permitting amicus participation. There was also little precedent among international courts for such participation; indeed, the International Court of Justice had traditionally expressed reluctance to accept such submissions. Finally, the Methanex arbitrators could hardly claim that acceptance of amicus briefs was a general principle of law common to most national courts, because even as among the three NAFTA parties, Mexican courts did not accept such non-party submissions.[14]

Despite all of this, the Methanex arbitrators decided that their general authority to conduct the proceedings as they deemed appropriate gave them the authority to admit amicus briefs from NGOs. The most striking passage, stating their rationale, was the following:

> There is an undoubtedly public interest in this arbitration. The substantive issues extend far beyond those raised by the usual transnational arbitration between commercial parties. This is not merely because one of the Disputing Parties is a State: there are of course disputes involving States which are of no greater general public importance than a dispute between private parties. The public interest in this arbitration arises from its subject-matter, as powerfully suggested in the Petitions. There is also a broader argument, as suggested by the Respondent and Canada: the Chapter 11 arbitral process could benefit from being perceived as more open or transparent; or conversely be harmed if seen as unduly secretive. In this regard, the Tribunal's willingness to receive amicus submissions might support the process in general and this arbitration in particular; whereas a blanket refusal could do positive harm.[15]

As this passage strongly suggests, investor-state arbitrations are not immune from public pressures. The arbitrators' decision in the Methanex case to admit amicus briefs undoubtedly had an impact on the legal arguments that the claimant investor was forced to answer and may have played a role in defeating its claim.[16] The Methanex case is not likely to be an aberration; it is a harbinger of much greater public participation and transparency with respect to the investment regime as a whole. It is likely that NGOs and other representatives of the public will only seek more, not less, involvement in states' future decisions to negotiate or to ratify investment agreements and states' defenses of investor-state claims. To that extent the investment regime may be emulating the WTO—where amicus briefs are, to a certain extent, now admitted in WTO dispute settlement and where NGO briefings by WTO staff are no longer a rare event.

Why are these issues not higher on the agenda of emerging market MNEs? It may be the case that some emerging market MNEs have far better relationships with civil society than is the case as with respect to at least some U.S. or European multinationals. It may also be the case that NGO networks are not yet as developed in the home countries of many emerging market MNEs and at least some of those companies have not yet felt a need to address these issues either as a matter of outreach or public relations. But even if this is currently the case, my suspicion is that emerging market MNEs will not long remain immune from having to consider how they are viewed by both NGOs at home and by transnational NGOs—or immune from having to decide what, if anything, to do about it.

22.2.5　Do Emerging Market MNEs Engage in Strategic Behavior to Take Advantage of International Investment Law?

As investment lawyers have pointed out, the investment regime is characterized by forum shopping of various kinds. An investor from state X who suffers a loss at the hands of country Y can choose to approach state X for diplomatic assistance, attempt to sue in country Y's own courts, make a claim under political risk insurance (whether issued under the United States' OPIC or through other mechanisms), or submit an investor-state arbitration claim under the X-Y BIT. To the extent that an investment dispute overlaps with a trade complaint, the investor may also have other remedies at his or her disposal, as under chapter 19 of the NAFTA, country X's domestic law, or in the WTO (where state X might be enticed to file a claim to protect its investors/traders' rights). To the extent the corporate or shareholder structure of our injured investor permits, it may also be possible to have its different foreign affiliates or even shareholders with distinct nationalities file separate claims against state Y under different BITs concluded by state Y with other states. These diverse possibilities are not figments of the academic imagination. There have been a number of claims filed in multiple forums involving the same underlying facts.[17] Moreover, even prior to investing, an investor might make a strategic decision on how to organize or locate his or her company based on the existence of a favorable BIT between his or her place of incorporation and host country Y. If the investor chooses to bring an investment dispute under a BIT, there is also the possibility of attempting to draw from guarantees provided under any other investment agreements concluded by country Y under the X-Y BIT's most-favored-nation clause. As all of this suggests, "adjudicatory competition" exists among a number of competing international and national dispute settlers capable of hearing investment disputes; investors are in a position to take advantage of the proliferation of investment agreements and dispute settlers (Bjorklund 2007b, 241–307).

The investment regime provides great potential for strategic behavior by foreign investors, both before an investment occurs and after a problem arises with respect to their investment. How aware are emerging market MNEs of these possibilities? Do they engage in BIT (or dispute forum) shopping? If not, is this due to lack of information or other circumstances?

Of course, strategic options can be created. Are emerging market MNEs attentive to the possibilities that may be accorded to them when their home countries formulate their BIT policies? Are they attempting to influence which countries will be approached by their home countries to negotiate a BIT or what the scope of the most-favored-nation clause in such BITs will be? Do they consider the availability of investment agreements when they choose where to incorporate? Is it important to emerging market MNEs to have multiple options for asserting their rights?

Conclusions

Lawyers trying to answer the question "what do emerging market MNEs want?" face nearly as many difficulties as Sigmund Freud did when he sought the answer to a comparable question. The complexity of this inquiry is exacerbated by five background facts. First, by the alleged differences that appear to distinguish emerging market MNEs from their developed country counterparts. Second, by the rising levels of political risk that threaten foreign investment for all companies. Third, by the rising incidence of regulatory risks, including more cautious attitudes toward foreign investment flows by governments such as the United States. Fourth, by the increasing number of investor-state disputes and the increased complexity of the resulting case law. And, finally, by resistance to the emerging investment law, including by some NGOs in the West. Lawyers attempting to advise emerging market MNEs given these background facts are likely to want to know whether these MNEs worry about either the national or international legal regimes in place, whether these companies are more or less likely to arbitrate their disputes with host states, whether these companies concern themselves with civil society, and whether these enterprises strategically engage with the international investment regime.

Notes

1. The Foreign Investment and National Security Act of 2007 (FINSA), which became law in the United States on October 24, 2007, reformed the CFIUS process in the wake of the Dubai Ports incident. Senate hearings on that legislation suggest the various concerns that gave raise to that legislation.
2. Without the need to have recourse to one's government as would be the case under the WTO dispute settlement system.
3. Gantz (2003, 943) discusses Canada's argument that the NAFTA's "fair and equitable treatment standard" required, in accordance with old cases interpreting customary international law, "egregious" government conduct for a violation of that standard.
4. Compare Article III(1), 1984 model to Annex B, U.S.-Uruguay BIT.
5. See *Penn Central v. City of New York*, 438 U.S. 104 (1978).
6. See Article X(1) (entitled "measures not precluded"), 1984 model BIT.
7. International Centre for Settlement of Investment Disputes (ICSID) (2005), *CMS Transmission Co. v. Argentine Republic*, ICSID Case No. ARB/01/8, Award (May 12), available at http://icsid.worldbank.org/ICSID/FrontServlet?requestType=CasesRH&actionVal=showDoc&docId=DC504_En&caseId=C4, last visited May 24, 2009; ICSID (2007), *Enron Corp., Ponderosa Assets, L.P. v. Argentine Republic*, ICSID Case No. Arb/01/3, Award (May 22), available at http://ita.law.uvic.ca/documents/Enron-Award.pdf, last visited May 24, 2009; ICSID (2007), *Sempra Energy Int'l v. Argentine Republic*, ICSID Case No. Arb/02/16, Award, P 391 (September 28), available at http://ita.law.uvic.ca/documents/SempraAward.pdf, last visited May 24, 2009. In a fourth case, the arbitral tribunal found that Argentina's economic crisis in 2001 excused that state from paying the injured investor for damages incurred while that crisis was occurring. See ICSID (2006), *LG&E Energy Corp. v. Argentine Republic*, ICSID Case No. Arb/02/1, Decision on Liability (October 3), available at http://icsid.worldbank.org/ICSID/FrontServlet?requestType=CasesRH&actionVal=showDoc&docId=DC627_En&caseId=C208, last visited May 24, 2009.

8. The 2006 U.S.-Peru Trade Promotion Agreement includes a non-precluded measures clause, Article 22.2, which is like the one in the U.S. 2004 model BIT (which makes a state's invocation of "essential security interests" self-judging). Footnote 2 to that provision states: "[f]or greater certainty, if a Party invokes [the non-precluded measures clause] in an arbitral proceeding…the tribunal or panel hearing the matter shall find that the exception applies." For text of the agreement, see http://www.ustr.gov/trade-agreements/free-trade-agreements/peru-tpa/final-text, last visited May 6, 2010.

9. See latest Canadian Model Treaty for the Promotion and Protection of Investments at http://www.naftaclaims.com/files/Canada_Model_BIT.pdf, last visited May 24, 2009.

10. See UNCTAD's online tracking of these disputes at http://www.unctad.org/Templates/Page.asp?intItemID=3775&lang=1.

11. U.S.-based MNEs, for example, strongly urged the U.S. government to negotiate anticorruption agreements within the OECD and elsewhere, in large part because U.S. national legislation had already imposed anticorruption measures on them, and without international regulation U.S. companies operating abroad would be at a disadvantage.

12. Thus, even current officials in the U.S. Trade Representative's Office acknowledge that we are now living in an age of trade "anxiety."

13. See Methanex Corporation and USA, "Decision of the Tribunal on Petitions from Third Persons to Intervene as 'Amici Curiae'" (January 15, 2001), available at http://www.iisd.org/pdf/methanex_tribunal_first_amicus_decision.pdf, last visited October 11, 2009.

14. Ibid., para. 9.

15. Ibid., para. 49.

16. For examples of the innovative legal arguments submitted by amicus in that case, see Methanex Corp. and USA, "Submission of Non-Disputing Parties Bluewater Network, Communities for a Better Environment, and Center for International Environmental Law" (March 9, 2004), available at http://www.ciel.org/Publications/MethanexAmicusSubmission_Mar04.pdf, last visited May 6, 2010.

17. See, e.g., UNCITRAL (2001), *Lauder v. The Czech Republic*, Final Award (September 3); and UNCITRAL (2003), *CME Czech Republic B.V. v. The Czech Republic*, Final Award (March 14).

References

Abbott, Kenneth W. (2001). "Rule-making in the WTO: lessons from the case of bribery and corruption," *Journal of International Economic Law* 4 (2), pp. 275–96.

Atik, Jeffery (2004). "Repenser NAFTA Chapter 11: a catalogue of legitimacy critiques," *Asper Review of International Business and Trade Law* 3, pp. 215–34.

Bjorklund, Andrea K. (2007a). "Adjudicatory competition in international economic law," Columbia Program on International Investment, Foreign Investment & Globalization Speakers' Series, Columbia Law School, New York (March).

——— (2007b). "Private rights and public international law: why competition among international economic law tribunals is not working," *Hastings Law Journal* 59, pp. 241–307.

Bottini, Gabriel (2008). "Protection of essential interests in the BIT era," in T.J. Grierson Weiler, ed., *Investment Treaty Arbitration* (Huntington, NY: JurisNet), pp. 145–64.

Council of European Union (2008). "Council of European Union: sovereign wealth funds—report on the outcome of discussion in the Ecofin Council of 4 March 2008," *ECOFIN 107, EF 19, AG 26, FELEX 152, 7302/08*, March 5.

Forcese, Craig (2006). "Does the sky fall?: NAFTA chapter 11: dispute settlement and democratic accountability," *Michigan State University Journal of International Law* 14 (315), pp. 315–43.

Gagné, Gilbert and Jean-Frédéric Morin (2006). "The evolving American policy on investment protection: evidence from recent FTAs and the 2004 model BIT," *Journal of International Economic Law* 9 (2), pp. 357–82.

Gantz, David A. (2003). "International decisions: Pope & Talbot, Inc. v. Canada," *American Journal of International Law* 97 (4) October, pp. 937–50.

——— (2003–2004). "The evolution of FTA investment provisions: from NAFTA to the U.S.-Chile Free Trade Agreement," *American University International Law Review* 19, pp. 679–67.

Ginsburg, Tom (2005). "International substitutes for domestic institutions: bilateral investment treaties and governance," *International Review of Law and Economics* 25 (1), pp. 107–23.

Graham, Edward M. (2000). *Fighting the Wrong Enemy* (Washington, DC: Peterson Institute for International Economics).

Montt, Santiago (2007). "What international investment law and Latin America can and should demand from each other," *Res Pública Argentina*, No. 3, October–December (Ediciones RAP: Buenos Aires), pp. 75–106.

Mostaghel, Deborah M. (2007). "Dubai ports world under Exon-Florio: a threat to national security or a tempest in a seaport?" *Albany Law Review* 70, pp. 583–624.

Moyers, Bill (2002). "Bill Moyers reports: trading democracy," *Public Broadcasting Service*, February 5.

Muchlinski, Peter (2008). "Corporate social responsibility," in Peter Muchlinski, Federico Ortino, and Christoph Schreuer, eds., *The Oxford Handbook of International Investment Law* (Oxford: Oxford University Press), pp. 637–90.

Newcombe, Andrew (2007). "Sustainable development and investment treaty law," *Journal of World Investment & Trade*, 8, pp. 357–407.

Salacuse, Jeswald W. (2007). "Is there a better way? Alternative methods of treaty-based, investor-state dispute resolution," *Fordham International Law Journal* 31, pp. 138–85.

——— (2008). "Explanations for the increased recourse to treaty based investment dispute settlement: resolving the struggle of life against form?" in Karl P. Sauvant, with Michael Chiswick Patterson, eds., *Appeals Mechanism in International Investment Disputes* (New York: Oxford University Press), pp. 105–25.

Sauvant, Karl P. (2006). "A backlash against foreign direct investment?" in Laza Kekic and Karl P. Sauvant, eds., *World Investment Prospects to 2010: Boom or Backlash?* (London, UK: Economist Intelligence Unit and Columbia Program on International Investment), pp. 71–77.

——— (2009). "Driving and countervailing forces: a rebalancing of national FDI policies," in Karl P. Sauvant, ed., *Yearbook on International Investment Law and Policy 2008/2009* (Oxford: Oxford University Press), pp. 215–72.

Sikkink, Kathryn (1986). "Codes of conduct for transnational corporations: the case of the WHO/UNICEF code," *International Organization* 40 (4) September, pp. 815–40.

UNCTAD (2000). *International Investment Agreements: Flexibility for Development* (New York and Geneva: United Nations).

——— (2005). "Research note: recent developments in international investment agreements," UNCTAD/WED/IIT/2005/1, *Transnational Dispute Management* 2 (5) November, p. 1.

U.S. Senate (2005). "A review of the CRIUS process for implementing the Exon-Florio amendment, hearings before the Committee on Banking, Housing and Urban Affairs," *S. HRG,* October 6 and 20, pp. 109–805.

Van Harten, Gus (2007). *Investment Treaty Arbitration and Public Law* (Oxford: Oxford University Press).

Veroneau, Ambassador John K. (2007). "Trade in the age of anxiety," speech at the National Association of Business Economists in San Francisco, California, September 11, available at http://www.ustr.gov/sites/default/files/uploads/speeches/2007/asset_upload_file948_13308.pdf, last visited May 6, 2010.

Weisman, Steven R. (2008). "U.S. security concerns block China's 3Com deal," *New York Times,* February 21.

White and Case (2007). "FINSA: raising the risks for foreign investments in the US, a Q&A discussion with White & Case's Christopher Corr," August 3.

World Bank (2007). *Doing Business 2008* (Washington, DC: World Bank).

Conclusion

Chapter 23

Emerging Market Investment: Continuity or Change?

Stephen Thomsen

Introduction

The growing list of multinational enterprises (MNEs) from emerging market economies is attracting increasing attention in both government and academic circles. It is one of the least expected aspects of the rising importance of emerging markets within the global economy. The speed with which events are unfolding, as emerging market investors acquire western corporate icons or establish operations in distant markets, means that our understanding of the driving forces and of the likely implications is still in its infancy. Our understanding also often lags behind policy reactions in home and host countries.

The Vale Columbia Center on Sustainable International Investment has been at the forefront of efforts to measure and explain the causes and effects of this new wave of foreign direct investment (FDI). A first Columbia International Investment Conference was held in October 2006. In 2008, a second conference looked again at these new investors from an academic, policymaking, and business perspective. It was followed, in 2009, by a conference examining the future of transnationalization for emerging market companies, organized by Fundação Dom Cabral (Brazil) with subsequent conferences planned in Russia, India, and China over the next three years. The aim of this conference cycle is not simply to rejuvenate existing theories or postulate new ones but also to provide hard data with which to inform future discussions and to outline possible policy responses.

This chapter will try to tie together the various themes in the different chapters, drawing on some of the dozens of presentations and the wide-ranging discussions at the two-day conference. It will also discuss some methodological issues and suggest areas for further research.

23.1 What Do We Know About Outward FDI from Emerging Markets?

Balance-of-payments data on outward foreign direct investment (OFDI) from emerging markets are unreliable in many respects. Fiscal considerations often mean that investment is channeled through offshore tax havens or passes through other foreign destinations. Thus, FDI data often provide little information about the ultimate destination of the investment which, in some cases, could be the home country itself.[1] Chinese firms, for example, invest heavily in Hong Kong (China), the British Virgin Islands, and the Cayman Islands; Indian firms in Mauritius; and Russian ones in Cyprus. Host country reporting of inward investment from emerging markets is not much more useful because of the lack of detail on these new investing countries.

Faced with these inadequacies, the chapters contained in this volume provide very useful microlevel details on the largest MNEs from the BRICs and from such a small country as Slovenia. The country surveys show how much this new trend in OFDI sometimes depends on a handful of the largest firms in each country, particularly in natural-resource sectors. In Russia, one-half of the foreign assets of the top twenty-five Russian MNEs is represented by Lukoil and Gazprom. Similarly, oil and gas operations account for 59% of the foreign assets of the twenty-five top Indian MNEs. But at the same time, the rise in OFDI from emerging markets is not just a result of these large firms and of the dynamics of natural-resource sectors. Both manufacturing and services also figure prominently in these new outflows and, as Yair Aharoni argues, the universe of MNEs—including from emerging markets—comprises mostly small and medium-sized enterprises.[2] Heather Taylor and Andreas Nölke found that many Indian SMEs are also undertaking OFDI.

Some emerging markets now find themselves in the unusual position of being net outward direct investors on an annual basis. Brazilian outflows vastly exceeded inflows in 2006 for the first time. Slovenian outflows have surpassed inflows in three of the past four years. Russian outflows have grown rapidly in recent years, only slightly less than inflows. Only India and China are still net recipients, which is not surprising given their size and level of economic development, but their outflows are growing very quickly.

The extent to which these new investors enter foreign markets through greenfield projects or mergers and acquisitions (M&As) has yet to be established properly. Taylor and Nölke reported the preference of Indian investors for M&As, while Henry Loewendahl asserted that the primary growth engine for developing country FDI has been through greenfield investment. This divergence in opinion seems to be more than simply a question of investment values versus the number of projects. More research is clearly needed to establish the mode of entry of these new investors and whether it differs by home and host country.

23.2   Why Are Emerging Market Firms Investing Abroad?

Emerging market firms invest abroad for many different reasons, depending on the sector and destination. The surveys of their motives presented at this conference and elsewhere suggest that the range of motives behind their OFDI is as wide as for developed country MNEs. The same need to access markets, natural resources, technologies or know-how, other assets such as brand names or distribution channels, or skilled and unskilled labor arises for emerging market MNEs as much as it does for their developed country rivals. The weight of each motive will differ across home and host countries and over time, but the generic corporate strategies remain basically the same. Emerging markets are on the same planet as developed ones.

Several surveys of investors contained in this volume attest to the importance of market access for these new investors. Market access ranks first as a motive for Brazilian investors in a survey by Paulo Resende, Andrea de Almeida, and Jase Ramsey, and dominates as a motive for Russian OFDI according to Kalman Kalotay. A World Bank survey of OFDI by Chinese firms reports that market access is also first on the list of motives, with 85% of respondents listing it as important or very important (Yao and He 2005). In an empirical study of Chinese OFDI, Peter Buckley et al. concluded that "general market-seeking motives underpin much Chinese investment behavior" (2008, 136). Loewendahl cited a survey of 1,577 FDI projects by emerging market MNEs over the past five years in which almost one-half of respondents cite the growth potential of the host market as a motive for investing, and another third mention proximity to markets or customers.

Market access also routinely ranks as most important for developed country investors as well, but clearly it is not the only consideration behind OFDI from either region. Firms also invest abroad to access technology or other intangible assets. One-half of Chinese firms responding to the World Bank survey mentioned earlier, replied that they were investing abroad partly to acquire strategic assets. The survey by Paolo Resende et al. of Brazilian motives for OFDI showed that these firms attach a relatively high importance to the benefits of OFDI for their overall competitiveness and to the access to technology, know-how, and management skills that it provides. Western and Japanese firms are more likely to see FDI as a reward for competitiveness at home than as a way to enhance parent company competitiveness, although strategic asset seeking has certainly characterized some Japanese and Korean investment (Caves 1982, 198).[3]

Huaichuan Rui, George S. Yip, and Shameen Prashantham argued in their study of three major Chinese investors that strategic asset seeking can operate at many levels. For these firms, according to the authors, OFDI is partly seen as a way to put pressure on foreign joint venture partners in China to transfer more technology for fear of losing out to the newly acquired firm. It is an intriguing hypothesis, but it is equally possible that the joint venture partner will become even more hesitant to share technology as the Chinese firm asserts itself increasingly in global markets.

Emerging market firms can be influenced by both push and pull factors when investing abroad. Whereas access to foreign technologies or markets is the most common pull factor, one domestic element frequently associated with pushing emerging market firms abroad is the threat of greater competition at home. In a survey of three of the largest Chinese outward investors (Huawei, Lenovo, Nanjing), Rui et al. found that the most common push factor for all three firms was the fierce competition in their own domestic market. Taylor and Nölke argued in a similar vein that increased competition in the Indian market, following liberalization after 1991, forced local firms to venture abroad in search of not only profitable opportunities but also new skills, products, brands, knowledge, and technology.

Another push factor that is mentioned by several contributors to this volume is the need to escape a burdensome legal and regulatory framework at home, which figured tenth on the list of most important factors for Brazilian MNEs. It was also mentioned by Andreja Jaklič and Marjan Svetličič for Slovenian MNEs, by both Art Durnev and Kalotay for Russian ones, and by Taylor and Nölke for Indian firms. It also possibly figures as a motive for some private Chinese investors abroad given that, until recently, foreign firms have been granted more favorable treatment than domestic private firms. Rob van Tulder mentioned other studies that document this escape motive for emerging market firms.

More research is needed to explain precisely how outward investment allows firms to avoid burdensome regulations at home. In addition to cases of tax planning and positive discrimination in favor of foreign firms, Durnev suggested that predatory governments might find it slightly more difficult to expropriate the assets of MNEs that have a greater international presence and will be unable to expropriate those assets held abroad. Presumably the same protection could be achieved by selling a share of the Russian company to a foreign investor.

A question that arose at the conference and that is a frequent topic of discussion in international business journals is whether a new FDI theory is needed to incorporate emerging market MNEs (see, for example, Mathews 2006). Several participants argued, along the lines of Alan M. Rugman in his chapter, that existing theories of FDI are sufficiently elastic to accommodate outward investment by emerging market firms. Strategic asset seeking motives could be given greater prominence, but they are neither new as an explanation for FDI, nor do they appear to be the main motive overall. Harry G. Broadman argued that a new theory is only necessary if it can be demonstrated that there is a fundamental difference between emerging and advanced countries as home markets. Van Tulder made the case that, rather than developing a new theory, some of the old insights into the study of international business should be dusted off, and current theories should be expanded to incorporate both state- or family-owned enterprises and the role of home governments. Broadman found many similarities between this new OFDI and the traditional product life cycle theory.

23.3   What Are the Ownership Advantages of Emerging Market Firms?

Even though most scholars can accept a plurality of motives behind emerging market OFDI, the debate surrounding the ownership advantages or firm-specific assets (FSAs) possessed by emerging market firms is more contentious. In the market for ideas, academics are often keen to protect the value of their "brand." Rugman argued strongly in his chapter that the new investors are building on country-specific assets in their country of origin.

Other contributors maintained that FSAs for these firms might well be in places in which traditional FDI theorists have never thought to look. Flexibility, adaptability, and being better able to cope with economic crises (such as high inflation) or institutional voids (Khanna and Palepu 2006)[4] are likely to confer an advantage on emerging market investors—at least in other emerging markets. This notion is now a common feature of the management literature on emerging market MNEs and is mentioned in many of the country chapters of this volume and also cited by some emerging market firms themselves.

Kalotay contended that Russian MNEs might not have technology-related FSAs but they do have certain organizational advantages in operating in less-than-perfect business environments. Taylor and Nölke argued that Indian firms have experience in managing in a multicultural setting derived from the cultural diversity of their own home country. Rui et al. claimed that Chinese firms have a superior ability to cope with institutional barriers. In a similar vein, the Multilateral Investment Guarantee Agency (MIGA) suggested that one reason emerging market MNEs might be less sensitive to political risk is the fact that they are already based in countries in which there is often a high perception of political risk. Some of these companies, responding to a MIGA survey, cited their ability to operate in a domestic environment with frequently changing regulations as their reason for greater tolerance for political risk abroad. Rugman, in contrast, argued that skills in adjusting to a volatile environment at home do not constitute FSAs.

Rui et al. listed several sources of competitive advantage for Chinese MNEs. These include: innovative products for niche markets using applicable technologies; tremendous cost advantages in terms of manufacturing, labor, and overheads; highly centralized management systems characterized by entrepreneurial leadership; innovative and effective marketing and service; and institutional advantages in terms of state support and a superior ability to cope with institutional barriers.

Another feature of some recent investors from emerging markets is a high proportion of state- or family-controlled firms. Many contributors reasoned that this might provide an advantage to local firms when investing abroad, primarily through a lower cost of capital. According to Taylor and Nölke, Indian firms rely more on internally generated funds or family connections to raise capital for acquisitions, which the authors maintain is more patient than debt and equity raised in international capital markets. Resende et al. pointed out that many of the largest Brazilian businesses are family controlled. Chinese and Russian investors, in contrast, are more likely to be state owned or controlled, as Kalotay demonstrated in the case of Russian firms and Qiuzhi Xue and Bingjie Han for Chinese firms. State ownership reduces the cost of capital both through privileged access to the state banking system or other government funding and through any monopoly profits that might accrue to the favored firm. Judith Clifton and Daniel Díaz-Fuentes reported that the Russian energy giant Gazprom has used its excess profits at home to acquire downstream assets abroad.

The discussion of FSAs is of more than passing academic interest. If emerging market MNEs do not possess the necessary firm-specific or ownership advantages, it is unlikely that they will be able to compete effectively against sophisticated rivals in developed markets or to integrate acquired, and often unprofitable, western firms. Only time will tell, but it should not be assumed that all of the recent OFDI from emerging markets into developed ones will necessarily succeed. A common theme of the conference discussion of the OFDI experience of individual countries was the managerial and organizational burden imposed by OFDI, especially in cases of foreign acquisitions. Cross-border M&As have a high failure rate in general, and it is probable that acquisitions by emerging market firms are even more difficult given the wide cultural gap that often exists with western firms and the speed with which internationalization is taking place.

Van Tulder asked whether these new investors have the managerial capacities to digest their new acquisitions. During the conference, Boris Kheyfets (Institute of Economics, Moscow) spoke of the low competitive capacity of Russian companies in the international M&A market, citing examples of failed foreign mergers. Jaklič and Svetličič concluded that in the long run human capital seems to be the biggest barrier to internationalization for Slovenian enterprises, together with a lack of cultural management knowledge. Some Chinese acquisitions in Europe and North America, such as the TCL acquisition of Thomson's television business, have failed partly for these reasons. In a World Bank survey of Chinese MNEs, 85% of CEOs cited differences in management styles and corporate cultures as the main reason for failure in foreign ventures (Yao and He 2005). One speaker at the conference mentioned that few Chinese MNEs have formalized a governance process for cross-border M&As.

Not all contributors saw emerging market firms as lagging behind western rivals in this area. Drawing on his knowledge of Israeli MNEs, Aharoni asserted that FSAs of emerging market MNEs appear to be their ability to identify candidates for acquisition, acquire them and absorb them into their networks.

23.4   Does OFDI Improve Corporate and National Competitiveness?

The notion that OFDI might be beneficial for both the investing firm and the home country is becoming common currency in academic and some government circles if not yet among the public at large.[5] Competitiveness is improved not just through greater inputs of technology and other factors but also through improvements in a firm's overall efficiency as a result of the discipline imposed by competing in more sophisticated and contestable developed country markets. In this way, OFDI serves as a kind of vaccination against competitive threats at home.

Many studies have found that MNEs perform better than strictly national firms, though it is often difficult to disentangle cause from effect. A recent Organisation for Economic Co-operation and Development (OECD) review of the literature found that "outward FDI tends to increase output, employment and exports in the parent firm in the home country, in part because of the positive impact on the parent's competitiveness...The academic literature is divided over the degree to which these benefits accrue to a broader segment of the home economy through spillovers and other externalities" (Thomsen 2006, 116). Jaklič and Svetličič found that Slovenian MNEs have outperformed national firms in terms of profitability, sales, and productivity. Other country studies do not provide the same comparison.

De Beule and Van Den Bulcke, along with several commentators at the conference, cautioned against assuming an automatic link between OFDI and competitiveness. They argue that recent UNCTAD work on the subject (such as UNCTAD 2006) "presents little hard evidence on the issue of improved competitiveness as a result of outward investment or its promotional policies...It would seem that the link between competitiveness and OFDI is an underresearched area" (chapter 14, 300). As with studies of the economic impact of inward FDI (IFDI), it is more difficult to show economywide effects of OFDI than it is at the level of the firm. This area also merits further investigation.

23.5   How Much Should Home Governments Promote OFDI?

Given the risks associated with OFDI and the difficulty in finding evidence of spillovers to the home economy, how much should home governments promote OFDI? This question was much discussed at the conference. One participant summarized the discussion as follows: "No case was made against OFDI. Most were for a neutral stance and a few were for active promotion—although it remains to be seen whether it will be fruitful."

At present, very few emerging market governments actively promote OFDI although most are removing existing restrictions. At one extreme, many Latin American governments seem to be lodged in what some might consider an earlier development paradigm in which what matters is inward investment. According to some representatives from the private sector at the conference, the Brazilian government does not actively support OFDI, although it might occasionally help local firms achieve access to foreign markets or technologies. MIGA pointed out that the Brazilian government does not even offer political risk insurance to Brazilian firms investing abroad.

The role of the Indian government behind recent OFDI seems harder to pin down. Taylor and Nölke argued that "regulatory protectionism and supportive industrial and technological policies, from the 1950s onward, helped considerably in allowing firms to accumulate the technological capacity to expand abroad in the post-liberalization period" (chapter 9, xxx). Others might argue that these firms prospered despite, rather than because of, the license raj. Rui et al. also saw the visible hand of the Indian government behind recent outflows, although liberalization of the investment regime and promotion of OFDI are not necessarily the same thing. The Indian government seems to bask in the reflected glory of Tata or other Indian MNE takeovers of corporate icons in Europe or North America, but its exact role in the promotion of OFDI still needs to be established.

In recent years, Russia has moved toward a more proactive policy toward OFDI in the expectation that it will translate into improved competitiveness for Russian firms, which in turn will generate spillovers for the home economy more generally. Slovenia is also moving in this direction with its Act on Attracting FDI and Internationalization of Companies (August 2004) and following on from an "enterprise and competitiveness development" policy introduced in 1999. As Xue and Han demonstrated, China has initiated its "Go Global" policy to encourage the overseas expansion of its state-owned national champions but has also introduced other policies to encourage OFDI more generally. Most governments that promote OFDI explicitly mention national firm competitiveness as a motive.

The promotion of OFDI is conditioned in part by the broader macroclimate. De Beule and Van Den Bulcke demonstrated in their review of developed country government OFDI policies in earlier decades that balance-of-payments considerations were a key influence on the treatment of OFDI. While the United States restricted outflows when faced with a deteriorating balance of payments, Japan and Germany encouraged OFDI in order to alleviate upward pressure on their currencies. This relationship is perhaps even stronger today, particularly for Asian governments for both reasons mentioned above. As the authors argued, "improvements in the balance of payments of countries and the buildup of foreign exchange reserves were often necessary, but not sufficient conditions, to reevaluate the OFDI policy" (chapter 14, 295). Kheyfets mentioned this as an element for the Russian government, and it is well known to be a consideration behind some Chinese OFDI, particularly by the sovereign wealth fund, the China Investment Corporation.

Discussions of home country policies need to distinguish between those policies that seek to enable greater OFDI by removing home government impediments and by lowering transactions costs and those that actively seek to promote outward investment by local firms, whether private or public. Some of the presenters from the private sector and some of the survey results from individual emerging economies suggest that policy neutrality might be more important for investors than actual help. Of particular importance is fiscal neutrality, including allowing foreign tax credits, signing double taxation treaties and bilateral investment treaties, or even participating in a multilateral agreement on investment.

Some in government might favor OFDI promotion as a modern form of industrial policy, more in keeping with an age of globalization, but implementation requires popular support. Unlike the promotion of inward investment which, rightly or wrongly, is welcomed for its impact on employment, OFDI is more likely to be viewed as a policy that favors capital over labor.

Are we likely to see a generalized attempt to encourage OFDI by developed and developing countries? As Buckley et al. pointed out in their contribution, OECD governments have been fairly reticent about supporting

OFDI. As the United Kingdom House of Commons argued, such policies tend to support the firm and the host economy more than the home one. For this reason, OFDI support by OECD governments has tended to be restricted to projects in the least developed countries. Until recently, this was also the only type of OFDI actively supported by the Indian and Chinese governments as well, particularly where it dovetailed with wider foreign policy interests.

Active promotion of OFDI is unlikely to gain much popular legitimacy in developed countries, especially in sectors in which it might be construed as encouraging outsourcing. De Beule and Van Den Bulcke suggested that even the Republic of Korea has had to temper its promotion of OFDI with measures to counter the risk of hollowing out its industries. The authors lamented the absence of information about how the public in other emerging markets reacts to OFDI by local firms and to government measures to encourage it. Where information is available it does not suggest an accommodating view. Kheyfets cited one survey finding that only 21% of Russians responding support foreign expansion. In Slovenia, anecdotal evidence suggests that investing abroad was considered as unpatriotic in the past because "capital was needed at home" (cited in chapter 11, 197). This fear that OFDI could substitute for domestic investment was echoed by Kheyfets in the Russian case.

Policy makers wishing to promote OFDI still need to decide how and how much. Should all firms receive assistance or only in certain sectors or public enterprises? Many governments, for example, now see an advantage in allowing state-owned enterprises (SOEs) to invest abroad. Clifton and Díaz-Fuentes argued that some utilities in European Union countries have benefited from delayed opening up at home to pursue aggressive expansion abroad. Acquiring foreign rivals is seen as a better alternative than being acquired by those same firms.

Nowhere is the link between state ownership and OFDI promotion more pronounced than in China where, as Karl P. Sauvant demonstrated, 83% of outflows are by SOEs. But at the same time, the evidence on Chinese OFDI policies outlined by Xue and Han suggested the need to avoid overly simplistic notions of monolithic policies. Chinese SOEs face a complex approval and regulatory process for OFDI involving many agencies with overlapping responsibilities. Furthermore, as Trevor Houser argued in a study of Chinese SOEs in the energy sector, "policymaking…is much more fragmented than outsiders generally perceive…[C]ompanies, ministries, and individuals all vie for influence. Given their quasi-governmental status and the political rank of their leadership, China's [national oil companies] are able to operate abroad largely free of government oversight" (Houser 2008, 161).

23.6 How Have Host Governments Responded?

Potential host countries, especially developed ones, have evinced an ambivalent attitude toward these new investors. Host country governments generally welcome FDI for the expected benefits in terms of technology, employment, and competition. But acquisitions of local firms by SOEs or by firms that are protected from takeover in their own market are more problematic. After an extended absence, this issue has returned to the heart of the international political agenda.

Loewendahl discussed the implications of emerging market OFDI for investment promotion agencies (IPAs) in host countries. Compared to the profile of earlier international investors, these new MNEs have greater government involvement in their activities and less experience in overseas investment. They are also characterized by a relatively greater importance of business and personal networks. The rise of these new investors is closely related to other emerging trends, including the growing share of FDI that is intraregional and the rise of services. To be effective in this new environment, IPAs need to look at M&As as well as greenfield projects, to integrate more closely trade and investment agencies, and to focus on selling specific projects rather than more general locational aspects.

Gary Hufbauer and Matthew Adler focused on the policy challenges ahead for both emerging market MNEs and for home and host governments. For host developing countries, even though many authors assume that South-South FDI might offer certain advantages compared to the traditional North-South equivalent, Hufbauer and Adler raised certain potential concerns. Emerging market FDI might be easier to entice in some cases, but—compared to investors from developed countries—emerging market MNEs might be less likely to transfer technology and more likely to impose unfavorable working conditions and layoffs on their workers. Their investments in natural-resource sectors might also be less concerned about sustainability. None of these outcomes is preordained, but they speak to the need for a better understanding of emerging trends.

For developed host economies, emerging market OFDI raises questions of technology leakage, as well as of national security and geopolitical issues. From a home country perspective, governments will need to judge whether the possible benefits to the home economy from domestic MNEs outweigh the perceived costs in terms of tax avoidance and job outsourcing.

Where the investment takes the form of an acquisition of a local company, the reaction is likely to be less welcoming. Examples of host government hostility are still few in number but this belies their impact on policymaking and on FDI worldwide. The cases of Dubai Ports World or China National Offshore Oil Corporation (CNOOC) in the United States and Chinalco in Australia, or of the reaction to the takeover of Arcelor by Mittal in Europe, attest to hostility that emerging market investors sometimes face in their acquisitions of western companies. In some cases, host governments object to the degree of state ownership of the investor; in others, it is the lack of reciprocal access to takeovers of firms in the investing country. In some cases, as suggested by Clifton and Díaz-Fuentes, the characteristics of the investor or the investing country are of secondary importance compared to the desire to retain local ownership in an industry deemed to be strategic.

23.7   Corporate Social Responsibility as a Key to Host Country Acceptance

Participants at the conference generally agreed that improved corporate governance, greater transparency, and an adherence to codes of corporate social responsibility (CSR) could all help defuse tensions. CSR practices vary greatly from one emerging market to another and from one firm to another in these markets. Van Tulder argued that one "liability of foreignness" for emerging market MNEs is their position on CSR and that the success of BRIC MNEs will increasingly be influenced by their position on CSR. Many contributors considered that CSR will be—or has been—a significant factor behind both political and popular acceptance in host countries. Taylor and Nölke argued that, when the Indian pharmaceuticals company, Dr. Reddy's, acquired Betapharm in Germany, a crucial element allowing the smooth transition of ownership was Dr. Reddy's active CSR policy. Sauvant talked of the importance of stakeholder management for Chinese MNEs, involving policy makers, labor, investors, local communities, and the public.

Governments can do much to promote CSR among its firms, as can be seen from the OECD Guidelines on Multinational Enterprises. A recent OECD Investment Policy Review of China focusing on CSR reported that "Chinese authorities are striving to ensure corporate compliance with laws relating to [CSR] and are also promoting [CSR] in overseas operations of Chinese enterprises. China has signed and ratified international agreements relevant to promoting [CSR]" (OECD 2008, 9). The report goes on to argue that, even though Chinese firms are seeking to learn about CSR standards, these firms are still largely unaware of what CSR entails and have not organized themselves to promote it.

23.8   Is It a Propitious Time to Reconsider Multilateral Rules for Investment?

Many emerging market governments were hostile or at best indifferent to the proposed Multilateral Agreement on Investment (MAI), negotiated in the 1990s at the OECD, and to any discussion of Singapore issues relating to investment in the World Trade Organization. What does the rise of OFDI from emerging markets imply about multilateral rules for investment? As emerging markets become outward investors, sometimes even on a net basis, the possibility arises that this new symmetry in global FDI flows will break the deadlock on issues relating to a multilateral investment agreement.

One participant felt that the lack of progress to date suggests that one should be pessimistic about any future agreement. Several presenters and commentators nevertheless asked whether the need to protect emerging market investors against rising hostility in some markets might not persuade their home governments that they have an interest in a global agreement. At least one of the country studies revealed a majority of investors in favor of such an agreement.

More needs to be studied about what issues are of most interest to these new investors. Which obstacles are most important, and what are the greatest policy risks? What kind of dispute settlement would these new MNEs favor? How far would they be willing to go in accepting obligations in investment agreements? Hufbauer and Adler argued for an international agreement that places proper limits on M&A subsidies.

Jeffrey D. Sachs linked FDI to the issue of global resource constraints and the recent economic crisis. Keeping markets open, he argued, will not only contribute to growth and prosperity but will also help to disseminate a new generation of sustainable technologies. Anthony O'Sullivan highlighted the role of the Freedom of Investment (FOI) process at the OECD in keeping markets open to investment. He suggested using the FOI process to encourage better corporate governance, CSR and increased transparency for emerging market MNEs.

José E. Alvarez argued from a legal perspective that rule making concerning FDI is in retreat. Investors face increasing political and regulatory risks and home and host governments are retreating from earlier negotiating positions: bilateral investment treaties are still being negotiated but fewer are ratified; foreign investors in the United States are increasingly filing for advance approval with the Committee on Foreign Investment in the United States; "fair and equitable" treatment for investors has been eviscerated; "essential security interests" have become self-judging; and investor rights have been restricted in the case of regulatory takings.

Most of the examples Alvarez provided are based on the U.S. experience. To the extent that this retrenchment is universal, it suggests that whatever impact OFDI might have on the negotiating positions of emerging market governments concerning international investment is dwarfed by the protectionist sentiment aroused by these new investors in major host markets. As Edward M. Graham (2008) argued based on the experience of the MAI, most governments tend to adopt negotiating positions based on their role as host rather than home countries for FDI. Rugman concurred that it is unlikely any major new multilateral initiatives to liberalize FDI (either inward or outward) will be successful.

23.9   Emerging Market Economies: The Broader Perspective

With so many firms from emerging markets starting to invest in both developed and developing countries at the same time, there are deeper forces at play than the simple aggregation of trends in individual industries or even countries. The rise of emerging market OFDI is a direct consequence of the rise of emerging market economies themselves. This broader picture was presented with an almost infectious enthusiasm by Antoine Van Agtmael (Emerging Markets Management LLC).

It would be interesting to see how the growing relative size of emerging markets has shifted the global balance of competitiveness between emerging and developed market firms. Does the rise of billions of less discerning consumers (in terms of differentiated products and technological sophistication) create competitive advantages for emerging market firms in global markets? While broader discussions of emerging markets can sometimes border on hyperbole, there are clearly demand- and supply-side implications for firms in global markets from what Van Agtmael labeled the "emerging markets century." Case studies of individual countries or sectors are important, but we need to look at the forest as well as the trees.

Conclusions

The conference discussions and the chapters in this volume suggest a good deal of continuity between emerging market OFDI and that by developed country firms in earlier decades. Differences exist, but they need to be put in context. Recent OFDI by emerging market firms is unprecedented in its scale, given the level of development of many emerging markets and the fact that many investors do not yet appear to have an endowment of technology or other proprietary assets with which to compete effectively abroad. It is also progressing at a rapid pace rather than incrementally as in the past. But in all other ways, emerging market OFDI is different only by degree. Some emerging market governments are relatively more proactive than developed country governments are in promoting OFDI, either through a share of ownership in the investing firm or through promotional measures directed at private local firms. But it is not yet clear how much impact this policy stance has had on OFDI by local firms. Emerging market firms are also driven, to a greater extent than for developed country MNEs, by pressures to improve competitiveness; but here, too, strategic asset seeking has always been an explicit or implicit aim of foreign investors, even if it was under-played in many existing FDI theories until recently.

The rapid growth of outward investment by emerging market firms is a small step for global FDI but a giant step for the firms themselves and for the governments at home. While the potential rewards are high, so too are the risks. These new investors will need to develop new organizational skills as well as political ones. Political skills were mentioned by one participant as a factor behind the successful acquisition of the personal computer division of IBM by Lenovo. Investors from some emerging markets also lag far behind their western counterparts in adhering to principles of good corporate governance and of corporate social responsibility.

Emerging market governments will also need to adapt, by reconsidering their policies concerning the promotion or restriction of outward investment and the treatment of foreign investors in their own economies. How much should they promote OFDI? Will there be greater pressure to liberalize IFDI policies in the face of demands for reciprocity from countries that are now hosts to emerging market OFDI?

No private sector participant at the conference clamored for subsidies for OFDI, but many suggested ways in which their home governments could be more helpfully neutral. At present, lingering capital controls and other administrative impediments, as well as the absence of double taxation treaties, are sometimes as much an obstacle for outward as for inward investment.

To what extent have international organizations started to give the same assistance in removing regulatory barriers to OFDI as they currently do for IFDI?

To understand better the causes and effects of emerging market OFDI, we need to spend less time looking for differences between emerging and developed economy firms and more time examining the many differences among emerging markets themselves. The papers presented at this conference and the discussions they sparked all highlight a high degree of continuity between the current wave of OFDI and preceding ones. It has yet to be proven that emerging market firms have invented a new business model. What is more interesting is the variety of approaches taken by emerging market firms and their home governments to the question of OFDI.

Firms from countries such as the Republic of Korea, for example, have been investing abroad for decades, while firms from other emerging markets have started only in the past five years. Some are market economies and some, like China, are in transition. In some, state-owned firms figure prominently (China or Russia); in others they are largely absent (Brazil or India—except in natural resources). Some emerging market governments actively promote OFDI; others only grudgingly accept it. Some received massive inflows of FDI as a prelude to OFDI; others restricted inflows.

Even within individual emerging markets, there are differences in the experience of outward investors. Samsung, for example, was considered by Van Agtmael to be a world-class firm. How is its story different from that of Daewoo, which has sold large parts of its company to foreign investors, including from other emerging markets? At a country level, it might also be useful to consider some developed country experiences. One participant suggested that Spain might be an interesting case study because its firms had no obvious competitive advantages when they embarked on overseas expansion and met with considerable hostility in Latin America. How have they managed to become among the largest foreign investors, with a substantial presence throughout Latin America and increasingly in the rest of the world as well?

We also need to be cautious in extrapolating based on current trends. Emerging market OFDI is growing quickly and is likely to continue to do so in the future, but there will likely be many setbacks and about-turns along the way. Some investors will collapse under the organizational burden of running an MNE. Others will decide that the best hope for future profits is to sell to a suitable partner from a developed country. After several years of aggressive expansion in Europe and North America, Ranbaxy decided to sell a large stake to Daiichi Sankyo of Japan. The move was unexpected, but it will not be the last.

We also need to move beyond assertions. We need to understand better both the advantages and disadvantages of state ownership for emerging market MNEs. The same goes for family connections and for the notion of social capital (*guangxi* in China or *kankei* in Japan and *inmak* in the Republic of Korea), which is considered to bestow competitive advantages on Asian firms compared to their western rivals.[6] We need to ascertain the importance of strategic asset seeking behind emerging market OFDI, whether it provides the expected benefits both to the investing firm and to the home country, and how it affects research capacity in the host country. We also need to look behind the notion of institutional voids to examine whether transaction costs are really lower for emerging market investors in other emerging markets than they are for OECD investors. And to the extent these newer MNEs do have some transferable advantage, what does it imply for host developing countries eager to attract and benefit from such investment? This conference raised many interesting questions and provoked a lively discussion, but future conferences will still have much to talk about.

Notes

1. Such round tripping for fiscal and other reasons is frequently associated with Chinese outward and inward investment, but Kalman Kalotay also found in the case of Russia that, in one out of ten cases, cross-border M&As targeted firms abroad that ultimately invested in Russia.
2. Aharoni's recent work on Israeli MNEs (Aharoni 2009) would be a useful addition to the Five-Diamond Conference series.
3. Caves (1982) cited early Japanese investment in the United States and Germany that was intended "to improve their access to technology flows after companies in those nations, conscious of the burgeoning Japanese competition, grew more reluctant to license." A more recent study of Japanese investors by Branstetter (2002) found that technological access still matters.
4. Institutional voids refer to the absence, or poor functioning, of the specialist intermediaries needed to bring buyers and sellers together in markets.
5. The notion of OFDI as a way of building competitiveness parallels in many ways the discussion of "learning-by-exporting," whereby firms learn to improve the quality of their products and production processes through contact with more advanced foreign competitors and customers in global export markets. This view is not universally shared: a recent OECD report on trade policies in Indonesia argued that "it is not export competition that drives productivity but rather import competition" (2008, 355).
6. For a discussion of social capital and Asian firms, see Hitt, Lee, and Yucel (2002).

References

Aharoni, Yair (2009). "Israeli multinationals: competing from a small open economy," in Ravi Ramamurti and Jitendra Singh, eds., *Emerging Multinationals from Emerging Markets* (Cambridge: Cambridge University Press), pp. 352–96.

Branstetter, Lee (2002). "Is foreign direct investment a channel of knowledge spillovers? Evidence from Japan's FDI in the United States," Working Paper No. 8015 (Cambridge, MA: NBER), November, mimeo.

Buckley, Peter, Jeremy Clegg, Adam Cross, Hinrich Voss, Mark Rhodes, and Ping Zheng (2008). "Explaining China's outward FDI: an institutional perspective," in Karl P. Sauvant with Kristin Mendoza and Irmak Ince, eds., *The Rise of Transnational Corporations from Emerging Markets: Threat or Opportunity?* (Cheltenham, UK: Edward Elgar), pp. 107–57.

Caves, Richard (1982). *Multinational Enterprise and Economic Analysis* (Cambridge: Cambridge University Press).

Gammeltoft, Peter (2008). "Emerging multinationals: outward FDI from the BRICs countries," *International Journal of Technology and Globalization* 4 (1), pp. 5–22.

Graham, Edward M. (2008). "Will emerging markets change their attitude toward an international investment regime?" in Karl P. Sauvant with Kristin Mendoza and Irmak Ince, eds., *The Rise of Transnational Corporations from Emerging Markets: Threat or Opportunity?* (Cheltenham, UK: Edward Elgar), pp. 299–318.

Hitt, Michael, Ho-Uk Lee, and Emre Yucel (2002). "The importance of social capital to the management of multinational enterprises: relational networks among Asian and western Firms," *Asia-Pacific Journal of Management* 19, pp. 353–72.

Houser, Trevor (2008). "The roots of Chinese oil investment abroad," *Asia Policy* 5, pp. 141–66.

Khanna, Tarun and Krishna G. Palepu (2006). "Emerging giants: building world-class companies in developing countries," *Harvard Business Review* 84 (10) October, pp. 60–69.

Mathews, John (2002). *Dragon Multinational: A New Model for Global Growth* (New York: Oxford University Press).

OECD (2008). *Investment Policy Review—China: Encouraging Responsible Business Conduct* (Paris: OECD).

Sauvant, Karl P., with Kristin Mendoza and Irmak Ince, eds. (2008). *The Rise of Transnational Corporations from Emerging Markets: Threat or Opportunity?* (Cheltenham, UK: Edward Elgar).

Thomsen, Stephen (2006). "Outward direct investment: what benefits to the home countries?" *International Investment Perspectives* (Paris: OECD).

UNCTAD (2006). *Global Players from Emerging Markets: Strengthening Enterprise Competitiveness through Outward Investment* (New York: United Nations).

Yao, Yang and Yin He (2005). "Chinese outward investing firms: a study for FIAS/IFC/MIGA," Beijing: China Center for Economic Research, Peking University, mimeo.